Roger's Profanisaurus
THE MAGNA FARTA

VIZ ROGER'S PROFANISAURUS

THE MAGNA FARTA

Dennis

First published 2007 by Dennis Publishing Ltd
30 Cleveland Street, London W1T 4JD

This edition September 2008

Distributed by Pan Macmillan Ltd

ISBN 0 9548577 8 X

Note to Oxfam bookshop pricers: We're not sure which printing this is, exactly, but it certainly isn't a first edition, so it's not fucking 'collectable'.

A CIP catalogue record for this book is available from the British Library.

Compiled and edited by Graham Dury, Davey Jones & Simon Thorp.

Production Managed by Stevie Glover.

Designed by Wayne Gamble.

Printed and bound in the UK by CPI Mackays, Chatham ME5 8TD

This book has been made possible by the hard work of one man ~ my solicitor, Ronnie 'Slippery Eel' Wragg.

Last year, I was unfortunate enough to drive through a small bus queue after having one over the eight. But for the many hours Ronnie spent reading and re-reading legal documents looking for loopholes in the law, I would now be sewing mailbags.

It is to him that this book is dedicated.

Roger Mellie, OBE
Fulchester, 2007

P.S. And thanks too to all the Viz readers who have sent in their contributions. Keep them coming.

A Foreword by Brigadier Sir Hercules Lethbridge-Stewart, KG, GCVO, CB, CBE, MC, LNER.

THE ENGLISH LANGUAGE is without doubt the most beautiful in the world. Free of the the guttural clicks of the Germanic tongue or the hideous, phlegmatic back-of-the-throat rumblings that the French insist on doing, it has become the language of poetry and song throughout the entire right-thinking world.

Moreover, it has an extraordinarily rich vocabulary, boasting almost one million words. In comparison, the French can lay claim to just 400,000, even including all their stolen utterances such as "le week-end", "le sandwich" and "le pop music". And whilst the Germans don't shy away from starting wars, they seem ill-inclined to think up new words; their vocabulary consisting as it does of a mere 45,000 very long, but largely similar-sounding words.

If we look at the numbers of people who use our mother tongue as their first language, the figures are equally impressive. Our planet currently boasts over 370 million English-speakers, (not including the countless millions who use it as a second language); more than twice the number who speak French and German put together. Let the barmy Brussels bureaucrats stick that in their pipes and smoke it.

But the real beauty of English lies neither in the number of words in its lexicon nor in the number of people who speak it. It lies in its constant evolution ~ its ability to adapt itself to our changing times; its perennial willingness to absorb new words and phrases.

When I was a young man, if I met a fellow in a lavatory who told me he was "gay", I would have congratulated him and shaken him by the hand. These days, I imagine an altogether more sordid event would take place. Similarly, if during my youth I had asked a lady if she would like to "split a kipper" with me, she may indeed have joined me for breakfast. Today she would, quite rightly slap me across the face and call the police. And if during the war I had ordered one of my men to "rim my helmet", I would expect him to ensure that my military headgear was in good order for a forthcoming parade. Were I to issue the same command today, I expect that his eyes, and indeed mine, would pop out of their sockets.

So you can see that in order to avoid such awkward and unnecessary misunderstandings, it is important to keep up with all the changes that take place in this constantly-evolving language of ours. And that is where this book comes in.

The Magna Farta is an up-to-the-minute reference collection of all the newly-accepted words and terms that have been welcomed into the ever-changing fold of our vocabulary, and I cannot recommend it highly enough. I carry a copy with me wherever I go, and it has helped me out of many embarrassing situations in shops, on buses and in homosexual nightclubs around the world.

Bdr. Sir Hercules
Lethbridge Stewart

Brigadier Sir Hercules Lethbridge-Stewart,
KG, GCVO, CB, CBE, MC, LNER.
Marrakesh, October 2007

Aa

aardvark's nose *n.* An uncircumcised *zucchini.* An *anteater, tickle tackle. 'Then God spake unto Abraham in a loud voice, saying, Any uncircumcised male, who has still got an aardvark's nose, will be cut off from his people; he has broken my covenant.'* (*Genesis*, Ch. 17 v 14).

abattoir floor *n.* A particularly untidy *snatch*. Slightly *grimmer than a butcher's dustbin;* much grimmer than a *butcher's window*.

ABC *abbrev.* The Anus Bollock Connector. See *barse, tintis, notcher, Finsbury Bridge, taint etc.*

Abdul's special sauce *n.* A thin, red, oddly metallic-tasting liquid occasionally found in *badly-packed kebabs,* which usually ends up smeared round the mouths of hungry gents after closing time on Saturday nights.

Aberdare tic-tac *n.* An anabolic steroid tablet, after the South Wales town where every young man between the ages of nineteen and twenty-four eats them like sweets.

abfab *1. abbrev.* Common contraction of the title of the TV comedy show *Absolutely Fabulous. 2. n. acronym.* A lady who has such a *lovely personality* that, when she is viewed from the waist down, it is impossible to tell which way she is facing. Unless you can see her feet. Arse Both Front And Back.

a bit more choke and she would have started *exclam.* Humorous expression to be used after one has just launched a particularly loud and/or prolonged *air biscuit.* Also *a confident appeal by the Australians there.*

abnormal load *n.* An *arse* so large it necessitates a motorcycle outrider.

abra-kebabra *n.* A magical illusion performed after a night on the *piss*, whereby a kebab is made to disappear down the performer's throat, only to reappear a short time later on the back of a taxi driver's head.

abrowsal *n.* Embarrassing state of penile semi-hardness seen in the trousers of gentlemen casually flicking through *jazz mags* whilst ironically laughing and shaking their heads or when browsing the top shelf *art department* in a newsagents or motorway services.

abseiling *n.* The act of masturbating whilst using a *dildo* in one's *anus.* From the similar coordinated two-handed action required, not to mention the fact that there is a good chance the emergency services may have to be called out to rescue you at any moment.

ACAB *acronym.* All Coppers Are Bastards. Popular knuckle and forehead tattoo amongst members of the urban underclasses.

accessories *n. Tits. 'Miss Jolie's outfit is set off with a lovely set of accessories.'*

access time *1. n.* In computing, the time taken between requesting and receiving data. *2. n.* In foreplay, the time taken for a woman's *blip tap* to produce sufficient *moip* to allow a gentleman to penetrate her smoothly without feeling like he is scraping his *giggling stick* on the Great Barrier Reef.

ace of arse *n.* The patch of dark skin around the *anus,* frequently shaped like the ace of spades symbol, which forms the target of cosmetic bleaching.

ace of hearts *n.* A sheet of used *bumwad* that informs the wipee that his *nauticals* have been ruptured by an excessively large or firm *Bungle's finger.*

acid splashback *n.* The subject of a fleeting, paranoid sensation experienced by a person sitting on a recently disinfected *khazi,* fearful that a sudden spout of *turd*-propelled bleach might dissolve their *anus.*

Acker Bilk *1. n.* Neatly-goateed yokel clarinettist who rose to prominence during the trad boom of the 1960s, releasing eleven Top 50 singles, including the plaintive, chart-topping *Stranger on the Shore,* and who won the 1962 Best Actor Oscar for his part in the classic film *Band of Thieves. 2. n.* A meticulously well-kept *minge* of the sort often seen in *jazz mags.* A *fanny* that is trimmed to a sharp point and wears a striped waistcoat and bowler hat.

acne carriage *n.* The preferred conveyance of the sort of spotty-complexioned gentlemen who effect backward-facing caps. Usually an Escort Cabriolet or Citroen Saxo.

a confident appeal by the Australians there *exclam.* Phrase which should be amusingly delivered in the voice of Richie Benaud following a raucous *shout from down under.* An antipodean twist on *a bit more choke and she would have started; you're only supposed to blow the bloody doors off.*

acorn *n.* A little *bell end* nestling forlornly in the *pubage* of a fat German naturist.

acrotwat *n.* One who, after copious consumption of *giggle water,* becomes possessed by the spirit of The Great Wallenda and is compelled to attempt feats of derring-do upon scaffolding, public statuary *etc.* Usually with comically fatal results.

action man's hand *n. medic.* A condition symptomised by manual paralysis, brought about by excessive or prolonged masturbation.

activitity *n.* A "hands on" style of *mammary management. Come in Tokyo.*

Adam Ant, give her an *1. v.* To inscribe a white line across a lady's face using one's *naughty paintbrush,* in a style reminiscent of the briefly popular eighties pistol-waving dandy highwayman's makeup. To *lob ropes* over the bridge of a *bird's* nose. 2. v. To lob a car starter motor through her front window.

Adam's bridge *n.* The bit of skin between a lady's *gash* and her *freckle.* The *tinter, carse, taint, twernt etc.*

address the speaker of the house *v.* To *suck* off the *honourable member for Pantchester.* To engage in *horatio.*

add-to-basket bride *n.* A lifelong partner and soul-mate acquired via a touchingly romantic and secure internet transaction. *'Have you met my add-to-basket bride, vicar? Her name escapes me for the moment, but I'm pretty sure it begins with a vowel.'*

admiral's in port, the *exclam.* Phrase shouted aloud when one finds that someone has left an unattended *dreadnought* at anchor in the *chod bin.*

adult *adj.* Something to have *one off the wrist* at, on or over *eg.* adult channel, adult magazine, adult phoneline, adult text messages.

ADW *abbrev.* All Day Wank. A 24-hour trip to the *Billy Mill Round-*

about with no hand signals. Something to do if you're a lighthouse keeper or Apollo Command Module pilot at a loose end or when an elderly and much-loved member of the royal family dies and they put the telly off.

aerial assault *n.* An act of *horatio* given to a man whilst he is standing on a chair, due to the lady being unable to kneel down, *eg.* when she is wearing party clothes, a wedding dress, a spinal brace *etc.*

aeroplane blonde *n.* A dark-haired female who dyes her hair blonde, *ie.* she is equipped with a "black box".

afterburner *n.* A pyroflatulatory *anal announcement.* A *blue streak, St. George's ruin.*

after dinner bint *n.* A *bird* you only lets you *fuck* her after you have taken her out to dinner.

after dinner speech *n.* A hearty bout of flatulence following a particularly large meal. Delivering an after dinner speech is considered good etiquette in some cultures, such as Humberside.

Agatha Christie *n.* A silent, putrid *fart* committed by someone in this very room, and only one person knows whodunnit.

aim Archie at the Armitage *euph.* To *point Percy at the porcelain.*

airbag *n.* A budget airline stewardess who looks like she's parachuted out of the ugly plane and hit every cloud on the way down.

air bags *n.* Huge breasts which can leave you temporarily deaf. *Oomlaaters.*

air biscuit *n. Fart, botty burp.* A floating body of *trouser gas.* *'Could you open a window, Your Highness? I think your mother has launched an air biscuit.'*

airbrakes, disengage the *v.* To discharge the first *horse & cart* of the morning.

air buffet *n.* A lingering, gaseous meal which is more nourishing than an *air biscuit*, and to which one may make several visits.

airburst *n.* A *jedi* that explodes on contact with the atmosphere, leaving the *pan* with the texture of a Wall's Feast ice lolly. A *flock of pigeons*, a *space shuttle.*

air lingus *n.* A sexual position adopted by soft porn *jazz mag* lesbians, where one is just about to lick the other one's *twat.*

air onion *n.* A *fart* that makes the eyes water.

air sitar *n.* A twangy *trouser cough* with a distinct Bollywood influence.

air tulip *n.* A delightfully fragrant *gut,* of the sort that would be *dropped* by Lady Di, Audrey Hepburn or Grace Kelly. But not Jocky Wilson.

airwolf *1. n.* Helicopter-based TV series indistinguishable from helicopter-based TV series *Blue Thunder. 2. n.* A terrible howling sound heard after a night *on the pop.* A particularly predatory *jam tart.*

air your guts *v.* To *puke.* To *shout soup.*

Alan Johnston's vegetable patch *n.* A *ladygarden* that isn't as bad as *Terry Waite's allotment* by any means, but would nevertheless benefit from an afternoon's work with the shears to bring it up to snuff. From the BBC journalist who was kidnapped in the Gaza Strip and spent several months chained to a radiator while his parsnips went to seed.

alans *rhym. slang.* Ladies' *undercrackers.* From Alan Whicker = knicker. *'Come on, love, fair's fair. I bought you six pints of Younger's and a bag of scratchings, so get your alans off.'*

alarm cock *n.* Apparatus which springs into action first thing every morning, and can be used by a man to wake up his spouse. Usually by sticking it up her *arse.*

albatross *1. n.* A large seabird with a 12-foot wingspan that is said to bring good luck to sailors. *2. n.* A *grumble flick* sexual position featuring five men and one woman flapping about.

Albers pitstop *n.* Leaving the toilet with your *cock* still hanging out of your trousers. From the farcical episode halfway through the 2007 French Grand Prix at Magny-Cours when Spyker driver Christijan Albers exited the pit lane with half the fuel rig hanging off his car.

alcofrolic *n.* A frivolous yet ultimately regrettable act of *carnival knowledge* which is embarked upon whilst *heavily refreshed. 'I'm sorry, love. She meant nothing to me. It was just an alcofrolic.'*

alcoholiday *n.* A sojourn from which one doesn't bring back any memories.

alcohologram *n.* A fascinating multi-dimensional optical illusion which usually occurs round about the eleventh pint of *wifebeater.*

alcopocalypse *n.* The morning after a smashing night *on the pop* feeling like one has just been strafed by helicopter gunships.

alcopoop *n.* The loud, smelly, life-affirming *shit* you have the next morning after a heavy night *on the razz,* which quite often contains your hangover. An escape sub.

alcopopscotch *n.* The nimble pavement-hopping required to avoid stepping in brightly-hued vomit when proceeding down Preston Road, Hull, or similar streets throughout the land, on a Friday night.

alcotroll *n.* A woman who looks *fugly* even through high-powered *beer goggles.*

al dente *1. adj.* From the Italian, meaning "to the tooth" or "to the bite". A poncy way of saying "just so", when referring to the precise way that one likes to cook one's pasta. Not a problem that arises, of course, if one gets one's spaghetti out of a dented tin, and eats it cold with a spoon because one's gas has been cut off. *2. adj.* Middle class, but well hard.

ale force winds *n.* The toxic siroccos which blow through *cack canyon* the morning after a night spent getting *hammered* on brown beer. Ale force winds which measure highly on the *Beaufart scale* may occasionally be accompanied by an unexpected fall of *ale stones.*

alehouse ball *n. sport.* In Sunday League football, a mindless punt which is lumped vaguely forward with no clear idea as to its purpose or intended recipient. *'And a right alehouse ball from Ronaldinho, there. A complete waste of... Fuck me! The buck-toothed cunt has scored!'* (John Motson, June 2002).

alehouse tan *n.* The healthy, florid complexion and broken facial veins sported by the dedicated *turps nudger, eg.* tramps, regional newsreaders and sundry eminent Premiership football club managers.

alements *n. medic.* Any symptoms caused by a night on the pop. *Binjuries.*

alesheimer's disease *n. medic.* Premature senility and memory loss of memory brought about by excessive imbibition of beer.

ale stones *n.* A downpour of marble-sized *tods* after a night spent quaffing Younger's Scotch Bitter.

Alfred *n.* An itchy *cock.* Named after the "master of suspense" film director Alfred Hitchcock, who was well known in Hollywood for having an itchy *cock.*

Alf's nose *euph.* Term used to describe the state of a fellow's *giggle stick* following prolonged immersion in water. From the sad, wrinkled proboscis of the TV alien puppet. *'I've got a right Alf's nose after that swim, I can tell you.'* (Captain Matthew Webb, Calais, 25th August 1875).

Alka-Seltzer *n.* The involuntary fizzing of a female's *parts* when she becomes aroused.

all at sixes and fours *adj.* Descriptive of a mixed up chap who is equally happy with *rice or chips.* Bisexual, derived from the scoring opportunities available to a snooker player who doesn't really care whether he pots the *pink* or the *brown.*

allotment *n.* Anywhere that isn't the allotment, *eg.* the pub, the bookies, the dog track. *'I'm off to the allotment, love. Have you done me a clean shirt?'*

all cisterns go *exclam.* A hearty cry from the toilet cubicle after the launch of a particularly hefty *escape sub.* Often to be heard the day following a heavy session *on the hoy.*

all threes *n.* Naturally-assumed *self abuse* position, balanced on one hand and two knees, adopted when one's *noddy book* is placed on the edge of a bed or sideboard.

almond *1. rhym. slang.* Penis. From almond rock = cock. *2. rhym. slang.* Socks. *3. n.* An imperial measure of *spongle*, approximately one stomach full. Derivation unknown.

almond flakes *n. Mandruff, dried taddies.* Also *mammary dandruff.*

almosturbate *v.* To stop halfway through an act of sinful *self-pollution,* either to avoid being caught or as part of an attempt to summon up a modicum of enthusiasm for a *poke* when one really isn't in the mood. To practise *wankus interruptus,* to *stir the tanks.*

ambassador's hedge *n.* An immaculately-trimmed *bush.*

ambassador's reception *euph.* A visit to the toilet involving the expulsion of a pyramidal pile of small, nutty *rabbit tods,* similar in appearance to the famous all-night-garage-gift chocolates which were popular with visiting foreign dignitaries in the 1980s.

ambisextrous *adj.* Descriptive of a happy shopper, that Is to say one who is able to *bat for both teams.* Half rice half chips.

American tip *1. n.* A piece of advice given by someone from the USA. *2. n.* A short *rubber johnny* that just covers the *herman gelmet* and prevents the *wanked-up spunk* going on the hotel sheets.

American trombone *n.* A *spit roast.* A horny trio of two men - usually Premiership footballers - and one woman, who plays the *pink oboe* of one of the men, whilst the other strikes up the *double bass*.

amidships *euph.* A polite term used by cricket commentators, vicars and public school nurses to describe the *knackers* and *cock*. *'Ooh, Aggers! That delivery was pitched long, swung back in from middle and off and caught him squarely amidships.' 'Yes, Johnners. The poor cunt must be in fucking agony. More cake?'* (*Test Match Special*, Radio 3).

anal announcement *n. Fart, chuff, beefy eggo, trouser trumpet.* A *rumpet voluntary*.

anal boot *n. milit.* An army barracks forfeit whereby members of a platoon spit into a glass of beer before another stirs it with his *cock*, after which it is poured down the cleft of another's *arse* into the mouth of the unlucky loser of a bet.

anal delight *1. n.* A soft, light, fluffy chocolate or butterscotch-coloured pudding served in a large porcelain bowl. *2. n.* Pleasures taken in *tradesman's practices*.

anchor man *1. n.* A puce-faced, be-wigged alcoholic who reads the news from behind a desk because he is in no fit state to leave the studio and file a report whilst standing up. *2. n.* The first link in a multi-person *bum chain*.

anchovy's fanny *n.* The *fishiest* of all possible *suppers*.

and Bully's special prize *exclam.* Comical preamble to announce the impending arrival of something that sounds more like a motorboat than it does a caravan.

and if you've just joined us *exclam.* Said as if addressing an unseen camera on a topical chatshow. A convenient phrase which can be used to fill in awkward conversational silences, for example during a tea party to which Chrissie Hind, Bernard Matthews, Simon Weisenthal, David Irving, Germaine Greer and John McCririck have been invited.

Andrex runway *n.* The long strip of *arsewipe* stretching from *pubes* to throat on a *relaxing gentleman's* prone body that provides a landing strip for his airborne *jizz*. A *wank runway*.

an excellent theory, Dr Watson *exclam.* A humorous quip which can be used immediately after someone has *dropped* a very loud *Exchange & Mart*. Also *a confident appeal by the Australians there; you'll have to buy that now, you've ripped it*.

angel *1. n.* Spin-off series from *Buffy the Vampire Slayer. 2. n.* A passive *puddle jumper*. A *buggeree*.

anger jam *n.* The sticky substance ejected from the *slag hammer* whilst watching a German *art film* with one clenched fist, a red face and gritted teeth.

angry *adj.* Of a gentleman, to be aroused into a state of tumescence. To have a *bone on*. *'Exhausted by writing of the Great Fire of London, I decid'd to retire early to my bedchamber, whenceforth I perchanced upon Flossy the maid, bent over the counterpane of my four poster bed. The sight of her thus did inflame the most base of my passions, and I fast became as angry as a rolling pin.'* (*The Diary of Samuel Pepys*, 1666).

angry pirate *n.* An unlikely sounding and quite possibly illegal sexual act whereby a fellow *shoots his mess* into his ladyfriend's eye and then kicks her in the shin. For some reason.

ankle chaingang *n.* A crowd of middle-aged ladies out on the town.

ankle spanker *1. n.* An extremely long *cock. 2. n.* A normal-sized *cock* on a man with extremely short legs.

annabels *rhym. slang. Chalfonts,* haemorrhoids. From thin former semi-personality Annabel Giles = farmers. *'Jesus your holiness, I'm getting some gyp off me annabels today, I can tell you.'*

Anne Frank *rhym. slang.* To masturbate. Whilst hiding in a cupboard for five years.

Anne Frank's drumkit *sim.* Used to describe something utterly useless that merely takes up space. *'That (insert name of over-priced footballer here) is about as much use as Anne Frank's drumkit.'*

Ant & Dec *n.* A popular *art pamphlet* photographic study, whereby the model displays her well-trimmed *minge* and *anus, ie.* a half-bald *twat* and a little *arsehole. 'Right love, that's the hamburger shots finished. Now roll over and I'll take a couple of Ant & Decs to finish off the film.'*

anteater *n.* An *aardvark's nose,* eager to get stuck into a mound.

anticibation *n.* The hopeful, *half-a-teacaked* wait of an excitable young man whilst he is watching a late night foreign film on BBC2 or Film 4, in the knowledge that these minority channels aren't averse to showing *tits, bums* and *fannies* as long as they are integral to the plot.

anus *n.* An offensive term for the *council gritter, brass eye or nipsy.*

anus horribilis *n.* An *arse* that looks like it hasn't been wiped for a year, *eg.* HM The Queen's, during the notorious twelve-month butlers' strike of 1992.

anybody injured? *exclam. interrog.* Humorous interjection following a particularly loud *horse and cart.* See also *an excellent theory, Dr Watson; what's that, Sweep?*

Anzac biscuit *n. Aus.* A *turd* full of disturbingly-recognisable lumps of food, slightly less appetising than the oat comestible of the same name.

apache *1. n.* Sex without a condom, riding *bare-back. 2. n.* Popular instrumental hit by 60s guitar combo The Shadows.

apeshit *1. n.* That which is flung at your granny in a zoo. *2. adj.* State of mental perturbation. *Fucking radgy.*

appendix tickler *n.* A *kidney stroker.* A bout of *backdoor work* up the missus's *chamber of horrors. 'Roll over, love. I fancy an appendix tickler tonight. You'll like it. Not a lot, but you'll like it.'*

apple catchers *n.* Generously-proportioned *dunghampers* for the more generously-*arsed* lady.

apple daft *adj.* Descriptive of the state of cerebral confusion achieved by *Harry Ramps* following *al fresco* consumption of cheap white cider.

apple grumble *n.* American *tug pamphletry.*

approach Dresden *v.* To experience a strong feeling in the *back body* that one will shortly be opening the *bomb bay doors,* in the style of a World War II pilot flying a fully-loaded Avro Lancaster towards the popular RAF target city. Possibly accompanied by the ominous sound of ack-ack and a certain amount of shrapnel.

Aquafresh *1. n.* A *skidmark* created on the inside of the trousers of someone wearing a G-string, *ie.* three stripes of two different colours. *2. n.* The thin red stripe down the length of a *tom tit*, caused by a bleeding *clackervalve*.

arabians *rhym. slang.* To have the *Gladyses*. From arabian nights = Earthas. The *Brad Pitts*.

arab stallion, hung like a *sim. Donkey-rigged, well endowed.*

archaeologist *n.* A curious gentleman with a preference for poking his *tool* about in historical *trenches* belonging to women of a certain age. One who is not averse to *meating the ancestors. A biddy fiddler.*

are you in there, Mr Hill? *exclam.* A jocular remark made to put people at their ease when someone has *launched an air biscuit* which smells like the late Benny Hill's flat did after the police broke down the door.

Argos biro, hung like an *sim.* Of a gentleman, to be endowed with a *gut stick* the size and shape of one of the famous catalogue shop's customer-insulting ballpoint pens. Descriptive of a chap who has a *cock like a bookie's pencil. eg. The Rt Hon Jack Straw MP.*

Argos it *v.* After splitting up with one's significant other, to mentally leaf through one's back catalogue of past sexual relationships because you simply can't be *arsed* to go out *on the pull*. From the advertising slogan of the endlessly depressing high street store; "Don't shop for it, Argos it."

argosm *n.* A joyless, spirit-sapping orgasm achieved using a catalogue.

argue with the colonel *v.* To suffer from gastric complications following a visit to a famous Kentucky-based fried chicken restaurant. *'Are you okay, love? You've been in there nearly three hours.' 'I'll be fine. I'm just arguing with the colonel.'*

aris *rhym. slang.* Convoluted rhyming slang for *anus*. From Aristotle = bottle, bottle and glarse = arse.

arisola *n.* The darker patch of skin which frames the *rusty bullet hole*. The rings around your anus.

Ark Royal landing deck *n.* Descriptive of the state of the U-bend in a student house *crapper. The starting line at Brands Hatch.*

arkwright *n.* A lady of easy affections and loose knicker elastic. One whose *twat*, like the South Yorkshire/Lancashire corner shop in the popular sitcom, is "open all hours".

Arkwright's till *euph.* Descriptive of an unpredictable and over-aggressive woman, who snaps at the slightest provocation and takes all one's money. Named after Ronnie Barker's dangerous-looking prop in *Open All Hours*.

arm and hammer *1. n.* Trade name of a brand of inexplicably expensive toothpaste which contains baking powder, for some reason. *2. n.* The two components required by a *wanksmith* before he gives a length of hot *pink steel* what-for on his scrotal anvil.

Armani & Navy *n.* Poorly-made imitation designer clothes purchased from a scouser in a street market.

armbreaker *euph.* A particularly vicious *hand crank*. *'What with* *excellent browsing and sluicing and a couple of armbreakers and what-not, my afternoon passed quite happily.'* (from *Wooster Wanks Himself Daft,* by PG Wodehouse).

armchair angler *n.* One who gets his tackle out in order to enjoy a spot of indoor fly fishing.

armtits *n. Bingo wings, dinner lady's arms.*

army and navy *adj.* Descriptive of one who likes his *bread buttered both sides. Half rice, half chips. 'Birthdays: Elvis Presley, swivel-hipped toilet-death rocker, 69; Shirley Bassey, fling-titted entertainer, 67; David Bowie, wonky-eyed army and navy pop star, 57.'* (*The Times*, Jan 8th 2004).

around the world *n.* Sexual practice which lasts considerably less than eighty days and costs about £25. *Anilingus.*

arrange the orchestra *v.* To make adjustments to one's *horn, wood-wind, string* and *brass* sections. To rearrange your *fruitbowl* through your trouser pockets. *Wind the clock, nip and roll, sort out the boys, tune the banjo, stir the stew, pop the mouse back in the house.*

arse *1. n.* The *Gary Glitter*, the *chuff*, the *nick*, the *tradesman's*, the *chamber of horrors*. The *an*s.* *2. exclam.* A negative reply, expressing denial. *'Did you or did you not, on or about the night of June the twelfth 1994, feloniously and with malice aforethought murder Nicole Brown Simpson and Ronald Goldman?' 'Did I arse'.* *3. v.* To *do*, up the *arse. 'Have you seen the new girl in accounts? I'd give her a right good arsing, I would.'*

arse about *v.* To have a bit laugh and carry on.

arse angel *n.* The dark, spread-winged patch of perspiration on the back of a jogger's shorts, or a driving instructor's trousers.

arse antlers *n.* That Celtic tattoo that dodgy *birds* seem to think is a classy thing to have growing out of the top of their *bum crack.*

arse baby *n.* A *ring ripper*, a *dread-nought.* A huge *turd.*

arse bar *n.* Unappetising *bum toffee* confection.

arse barnacles *n.* Unremovable *winnets* on which the fingers of the right hand can be keelhauled. *Miniature heroes.*

arsecons *n.* Of e-mails and phone texting, resourceful use of punctuation to illustrate the condition of someone's *jacksie*, *eg.* normal *arse* (-!-) lard *arse* (-!-) tight *arse* (!) sore *arse* (-*-) slack *arse* (-0-) etc. *Arse* icons.

arse cress *n.* Spindly anal vegetation that doesn't get much light. The hairs that attach the *winnets* to *Dot Cotton's mouth.*

arsed *adj.* The state of being bothered. *'CEDRIC: Come onto the balcony, Lavinia. The moon is so terribly, terribly enchanting this evening. The stars are twinkling like the lights in your eyes when you laugh. LAVINIA: (off stage) In a bit. I can't be arsed at the minute.'* (from *Don't Put your Daughter on the Game, Mrs Worthington* by Noel Coward).

arse fairy *n.* A bit like the tooth fairy, only instead of removing milk teeth from under your pillow and leaving small amounts of cash wrapped in toilet paper behind, she miraculously changes the missus's smashing, firm bottom into a flabby wide one when you're not looking. *'Bloody hell, love. The arse fairy's been, so I'm leaving you.'*

arse feta *n.* The barely-edible cheese that forms inside Clive James's trousers on hot days.

arse fuse *n.* The first tab of the morning, the lighting of which precipitates a sudden and breathtaking pyrotechnic display.

arse glue *n.* A particularly spicy cuzza that, once eaten, has the unique property of sticking one's buttocks to the *chod bin* for most of the following day.

arse grapes *n.* Haemorrhoids, *farmers, Chalfonts, Emmas, ceramics.*

arsehole *1. n.* The *dirtbox,* the *tea towel holder. 2. sim.* Measure of the roughness of someone or something. *'That Jordan is as rough as arseholes without her make-up on. When she's got it on she's as rough as fuck.' 3. n.* Descriptive of a person with a character comparable to that of Jimmy Carr or Dave Lee Travis.

arseholed *adj.* Completely *wankered. Shit-faced.*

arsehole farm *n.* A golf course.

arse ker-plunk, play *v.* To squeeze an *Exchange & Mart* out when you know there is a danger of *following through* at any moment. To *pull out a straw* and hope you don't *drop a marble.*

arse labour *v.* The agonising cramps which indicate it is time to give birth to *Meatloaf's daughter. 'Was I really going that fast, officer? I'm terribly sorry, only we've been out for a couple of arse glues at a well-known Newcastle upon Tyne curry restaurant, and my wife has gone into arse labour.'*

arse like a brake light *sim.* Of one's *ringpiece,* to be enjoying the benefits of last night's *Ruby Murray. 'Come to the Curry Capital, Bigg Market, Newcastle upon Tyne. You'll get a warm welcome, a hot curry and an arse like a brake light the next morning - or your money back!'* (Speech to the United Nations, Abdul Latif, Lord of Harpole).

arse like a Tetley tea bag *sim.* Descriptive of a *ringpiece* the morning after sinking a powerful vindaloo. From the old television advert in which, to the accompaniment of a voiceover by Barnsley's greatest son Brian Glover, a tea bag was suspended in mid-air, boiling water was poured onto it, and red hot, steaming brown liquid flooded out. An *arsehole* that feels like it's got two thousand perforations.

arse like a wind sock *sim.* A well-*bummed shitter.*

arse like the top of a sauce bottle *sim.* A less-than-clean rectum. A *nipsy* where slight spillages and leaks have dried *in situ,* and which will have to be picked clean.

arse mail *n.* A miasmatic special delivery which may take two or three minutes to reach each person in the room. The contents of one's *whiffy bags.*

arse man *n.* One whose *boat* is *floated* by ladies' *buttocks* in preference to their *gams* or *thruppennies.*

Arsenal are at home *euph.* Of a *bird,* to be *up on blocks, chasing the cotton mouse, dropping clots, smoking short cigars* etc. Arsenal can be replaced by any football team who play in red.

Arsenal sock, fanny like a *sim.* Descriptive of one of those 2-foot long, bright red, knitted vaginas that smell of feet and liniment.

arse on, to have a *v.* To have a *monk on*. To be in a huff or bad mood. *'There once was a man with an arse on / Who went to take tea with the parson / He was in such a mood / He refused all his food / That stroppy old cunt with an arse on.'* (from *The Book of Fucking Nonsense* by Edward Lear).

arseovoir *n.* The little indent just above a builder's *arse* that holds about half a pint of sweat. The *bum cruet*.

arse pips *n. Winnets, tagnuts, dangleberries.*

arse piss *n.* Diarrhoea, *rusty water, anal fire water, Jap flag juice*.

arse-ritis *n. medic.* Affliction affecting long-term jobseekers which is characterised by stiffness in the buttocks and legs. Usually caused by sitting down all day watching *American Chopper, Mega Machines, Monster Garage* and *Massive Engines* on the Discovery Channel. And then again an hour later on Discovery +1.

arse spider *n.* A tenacious, well-knotted *winnet* that cannot be removed without bringing eight spindly hairs with it.

arsetex *n.* Public lavatory bowl render. Also known as fartex.

arse Tourette's *n. medic.* Comedy disorder of the lower alimentary canal characterised by sudden, repeated bowel movements and uncontrollable, involuntary anal vocalisations. Particularly prevalent amongst the elderly, the infirm, and recent visitors to the Curry Capital, Bigg Market, Newcastle upon Tyne.

arse tramp *n.* A *cleft*-dwelling vagrant who hangs around in the bushes long after his pals have been moved on by the prudent use of *bumwad*. A tenacious *dangleberry*.

arse vinegar *n.* The acidic contents of the *arseovoir*.

arse wasps *n.* A swarm of aggressive, imaginary insects that attack and sting your *anus* after a particularly spicy meal. Indian killer bees.

arse weasel *n.* A long, flowing *cack* that tickles the *nipsy*.

arse whisperer *n.* One who has the magical and rare ability to quieten down a lift full of people by silently *dropping a gut*.

arse wig *n.* The *tagnutty* halo of hair around the *gammon ring*.

arsewipe *1. n.* Bathroom tissue, *bumwad, shit scrape. 2. n. pej. US.* Contumelious epithet for a *tosser*. Often pronounced as "asswipe", because they're not very good at English.

art department *n.* The newsagent's top shelf, where the proprietor keeps magazines which are of particular interest to connoisseurs of the undraped female form.

artful as a supermarket butcher *sim.* Descriptive of a woman who makes the best of her limited visible assets by presenting herself appealingly packaged whilst simultaneously concealing what lies beneath. From the similar skills of a superstore butcher, who takes a slab of old mutton and, with careful manipulation, disguises the fat, hairy bits and gristle so that it looks like an unblemished morsel of tasty lean meat.

art pamphlet *n.* A *jazz magazine, bongo periodical* or *noddy book*.

Any one-handed reading material.

artichoke *n. Aus.* Ugly *slapper*.

asbopolis *n.* A claimant-rich conurbation such as Liverpool or Manchester, which boasts a vibrant youthful culture of noncomformist behaviour.

Asda rollback *n.* A crafty *self-harm* opportunity taken advantage of by a *tescosexual* during the *wank window* whilst his missus is out at the supermarket buying his tea.

asdas, legs like *sim.* Expression which can be used waspishly when referring to a lady who is generous with her favours, *ie.* one whose legs, like those of the sexually promiscuous supermarket, are "open twenty-four hours".

aslan *n.* Typically sexist, male description of a woman who has the hair of a lion, the face of a witch and the body of a wardrobe, *eg. fugly,* frightening, feminist icon the late Andrea Dworkin.

Aslan is on the move *1. exclam.* A popular line from one of them Narnia books, in which the presence of a big lion is announced. 2. *exclam.* Something to say the day after a big curry, when your stomach emits a huge roar and you have to run to the *crapper* before your entire digestive system ends up in your underpants like a big steaming pile of wildebeest entrails.

ass *n. US.* That part of the body the *whupping* of which indicates a comprehensive victory, and of which the invitation to kiss is often rhetorically made.

assets *n. journ. Charms.*

asstrash *n. US.* Rectal garbage.

ASWAD *1. n.* Lightweight 80s reggae band formed by Doughnut or somebody off *The Double Deckers. 2. acronym.* A Slash, Wank And Dump. A multi-tasking *chod bin* visit.

at a loose end *adj.* Descriptive of a fellow who is *relaxing in a gentleman's way. 'Why is there spunk all over the walls, floor and ceiling, Jeffrey?' 'Sorry Mary, I was at a loose end.'*

at it *adj.* To be engaged in copulation like knives. The use of this term is restricted to disapproving neighbours. *'Tssch. Sounds like those two next door are at it like knives again.'*

ATM *1. abbrev.* A cashpoint. Probably an abbreviation of Automatic Till Machine or something like that. *2. abbrev.* Anal To Mouth. A self-explanatory activity apparently much-favoured by aficionados of the sort of *grumble flicks* which rarely get shown on Channel Five. *3. abbrev.* Similarly, a dirty lady. From Arse Then Mouth. *'Blimey. That Fiona's a right ATM, isn't she?'*

atomic mutton *n.* A mature woman trying to look younger than she obviously is and ending up looking like a *tart* in the process, *eg.* Liz McDonald out of *Coronation Street* or Floella Henshaw in *Two Pints of Lager and a Packet of Crisps*.

auditioning the finger puppets *n.* A single act, one woman show which is not suitable for children. *Gusset typing, Kit-Kat shuffling.*

augustus *n.* A homosexual. A *botter.* From *Charlie and the Chocolate Factory*, where Augustus Gloop got stuck up the chocolate pipe.

auld lang syne *n.* A frankly unlikely crossed-hands *circle jerk* in a porn cinema.

auntie *1. n.* Affectionate term for the BBC coined by the BBC. *2. n.* An elderly *gentleman who is good with colours.*

auntie's round *exclam.* Euphemistic reference to *a visit from Aunt Flo.*

aunt mary *n.* A lady's hairy *fadge. A judith.*

Aussie kiss *n.* Similar to a *French kiss* but performed *down under.*

autograph the gusset *v.* To allow the newly-born *turtle's head* to countersign one's *bills.*

avril *n.* The lavatory. Named after the popular singer Avril Latrine.

awaken the bacon *v.* To sexually arouse a lady's *puh-seh.* To turn on the *blip tap* prior to a *Dutch breakfast.*

away win *n.* An adulterous episode which happily goes undetected.

axle grease *n.* A budget lubricant used in *grumble flicks. Hockle flobbed* onto a *herman gelmet* before it gets pushed in.

Aztec two-step *n.* Diarrhoea dance along the lines of the *Tijuana cha-cha* or *Turkish two-step. Sour apple quickstep. 'Tonight, Bruce, Anton will be performing the Aztec two-step, as he had some dodgy boil-in-the-bag prawn chimichangas he bought at a car boot for his lunch.'*

Bb

babia majora *exclam. US.* Phrase uttered by Americans upon sighting a gaggle of *flange* or a *flange* of *quim* at a public gathering, such as a clambake or lynching party.

baby birding *n.* In the world of *grumbular* cinematography, the jostling of two or more *stick vid* starlets hungry to get a mouthful of the same tasty *worm*.

baby gravy *n. Spaff, speff, spongle, spungle, spangle, heir gel.*

baby's arm *n.* Descriptive of a substantial penis, *ie.* one that is a good ten inches long with a bend in the middle. Sometimes covered in jam and usually holding an apple.

baby's dinners *n. Assets, air bags, norks.*

baby-sham *n.* The weedy ejaculate of a vasectomy victim. *Decaff jitler.*

bacardi bruiser *n.* An inebriated lady who elects to fight rather than to cry.

bacardigan *n. Tart fuel* version of the *beer coat. 'Are you sure you'll be warm enough walking along Whitley Bay seafront during a blizzard in November wearing just those skimpy Kylie shorts and a spangly boob tube?' 'Oh yes. I don't notice the cold when I've got me bacardigan on.'*

Bacardi geezer *n.* A bloke who quite inexplicably chooses to quaff *tart fuel* as his favourite tipple.

Baccus Marsh *n.* A *dobber, lazy lob-on*. From the spongy area halfway between *Melbourne* and *Ballarat.*

baccy pouch *n.* An overgrown *mapatasi.* A *pant moustache*, a *St. Bruno.*

bachelor's boomerang *n.* A rock-hard sock found under the bed or sofa cushion of a gentleman who is not in a steady relationship. *A midget's surfboard, Mother Shipton's sock.*

bachelor's collar *n.* Unbroken ring of *cheese* round the neck of the *bell end,* indicative of enforced sexual continence, poor genital hygiene, or most likely a combination of both. *Cliff's ruff.*

bachelor's newsletter *n.* A *tug pamphlet.*

backbench rebellion *n.* A rectal revolt, often experienced following a night at the Curry Capital, Bigg Market, Newcastle upon Tyne. *'I thought you said you were ready to leave.' 'Sorry love, I've just had an unexpected backbench rebellion. I might be another ten minutes.'*

back beauty *n.* A woman who appears to be attractive from behind, but when seen from the front is a bit of a horse. *Back beauties* form a staple joke in Benny Hill's oeuvre. A *backstabber, golden deceiver.*

back brace *1. n. medic.* A *Meatloaf's daughter* of such length, girth and consistency that, prior to its delivery, you are unable to bend or flex your spine and are forced to adopt a standing posture and facial expression reminiscent of an outraged Frankie Howerd. *2. n. medic.* Gentleman's orthopaedic device employed in order to rectify the debilitating effects of over-optimistically attempting a *thirty-four-and-a-halfer. 'Excuse me, do you have any back braces in stock?' 'I'll just go and have a look, Lord Archer.'*

back catalogue *n.* Material which one has brought out before. And is plastered all over the bowl of one's *chod bin* with loads of flies buzzing round it.

backdooral *n.* A type of unhygienic behaviour involving bottoms and mouths. *Around the world.*

back door boogie *1. n.* In heterosexual relationships, the ritual dance which accompanies a game of *hide the salami* when observing *canine rules*. *2. n.* In homosexual relationships, the theme tune for *Pot Brown.*

backeye *n.* The *brown eye.*

backfire *v.* To *fart* with sufficient volume to startle a police horse.

back garden *n.* That place, situated at the rear of the premises, where the more vertiginously-inclined horticulturalist may till the soil, sow his seed and keep a selection of rusty bicycles. The *podex* or *council gritter.*

back gwats *n.* See *back tits.*

back on 3s and 4s *adj. medic.* Assessment of one who has returned to a state of defecatory normality following a (possibly curry-induced) period of gastric upset. This is based on the Bristol Stool Form Scale, which doctors use to fit *Brads* into one of seven categories. 3 and 4 are considered healthy and normal.

back on solids *adj.* Descriptive of a woman who has recently been *drinking from the hairy goblet*, but who is now back eating *beef on the bone*. A cured lesbian.

back one out *v.* The act of *reverse parking your breakfast*, usually involving much looking over the shoulder, grunting and sweating.

back passage *n.* Rear exit and/or entrance.

back pocket rocket *n.* A *turd* that shoots out of your *arse* at speed and disappears round the bend, leaving no trace whatsoever and making you wonder whether you did a *crap* at all or if you just imagined the whole thing. A *ghost shit.*

back scuttle *1. v.* To *scuttle* from the back. *2. n.* A *scuttle* from the back.

back seat driver *1. n.* Car passenger who offers useful advice and helpful tips to the driver. *2. n.* Gentleman who puts his *sixth gearstick* up someone else's *exhaust pipe*. A *botter* rather than a *bottee.*

backstabber *n.* A *stegular* woman who practices a cruel deception on men. A *back beauty.*

backstage pass *1. n.* In the showbiz world, a token which allows one privileged access to the behind-the-scenes areas of a theatre or similar place of entertainment, usually obtained by *sucking off* a fat, bearded man in a Hawkwind T-shirt. *2. n.* Permission from one's ladyfriend to give her an *appendix tickler. 'I don't know why she's got the hump. The way she was acting, I was sure I had a backstage pass.'*

backter *rhym. slang.* A lady's *front bottom*. From back to front = cunt. *'Oi, Fatty. Careful near me backter with that champagne bottle.'*

back tits *n.* On the more pie-loving lady, the folds of fat which spill over the rear panels and fastenings of her bra, giving her the appearance of having *knockers* on her back.

backwards burp *n. Fart, air dump, tree monkey.*

backwards compatible *1. adj.* In the world of computers, a term guaranteeing that one bit of equipment or software will work with another, older piece of equipment or software. Not that it will. *2. adj.* In the world of *uphill gardening,* prepared to be the wheelbarrow rather than the earthy chap pushing it from behind.

back wheels *n. Bollocks, balls. 'What a gob, Your Royal Highness. You've even managed to get my back wheels in.'* (Peter Sellers overheard behind a hedge at Kensington Palace).

bacne *n. medic.* Dorsal pustules, spinal zits. *'Excuse me, Lord Archer. Would you like me to scrub your bacne for you?' 'No thank you, Mr Big.'*

bacon bazooka *n. Pork sword, spam javelin, mutton musket.* The penis.

bacon belt *n.* The perennially unstylish lardy spare tyre visible between the fashionable hipster jeans and modish crop top of a fat *bird. Muffin tops.*

bacon strips *n.* Female external genitalia, presumably with the word 'DANISH' printed on in blue ink. A *ragman's coat.*

badass *1. adj.* A street term descriptive of the sort of splendid moves made by an accomplished dancer. *2. adj.* A street term descriptive of the excellence of a *motherfucker. 3. n.* Street term describing an *arse* afflicted with *farmers.*

Bader *v. medic.* To suffer temporary legular paralysis brought on by sitting reading the *Autotrader* on the *chod bin* for an excessive time. A complaint named after the tin-legged World War II fighter pilot Sir Douglas Bader. Often accompanied by *Bombay birthmarks.*

Bader's balance *n.* The semi-leaning, stiff-legged posture adopted by a *relaxing gentleman* as he approaches the successful climax of a *Hilary.*

badger *n. Minge.*

badger loose *euph. RAF.* An air force issue *air biscuit. "I say, Ginger,' cautioned Biggles, sniffing the air. 'Smells like number two engine is on fire.' 'No, that's me,' confessed Algie. 'I've just let a badger loose."* (from *Biggles Follows Through,* by Capt. WE Johns).

badger the witness *v.* To *wank.* During a recess in court.

badger's ballbag, face like a *sim.* Phrase used to describe something or someone not very attractive. *'I wouldn't say my wife's ugly, ladies and gentlemen, but when they were designing the Royal Wedding stamps, the Post Office accidentally printed a picture of a badger's ballbag on them instead of her portrait, and no-one noticed.'* (HRH the Prince of Wales addressing the Royal Institution of British Architects Annual Dinner, Mansion House 2005).

badger's drift *n.* The *smelly bridge, notcher* or *taint.*

badly-packed kebab *n.* An untidy vagina that only starts to look appetising after 10 pints. A *butcher's window,* a *ripped sofa.*

bad thrower *n.* A *puddle jumper,* one who is *good with colours, not the marrying kind.* A *heemasex.*

badunkadunk *n. onomat.* A big *arse.*

bag ladies' period *sim.* Unpalatable. *'Don't buy Mrs Timpkin's home made jam, vicar. I've tasted nicer bag ladies' period.'*

bag *n. Slapper, boot.*

bagbird *n.* An attractive young *bag lady.*

bag for life *1. n.* A grubby old sack picked up at a supermarket which will accommodate your meat and veg for the foreseeable future. *2. n.* A grubby old *bird* picked up at a nightclub who doesn't mind accommodating your *meat and veg.* The wife.

baggage boy *n.* Of *pooves* and *poovery*, the opposite of a *pillow biter.* A *backseat driver.*

baggage handler n. Unpleasantly sexist term for a fellow who is not too fussy about the quality of his *cockwash* arrangements. Also *dog handler.*

baggage handler's arm, cock like a *sim.* To have a *chafed chap* due to excessive *self discipline* or sexual intercourse. From the similarity to the injuries suffered by airport luggage operatives as they poke their forearms through the zips of partly-opened suitcases feeling for cigarettes, booze, cameras, wallets, porn, ladies' underwear etc.

bagging *v.* Discreet public lavatory *cottaging* technique involving one participant standing in a shopping bag to mislead any *tit-head* peering under the cubicle door.

bag it up *v.* To perform the preliminary preparations for a *posh wank* on one's *old fella*; that is to say, to don a *jubber ray* or *American tip.*

bag of slapped twats, ugly as a *sim.* Not conventionally attractive, facially inept. Descriptive of one who looks like *she's fallen off the bells at Notre Dame.*

bag of slugs *n.* A particularly slimy *mingepiece. 'Jeeves answered on the first ring. 'What-ho, old chap,' I said. 'Fish out those French letters from my dressing table, there's a fellow. I'm out with the Duchess of Worcester and I've just got my fingers off her. By Jove, it was like putting my hand in a bag of slugs."* (from *I'm Coming, Jeeves!* by PG Wodehouse).

bagpeel *n. medic.* The condition suffered by men on hot days, symptomised by the *ball bag* glueing itself to the inner thigh, necessitating awkward, Jack Douglas-style leg spasms to separate the two.

bagpipe *v.* To ignore the *pink* and the *brown*, and instead shove the cue straight into the top corner pocket. To have armpit sex, *Hawaiian muscle fuck.*

bagpuss *n.* An old, fat, furry *cunt.*

bagsy *v. legal.* An make an assertion of claim upon something, based solely upon the legal precedent that the one who speaks first has primary rights of ownership. *'Right. Bagsy me the Sinai. Yous lot of had it since the Six Day War in 1967. It's not fair.'* (Anwar Sadat, Israeli-Egyptian Summit, 1978).

bahdumb bahdish *1. n. onomat.* The sound of a drummer pointing out where the jokes are in Jay Leno's script on the *Tonight Show.* 2. *n. onomat.* The sound of a *Sir Douglas Hurd* leaving your *nipsy* and momentarily later hitting the water in the *pan.*

bahookie *n. Scot. Arse.*

baibhe *n. Gaelic.* Rough old *slapper. Bag.*

Bailey's mouthwash *n.* Of a lady, to *horate* a gentleman friend with her gob full of ice cubes.

Bailey's moment *n.* A situation whereby an otherwise straight gentleman chooses to indulge in an act of *puddle jumpery.*

bairn brine *n. Baby gravy.*

bairn's sock, it's like trying to get a roll of carpet into a *sim.* Gentleman's generally somewhat hyperbolic excuse for not wearing a *jubber ray*.

bake one *v.* To not go for a *shit* when you really ought to. *'How was Glastonbury, dear?' 'I'll tell you when I come out the shitter, mum. Only I've been baking one since last Wednesday'.*

Bakerloo breeze *1. n.* The pungent wind that precedes the London underground train moments before it exits the tunnel. *2. n.* The pungent *wind* that precedes the *cocoamotive* moments before it exits the *bonus tunnel.*

baker's impatience *n. Potter's wheel.*

Bakewell *rhym. slang.* A *dropped hat.* From Bakewell tart = Exchange & Mart.

bald-headed hermit *n.* A long-winded way of saying *cock*. Also *bald man.*

bald man *n. Kojak, Captain Picard, Spurt Reynolds* etc. The penis, the *old man,* the *chap.*

bald man in a boat *1. n.* A lady's *clematis*. The *wail switch*. *2. n.* A hairless fellow esconced in a waterborne craft.

Balham ballet *n.* The intricate, yet graceful movements of an inebriated tramp on any South London high street.

Balkans *n.* In British *Carry On* films, a vague euphemism for the testicles, *bollocks.* Also the *Urals*, the *Balearics*.

ball *v. US.* To *poke, nob, bang.*

Ballarat *n. Aus.* A fully-erect penis. See also *Lake Wendouree, Baccus Marsh*. *'Are you ready yet Bruce?' 'Almost there, Sheila. I'm nearly at Ballarat.'*

ball bag *n.* Bag in which *balls* are kept. The *nadsack, knackersack* or scrotum.

ballbearings in a condom *sim.* Descriptive of an older woman's saggy *knee shooters* whilst she's on top.

ball bumpers *n.* Cosmetically enhanced lips, as worn by Brian's late mum off *Coronation Street* and, less attractively, by former Homebase ad queen Leslie Ash.

ball buster *1. n.* Unpleasant neighbour who puts a garden fork through your football when you kick it over the fence. *2. n.* A sexually-aggressive female. A *cock chomper*.

ball glaze *n. medic.* The clear, colourless solution secreted by the *clockweights* which gives the tadpoles something to swim in. Also *guardsman's gloss, perseverance soup, dew on the lily.*

balloon animal boobs *n.* Amusing, squeaky, odd-shaped breasts.

balloon knot *n. Ringpiece, chocolate starfish, Dot Cotton's mouth.* A puckered *gazoo.*

ballrooms *rhym. slang.* Diarrhoea. From the Sweet song Ballroom Blitz = Brads.

balls *1. n.* Testicles, those miniature, spherical *spunk* factories a gentleman keeps in his *chicken skin handbag.* *2. n.* Courage, guts. *'I like him. He's got balls.'* *3. exclam.* Denial. *'Has he balls got balls!'* *4. exclam.* Rubbish, nonsense, poppycock. *'Balls! Of course he's got balls.'* *5. n.* Round things you play football with.

balls deep *adj.* Of a *pork sword,* buried up to the hilt. The maximum *length* which it is possible to *slip* someone. In a *sausage and doughnut situation*, the greatest extent to which the *sausage* can *fuck* the *doughnut. In up to the apricots, in up to the maker's nameplate* etc.

ballseye *exclam.* Director's cry of approbation heard on pornographic film sets, coinciding with the starring male thespian managing to successfully *chuck his muck* directly into the eyeball of his lady counterpart. *'Well done, Gunther. Ballseye!'*

balls like bats' wings *sim. medic.* Descriptive of deflated, leathery testicles, a condition often accompanied by insanity, blindness and stunted growth. *Knackers* that have been *wanked* flat.

balls-on *advb.* Used primarily as the adverbial function of adjective modifier, usually in the superlative, *eg. 'My Porsche is balls-on fast.'* or *'Have you tried Red Bull? Man, that shit is balls-on!'*

ballsworth *n.* An imperial measurement of *spunk* volume, approximately half an ejaculation or one-fortieth of an *almond* avoirdupois.

ball tampering *1. n.* Evil, despcable act performed upon the seam of a cricket ball which could well lead to the downfall of civilization. *2. n.* Evil, despicable act performed upon the seam of a scrotum which could well lead to being placed on the sex offenders' register.

bally heck *exclam.* Wartime form of *bloody hell used* when swearing was rationed. Strong expletives and eggs were reserved for soldiers on the front line.

baloobas *n.* See *bazoomas.*

balsa *n.* A semi-erect penis, resembling the soft texture of the popular model aeroplane construction material, opposite of *hickory dick.*

bampot *n. Scot.* Survivor of the mental health system. A *mentalist*, a *headbanger*, a *heed-the-baall.*

banana *rhym. slang.* Hampshire rhyming slang for *feeshus.* From banana split = shit.

banana hammock *n.* Skimpy *undercrackers* or swimming trunks. The male equivalent of *genital floss.*

banana yoghurt *n.* Not particularly healthy breakfast alternative to *porridge*, to either *swallow* or *spit.* Rich in *Vitamin S.*

B&Q *n.* A hurried act of furtive intercourse enjoyed in the spare room of one's girlfriend's parents' house. A *B&Q* is performed with a sock inserted in the lady's mouth, with a view to maintaining radio silence during the entire sorry, sordid business. From Brief and Quiet.

B & T *abbrev.* Cheap thrills which may be taken with a slice of lemon. *Bum* and *Tit.*

bandy *adj.* Of a female, to have a bit of a *froth on. 'That Issey Miyake after-shave stinks like shite, but it knocks the birds bandy, I can tell you.'*

bang *v.* To copulate like a *shithouse* door in the wind.

banger hangar *n. Sausage wallet, cock wash.*

bangers *1. n.* Things you stick up cats' *arses. 2. n. Carry On*-style *tits.*

bangers and mash *1. n.* The heaps of half-dissolved bumwad, human excrement, used *fanny nannies* and what-have-you which are often to be seen adorning the tracks at railway stations. Not, as a passenger, that you get the impression that anyone has ever managed to successfully flush a train toilet. *Rat's banquets, Radcliffe's sleepers. 2. n.* The contents of a well-used but badly-flushed *bog*, the *bangers* being the *turds* and the mash being the *bumwad*. Usually found in the public conveniences of pubs, campsites and non-stop coaches to Spain. *"Cinders and ashes, Thomas, your coaches are a disgrace,' cried the Fat Controller. 'There are used tickets on the floor, soot all over the windows and Clarabelle's cludgy is full of bangers and mash."* (from *Thomas and the Dyno-Rod Man* by Rev W Awdrey).

Bangladeshi bagpipes *n.* A musical instrument played in curry house toilets throughout the land. Also *Bombay bagpipes.*

bangles *1. n.* All female pop group consisting of one *fox* and a pack of *hounds*. *2. n.* Particularly delicate parts of the *crown jewels*. The *orbs*, rather than the *sceptre.*

bangover *n.* The hangover headache that, temporarily vanquished by the act of love, returns with all its mates at the moment of *stackblow.*

banjo *1. n. US.* Musical instrument played by inbreds in the deep south, that makes a twanging sound when plucked. *2. n.* The thin ridge of skin on the penis connecting *Kojak's roll-neck* to the *bobby's helmet*, that makes a twanging sound when plucked. The *guy-rope*.

banjo cleaner *n.* Of ladies' dentition, that gap between the two upper front incisors which effectively scrapes detritus from a gentleman's *banjo* during *horatio*. Guy Ritchie has one of the cleanest *banjos* in showbusiness.

banjoed *adj. Pissed-up, wankered, arseholed, shitfaced, rat-arsed.*

banjo pills *n. medic.* Viagra. *Cock drops, mycoxafloppin.* Also *blueys, Bongo Bill's banjo pills.*

banker *n.* A lady, spotted upon entry to a nightclub, who one thinks will be a certainty should all other attempts to *pull* fail.

banker's draught *n.* Eminently-civilised flatulence emitted from the bottom of a pinstriped city gent. A *dropped bowler hat.*

bannistered *adj.* To be in a state of extreme *refreshment,* to the extent that one has to be carried home by two friends. Derived from the state that record-breaking athlete Roger Bannister got himself into after crossing the finish line after running the world's first sub four-minute mile.

bannocks *1. n.* Unappetising Scottish bread buns. *2. n.* Unappetising Scottish *knackers. 3. exclam.* Expression of anger or frustration. *'Aw Bannocks! A've just dropped a fuckin' ha'penny doon the drain. Bang goes oor dinner, children.'* (Cartoon by Phil May, *Punch*, 1896).

BANT *acronym.* Big Arse No Tits.

banty *n.* One who nods at *stoats*.

bapdog *n.* An ugly *bird* with a cracking pair of *tits, ie.* one who has *hefferlumps.*

bap happy *adj.* The stunned, bemused state that one enters having overdosed on *meat vids, bongo mags* or the Bravo Channel.

baps *1. n.* Soft bread rolls. *2. n. Tits.*

baptism *1. n. Chestular rope-lobbing.* The act of *bespangling* a pair of lady's chests. *2 . n.* Psychological term for a defining stage in the development of a chap's *headlamp* fixation. *'Patient Z first developed his taste for large breasts during lactation, and has thenceforth gained excitation throughout his life from both seeing, sucking and fondling large breasts. I call this moment his 'baptism' as a bubby man or bap-fancier.'* (from *Das Psykologikken Geprinkipelschaft auf den Stonkenjubblies* by Sigmund Freud).

barber's floor *n.* A particularly hairy *quim.*

barber's lather pot *sim.* A generously filled *snatch.* Also a *billposter's bucket,* a *St. Bernard's chin.* A very, very, very *well-buttered bun. 'My daughter is a groupie for So Solid Crew.' 'Good heavens! She must have a twat like a barber's lather pot.'*

barber's lolly *1. n.* In childhood, a reward given for sitting still whilst one's hair is cut. *2. n.* In adulthood, a reward given in return for performing any unpleasant task. *'Suck that? Alright, but you'll have to buy me an expensive barber's ticket afterwards, your Grace.'*

barber's pole *n.* The stripy result of *parting the whiskers* while the *painters are in*. An *eggy soldier*.

barber's sandwich *n.* A badly-pruned *muff,* from its resemblance to a buttered bap inadvertently dropped onto the unswept lino in a hairdresser's.

Barclay's *rhym. slang.* A *J. Arthur.*

barf *v.* To *vomit, huey, puke, bowk, yoff*.

barf bag *n.* Sick bag, as found on an aeroplane. Also a useful alliterative insult.

bargain *rhym. slang.* A *cuntish* fellow. From the popular daytime TV show, *Bargain Hunt*, which was originally hosted by popular orange *bargain* David Dickinson although it's now hosted by that spivvish *cunt* with a bow tie.

bargain bucket *n.* An over-employed and overstretched *clopper*. A *mary* like a *welly top*.

bargain munter *n.* Term for a lady who is yours for as little as one or two drinks, *ie.* one who is literally "cheap as chips".

barge-arse *n.* A lady of rotund posterior aspect.

bargoyles *n.* Hideously ugly female pub fixtures.

bark at the ants *v.* To *yoff.*

barker's egg *n.* Poodle *shit*. A dog *turd* so old that it has gone white.

bark carrots *adj.* To *park a tiger*, to *vomit, puke, sing a rainbow, barf.*

barking spider *n.* The *ringpiece, freckle, chocolate starfish, rusty sheriff's badge, nipsy*.

barn door gentleman *1. n. Aus.* Term used by early antipodean settlers to describe clumsy fellows. *'In Sydney, the idea of some barn door gentleman, an untutored hayseed, big-booting nervously about the drawing-room and breaking the china, filled the matrons with horror.'* (from *The Fatal Shore* by Robert Hughes). *2. n.* A *heavily refreshed* gent who dispenses with the customary niceties on his return home, braying through the letterbox, punching walls, throwing his tea at the wall, *pissing* in the sink *etc*.

Barnes Wallis *n.* The type of *turd* released from the *bomb bay* which sends a splash of water onto your *undercarriage*. A *panbuster*.

barney rubble *n.* That which, in a good natured protest, is torn up from pavements, walls *etc.*, and *hoyed* at the *tit-heads*.

Barney Rubble's car *n.* An enormous pile of *logs*.

Barnsley briefcase *n.* A Netto, Aldi or Kwiksave carrier bag carried into work each day by one who is employed as a professional call-centre operative in the salubrious South Yorkshire hell-hole. The typical contents of a Barnsley briefcase include a triangular, prepacked sandwich, a bottle of Oasis, a copy of the Sun and a biro which pokes out the bottom of the bag. Not to be confused with a *Basingstoke briefcase*, which is a carrier from Waitrose, Sainsbury's or some other upper class establishment.

Barnsley moustache *n.* A tide mark of *fanny batter* resembling the facial hair sported by youths of the eponymous northern beauty spot. Caused by an accumulation of *blip* during vigorous *cumulonimbus*.

Barnsley shag *n.* An act of sexual intercourse which climaxes not with an orgasm, but with the bloke falling asleep *on the job* due to a surfeit of booze.

Barry Gibb *n.* The *carse*. Because it is situated between a *cunt* and an *arsehole*.

barse *n.* The little bit of skin between a chap's *bannocks* and his *freckle*. The *great*.

barse mallow *n.* A light, pink fluffy substance that forms spontaneously in a *salad dodger's tintis*. A sweet-toothed counterpart to the more savoury *arse feta*.

bar stool *n.* An habitual drinker's *turd*, typically a thin, sickly *arse weasel* that slides out and lies forlornly in the water feeling very sorry for itself.

Barthez *1. n.* Former Manchester United goalkeeper. *2. n.* A bald *twat*.

Bartlett's dilemma *n.* A gentleman's happy bedtime conundrum. From the scene in *The Great Escape* when Bartlett (played by Richard Attenborough) has to decide which of the three tunnels to send his chaps down.

barumph *v.* To sniff a lady's bicycle seat. To *snurgle*.

base pissing *n.* The extreme sport of urinating from a great height for the purposes of entertainment, *eg.* off a cliff into the sea, off a bridge into a river or out of a tree onto a cow.

bash *n.* A woman's *fanny*.

bashing booth *n.* A small room or cubicle where a gentleman may sit in quiet, solitary contemplation of a live *jazz* performance. The working environs of a *jizz mopper*.

bash the bishop *v.* To *pull the Pope's cap off*, to *box the Jesuit*. To *bank with Barclay's*.

Basildon bagpipe *n.* An Essex-based development of the *trombone*, whereby the lady sucks the gentleman's *clockweights* whilst *tossing* his *charlie* with one hand and fingering his *freckle* with the other, causing him to emit a series of shrill squeaks and an unpleasant droning sound.

basket making *v. arch.* Medieval sexual intercourse. *Coccupational therapy*.

bastard *n.* A football referee.

baste the turkey *v.* Of dirty ladies,

to squeeze men's *bulbs* so that *hot fat* shoots out the end of their *cocks*.

bateau mouche *n. Fr.* A *dreadnought* that is so satisfyingly large one could easily imagine it being used to to take tourists along the Seine. A *pleasure steamer.*

bath bomb *1. n.* A ball of effervescent salts which fizzes when dropped into the water. *2. n.* An unfortunately-timed *evacuation* which can quite take the shine off an otherwise pleasant soak in the tub.

bathroom broadband *n.* The installation of a lengthy and unsightly dark brown or black *cable* in the bottom of the toilet bowl. A substantial *download.*

bathroom origami *n.* The ancient and beautiful oriental art of folding *bumwad* into complex geometric folds, pleats and creases in order to avoid getting all *shit* on one's fingers.

bathturbate *v.* To *polish the lighthouse, wax the dolphin,* play *up periscope.* To masturbate in the bath. Derivation unknown.

bat in the cave *n.* A precariously-suspended *bogie* that hangs upsettingly in someone's nostril.

Batman on the side of the Palace, like *sim.* Descriptive of something which sticks out a mile, such as Sharron Davies's splendid nipples during the Athens 2004 Olympic coverage.

batman's cave *euph.* A lady's *secret entrance* which is difficult to locate due to an over-abundance of *bush.*

batmobile *n.* Descriptive of the state of one's *brass eye* after a particularly hot *Ruby Murray. 'I had a real ring stinger at the Curry Capital last night. My arse is like the back end of the fucking batmobile this morning. Five stars.' (Guardian* food critic Victor Lewis-Smith, 2005).

bat on a sticky wicket *v.* To stir another gentleman's *porridge.* To partake of a *buttered bun.*To have *sloppy seconds.*

bats at dusk, to come out like *sim.* Of loose stools, to exit the *clay pit* at a ferocious rate. Descriptive of a *flock of pigeons* or the *splatters.*

batter catcher *n.* That small tuft of hair tucked under the bottom lip, for example the one sported by Sir Trevor McDonald or Tom Waits, which enables its owner to trap some of that pungent fishy juice for later.

battered kipper *n.* A frothsome *gash* on your old *trout.* A *blippy mackerel.*

battery tits *n.* Affectionate epithet for a *bird* with tiny *knockers.* From the battery and comedy bra size AA.

batting for both sides *euph. Bowling from both ends*, as opposed to just the *gasworks end.*

batting on a wet wicket *n.* Not being the *first man in. Stirring the porridge. Sloppy seconds.*

battleship rivets *n. Chapel hat pegs, JCB starter buttons, blind cobblers' thumbs.*

batty-boy *n. W. Indies. A tail-ender* who habitually serves his balls up from the *pavilion end.*

batty crease *n.* The line of whiting or chalk on a cricket pitch which defines the position of the batsman.

bat wings *n.* Thin, leathery, nocturnal flaps. *Beef curtains.*

baw bag *n. Scot.* Oor Wullie's scrotum. A tartan *chicken skin sporran.*

bawd *n. arch.* Old fashioned term for a *rub-a-tug shop* proprietress.

bawhair *1. n. Scot.* A single pubic hair. *2. n. Scot.* A *de minimis* unit of measurement. *'A quick look oer the shoulder a'fore ye pull awa frae the kerb, indicate tae pull oot, let the clutch oot a bawhair an' awa' ye go.'*

bay window over a tripe shop *n.* The *gunt.*

bazongers *n.* Gravity-defying, surgically-enhanced, hemispherical breasts that explode in aeroplanes. *'Look out the window, Pete. The people on the ground look like ants. Oh shit, me bazongers of exploded.'*

bazoomas *n.* See *begonias.*

BBBA *abbrev. medic.* The Bit Between the Bollocks and the Arse. The *barse,* the *ploughman's,* the *scruttock,* the *ABC.*

BBC *abbrev.* Big Brother Contestant. A person who appears pleasant enough at first, but who quickly turns out to be a right *spastard.*

BBLB *1. abbrev.* Big Brother's Little Brother. Television show fronted by Dermott O'Leary designed to wring the last dregs of phoneline money out of Channel 4's bovine reality show viewers. *2. abbrev.* medic. The painful result of sitting cross-legged in tight-fitting trousers for a significant time whilst fantasising about noshing the *tits/bush* off Orlaith from *Big Brother* 6, to pick an example entirely at random.

BDF *abbrev.* A festive *own goal,* brought about by excessive consumption of rich foodstuffs and ale. A Boxing Day Fart with all the trimmings.

bead curtains *n. Dangleberries, toffee strings, mud-buttons, tagnuts.* Also *beaded curtain.*

bead *v.* To exude pre-ejaculate during moments of arousal. *To perspire out of one's hog's eye. 'I tell you, Alan, I was that excited I was beading before I'd even parked the car.'* (Stan Collymore, Radio 5Live).

Beadle *1. n.* A *cunt* with a neatly-cropped bikini line. A *bushell,* a *Californian wax.* *2. v.* To fondle a pair of *Kelly Brooks.*

Beadlehands *exclam.* Alternative exclamation to *butterfingers.*

Beadle pint *n.* A half. Also known as a *Jeremy* of lager.

Beadle's fist *n.* A tightly-shrivelled or retracted scrotum.

beagle break *n.* A five-minute recreational interval at one's place of work which is spent on the *cancer verandah.*

Beaker's mouth *n.* The involuntary movement of a *bird's* vaginal lips when she is being taken up the *bonus tunnel,* as seen in many a *grumble flick.* Reminiscent of the movements of the Muppet character Beaker "me-mo-ing".

beanfeast *n.* A lesbian orgy. A *carpet munchers'* all-you-can-eat buffet.

bean flicker *n.* A lady of lesbicious tendencies. A wearer of *comfortable shoes, tennis fan, lady golfer.*

beans on toast *1. n.* A quick and yet satisfying snack. *2. n.* A quick and yet satisfying *tug. 'I'm just going to nip home for beans on toast.'*

bear bile *n.* Descriptive of any food or drink that is particularly unpalatable. *'Betty, this hotpot is* *like fucking bear bile, I said bear bile.'*

bear claw *n.* Late night, drunken, clumsy pawing at a ladyfriend's *honey pot,* possibly resulting in torn garments.

beard *1. n. arch.* Fulsome *twat-thatch, mapatasi. 2. n.* A woman who is married to a *batty-boy* in order to conceal his true sexuality. See *whiff of lavender. 'Do you reckon that Sophie's a beard then, or what?'*

bearded clam *1. n.* An edible mollusc. *2. n. Aus.* An edible *fish mitten.*

bear trap *n.* A big *cludge,* strong enough to snap a man's ankle if he put his foot into it. One might imagine that Pat Butcher out of *EastEnders* has a bear trap in her knickers, for example.

bear trapper's hat *n.* An excessively hairy *front bottom.* A *biffer,* a *Davy Crockett hat. 'Put my ladder up to the flat / Saw a nun with bear trapper's hat / I get a wank out of things like that / When I'm cleaning windows.'* (from *The George Formby Song Book,* 1945).

beast with one back, make the *v.* To perform an act of sexual intercourse whilst experiencing a fifty percent staff shortfall.

beast with two backs *n.* A strange, grunting animal with two heads and four legs, commonly found in Newcastle bus shelters, back alleys and taxi queues after midnight.

beat a donkey out of a bog *sim. Ulst.* A Northern Irish expression useful when describing something with roughly similar dimensions and proportions to a shillelagh. *'Have ye seen the size of the Pastor's cock? You could beat a donkey out of a bog with that fucker, so ye could.'*

beaten like a ginger step-child *adj.* Descriptive of a particularly ferocious and merciless thrashing, for example, off a bouncer at a nightclub, a policeman in a cell, or Bjork at Bangkok Airport. *'This is dreadful. I don't think Hawking can take much more of this punishment. Bruno's raining the blows down now, left right left right. I can't look, this is terrible. Hawking's being beaten like a ginger step-child.'* (Harry Carpenter, commentating on charity boxing match, *BBC Children in Need,* 1998).

beat the buzzer *v.* To impregnate one's wife in the week prior to the divorce coming through.

beat the meat *v.* To avail oneself of a *ham shank,* perform the *five-knuckle shuffle, pull your pud, fire the one o'clock gun etc.*

beaver *1. n. US.* Female pubic hair. *Gorilla salad. 2. n. coll. US.* An offensively sexist term used when referring to a group of *birds.* Also *blart, mackerel, fanny. 'Heavens to Murgatroyd. Check out the beaver in here, dudes.'*

beaverage *n.* That which is quaffed from a *hairy goblet.*

beaver cleaver *n.* Primitive male wooden weapon for splaying *beaver.*

beaver dam *n.* Ladies' personal feminine hygiene requisite. *Jam rag, fanny nanny, blobstopper,* large pile of tree trunks.

beaver lever *n.* A *flapjack.*

beaver paddle *n.* Bizarre act performed by a man mid-way through committing sexual intercourse with a lady, when he unexpectedly pulls out his *meat flute*, grips it in his hand and then slaps it repeatedly against his partner's *bodily treasure*. From the similarity to the way that the eponymous Dodd-toothed tree-noshing rodent of the genus *Castor* slaps its scaly tail against the water for a cheap sexual thrill.

beaver dam *n.* A bath plughole, when blocked up with the flotsam and jetsam of the wife's *minge*.

beaver's guts *n.* In the world of *art pamphlet* photography, that which is visible in a *close up pink* study. A *nipped sofa*.

beaver tails *n.* Long, flat *thrupenny bits* which resemble the unerotic, scaly tails of the eponymous wood-chomping animals. Also known as *socktits, spaniels' ears, NGTs*.

because you're worth it *exclam.* Waggish phrase to be used by a gentleman as he rubs his recently dropped *spooge* into his lady-friend's hair.

Beckham, do a *v.* To fail to *score*, despite every opportunity to do so.

Beckham penalty *n.* A *piss* which combines high speed and inaccuracy, hitting everywhere except its intended target. Often results in a *Queen Mum's smile*.

becksfart *n.* Brand-specific lager hangover flatulence. Has an aroma a bit like egg mayonnaise.

bed *v.* A tabloid term, to *fuck*. *'I went out with Tracey last night and ended up bedding her up the arse in the bus shelter.'*

bed bellows *n.* After dropping a post-bedtime *air biscuit*, the thoughtful act of wafting the quilt or blankets with one's leg in order to create a flow of air towards one's partner so that they may share its savoury aroma.

Bedford diff *euph.* A female rear end that has succumbed to the ravages of time. *'Bloody hell Fred, did you see that lass's arse? It was hanging down like a Bedford diff.'*

bed flute *n.* Woodwind instrument closely related to the *pink oboe* that responds well to double tonguing.

bed glue *n.* Liquid that adheres people firmly to their mattresses, especially students. Beer.

bedknobs and broomsticks *1. n.* Film starring her out of *Murder She Wrote* and that bloke out of *Mary Poppins* that looks like her out of *Murder She Wrote* wearing a false moustache, which stirs up Pavlovian feelings of boredom, resentment and uninterest in anyone who ever sat through an episode of fucking *Screen Test* in the 1970s. *2. n.* The early morning result of a low fibre diet.

bed muscle *n.* The *old fella*.

bedroom popadoms *n.* Large, dried *wankerchiefs*. *Porn crackers, wankers' crisps*.

Bee Gees bite *n.* The first mouthful of an extremely hot foodstuff, such as a Pop Tart or McDonald's apple pie, that causes the eater to involuntarily perform the falsetto "ah-ha-ha-ha-" intro to *Stayin' Alive*.

beef *n.* A hearty *brew*. A *beefy eggo*.

beef bayonet *n.* *Bacon bazooka, mutton musket, lamb cannon, luncheon meat howitzer*.

beef box *n.* A container into which *sausages* are put.

beef cloud *n.* A *fart* that smells like one has just opened a very old tin of Butcher's Tripe Mix dogfood or a fresh packet of Bernard Matthews' honey roast ham.

beef curtains *n. medic.* Of women's genitalias, those folds of skin known as the *labia majorcas*, or big lips. Or indeed *piss flaps*.

beef dripping *n.* The spreadable extract found in a *butcher's window*, traditionally used in the preparation of *fish suppers*.

beef encounter *n.* A romantic, one-off *bang*. A *hit and run*, a *none night stand*.

beef or salmon *1. n.* Name of the much-fancied horse which nevertheless ran a nightmare in the 2006 Cheltenham Gold Cup. *2. n.* Question asked of a person of indeterminate alignment in order to ascertain whether they eat *meat* or *fish*.

beef wellington *1. n.* Popular dish originally popularised by 19th century military hero the Duke of Beef. *2. n.* A rubber prophylactic device placed over a gentleman's *meat flute* to prevent babies and/or *the clap*. *3. n.* A *wizard's sleeve*, a *clown's pocket*. A voluminous *mary*.

beefy eggo *n.* A pungently carnivorous *Exchange & Mart*.

beerache *n. medic.* The painful afliction of the eardrum usually experienced after returning home *pissed* and late. Like tinitus, but with an annoying woman's voice instead of bells.

beer angel *n.* The unseen guiding force that watches over and keeps safe the inebriated as they stagger across all six lanes of the North Circular at chucking out time.

beer armour *n.* The invisible protective clothing that prevents injury on the way home from the pub by shielding the body from all sensation of damage on contact with the pavement.

beer baby *n.* A large booze-induced gut. A *Foster's child, verandah over the toyshop*.

beer callipers *n.* Miraculous leg splints which enable *wankered* stragglers to make their way home at closing time.

beer cancer *n. medic.* The sort of hangover that not only makes you feel utterly *shit*, but lasts so long that you suspect you may be genuinely ill. Shane McGowan has now been fighting a brave battle against terminal beer cancer for over twenty years.

beer coat *n.* An invisible, yet warm outer garment worn when walking back from a club at three in the morning.

beer compass *n.* A homing device that ensures your inexplicably safe arrival home after a night *on the pop*.

beer cones *n.* Invisible contraflow system surrounding a drunkard meandering up the road, allowing traffic to move freely around him.

beer degree *n.* A qualification attained after a sufficient intake of alcohol, which enables one to talk at length and with complete authority on any given topic.

beer facelift *n.* Subjective cosmetic surgical procedure which is only visible to *pissed up* men. *'Have you seen Bazza's new bird? He met her when she had a beer facelift and now he can't shake her off.'*

beer goggles *n.* Booze-fuelled optical aids which make *hounds* look like *foxes*.

beer graduate *n.* One who has

moved onwards and upwards in the beverage world. A gentleman who drinks such strong ales that his wife wakes up with two black eyes and a headache as well.

beer halo *n.* Alcohol-induced self-righteousness.

beer hunter *1. n.* A jolly drinking game whereby Chris Evans's employees are forced to open cans of beer into their ears from a six-pack, one tin of which has been shaken vigorously. *2. n.* A demented person who searches the house for a drop of booze in the early hours, *eg.* as Chris Evans has been known to do.

beeriod *n.* Twice-weekly malady suffered by men after a night *on the lash.* Symptoms include headache, mood swings and a bloated stomach. *'Leave me alone, woman, me beeriod started this morning.'*

beer lag *n.* The disruption to human sleep patterns encountered after intense lunchtime drinking which leaves one unable to keep one's eyes open for *Heartbeat*, but wide awake at two in the morning.

beerlarious *n.* Amusing only when drunk; specifically, putting a traffic cone on a statue's head.

beerloom *n.* Any item that one wouldn't ordinarily touch with a bargepole, but which suddenly seems irresistible when you go on eBay *pissed* out of your skull in the wee small hours. *'A Madness fruit machine? What on earth possessed you? How much did you pay?' 'Nearly three hundred quid. It's a fucking beerloom.'*

beero *n.* One who, fortified by several pints, is prepared to engage in acts of incredible heroism, *eg.* squaring up to doormen on the other side of the street, gesticulating at others in an abusive manner from inside a car travelling at speed.

beer miles *n.* Easy, cheap, long-distance travel made possible by the consumption of large quantities of ale.

beer monkey *n.* A mythical simian creature which, during a drunken slumber, sneaks into your bed, ruffles your hair, steals your money and *shits* in your mouth.

beer muffs *n.* Invisible ear defenders that attach themselves to a man's head after several pints, rendering him unable to hold a conversation without shouting or to watch TV at anything but full volume.

beer mugger *n.* The man you discover has hit you over the head and taken £35 out of your wallet the morning after you "nip out for a couple of pints".

beer pressure *n.* A benevolent psychological influence applied by drinking companions, encouraging one to consume more alcohol than one feels comfortable drinking.

beer queer *1. adj.* Of a normally heterosexual person, to be tempted to go *half rice half chips* when fuelled by sufficient quantities of *dizzyade. Booze bent. 2. n.* One who takes his drink the other way. A *teapot sucker.* A teetotaller.

beer scooter *n.* Miraculous method of transport employed when leaving the pub after drinking an elegant sufficiency of alcohol. So-called because one returns home seemingly in no time and at incredible velocity.

beer shoes *n.* Gloves

beer sniper *n.* An invisible marksman who silently "takes out" drunkards causing them to unexpectedly collapse in the street, fall off bar stools, *etc*.

beer stretcher *n.* A magical post-pub St John's Ambulance service. When *fully-refreshed* and lying down in the *Scotsman's lounge*, ditch or on the pub toilet floor, one is immediately whisked home on the *beer stretcher* to the comfort of one's own bed, to awaken in the morning with absolutely no memory of the journey. *'I came home on the beer stretcher, only I must have stopped off at the all-night garage because when I woke up there was a 50+ wank mag and an empty packet of scotch eggs on the bed.'*

beer thinners *n.* The pint of water one forgets to consume at the end of a long evening *on the pop*.

beer tent *n.* Jocky Wilson's shirt.

beer whistle *n.* At a football match, the signal given 10 minutes before half time that causes a mass exodus of gentlemen going for a pint, a pie, a *piss* or any simultaneous combination of the three.

beerwolf *n.* One who wakes up in unfamiliar surroundings with torn clothes, aching limbs, the taste of blood in his mouth and suffering from nightmarish flashbacks to terrible events which occurred the previous evening.

beer wood *n.* The thing that feels like an erection, but isn't, whilst attempting sexual congress under the influence of alcohol.

bee's dick *n.* The incredibly small distance, or period of time, which is needed in order to achieve an important outcome. *'I nearly finished the exam. I was a bee's dick short of finishing the last two questions.'*

bee stings *n.* Small *tits*. *Chestnuts, stits, tisn'ts*.

Beethoven's fifth *n.* A large, stirring movement of the bowel which may leave the performer deaf.

beetle bonnet *n.* Female pubic mound as viewed through tight garments. From the design of the VW car. *Camel's foot, camel's lip*, visible *knicker sausages*.

begonias *n.* See *bejonkers*.

behind with the rent *euph.* A polite way of explaining that one is a *good listener*. *'Mum, dad, I've got something to tell you. There's no easy way of saying this, so I'm just going to come straight out with it. I've had an idea for a television programme - It's a Royal Knockout. Oh yeah, and I'm behind with the rent.'*

bejonkers *n.* See *bouncers*.

Bela Lugosi's gob *n.* An *axe wound* which drips with fresh blood on a regular basis. A *jam sandwich*.

Belfast taxi *n.* Battery-powered shopping scooter for old people too fat or idle to walk. A *Disneyworld dragster*.

Belfast tickle stick *n.* A baseball bat, iron bar, length of four-by-two, *etc*.

Belgian *1. adj.* Of chocolates, twice as expensive as normal. *2. n.* In the world of sex, a spot of *ESD* or *ATM*. *Hot karl*.

Belgian biscuit *n.* Sexual practice of Flemish origin and costing over £100. Not to be confused with *Belgian bun*.

Belisha beacon *n.* Flashing orange globe on a black and white pole, named after the British Transport

Minister in 1934.

Belgian bun *n.* Walloon-based deviant behaviour which comes in at about £75. Not to be confused with *Belgian biscuit.*

bell *n.* A lady's *clit.* The *devil's doorbell,* found just above the *snail's doorstep.*

bell clapper *n.* An humungous dangling *turd* that tolls the *bummocks* as one tries to swing it loose.

bellefire *1. n.* A crappy manufactured girl group. *2. n. medic.* A *herman*-based symptom of *cock rot.*

bell end *1. n.* An amusingly-named tent. *2. n. medic.* The *bobby's helmet, bobby splithead.* The glans of the penis.

bell end brie *n. Brimula, fromunder, knacker barrel.*

bell housing *1. n. mech.* The flywheel/clutch cover on a car. *2. n.* The *fiveskin* on a gentile's genital.

bell rag *n.* A cloth with the specific designated purpose of removing *spodge* from under the *bridge.* The raw material from which *bedroom poppadoms* are forged by *wanksmiths.*

bell-swagged *adj.* To be endowed with a large *bishop's hat* on a contrastingly-small *jesuit. Mushroom-rigged.*

bell tower *n. Knob* shaft. *Bean stalk.*

bell wringing *v.* A harmless pastime that builds up the arm muscles, and has been popular with monks for the last two thousand years.

belly flopper *n.* A clumsy *brown trout* whose graceless entry into the water causes splashing of the *arse.*

belly warmers *n.* Big, droopy *tits. Overblaaters.*

belongings *n.* Word used in the badly-translated subtitles of an un-named Dutch/German *bongo vid* to describe the leading gentleman thespian's nether parts. *'That's right you whore. Take his belongings and put them in your mouth.'*

belt-fed mortar *sim. milit.* A measure of the sexual enthusiasm of a lady. See also *shithouse door in the wind, kangaroo shagging a space hopper. 'I bet she bangs like a belt-fed mortar.'*

Ben Jones *euph.* An act of *horatio.* A *chewie,* a *BJ.* Named after the Virgin Radio presenter. Also *Billy Joel.*

bender *1. n.* A prolonged drinking spree. An *all-dayer,* or *Leo Sayer. 2. n.* A crustie's tent. *3. n.* A *pinch of snuff.*

bender like Beckham *n.* A fellow who tries to emulate the fashionably androgynous mien of the publicity-hungry LA Galaxy midfielder, *eg.* wearing ladies' earrings, sarongs, makeup *etc.*, but who merely ends up making himself look like a right *puff.* A bit like David Beckham does.

bend one in *v.* To manage to commit sexual intercourse up a lady. *'She's well fit. I'd like to bend one into her, Cilla.'*

bend the elbow *v.* To go for a *beer goggles* fitting.

benefactor *n.* Of *farts* and *farting,* the selfless altruist who supplies it. Also known as the *donor.*

beneficiaries *n.* Those who benefit from the smelly largesse of the *benefactor's custard.*

benefit buddies *n.* The group of lonely OAPs and unemployable misfits who gather outside the

Post Office half an hour before it opens in the morning just to talk to one another.

benefit buffet *n.* In supermarkets, the shelves situated close to checkouts that bear a mouth-watering array of dented tins, loaves of bread with torn packaging, crushed crisps and almost out of date meat.

Benny Hill *rhym. slang.* A form of contraception. *'It's nothing to do with me, Mrs Gamp. You told me you was on the Benny Hill.'* (from *Nicholas Nickelby*, by Charles Dickens).

bent *1. adj.* Descriptive of a fellow who prefers not to walk through puddles. *Good with colours as a nine bob note. 2. adj.* Descriptive of a dishonest *scuffer.*

bentertainment *n.* The sort of TV programmes that only girls and *botters* watch, *eg. What Not to Wear, Sex & the City, Coronation Street etc.*

bepalmed *adj.* Of a jobseeker or student, to be marooned in that awkward hour or so when he's already *wanked* his *knackers* flat as a pancake, but it's too early for a drink. *In colimbo.*

Beppe's beard *n.* A severely but neatly-trimmed *bush*, named after the severely but neatly-trimmed chin growth of the former *EastEnders* character. A *clitler, Mugabe muff.*

Berkeley Hunt *rhym. slang. Quim.*

Berlin Wall *1. n.* Heavily-policed strip of no-man's land formerly dividing the forbidden East and free West halves of the German city. 2. *n.* The *taint, tinter, notcher, carse, biffon, scran, twernt, Humber Bridge etc.*

Bermuda triangle *n.* A mysterious area where *skin boats* full of semen seem to disappear. For two or three minutes.

berry *1. n.* A sexual deviant, a kinky person. A goddam prevoit. *2. n.* One who has *carnival knowledge* of animals. 3. *n.* A lady with a great body, but a less-than-pleasing face, *ie.* one who has the body of Halle, but the face of Chuck. *eg.* Sarah Jessica Parker. A *bobfoc.*

bertie *1. n.* A male homosexual. *2. n.* A *charlie. 3. adj.* Of a woman, to be blessed with morals as *slack as a brewer's cock.* From the spoonerism Bertie Ditch = dirty bitch. *'...or should he go for saucy number three, who sounds well bertie and takes it up the council?'* (Graham Skidmore, voiceover on *Cilla's Blind Date,* LWT).

Bertie Bassett's hat *n.* The small, unsatisfying, sticky nugget of dark excrement that drops to the bottom of an otherwise empty toilet bowl. *'No sign of Bertie, but he's dropped his hat.'*

Berwick Rangers' goalmouth 1. *n.* The badly churned-up sea of mud between the posts at Shielfield Park. 2. *n.* The badly churned-up sea of mud in the back of a pair of badly-*shitted undercrackers.*

bespectable *adj.* Respectable in glasses.

bet she can shit! *exclam.* Uttered to your mate under your breath as you pass a particularly keen *avoider of leaf vegetables.*

Betty Both *n.* A *happy shopper,* a *switch hitter. 'Yes, he is. I've heard he's a Betty Both and so is his wife.'* (Paul Lavers, unintentional live broadcast, Friendly TV, 2003).

Betty Swollocks *n.* Polite term for *knacker* discomfort. *'Forgive me, Your Majesty, whilst I adjust my doublet and hose. I have sailed the oceans these last six months and have not changed my codpiece since we left the New World. I fear I have the most awful Betties.'* (Sir Walter Raleigh, Audience with Queen Elizabeth I, 1584).

beverley *n. rhym. slang.* A lady's rigorously-depilated *bush.* Named after the formerly popular singer Beverley Craven = shaven haven. *'I couldn't believe my luck, nan. When I stuck my hand up her dress she wasn't wearing any knickers. And she'd got a beverley.'*

beverly hills *n.* Ridiculous, Californian-style silicon-stuffed *churns.*

bevvy *1. n.* A portion of *booze.* A quantity of drink. *2. n.* A number of beauties, although that might be spelled differently, come to think of it.

bezzing *1. n.* Vigorous chewing of the face after taking one too many *disco biscuits. 'Shit, these beans are good. I'm bezzing me tits off!'* *2. n.* The act of dancing like a drunken gibbon, in a similar fashion to Mr Bez out of the Happy Mondays pop group.

biddeos *n. Scud videos* in which the actresses look somewhat younger on the packaging than they do in the film itself.

biddy fiddler *n.* A fellow who prefers the company of ladies who are of sufficient maturity that they can ride the bus for free during off-peak periods. A *granny magnet.*

biff *n.* Poetic epithet for a lady's *bodily treasure. 'Cross your legs again, will you Sharon. The camera missed your biff that time.'*

biffer *n.* A particularly hairy *minge. 'Gaw, you've got a right old biffer on you there, Mother Superior.'*

biffie *n. Bog, shitter, dunny, cludgy. 'I'd give the biffie ten minutes if I was you.'*

biffin *n.* Perspiration which condenses in the *biffin bridge* area during coitus.

biffin bridge *n.* See *barse.*

biffing plate *1. n. Beetle bonnet, monkey's forehead. 2. sim.* That which is flat. *'Christ! This lager's as flat as Kate Moss's biffing plate.'*

biffon *n.* That part of the female anatomy between the *council gritter* and the *fadge,* which the man's *clockweights* "biff on" during intercourse. The *taint.*

big bamboo *1. n.* A chap's *old man.* *2. n.* In the film *Chitty Chitty Bang Bang,* a song performed by Dick Van Dyke. About his cock.

Big Ben *1. n.* A large bell in St. Steven's Tower, London. *2. n.* An enormous *erection,* possibly with Robert Powell hanging off it.

big boned *1. adj.* Of thin people with corpulent skeletons, suffering from an unfortunate medical condition that makes it look like they eat forty cakes a day. *Glands.* *2. adj.* What *donkey-rigged* men are, when they've got a *horse's handbrake.*

big brother is watching you *phr.* The *wood*-felling realisation, whilst watching a *scruff* video, that there is a photo of a grinning sibling on top of the TV set which must be laid face down before one can continue *relaxing in a gentleman's way.*

big cock day *n.* A day, quite possibly in spring, the arrival of which is greeted with the *dawn horn*, and throughout which the sap continues to rise. *'As he wrestled himself into his shreddies, D'Arcy knew it was going to be a big cock day.'* (from *Pride And Prejudice* by Jane Austen).

biggie smalls *n.* Fat lasses' knickers.

big mac *1. n.* A disappointing *hamburger*, consisting of two tired, grey pieces of meat, random, sorry-looking vegetation and traces of unidentified mayonnaise-like liquid. *2. n.* A high street fast food that looks and tastes like *1.*

bike *n.* A frequently-*ridden* woman, one who has had thousands of gentlemen swing their legs over her. Often prefixed with a location. *'You don't want to go near her, mate. She's the office/factory/ London Symphony Orchestra and Festival Chorus bike.'*

biker's highway code, thin as a *sim.* Reference to something which is notably slight. *'Strewth Marvin, I saw Tim Henman's grand slam record today, and it is as thin as a biker's highway code.'*

bikini burger *n.* A *vertical bacon sandwich*. See *hairy pie*.

Bilbo Baggins' foot *n.* An hirsute vagina, resembling the hairy toes of a hobbit.

bile mile *n.* The finishing straight of a marathon *spewing* session, where one's gallbladder is going flat out to produce something worth *yoffing*, but is frankly fighting a losing battle.

bilge tanks *n.* The "double gut" effect caused by an overly-tight belt on an overly-large belly, *eg.* Simon Bates.

Bill Grundies *rhym. slang. Undies, trolleys, dunghampers.*

Billingsgate banjo *n.* Something that a lady strums and which smells of fish. That'll be her *twat*, then.

Billingsgate box *n. Minge.* Based on a comparison between the smell of a cockney seafood market and a cockney *fadge*.

billposter's bucket *sim.* Large paste-filled *snatch. 'I was stationed in Scutari Hospital for six months, the only woman amongst thousands of soldiers. By the end of my first shift I had a twat like a billposter's bucket.'* (from *My Poor Cunt - The Crimean Wartime Memoirs of Florence Nightingale*).

bills *n. Shreddies, bills, dunghampers*.

Bill Wyman *rhym. slang.* A lady's *virgin string*. From Bill Wyman = hymen.

Billy Connolly's beard *n.* A *ragweek fanny*.

Billy Dainty *n.* The awkward, foward-leaning posture that a chap has to adopt in order to mask a *bone on* when making his way, for example, to the pub bogs. Named after the priapismic Happy Shopper Max Wall who played the cameraman on *Emu's Broadcasting Company*.

billy goat's mouth *n.* An exceptionally loose vagina. With bits of the Mayor's hat sticking out.

Billy Mill roundabout *n.* Climactic point of a bout of masturbation. From the climactic point of the A1058 Coast Road near Newcastle. The *vinegar strokes*. *'My mum walked in just as I was coming up to the Billy Mill roundabout.'*

Billy no mates *1. n.* A lonely little buoyant *turd* that remains hanging around in the *chod bin* after all the others have gone to the beach. *2. n.* A person bereft of close acquaintances.

Billy Two-Mirrors *n.* Affectionate nickname for one whose bones are so big that they need two mirrors in order to fully encompass their reflection. Also *Bessie Two-Mirrors. 'Oi, Billy Two-Mirrors. You forgot my McFlurry, you fat cunt.'*

Billy Wright *n.* Legendary Wolverhamtpon Wanderers footballer who married Vera Lynn or the andrews Sisters or someone, latterly immortalised as rhyming slang for *shite.*

bilp *n. Blip.*

biltrum *n.* The *chin rest.* See *wannocks.*

bimbo *n.* The likes of Jordan or Joanne Guest. A *tit-for-brains.*

bimboid *adj.* Appertaining to the likes of Jordan or Joanne Guest.

bingo armour *n.* The excessive amounts of tawdry jewellery worn by flabby-armed ladies enjoying a night frantically crossing out numbers in a former cinema. *Blingo, bingo clink.*

bingo bongo *1. exclam. zool.* The mating call of the male silverback western lowland gorilla *(Gorilla gorilla gorilla). 2. n.* Granny porn. *'Oi, mister. Give me a pack of Scotch eggs and a bingo bongo mag, will you? I'm off me face.'*

bingo partner *n.* A man who is engaging in a romantic dalliance with a somewhat older lady.

bingo top *n.* A lady's upper body garment, cut in such a way as to encourage men to cast their "eyes down" in the hope of a glimpse of *nork* and/or *Bristol Channel.*

bingo wings *n.* Upper arm adipose underhang found on post-menopausal ladies of a common bent. *Arm tits.*

binjuries *n.* Ailments acquired whilst in a drunken stupor, *eg.* griddle burns on the *arse* cheeks caused by falling onto an electric fire, to pick an example entirely at random.

Bin Laden's beard *n.* A particularly luxuriant, yet unruly *stoat.* The antithesis of a *Hitler tash.*

bin lid penny *euph.* A more extreme version of *half a crown thru'penny bit* for the more anally-flexible frightened person. *'I bet it was bin lid penny for Nick Ross every time the doorbell rang until they arrested Barry George. And after that too.'*

bin lids *n.* The areolae round a lady's nippular bits.

binorkulars *n.* Sunglasses as worn by the observant fellow at the beach. *Perv windows.*

bin ripper *n.* An *alcoholic womble.* One who finds his treasure amongst the things everyday folk leave behind. A *Harold Ramp.*

bint n. Derogatory term for a daft *slapper*, *eg.* Jordan or Joanne Guest.

binternet *n.* The world-wide electronic network which can apparently be used to view titillating pictures of young ladies in various states of undress.

bint imperials *n. Rocks* so hard that your *bird* could break her molars on them. But without the breath-freshening qualities of their confectionery almost-namesakes.

bio bling *n. Jelly jewellery. Pearl necklaces, spunky earrings* and the like. Also *Jizzie Duke*.

bird *n*. Outdated, offensively sexist way of referring to a woman. *'Phoar! Is this your new bird? She's a bit of alright, ain't she. Fantastic tits. What does she go like, then?'*

bird flu *n. medic.* Pre-*women's things* irritability. *Pre-rag radge, strawberry mivvie.*

bird sanctuary *n.* A place where women of the opposite gender can congregate, safe from the reaches of male gentlemen, *eg.* the bingo, the hairdressing salon, the cleaning products aisle at Tesco's.

birds' custard *1. n.* A sweet, gloopy substance that comes out of a tin. *2. n.* A savoury, gloopy substance that comes out of a lady's *clout. Blip, bilp, fanny batter.*

birdseed *n. derog.* Nickname for a henpecked fellow.

bird's trifle *1. n.* Popular proles' dessert containing several fingers and a lot of jelly, topped with custard and cream but frequently missing the cherry. *2. n.* A dirty lady's *letterbox.*

birdstrike *1. n.* In pilot circles, a high altitude pigeon or similar avian hitting the whirring fanblades of a jet engine, leaving everything covered with blood, minced guts and feathers. *2. n.* One's wife or girlfriend's monthly *moon juice* session, when she wheels her *fanny* into the hangar for a week's essential maintenance.

Birkenhead confetti *n.* Gravel.

Birmingham botox *n.* Budget cosmetic procedure, available in most Black Country pubs, which leaves one's face looking not unlike that of Sylvester Stallone's mum. A sound *pasting.*

biscuit *n.* A *turd.*

biscuits *1. n. UK.* the contents of the stomach after a heavy night's drinking. *'Get me a bucket, quick, Your Honour, I'm gonna chuck me biscuits.' 2. n. US.* Tight *buns.* Attractive *ass cheeks.*

bishop rage *n.* A *monkey spanking* performed with such vigour that one takes on the appearance of one of Francis Bacon's screaming Popes.

bishop's dick, stiff as a *sim.* Descriptive of the muscular and joint rigidity experienced after a 20-mile walk. *'With Striding Edge safely negotiated, I wearily descended the Victorian pony track down Birkhouse Moor with its fine views across to St. Sunday Crag. At the foot of the slope I crossed Grisedale Beck and joined the tarred road for the difficult last eight miles, finally entering Patterdale as stiff as a bishop's dick.'* (from *Coast to Coast the Miserable Way* by Alfred Wainwright).

bishop's licence *n.* That which is granted to a man left home alone by his wife, enabling him to *wank* himself blind at his leisure.

bishop's mitre *n.* A *bobby's helmet.*

bishop's waltz *n.* The practice of keeping one's threadbare old t-shirt held up over the chest with the chin and one's soiled tracksuit bottoms held out at the waist with the thumb of one hand, the other wrist dripping with fresh *kebab fat,* whilst waddling awkwardly to the toilet following an act of mid-morning *self pollution.* Also known as a *spangle dash.*

bismarking *n.* An act of love where a man strikes a lucky lady repeatedly around the chops with his *cock* for their mutual pleasure. Also *colting, salami slap.*

bisto skids *n.* The beefy stains left down the back of the *pan* after a night *on the sauce. Toilet snail* trails.

bit, a *1. n.* An imperial unit of *the other*, slightly less than an entire *portion. 2. n.* Unspecified quantity of sex, usually partaken *on the side.*

bitch piss *n.* Alcopops. *'A pint of Timothy Taylor's Landlord please, barman, and a bottle of bitch piss for the missus.'*

bitch tits *n.* Large, flabby breasts found on overweight males of any age. Particularly amusing when sported by obese American children on *Oprah. Triple-hearters, dog udders, moomlaaters.*

bitchwhore *n.* A woman who is not only a bitch, but is also a whore.

biting point n. The first tingly inklings down amongst the loins that a prolonged bout of *self help* might just possibly be about to prove worthwhile after all. *Fringles.*

biting the butter *n.* Going down to commit an act of *cumulonimbus* on a *plumper's clunge,* only to find the experience akin to that of biting into a warm, salty slab of Lurpak.

bit of fluff *n.* A singular piece of *totty*.

bit of rough *n.* A sexual partner, usually male, from a lower social echelon. One who would wipe his *cock* on a *bird's* curtains, *eg.* Mellors in *Lady Chatterley's Lover,* or HM The Queen's *tit*-feeling bedtime interloper Michael Fagan.

bitten by the brewer's horse *euph.* To be as *refreshed* as a Space Shuttle pilot.

bitterflies *n.* Mythical intestinal insects that flutter in the stomach when it's knocking off time and one can almost taste the first pint.

BJLs *abbrev.* Blow Job Lips. See *DSLs*

blaaters *n. Oomlaaters.*

black and blue menstrual show *n.* An unprovoked assault accompanying a particularly disputatious *tammy huff.* A bruising *blobstrop* encounter of noteworthy pugnacity, tempestuousness or excitability.

Blackbeard's ghost *n.* A triangular, white, spooky apparition occasionally glimpsed by the *one-eyed lookout* in one's *crow's nest.* A mature lady's once-raven *mapatasi*. A *fanny badger*.

black country urgency *n.* The performance of a task with dizzying slowness and ineptitude, in the style of a denizen of the West Midlands.

black forest shateau *n.* An overly-rich mountain of *feeshus* of the sort produced the morning after a night out on the Guinness.

Blackpool cock *n.* A pink, sticky erection upon which one's *bird* could break her teeth. And which would make her sick half way through.

blacksmith's apron *n.* A lady's substantial, leathery *front bottom.*

bladdered *adj.* See *blitzed.*

bladdertorial combat *n.* Vicious man-to-man duel, whereby a man attempts to drink more pints of booze than his comrades before having to relieve himself.

bladdiator *n.* A fellow who engages in *bladdertorial combat.*

bland job *n.* Being *tossed off* by a lass whilst so *pissed* that one can hardly feel it. See *no job*

blanket drill *n. Milit.* An early morning *mutton musket* practice that results in the loss of the *officer's mess*.

blanket ripper *n.* Back-draught in a *Dutch oven*.

blanket welding *n.* Under the covers heavy manual work involving *pink steel*, which may lead to blindness.

blart *1. n.* Vagina. *2. n. coll.* Women, *totty*. *'Golly gosh! This nunnery is heaving with blart'*.

blart attack *euph.* A strange feeling, starting in the *pills* and spreading down the right arm, upon finding oneself surrounded by a large quantity of top flight *cabbage*. *Acute vangina*.

blart gallery *n.* A pub containing wall-to-wall *totty*.

blarticulate *adj.* Silver-tongued; able to charm the *dunghampers* off the ladies. *'Blimey, that Russell Brand isn't half blarticulate. He stopped to ask me granny for directions and her knickers fell off.'*

blartist *n.* One who demonstrates unrivalled skills in the field of *blartistry*. *'Titian remains among the foremost blartists of his era, and few would dispute that the sublime nudes of his oeuvre constitute an unrivalled array of proper little minge winkers.'* (Brian Sewell, *Titian's Tiffins*, Evening Standard, August 2002).

blazing saddles *1. n.* Title of Mel Brooks's spoof Western, one scene of which involved a great deal of farting. *2. n.* The *ringpieces* of a group of men who have enjoyed a surfeit of *Edwina* the previous night, for example at the Curry Capital, Bigg Market, Newcastle upon Tyne, and consequently do a lot of farting. And *shitting* blood.

bleed the lizard *v.* See *siphon the python*.

bleed the radiator *v.* To commit an act of flatulation in which one would be well advised to hold a rag over one's *brass eye* to prevent sludge going all over the wall. A bit like when you have to sort out your central heating, only you don't have to spend twenty minutes emptying out the kitchen drawer looking for that little brass key.

Bleep & Booster *1. n.* Vaguely- remembered black and white *Blue Peter* science fiction series, voiced by the same bloke who did *Captain Pugwash*. *2. n.* The *ringpiece*.

bletherskate *n. Scot. Shit-for-brains, fuckwit, twat*. Literally meaning *bag of shite*.

blick *n.* Pubic scurf, *muffdruff*.

bliff mag *n. Rhythm journal, art pamphlet, noddy book*. A pornographic magazine.

bliff *n. Minge, front bottom*.

blimp *v.* To surreptitiously ogle ladies' breasts and *arses* from behind a pair of mirrored sunglasses.

blimplants *n. Knockers*, surgically-enhanced to comic proportions, as sported by the likes of Jordan and the late Lolo Ferrari. *Bazongers*.

blind cobbler's thumbs *n.* Large, well-hammered *nipples*. *Pygmies' cocks, chapel hat pegs, fighter pilots' thumbs*.

blind dirt snake *n.* A malodorous, legless lizard inhabiting *cak canyon*, which migrates south every morning. A *Richard the Third*.

blind man's buffet *n.* A *fanny* that can be located by the olfactory senses alone. *Blind man's muff.* A stanksome *snatch.*

blind man's porn *n.* Sexual noises, usually coming from an adjacent room or house. A *horn chorus.*

blinglish *n.* Street language spoken by rappers and bishop's son DJ Tim Westwood.

blip. *n.* The watery substance of female love. *Fish cream, nog juice, moip, bilp.*

blip fountain *n. medic.* The Bartholin's gland that secretes vaginal lubrications. The *batter tap.*

blistered pisspot, face like a *sim.* Useful phrase to describe the appearance of a woman who has fallen out of the ugly tree and hit every branch on the way down. And then landed in a pile of broken glass, *eg.* Sonia from *EastEnders*. *'Ladies and gentlemen, here to perform her latest single is a singer who needs no introduction. Her debut single Lost in France went straight into the Top Ten; her follow up, Total Eclipse of the Heart, went platinum in eight countries. Ladies and gentlemen, she sings like a cat having barbed wire pulled out of its arse and she's got a face like a blistered pisspot so let's give a big Summertime Special welcome to Bonnie Tyler.'*

blit *n.* See *blivvet.*

blitzed *adj.* See *wankered.*

blivvet *n.* coll. *Mackerel, blart, fanny, tussage.*

bloatee *n.* The type of carefully-toped beard favoured by the chubbier male, in the vain hope that it will demarcate his chin from his neck and thus indicate where his face stops. As sported by hopelessly optimistic *pie shifters* such as Chris Moyles, Johnny Vegas, Rik Waller, Lisa Riley *etc.*

blob *1. n.* Condom, *French safe, French letter, rubber Johnny. 2. v.* To inadvertently make pregnant. *"You look a little green around the lemon, old chap. Bad news is it?' I asked as Jeeves continued to study the letter. 'I'm afraid so Sir,' he replied. 'I attended a party of the downstairs staff of Brokenbury Manor, and I am afraid things got a little out of hand. To cut a long story short, Sir, it appears that I have blobbed the cook."* (from *Use the Back Door, Jeeves* by PG Wodehouse).

blob blimp *n.* A post-coital cabaret in which a used *jubber ray* is inflated and knotted for the amusement of one's ladyfriend.

blob it *v.* To oversleep. *'Jesus, Phil, look at the time. Get up, quick! I'm being coronated in half an hour and we've blobbed it.'*

blob jockey *n.* A gentleman with a penchant for the fuller-figured lady, *eg.* Lenny Henry. A *chubby chaser.*

blobsleigh *n.* Unexpected barefoot skid on last night's discarded prophylactic. The *spunky-footed luge.*

blobstopper *n.* A *fanny mouse,* a *slim fanatella* or *jam rag*. Put crudely, a feminine hygiene product.

Blofeld brunette *n.* A natural blonde who dyes her hair dark to feign intelligence. However, inspection of her lap reveals a white *pussy.* And draft plans for world domination.

blonde bombsite *n.* The distressing prospect that often greets a chap upon waking after a night of loud *banging* in the dark. The very antithesis of a blonde bombshell; more Marilyn Manson than Marilyn Monroe, if you will.

blonde herring *n.* A woman who looks like she ought to be a nice bit of *mackerel* from the back, but who turns out to be an *old trout* from the front.

blongle *n. medic.* Seminal fluid containing traces of blood. *Blunk, blism, blimphet.*

blood and custard *1. n.* Humorous, sex-case/train-spotter parlance for the cream and maroon livery in which British Railways coaching stock was painted in the 1950s and 1960s. *2. n.* The sort of curse that a soft pirate like Captain Pugwash might have uttered when he discovered that Cut-throat Jake had beaten him to the treasure of the San Fandango. *3. n.* The evidence left on the sheets after one has *done* it with a lady during her *unclean time.*

blood bachelor *n.* Married man undergoing the monthly interruption to his rightful conjugal privileges whilst his missus is *on the mop.*

bloodhound's jowls *1. n.* Oversized *beef curtains* which could track an escaped convict across Dartmoor. *2. n.* A mature *bird's funbags* during the later stages of collapse.

blood in your undies, here's *exclam.* Heart-warming oath in the style of "bottoms up" or "cheers" which can be used when raising a glass amongst company. A simple way of toasting the health and future happiness of those about whom we care. *'And now I would like to propose a toast: To the President of the Arab Republic of Egypt, Anwar al-Sadat, and to the Prime Minister of the State of Israel, Menahem Begin; to the great peoples they serve, the people of Egypt and the people of Israel, now joined together in hope; and to the cause we all serve: here's blood in your undies.'* (Former US President Jimmy Carter, on the occasion of the signing of the Egyptian-Israeli Peace treaty, March 26th 1979).

blood muppet *n. Jam dam, cotton mouse, gash mop, Dracula's teabag.* A *women's things* thing.

blood orange *n.* The *arsehole* after it has been savaged by a particularly vicious *chocolate shark. Japanese flag.*

bloodsports *n. Salsa dip.*

bloodstick *n.* A fellow's erectivitated *membrum virile.*

blood wank *n.* The ill-advised and possibly life-threatening act of *gentlemanly relaxation* that takes the day's tally into double figures. Regularly achieved by certain second year physics students at Manchester University and all bus drivers.

bloody *adj.* Swearword.

bloody sundae *1. n.* An act of *cumulonimbus* performed on a lady *up on blocks. 2. n.* A U2 song about an act of *cumulonimbus* performed on a lady *up on blocks.*

bloomers *1. n.* A voluminous item of women's underwear. *2. n.* Large loaves of bread. *3. n.* Unfunny and self-indulgent "mistakes" made on camera by a BBC employees which are later transmitted as part of tiresome "comedy" compilations.

blooper *1. n.* ITV version of *bloomer*. An actor's mistake which provides Dennis Norden with something to do while he waits to die. *2. n.* A sub-aquatic *trouser cough.* A *tottle*, an *Edward Woodward.*

blootered *adj. Blotto.*

blot bang rub *1. phr. milit.* Skin

decontamination procedure used by HM armed forces following a nuclear, biological or chemical attack. *2. phr. milit. Nipsy* decontamination procedure used by HM armed forces the day after a particularly delicious curry from the Curry Capital, Bigg Market, Newcastle upon Tyne.

blotto *adj.* B*lootered.*

blottopilot *n.* Inbuilt male homing device which secures a safe return to one's house after a night *on the sauce,* whatever one's level of inebriation. Often fitted to one's *beer scooter.*

blouse hounds *n. Shirt puppies* which are getting a bit long in the tooth.

blow a dog off a chain *v. Aus.* To *let off* with a severity sufficient to strip canines from their moorings.

blowback *1. v.* Of drug addicts, to puff smoke from a marijuana joint into another drug addict's mouth. *2. n.* A gobful of one's own *spangle* thoughtfully passed on by a *nosher.* A *snowball. 3. n.* A potentially fatal *blue dart* ignition mishap.

blowd *n.* A strange brown haze at the bottom of the *lavvy* made by a *turd* that has successfully resisted the flushing process. *Poo tea, PG shits.* From brown + cloud.

blow dry *v.* Of a dirty lady, to repeatedly *suck off* a fortunate gentleman until his *pods* are exhausted of *men's spendings.*

blow hole *1. n.* A whale's nose on top of its head. *2. n.* The *hog's eye* or *meatus.*

blow job *n.* Dangerous sex act whereby the female inflates the male's testicles like balloons by blowing air into his penis.

blow job off Emu *n.* A *wank.*

blow job week *n.* A once-monthly, seven-day *nosh fest.* A lady's *unclean time. 'Now your life doesn't have to stop just because blow job week starts.'* (Advertising slogan for Vespray Ultra *cunt rats*).

blowlamp *n.* A *fart* which is strong enough to fetch paint off a door or caramelise the sugar on a crème brûlée.

blow mud *v.* To noisily expel a loose stool, *crop spray, pebbledash,* release a *flock of pigeons.*

blow off *v.* To trumpet through the trousers, *parp* in the pants.

blow sisters *n.* Lesbian nuns, often seen in candle shops, sharing baths and cycling along cobbled streets.

blow your biscuits *v.* To *puke, yawn in technicolour, yoff.*

blubber beret *n.* Fleshy, Frank Spencer-style headwear worn by a man *licking out* a lass equipped with a *pie-hider.* A *fat hat.*

bludger *1. n.* One of two balls in the Harry fucking Potter bollocks broomstick cricket game Quidditch. *2. n.* A *stool* of the very firmest consistency imaginable. A *pan-cracker.*

blue *1. adj.* Of comedians and jokes, to be a little bit near the knuckle. *''Ere no, lady. This one's a little bit blue. I was up a mountain last week, walking along a narrow path and I met a gorgeous naked woman coming the other way. Well, I didn't know whether to wank myself off or fuck her up the cunt.'* (Max Miller, *Max at the Met*, 1951). *2. adj.* Of films, to have a different relationship to the knuckle altogether.

blue balls *1. n. Bollocks* which are fit to burst through lack of use.

DSBs, Sir Cliff's plums, nuts like two tins of Fussell's Milk, monks' nuts. 2. n. medic. Painful medical condition in young men caused by not *getting any* off their *birds.*

bluebottle banquet *n.* A freshly-laid *al fresco tom tit,* which instantly attracts a swarm of ravenous flies. Familiar to farmers, festival-goers, boy scouts and 1982 World Professional Darts champions.

bluecoat *n.* A lady who favours sex in the *tradesman's entrance.* From the practice in greyhound racing whereby the dog in the blue coat is traditionally run from trap two.

blue dart *n.* That brief but exciting pyrotechnic display achieved by igniting one's *air biscuits.* An *afterburner, blue streak.*

blueloon *n.* A raving street crazy having a loud conversation with his imaginary friend while a little blue light flashes in his ear. Could be seen choosing the filling for his sandwich at the counter of Subway in the centre of Newcastle upon Tyne, to pick an example completely at random. Also *bluetwat, blueannoyingfuckingarsehole.*

blue notes *n.* The mellifluous, jazzy sounds produced by a fellow the moment a dirty lady starts to blow a few double-tongued arpeggios on his *purple-reeded sex clarinet.*

Blue Peter bird cake *1. n.* Half a coconut shell filled with a solid paste of lard and old seeds. *2. sim.* Descriptive of a right full old *growler. 'Up betimes and feeling heavy of nodgers I made my way to Mrs Fitzgibbon's bordello on Threadneedle Street to see darling Bess. However, to my dismay I found she had done good business this day, and indeed, when I remov'd her scads did find that her cunny resembled naught but a Blue Peter bird cake. I was forced to demand back my shilling.'* (from *The Diary of Samuel Pepys*).

blue spinach *n.* Slang term for the blue pills that have the same effect on the *trouser muscle* as the eponymous stringy vegetable used to do on Popeye's arms. *Bongo Bill's banjo pills. 'Bloody hell. Look at your cock, Edson. There's big anvil shapes bulging out the side and the bell end is ringing like a Test Your Strength machine.' 'Aye pet. I've just had me blue spinach, you see.'*

blue-veined piccolo *n.* A tiny, high-pitched *cock.* Like a *bed flute,* only smaller.

bluey *1. n.* A *bongo vid. 2. n.* A *mycoxafloppin* tablet. *'Are you going to be much longer on the shitter, love? Only I popped my bluey half an hour ago and it's starting to wear off.'*

blumpkin *n. US.* An American rock groupie speciality. To administer a *gobbie* to an artiste whilst the latter is *dropping his kids off at the pool.* Being *duggled,* or indeed *duggling.*

blunderbarse *n.* A *nipsy* which sprays a cone of high-speed feculant matter out in every direction, rather in the style of one of them old-fashioned Elmer Fudd-style farmer's shotguns with the end of a trombone welded onto the barrel. A *twelve bore shitgun.*

blunderguff *v.* To expel an horrendous-smelling *fart* only to realise that the tastiest *bird* in the office is fast approaching.

blunk *1. n. Blongle. 2. n.* Scabrous, multi-layered jewellery of the type purveyed by Elizabeth Duke *etc.* From bling + junk.

Blunkett *n.* Facial expression adopted when two oncoming attractive ladies are forced to pass you, one on each side.

Blunkett's kiss *n.* An inaccurate show of affection, *eg.* When a pet dog licks one in the eye socket at 5am to welcome in a new day.

blurt *n. Splod.*

blurtch *n. medic.* The female reproductive organs. *'Congratulations, Your Majesty. You have been delivered of an heir to the throne of England, Great Britain, and her Commonwealth Dominions. I'll just stick a couple of stitches in your blurtch and you'll be as right as ninepence.'*

blurter *1. n. Aus. Chocolate starfish, ring.* 2. *n.* A little fishy that thou shalt have on a little dishy, when the boo-ert comes in.

blut *n. medic.* A lady's *mingepiece.*

boabie *Scots.* Glaswegian term for the male *member. 'Och, Wullie. Stop bein' such a boabie, an' poot on yir sporran.'*

boak *v.* See *bowk.*

boarding house tap, arse like a *sim.* A *nipsy* with an intermittent supply of hot, rusty water. Also *arse like a Tetley tea bag. 'I went to the Curry Capital, Bigg Market, Newcastle upon Tyne for my tea on Tuesday night. It's now Saturday and I've still got an arse like a boarding house tap.'*

boatswain's whistle *n. nav.* Stiff pipes that sailors blow into whilst cupping the spheres below with their hands. An act customarily performed as a rear admiral comes onto their poop deck. Also *bo'sun's pipe.*

bob *n.* A *neck massager,* a *dildo.* From Battery-Operated Boyfriend.

bobbery *n.* Female-on-male *strap-on*-assisted *arse-banging.*

Bobby Charltons *n.* Rogue pubes trapped under the foreskin that stick themselves across the dome of your *bell end,* in the manner of the erstwhile centre-forward's last few remaining hairs.

Bobby Davro eyes *n.* Descriptive of a cold, souless, miserable stare on the face of one who is doing something that is meant to be fun.

bobby dazzler *1. n.* Any item of pottery bought at an antiques fair with £100 of licence payers' money which is later sold for £3 at an auction. *2. n.* A rather gorgeous young lady who, when in one's hotel room, turns out to be a *babylicious* man. A *tiptop.*

bobby splithead *n.* Affectionate term for a *herman gelmet.*

bobby's anorak *n. Kojak's roll-neck, fiveskin, cock collar, Wilfrid's jumper.*

bobby's helmet *n. Bell end.* From the distinctive shape of the British police constable's hat which manages to look like a *tit* and a *cock end* simultaneously.

bobfoc *acronym.* Body Off Baywatch, Face Off Crimewatch. Having a *welder's bench* inexplicably mounted on a finely carved *rack and pegs, eg.* Sarah Jessica Parker.

bobfok *acronym.* Inter-changeable variant of *bobfoc* (see above), to describe a woman blessed with a comely figure but cursed with a *boat race* resembling Fred Dibnah *shitting* a coathanger. Body Of Barbie, Face Of Ken.

bobhouse *n.* The *shit box. 'My dar-*

ling Bobo, I will not take no for an answer - you simply MUST come to Chatsworth. The gardens are too divine at this time of year and the house is wonderfully enormous. Just imagine, the ballroom is the longest of any house in Europe! the dining room has a table that can seat 200! And there are 120 bedrooms! Can you believe it? And each one with its own ensuite bobhouse.' (Letter to Jessica Mitford, from her sister Deborah, Duchess of Devonshire).

boff *v.* See *bonk.*

boff licence *n.* A shop vending an intriguing and comprehensive selection of international *art pamphletry. 'I'm just popping down the boff licence. Anyone want anything?'*

bog dice *n.* The small cubes of disinfectant that are rolled down the trough using *piss* instead of a croupier. Used to replace the smell of stale urine with one of stale urine and disinfectant. *Kola cubes.*

bog *n. The shit house* or lavatory.

bogey spoon *n.* A fingernail.

bog library *n.* Reading material that builds up around the toilet of a bachelor. *Shiterature.*

bog-mess monster *n.* A legendary brown beast that curls its body out of the water in at least two places. May be a *brown trout* or a *dead otter.*

bog salmon *n.* An agile *turd* that, despite being flushed down river, manages to swim against the current back to its birthplace.

Bogside barbecue *n. NI.* From the salubrious Bogside area of Derry. A social gathering of locals enjoying cans of lager around a smouldering Ford Escort.

bog snorkelling *n. Around the world* or *dirtbox diving. Anilingus.*

boh! *exclam.* The noise made by a man after a particularly heavy woman has bounced up too far and sat down hard on his *gut stick*, breaking it in two. Reportedly Prince Albert's last word.

boiled eggs for four *n.* Visual impairment enjoyed by two reciprocating *homo horatiolists* in the 69 position. *A double Dutch blindfold.*

boiler *n.* An ugly woman who is lucky to get *serviced* once a year.

boilerdom *n.* The state of being a *boiler* into which many ugly ducklings pass directly upon reaching puberty.

boilersuit *n.* The charge that you did wilfully, and with phallus aforethought score with a *pig ugly* lass on Friday night. Usually brought by a kangaroo court convened in a pub on Saturday.

boiling beetroots *euph.* Of a lady, to be *up on blocks. 'Sorry, not tonight, love. I'm boiling beetroots.' 'Oh. Can I kick the back doors in instead, then?'*

boil your eggs *v.* To place your testicles over the anus of a farting naked woman that is standing on her head, for three minutes or so. A sexual practice that, if anyone has ever performed it, which let's face it is frankly unlikely, will undoubtedly have proved to be not worth the fucking bother.

bolitics *n.* The practice of talking utter *bollocks* about politics. Often performed by drunks in pubs, students in halls of residence and Hazel Blears.

bollock goatee *n.* The fashionable, jazz-style beard of testicles apparently grown by a woman whilst she is *smoking a gadgee.*

bollock jockeys *n.* See *bollock rats.*

bollock rats *n.* See *willipedes.*

bollocks *1. n.* Nonsense. *'That's utter bollocks, that is.' 2. n.* Knackers, balls. *'Oi, missus. Look at me bollocks.' 3. exclam.* Denial. *'Did you expose your bollocks to Mother Teresa?' 'Did I bollocks.'*

bollock service *n.* To make a withdrawal from *Barclay's. 'Tell you what, Hank, my balls are blue. It's about time I had them in for a bollock service.'*

bolt from the blue *n.* A nostalgic, Viagra-fuelled ejaculation.

Bolton alarm clock *n.* The convoy of police cars, ambulances and fire engines which charges through the streets of the delightful Lancashire resort at precisely 9.05 each morning.

Bolton dipstick *n.* The middle finger of a gentleman's right hand.

Bolton dip test *n.* A quick check of a lady's *undercarriage* to make sure that she is well-oiled and ready for sexual intercourse. *'Heliotrope could smell Fandango's musty male aroma as he held her in his muscular Cruft's judge's arms. She could feel his hands explore every inch of her lithe pedigree labrador breeder's body. Then he reached down for a quick Bolton dip test.'* (from *Pedigree* by Jilly Cooper).

Bolton shotput *n.* A sport played by nightclub bouncers in which their clients are grabbed firmly under the chin and shoved as hard as possible into the road, against a wall or through a shop window.

Bombay birthmarks *n.* The red patches evident just above the knees of someone who has spent the last hour ensconced on the *shitter.* Reading the *Autotrader* from cover to cover. Twice.

Bombay roll *n.* Like a sausage roll, but with *tits* instead of pastry and a *cock* instead of a sausage. And it costs £25 instead of 30p. But you could probably still get it at Greggs if you asked nicely.

bomb bay *n. medic.* The last lock on the alimentary *shit* canal. The *turtle's parlour* or rectum.

bomb bay bedbath *n.* A *shitted* bed following a pleasant night of curry and lager. *Mrs Chegwin's facepack.*

bomb bay duck *n.* A *dog's egg* that quacks to let one know it wants to come out.

bomb bay mix *n.* A single lavatorial sitting that produces a pot-pourri of stool consistencies; everything from *copper bolts* to a *rusty water geyser,* and all points in between. *Shitterish Allsorts, variety cack.*

bomb bay sapphire *n.* A *turd* which has been baked for so long in the *shit pipe* that it exhibits a hardness comparable to that of a precious stone.

bomb China *v.* To release your *payload* over the *Yellow River.* To have a *Billy Wright.*

bomb on a short fuse *n.* The *shit* that causes one to sprint around looking for a *chod bin* in the manner that Adam West ran around the pier looking for a safe place to throw the incendiary device in the 1966 film *Batman.*

bone *v. US.* To *fuck.*

boneless box *1. n.* A last resort family meal purchased from a popular fake-colonel-based high street chicken franchise. *2. n.* A *lezzer's cludge,* because it contains plenty of *batter* but rarely has a *bone* in it.

bonemeal *1. n.* A white fertilizer made from ground-up cattle skeletons which is used to grow vegetarians' food. *2. n.* A nourishing, meaty snack for the ladies, served with a cheese topping on a bed of nuts.

bone of contention *n.* A *stonk on* that causes an argument, *eg.* one that arises whilst watching beach volleyball with the wife.

bone on *n.* A *panhandle, wood, string.*

boner *n. US.* That which is used to *bone* with. A *bone on*.

bonersaurus *n.* An erection of such gargantuan magnitude that it wouldn't look out of place on a plinth in the foyer of the Natural History Museum.

boneshaker *1. n.* An unsprung Victorian bicycle, named for the teeth-loosening progress that it would typically make along cobbled streets. *2. n.* An act of sexual intercourse that has to be finished by hand.

bone xylophone *n. medic.* Gynaecological term for the interior of a woman's rib cage. Her *slats.* *'Oi, Heather. Let's go play the bone xylophone.'*

bongo bush *n. bot.* A plant which bears torn-up pornographic fruits.

bongo mag *n. Rhythm literature, spangle book.*

bonk *1. v.* Soft tabloid term for *fuck*. *2. n.* Soft tabloid term for a *fuck*. *3. n. W. Mids.* Obscene term meaning hill.

bonk on *n.* A splendidly tumescent member. *'A copy of Splosh and a box of tissues please, Mr Newsagent. I've got an almighty bonk on and I fancy a wank.'*

bonobo's breakfast *n.* An early morning *lamb shank.* From the famous sex maniac chimpanzees you sometimes see *wanking themselves off* left, right and centre on TV nature documentaries.

bonus ball *n.* The unheralded faecal pebble that drops in the gusset after an unsuccessful gamble on the *fart lottery.*

boobies *n.* See *boobs.*

boobs *n.* See *boobies.*

bookends *n.* The fellows at either end of a *spitroast.* *'It is estimated that up to 85% of professional footballers have, at some time in their career, been bookends.'*

bookie's biro *sim.* Descriptive of the chewed-up state of one's *old man* after a prolonged session of *horatio.* A *well-chomped chopper.* *'I came back from my weekend in Amsterdam with a suitcase full of souvenirs, a head full of happy memories and a charlie like a bookie's biro.'* (Jim White, *BBC Holiday Programme*).

bookie's bog *euph.* Descriptive of something that is a right old mess. *'Beckham now. Steps forward to take the penalty that could see England go through to Euro 2004. He looks composed, but he must be feeling the pressure. Starts his run up and oh my word. He's made a complete bookie's bog of that one.'*

bookie's pencil *n.* Descriptive of a dismally short, stumpy *cock.* *'He sings, he tells jokes, he does impressions and he's got a cock like a bookie's pencil. Ladies and gentlemen, put your hands together and give a warm welcome to Mr Bobby Davro.'* (Jimmy Tarbuck, 1988 Royal Variety Performance).

bookie's tip *n.* A John McCririck-style sequence of tic-tac twitches, flinches and flapping arms that signals to a *fellatrix* that it's odds on she's about to get a mouthful of *spooge.*

book reader *euph.* In the days before our present frank, outspoken terminology, *book reader* was Hollywood gossip column code for an actor who was *good with colours.* Also *sensitive.*

boomerang *n.* A sock that has been masturbated into so many times that it is hard enough stun a passing wallaby before returning to the masturbator's hand. A *womble's toboggan.*

boot *n. Can.* A woman who is too easy to *shag.*

booze flu *n.* A non-viral ailment that strikes suddenly after an evening at the pub and causes the sufferer to take the next day off work. Symptoms include staying in bed and feeling like *shite. Beer cancer.*

booze snooze *n.* An alcohol-induced siesta taken in the pub, the pub toilets or in a layby.

booze tardis *n.* A four-dimensional *beer scooter.*

boozoms *n.* Self-inflicted, public house-induced *man breasts. Beer-jugs, daddaries.*

boregasm *n.* A disinterested act of *self-pollution* for want of anything else to do.

Boris *1. n.* An act of premature *spangulation.* Named after the incident in a restaurant cupboard that turned out to be the most expensive five seconds tennis ace Boris Becker ever spent. *2. n.* Term used by females for their *farmyard area*, apparently.

born again fistian *n.* One who has recently become single and is once again spending a lot of time *praying for milk.*

Boscastle hall carpet, wetter than a *sim.* A no-longer-topical phrase used to describe the moistness of a sexually keen young lady's *clopper.* Also *wetter than a Tewkesbury doorstep* at the time of going to press.

bosch *v.* Of bishops and farmers - to drill a hole between cubicles in a public lavatory for the purpose of spying on, or making your penis available to the farmer or bishop in the adjacent *trap.*

bosphorus *n.* The bit that connects the fishy pleasures of the Mediterranean with the exotic mysteries of the Black Sea. The *taint, tinter, notcher, biffon.*

boswellox *1. n.* An unlikely sounding wrinkle-cream ingredient. *2. n.* Utter bollocks, *eg.* the claims made in wrinkle-cream adverts.

botcaps *n.* Plugs of *shit roll* worn in the *anus* to prevents *skids* on hot days.

Botley Interchange *1. n.* Section of Oxfordshire thoroughfare, connecting the A34 to the A420 and thus *2. n.* The section of the female anatomy which separates the *front* from the *back bottoms.* The *carse, tinter, snarse, Humber Bridge, Barry Gibb, bosphorus etc.*

bott *v.* To commit the sex act performed by *botters.*

bottee *n.* One who is *botted* up the *bottom* by a *botter.*

botter *n.* One who *botts* a *bottee up the bottom.*

bottery barn *n.* Any public convenience frequented by gentlemen who are *good with colours.* A *cottage.*

bottled Bass, frothing like *sim.* Descriptive of the lubricity of a *stoat*. *'You may be knocking on a bit, love, but your granny's oysters are frothing like bottled Bass.'*

bottle of olives *onomat.* The sound a *fart* makes in the bath. Named after the actor Edward Woodward. A *tottle.*

bottle opener *n.* A particulary strong and robust *blurtch*. Presumably with a little metal hook at the top.

bottom *n.* That part of the *bottee* which is *botted* by a *botter.*

bottom cork *n.* The last firm stool passed before the torrent of beer slime pours out.

bottom feeder *n.* An *anal linguist, rimmer.*

bottomist *n.* A chap who studies and performs experiments on, other fellows' *bottoms*. A student of *bumcraft*.

bottom log *n.* A scuttled *dreadnought* that hits the sea bed whilst still exiting the *windward passage*. Also *bridger, earthing cable.*

botto voce *adj. Lat.* Descriptive of a barely-audible *anal aside*. From the 18th century Italian; voce = voice & botto = nipsy.

botty burp *n.* A burp from the *botty*, *trouser trumpet, fart.*

bouncers *1. n.* Unsportsmanlike, short-pitched deliveries in cricket aimed at intimidating the batsman. *2. n.* Muscle men, *ripped to the tits* on *Aberdare tic-tacs*, who keep the riff-raff out of pubs and clubs. *3. n.* Big, wobbly *tits*.

bouncy castle *1. n.* A large, fat, rubbery *snatch* that one has to remove one's shoes before having a go on. *2. n.* A larger *bird*, endowed with *tits* like floppy turrets, who is fun to jump onto after spending the afternoon drinking cider.

bourbon *n.* Someone who is good at *horatio*. A "fancy licker".

Bourneville boulevard *n. The arse, fudge tunnel. 'I believe he strolls down the Bourneville boulevard'.*

Bovril bullets *n.* Stools, excrement. *Feeshus.*

bow Derek *n.* A *bird* who looks like a perfect ten only after one has imbibed a surfeit of cider.

bowel bugle *n.* A *trouser trumpet*.

bowel howl *n.* Fearsome wailing of the *anus*, the *sound of your supper*.

bowel jowls *n.* The hangdog *dirt curtains* of a *mud-plugger.* An *arse* that could do a good impression of Sir Clement Freud, the bloodhound-faced former Liberal MP for Ely and erstwhile *Punch* magazine food columnist, if you drew some eyes on it with a marker pen.

bowel trowel *n.* One of a selection of tools at the disposal of the *uphill gardener*. See also *cheesy wheelbarrow, trouser rake, one-eyed purple-headed blue-veined hairy secateurs.*

Bowie stare *n.* The unsettling sight of a knickerless stripper's *brown eye* and *pink eye* as she turns her back on a chap and bends over. Named after the famous wonky-eyed *half rice-half chips* crooner David.

bowk *v.* To *barf, vomit, spew, yak, hoy up, bake a pavement pizza.*

bowl constrictor *n.* An enormous *blind dirt snake* that kills its victims by choking the breath out of them.

bowl from the pavilion end *v.* To *bott*, travel on *the other bus*.

bowling shoe, fanny like a *sim.* A particularly well-worn and ill-fitting *clopper. 'Leia was powerless to resist. C-3PO's eyes burned into hers like light-emitting diodes. His strong metal arms enfolded her body as she felt herself being swept away on an Imperial battle cruiser of passion. After they had made love, and he had shot his electronic muck, they lay together in the twin moonlight. 'How was it for you?' she asked. 'To be perfectly honest, highness,' answered the droid, 'it was a bit of a let down. Jabba the Hut was right. You've got a fanny like a fucking bowling shoe.'* (from *The Space Princess and the Gold Protocol Droid* by Barbara Cartland).

bowl mole *n.* A small Cindy Crawford-style beauty spot on the side of the lavatory pan that resists all attempts at removal by *yellow toilet brush* and has to be picked off with a fingernail.

bowsprit *1. n.* In the maritime world, a mast or spar running forwards from a ship's bow, to which are fastened stays. *2. n.* In the world of *bone ons,* the sort of *diamond cutter* which points ahead as one walks and could, if one weren't careful, *poke a hole in a cheap door.*

box *1. n.* The vagina. *'I wouldn't mind getting into her box.' 2. n.* In cricket, a gentleman's protective device worn around the *undercarriage. 'Ooyah me pods! I wish I'd worn a box.'*

box doc *n. medic.* A gynaecologist. A *fanny mechanic.*

boxer's eye *n.* A puffed-up, swollen *fanny* whose owner ought to throw in the towel.

boxer's punchball *n.* The acorn of *shit* that hangs off the *toffee strings* and resists all attempts to *tap the ash off,* simply bouncing around like a pugilist's exercise equipment.

box of assorted creams *n. Aus.* She who has recently been over-accommodating to a number of gentlemen. A promiscuous female with a *fanny like billposter's bucket.*

box the Jesuit *v. 17thC.* How Friar Tuck may have referred to *strangling the parson* behind a bush in Sherwood Forest.

Boycott shits *n. medic. The runs.* It just takes you longer to get them.

boyner *n. NI.* A lady who appears to be about sixteen when seen from the back, but looks ninety when viewed from the front. From the Battle of the Boyne, the pivotal military engagement during the Irish Williamite Wars fought between the armies of King James and King William in July 1690. Twenty-six years worse than a *Kronenberg.*

brace *rhym. slang.* To defecate. From brace and bit = tom tit.

Brad *rhym. slang.* A *dump.* From Brad Pitt = English Lit. *'Give me the paper, I'm off for a Brad.'*

Brads, the *n. medic. The Earthas. 'Can you pass me some moist wipes in? I've got a bad case of the Brads.'*

Bradford dishwashing *n. Pissing* in the sink.

Bradford street carnival *n.* A traditional, city-wide riot that celebrates the popular West Yorkshire city's cultural diversity.

Bradman *1. n.* An extended session of *relaxing in a gentleman's way,* involving a lot of stroking one's *balls* under the covers. *2. n.* A prolonged *cumulonimbus* marathon. A long time at the *crease.* From the famous Australian cricketer Sir Donald Bradman (1908 - 2001), who used to spend a lot of time *wanking* and *licking out* his missus.

Brahms and Liszt *rhym. slang. Shitfaced.*

braille tits *n.* Tiny, raised *knockers* that allow a blind man to read a woman's chest over and over again. *Stits, fried eggs, chest warts, bee stings.*

brain donor *n.* An intellectually-challenged person.

brandy snap *n.* The *pubal area* of a russet-haired lady. A ginger *minge.*

Bransholme lighthouse *n.* Nickname for the Humberside Police helicopter, owing to the fact that it spends most nights hovering over the exclusive Bransholme Estate in Hull.

brap *n.* The volume rating of a *fart (Bp)* governed by three variables - rectal pressure *(r)*, buttock friction *(f)* and sprouts consumed *(SpC)* such that *Bp = f x SpC/r.* Buttock friction *(f)* can be reduced to zero by pulling the *ringpiece* open wide during emission.

brass eye *n. Hog's eye, brown eye, red eye, chocolate starfish.* The *fifties tea towel holder.*

brass rubbings *n.* Rusty, finger-end-shaped tracings found in a gentleman's *undercrackers* following a good scratch of his poorly-wiped, sweaty *arse crack.*

bratmobiles *n.* People carriers.

Brazilian rocket *n.* A gentleman who explodes whilst still on the launchpad. One who *stamps on the toothpaste* before he's got his pants off. A *no-push charlie.*

Brazilian wax *n.* A bald *monkey's forehead.* A *shaven haven, Beverley Craven, Barthez.*

breach of the peach *n.* A *kicking in* of a lady's *back doors.*

breach the hull *v.* To push one's digit through inferior quality *bumwad* when wiping one's *arse. Push through. 'Day 82, and the men are getting restless. Squabbles are beginning and tempers are short. John Norton handed out the ship's biscuits, but Mr Christian refused to eat, accusing him of breaching the hull and then not washing his hands.'* (from *The Log of HMS Bounty* by William Bligh, 1764).

breadlocks *n.* The nutritious foody entanglements of a tramp's beard.

break America, trying to *1. euph.* Phrase used by PR companies and showbiz columnists to describe that phenomenon whereby British celebs like Robbie Williams, Chris Evans and Lieutenant Pigeon vanish to LA for six months and signally fail to get arrested. *2. n.* Signing on. *'What are you doing in William Hills at three in the afternoon?' 'I'm at a bit of a loose end at the moment, I'm trying to break America, you see.'*

break company *v.* To disrupt a gathering of *beneficiaries* by the release of a *McArthur Park.*

breakfast in bed *n.* An early morning *fart* that sets one up for the rest of the day. A *dawn chorus.*

breakfast maker *n.* An early morning *fart* which is so smelly that the missus has no choice but to get out of bed and make the breakfast.

breakfast of champions *n.* A *beef dripping*-rich *fanny fry-up* eaten the morning after *putting the wife to the sword.*

breakfast podcast *1. n.* Helpful community service provided by the BBC, whereby it is possible to download news content onto one's MP3 player. *2. n.* A sordid act of ante-meridian *self pollution* brought to a successful conclusion whilst *horny* BBC Breakfast Programme presenter Kate Silverton is on the screen.

break for the border *1. n.* A risky dash made by one's hand for a woman's knickers when one is uncertain of her reaction, half expecting a slap. *2. v.* Of a *shit,* to catch one unawares by suddenly *darting south, eg.* when one is looking for something to read. A *charge of the shite brigade.*

break the seal *v.* To partake of one's first *piss* at the pub, usually after three or four pints. Return visits to the toilet are thereafter required every fifteen minutes throughout the evening.

break the crust *v.* The morning after an evening fuelled with hot food and brown beer, to *pinch off* the day's first *loaf,* an act which is shortly thereafter followed by an uncontrollable Krakatoa-style pyroclastic flow of hot brown lava from the *jacksie.*

break the siege *v.* To enjoy a long overdue *dump* following a bout of constipation.

breast fest *n.* Those summer months during which women sunbathe topless.

breasticles *n.* Particularly small, wrinkly bosoms of the type you'd expect Dot Cotton to have.

breastitute *adj.* Descriptive of a lady who hasn't got two *thruppennny bits* to rub together, *eg.* Tara Palmer-Tomkinson.

breather ring *n.* An anular indentation on a long *turd,* indicating where the *cable layer* has had to pause for breath, allowing the *nipsy* to partially contract. A faecal aneurism. *'Fuck me! That was a bastard to part with. I left it with three breather rings on it.'*

brew *n.* A refreshing *air biscuit* to dunk in one's tea.

brewer's droop *n. medic.* Marshmallowing of the penis due to excessive *turps nudging.*

brewer's fart *n.* A particularly sulphurous *bowel howl. 'Jesus, he's just dropped a brewer's fart, grains and all.'*

brewer's flu *n.* A nasty hangover.

brew one up *v.* To be *burbulent,* to bake an *air biscuit. 'For your own safety step back please ladies, I'm brewing one up over here.'*

Brian May's plughole, a fanny like *sim.* A lady's *bush* which is so hirsute that it resembles the bath drainage outlet of the erstwhile Queen plank-shredder-turned-astronomer.

brice *v. Vict.* To engage in a sexual act in which one party is tied to a large stake known as the *bricing post.*

bricing post *n.* Stake to which a person who is to be *briced* is tied.

Brick Lane *1. n.* Bustling London thoroughfare running between Whitechapel High Street and Bethnal Green Road, which includes many exotic eateries amongst its attractions. *2. n.* The narrow skin isthmus connecting the *ringpiece* with the *knackers,* which generally experiences peak traffic flow shortly after visits to the aforementioned spicy comestible establishments. Also *tornado alley,* *smelly bridge, tintis etc. 'Emergency hotline. Which service do you require?' 'Ambulance please, operator. There's been a terrible accident on Brick Lane.'*

bricks and mortar *n.* A sit down toilet visit of miscellaneous consistencies. *Bomb bay mix.*

brick shithouse, built like a *sim.* Resembling a Leeds Rhinos prop forward. Heavy set, stocky. *'Is that your missus? Fucking hell, she's built like a brick shithouse.'*

bridge the gap *v.* See *TUBFUF.*

bridger *n. Bottom log.*

brigadier *1. n.* Military officer ranking immediately below a Major General. *2. n.* A three-course meal for one's *cock* consisting of the *pink,* the *brown,* and a *chewie,* in that order.

Brighton *rhym. slang. On the other bus.* From Brighton pier = ginger beer.

Brillo pad *sim.* Coarse vaginal foliage. A red-headed Scottish lassie might be described as having *'a mott like a rusty Brillo pad.'*

brim *n.* That wainscotting around the base of the *helmet.* The *wankstop,* the *sulcus.*

brimula *n.* Spreadable *knob cheese.*

bringing the safety car out *1. v.* The spoilsport action of Formula 1 organisers attempting to prevent exciting high-speed pile-ups in dangerous conditions. *2. v.* A gentleman's attempt to prevent early *crashing of the yoghurt truck* in an exciting situation, *eg.* by thinking about abandoned puppies, football scores or Rovers Return barmaid Betty Turpin. *Summoning Moira.*

bring off *v.* To cause to have an organism.

brink *n.* The *taint, tinter, carse, Humber Bridge, crontis.* So called because it rests between the *brown* and the *pink.*

Brinks job *n.* To successfully *bang* the boss's wife without getting caught.

Bristol Channel *n.* The cleavage.

Bristols *ryhm. slang. Tits.* From Bristol Cities = titties. And Bristol dockers = knockers. And Bristol fig slugs = big jugs.

Bristol therapy *n. medic.* Alternative holistic treatment whereby an ailing man is revived and soothed by exposure to a massive pair of *oomlaaters.*

Britney's chuff *euph.* A situation when a much-anticipated reality in no way matches up to what you'd imagined it would be like, to the point that you begin to wish you'd never seen it. *'I got the Sky Sports so I could watch the Ashes series. A right Britney's chuff that turned out to be.'*

broadband blister *n.* A callus that appears on a chap's *stench hammer* shortly after his internet download speed increases.

broat *n.* See *vurp.*

brobs *n.* Overwhelmingly large *tits.* From the giant Brobdingnabians in *Gulliver's Travels.* Opposite of *lils.*

broken ice cream machine, arse like a *sim.* Symptom of major gastro-intestinal meltdown which results in a day spent off work, sitting on the *chod bin* reading the local *Autotrader* and moaning.

Bronx cheer *n. arch.* Obsolete term for a *fart* used exclusively by Whoopee Cushion manufacturers.

broomstick *n.* Any small runaround car aimed specifically at the ladies' market, *eg.* Renault Clio, Ford Fiesta, Nissan Micra.

brothel sprouts *n. medic.* An attack of genital herpes following a visit to a house of ill repute. *'What's that on your cock, Lord Archer?' 'Oh that? It's nothing, just a few brothel sprouts, that's all. I've got them all up my back as well, you know. And I'm a thief.'*

brother *n. Bean flicker, tuppence licker, carpet muncher.* A lesbian.

brother, email my *euph.* To masturbate. From the US baseball player Carlos Zambrano, who was put on the Chicago Cubs injured list because of a wrist injury caused by spending four hours a day on the internet "emailing his brother".

brown admiral *n. zoo.* The common and far from beautiful butterfly that can be found in the pants of someone who has failed to *draw an ace.* A *gusset moth.*

brown ballerina *n.* The "tutu" effect achieved when one's index finger pierces cheap bathroom tissue whilst wiping one's *ringpiece. Also Kermit's collar.*

brown bear's nose *n.* A cute little round *turd* that hibernates at the bottom of the *grizzly bear pit.*

brown Betty *n.* The mess that can result from *back door love* with someone with a full or disturbed bowel.

brown bullet-hole *n. Bumhole, barking spider.*

brown daisy *n.* An unpleasantly-scented flower which attracts flies instead of bees and butterflies. A *bronze eye.*

brown drought *n. medic.* Constipation.

brown dwarf *n.* The tiny, super-dense, hard-to-find nugget of highly-compressed *barker's egg* hiding somewhere on the sole of one's shoe.

brown extender *n.* At B&Q, a device for raising the height of an existing fence.

brown eye *n.* The *ring* through which the *brown trout* jump on their daily migration to the sea.

browneye lashes *n.* Glamorous hairs that surround the *balloon knot.* Often caked in a brown, mascara-like substance.

brown finger poncho *n.* The square of *arsewipe* through which the digit pushes when one *breaches the hull.*

brown flower in the window, have a *euph.* Expression of one's need to defecate. *'Sorry, love, I'll get a fire engine off to you as soon as I can, but I've got a brown flower here and it needs to be put in some water.'*

brown hatter *n.* A *bottsman* with *shit* on his helmet.

brown helmet *n.* An award presented to a man by his girlfriend or wife to commemorate the day she leaves him, *ie.* metaphorically *shits* on his head. *'And it came to pass that Naboth had journeyed to the shops and his wife Bathsheba was left alone in his tent. And David came unto her in the tent of Naboth and knew her twice. And she took up her chatels and went to live in the tent of David amongst the Gibeonites. And Naboth did return to his tent and found that Bathsheba was gone. And he went to the inn with his mates Mephibosheth and Jonadab son of Shimeah, and he wailed and gnashed his teeth saying, I always did my best for her,* *no man could have done more. Yet she gives me the brown helmet. And great was his sorrow, even unto the twelfth pint.'* (from *Epidydimis,* Ch. 6 vv12-16).

brownhouse gases *n.* Environmentally harmful emissions from a *tail pipe.*

brownian motion *1. n.* The apparently random movements of minute particles immersed in a fluid, discovered by physicist Richard Brown. *2. n.* The frequent and painful visits to the *throne room* experienced by one who has recently enjoyed a delicious meal at the Curry Capital.

brown jewels *n.* The Queen's *winnets*. The *dangleberries* of state.

brown laser *n.* A beam of hot, liquid *shite* that exits the *brass eye* at the speed of light, and which could easily cut a secret agent in two.

brown light's flashing *euph.* Emergency warning sign of a toiletry nature. *Umber alert. 'Can you hang the washing out for me, dear?' 'Sorry love. Brown light's flashing, with you in five.'*

brown lilo *n.* A buoyant *tom tit* that, left alone, will eventually float out to sea and be eaten by a cod.

brown men on swings *n.* See *miniature heroes.*

brownout *n.* After a heavy night on the tiles, the distinctly unpleasant consequence that is one stage further than a blackout. *'Aw, bloody hell Maggie. The dog must've climbed in the bed and done a dirt in my pyjama bottoms last night, look. Again.' 'You can't fool me, Keith. We haven't even got a dog. You've had another one of your brownouts, haven't you.'*

brown owl *n.* A sizeable *log. Meatloaf's daughter,* a *dead otter.*

brown pipe engineer *n.* An *arse mechanic* who always calls at the *tradesman's entrance.*

brown pocket *n.* A smuggler's receptacle that allows him to spirit contraband through customs. *'Did you bring anything back from Amsterdam, Phil?' 'Yes. I've got some clogs and cheese in my suitcase and a lump of squidgy black in my brown pocket.'*

brown roulette *n.* A game of chance with potentially disastrous consequences whereby one *shoots rabbits* through an *arse* over which one has little control. To risk a *fart* whilst suffering with the *squits. Twisting on nineteen.*

brown sunrise *n.* Whilst ensconced on the *throne,* the majestic sight of a *Thora Hird* gradually emerging from behind the knackers as one watches with the head between the knees. A sign that it's time to buy some Bill Tidy books to keep on the cistern.

brown-tak *n.* A pliable, adhesive compound used by prisoners to stick posters to the wall. Also known as *scat-tak.*

brown tap *n.* A particularly non-viscous bout of the *Mexican screamers*. The *gravy rocket.*

brown ticket *n.* Secret prize hidden inside certain Cadbury's chocolate bars in recent months. The lucky winner of a *brown ticket* receives a day-long trip to the *chocolate factory. Salmonella serovar Montevideo.*

brown tie *n.* The dirty mark left between a lady's *jugs* by a man having a *sausage sandwich* immediately after taking her up the *council gritter.*

brown trout *n.* A *turd, big job, shite.*

brown trout pond *n.* The lavatory bowl.

brown wings *n.* The honour bestowed on who has performed *bumilingus* on a lady Hell's Angel.

brown zombie *n.* A *Douglas* that refuses to be flushed away and keeps on coming back.

brummie orgasm *n.* A plangent, discordant and ultimately deafening sound. *'As the giant iceberg tore through the mighty liner's hull, in that same dread moment the ship's cat was tipped into the cooking fat and the palm court orchestra was caught in the deadly whiplash of the broken cables. It sounded like a brummie orgasm.'*

Bruce Lees *n.* Firm nipples. A somewhat racist and inaccurate reference to the San Francisco-born kung fu master of Chinese descent. *Hard nips.*

Brucie *n.* A *fart* which is performed whilst adopting the silhouetted "Thinker" stance made famous by Bruce Forsyth on *The Generation Game*, followed by a camp little kick forwards.

brush up on one's Punjabi *v.* To lick a lady's *bodily treasure. 'Virginia looked resplendent as she descended from the Sao Paolo steamer, quite bronzed and elegant in the London mist. After taking tea at Claridge's we took the charabanc to my rooms at Oxford, where I relished the opportunity to brush up on my Punjabi.'* (from *The Diaries of Evelyn Waugh*).

brut *1. n.* Great-smelling man musk peddled by an unlikely alliance of bald former prize-fighters and unstable future football managers who found themselves sharing a bathroom mirror in the 1970s. *2. n.* The predictable end scene of a *grumble flick* when the lady participant encourages her male co-star to "splash it all over". And she's not talking about his aftershave. She's talking about his spunk.

BS *abbrev. US.* Booooool-shee-it.

BSH *abbrev.* British Standard Handful. The imperial unit by which *knockers* were measured in the good old days.

bubbies *n.* Coy term for *breasts*, much beloved of writers of cod-Victorian pornography. *''Ooh, zur! What does you think of moi bubbies, then?' asked Molly the Milkmaid, as she unzipped the Squire's heaving breeches.'* (from *A Roll in the Hay*, by Jeffrey Archer).

bubble poo *n. Fizzy gravy.*

bubblebum *n.* An unfortunate release of *burbulent gas* through moist *buttocks,* the resulting sound being eerily reminiscent of Leonardo di Caprio's final words in *the film Titanic.*

bubblyduck *n.* A particularly loud, prolonged and wet *fart.* Named because the sound is identical to that of an agitated mallard being drowned in a bucket of custard.

bucket fanny *n.* A spacious or roomy vagina. *Tardis twat, cathedral, welly top.*

Buckfast breakfast *n.* The first meal of the day for many a Scottish *professional outdoorsman.*

buckie *n. Scots.* Affectionate nickname given to the tonic wine traditionally produced for Glaswegian tramps by the monks of Buckfast Abbey, Devon.

buckle bunny *n.* US. A *cock*-hungry *bird.*

buddy breathing *1. n.* In SCUBA

diving, of two divers to share a mouthpiece in an emergency situation, taking it in turns to suck on the same oxygen supply. *2. n.* In *jazzular cinematography,* of two actresses to share a genital, taking it in turns to suck on the same *spongle* supply. *Baby birding.*

budget spunk *n. medic.* The fluids that a gentleman expels after undergoing a *walnut whip. Decaff spaff.*

budgie smugglers *n.* Extremely tight gentlemen's bathing trunks. *Noodle benders.*

budgie supping *v.* The act of pitiful beer drinking performed by men who aren't used to it, *eg.* a terrified Tony Blair pecking at a pint for the benefit of TV cameras in Sedgefield Labour Club.

budgie's tongue *n.* Descriptive of the female erectile bit, particularly when her *fanny* has climbed a little plastic ladder to ring a bell.

budmiser *n.* The unusually quiet member of a lad's night out who waits until he has downed four rounds of drinks before revealing that he has come out without any cash.

buff, to *v.* To engage in the removal of the *poo*/sweat mix which accumulates in a chap's *arse cleft* during a long drinking session, or perhaps whilst moving filing cabinets down a fire escape on a hot and humid day, by the vigorous application of copious amounts of *bumwad.*

buffage *n. US.* Highly offensive and sexist term used by women to describe men. *'Hey girls, check out the buffage in here.'*

buffeting *n.* The disturbing half-gulping, half-choking carry-on that precedes a *psychedelic yawn.* A *frogs' chorus.*

buffet slayer *n.* A female *lard of the manor.* A lady with a penchant for eating more than her fair share of free food.

buffing *n. Gusset typing.* The act of female masturbation.

buffty *n. Scot.* A gay fellow. A *Gordon.*

BUFFY *1. n. prop.* That tasty piece of young *blart* who fights vampires on Sky One. *2. acronym.* The complete opposite of *1.* A Big Ugly Fat Fucking Yeti. A lady who's been beaten senseless with the *nice personality stick.*

bugger *1. n.* He who pokes animals, *arseholes* or animals' *arseholes.* A *berry. 2. v.* To break or damage. To *fuck. 3. exclam.* A cry of dismay. *'PC World phoned up while you were out. They said they'd managed to get your laptop going again, and you can pick it up any time tomorrow from the Police Station.' 'Bugger.'*

bugger all *n. Nowt, fuck all.*

bugger's grips *n.* Sideburns. Any tufts of facial hair on the cheeks. *Bugger's handles, face fannies.*

Bugner's eye *n.* Flapless female genitalia, resembling boxer Joe Bugner's closed-up eye in every fight he had.

build a log cabin *v.* To pass a series of sturdy stools.

builder *n.* A sexually unresponsive ladyfriend, *ie.* One that "never *comes*". Also *plumber, gasman, Initial City-Link van driver.*

builder's bum *n.* The protrusion of fat, sweaty *arse* cheeks above the sagging waist of the jeans. Common amongst bricklayers, council workmen and top fashion designer Alexander McQueen. *Bricky's crack, Dagenham smile.*

bukhaki *n. milit.* Nocturnal military manoeuvre involving a billetful of other ranks masturbating onto the face of their sleeping brother in arms, who has returned to his barracks in a state of critical *refreshment. 'Bukhaki's happened in the night / The soldier wakens in his bunk / His eyes don't open to the light / They're all gummed up with squaddies' spunk.'* (from *Conscious* by Wilfred Owen).

bukkake *1. n.* Saucy carry on whereby a load of randy blokes *tip their filthy concrete* onto a delighted *plasterer's radio.* From the noun form of the Japanese verb *bukkakeru*, meaning "to dash water". *2. adj. Jap.* Descriptive of dishes, such as bukkake-udon and bukkake-soba, where fresh soup-like toppings are poured on top of noodles. *3. adj.* In Britain, descriptive of dishes about to be served to *Sunday Times* food critic Michael Winner, such as soup and macaroni cheese, into which a group of kitchen employees - not to mention other customers - *empty their nuts.*

bulimia amnesiac *n. medic.* One suffering from a condition whereby they binge eat, then forget to throw up. A *salad dodger, lard arse,* one who is a martyr to their glands.

bull *abbrev. US. BS.*

bulldog chewing a wasp *sim.* Descriptive of a lady's face that does not conform to conventional ideals of beauty. Also *bulldog licking piss off a nettle, welder's bench, stripper's clit.*

bulldog eating porridge *sim.* Poetic term describing a *lady's bodily treasure* in the aftermath of an act of love. *'When I'd finished with her, she had a fanny like a bulldog eating porridge, I can tell you.'*

bulldog's tail *n.* A *turtle's head.*

bulldyke *n.* A butch, masculine or aggressive *lezza. Diesel dyke.*

bullet-proof vest *1. n. milit.* Armoured clothing designed to minimise injury from incoming gunfire. Usually worn by TV reporters trying to look butch in conflict zones. *2. n.* Reinforced clothing designed to minimise the impact of outgoing nipples. Usually worn by females in cold conditions.

bullet train *n.* A *ride* that is over far too quickly.

bullfrogging *1. n.* A specialised variation on the act of *horatio,* whereby the *nosher* takes not only the *noshee*'s *tallywhacker* but also both his *magic beans* into his or her mouth, thus creating the effect of the state amphibian of Missouri (*Lithobates catesbeianus*) complete with its swollen throat and guttural retching call. *2. n.* The act of *farting* against a closed door from the outside, so that the occupants of the room believe that a large bullfrog is about to enter.

bullfruit *n.* A *tailgunner* who is a bit *rock.* A canny hard *puff.*

Bullimore *n. prop.* An extremely buoyant bit of *cack,* which refuses to drown. Named after extremely buoyant round-the-world yachtsman Tony Bullimore, who spent three days being lashed by storms under his capsized boat.

bull queen *n.* A large, butterfingered prison inmate who cannot keep hold of the soap in the shower, and who instructs other, smaller, prisoners to bend over and pick it up for him. Then he sticks his *cock* up their *arse*.

bull's dick, thick as a *sim.* Somewhat unintelligent, *fuckwitted*. *'That turd serving me in McDonald's was as thick as a bull's dick.'*

bullshit *1. n. Feeshus* of male cattle. *2. n.* Rubbish, nonsense, *bollocks*. *3. v.* To lie, deliberately mislead, talk rubbish to. *'Don't you bullshit me now, you hear, bitch, or I'll cut yo' jive-ass face wide open.'* (Sir Neville Chamberlain to his wife, after she informed him that Hitler had invaded Poland).

Bully's Prize Board *1. n.* Part of the popular darts gameshow *Bullseye*, where guests could win various prizes announced by Tony Green in the following distinctive manner: *"HHHHIN One!...HHHHIN Two!..." etc.*, and thus *2. n.* An ultimately unsatisfying and prolonged toilet visit whilst suffering from a *log jam*, when it would be a good idea to settle down, find your rhythm *etc*. *'Sorry I'm late, ladies and gentlemen. I've been stuck on Bully's Prize Board.'* (HRH Prince Charles, addressing the Board of Architecture and National Heritage, 1987).

Bully's special prize *1. n.* A speedboat. *2. n.* An extra large, beefy *shit*. *'I'd give it ten minutes before you go in there, Your Majesty. I've just won Bully's special prize.'*

bum *1. n. Arse, bottom, poop-chute. 2. n. US. Harold Ramp, pan handler.* A homeless person. *3. v.* Of cigarettes, to scrounge, scavenge. *4. v.* To *bott*. *5. adj. US. legal.* Of *raps*, to be unjust, unfair. *6. n.* Trebor mint preservation apparatus.

bum bandit *n.* A robber, outlaw or highwayman who steals people's bottoms.

bum bar *n.* A richly-textured item of *arse chocolate*. *'Take the helm, Captain Hardy, I'm off down the poop deck for a bum bar.'*

bum baubles *n. medic.* Big, round, shiny *farmers* that your missus and the doctor can see their faces in.

bum beaver *n.* An *arse* where the *cress* has grown out of control. A *botty beard*, a *DLT*.

bumblebee dance *1. n.* Action performed by bees in which they shake their abdomens to indicate to other members of the hive in which direction the pollen lies. *2. n.* The waggling of the buttocks in order to dislodge a reluctant *geetle* from the *dot*. A *logarhythm*.

bum brake *n.* The *cigar cutter* or *nipsy*.

bum brusher *n. Vict.* A schoolmaster. From the good old days before political correctness when there was nothing wrong with a spot of wholesome, *arse*-based corporal punishment which never did red-faced ex-military men who write to the *Daily Telegraph* any harm. A phrase which is quite possibly still in current usage on the Isle of Man.

bum chain *n.* A rather intimate version of the Conga, danced around the streets at the end of a gay party.

bum chums *n.* Primary school term for any two boys who always sit next to each other.

bum cigar *n.* In after dinner conversation, a stool. *'Well, if you'll excuse me ladies, I think I shall retire to the bathroom and light a bum cigar.'*

bum conkers *n.* Shiny, brown, spherical agglomerations which hang off the *arse strings*, and can be baked in the oven or soaked in vinegar.

bumcraft *n. Uphill gardening, cable laying, stepping on ducks.* The wholesome enjoyment of all things *bum.*

bum crumbs *n. Kling-ons* which have ceased to cling on. Usually found in the bed or in the gusset of the *trolleys*.

bumdruff *n.* The *anal scurfage* and general buttock effluvium left on the back of the *bog* seat after one has been for a *digestive transit.*

bum drummer *n.* A *puddle jumper.*

bum fluff *n.* Risible pubescent attempt to grow a moustache.

bumfoolery *n.* Light-hearted action centred loosely around the *Bleep & Booster. Carry On* film-style *poovery.*

bum goblin *n.* A gnarled, malevolent *turd* that jumps out from behind you, casting a painful spell on your *ringpiece.*

bum grapes *n.* Agonising, juice-filled, seedless, purple fruits which grow well in the moist, shady regions of the *Khyber Pass.*

bum gravel *n.* A scree-like accumulation of anal detritus found in the bed after one has *raked one's arse out.*

bum gravy *n.* Diarrhoea, *rusty water*.

bum jumble *n.* Bits and bobs of excrement. *'Fucking hell, Brendan. Paula's left some bum jumble in the road again.'*

bum lungs *n.* Additional, apparently rectally-situated, breathing apparatus which allows members of the fairer sex to speak continuously without pausing for breath.

bummange *n.* A light, fluffy *arse* dessert. *Anal delight*.

bummer *1. n.* One who *bums. 2. n.* A disappointing situation. Such as being stuck on a beach for the whole summer, after missing a charabanc.

bummocks *n.* The buttocks of the *bum*.

bummy mummy *n.* A *milf* who could well benefit from having her *back doors* kicked in. A *milb.*

bumnugget *n.* A *number two,* consisting of an accretion of many smaller *number twos.*

bumpies *rhym. slang. Fun bags.* From bumpy bits = tits.

bump the kerb *v.* Of a *heavily-refreshed* gentleman, to make a series of ineffectual attempts to get his *cock* into the *hairy parking space.* A repeated failure to score a *hole-in-one. 2. v.* To deliberately on purpose nudge the wife's *wrong 'un* with the *pit prop. 'Sorry love. I seem to have bumped the kerb there.'*

bum rope *n. Shit. 'Has anybody seen the Autotrader? I'm just going to cut some bum rope.'*

bumscare *n.* Severe pressure in the lower abdominal region prior to a controlled explosion.

bumshee *n.* A blood-curdling howl of anguish coming from a lavatory cubicle.

bum sink *n.* The toilet.

bumsong *n.* A long, tuneful and mellifluous *botty bugle.*

bum spuds *n.* Faecal tubers. Human stools.

bumtags *n. Dangleberries.*

bum tongue *n.* A large piece of *shit* hanging from *Dot Cotton's mouth* just before it licks the bowl.

bum vinegar *n.* The sweat found between the *arse* cheeks in general, and in particular during or after exercise. A condiment that goes well with *arse feta*. *Sarsehole.*

bumwad *n.* Lavatory tissue.

bun-chukas *n.* Saggy *lils* that can be swung around the waist and shoulders, and used *in extremis* as offensive weapons. Extra-mobile *knee shooters. Socktits* with a billiard ball in the end.

bung hole *n.* The vagina, at which a dirty lady *fizzes.*

bunglasses *n.* Like *binorkulars*, but pointing slightly lower down.

Bungle's finger *n.* A short, stocky *turd*, named after the ursine simpleton from the 70s children's show *Rainbow.*

bun in the oven, to have a *v.* To be pregnant, *up the stick, in the club, in trouble, up the pasture. 'Guess what love. I've got a bun in the oven.' 'That's nice. Is my tea ready yet?'*

bunion ring *n.* An old lady's *jacksie.*

bunko booth *n.* Paul Daniels's *shithouse*. A water closet cubicle.

bunk up *1. n.* A utility poke. *'Darling, you look beautiful tonight. Any chance of a bunk up?' 2. n.* Assistance in climbing. *'Shit. I'm so pissed I can't get onto the bed. Any chance of a bunk up?'*

bunk-up badge *n.* A love bite, usually found on really ugly people's necks to prove they have a love life. Or a at least access to a bicycle pump. A *hickie,* a *bub,* a *shag-tag.*

bunnet brie *n. Scot. McHelmetdale. 'Whit's yon stink, maw?' 'Och, Wullie. It's jist Granpaw's bunnet brie, son.'*

bunny-boiler *n.* A determined woman who misinterprets a one-off drunken *scuttle* as the overture to a deep and lasting relationship, then tries to win your affections when you go back to the missus by boiling your kids' pets. *A pork 'n' stalk.*

bunny rub *n.* A *tit wank, diddy ride, Bombay roll.*

buns *1. n.* Regional variation of *baps. 2. n. US. Ass* cheeks.

bunt *1. n.* A disease of wheat caused by the *Tilletia* fungus. *2. n.* The bulging part of a fishing net or a ship's sail. *3. v.* To block a ball with a bat. *4. v.* To greedily steal hampers of tuck from one's fellow public schoolboys. *5. n.* On a *salad dodging* lady, where the stomach seamlessly merges into the pudendums. From belly + cunt. Also known as the *super-poond* or *gunt.*

bunting *n.* Church fete-style strings of *jizz* looped around a *grumble flick* actress's face.

Burberry apes *n.* Designer-clad football hooligans.

Burberry shitbomb *n.* The delightful smell of perfume in the water closet after one's girlfriend or wife has been in to *drop the kids off at the pool.* Air freshener on lead guitar and vocals with excrement on bass and drums.

burbulence *n.* The uncomfortable alimentary rumbling which precedes the breakage of wind. *'Over Nova Scotia I finished the last of my egg sandwiches. Half an hour later I hit a pocket of burbulence, and had to fasten my seat belt and extinguish all lights.'* (from *My Flight Across the Atlantic* by Amelia Earhart).

burglar's dollop *n.* An episode of trouser-soiling through fear or nerves. *'David Cameron takes the stand for his keynote address to the Blackpool Conference. It's a real burglar's dollop moment for the embattled Tory leader.'* (Nick Robinson, BBC News 24).

burial at sea *n.* The dignified delivery of a stool, without *splashback*. The opposite of a *depth charge* or *belly flopper.*

burly *n. Bum wipe,* toilet paper, *chocolate shark bait, turd tokens.*

BURMA *acronym.* Secret code used on military correspondence - Be Upstairs Ready My Angel.

burn bad powder *v. arch. milit.* Of *trouser trumpetry,* to *light a tyre,* emit a *fyst.*

Burnley taxi *n.* A police car.

burnout *1. n.* In the world of dragster racing, a short burst of wheelspin on the starting line which is intended to warm up the racing slicks and which leaves impressive, black, smoking stripes on the tarmac. *2. n.* In the world of *diddy-riding,* an unfortunately exposed *arse crayon* which leaves a thick stripe of brown residue on one's ladyfriend's torso. And a strong smell of burning tyres.

burn out the arse clutch *v.* To fail to avoid defecating into one's *hoggers* whilst standing up having a *piss.*

burnt tyre *n.* An acrid, black, semi-vulcanised *Peter O'Toole* passed through the *back body* following a night on the Guinness.

burp the worm *v.* To *choke the chicken.*

burtains *n. medic. Labia majorcas. Gammon flaps, Keith Burtons.* From the contraction of beef + curtains.

bury a quaker *v.* To dispense with the contents of one's rectum. *To crimp one off, lay a cable,* release a payload from the *bomb bay.*

bury the hobbit *v.* To lose *Bilbo Bellend* in the *wizard's sleeve.*

bus bender *n.* A *bird* who is so *well-nourished* that, if she were to be involved in a road traffic accident, she would cause more damage to the vehicle that ran into her than she would incur herself.

bus driver's knob *n. medic.* A state of almost permanent semi-priapism suffered by bus drivers who sit on a vibrating seat all day, eyeing up their *horny* female passengers. A long lasting *semi-on, Varney's teacake.*

bush *n. Gorilla salad, ladygarden, mapatasi.* Female pubic hair.

bushcraft *1. n.* Survival techniques employed in the Australian Outback. *2. n.* Recreational techniques employed in the *Tasmanian Outfront.*

bush meat *n.* Meat found under *bushes.* Usually *vertical bacon.*

bush pig *n.* A slightly more polite term for a *swamp hog.*

bush tents *n.* Ladies' *applecatchers.*

bushell *1. n.* An imperial measure of grain equivalent to 2219.36 cubic inches, under which one can hide one's light. *2. n.* A hairy *cunt.*

bushman's hankie *n. Aus.* Term given to the process whereby mucus is expelled from the nose by placing a finger over one nostril and blowing. Popular amongst professional footballers. A *single barrelled snot gun, oyster.*

bushmonk *n.* A saucy chap who hides or secretes himself in an item of shrubbery for the purposes of *boxing the Jesuit,* especially near the bowling green in Heaton Park, Newcastle upon Tyne.

bushtucker *n.* Anything on the menu when *eating out* in Tasmania.

bushtucker challenge. *n.* Particularly unpalatable *hairy fish and chips.*

busker's hat *n.* The pocketful of change left over from a night *on the lash,* that feels like about twelve quid, but when emptying it into one's hand to buy Lucozade the next morning, turns out to be about thirty-six pence worth of one and two pees.

bustman's holiday *n.* A topless beach.

bust off *v.* To masturbate.

butcher's daughter *1. n.* A woman who has had unlimited access to the pastie counter. A *salad dodger. 2. n.* A woman who has had more than her fair share of *sausages, eg.* her late Royal Highness, Princess Margaret. A *slapper.*

butcher's dishcloth *sim.* A delightful expression, descriptive of the *sump* of a lady's knickers when *the fleet is in.*

butcher's dog, to lie like a *sim.* Descriptive of the bedtime arrangements of a married man. To sleep within reach of the *beef* whilst forbidden to touch it.

butcher's dustbin *n.* A sight grimmer than a *butcher's window.*

butcher's kiss *n.* Evidence left on the bedsheet that a fellow has been *doing it* to his wife during *cricket week.*

butcher's string *n.* Skimpy underwear on a fat lass.

butcher's turd *sim.* Descriptive of the richness of something. *'Do have some more gateau, Mr D'Arcy.' 'Well perhaps just a little slice, Mrs Bennet. It's as rich as a butcher's turd.'* (from *Pride and Prejudice* by Jane Austen).

butcher's window *n.* An appetizing display of raw female genitalia.

butfer *n.* An amusing term for the female perineum. The *carse,* the *tinter. 'NORFOLK: Anon, Sir, she has the most agreeable butfer. BISHOP: The butfer, my liege? Wherefore is it called thus? NORFOLK: Why, Sir, butfer that, thou wouldst be in the shit.'* (from *The Merry Readers' Wives of Windsor* by William Shakespeare).

butler in the pantry *n.* A polite *Brad* which knows its place, remaining below stairs, occasionally coughing discreetly until summoned.

butler's cuff *n.* A tightly-buttoned vagina, the opposite of a *wizard's sleeve.* A *fanny like a mouse's ear.*

butler's revenge *n.* A silent but deadly *fart. SBD.*

butler's ringpiece *adj.* Descriptive of something that is nipping clean. *"What can you see, Holmes?' I expostulated, as the great detective peered into his microscope. (I need not remind you of how in the past, he had solved the mystery of the Pope's cap when he found gibbon's tooth marks on the cardinal's walking stick.) 'I'm examining the handle of this dagger of unusual oriental design in the hope of finding a speck of tobacco, only available from one shop in London, or a hair from a rare species of Patagonian chinchilla,' he replied. 'However, I fear our murderer has wiped it as clean as a butler's ringpiece."* (from *The Brown Hatted League* by Sir Arthur Conan-Doyle).

butt cutlet *n.* A wholesome organic *loaf* cooked up in the *dirt bakery.* A vegetarian's *turd.*

butter your cheeks *v.* To *fart* and *follow through.*

buttered bun *n.* A well-used *snatch.* A *box of assorted creams.*

butterface *n.* A woman with a great figure, but the physiognomy of a darts player's wife. From the phrase "A good body, but her face..." A *bobfoc.*

butterfly with tits *euph.* Hyperbolic figure of speech pertaining to a particularly unlikely state of events. *'You'll never guess who come in the Dog and Duck for the meat draw on Friday, Dave. That Stella McCartney.' 'Oh yeah? Well I was in the park yesterday and I seen a butterfly with tits.'*

buttflood *n.* The *squirts,* the *Earthas.*

butt nuggets *n. Annabels.*

buttock *n.* Fifty percent of an *arse.*

buttock broker *n.* A controller of prostitutes, a pimp. A *titty farmer, pussy farmer, gash baron.*

buttock hall *n. Meat market.* A pub or club frequented by *slappers.*

buttock jig *n.* A close, horizontal dance that takes place after chucking out time. *Making the beast with two backs.*

button *n. Clitty.* The *devil's doorbell, wail switch.*

button groove *n. Hairy axe wound,* the *snapper.* The vulva.

button view *n.* The tantalising *sneak-peek* of a woman's *ta tas* and/or *tit pants* viewed through the gap in between the buttons of her shirt or blouse.

butt plug *n.* A medical appliance used to prevent water from the bath going up your *arse.*

buttress *n.* A *grumble flick* actress who makes a speciality of performing in *back door action* productions.

butt slammers *n. US.* Members of the gay community, who tend to accidentally catch their bottoms in the door in their eagerness to go out and be homosexual.

butt sneeze *n. US. Fart.*

butt's fizz *n.* Celebratory *bubble poo.*

buy a headache *v.* To purchase a strong alcoholic beverage.

buysexual *n.* A fellow who pays for *it.* Buysexuals in their natural habitat can commonly be observed in the Zeedyjk area of Amsterdam. And again two weeks later, sitting on uncomfortable plastic chairs outside the GUM clinic of your local hospital.

BVH *abbrev.* Blue Veined Hooligan. A hard, six-inch tall, one-eyed, purple-faced skinhead.

BWR *abbrev.* Beeps When Reversing. Code used between considerate men to identify, yet save the feelings of, a lady who has failed to achieve an acceptable level of thinness. A *barge arse,* a *double sucker.*

Byker plug *n.* An anally-inserted wad of *bog paper* reputedly favoured by habitual drinkers of Newcastle Brown as a means of preventing spontaneous bowel evacuations.

Byker tea cake *n.* A *Glasgow kiss.* A headbutt. *'Fuck me! Did you see that? Fucking Zidane just give fucking Materazzi a fucking Byker tea cake!'* (John Motson, commentating on the 2006 FIFA World Cup Final).

Cc

cabbage *n. coll.* Girls, *totty, blart, tussage. "What-ho, Jeeves!' I ejaculated. 'I've just been down to the Pink Flamingo club. Never seen so much cabbage in all my born pecker."* (from *Achtung, Jeeves,* by PG Wodehouse).

cabbage fart *n.* An *old dog's alarm clock.* A *dropped back* that smells of rotting vegetation.

cabbage gas *n.* Naturally-occurring renewable fuel which powers *Dutch ovens.*

cabbie's doorbell *n.* A car horn, used to inform a street that their neighbour's 3.00 am taxi has arrived.

cab hookers *n.* Taxi drivers who walk the streets outside nightclubs in the early hours, soliciting for business.

cabin crew doors to manual *exclam.* Phrase shouted as you run to the toilet upon sensing the onset of a severe attack of diarrhoea. From standard aircraft taxiing procedure (British Airways Pilot's Manual Section 4: What to shout when the pilot's about to shit his trousers).

cabinet re-shuffle, carry out a *v.* To sort out one's testicles, *wind the clock. 'Your honour, my client was merely carrying out a cabinet re-shuffle when he was caught in the bushes behind the nurses' home.'*

cable laying *n.* The excretion of lengths of *copper bolt.*

cab man's rests *rhym. slang. Bristols, thrupenny bits.*

caboose *n.* The *anchor man* in a *bum train. Lucky Pierre's* rear attendant.

cacafeugo *1. n. prop.* A Spanish ship captured by Sir Francis Drake on March 1st 1579. *2. n. Shit fire.* Red hot *squirts,* often experienced following a deliciously spicy repast at the Curry Capital, Bigg Market, Newcastle upon Tyne.

cack *1. n. Shit,* excrement, *feeshus. 2. v.* To *papper,* usually one's *trolleys.* Also *cacka, cak. 3. exclam.* Expression of disappointment. *'Mr President. The House Judiciary Committee has instigated articles of impeachment against you for obstruction of justice, abuse of power and contempt of Congress.' 'Oh cack.'*

Cadbury alley *n. Bourneville Boulevard.*

cafe hag *1. n.* A popular brand of decaffeinated coffee. *2. n.* A *fit* woman whom, upon returning to your flat for coffee following a night out, under the harsh fluorescent lights of your kitchen whilst waiting for the kettle to boil, appears neither *fit* nor womanly.

cafetiere, the *n.* The motion of pushing a lady's head *south* against a certain amount of resistance.

cajooblies *n. Oomlaaters.*

cake detector *n.* A portly person. One who does need to ask directions to the bakery. A *salad dodger,* a *piabetic,* a *double fare,* a *barge arse.*

cakeover *n.* That staple of daytime television where they take a plain, fat lass, give her new clothes, make-up and hair, and she comes out at the end of the show looking like a plain, fat lass with new clothes, make-up and hair. *'I see that Jade Goody's had another cakeover, then.'*

Calcutta rinse *n.* The act of using an inverted showerhead to cleanse one's *rusty bullethole* when bereft of *shit tickets.*

Calcutta splutter *n.* A rousing, Neddy Seagoon-style *ringpiece raspberry* blown the morning after an inadvisably piquant *cuzza.* Also *Bombay spray.*

call down for more mayo *v.* To *jack the beanstalk.*

call Huey *v.* To vomit, *puke.* Also *call Ralph, call Ruth, call God on the great white telephone etc.*

call Radcliffe *n.* To leave halfway through something you know you won't be finishing, *eg.* a crap pint, a bad relationship, an Olympic long distance race. *'How did you like Vera Drake?' 'Jesus Christ. I called Radcliffe on it after the first half hour, mate. Went to see Spongebob instead.'*

call to prayer *n.* An early morning, wailing *horse and cart* which indicates that it is time to rise. A *breakfast mecca.*

calve *v.* To have a difficult delivery on the toilet. To attempt to pass an exceptionally toublesome stool where, in extreme cases, it may be necessary to tie a rope around it and get someone to pull it out. A *Herriot turd.*

camel's foot *n. Twix lips. Beetle bonnet.* The pediments of the *toblerone tunnel.*

Camillas *n.* The bowels. Named after equine-featured former Prince's *spunkbucket,* now her Royal Highness the Duchess of Cornwall and Queen-in-waiting Camilla Parker-Bowels.

camp *adj.* As butch as Kenneth Williams.

Campbell's condensed *n.* A small volume, double-strength *brew* which, when diluted with air, can feed a whole room.

can *1. n. US. Bottom. 2. n. US.* A quantity of *Bob Hope, marijuana. 3. n. US.* Prison. *4. n. US.* Toilet, *shithouse. 'They put me in the can after I was caught in the can sticking a can up my can.'*

canary killer *n.* A *fart* that smells like a 60s cokeworks.

canary, send in the *exclam.* Old mining term now appropriated by folk who have just befouled the air in the bobhouse. *'Fuck me. Send in the canary before you use that shitter, your Holiness. I just done a right smelly dump in there.'*

cancer shop *1. n.* A charitable retail outlet selling corpses' trousers, Mantovani records and damp, mouldy copies of *Readers' Digest. 2. n.* A high street tanning studio.

cancer veranda *n.* The *al fresco* area around an office door to which *snoutcasts* are exiled.

c and c *abbrev. Clips and cunts.* Generic term for any television programme consisting of nothing but clips from other televison shows/films/ads/videos interspersed with hilarious, insightful and profound comments from assorted *cunts* whose only reason for existing appears to be appearing on *c and c shows.*

candy floss *1. n.* A large, fluffy fairground snack which is impossible to finish, damages the teeth and invariably leaves one feeling slightly nauseous. *2. n.* A large, fluffy *bush* which is impossible to finish, damages the teeth and invariably *etc., etc.*

cankle *n.* On a lady with a lovely personality, where the calf is indistinguishable from the ankle.

cannonball *v.* Of a fortunately flexible gentleman who never leaves the house, to perform a *thirty-four and a halfer.* To administer *self-horatio.*

cannon wheels *n.* The testicles. *'Are you in yet?' 'Aye, I'm in up to me cannon wheels you cheeky cow.'*

canoe *n.* A streamlined *poo* which is shaped perfectly to ensure anal comfort throughout its expulsion from the *dirt bakery; ie.* one that tapers to a point at both ends like a shuttle off a powerloom.

can tan *n.* The healthy, bronzed skin tone achieved by gentlemen who sit on the *shandy sunbed* all day, supping from tins of 9% lager. *Tramp's tan.*

can't understand new technology *exclam. acronym.* Phrase which can be usefully dropped into the conversation during meetings with patronising IT personnel, or encounters with smart-arsed salesmen in electrical stores, when you are being bombarded with technical bullshit. *'Yeah, the Canon EX-t 677 has nine million pixels. That's with the super hybrid aspheric inkjet CCD of course. Now the Bang and Olufsen B3 X-Z66 has a signal to noise ratio of three hundred, so obviously you're going to see a fall off in your mid-range transients on your hard disk especially since its only got an ISO range of 100-1600kHz. This button toggles through the various modes; shuffle play, flatscreen DVD, wireless bluetooth. Obviously, it's your money, but if it was me I'd go for the Samsung GR 88X-Z23232323b, because it's got the tiltable USB. Do you want to take out the five year extended warranty?' 'Eeh, sorry. Can't understand new technology.'*

canvas cashpoint *n.* On a festival campsite, an illicit source of money, cameras, mobile phones, car keys, iPods *etc.* Someone else's tent.

captain *n.* Penis. *'Don't be shy, love. Go below deck and say hello to the captain.'*

captain, do a *v.* To display one's *buttocks* through the back window of a coach, usually to a couple of nuns in a Morris Minor. To do a *moonie.*

Captain Caveman *n.* A yodelling *biffer.*

Captain Hogseye *n.* Curly-bearded seafarer with a shiny, bald, purple head who trawls in *cod cove.* And spits a lot.

Captain Hook *n.* A fellow proficient in the gentle art of using his crooked index finger to haul the gusset of his ladyfriend's *bills* safely out of the way, for whatever reason.

Captain Oates, to do a *v.* To altruistically leave the pub early when struggling with the pace, so as not to hold your more manly fellow drinkers back.

Captain's pie *1. n.* Tasty *slice* caught fresh by Captain *Hogseye. Haddock pastie. 2. n. milit.* Of naval catering, that pie which belongs to the captain.

capuccino fanny *n.* When the *furry cup* has reached its maximum froth.

caramel keg *1. n.* A much-loved, self-explanatory chocolate in a box of Cadbury's Roses. *2. n.* A lady with a *pint glass figure, eg.* her with the red face and the glasses who used to show off at the front of Les Dawson's Roly Polys tap-dancing troupe.

caravanner *n.* A slender gentleman hitched to a distinctly more sizeable spouse, *ie.* One who is used to towing a large, ungainly *load* around. *'Today's Birthdays: George Ellery Hale, American astronomer, 1868; Giacomo Leopardi, Italian poet, 1798; Christos Papakryiakopoulos, Greek mathematician, 1914; Ben Ofoedu, Celebrity Wife Swap caravanner, 1972.'*

carbon dating *n.* Of a young gentleman, the act of going out with a somewhat more mature lady friend.

carbon dibaxide *n.* Chemical name for *arse gas.*

car bootylicious *adj.* Descriptive of those rough *bints* one sees in *saggy-arsed* velour tracksuits and *bingo clink.* Also *aldilicious.*

cardie muffins *n. Tits* of the sort you would expect a spinster librarian to have.

Cardiff grandmother *n.* A lady whose own children have left the nest and who is now, at the age of twenty-eight or so, out *on the pull* again.

cardinal's cap *n. medic.* A swelling and reddening of the *herman* brought on by chronic *bishop rage. Fireman's helmet.*

cardswipe *n.* The groove on a *bird's* frontage.

card table *n.* A position whereby a lady engages in simultaneous oral/vaginal pleasures with two gentlemen who, should they wish, could play a game of cards on her back. A frankly unlikely scenario. A *spit roast.*

cargle *v.* Of a *dirty lady,* to gargle with a gentleman's *erotic spendings.* Like they do. From cum + gargle.

cargoyle *n.* A lady with such *a lovely personality* that all dates with her are spent in the car to avoid the possiblity of being spotted in her company.

Carling darling *n.* A lady whose attractiveness only becomes apparent after one has had a few. A *ten pinter, gallon girl.*

carnival *n.* A sexual game where a woman sits on a man's face and he has to guess her weight.

carnival knowledge *n.* Biblical phrase meaning to have sex. *'And it came to pass that Mary was up the spout, yea though Joseph had not lain with her, and certainly had not carnival knowledge of her.'* (from *St. Paul's Letters to the Gas Board,* Chapter 6, v. 3-5).

carniwhore *n.* A speciality film actress with a real taste for meat.

Carolgees' cuff *n.* Having one's *wanking spanner* wrist deep in a *biffer.*

car park, to *v.* To kick the *Brad* out of someone. To *take them outside.*

car park karaoke *n.* A post-drink entertainment where women *pissed up* on bacardi breezers take turns on the *purple-headed microphone.*

carpark sutra *n.* The ancient mystical art of gymnastic *screwing* on the back seat of an Astra. Usually whilst parked round the back of Shire Oak Miners' Welfare and surrounded by a crowd of enthusiastic onanists staring through the windows.

carpenter's dream *n.* A sexually promiscuous woman. From the fact that she is "flat as a board and easy to screw". A *boot.*

carpet duster *n.* A dense, heavier-than-air cloud of *carbon dibaxide* which forms a thin layer over the whole floor surface.

carpet muncher *n.* A lady who enjoys *gorilla salad,* but turns her nose up at *meat and two veg.*

carpet tiles *rhym. slang. Bumgrapes.*

carrot bladder *n. medic.* Secret internal organ situated just beside the pyloric sphincter from where diced carrots magically appear when you vomit. (© Billy Connolly Ltd. 1978).

carrot knackers *n.* Affectionate term for a ginger-haired fellow. *'Oi, carrot knackers. There's a picture of you in a nazi armband on the front of the Sun.'*

carrot snapper *n.* A lady with the sort of protruding front teeth that would do a rabbit proud. A *bunny girl. 'Famous people born on the 27th December: Johannes Kepler, astronomer who correctly explained planetary motion, thereby becoming the founder of the science of celestial mechanics, 1571. Louis Pasteur, scientist and discoverer of the theory that infectious diseases are caused by germs, whose pioneering work became the foundation of the science of microbiology, and hence a cornerstone of modern medicine, 1822. Janet Street Porter, screeching carrot snapper, 1946.'* (from *Schott's Oh Fucking Hell, What Am I Going to Put in it This Year Book, 2006*).

carry out, to have a *v.* To *cack* oneself and have to walk to the nearest convenient spot for a *scrape out.*

carry your bat *1. v.* In the world of cricket, to return to the pavilion, having remained at the crease throughout the team's entire innings without getting out. *2. v.* In the world of *having it off,* to terminate a drunken act of sexual intercourse after failing to *drop your filthy yoghurt* up a lady due to the effects of strong liquor.

carse *n.* The female equivalent of the *barse. Biffon.*

Carsten Janker *rhym. slang.* A *wanker.* From the bullet-headed footballing kraut who taunted the crowd after putting Germany 1-0 ahead at the start of their 5-1 trouncing by En-ger-lernd, En-ger-ernd, En-ger-lernd! En-ger-lernd, En-ger-lernd, En-ger-lerrr-ernd!

cartman *n. medic.* A small *stool.* From the little shit in the popular children's cartoon series *South Park.*

carwash *n.* View of the vagina whilst performing *cumulonimbus.* The hair of the *muff* looking like them big whirly brush things that knock your wing mirrors off.

Casanova's rubber sock *n.* Condom, *blob, dunky, French letter, Coney Island whitefish.*

cashanova *n.* One who doesn't waste his money, but spends it wisely on prostitutes. A chap who pays for his love. A *punter,* a *John,* a *buysexual.*

cash crash *n.* A deliberate car accident intended to enrich the perpetrator by insurance and injury claims.

cash in the attic *1. n.* Vile daytime TV programme in which gullible homeowners are bullied into selling their worthless heirlooms for the entertainment of semi-comatose students, professional comedians and the unemployed. *2. v.* To perform a *money shot* into a *bird's* mouth.

cashpoint cripple *n.* See *video cripple.*

casting Churchill's reflection *euph.* A political impression involving a porcelain bowl with water in the bottom, your *arse* and a *bum cigar.*

castle on the queen side *1. v.* In chess, to perform the risky strategy of castling on the opposite side of the board from the usual default manoeuvre of castling on the king's side. Whatever that means. *2. v.* Of a man, to be prone to a spot of *airborne puddle avoidance. 'You see him over there? That bloke with the bushy moustache and the leather motorcycle cap, grinning from ear to ear in the middle of that writhing, sweaty, naked homosexual bumchain? Well, I have it on very good authority that he castles on the queen's side, if you know what I mean.'*

Catalan custard *n.* Strange, viscous deposit found in the gusset of one's *grundies* after a heavy night *on the piss* in Barcelona. A discovery which is accompanied by unnerving, nightmarish flashbacks to an unpleasant interlude set on a seedy strip club stage which involves a blindfold, a man dressed in a monkey suit and a cheering crowd. *'What's up, Bill?' 'I've found some Catalan custard in my gusset, Marge.'*

catbab *n.* An exotic snack containing unidentifiable meat of questionable provenance, usually sold out of the window of an old ambulance.

catcher's mitt *n.* A contraceptive diaphragm, a *fuck-plug, babe roof.*

cat five *1. abbrev. RAF.* Classification of an aircraft that is considered beyond repair following a crash. *2. abbrev. RAF.* Classification of a *chod bin* that is considered beyond use following a *dirty bomb.*

cat flaps *1. n.* Means by which a cute little pussy can enter the house. *2. n.* Means by which a *cock* can enter a cute little *pussy.* Labia minora, *beef curtains.*

Catford bunch *n.* An inexpensive floral offering to a ladyfriend, hand made from the flowers taped to the railings and lamp-posts of South London in memory of the recently-stabbed.

cathedral *sim.* Describing an oversized vagina which is too echo-y for a satisfactory *organ recital.* A *bucket fanny.*

catholic tastes *1. n.* Wide-ranging interests, from the word "catholic" meaning "universal". *2.n.* Narrowly-focused interests, specifically those pursued by certain members of the left-footed clergy which revolve principally around the contents of their prepubescent choirboys' surplices.

cat on the bed *euph.* Descriptive of the sensations transmitted through the mattress that a gentleman feels when his fellow bedlady is *playing the invisible banjo. 'Can you feel something, Your Majesty?' 'It's just a cat on the bed, Mr Fagan. Now go back to sleep.'*

cat scarer *n.* An unsuccessful haircut. A coiffure so bad that the victim's own moggy doesn't recognise them and runs off.

cat's face *n.* Mrs Slocombe's *cunt.*

cattle *rhym. slang.* To engage in coitus. From cattle truck = fuck. Also *trolley* (& truck), *Friar* (Tuck) or *Russian* (duck).

cat with a strawberry-flavoured arse, like a *sim.* Descriptive of the happy demeanour of those who cannot believe the extent to which Heaven appears to have smiled upon them, *eg.* A rollover lottery winner, a dog with two *cocks* or whichever ne'er-do-well is *banging* Charlotte Church.

caught white handed, to be *v.* To lose a game of *rushin' roulette.*

cauliflower *1. n.* Sex. *'Hey! Your missus gave me a bit of cauliflower while you were at work last night.' 2. n. 18thC. Lettuce.*

cauliflower biff *n. medic.* A *clout* that has had a right good *banging.* A blurtch that looks like one of Bill Beaumot's ears.

cauliflower cheese *n. Smegma.*

cavalier *n.* An uncircumcised penis. With a big smile and a feather stuck in the top.

cavalry caviar *n.* A highly-prized, piquantly-flavoured salty delicacy, traditionally served in armed forces circles on a digestive biscuit or cream cracker. *Officer's Mess.*

cave paintings *1. n.* Mysterious and multicoloured daubings of dinosaurs, which date from the upper Palaeolithic period after the last ice age. Found extensively decorating the inside walls of limestone caves in France and Spain during the 19th century. *2. n.* Mysterious and multicoloured daubings dating from a night after protracted consumption of draught Bass. Found comprehensively decorating the insides of *undercrackers* and bed linen the length and breadth of the UK on most weekend mornings.

caviar *1. n.* Expensive delicacy made from fish periods. *2. n.* Webspeak for scatalogical *grumble,* apparently.

cedar burp *n.* A small outbreak of *chocolate thunder.*

cemetery gates *n.* An old lady's *muff minders. Granny's oysters.*

centre parting *n.* Highly enjoyable form of solo *balloon knot* sport whereby the practitioner sits on a sturdy, solid chair or bench and then forcibly breaks wind whilst leaning forward at an angle of forty-five degrees, thus causing the emitted *trouser cough* to shoot straight up the middle of his or her back, like a sort of gaseous Evel Kneivel going up a ramp. HRH the Duchess of York is said to be an enthusiastic *centre parter* and, during Christmas dinners at Balmoral often demonstrates her skills by knocking a paper crown off the top of her own head.

cervix charge *n.* The hidden costs incurred in the *getting over of one's leg, eg.* flowers, meal, taxi home, changing locks *etc.*

CF Bundy *abbrev. medic.* Doctors' shorthand written on the charts of terminally ill patients. Completely Fucked But Not Dead Yet.

CFN *abbrev.* A *ringpiece* which flies in the face of the Kyoto agreement, and burns at tremendous temperatures, belching out toxic fumes and clouds of particulates which are harmful to the ozone layer and one's underpants. A *heavy smoker,* an *arse* with a huge *carbon dibaxide* footprint. Coal Fired Nipsy.

CGI *1. abbrev.* The City and Guilds Institute. *2. abbrev.* Cunt Gap Index. A measurement on a scale of finger widths of the size of a woman's *Toblerone tunnel.*

Chalfonts *rhym. slang.* Piles, *bum*

grapes. From the town of Chalfont St. Gemerroids, Buckinghamshire.

challenge oneself *v.* To engage in a bit of *five against one.* To *knock yourself about a bit.*

champagga *n.* A fight fuelled by expensive beverages, as opposed to Special Brew. A brawl one may see once in a blue moon outside a brasserie.

champagne corks *n.* Bullet-hard *nipples* that pop out of the *tit pants* with enough force to take your eye out. *Organ stops.*

champagne shit *n.* A sit down toilet visit where one strains for some time to *pop a cork,* but once it goes it is followed by a magnum of fizzy brown liquid. A *champoo.*

change ammo *v. milit.* To empty one chamber of the *mutton musket,* readying the firing piece for the next shot. To take a last minute *gypsy's kiss* prior to a *poke.*

change at Baker Street *v.* During intercourse, to decide to *play the B-side.* From the only station on the London Underground where it is possible to change from the Pink line (Hammersmith & City) to the Brown line (Bakerloo).

change at Oxford Circus *v.* Similar usage to *change at Baker Street,* but for monthly ticket holders. *Going from red to brown.*

change lanes *v.* To switch, mid-romp, from vaginal to anal penetration or vice versa. *'Just like when on the road, when on the job it is good practice to signal one's intentions before changing lanes so as not to take anyone by surprise.'* (from *The Joy of Sex* by Dr Alex Comfort).

change rain *n.* A shower of coins which falls from the trouser pockets when a gentleman is attempting to undress quietly and not wake his slumbering wife.

changing the washer *n.* Remedial action required to address the issue of post-curry *ring* leakage. In the event of the *balloon knot* failing to keep one's *rusty water* sufficiently at bay, furtive trips to the water closet are required to make good the faulty orifice using an index finger swathed in toilet tissue.

chan it *v.* To take unnecessary risks in mundane situations whilst under the delusion that if the short-arsed 80s martial arts hero Jackie can do it, then so can you. Examples include running between two buses, escaping an attacker on your bicycle and fending someone off with an umbrella *etc*.

chanson *n.* Any tacky trinket or ornament adorning an elderly person's mantelpiece. From the Manhattan Transfer song, which seemed to be performed on *The Two Ronnies* every week for about fifteen years, whose lyrics went; "Chanson d'amour / Tat! Tat! Tat! Tat! Tat!"

chap *1. n.* The *charlie*. *2. v.* To gently slap your *chap* in the face of your sleeping wife, girlfriend or party guest, take a Polaroid photograph and leave it in a place where they are bound to come across it, *eg*. fridge door, car windscreen, internet.

chapel hat pegs *sim.* Large, erect *nips*. *Pygmy's cocks, Scammell wheel nuts, JCB starter buttons*.

chapkin *n.* A protective cloth placed over a fellow's stomach and chest in order to soak up any salty spillages which may accidentally occur for any reason whilst he is lying on his back.

chap's eye *n.* A politically correct alternative to the outdated, offensive term *Jap's eye*, which can be used to describe the male urethral opening when in polite, right-on company. Usefully, in the event of an outraged reaction to an accidental slip, the speaker can claim to have said "chap's eye" in the first place, thus making his accusers feel like racials.

chapstick *n.* An implement with which a lady moistens dry lips.

charge of the light ale brigade *n.* The Friday 2pm stampede of builders, roofers and scaffolders to the pub. Or any other day that a drop of rain has fallen. Or it looks like it might rain later.

charioteer, the *n.* Self explanatory sexual position involving a woman with long hair who's down on all fours and a man with very short legs pretending to be Charlton Heston. A *ben her.* Also *attempting to enter the gates of Rome.*

charity work *n.* The altruistic act of buying a drink for, or flirting with, an aesthetically challenged woman out of pity. *'Where are you off to, John?' 'I'm just going to go on the dance floor to do a bit of charity work with fat Lisa from accounts.'*

charlie *1. rhym. slang. Cunt.* From "Charlie Hunt". *'You look a right charlie'. 2. n. Showbiz sherbert. 3. n. Hampton Wick*, the penis.

Charlie Cairoli's hat *n.* A lady's *minge*, brimful of *spoff*. From the erstwhile clown's blancmange-filled bowler.

Charlie Dimmock's nipples *n.* Term used by vicars to describe the hat-pegs in their chapels.

charlie in the chocolate factory *n. Bolivian marching powder* snorted in a public *shithouse eg.* the *crappers* at the Groucho Club.

Charlie Potatoes *n.* One who labours under the misapprehension that he all that when he ain't. Someone who thinks he's the *bollocks, eg.* Richard Blackwood, Chris Moyles. *'Look at that cunt swaggering about like he's Charlie Potatoes.'*

charlies *n.* 1970s *assets.*

charlies' angels *1. n.* See *tit fairies. 2. n.* Women who appear attractive to a man as a consequence of him having taken a quantity of *showbiz sherbet* on board. A Class-A variation on the term *five pinter.*

Charlie two-dinners *n.* A gentleman whose glands eschew salads in favour of pies, sausages and more pies. A *double sucker.*

charms *n.* In British tabloid journalism, the breasts. Usually prefixed "ample".

charva *n.* See *charver, chav.*

charva cava *n.* Substandard *trampagne.* White cider.

charver *1. v. US.* To have sex, *shag. 2. n.* Boy, lad, adolescent. *3. n.* Aerosol-snorting, be-tracksuited *twocker, borstal boy, car radio removal mechanic. 4. n.* A 10-year-old mother of several *pastie babies.* Also, *charva, chav.*

chase the dragon *1. v.* To "snort" a syringe full of marijuana cigarettes up your bottom through a burnt spoon. *2. n.* To attempt to get a good whiff of one's own *dropped back* in an attempt to acheive the ultimate high.

chase the cotton mouse *v.* To have the *painters in, flags out,* to *surf* *the crimson wave,* be *up on blocks.*

chastity patch *n.* A small smear of excrement surreptitiously wiped on the back of one's girlfriend's neck before she goes on a lasses' night out, the aim of which is to deter any would-be suitors.

Chatham crow *n.* The classy corvoid tattoo that ladies of the eponymous Kent Olympic village typically sport on their lower backs just above their *arse cracks.* Chatham crows are usually displayed to best advantage by a pair of jeans or sweatpants that are three sizes too small. *Arse antlers.*

chauffeur's glove *n.* A tight-fitting *flunkey*. Possibly with three buttons on the back.

chav *n.* A member of the lower orders. The sort of person who would have been unlikely to turn up on *Ask the Family* in the 1970s.

chavalanche *n.* A terrifying Burberry-clad cascade of *scratters.*

chavalcade *1. n.* A town centre procession of souped-out, clapped-up Astras, Corsas and XR3is driven by a motley assortment of *scratters, neds, pogs, ratboys* and *Burberry apes. 2. n.* A pram-pushing convoy of the above on their way to Greggs.

chavalry *n.* Mobile units of these halfwit *ratboys* on toddlers' BMX bicycles you get on the pavements these days, easily recognised by their uniform of shellsuit trousers, hoopy pullovers, leather gloves and peaked caps.

chavelin *n.* Semi-olympian sport played by denizens of the urban underclass. Darts.

chavel inn *n.* A low quality hotel, with its bar populated by *burberry apes,* aggressive manual workers and, unfortunately for themselves, sales managers working for tight-arsed companies.

chavellers' cheques *n.* Giros.

chaviar *n.* Supermarket own-brand "value" baked beans.

chavrolet *n.* A *scratter's* motor vehicle, normally a lower-end production model souped up to *bloody fuck* with alloy wheels, blue downlights, spoilers, tinted glass, laughably loud sound systems *etc.*

chaviot of fire *n.* A burnt out Clio, Astra or Citroen AX on a rough estate. A *fourth party insurance* write-off.

chav-nav *n.* Ankle-mounted hi-tech electronic device which ensures that *scratters* can find their way home before 8pm each evening.

chavrons *n.* The trendy, angular shapes cut into the Action Man-style hair on a young ASBO laureate's head.

cheapies *n.* Schoolboy sexual thrills. *'Miss Pollard bent down to pick up the chalk and gave William his cheapies.'* (from *William Stirs Below* by Richmal Crompton).

chebs *n. Tits, norks, headlamps.* Breasts.

check the oil *v.* To put one's *cock* in some *bird's dirtbox* before pulling it out, inspecting, it and wiping it with a cloth.

check the roast *v.* To see whether what you've been baking is ready to come out. To go for a *shit.*

check one's emails *v.* To search for *grumble* on the interweb, for the purpose of fuelling a sordid and shameful act of *self harm. 'Hurry up there, son. I want to check my emails. Into a sock.' 'Alright dad. Can I just finish off my homework* *first, though? Into a sock.'*

check on the scones *v.* To *turn one's bike around,* have a *Chinese singing lesson, strain the potatoes, see a man about a dog.* To relieve oneself, *have a slash.*

checkout time *n.* The period that elapses whilst the heady aroma of an *air biscuit* permeates its way out through the layers of one's clothing.

cheddar apple *n.* A very large, cheesy *bell end.*

cheek flapper *n.* A *fart* which registers highly on the *brap scale.* A *clapper rattler,* a *drive on the cats' eyes.*

Cheeseboard Charlie *n.* Amusing pejorative term used to describe an individual who is excessively accustomed to big restaurant sessions. *'Oi, Cheeseboard Charlie, shut your fucking pie hole. Let Shirley Maclaine get a fucking word in edgeways, will you, you fat twat.'* (Michael Parkinson interviewing Peter Ustinov, BBC TV, 1978).

cheese cracker *n.* A savoury, pungent *custard tart.* An air *snack* rather than a *buffet.*

cheese cutter *n. medic.* A rogue *pube* caught in the *fiveskin,* whilst still attached to the body. Results in two-fold agony; simultaneously cutting into *Captain Picard's head* whilst trying to tear itself out at the root. A *Bobby Charlton.*

cheese map *n.* Protein-based staining often to be found on the front of a young man's lower nightwear. *'Mums know that new Azox 2-in-1 will remove 99% of all household stains even on the cold water cycle. Dried-on food on the baby's bib, grass and mud on Janet's hockey skirt, oil and grease on dad's overalls or cheese maps on Jimmy's pyjama bottoms ... none of them can stand up to Azox's magic new non-bio formula.'*

cheesepipe *n.* The tubular organ that secretes *chucky cheese.*

cheesepipe clingfilm *n.* Condom, *rubber johnny.*

cheese ridge *n.* The fertile area of the *cheesepipe* where *knob cheese* is matured for weeks and months. The *brim* of the *lid.* Your sulcus.

cheese whistle *n.* The marvellous musical instrument kept in a fellow's tweeds. The *pink oboe.*

cheesy wheelbarrow *n.* A self-explanatory sexual position utilised by two *uphill gardeners.*

cheezer *n.* That which is a cross between a *chick* and a *geezer, eg.* Julian Clary or Richard Branson.

chef's arse *n.* An uncomfortable, perspiring, smelly *bum cleft.* From the condition's prevalence amongst catering professionals, *eg.* Gordon Ramsay, Anthony Worrall-Thompson and Nigella Lawson.

chef's special sauce *n. Spunk. 'Here is your steak, Mr Winner. And chef wanted you to know that he enjoys your Esure adverts so much, he's put you an extra helping of his special sauce on there.'*

cheggered *adj. Pissed* as an *Exchange & Mart.* Derivation unknown.

Chelmsley Wood foreplay *n.* Any form of domestic violence or spousal abuse. Named after the Chelmsley Wood area of Solihull, West Midlands, which is known to be somewhat rough.

Chelmsley Wood lie detector *n.* A West Midlands Police Force truncheon.

Chelmsley Wood pill *n.* Anal sex. *UTBNB.* One up the bum, no harm done. A *Colchester condom.*

chemi-khazi *n.* What one commits when entering a portable lavatory cubicle at a music festival. *Poo-icide.*

cheps *n. Chebs.*

Cherie Blair *n.* A mouth conducive to group fellatio. A *Carly Simon,* a *three-dick gob, Wallace.*

Cherie Blair's cake hole *n.* A strangely convoluted and, frankly, frightening *fanny.*

Cherie's smile *n.* Scary-lipped part of the anatomy of a lady who's been around a bit, for example one of those not-particularly-good time girls commonly to be seen disporting themselves in windows near the Holiday Inn, Nuremburg.

cherry *1. n.* An intact *virgin string.* One that has not been *popped. 2. n.* One's virginity generally.

cherry boy *n.* A crimson, hormone-filled adolescent male with an intact *virgin string,* on whom a dampened finger will sizzle.

chest furniture *n. Tits, hooters, sweatermeat.*

chestnuts *n. Stits, juglets.*

chest pillows *n. Chebs again.*

chest tuners *n.* The symmetrical dials on a lady's *frontage* that enable a gentleman to find Radio Luxembourg. *Nips.*

Chewbacca after a fight *sim.* Descriptive of a particularly untidy *biffer.*

Chewbacca's calling *exclam.* A long, protracted *fart* similar to the strangulated guttural mewings of the famous *Star Wars* dog.

Chewbacca's growl *n.* The involuntary shrieks and groans released when one passes a *bum spud* as *wide as a footballer's tie knot.*

chewie *n.* An act of *horatio,* a *sucking off,* gobbie, *nosh.*

chewing a toffee *n.* The unpleasant sensation of anal chafing and squelching when walking out of the *bog* following insufficient wiping of the *freckle.*

chewing on a brick *n.* Of *logs* and *logging,* that desperate point when the *turtle's head,* and indeed *shoulders* protrude, and the *arse* is left gumming away at a *dirt.*

Chicago shuffle *n.* An entirely imaginary sexual act whereby a lady traps a gentleman's *member* under her arm before shuffling a pack of cards. A *Las Vegas bagpipe,* an *Monte Carlo musclefuck.*

chichis *n. Mex. Tits,* breasts.

chicken *n.* Young gay male. A *botter's apprentice.*

chickenhawk *n.* The time-served *botter,* to whom several *botter's apprentices* are apprenticed.

chicken skin handbag *n. Scrot, nadbag.*

chicken wings *n. medic.* The anatomical spare skin underneath the upper arms of a *Duchess of Giblets,* so called as they resemble the contents of a KFC Zinger burger. *Bingo wings, dinner ladies' arms.*

chill the husband's salad *v.* Of a lady, to position herself such that a cold blast from the air conditioning goes up her skirt, thus keeping her *lettuce* crisp and fresh. The opposite of *warming the husband's supper.*

chimbonda *n.* A lady with oversized *pins* wearing leggings that are far too tight. Named after the diminutive, muscly-legged, Guadeloupe-born Tottenham Hotspur right back Pascal Chimbonda, who has a penchant for wearing tights under his shorts. *Two pounds of shit in a one pound bag.*

chimney sweep *1. n.* A soot-covered man who cleans your chimney. *2. n.* A soot-covered man who *bangs* you up the *dirtbox.*

chimney sweep's brush *n.* Dick Van Dyke's penis.

chimping 1. n. *Spanking the monkey* whilst grinning from ear to ear. And having a cup of PG Tips. *2. n.* The frankly unlikely (though you wouldn't put it past the Germans) act of shitting into your hands and throwing it at your partner, for your mutual pleasure. *'Mature professional gentleman, married, 52, seeks discreet, elegant, educated lady, 35-45, for long walks in the country, fine wine and food, trips to the theatre and sophisticated classical music concerts. Must be into chimping.'*

chimp oneself red *v.* To furiously *relax in a gentleman's way,* to have *one off the flipper.*

chimps' fingers *n.* Particularly dry, thin stools, often with distinct knuckles. *'Twenty six days at sea, and the men are wracked with stomach cramps. Regular bowel motions are naught but a memory. I myself have not passed solids for nigh on two weeks, and that was but a couple of chimps' fingers 200 miles SSE of Christmas Island.'* (from *The Journal of William Bligh,* 1765).

chin airbag *n.* A phantom double chin on a non-fatty. Usually associated with *pissed,* impromptu group photographs on a night out, especially common late on during wedding receptions when wearing a collar and tie and leaning slightly backwards. A *pelican's beak. 'Fucking hell! It's a great photo of everybody, but look at me! Looks like my chin airbag has gone off.'*

Chinese algebra, harder than *sim.* Descriptive of the magnificent tumescence of a right *diamond cutter. 'You're a lucky lady tonight, love. This bugger's harder than Chinese algebra.'*

Chinese fire drill *n.* A scene of utter disorder and pandemonium. *'Emergency services were today called out to the Dover branch of Netto after staff reduced to price of own brand baked beans to 1p a tin. In the Chinese fire drill that followed, 17 people were trampled to death and another 68 were detained in hospital, suffering crush injuries'.* (BBC News 24, Jan 3rd 2003).

Chinese firework *n.* The *cock* of a *one pump chump, ie.* one that *goes off* almost instantaneously.

Chinese gravy *n.* Something with a foul flavour. *'I was dining at the Y the other night and my fish supper tasted worse than Chinese gravy.'*

Chinese helicopter pilot *sim.* A bloke sitting up and operating his *chopper.*

Chinese junk *rhym. slang. Jitler, pineapple.*

Chinese mouse, hung like a *sim.* Opposite of *hung like an Arab stallion.*

Chinese singing lesson *n.* A *gypsy's kiss.* A *piss.*

Chinese tool *n.* A feeble penis, *ie.* one that is barely up to the job in hand.

Chinese wicketkeeper *euph.* One who gamely adopts the bending stance of a stumpsman whilst grimacing. A *pillowbiter,* an *uphill* *gardener's cheesy wheelbarrow.*

Chinese wordsearch, hard as a *sim.* A good way to describe a particularly tumescent erectipulation of the *gentleman's parts;* that is to say, when one's *on* is very *hard* indeed. *'I woke up this morning and I was as hard as a Chinese wordsearch, Your Majesty.'*

chin music, play a little *v.* To give some wiseguy a fourpenny one up the bracket.

chinook position *n.* Coital congress arrangement often practised behind skips, up back alleys and round by the wheelie bins at the back of the kebab house, wherein the female participant is supported betwixt her partner's virile member and a wall. So called because it involves being lifted off the ground by a powerful *chopper.* Also known as a *fork lift truck* or *flying buttress.*

chin rest *n. Duffy's bridge.*

chinstrap n. The small piece of skin which holds the *German helmet* safely in place. The *banjo.*

chin splash *n.* Condition caused by trying on a *pearl necklace* in a clumsy manner.

chin tinsel *n. Sloom*-based decorations dangling from the mandibles of a *messy eater.*

chin varnish *n. Perseverance soup.*

chinwag *n.* The side-to-side use of one's lower mandible, preferably with a few days' growth of stubble, in the style of a ruminating heffer, to stimulate a lady's *barnyard foliage.*

Chip Pan Alley *n.* The sort of High Street which only contains chip shops interspersed with the occasional tattoo parlour.

chipperfield *n.* A proper leathering you get off a bouncer for no good reason.

chippie's toolbag *n.* Of women's *bodily treasures,* the *labia majorcas.* The *beef curtains, mutton shutters, Deputy Dawg's ears.*

chippopotamus *n.* A generously-proportioned lady who honestly just eats like a mouse but whose glands scoff vast quantities of deep-fried spuds.

chippy lippy *n.* Tell-tale traces of tomato sauce on one's face and clothing after a night on the town. *'Me missus went nuts because she thought I'd been gobbing off with some bird. Turns out it was just chippy lippy.'*

chip shovels *n.* The hands of a fat lass.

chips 'n' hame *phr. Scot.* The observed state of someone's failure to *score* and their resulting departure from the pub or club. *'Wee Angus has had nae luck the neet.' 'Aye, Hamish. It's chips 'n' hame for him.'*

chipwreck *n.* A person who has unaccountably failed to lose weight despite clearly putting a lot of time and energy into nimbly *dodging salad.* Ironically, chipwrecks typically adhere to the government's healthy eating injunction to eat five or more portions of fruit or veg each day, concentrating particularly on regular portions of the vegetable *Solanum tuberosum.*

chirp on *n.* The sort of good-natured, non-threatening erection that Kenneth Connor would have got in *Carry On Cruising* when Liz Fraser bent over to pick up a quoit. A *stiffy* that causes one to slap the back of one's neck and pull one's collar out whilst rubbing one's right leg up and down one's left calf.

choad *n.* A *cock,* specifically one that is wider than it is long.

chocnose *v.* A traditional end of party trick whereby a guest drops his trousers and rubs his *arse* on the nose of a comatose friend for the amusement of the other guests. *'August 3rd. Opening night party for Cavalcade at The Savoy. Kit (Hassall), Gerty (Lawrence) and Fanny (Brice) were all in attendance. Ivor (Novello) passed out on the chaise longue after drinking far too much Bolly, and Jimmy (Clitheroe) chocnosed him, poor dear. How we laughed!'* (from *The Diary of Noel Coward*).

chocolate cha-cha *n.* Unlikely-sounding rooftop dance in the style of Dick Van Dyke, but performed by *chimney sweeps* of the *chocolate* variety.

chocolate chimney sweep *n.* A soot-covered man who is not interested in cleaning ladies' flues.

chocolate chip *n.* Special type of dark, shiny residue which is only found spattered on the bowls of the lavatories at international airports. *Chocolate chip* can only be removed using products which are so astringent that they can not be sold to the general public.

chocolate eclair *n.* A *Cleveland steamer*.

chocolate eye *n.* The *bronze eye, brass eye, red eye, brown eye.* The *bumhole.*

chocolate fountain *n.* A spectacular anal, upside-down firework ignited in the lavatory to celebrate having a belly full of beer and a dodgy curry the night before.

chocolate iceberg *n.* Giant *turd* sitting in the pan, nine tenths of which remains below the surface. A *growler.*

chocolate knob, to have a *v.* Of a fortunate fellow, to experience little or no difficulty in persuading ladies to perform *horatio.*

chocolate quilting *n.* The considerate public lavatory practice of covering a floating *Bullimore* with a duvet of toilet tissue so as to avoid startling the next occupant.

chocolate sandwich *n.* A sexual act performed in the presence of Arthur Lowe in the film *Oh Lucky Man!* involving a black man and two white lady strippers.

chocolate speedway *n. Bumhole, poop chute.*

chocolate speedway rider *n.* Purple-helmeted star of the *dirt track.*

chocolate starfish *n. Rusty sheriff's badge, Bovril bullet hole.* The *clackervalve.*

chocolate thunder *n. Tail winds,* a *trouser typhoon.* Also *under thunder.*

chocolate wink *n.* A gentleman's cheeky treat for the special lady in his life whereby, when exiting the shower, he bends forward, reaches back and parts his buttocks, momentarily exposing his *bronze eye.*

chod bin *n.* The lavatory bowl.

chod hop *v.* To move with increasing desperation from cubicle to cubicle in a municipal *crapper,* searching for an acceptable toilet to use, *ie.* one which is not covered in diarrhoea, has no *piss* on the seat, has a lock on the door *etc.*

choir of angels *n.* A cloud-parting zephyr of heavenly *wind* that rises in pitch, timbre and volume, bringing a lump to the throat and a tear to the eye.

choke a brown dog *v.* To apply the *bum brake* too early. To nip a *shite* halfway through.

choke the chicken *v.* To masturbate.

choke the goose *v.* To masturbate again.

cholesterol special *n.* A Byronic breakfast, *ie.* one that is "swimming in grease".

chommie *n.* The *barse.*

chooza *n. NZ.* A *choad.*

choozies *n. Aus.* Breasts.

chop *v.* To *wallop your wood*, practise karate whilst holding a weapon in the hand. To *turn Japanese.*

chopper *1. n.* Penis. *'That (insert name of striker currently having a run of bad form) couldn't score in a brothel with a £50 note wrapped round his chopper.' 2. n.* Fancy orange bike that fat kids owned in the 1970s. *3. n.* Helicopter. *4. n.* Axe. *5. n.* Nickname of anyone with the surname Harris.

choreplay *n.* Tiresome pre-sex ritual required by selfish women. *Frigmarole.*

chorus from Mama Jo's bongos *n.* An early morning *fart* that sounds like someone from *Scooby Doo* running on the spot before scarpering from the ghost. *Morning thunder.*

Christmas 1914 *euph.* A period of unnatural calm and tranquility between the beginning of something and the moment when the full horror of what has been set in motion becomes apparent. The *grace period* between the consumption of a hot meal and the inevitable bloody trauma that ensues.

Christmas spirit *n.* An essentially altruistic approach to oral sex adopted by generously-inclined ladies. *'Henry rather liked his new bird as she displayed the Christmas spirit in abundance, noshing him off three times a day and never asking for anything in return.'*

chrome-dome *n. Slap head, baldy.*

chubblies *n.* A fat *bird's choozies.*

chubby bullet, take the *v.* To distract and occupy the fat mate of a fit *bird* your friend is attempting to chat up. To act selflessly, like a soldier who throws himself on a grenade to save his comrades, or a CIA agent who dives stupidly into the path of an assassin's bullet. *'Thanks for taking the chubby bullet, mate.'*

chubby checker *n.* A pornographic film-set technician responsible for monitoring and maintaining the leading man's state of penisular tumescence. A *fluffer. 'Cut! Either we've got the wrong lens on or Gunther's losing string. Quick, somebody fetch the chubby checker out the pub.'*

chuck flick *n.* An artistic cinematographic production that eschews plot and dialogue in favour of action, eg. *European Cum-Bath 26.* A *stick vid,* a *grumble flick.*

chuckle vision n. The stirring view of rolling *cuntryside* experienced whilst taking a breather during an act of *cumulonimbus* on a fat lass.

chuck out special *n.* Large quantities of leftover fried chicken that have been sweating all day, which are available for next to no money from USA Fried Chicken in Witney, Oxfordshire at around 2am.

chuck salt *v.* The consequences of masturbating again, after already masturbating oneself dry.

chuck up *v.* To vomit, *honk up, barf.*

chuck your muck *v.* To *lose your mess, spend your wad, tip your filthy concrete.* To ejaculate.

chuckies *n.* Balls.

chuckle Brother *n.* Either of the male participants in a *spit roast.* From the children's TV comedy northerners' catchphrase "*To you, to me*".

chucky cheese *n.* Vomit-inducing tangy cheddar matured in unwashed *brims.*

chudleighs *n. Chuds, chebs, charlies, charms, chichis, choozies.* Ladies' *tits.*

chuff *1. v.* To *pass wind, shoot a bunny rabbit. 'Oops! Best open a window vicar. I'm about to chuff.'* *2. n.* Vagina, lady's *front bottom.* *3. n. zoo.* A parsimonious *anus,* usually of a gnat.

chuffage *n.* coll. A *rats' banquet, bangers and mash, Radcliffe's sleepers.* Railway track faecal detritus.

chuff chowder *n.* A pungent soup served as a first course when *dining at the Y.* Hopefully without croutons.

chuff mountain *n.* Surplus of *cabbage* at a party.

chuff muncher *n.* A *woman in comfortable shoes* with a penchant for chowing down on other ladies' *Jacky Dannies.*

chuff-nuts *n. Dangleberries.*

chuffdruff *n. Muffdruff.* Residual flakes of desiccated *mess* and *fanny batter* found on the *mapatasi.* Pubic equivalent of *mammary dandruff.*

chufflink *n.* A piece of over-elaborate *clitoral* ironmongery of the sort often sported by loose women in *bongo vids.*

chuftie plug *n. Cotton pony.* Tampon.

chug *v.* To *choke the chicken, spank the monkey, burp the worm.*

chugger *n.* A clipboard-wielding charity collector who stalks Britain's pavements wearing a luminous bib and relieving passers by of their valuables, loose change, spare time *etc.* From charity + mugger.

chugnuts *n.* Extremely big piles. *'A cushion, Mrs Bennet, a cushion! I fear the frivolities at Lady Marchmain's ball have brought down my chugnuts no end.'* (from *Pride and Predudice*, by Jane Austen).

chumbawumbas *onomat.* A rather predictable use of a pop group's name as slang for breasts. Other examples of this phenomenon are; *Bananaramas* (penises), *Wurzels* (testicles) and *Bee Gees* (hairy twats).

chumblies *n medic. Nuts, knackers, clockweights.*

chum bucket *1. n.* Underwater fast food restaurant in the children's cartoon series *Spongebob Squarepants,* which specialises in the provision of crabby patties. 2. *n.* A lady's *snatch* with all the aromatic qualities of a bucket of live fish bait.

chumley warning *1. n.* The signal a gentleman gives to a fussy *nosher* to tell her that *Elvis is about to leave the building. 2. n.* The signal a lady gives to a *nosher* to warn him that she is about to *step on a frog.*

chunder *v. Aus.* To *chunk, shout soup.*

chunderbirds *n.* Binge-drinking teenage girls full to the brim with *tart fuel* and screwtop wine, who stagger around parks and town centres vomiting and crying. *'It's seven pm on a Friday and Chunderbirds are GO!'* (voiceover from Police surveillance video footage of Chappelfield Park, Norwich on Fair night).

chunk *v.* To vomit. Also chunder, *blow chunks*.

Churchill bulldog *n.* An ugly, overweight *10-pinter.* After her resemblance to the TV insurance advert canine. A girl who loves to say "Oh, yus" in the back of a car.

churchilling *n.* Nodding in agreement and pleasure whilst shouting the phrase "yus!" like a cross between Arthur Mullard and Derek Guyler, for example whilst being *ministered to* by the missus. From the loose-necked motor insurance company advert computer-generated parcel shelf bulldog.

churns *1. n.* Breasts. *2. n.* Testicles. *3. n.* Seemingly any vessel containing white fluid.

chutney Chuckle brother *n.* A *dirty Sanchez.* Also *Stinky Selleck*.

chutney ferret *n.* A *chocolate speedway rider*.

chutney locker *n. medic.* The *bomb bay*, rectum. Also *date locker*.

cidercafe *n.* A town centre bench or war memorial from which *ciderspace* can be accessed.

ciderspace *n.* A virtual multidimensional world, accessible to tramps.

cider visor *n. Beer goggles* for the younger street drinker.

cigarbutts *n. JCB starter buttons, blind cobblers' thumbs, Bruce Lees.*

cigar clipper *1. n.* An exceptionally tight *clopper.* A *mouse's ear,* a *paper cut. 2. n.* The *nipsy.*

circle jerk *n.* A communal *hand shandy* session. A *milk race, daisy chain.*

cistern chapel *n.* The porcelain font where *Meatloaf's daughter* is baptised.

clabby *adj.* Exceptionally pink. Used to describe *bacon strips. 'Fuck me, love. You've got some clabby bacon strips on you, I'll give you that. And I've seen a few cunts in my time, what with being a consultant gynaecologist and obstetrician.'*

clacker *1. n.* One half of a dangerous, finger-breaking 1970s toy. *2. n.* The *fanny. 3. n. coll. Blart, tussage, mackerel. 4. n.* Fifty percent of the contents of the *clackerbag.*

clackerbag *n.* A leathery receptacle for *clockweights.*

clacker lacquer *n. medic.* Shameful secretion from the *blip tap* up a lady's *snapper. Love juice, moip, fanny lube, bilp, parsley sauce.*

clackervalve *n.* The *nipsy,* the *ringpiece,* the *arsehole. 'Porphyria was powerless to resist. His eyes burned into hers like sapphires. His muscular arms enfolded her body as she felt herself being swept away in a whirlwind of passion. Tenderly, Sven lay her down on the ottoman, whipped off her scads and stuck his thumb up her clackervalve.'* (from *The Lady and the Football Manager* by Barbara Cartland).

clackweed *n.* Perennial pubic hair.

Clacton chinwag *n.* The oral intercourse that takes place between a man and a kneeling woman who has had a couple of bottles of *tart fuel.* A *blow job.*

clagnet *n.* A net-like tangle of *arse cress* which forms over the *freckle,* leading to a sensation similar to that felt when one defecates through a pair of fishnet tights. One would imagine.

clagnuts *n. Dangleberries, tagnuts. Miniature heroes.*

Claire Goosebumps *n.* Smashing *Gert Stonkers* of the type sported by the popular former *Casualty* actress. *Tits* which are capable of "*Waking the Dead*".

clamateur *n.* A clumsy, naive male who is inexperienced in the workings of the fairer sex's *farmyard apparatus.* A *batterfingers. 'Honestly Jet, it was nothing. He had no idea what he was doing down there. He was a total clamateur.'*

clamchop *n.* The tasty cut of fish-like mutton found in a lady's knickers.

clamdruff *n.* The dried *jitler, fanny batter* and general downstairs effluvium and detritus that accumulates around the *bodily treasure* of a lady who is less than attentive in the ablutionary department. *Pornflakes, chuffdruff.*

clam dunk *n.* A spectacular shot at the *furry hoop.* A *break for the border.*

clamembert *n.* Female equivalent of *helmetdale. Fanny cheese.*

clam jousting *n.* A *fur-bumping* encounter between two *scissor sisters* afflicted with lesbism. Also *velcro fastening.*

clamouflage *n.* Thick, impenetrable *bush* which makes the target impossibly hard to spot at first glance. The *pubes* on a *biffer.*

clam ram *n.* A *gut stick, cock, cheesepipe.*

clam shandy *n.* A lady's version of a *hand shandy.* A few scales on the *invisible banjo.*

clam smacker *n.* A *bean flicker.*

clankers *n. onomat.* The same as *clinkers*, only louder.

clap, the *n. medic.* Any sexually transmitted disease, but usually gonorrhoea. Or syphilis. *Cock rot.*

clapometer *n.* Imaginary medical instrument used by doctors to diagnose the *clap. 'Don't touch her. I hear she scores ten on the clapometer.'*

clappers *1. n.* In *farting,* the buttocks. *'Christ! That one didn't half rattle the clappers.' 2. n.* That part of a bell like which a lady *goes.*

clapping fish *n.* Female genitalia.

Clapton *n.* A nicely-paced *Jodrell,* such as a gent might enjoy when his wife is out for the evening, or in hospital. After plank-spanker Eric's nickname "Slowhand". *'It was a normal Thursday night, your Honour. The missus had gone out with the girls so I put Jenna Jameson on the video, opened the hand cream and settled down for a Clapton.'*

Clara Dawes *n.* An extremely hairy *mott.* A *judith.* From the parts of the actress playing the part of Clara Dawes in the recent TV adaptation of *Sons and Lovers.*

claret mouse *n.* A *Dracula's tea bag.* A spent *jamrag.*

Clarkson's cock *n.* Anything small, based on the commonly-held assumption that men, such as the outspokenly irreverent, curly-topped *Top Gear* presenter, only feel the need to drive round in big-engined sports cars in order to mask some deficiency in their *trouser departments. 'You couldn't even swing Clarkson's cock in here.'*

clarts *n.* Tacky excrement, such as would cling to the lavatory bowl above the water line rather than slip below the surface.

clarty goalmouth *n.* A *muff* one could lose a boot in.

Clattenburg *n.* Heavily-edited hardcore pornography *ie.* where it obviously *goes in,* but you don't see it. Named after the hapless referee in the famous Mendes goal incident, where it obviously went in, but he didn't see it.

clatter *v.* To *pleasure* a lady, esp. from behind. *'I'd love to spend a minute or two clattering into the back of that.'*

claw, the *n.* The bizarre contortions of a semen-covered hand that a fellow is forced to employ in order to avoid spilling any *splinkle* onto his mum's soft furnishings whilst making his way to the toilet following a successful bout of *self help.*

claypit *n.* Source of the raw material for making *coil pots.* The *arse.*

cleach *n.* The small strip of skin between a *bird's front bottom* and her *back bottom.* Scientifically referred to as the *taint, tinter, carse, snarse, Niftkin's bridge, clutch* or *biffon,* but more crudely called the perineum.

clean and jerk *1. n.* Standard sort of weightlifting method, also sometimes known as the clean and press. *2. n.* Seizing the opportunity for a spot of *self improvement* whilst taking a bath. *Waxing the dolphin, polishing the lighthouse, up periscope, burping the sea slug.*

clean behind the curtains *v.* To perform thorough *cumulonimbus* on a young lady's floppy *bits and pieces.*

clean the au pair's teeth *v.* To receive the oral sex.

clean workspace *n.* A shaven *fanny.*

clear the custard *v.* To have a long overdue *wank. 'I've got ten minutes before I have to take mass. I'll just nip upstairs and clear the custard.'*

clems *n.* The *clockweights, swingers, nads, cods.* Testicles.

Cleveland steamer *1. n.* A merchant cargo vessel operating on Lake Erie. *2. n.* A sexual act much favoured by your average Teuton that doesn't bear thinking about. A *chocolate eclair.*

cliffclangers *n.* Heavy, swollen *bollocks, eg.* the sort that might be owned by an ageing Christian rock and roll singer who has yet to find the right girl. *Cliffhangers.*

climb on *v.* The culmination of a romantic evening. *'Lavinia was powerless to resist. His eyes burned into hers like rubies. His strong arms enfolded her tender body as she felt herself being swept away on a tidal wave of passion. Then he dropped his trolleys and climbed on.'* (from *The Lady and the Gentleman* by Barbara Cartland).

clinkers *n. onomat. Aus.* Tenacious particles of feculant welded onto the *arse spider's* legs; *toffee strings, winnets, kling-ons, dangleberries, bum conkers.*

clit car *n.* A once desirable motor vehicle that has been rendered undesirable as a consequence of its own popularity, *eg.* the Subaru Impreza or them new Minis. From the fact that, like a *clematis,* "every *cunt's* got one".

clit and run *n.* A light-hearted indecent assault whereby one makes a playful grab for *Captain Caveman's nose* followed by a swift getaway into the crowd.

cliterati *n.* A dazzling array of *grumble vid* starlets. Perhaps attending some sort of *bongo* convention on the Bravo channel.

cliterature *n.* One-handed reading matter.

clitler *n.* A fashionable *downstairs* moustache, as seen on female *grumble* artistes who leave a daft little tuft. A *toothbrush muff, mufftache, muffgabe.*

clitoris allsorts *n.* The array of delicacies on display in the windows along a typical Amsterdam street.

clitty litter *n.* Vaginal flotsam and jetsam in the *drip tray* of a lady's *dunghampers*.

cloacal chords *n.* The organs of anal speech which are located in the *nether throat* and occasionally, particularly after a visit to the Curry Capital, Bigg Market, Newcastle upon Tyne, manage to achieve a high falsetto which could shatter a crystal wine glass.

clock *n.* One who swings like a pendulum do. A *happy shopper,* a *switch hitter,* one who is *half rice half chips. 'Birthdays: David Bowie - musician, artist, film actor and right fucking clock, 55.'* (*The Times*, 8th Jan 2002).

clock springs *n.* Very strong, curly pubic hairs usually spotted on the *clockweights* or coiled tightly around the top of the *belltower.* Often found stuck onto bars of soap.

clockweights *n.* Large, metal, adjustable testicles that have to be *cranked* at least once every eight days.

clodge *n.* The *spadger*.

clogmaker's hammer, arse like a *sim.* Descriptive of the buttocks of a 33rpm gentleman who appears to be *banging* his *old boot* at 78.

clopper *n.* A romantic term for the female genitalia. *'Ocarina was powerless to resist. His eyes burned into hers like topazzes. His strong arms enfolded her body as she felt herself being swept away on a hailstorm of passion. 'Take me, Abdul, take me', she gasped. 'I'm fizzing at the clopper''.* (from *The Dowager and the Sheik* by Barbara Cartland).

close the deal *v.* To *scuttle* a *bird*.

close-up pink *n.* Medically-explicit *clabby cliterature.* Erotica that wouldn't look out of place in a gynaecology textbook.

closing time donner *n.* A well-worn *grotter* that looks like a rushed and messily-prepared Turkish cat sandwich. *'Lady Emma was powerless to resist. His eye burned into hers like a marble. His muscular arm enfolded her body as she felt herself being swept away in a gale of passion which measured a good five on the Beaufort wind force scale. She felt a thrill of forbidden pleasure as the Admiral pulled down her bloomers. 'Take me, Fellatio,' she cried. 'Take me now!' 'Bloody hell, love,' said Lord Nelson, peering at her fanny through the wrong end of his brass telescope. 'What have you been up to whilst I've been away at sea engaging Napoleon's war fleet at Aboukir Bay in the Battle of the Nile? Your blurtch looks like a closing time donner.''* (from *The Wife of the Ageing British Envoy and the 18th century Naval Hero* by Barbara Cartland).

clot mops *n.* Feminine napkins. *Dangermice.*

cloth tit *n.* The least far a gentleman

can get in a sexual encounter with a lady. *Outside tops. 'Did you fuck her?' 'No, I only got my cloth tit.'*

clout *1. n. Clunge. 2. n.* South African lesbian rock band.

cloven hoof *n. Camel's foot, camel's mouth, camel's lips.* In fact, any part of a camel. *'Did you see Madonna at Live Earth? I was right at the back of the stadium and I couldn't get a view of the big screen, but even I could see her cloven hoof. And I've got cataracts.'*

clowns' buckets, spunk *v.* Of single gentlemen who have spent the day *challenging themselves* repeatedly, to eventually conjure forth nothing more than a wince upon ejaculation.

clown's hat *n.* A *bald man in a boat.* A *clematis* with all wallpaper paste shooting out of the top of it.

clown's pie *n.* A very, very wet *clodge. 'Finding ourselves alone in the shooting lodge at Balmoral, Her Majesty bade me descend to her ladygarden. After fifty years of widowhood, I found her to be be considerably aroused. It was like being hit in the face with a clown's pie.'* (from *The Memoirs of Queen Victoria's Ghillie* by John Brown).

clown's pocket *sim.* To describe the bigger, baggier and perhaps yellow and red checkered vagina. *'May I introduce my wife, Your Worship? She has a fanny like a clown's pocket.'*

clown's smile *n.* Facial make-up donned when performing at the *red ring circus. Mexican lipstick, pasata grin.*

clubbed seal, raw as a *sim.* The state of a *bird's nether pelt* after she's been *banged* senseless with a substantial *giggle stick.*

cludger *n.* A lower class lady from the north west of England, specifically Bolton.

cludgy *n. Shite house,* lavatory, *thunderbox.*

clump *n. coll. Blart, fanny, tussage. 'I tell you what, Mother Superior, this place is absolutely fucking crawling with clump.'*

clumper *n.* The *nipsy, clackervalve, cigar cutter.*

clumsy beekeeper, face like a *sim.* Descriptive of a lady with a *lovely personality.* She who has a mug like a *stripper's clit.*

clunge *n.* A *clout,* a *furry hoop, hairy goblet.*

clusterfuck *1. n.* A group of people unable to make a simple decision, *eg.* friends standing on a pavement outside a pub wondering where to eat, or a group of PC World salesmen on a team-building course trying to construct a raft out of oil drums, planks and rope. *2. n.* A *gang bang.*

clutch *n.* The piece of skin between the anus and the vagina. So called because it works like its namesake component on a car, *ie.* it helps you to hit the right *hole.* The *carse, tinter, notcher, Humber Bridge etc.*

coal hole *n.* Any grubby little aperture around the back of something. A popular entry point for burglars and tradesmen.

coal scuttle, polish the *v.* To indulge in a foul act of *self-pollution, bleed the hydraulic system, stab the cat etc.* To have a *wank. 'Bless me holy father, for I have sinned. On Friday, I committed the sin of envy* *when my brother bought himself some new shoes. On Saturday I committed the sin of sloth when I fell asleep during the qualifying session for the Grand Prix. Then this morning I'm ashamed to say I had impure thoughts about polishing the coal scuttle over the bra pages of the Freeman catalogue.' 'Sorry my son, what was that again? I was just busy polishing the coal scuttle over the bra pages of the Freeman catalogue.'*

coat hangers *n.* Large erect *nipples* that can double up as an emergency car aerial.

cob on *n.* A foul temper, usually displayed by *werecows*. A *blob strop.*

cobblers *ryhm. slang. Bollocks.* From cobbler's awls = balls.

cobs *n. Nads, pills, pods.* Testicles. *'Ooyah! Go and fetch a cloth our Ashley. I've caught me cobs, I say me cobs, in the bacon slicer again.'*

coccupied *adj.* Of a desirable woman, to already have a boyfriend. *'Phwooar, I really fancy that Sienna Miller. If she wasn't already coccupied and if I didn't have another 60 hours of my community service nightshift at the offal plant to go, I'd be up her like a rat up a drainpipe, I'm telling you.'*

cock *1. n.* Penis, *willy, knob. 2. n.* A person to whom a chirpy cockney wishes to speak, often prefixed by "Wotcha..." *3. n.* A gentleman chicken. *4. v.* Something that you can do to a snook.

cock-a-doodle-poo *n.* The *shit* that, needing to come out, wakes you up in the morning. *Alarm cack.*

cock-a-fanny *n.* The act of hiding one's *wedding tackle* between one's legs to give the appearance of having female genitals. Popularised by Captain Sensible and East German female shot-putters of the 1970's.

cock-a-hoop *1. adj.* The metaphysical state of mind produced by advantageous circumstances. *'I just won a million on a scratchcard. I'm cock-a-hoop.' 2. adj.* The state of one fellow who is engaged in an act of *brown love* with another. *'I just managed to get my glans up your nipsy. Frankly, I'm cock-a-hoop.'*

cock block *n. Shag slab, wanking chariot,* bed. *'I wouldn't mind lying that on me cock block.'*

cock book *n.* Literature which encourages a chap to whip up a quick *cheese-based white sauce.*

cockbuster *n.* A video shop, or indeed work colleague, specialising in the commercial hiring of *grumble vids.*

cockchops *n. pej.* A pernicious, malicious, seditious fool. A *fuckwit,* an *idiot. 'Armstrong: 'That's one small step for man, one giant leap for mankind.' (Beep) Aldrin: 'Oi, cockchops. That should have been 'one small step for A man.' I knew they should of let me go fog out the rocket.''*(from NASA transcript of Apollo 11 mission, 1969).

cock clamp *n.* A *'v' clamp,* a *mouse's ear.* A tight *muff.*

cock collar *n.* The *fiveskin.*

cock drops *n. Blueys.* Viagras.

cock duster *n.* A handlebar moustache sported by the sort of leather-clad *Village People*-style *puddle jumpers* who people Richard Littlejohn's graphic nightmares. Also *scrotum tickler.*

cock eggs *n. medic. Clems, swing-*

ers, clockweights. Testicles.* Also *knob eggs. 'Vasectomy is a simple routine procedure. The surgeon makes a small inscision in the scrotal sac, through which he severs the cock eggs from their clacker strings. All this is carried out under a local anaesthetic.'* (Family Planning Leaflet, The Marie Stopes Foundation).

cockfest *n.* A pornographic film featuring quantities of *skinclad tube.*

cock had been caught by a fisherman, like his *sim.* Description of the buttock-clenched, pelvis-thrust-forwards way a chap sprints to the khazi during a sudden *shit rush. "Heathcliffe must have the runs again,' sighed Cathy. 'Only this morning I saw him running to the crapper like his cock had been caught by a fisherman."* (from *Wuthering Shites* by Charlotte Bronte).

cock hair *n.* Imperial unit of measurement used in engineering, equivalent to 2.32 *gnat's cods. 'It seems that the O-ring failed 45 seconds after take off, allowing a jet of superheated gas just a cock hair wide to penetrate the main solid fuel booster, leading to the loss of the Challenger.'* (NASA Official Accident Inquiry Report, 1987).

cock heavy *adj.* Descriptive of a drinking establishment blighted with a serious lack of *buffage.*

cock holster *n.* A romantic term for a lady's mouth. *'Felicity was powerless to resist. His eyes burned into hers like amethysts. His strong arms enfolded her tender body as she felt herself being swept away in a whirlwind of passion. Then, she knelt before him and he stuck his eight-inch charlie into her cock holster.'* (from *The Officer and the Gypsy Duchess* by Barbara Cartland).

cock in a top hat, sticking one's *v.* Unfulfilling *futtering* in a slack *snapper. 'How was it for you, Mr Deayton?' 'Like sticking my cock in a top hat, you whore. Now slag off.'*

cocking her into it *v.* The gentleman's art of cajoling a lady with whom he is sharing a bed into coitus by means of persistent and relentless nudging and frottering. To annoy a woman with one's genitals so much that she eventually lets one *on the nest. 'She told me she had a headache, but I managed to cock her into it anyway.'*

cockjaw *n.* The open-mouthed expression adopted by porn queens after they've quaffed a gobful of *manpop.*

cock knocker *n.* A gentleman who *bangs* at the *back door.*

cock knot *n.* The machine head of the *one stringed banjo,* the *frenum.*

cockless pair *n.* A particularly athletic looking lesbian couple.

cock lodger *n.* An idle man who persuades a gullible single mum to let him move in and sit on her sofa all day watching DVDs in exchange for the odd *scuttling.*

cock mess monster *1. n.* A *grumble flick* actress, transformed by a small fortune in *money shots.* A *plasterer's radio. 2. n.* A cryptozoological beast occasionally sighted floating round the bath after *playing up periscope.*

cock monkey *1. n.* A lady who does a lot of jumping about, squealing and general circus-like activity in the *fart sack,* especially when presented with a banana. *2 n.* A film set technician who keeps the gentleman lead thespian erect during set changes, drug runs, *spunk* mopping *etc*. A *fluffer.*

cockney *1. n.* A pearly-buttoned, colourfully-opinionated person born within the sound of Big Ben, who either drives a taxi or sells fruit on a market. *2. n.* A person of indeterminate gender. From cock + fanny.

cock nostril *n.* A term for the *Jap's eye* which can be used by the more politically correct.

cocknuckle *n.* The sixth knuckle, that always comes at the top of the deck in a *five knuckle shuffle*. The *glans.*

cockofadge *n.* A very butch woman, or possibly a slightly effeminate man. *'Did you see that, Tommy? Couldn't tell if it had a cock or fadge.'*

cock off *v.* To suspend one's working day in order to enjoy a protracted recess of *gentlemanly relaxation. 'Fiona, where's Huw gone? He's supposed to be reading the closing headlines in three minutes.' 'I'm sorry, Moira. I think he cocked off during the local news.'*

cockoholic *n.* One who is addicted to cockohol. *'Mate of mine used to work as a roadie for Abba. Reckoned the blonde bird was a fucking cockoholic.'*

cock or ball? *n.* Name of a game, similar to Hangman or I Spy, which can be used to pass the time during long train journeys or dull wedding services, whereby the interlocutor requires their neighbour to identify a flap of nondescript skin poking through his trouser fly.

cock patience *n.* A solitary pursuit whereby one whiles away the hours with one's favourite *Gash 'n' Gary* mags arranged in a circle around oneself.

cockpit *n.* The piece of skin between the *devil's bagpipes* and the *German shepherd's winkhole.* The *barse.*

cock porridge *n.* Messy load fired from the *porridge gun.*

cock puppet *n.* A petite lady. A *throwabout.*

cock rock *1. n.* A variety of popular music performed by *rock poodles* such as *Whitesnake, Van Halen etc. 2. n.* The substance that *knobs* are made of that is able to go from marshmallow limp to diamond hard at the thought of a pair of *tits.*

cock rot *n. medic.* VD, a *dose.*

cock smoker *n.* A lady who doesn't mind a puff on one's *Whitehouse cigar*. A *fellatrix.*

cock snot *n.* Semen, sneezed out of the *cock nostril.*

cock sucker *n.* A motorist who cuts you up.

cocksucker's doormat *n.* Facial hair growth favoured by the ageing male attempting to hide his jowls. A goatee beard, *bloatee.*

cock tease *n.* A woman who wears *fuck me shoes* and then changes into *fuck off slippers* when you get back to her place.

cockumentary *n.* A serious-minded factual film exploring issues surrounding the adult entertainment industry broadcast at 11 o'clock on Bravo in order to educate and inform the viewers. While they *wank*. The sort of programme that should be sponsored by Kleenex. A *masturmentary, sockumentary, rudimentary.*

cockusoap *n.* A television serial drama, the cast of which contains a disproportionate amount of high quality *tussage, eg. Hollyoaks* but not *Last of the Summer Wine.*

cock venom *n. Spaff, spodge, spooge, etc. Spunk.*

cockwash *n.* The *punani.* See also *token for the cockwash, municipal cockwash. 'My charlie's absolutely filthy. I think I'll stick it through the cockwash on Sunday morning.'*

cockwasher *n.* A *fellatrix* who takes it to the *biffin bridge.* A *deep throater,* a *pork sword* swallower. A woman with a *bollock goatee.*

coco-pops *n. Winnets,* known briefly as Choco Krispies.

cocoa sombrero *n.* Mexican *brown hatter.*

coconut husk *n.* In erotic photography and nude police work, the soft mound of *clocksprings* which becomes visible when a lady *assumes the position.*

coconut minge-mat *n.* Pubic hair you could wipe your feet on. A *welcome twat.*

cod *adj.* Extremely *Swiss.* Fucking rubbish.

cod cove *n. Fish mitten.*

cods *n. Balls.* Often prefixed "a kick in the...".

cod's wetsuit, wetter than a *sim.* Descriptive of a woman's *bits and bobs* when she's *dripping like a fucked fridge.* Also *otter's pocket. As wet as a Tewkesbury doorstep.*

coffee bean *n.* The back view of a dirty lady's *Gareth* as she bends over on all fours. *Coconut husk.*

coffee turtle *n.* The first *turd* of the day, powered on its way by the first cup of Nescafe of the day.

coffin-dodger *n.* Affectionate term for an incontinent, elderly relative. An *oxygen thief.*

coilus interruptus *n. Lat.* Method employed by God to prevent the birth of *Meatloaf's daughter* whereby the Jehovah's Witnesses ring the doorbell just as you are laying the foundations of a *log cabin.*

coins of the realm *n.* Trouseral *piss spots* of various sizes sported by gentlemen leaving public house lavatories.

Colchester condom *euph. milit.* Anal sex, *one up the bonus tunnel,* a phrase used by squaddies in the garrison town. *'Please be careful, Field Marshal'. 'Don't worry, sweet tits, I'll be using a Colchester condom when I meet you behind the skip.'*

cold tea bag *n.* The feeling one gets in one's underpants a couple of minutes after a badly-diagnosed *trouser cough.*

colimbo *n.* That desolate time of day occurring in the afternoon and heralded by the appearance onscreen of Peter Falk's squint-eyed, dirty-raincoated supersleuth, when the jobseeker/person working from home realises that not only is there nothing new worth watching on Sky, but it's also as yet still too early to start drinking.

collagen biospheres *n. Knockers* which miraculously iron the wrinkles out of a fellow's *twig.*

collar and cuffs *euph.* Matching hair colour, up top and down below. *'See that blonde? Do you reckon her collar matches her cuffs?'*

collie's chest, fanny like a *sim.* Descriptive of the more hirsute ladygarden. *'This is the tale of Bertha Boot / Who's bought a brand new* *bathing suit / When she wears it in the water / You see things you didn't oughta / On the beach at Whitley Bay / Her knockers show up clear as day / But down below the view is best / Her fanny's like a collie's chest.'* (from *Odd Odes* by Cyril Fletcher).

colly wobbles *n.* The strange, unnerving feeling that one is being watched whilst having sex. Possibly by a *wanking* ex-Premiership footballer.

colon burger *n.* A *shit* weighing in at a quarter of a pound uncooked.

Columbian flush *n.* Tell-tale double or triple toilet evacuation procedure used by *showbiz sherbet* enthusiasts to conceal the preparation and consumption of their favourite powdery foodstuffs.

Columbo's coat *n.* A tatty and creased-up *fanny* that looks like an aged basset hound might use it for a bed. Not to be confused with a *Columbo's mac* which is, of course, a tatty and creased-up *fiveskin* that looks like an aged basset hound has spent the morning chewing it behind the sofa. *'Oops. I think my Columbo's mac has got caught in your Columbo's coat.'*

Columbo's mac *n.* A rumpled prepuce that is much too long for the *one-eyed bobby* it covers. *Delaney's overcoat.*

Colwyn Bay *1. n.* Welsh seaside resort famous for its multi-storey Safeway's and its elephant-less zoo. *2. rhym. slang.* Homosexual. *'This is your cellmate, Lord Archer. Try not to drop anything on the floor, only he's a bit Colwyn.'*

combo *n. One* in the *goo*, then *one* in the *poo*. To *pot the brown* after the *pink*, though not at the Crucible.

combover *n. Swope.*

combustoflatulation *n.* Anal flamethrowing. *Pyroflatulation, blue streak.*

come *1. v. Cum. 2. n. Cum.*

come in Tokyo *n.* Manipulating both a lady's breasts at the same time in the manner of a World War II radio operator. *Finding Radio Luxembourg.*

come like a bishop *sim.* Of a man, to ejaculate in an explosive style, as one would imagine a long-term celibate does every now and again.

come to bed pies *n.* Pastry-based foodstuffs presented to a fat lass in exchange for a *bunk up. Pork for pork.*

comforts *n.* Casual visitors, because they just "come for t'day".

command module *n. Bell end*, glans, *bishop's mitre.*

commercial sex *n.* An act of penetrative congress enjoyed during the advertisement break in a television programme, usually the three-minute long intermission halfway through *Coronation Street.*

committee shitty *n.* A *motion* that is seconded after the paperwork is complete. A *council dump.*

community chest *n.* A pair of *charlies* that the whole estate has had a go on.

communting *n.* Choosing to live in an area within a convenient distance of a place where one confidently expects to find ugly women to *tup*. *'We are delighted to welcome to the market this deceptively delightful 1 bedroom studio flat which would make an ideal starter home for the single, semi-*

skilled gentleman, and is deceptively delightfully situated within easy communting distance of the Bigg Market. £95,000 ono.'

competitive advantage *euph.* Big *tits, first impressions, qualifications,* high capacity *juggage. 'I know her criminal record, history of drug use and non-existent educational attainments perhaps count against her, but I felt as soon as she walked into the room that she had a competitive advantage over the other candidates.'*

compliments to the chef *n.* The drunken, unintelligible, Marlon Brando-style ramblings of a lucky woman immediately after she has completed a successful act of *horatio* on an accommodating gentleman friend.

compliment the chef *v.* To *drop one's guts* after a meal. Good manners in some countries, but it's probably best to check first with your host.

compose one's thoughts *euph.* Polite phrase often used by snooker commentators to describe the actions of players who leave the table in between frames. To defecate, take a *shit, drop the kids off at the pool, light a bum cigar, crimp one off etc. 'It's all square in the Embassy World Snooker Championship finals and you could cut the atmosphere here at the Crucible with a knife. And as referee Len Ganley prepares the table for the all-important deciding frame, Ray Reardon's just leaving the arena for a moment to compose his thoughts. Let's hope he washes his hands after he wipes his arse.'*

con *n. Fr. Cunt, fanoir.*

Conanism *n.* The act of *wanking* oneself *off* so frequently that one develops a right arm like right wing muscle-bound shit actor, execution-happy California State Governor and right *wanker* Arnold Schwarzenegger.

con artiste *n. Fr.* A *cunning linguist, muff diver*, a *Jacky Danny Cousteau*, a *puba diver*.

concrete donkey *n.* A *horse's handbrake*, a *diamond cutter*.

conduct the ragtime band *v.* To wave one's *baton* in a rousing performance of the Russian national anthem when *Arsenal are playing at home*.

cones *n.* Pointy, orange, dayglo breasts found alongside the M25 or in Madonna's vest.

cones are out *euph.* A warning that there is only one lane in use. *Blow job week*.

conflatulations *n. interj.* A term of praise accorded one by one's friends after one has *stepped on* a spectacular *duck*.

congrafellation *n.* The act of giving a lucky lady an appreciative pat on the head after she has performed a decent *blowjob*.

conjaptivitis *n. medic.* Occlusion of the male urethral opening due to a deposit of ossified *spangle*.

conkers *n.* See *hairy conkers*.

conkers deep *adj.* To be in a state of total intromission. *In up to the back wheels, in up to the maker's nameplate*.

conker water *n. Spangle, spooge, spadge, gunk*.

continental shelf *n.* Feature of foreigners' barbarian design *jobby engines*, providing a place in the *throne room* where one's *royal decrees* can pile up to be admired before being flushed away.

convent porridge *n.* Hot, steaming *spunk* ladled out of a cauldron by a smiling Mother Superior. *Nuns' porridge, jizz.*

convicts' shuffle *n.* The "chain-gang"-style gait one adopts when looking for *bumwad* whilst manacled round the ankles by one's lowered *grundies.*

convoy cock *n. milit.* A squaddie's *travel fat.*

cooch *n. US.* A Yankee *poon.*

cooint *n.* A variation on the popular rude word *cunt,* used in the quaint picture-postcard village of Barnsley, South Yorkshire.

cooking at both ends *adj.* Of the eater of a spicy *cuzza,* descriptive of the burning sensations experienced first in his throat and then, about an hour later, when his *bottom hob* gets lit. *'Come to the Curry Capital, Bigg Market, Newcastle upon Tyne, where we'll prepare you a meal that will have you cooking at both ends in no time.'*

cooking lager *n.* Utility pub booze, as drunk by Selwyn Froggatt. *Wallop.* Also *cookin'.*

cooter *1. n. prop. US.* A character from *The Dukes of Hazzard. 2. n.* The visible contents of Daisy Duke's shorts in the *Dukes of Hazzard.*

cooter cutters *n. US.* The type of shorts worn by Daisy Duke in *The Dukes of Hazzard,* in which she kept her *cooter.*

cop a feel *v.* To get one's *tops* or *fingers.* Or *tops and fingers.*

copper bolt *v.* A very heavy or dense *sweaty morph.* With a clockwise thread.

copper's torch *n.* A large, heavy, *bell-swagged schlong* dangling disturbingly between the legs of a skinny old man. A *schlepper. 'What's the matter, your holiness? Are you wrestling with an intractable theological conundrum, such as the concept of original sin?' 'No, cardinal. I've just went for a slash and I've been and caught me copper's torch in me zip.'*

copper wire *n.* A stray pube appearing in a handful of loose change.

copy twat *n.* An acquaintance that always gets the same clothes, car, phone, *bird etc.* as oneself.

cordless bone *n.* A *bobby's helmet* without the *roll-neck* and *cheese-slicer* apparatus.

cordon bleugh *n.* The sophisticated sort of food whizzed up on their bedsit mini-hobs by sad bachelors, *eg.* a pot noodle sandwich, bubble and squeak made from the remains of an uneaten pot noodle sandwich, a bubble and squeak leftovers sandwich, cornflakes and lager.

corgi *1. n.* A high class hound, such as those that accompany the Queen. *2. n.* A high class *hound,* such as the one that accompanies Prince Charles.

corridor of uncertainty *n.* The no-man's land encountered during a drunken act of congress, when one is unsure of where *John Thomas* is a-roaming. *'Hang on a minute, love, I've just entered the corridor of uncertainty. Stick us in the front door, would you?'* (from *The Night After We Won the Ashes* by Frederick "Andy" Flintoff).

corked *1. adj.* Of wine, to be contaminated with bits which render it unpalatable. *'Mr Winner's sent his 1978 Montrachet back. He* *says it's corked.' 2. adj.* Of *spaff,* to be contaminated with bits which render it unpalatable. *'Mr Winner's sent his soup back. He says the spunk in it is corked.'*

corks *1. n.* Nipples. *2. exclam.* 1950s schoolboy cry of surprise. *"Corks!', cried Darbishire. 'I've just seen Matron's corks. Anyone for a daisychain?"* (from *Jennings and the Sticky Sheets* by Anthony Buckeridge).

corn *rhym. slang.* The *chopper.* From corn on the cob = knob.

cornbeef cudgel *n.* Short, thick *trouser stick* the "taking up" of which relieves *gentlemanly tensions,* and so aids restful sleep. The *spam baseball bat.*

cornbeef lighthouse *n.* Big thing that flashes to attract sailors' attention.

cornbeef sandwich *n.* The contents of Daisy Duke's *cooter cutters.*

cornhole *1. n. US. Brass eye, ring, balloon knot. 2. v.* To shove one's *cock* up the same.

Cornish chuff *1. n.* A wrongly-spelled crow-like bird (*Pyrrhocorax pyrrhocorax*) which is native to the Cornish coast and characterised by its red beak, red legs and high-pitched, excitable "chiow" call, it says here. *2. n.* Pastie-powered act of flatulation which could cause a stampede in a tin mine.

corn on the cob *n.* A *spitroast,* where two gentleman revolve a hot lady in a shallow dish of melted butter.

corn on the nob *n.* A *niblet* on a *bottsman's lid.*

cornucopia *n.* A horn of plenty. A *cock* with all grapes, wine and fruit coming out of the end. *'Look at the size of the norks on that one, Dr Spillsbury. She's given me the cornucopia.'*

corybungo *n. Arse, fundament,* backside. *'The tomato boat's just docked, so you'll have to do me up the corybungo.'*

cosif *n. medic.* The *tinter,* the *taint.* The perineum. "'Cos if" it wasn't there, her guts would fall out.

costume drama *n.* The frantic behaviour of an hysterical woman who cannot decide what to wear for a party.

cottage *v.* To visit a thatched public lavatory with climbing roses round the door looking for a bit of *Colwyn Bay* action.

cottage cheese pastie *n.* A well-*shagged hairy pie*

cottage kex *n.* Type of gentlemen's trousers with an elasticated waist, enabling them to be lowered or raised at extremely short notice and with the minimum of fuss. Favoured by men who are *good with colours,* for some inexplicable reason.

cottage spy *n.* An inquisitive gentleman in a rain mac who stands uncomfortably close by whilst one is taking a *Chinese singing lesson* in a public lavatory. A *willy watcher.*

cotton bullet *n.* A cotton mouse.

cotton mouse *n. A cotton pony.*

cotton pony *n.* A *cotton bullet.*

cougar *n. US.* Sexist and offensive American slang term for a predatory older *slag,* usually sporting *tit tattoos* and bleached hair. Typically to be found reeking of alcohol on a bar stool near the men's room.

cough a dead rat *v.* To *drop a gut,* to *step on a duck.* To flatulate.

cough and drop nurse *n.* A comprehensive school health visitor who checks whether or not adolescent schoolboys' *nuts* wobble whilst they are clearing their throats.

cough cabbage water *v. To tread on the gloy bottle.*

cough your filthy yoghurt *euph.* A romantic expression for ejaculation. To do a *money shot. 'Ursula was powerless to resist. His eyes burned into hers like sapphires. His strong arms enfolded her tender body as she felt herself being swept away in a whirlwind of passion. Then he dropped his trolleys and coughed his filthy yoghurt in her hair.'* (from *The Gentleman and the Lady* by Barbara Cartland).

council *1. rhym. slang. The bumhole.* From council gritter = shitter. *2. adj.* General purpose dismissive term for anything or anyone deemed somewhat lacking in class. *'Mummy, can I go and play with Jade and Kylie?' 'No, sweetheart, you can't. They're a bit council.'*

council catwalk *n.* A public place in which *fugly birds* congregate or otherwise disport themselves, normally wearing skimpy tops two sizes too small, the better to show off their collections of prison tats.

council cock *n.* A genital which is unemployed and living on handouts.

council diamonds *n.* Sparkling pavement residue found, for example, following a collision between a *Vauxhall Chavalier* and a telephone box.

council futon *n.* Piece of dual-purpose street furniture which is used for sitting on during the day and sleeping on at night. A park bench.

council gritter *rhym. slang. Gary Glitter, apple fritter, pint of bitter, shitter*. The anal aperture.

council pop *n.* Water. Also *tapoline.*

council suitcase *n.* Binliner.

council tax *n.* A weekly levy paid in manageable £1 installments over the fag counter at the newsagent, which funds the Royal Ballet. Lottery ticket money.

council twat *n.* A scraggy, utility *clout.* Not very good quality, but it does the job.

country air *n.* The smell of a *fart* dropped whilst driving past a field. *'Mmmm. Just smell that country air, children.'*

coup de tat *n. Fr.* A sudden and unexpected takeover of a previously classy high street by pound shops, Wilkinson's and *scratter*-filled amusement arcades. *'Head for the hills, everyone. There's been a coup de tat in Leamington Spa.'*

court Madam Knuckle *v.* To woo your right hand. See *Madam Palm and her five daughters.*

Covent Garden nun *n.* A *fuckstress*. A *Fulham virgin*. A *ho'*.

covered wagon *1 n.* The method of holding the *tassel* in which the thumb is on the underside of the *shaft* and the fingers form a canopy like the top of a cowboy's wagon. A style much favoured by the street-urinating drunkard. *2 n.* To drive your old cow under canvas after you've had a bellyful of beans. A *Dutch oven*.

covering fire *n.* The act of waiting for someone in a public toilet to turn on the taps or hand-driers before defecating in order to conceal the appalling cacophony that accompanies the release of one's *bumload.*

cowboy walk *n.* Broad, rolling, John Wayne-style gait required when walking to the *bog* with the *turtle's head.*

cowgirl *n.* A sexual position popular with the choreographers of American *grumble flicks,* involving a lazy man and a bow-legged woman. A *fucking bronco.*

cow parsley *n.* The salad first course eaten by a *barge arse* as an antidote to the three-cake blowout she will shovel down her fat face for dessert.

cow's stomachs *n.* the effect of an ill-fitting bra on an over-endowed lady, giving the appearance of four udders instead of two.

coyote *euph.* A woman who you would chew your own arm off to get away from in the morning.

crabe *n.* A measure of *shite,* thought to equal about two crates full.

crab ladder *1. n.* The *gut stick,* penis. *2. n.* The hairy line that links the top of the pubes to the belly button. *Crab trellis, pubic footpath.*

crab paste *n.* A deposit of *fanny batter,* especially on a cucumber.

crabs *n. Bollock jockeys, mechanical dandruff,* pubic lice.

crack *1. n. Minge, fanny. 'Close your legs honey, folks will see your crack.'* (Ronald Reagan at his presidential inauguration, 1980). *2. n.* Pointless *bollocks* spoken after four pints of Guinness in Irish theme pubs. *3. n.* The cleft of the *arse* cheeks.

crack a fat *v.* To achieve a *bone on.*

crack a moistie *v. Aus.* Of a *rude lady,* to become aroused in the *downstairs department.* To get a *wide on.*

crack a stiffy *v.* To *crack a fat.*

crackerjacks *n.* Testicles. *'It's Friday, it's five to five, and I'm off upstairs to whack me crackerjacks.'*

crack hanger *n.* The inverted coat hanger-shaped triangle of thong visible on women bending over in hipster jeans. Also *top triangle.*

crackler *n.* A particularly satisfying *dump* that crackles like somebody gently crumpling a crisp bag as it exits the *nipsy.*

crackling *n. Totty, talent.*

crack maggot *n.* See *man overboard.*

crack one's back *v.* To commence a long overdue *Ingrid, ie.* where one's spine sounds like it is breaking up and is about to emerge through one's *clackervalve.*

crack one's nuts *v.* To *break one's eggs.*

cracksuit *n.* Convenient form of leisure clothing favoured amongst chemically dependant members of the urban underclasses. A *smacksuit.*

crack the flags *v.* A vigorous, no nonsense *gut drop* that makes a fresh, crisp sound.

craddock *1. n.* A *cock-a-fanny. 2. n.* An old *cunt* with wonky, bright red lips. Named after the famous TV chef of the 1960s and 1970s, Fanny Craddock, who was an old *cunt* with wonky, bright red lips.

CRAFT *1. acronym. medic.* Doctor's notes terminology for a geriatric patient exhibiting symptoms of the onset of senile dementia. Can't Remember A Fucking Thing. *2. acronym.* Term used by educationalists to describe the the learning potential of their less academically-gifted pupils on school records.

crafty ant *n.* Awkward instantaneous occurrence of *ringpiece* itchiness which happens at the exact moment when it would be most unsuitable to give it a good scratch. Generally occurs the morning after eating a mixed kebab from Abdul's, Manchester.

crafty butcher *n.* A male homosexualist, *ie.* a man who likes to *take his meat* around the back.

crafty fisherman *n.* An hermaphrodite, *ie.* one who carries around a spare set of *tackle.*

cranberry dip *n.* A special sauce for sausages only available during *rag week. Tomato boat ketchup.*

crane operator *n.* A *stick vid* actress with a *gut stick* in each hand, the motion of which gives the appearance that she is positioning a crane or wrecking ball. Also *Madam two-swords, downhill skier.*

crank *1. n.* Penis. *2. rhym. slang.* To have a *wank* in the style of someone attempting to start a vintage car. A *ham shank. 3. n.* A bathroom multi-tasking exercise. A *crap* and a *wank* performed simultaneously by someone with an extremely busy schedule. *4. v.* To cry and *wank* at the same time.

crap *1. n. Shit. 2. v.* To *shit. 3. adj. Shit. 4. exclam. Shit.*

craps *n. US. A* shit game with dice.

craparazzi *n.* Photographers assigned to the *shitterati, eg.* snapping former *Big Brother* contestant Cameron Stout leaving a launderette in Arbroath for a six page spread in *Heat* magazine.

crap flaps *n.* The doorstep of the *nipsy.* The insides of the buttocks of the *arse.*

crapidation *n.* In a public lavatory, the fear of the appalling horrors about to be exposed when lifting the lid. *'With a trembling hand and much crapidation, Roderick made to lift the lid. What he saw plastered in the bowl made the blood freeze in his veins. It was a sight that was to cast a black shadow over his soul for the rest of his life.'* (from *The Fall of the Shithouse of Usher* by Edgar Allan Poe).

crapier mache *n.* Those little bits of *bumwad* that gather around one's *dot* after a severe wiping. A *wasps' nest.*

crapitus *n. Lat. medic.* The creaking noise emitted by overstretched or broken *farting strings* as a *Meatloaf's daughter* forces its way out of the *chamber of horrors,* sounding similar to the noises made in days of yore by a galleon at anchor.

crapkins *n.* Fast food restaurant paper serviettes which, when pilfered in handfuls, act as free toilet paper. Popular amongst cash-strapped students.

crap nap *n.* An alcohol-induced siesta taken in a pub gents cubicle, when one is overcome with sudden tiredness at the effort of pulling down one's trousers and sitting on the *throne. Shitwinks.*

crapper *n.* The lavatory. Named after the inventor of the self-cleaning water closet, Thomas Shitehouse.

crappuccino *n.* A particularly frothy form of diarrhoea which one only gets whilst abroad. See *kexpresso.*

craptain Webb *n.* A long *turd* that "dips its toe" in the water before diving in. A *bridger* or *bottom log.*

craptivating *adj.* Descriptive of something completely *shit,* yet strangely fascinating, *eg. TV's Naughtiest Blunders,* presented by Steve Penk.

crash mat *n.* A *pap baffle*, a *turd raft, pilo.*

crash one's pants *v.* To momentarily lose control of one's *motions* leading to a *pile up* in one's *garnies. 'I was so scared when Derek went into his trance, I nearly crashed my pants, I can tell you.'* (Yvette Fielding, *Most Haunted Live,* Living TV, Oct 31st 2003).

crash the yoghurt truck *v.* To *shed one's load* at the *Billy Mill roundabout. Empty the wank tanks.*

crazy log *n.* A little *shit* that produces an annoying crescendo of high-pitched *ringtones.*

cream *v.* To *drop your yop*, esp. in your pants. To *milm.*

cream rinse *n.* A bubbly hair-care product that is often provided gratis with a facial. A *spermanent wave.*

cream tea *n.* A couple of generously -proportioned *nipplecakes,* topped off with a healthy dollop of *squirty cream. Iced baps.*

cream tea *n.* A posh *bird's* cuppa into which one has *jaffed.* Over the back of a spoon.

creme de la femme *n. Moip.*

creme de month *n.* Bi-fortnightly *egg nog* that tastes anything but refreshingly minty.

crepitate *v.* To discharge a noxious fluid accompanied by a slight explosive sound. How Stephen Fry would describe *following through.*

crescent wank *n.* To arrange one's favourite *jazz periodicals* in a half-moon display, before kneeling down to perform a five finger exercise on the *spunk trumpet.*

cricket week *n.* A five day test, when a gentleman must *bowl from the pavilion end* while his wife is *padded up.*

crimping off a length *n. milit.* Naval slang for *dropping a depth charge, laying a cable.*

crimson wave *n.* Also *crimson tide.* See *surfing the crimson wave.*

crinkle cuts *n. medic.* The large, crenellated *scallop lips* that protrude from a salty *bag. Real McCoy's, Nicki Lauda's lugs, turkey's wattles.* A *doctor's signature.*

cripple crapper *n.* A *chod bin* designated for the exclusive use of persons of restricted mobility. *'Fuck it. Look at the queue for the shitters. I'll just nip into the cripple crapper.'*

crone bone *n.* A state of somewhat unsettling sexual arousal brought on by an unlikely stimulus, *eg.* a picture of Camilla Parker-Bowels in jodhpurs.

crop spraying *v.* See *pebble dashing.*

crossword, teeth like a *sim.* Descriptive of the off-putting appearance of horrendous dentition, liberally strewn with gaps and cavities. Along with a sexy *bird* taking off her sunglasses to reveal that she was cross-eyed, and another one turning round and revealing herself to be Henry McGee with a bubble perm, a girl smiling and having teeth like a crossword was the third situation that Bob Todd encountered whilst trying to chat up women in unrealistic speeded-up discotheques on the *Benny Hill Show. English teeth.*

crotch broth *n. Scots.* Semen, *manfat etc. 'Och, help m'boab, Morag. Oor Wullie's got all crotch broth matted in his sporran again.'*

crotch crickets *n. Crabs.*

crotch eggs *n.* Hairy *knackers.*

Crouch's leg *n.* A long, thin, pale, pastie, sorry-looking penis with which its owner, contrary to all outward impressions, just keeps on *scoring*.

crouching tiger, hidden dragon *n.* Ancient Chinese sexual position. *Doggy-style* sex with a woman so *fugly* that one can't bring oneself to look her in the face.

crouton *n.* An erection that floats in one's soup.

crow *1. n. US.* That *muck* which has been *chucked*, esp. onto the *mapatasi*. Post-*porking* residue on the *hairy clam. Muffdruff. 2. n.* Nostril carrion. A *bogie, greb, greenie,* particularly when wiped on a wall.

crowbar *n.* An erection which is hard enought to force a sash window with. A *jemmy-on.*

crowd pleaser *n.* Unusual or noteworthy stool which one feels an urge to show to someone before flushing it away.

crown jowls *n.* The baggy bit of excess skin that hangs off the end of the *grub screw. Kenny's hood.* The *fiveskin.*

crow's nest *n.* A particularly ramshackle *snatch* in which a *one-eyed pirate* might feel at home.

Croydon national anthem *n.* The sound of sirens, which causes the denizens of the popular Surrey town to stand. A *Bolton alarm clock.*

cruiser and tug *n.* The common phenomenon of a stunning female who is always accompanied by an ugly little fat friend.

crumpa lumpa *n.* A tubby, *cake-worrying* lady with an orange hue that suggests that she frequents a cheap tanning salon or, alternatively, that she is exhibting the symptoms of a beta carotene overdose.

crumpet *1. n.* A traditional Scottish cake made of soft, light dough, eaten toasted and buttered, and much craved by the late Sid James. *2. n.* 1970s *blart.*

crumpet batter *n.* Gentleman's erotic spendings.

crumpeteer *n.* A fellow who has a way with the ladies. An expert in the science of *crumpetology. 'Birthdays: Curtis Mayfield, soul musician and corpse, 58; Charles R Drew, physician and blood plasma pioneer, 96; Allen Ginsberg, beardy poet, 74; Tony Curtis, actor and veteran crumpeteer, 75.'* (from *The Times*, June 3rd 2000).

crumpet trumpet *n.* An involuntary release of air from a young lady's *front bottom.* A *forward hat drop, queef, snatchaphone* or *Lawley kazoo.*

crunchie *1. n.* A tasty confectionary snack. *2. n.* A brittle sock worn on the foot the day after one has *wanked* into it.

crunk *n.* The *taint, barse, tintis, tinter.*

crusties *1. n.* Dog-on-a-string-owning soapophobes. *2. n.* Over-worn *bills* somewhat lacking in "April freshness". *Dunghampers* with a dirty *drip tray.*

Crystal Gayle *1. n. prop.* Long-haired, lightweight US country performer of the 1970s. *2. n.* A prison-based sexual act which may (in fact, almost certainly will) "make your *brown eye* blue". *'He walked into the shower block / Of Reading's dreadful gaol / And stooping to pick up the soap / The prisoner's face turned pale / As* *a voice behind him whispered / 'How about a Crystal Gayle?"* (from *The Ballad of Reading Gaol* by Oscar Wilde).

crystal maze, go *v.* To find oneself unable to perform a simple task due to pressure, *eg*. a learner driver being unable to get the car out of reverse gear during a test, Eamonn Holmes being unable to competently present a television programme when the cameras are on. To go all *cunty booby.*

CSB *abbrev.* Default hairstyle setting for young lady *scratters.* From Chav Scrape Back.

CT scan *n.* Act performed by men in public areas. A quick glance at passing ladies' *Toblerone tunnel* areas to check for the presence of *camels' toes.*

Cuban wank *n.* A *diddy-ride*, a *Bombay roll.* A *tit-wank.*

cubism *1. n.* A French school of painting typified by the works of Picasso and Braque which amalgamated multiple viewpoints into a complex surface of geometrical planes. *2. n.* A harmless gentleman's hobby which involves sneaking into a cubicle in the female toilets of a pub, club or department store and listening in to the action in the neighbouring "cubes".

cuckold *n.* A man whose wife allows another man to lay his *cock eggs* in her.

cuckoo *n.* A scoundrel who moves in on a *bird's nest* when someone else has nipped to the bar after doing all the groundwork.

cuff the dummy *v. US. milit. To wank, scrub the cook.*

cuff stinks *n.* The malodorous end result of an unfortunate sleeve mishap suffered when wiping one's *nipsy* following a messy *Brad.*

cum *1. v.* A sexiness-enhancing mis-spelling of *come* used by the authors of *bongular* literature to describe male ejaculation. *2. n.* A sexiness-enhancing mis-spelling of *come* used by the authors of *bongular* literature to describe male ejaculate.

cumbeard *n.* A white, coagulated sperminiferous goatee worn by a lady who has helped herself to a double portion of *spangle.*

Cumberland *1. n.* A long *turd* which forms a spiral in the *pan,* in the style of the popular helical pub grub sausage. *2. n.* A gentleman's *porky banger.*

Cumberland curl *1. n.* A somewhat off-puttingly designed Wetherspoon's pub sausage which presents a convincing simulacrum of a *shite. 2. n.* A somewhat off-puttingly designed *shite* which presents a convincing simulacrum of a Wetherspoon's pub sausage.

Cumberland gap *1. n.* A repetitive, annoying skiffle song by Lonnie Donegan which topped the hit parade in 1957. *2. n.* The triangular gap at the top of a lady's thighs which arouses curiosity as to whether the old *Cumberland* could fit through. The *Toblerone tunnel.*

cumbrella n. A *dunky.*

cumchugger *n.* A *bird* who enjoys guzzling *spadge.*

cumdown *n.* That feeling of soul-crushing worthlessness that follows a *sherman* as inevitably as night follows day.

cumster *n.* A small hamster-like female who fills her cheeks with your *nuts.*

cum to mind *v.* Of a person or favoured memory, to appear as a mental image in the imagination of one embarking on the *vinegar strokes. 'These days I find it's often Kylie Minogue who cums to mind when I'm poking the missus.'*

cum to one's senses *v.* To experience feelings of self loathing and disgust immediately upon ejeculation when, all of a sudden, one experiences a Damascene conversion and wearing the girlfriend's lingerie, *poking* a Bangkok *ladyboy* or *wanking* into Carol Decker's wardrobe *etc.*, no longer seem a such a good idea.

cumulonimbus *n. Lat.* Oral sex. Tongular stimulation of a lady's *clematis*.

cunch *n.* A satisfying midday snack furnished by, or comprising of, the secret *girly parts* of an obliging ladyfriend. Derivation unknown.

cunker *n.* Romantic term for one of a lady's *bodily treasures*. The *snatch*.

cunnifungus *n. Lat.* Female equivalent of *knob cheese 'n' mushroom*.

cunnimingus *v.* The act of orally pleasuring a lady with personal hygiene issues. *Licking a nine volter.*

cunny *n. Lat. Fadge*, vagina. From cunnus = shagpipe.

cunnylicious *adj.* Descriptie of any woman, or part thereof, demanding to be eaten.

cunshine *n.* The frustrating reflections which invariably hinder full enjoyment of the glossy *whacknicolour* photographs in *art pamphlets*. Also *porn glare, razzle dazzle.*

cunt *1. n. 14thC. medic.* Polite term for lady's genitals. *2. n. 21stC.* Impolite term for lady's genitals. *3. n.* A traffic warden.

cuntbitten *adj.* Of a gentleman, to have contracted *VD* from a dirty lady. To be struck down with a *dose* of clappage.

cunt book *n.* The *dog house. '16th August 1945. Went down the Feathers with Joe and Dwight to celebrate winning the War. Back to Downing Street 4am. Lost keys. Climbed up drainpipe and fell into bins. Woke kids up. Clementine came down to let me in. I reckon I'm in the cunt book for at least a fortnight.'* (from The Diary of Sir Winston Churchill).

cunt bread *n.* A yeast infection on a lady's *ninja's toe*.

cunt bubble *1. n.* An air lock up the *blurtch*, often leading to a *Lawley kazoo*. *2. n.* A traffic warden.

cunt buster *1. n.* An enormous erection. A *diamond cutter. 'Olivia was powerless to resist. His eyes burned into hers like sapphires. His strong arms enfolded her softly yielding body as she felt herself being swept away in a whirlwind of passion. Then he dropped his trolleys revealing a right cunt buster.'* (from *The Lady and the Gypsy* by Barbara Cartland). *2. n.* A large baby.

cunt candle *n.* An outstanding idiot amongst men, one who stands out like a shining beacon of utter imbecility, *eg.* The Rt Rev Graham Dow, Bishop of Carlisle, to pick an example entirely at random.

cunt corks *n.* A term used in chemist's shops when one is too embarrassed to ask for a box of *women's things*.

cunteen *n.* A number which is larger than twelve but smaller than twenty, and is used to describe the size of a group of something one dislikes, *eg*. *'There were cunteen fucking TV chefs.'*

cunt guff *n*. The *dropping forwards of a lady's hat*.

cunt grunt *n*. A politer term for a *fanny fart*. Also a *queef*, a *hat dropped forward*, a *Lawley kazoo, Seagoon's last raspberry, cunt guff*.

cunt hook *n*. Any stylish car such as a VW Lupo or Daewoo Matiz with oversized wheels, blacked-out windows and rear spoilers, which impresses discerning ladies. A *fanny magnet*. *'Fiesta XR2, red, D reg, 312k, 1 new tyre, some history, MOT October, a real cunt hook £120 ono. First to see will buy. No tyre kickers.'*

cuntinental *n*. Anyone who sits outside a cafe in Britain drinking coffee and eating croissants whenever the drizzle lets up for ten minutes.

cunting *n*. A lady's bestest knickers, brought out to decorate the *hairy goblet* on special occasions.

cuntitude *n*. A *cuntish* attitude.

cuntlashed *n*. Twice as drunk as *shitfaced*.

cuntlery *n*. Any utensil or digit used to assist when *dining at the Y*. For example, fingers, lolly sticks, clothes pegs or spoons *etc*. used to hold back the *beef curtains*.

cuntlifters *n*. An elderly lady's *dunghampers. Granny's bills*.

cunt mumps *n. medic*. That condition which causes a female to instantly reject the conversational gambits of a potential suitor.

cuntrified *adj*. Of a public house, to have been turned into a ritzy wine bar by the addition of a DJ, bowls of olives on the bar and a bunch of *twattish*, braying media types.

cunt ruffler *n*. A man who enjoys provoking ladies who have *fallen to the communists* because he finds their mood swings amusing. Easily recognised by his black eyes, missing teeth and stab wounds.

cunt rug *n*. A *muff*, a *merkin*. A pubic *syrup*.

cunt scratchers *n*. Humorous term for hands. *Wanking spanners*.

cuntsman *n*. *US*. A *cocksman, stickman*. A Don Juan type, highly skilled in the pursuit of *poontang*. *'Today's birthdays. Rod Stewart, singer, song writer, cuntsman, 73.'*

cuntstruck *adj*. Besotted, hopelessly in love.

cuntuppance *n*. Well-deserved humiliation following some sort of *fanny*-related behaviour. *Lust desserts*. *'I see Darren Day's got his cuntuppance in the News of the World again.'*

cuntwank *n*. A one-sided, loveless, no-nonsense bout of intercourse. A *hands free*. *'I've just seen that Victorian lesbo drama on the telly. Phwooar! So I'm off upstairs for a cuntwank off the missus.'*

cuntweep *n*. The custard-like mess found in a lady's *alans* after she has sat in the office all day chatting about Paolo di Canio's legs.

cunty booby *adj*. To be in a state of confusion. *'I don't pretend to understand the universe - when I start thinking about it I go all cunty booby, me.'* (from *Latterday Pamphlets Number 6*, by Thomas Carlyle).

cupcake *n*. Small quantity of *fart* gas caught between the palms of the hands and released in a person's face.

Cupid's measles *n. medic.* Victorian terminology for *cock rot.*

Cupid's toothpaste *n.* Oral *gunk.*

cup cracker *n.* A *cabman's rest* which is too large for the *titpant* to which it has been allotted.

curd *n. Jizz.*

curl one in *v.* To achieve a particularly skillful *fuck* from an impressively difficult starting position. *'Victoria Adams, the former Spice Girl, today refused to comment on allegations that her husband, transvestite advert star David Beckham, had curled one into his personal assistant, TV pig wanker Rebecca Loos.'* (BBC News 24).

curl one off *v.* To carefully deliver a *mudchild.*

curler *1. n.* A lump of excrement. *2. n.* Something in your wife's hair. *3. n.* A lump of excrement in your wife's hair.

curry hurry *n.* The increasingly-hasty homeward bound trot of one who has recently partaken of some sort of exotic foodstuffs which are already *touching cloth* in high-temperature, quasi-viscous form

curryoakie *n.* An enthusiastic but tuneless *fart* performed after a gallon of bitter and an Indian meal. A *blanket ripper.*

curry slurry *n.* The mixture of semi-liquified excrement, intestines and internal organs left in the pan of the *chod bin* the morning after a particularly hot madras. *'I'd give it ten minutes if I was you, dear. I just did a bit of a curry slurry in there. Oh, and can you call an ambulance. And a priest.'*

curtain *n.* Jason Donovan's foreskin. From his 1992 song about *wanking* entitled *Any Dream Will Do*, which contained the lines *"I close my eyes / Draw back the curtain (ah-ah-ahh)"*.

curtain call *n.* A return to the lavatory for an *encore dump.* A *second sitting.*

curtain drop *n. Cat flap* length. The size of a woman's *beef curtains.*

curtain rings *n.* Labial ironmongery.

curtain twitchers *n. Tennis fans, lady golfers.*

curvy *adj. UK. journ.* Of women, to have large breasts and/or *arses. 'Curvy Nigella Lawson cooked a right royal supper of cod and green ended chips for foreign dictator George W Bush when he recently visited the Queen and her brood of bisexual children.'* (*BBC Good Food Magazine*, November 2003).

cushion creeper *n.* An upholstery-muffled *Exchange & Mart.*

custard *1. n.* A sweet sauce made from eggs and milk that goes well with rhubarbs. *2. n.* Someone who is simultaneously a bit of a *cunt* and a bit of a *bastard, eg.* Tim Henman, Andy Murray. *3. Rhym. Slang.* A *bakewell.*

custard cannon *n. Lamb cannon, mutton musket, pork sword, beef bazooka, spam blunderbuss, etc, etc, et fucking cetera.*

custard cousin *n.* The relationship a fellow has with others who have shared the same *slice* of *pie. eg.* Bryan Ferry and Mick Jagger are *custard cousins,* as are Liam Gallagher, Ally McCoist, Jim Kerr and the 14th Batallion of the Royal Scots Dragoon Guards.

custard muscle *n.* Subcutaneous body fat.

custard pie *n.* A pre-*spoffed fadge.* Referred to in various blues songs, including 1947's *Custard Pie Blues* by Brown McGhee. Also forms the basis of the Led Zeppelin song *Custard Pie* which opens their 1975 double album *Physical Graffiti* in which Robert Plant exclaims: "Save me a slice of your custard pie", apparently implying that he would later like to re-*poke,* and indeed *nosh* on, his *bird's* aforementioned *jitler*-filled *clopper*.

custody tart *n.* An arrested woman who *sucks off* the duty sergeant, or performs similar act in lieu of bail.

customer service 69 aisle x *exclam.* Phrase called out over supermarket tannoys to alert male staff of the presence of a fit *bird* in aisle x, so they can go over and *sneak a peek* whilst pretending to run a price check or look at some tins or something.

cut and paste *1. n.* In the world of education, a process used by students when researching their essays and dissertations on Wikipedia. *2. n.* A method used by internet-surfing politicians when compiling telling dossiers in order to justify taking a country to war. *3. n.* In the world of motion picture *grumble* drama, the act of withdrawing from a lady's *minge* in order to deposit the contents of one's *clackerbag* on her face or *thrupenny bits*. *'Hurry up Gunther, we're running out of tape. It's time for a cut and paste.'*

cut a rug *1. v.* In World War II, to take to the dancefloor and impress onlookers by jitterbugging energetically, especially with an American airman. *2. v.* To *split a kipper, part the whiskers etc*. To make penetrative love to a lady.

cut 'n' shut *1. n.* A second hand car, skillfully engineered from the front and back of two insurance writeoffs. *2. n.* A woman, seemingly constructed of two ill-matched donor women, *eg*. a fantastic body, but a *minger;* a cutie, but built like a bus; or a flat-chested bonebag sat on a big *arse* and tree trunk legs.

cut price spice *n.* A lady who models herself on Victoria Beckham, but does so on a much tighter budget. Accompanies *David Peckham* on trips in his *estate car.*

cut the cheese *v.* To *drop some back*. Also *cut the brie, open the ham*.

cut the cord *v.* To break the link between one's *arsehole* and an invisible, yet highly noticeable cloud of recently expelled *gut gas* by means of rapid, short wafting motions of the hand.

cut through the red tape *v.* To ignore received wisdom and *swim when the red flags are flying.*

cutty sark *n.* A large *floater* that burns on its way out.

cuzza *n.* A *Ruby Murray.*

cyber clap *n.* The embarrassing situation whereby your home computer becomes riddled with viruses as a result of surfing the *binternet* whilst the missus is out.

cybertranny *n.* Man or woman who pretends to be of the opposite sex in internet chat rooms, *eg*. 16-year-old Brenda turns out to be a 35-stone tattooed American man called Jim-Bob. With his dead mother in a fridge.

Cyclops *n.* A legendary purple-headed monster with a single *hog's eye*. And two big hairy *bol-*

locks underneath.

Cyprus manoeuvre *n.* Removing the penis during *doggy sex* and re-entering "accidentally" up the *bonus tunnel.* The *Limasol slip.* Invented in 1972 by scientists in Cyprus.

Czech book *n.* A *twatalogue* featuring undraped studies of sultry young ladies from the former east european state. *'I fancy banking at Barclay's, but I can't find me Czech book anywhere, mum.' 'Have you looked on top of your wardrobe? That's where your dad keeps his noddy mags.'*

Dd

dab the wound *v.* Of a lady, to *audition the finger puppets.*

dad dressed as Brad *n.* The male counterpart of a *Whitney dressed as Britney.*

daddaries *n.* Male version of mammaries. *Mannery glands, mantits, moobs, moomlaaters. 'Phwoar. I bet you don't get many of those daddaries to the pound, Lord Owen.'*

daddy's sauce *n. Baby gravy, pineapple chunk, heir gel.*

Dagenham handshake *n.* Sexual practice whereby the gentleman inserts a finger in the *pink,* a finger in the *brown,* then uses a third to ring the *devil's doorbell.*

Dagenham smile *n. Builder's bum.*

dags *n.* Shepherd-speak for sheep's *dangleberries.*

dairy bags *n.* Proper old-fashioned *churns* of the sort Nurse Gladys Emmanuel would have stuck in Ronnie Barker's face whilst plumping up his pillows, causing him to blow his cheeks out and blink amusingly.

daisy chain *n.* Series circuit of *AC* or *DC* sex. The sort which only occurs in *bongo films,* Richard Littlejohn's most feverish imaginings and Stephen Fry's public school dormitory.

daisy cutter *n.* A heavyweight *fart,* in breach of the Geneva Convention, that leaves nothing standing within a wide radius.

dakkery doo *n.* A relaxing concurrent *shit* and cigarette. From the German word Dak = cigarette. *'His Holiness will be with us presently, Cardinal. He's just went for a dakkery doo.'*

dalek *n.* An erection which is reminiscent of a forehead-mounted sink-plunger, and best viewed from behind the sofa.

dalhoonies *n. Gazungas.*

daltons *n.* The *nuts. 'Ooh, me daltons!'*

damaging gusts *1. n. met.* In weather forecasting circles, a warning of wind likely to cause harm to buildings. *2. n.* In curry-loving circles, the onset of the sort of *nipsy* turbulence which could easily dislodge a nearby chimney pot or take the roof off the shed.

dance the blanket hornpipe *v.* To perform a sailor's jig in one's hammock. To have *all hands on dick.*

dancer's lance *n.* An unwelcome *dalek* that appears when dancing closely with a lady. A *Saturday night lever, St. Vitus pants.*

dancing bear *n.* A grizzly brown monster that stands on its end in the *pan* and refuses to be flushed away unless hit with a stick.

dancing on bubblewrap, like *sim.* Phrase descriptive of the snap, crackle, pop sound emitted by one's *chocolate starfish* following a particularly fruity *Ruby Murray. 'Jesus man. I spent most of last night sat on the bog sounding like S-Club 7 dancing on bubblewrap. I'm never going to Curry Capital, the Bigg Market, Newcastle upon Tyne again. Till Friday.'*

dancing with the captain *v.* To masturbate. Wearing a bowler hat. See *grandma's party.*

dang *1. n.* Penis. *2. exclam. US.* Expression of annoyance. *'Dang them pesky Al Qaeda varmints.'* (George W Bush, State of the Nation Address, 2002). *3. n.* A word which, together with ding and dong, features prominently in the lyrics of Eurovision Song Contest entries.

dangermouse *n.* A tampon or *slim fanatella*.

danger wank *n. Self-abuse* whereby you shout your parents from downstairs, and then try to *blow your tanks* before they get to your bedroom. A *dangerous spurt* for an adrenaline *jizz-junky*.

dangleberries *n. Winnets*; excrement adhering to the *arse cress* around an inefficiently-wiped *ringpiece*. *Fartleberries, toffee strings, bead curtains, kling-ons, clinkers, miniature heroes*.

dangler n. A dangling *donger, a copper's torch*.

danglers n. *Hairy conkers*.

dangly ham *n. Beef curtains, bacon strips*.

Danny Fishcharge *n.* Spooneristic vaginal *gleet*.

darb *v.* To *shag, bonk, bang*.

dark star *n.* Black, or rather brown hole from which the *pink Darth Vader* might emerge wearing a *shitty* helmet. *Uranus*.

darned hole in a jumper *sim.* Descriptive of a tightly-gathered *ringpiece*.

darted animal *n.* A *heavily refreshed* fellow who is reeling along and staggering from side to side, just prior to falling over in the gutter, in a style strongly reminiscent of a rogue rhinoceros which has just been shot with a tranquiliser gun.

Darth Vader's hat stand *n.* A sinister, six foot tall, wheezing *cock*.

Darth vulva *n.* The act of eating a *fish supper* with such gusto that it makes a sound not unlike Luke Sywalker's evil nemesis/long lost father trying to eat a squid without taking his helmet off.

dash for gash *n.* The desperate last half hour before chucking out at a night club. The *two am bin rake*.

date locker *n.* Rectum, *bomb bay*.

Dave Narey *rhym. slang. Scot.* A woman who would benefit from a major *waxing session, eg.* Anne Robinson and her who did 99 Red Balloons. Named after the Dundee United footballer who famously scored with a 25-yard toe-poke against Brazil in the 1982 World Cup.

David Peckham *n.* A young man who aspires to look like the England captain, but lives a very different lifestyle. ie, he has bleached, slicked-up hair, but wears *Armani and Navy* and drives a G-Reg Astra.

dawn horn *n.* Early morning *tent pole, bed flute*. See also *big cock day*.

dawn lumberjack *n.* A *woodsman* who is partial to taking his *chopper* in his hand early in the morning.

daylighting *1. n.* Construction industry term describing the appearance of a tunnelling machine or driven pipe emerging from a soil face. *2. n. Touching cloth, turtle's head*.

dead heat *n.* The situation whereby the urge to defecate comes to glorious fruition at the exact moment when the buttocks touch the *bog seat*.

dead heat in a zeppelin race *sim.* Large *tits, knockers, bazookas, oomlaaters, Gert Stonkers*.

dead herring *n.* A female woman in a pub or club who looks as filthy as a pornstar but turns out to be as frigid as a deceased fish.

dead man's handle *n.* The life-saving "Stop" button on a DVD remote control, over which a gentleman's left thumb constantly hovers whilst he is enjoying an artistic videographic presentation.

dead otter *n.* A single stool of immense proportions.

deal or no deal *n.* Gentleman's nightclub quandary; whether to turn down the offer of a certain *legover* from a below-par *boiler* early in the evening in the hope that he can get a higher calibre *box* later on, and thus risking ending up with *fuck all* at the end of the night. From the popular TV show for the housebound, where the constant question posed by tidy-bearded not-at-all-sinister host Noel Edmonds is: "Well, deal or no deal? Do you want to open the box?" *'Ayup. That scutter with the home-made tattoos is really giving you the glad eye, but there's some real quality blart over there. It's make your mind up time, is it deal or no deal?'*

dealt a Beadle, to be *v.* Whilst playing cards, to receive a totally *shit* hand.

dearotica *n.* Type of DVD ordered from a Nigerian porn site that costs the hapless purchaser the entire contents of his bank account. And his marriage.

death by chocolate starfish *1.n.* An incredibly disgusting *McArthur Park. 2. n.* A chronic attack of the *Earthas*.

death nest *n.* Estate agent speak for the smaller house that elderly people buy late in life.

death row *1. n. US.* A section of a prison where Texan authorities keep simple-minded black men prior to their execution for crimes which they have usually not committed. *2. n.* A retirement home or sheltered housing complex.

death star *n.* The *nipsy*.

debtors' dish *n.* Satellite television broadcast receiving apparatus. Term used by bailiffs and debt collectors who know that their indolent quarry will be at home watching advertisements for loan companies on the *shit pump*.

decafathon *n.* A gruelling day-long test of stamina, consuming only things that are good for you. *'Battered sausage, chips and soapy peas please love, and a big bottle of Tizer. I'm doing a decafathon tomorrow.'*

decrapitation *n.* The act of cutting the head off a *Richard the Third*, in order to answer the door, get the phone or present *Thought for the Day* on Radio 4.

deerstalker *n.* A lady's *bodily treasure* with tweedy *flaps*. Also known as a *Basil Rathbone*.

defarture lounge *n.* The vestibule of the *dirt bakery*, where *exhaust gases* gather in order to build up to maximum pressure. *'Fuck me, Your Majesty. I've got a right beauty brewing up in the defarture lounge, I don't mind telling you.'*

deflate *v.* To *suck off*. *'Oi, Gillian. Deflate this for me, will you?'*

de-ice the flaps *1. v.* In aeronautical circles, to carry out various procedures on an aeroplane which ensure that ice deposits on the wings do not impair the operation of the control surfaces and mechanisms. *2. v.* Of a frigid lady, to make use of her *muff* after a substantial layoff.

Deirdre's neck *n.* The knotted strings supporting the *nadbag* that are under immense tension.

Delhi belly *n.* Delicate stomach condition leading to the *Eartha Kitts.*

Delia *n.* At a social engagement, the cringeworthy performance of an embarrassingly loud and drunken partner. From tired and emotional TV chef Delia Smith's motivational half-time address at the Norwich versus Man City game on February 28th 2005. *'Oh Christ. She's had half a dozen Bacardi Breezers on an empty stomach. Give it ten minutes and she'll be doing a Delia on me.'*

Delilahs *n.* Stickily sweatsome *plums* which attach themselves to the side of the leg, and require hip-swivelling moves of the sort favoured by leather-trousered Welsh *scads* magnet Tom Jones to dislodge.

delivery from the coalman, take a *v.* To have a grubby chap empty his *sack* in your *back passage* on a regular basis.

dell *1. n. 16thC.* Prostitute, *tom.* 2. n. Original Hampshire venue of Southampton F.C.'s annual relegation battle.

Denis Norden, do a *v.* To chat up a piece of *clump* in an unnecessarily long-winded and tiresome way instead of just asking for a *poke.* From the way that the antediluvian *It'll be Alright on the Night* host bores the liver out of everyone for ten minutes before each batch of funny clips.

Deptford wives *n. Ankle chaingang* of women of uncertain breeding, staggering under the weight of their *bingo clink* on a night out. Often to be seen lifting their tops to expose their *noinkers* for the cameras of Bravo TV's hard-hitting documentary series *Booze Britain.*

depth charge *n.* A large or heavy stool, *copper bolt.* Also *belly flopper, Admiral Browning.*

derection *n.* The opposite of an erection, usually obtained by thinking about something unerotic. See *summoning Moira.*

derren *n. medic.* Of a man, to be sterile. From the mentalist magician Derren Brown who, in a TV Russian Roulette stunt, was found to be *firing blanks. 'No, we don't need a blob, love, I'm derren. But if you're really worried, I'll slip it in your brown pocket.'*

designer vagina *n.* Any *muff* which has been trimmed into an unusual shape, *eg.* a heart, a *Hitler tash* or Craig David's beard. *Armani fanny, Versnatche.*

desk lifter *n.* An attractive lady teacher who, on bending over to pick up some chalk can cause 30 desklids to be raised simultaneously.

desktop dusting *n.* A fellow's daily ritual of deleting the numerous *male interest* images and thirty-second video clips from his desktop, recent documents and internet history folders, and thus leaving his computer as *clean as a gay bloke's flat.*

desktop dykes *n.* The sort of aesthetically-pleasing *lipstick lesbians* found in huge quantities on a healthy young man's hard disk, but exceedingly rarely, if ever, encountered in real life.

devil's bagpipes *n.* A chap's *meat and two veg.*

devil's chimney *1. n.* Geological tourist attraction in the absence of anything else to look at on the Isle of Wight. *2. n.* The *shitter.*

devil's dumplings *n.* The *chesty substances* found on ladies' fronts.

devil's evacuate *n.* Piping hot *bum slurry* fermented in the depths of Hell. Diarrhoea.

devil's handshake *n.* A Roman Catholic *wank*. A means of reserving oneself a place in the eternal lake of fire.

devil's inkwell *n.* A gentleman's post *bust off* navel, brim-full with his onanistic yield.

devil's kiss *n.* A *fart* released during sex in the 69 position. *Hell's mouth*. On the plus side, it's probably not quite as bad as a *Satan's banquet.*

devil's kitchen *n.* The *chamber of horrors.*

dew on the lily *1. euph.* A lubricated *flange. 2. n. Knob glaze, pre-cum. Perseverance soup.*

dew south *n.* The condition of a young lady's *parts* when she is in a state of arousal, for example whilst watching Preston scratch his *nuts* on *Celebrity Big Brother.*

DFKDFC *abbrev. medic.* Used in patients' notes during diagnosis - Don't Fucking Know, Don't Fucking Care. *'Patient: Female. Age: 72. Presented: Hot flushes, swollen tongue, racing heart, low blood pressure, tingling down right side, loose finger nails. Diagnosis: DFKDFC. Treatment: Amoxyl 3 times a day.'*

diamond cutter *n.* The hardest erection known to man. *Pink steel.*

diamond in the muff *n.* A genuinely attractive woman in a *grumble flick.*

Diana, to do a *v.* To collide at a spot between two *tunnels* when having sex. To hit the *taint* with one's *bell end.*

dibble *1. v. 14thC.* To *shag. 2. n.* Cartoon police officer in Top Cat. *3. v.* To playfully prod around at the *hangar doors.*

Dibnah dick *n.* A sudden loss of erectile strength causing the *skin chimney* to collapse. Can be brought on by catching a whiff of badly-wiped *arse* when *changing at Baker Street.*

dick *1. n. US.* Penis, *pud, plonker. 2. n.* Idiot, *plonker. 'Rodney, you fucking dick.'* (*Only Fools and Horses' Christmas Special*, 1955) *3. v.* To *fuck.*

dick-do *n. US.* Light-hearted epithet used to describe a *salad-dodger*. Based on the assumption that "their gut probably sticks out more than their dick do". *'Deaths; Peter Ustinov, polyglot dick-do, 82.'* (from *The International Herald Tribune*, March 29th 2004).

dick docker *n.* A rabbi.

dick duster *n.* A hairy top lip on a lady.

dickhead *n.* Fool, *joskin, shit-for-brains.* An idiotic fellow.

dickhead dust *n.* White powder which, when snorted through a rolled-up banknote, turns even the nicest individual into a complete *twat.* Cocaine, *showbiz sherbert, Bolivian marching powder* etc. *'One of the Sunday newspapers reported that a Blue Peter presenter had been seen taking dickhead dust. I believe that he has not only let himself and the Blue Peter team down, including the dogs and tortoises, but he's also let all of you down badly. He himself agrees with me that, in the circumstances, he can no* *longer continue as a presenter on the programme. However, he'll be back in a couple of years doing phone-ins on Radio 5.'* (On-air apology by Lorraine Heggessey, head of BBC Children's Television, 1999).

dickie dido *n.* Something on a lady, the hairs on which come down to her knees.

Dickinson holiday *n.* A bottle of fake tan which makes the wearer look like a fucking satsuma. Named after bright orange cheeky ex-con TV auction wideboy David Dickinson.

dick skinners *n. medic. US. Wanking spanners, cunt scratchers.* Hands.

dick splash *1. n.* Urine on trousers or suede shoes caused by shakage or *splashback*. See also *forget-me-nots. 2. n. US.* Contumelious epithet for an unworthy person. Named after Senator Richard Splash, Vice President under Jimmy Carter.

Dick Turpin's hat *n.* A good old-fashioned three-cornered hairy *blurtch*.

dick van dyke *n.* A strap-on cockney. A lesbotic *twat* rattler, a dildo. A *mary pop-in*.

dick weed *n. US.* Goldang *melon farming fuckwit*.

dick wheat *n.* Male pubic hair.

dickwit *1. n.* Probably a character from a Charles Dickens novel. *2. n.* A bloke who thinks with his *charlie*. *3. n.* A foolish person.

diddies *n. Scot.* Ladies' *tits*.

diddy ride *n. Scot.* A deep-fried *sausage sandwich*.

diesel dyke *n. US.* A butch or masculine lesbian. Also *bulldyke, fanny nosher.*

diet choke *n.* A refreshing, low-calorie drink which is rich in *vitamin S*.

diet fart *n.* A loud clearing of the *nether throat* that sounds dangerous but actually has no smell and is harmless. *'No need to open the window, Your Majesty. It was just a diet fart.'*

difficult brown *n.* Tricky option in *bum games*. See also *Irish, snookered behind the red. 'I'd rather take the easy pink than the difficult brown.'*

difficult child *n.* One who, once *dropped off at the pool,* refuses to go into the water and clings onto the side.

digby *n.* A big, ugly woman. From the 70s children's film *Digby, the Biggest Ugly Woman in the World*.

digestive transit *1. n.* Advert-speak for a big, steaming *crap. 2. n.* Lightweight commercial vehicle which delivers biscuits.

dig in the whiskers *n. Aus.* A spot of *beard-splitting. 'Fuck me, look at that Sheila. She's worth a dig in the whiskers, wouldn't you say, Rolf?'*

dig up a badger and bum it *exclam.* Phrase used when in a state of extreme sexual frustration. *'I tell you what, Una. I'm that horny I'd happily dig up a badger and bum it.'*

dildo *n.* Practice version of the *pork sword.* A *bob*, *neck massager, dolly dagger*.

dill *1. n.* An unpleasant thing put in burgers by the staff at McDonald's. *2. n.* A type of pickle.

dillberries *n. Dangleberries, wufflenuts.*

dilm *n.* Unpleasant-tasting spermicidal lubricant on a *dunky*.

dilmah *n. Aus.* An amusing party trick whereby the performer of the trick bounces his *knackers* on the forehead of the first person to fall asleep. Named after an Australian brand of tea bag and the similar dunking action associated with them.

dimmock *1. v.* Of a lady, to create a *water feature*. See *squat 'n' squirt*. *2. v.* Of a lady's nipples, to pop out like a car cigarette lighter.

dine at the Marriott's buffet *v.* To succumb to a bout of alimentary unpleasantness. Named after Tottenham Hotspur's meek last-match-of-the-season capitulation to West Ham in 2006, after the team's players were (our lawyer wishes to make clear) definitely not poisoned by dodgy comestibles consumed at the plush five-star hotel the previous evening. *'Uh-oh, and if our helicopter camera high above Tower Bridge could just zoom in there....yes, it looks like Radcliffe's been dining at the Marriott's buffet again, Sue.' 'Yes, Steve. She's definitely shat herself alright.'*

ding-a-ling *n.* Chuck Berry's *cock*. With two silver bells hanging off it.

ding! dong! *exclam. arch.* Caddish expression of delight when Terry-Thomas spotted a woman with *dunce's hats*.

dingleberry roast *n.* A lighted *fart*, an *afterburner, a blue streak*.

dingo's breakfast *n. Aus.* A *piss* and a bit of a look around.

dining with the Askwiths *euph.* Illicit or surreptitious *puddle jumping*. From the deliberately misleading excuse offered to his missus by flamboyant Victorian playwright Oscar Wilde when he was late home for his tea; *viz.* that he was going for a meal with *Confessions* film actor and Patricia Hayes-lookalike Robin Askwith and his family.

dinner lady's arms *1. n. medic. Bingo wings. 2. sim.* Large, but nonetheless unhealthy-looking *cocks*. A penis that looks like it might have a heart attack at any moment.

dinner masher *n.* A *botter.*

dipping a worm in a bucket *v.* Engaging in unsatisfying sexual congress. *The last hot dog in the tin.*

dip 'n' dazzle *n.* A humourous epithet used to describe one whose ocular organs are so far out of whack as to be reminiscent of badly-adjusted headlights, *eg.* the late Marty Feldman. An *Isaiah.*

DIPS *acronym.* Paris Hilton's car wing mirrors. Drunken Impact Protection System.

dip your nib in the office ink *euph.* To partake in a romantic liaison with a female office colleague. To *shit on your own doorstep. 'What am I going to do, Tony? The News of the World's caught me dipping me nib in the office ink again.'*

dip your wick *v.* To slip your *dill* into the *hamburger.*

director's commentary *n.* The disconnected, self-obsessed ramblings of bitter-sodden tramps under their breath.

director's cut *n.* The point in an 18th generation *jazz video* where a previous *Chinese helicopter pilot* has inadvertently pressed "Record" instead of "Pause", leaving the viewer with a four-second clip of *Panorama* circa 1994.

dirt bakery *n.* That part of the human anatomy where *holemeal loaves* are freshly manufactured around the clock. The *chamber of horrors*.

dirtbox *n. Date locker,* rectum. Source of delights for devotees of *bumcraft*.

dirty Beppe *n.* A *dirty Sanchez*, but with coverage extended to the chin.

dirty bomb *1. n.* A crude explosive device containing radioactive material designed to contaminate an area, making it uninhabitable. *2. n.* A *dropped back,* the fallout from which makes the immediate vicinity uninhabitable for the foreseeable future, *eg*. one dropped by Jocky Wilson at a cocktail party. *3. n.* A *shit explosion* that peppers the bowl with bio-hazard shrapnel.

dirty Bristow *n.* A sexual act performed by a lady whereby she kneels behind a standing gentleman and licks his *anus* whilst reaching through his legs to stimulate his penis. Occasionally stopping to swig a pint of lager. *Tromboning*.

dirty dentist *n. Fanny mechanic, snatch doc, box doc.* A consultant gynaecologist. *'I'm having a bit of bother with me clopper, love, so I'm off to the dirty dentist for a scrape.'*

dirty devil *n.* An under-duvet *dropped gut* that tests one's relationship to breaking point. *'Sorry about that dirty devil, love. Anyway, it's your turn on top, isn't it.'*

dirty fart *n.* A *Lionel Bart* with delusions of grandeur. A *follow through*.

dirty lolly *n.* A girl whom one is tempted to pick up and lick, but who is probably covered in germs.

dirty onion *n.* The overture to an act of *backdoor romance* that is performed with such unexpected vigour by the *bummer* that it brings an involuntary tear to the eye of his *bummee*. *'Bloody hell, your lordship. That was a bit of a dirty onion, if you don't mind me saying so. Do that again and I'll take my story to the Mail on Sunday.'*

dirty Sanchez *1. n.* Television programe in which a group of educationally subnormal Welshmen dare each other to drink *piss*, set fire to their *bell ends*, nail their scrotums to double decker buses *etc*. *2. n.* Sticking one's finger up a lady's *back bottom* during *doggy style* sex. Then drawing a moustache on her top lip, apparently.

dirty secret *n.* A pungent *back biscuit* left by a surreptitious *benefactor* as he innocently sidles away from a group. *'I knew they weren't going to offer me the job. Mind you, at least I managed to leave a dirty secret as I got up to leave.'*

dirty spine, snip a length of *v.* To *lay a cable, drop a copper bolt.*

dirty ticket *n.* A very easy lady. *'I must say, when I first met Sarah at Klosters, I thought she was a bit of a dirty ticket. However, she's put all that behind her now, and I think she's going to make an excellent Duchess.'* (Prince Philip, wedding reception speech, 1986).

dirty Titchmarsh, do a *v.* To perform a rudimentary garden makeover without the owner's knowledge, a process that typically involves adding a used *jubber* and a pair of discarded *scads* to the existing landscaping arrangement. See *incapability brown*. *'You know that* *lass I was talking to in the pub? The one who was feeling sick so I took her outside for some fresh air? We ended up doing a dirty Titchmarsh in a garden round the corner.'*

dirty water *n. medic.* A medical term for seminal fluid. *Bollock bile.*

disabilitits *n.* Funbags which are so large that they become a hindrance. Faith Brown is apparently entitled to a parking permit because of her terrible disabilitits.

disco fanny *adj.* The full strength flavour achieved by a vigorous evening of giving it six nowt on the dance floor.

disfabled *adj.* To be claiming invalidity benefit on dubious grounds, *eg.* that copper who was off work with stress, but bravely managed to referee a Premiership football match.

dishonourable discharge *n. milit.* The shameful result of knocking the *little general's helmet* off.

disneyland *n.* A woman who takes an inordinate amount of time and a large amount of money to get into, although once you do, all the *rides* are free. Also *legoverland.*

display model *n.* A bit of *morning wood* that's just for show and, despite everyone's best efforts, refuses to *go off.*

ditch pig *n.* An affectionate, lighthearted epithet for an ugly fat girl.

divot *n.* A particularly hairy *placket.*

DIY *euph.* A single-handed job done around the house at the weekend using one *tool* and a bag of *nuts.*

Dizzy Gilespie *n.* A formidable blast on the *spunk trumpet* where the lady's cheeks puff out like a bullfrog's, and it would be a good idea for the man to stick a mute up his *arse* to keep the noise down.

dizzyade *n.* Beer. Also *dizzy pop.*

do *v.* To give someone *one*. *'No kissing, just cold, hard sex. And absolutely no simulation - these birds are really being done.'* (from an advertisement for erotic videos in the *Daily Express*).

do a West Ham *sim.* To *score* and *stay up* when you haven't really got it in you. Formerly *do a Southampton.*

dobber *1. n.* A *rubber johnny.* *2. n.* A semi-erect *dill*. A lazy *lob on.* *3. v.* To cheat someone out of something, to rip off. From a bloke called Dobber Bailey from Coventry who famously, twenty years ago, got ripped off buying an engine for his Triumph TR7.

dobgob *v.* To *spooge up* when only half *stonked.* Also *dobglob.*

Doc Brown, do a *v.* To delete all the *left-handed websites* from one's computer's history file, an act usually carried out between 12.30am and 1.00am, after the wife has gone to bed. Named after the eccentric inventor in the *Back to the Future* films, who was not averse to meddling with the past when the need arose.

dock *1. n. Arse.* The polite term by which horsey types refer to their steeds' *fudge tunnels.* *2. v.* To *shag.* Up a horse's *arse.*

docker's omelette *n.* A glistening gobbet of rubbery phlegm with remarkable anti-traction properties. A *gold watch*, a *rolex prairie oyster.*

docker's tea break *sim.* Descriptive of something very long. *"Oh, what a tiny little man,' laughed Verruca*

Salt as she saw the Oompa Lumpa. 'He may be small,' cautioned Mr Wonka as he turned briskly on his heel, 'but he'll have a cock as long as a docker's tea break." (from *Charlie and the Chocolate Sandwich* by Roald Dahl).

docker's thumbs *n.* Nipples so hard one could hang a soaking wet duffle coat off them. *Scammell wheelnuts, JCB starter buttons, Dimmocks.*

docking *n.* The rolling of one's *fiveskin* over another chap's hat. A *clash of heads.*

dockyard cat, fanny like a *sim.* Descriptive of a particularly unkempt semi-feral *snatch. Terry Waite's allotment, Alan Johnston's vegetable patch.*

dockyard rivets *n. Cigarbutts, pygmies' cocks.*

doctor's signature *n.* A particulary wiggly pair of *beef curtains* resembling a GP's scrawl at the bottom of a prescription.

Dodd job *n.* A *nosh* administered by the more toothsome lady, or perhaps one who likes to bite. *'Fancy another Dodd job, Normski?' 'No thanks, Janet. By the way, have you seen the TCP anywhere?'*

dodd *v.* To *shit* oneself in public. Named after a certain James Dodd who *shit* himself on the way to work and then phoned in to say he couldn't come in because he had *shit himself.*

dodger's conscience *n.* The ridiculous purchase of a diet drink after a *Duke* or *Duchess of Giblets* has ordered a large pie and chips, two pickled eggs, a battered sausage and "a saveloy while I'm waiting".

dog *1. n.* A woman who fails to reach an acceptable standard of attractiveness. A *steg, hound.* 2. *n.* A male prostitute. 3. *v.* To hang around in car parks at night, in the pretence of walking a dog, in order to spy on courting couples and watch it *go in* whilst *searching for loose change* in one's pockets.

dog at broth, like a *sim.* Descriptive of a desperate sexual act, usually *cumulonimbus. 'After returning from war service, Prince Philip was like a dog at broth when introduced to Her Majesty's front bum.'*

dog beers *n.* Any ale drunk by one who is unable to handle their beer. Drinking one *dog beer* leaves the average *two pot screamer* feeling and looking like he has drunk seven.

dog catcher *n.* A man who goes looking for unwanted *hounds* in a nightclub after all the pedigree *blart* has been collared. A *munter hunter.*

dog eating hot chips *sim.* A crude and voracious, yet effective, *horatio* technique. *'Lusitania was powerless to resist. His eyes burned into hers like garnets. His muscular arms enfolded her body as she felt herself being swept away in a force 10 gale of passion. Slowly, she fell to her knees and unzipped Giuseppe's breeches and went at his cock like a dog eating hot chips.'* (from *The Countess and the Lion Tamer* by Barbara Cartland).

dog eggs *n. Turds,* often laid on the pavement.

dog egg theory *n.* Scientific *blart* hypothesis; *viz.,* the older it is, the easier it is to pick up.

doggie chalks *n.* White canine excrements. *Poodle shit.*

doggies *n.* Intercourse performed in the position favoured by *hounds*, usually near some dustbins.

dogging *n.* The saucy behaviour of one who *dogs*.

doggy style *adj.* From the back. Or up against a visitor's trouser leg.

dog handler *n.* Offensively sexist term for a man who is prepared to go out with a right *fugly* old *ditch pig*.

dog in a bath *n.* A bedroom game like *rodeo sex*. *'The missus was setting the video last night and I was on me vinegar strokes when I called her by her sister's name. It was like trying to keep a dog in a bath.'*

dog lime *n.* *Dog eggs*, canine feculant.

dog-locked *n.* To be stuck in a compromising position due to muscular spasm, usually in the back of a car in a *Confessions* film. Also, *dog's lock-in*.

dognose *v.* To disturb one's slumbering wife following a *slash* in the small hours by touching her on the leg or buttocks with a cold, wet *bell end*.

dog section *1. n.* Division of the constabulary that uses highly-trained alsatians to apprehend people who run around with quilts tied to their right arm, firing starter pistols into the air. *2. n.* Sexist and offensive police station slang for the corner of the canteen where the pig-ugliest and *lesbo* WPCs (*ie.* the ones who least resemble strippagrams) congregate to eat.

dog slobber *n. Electric spaghetti.*

dog slug *n.* The act of licking around, and indeed inside, another person's *rusty sherrif's badge*. A *trip round the world*, a *rim job*.

dog toffee *n.* Tacky pavement deposit that readily adheres to the sole of a shoe or supports an upright lollipop stick.

dog toss *n.* Grinding against a woman's leg in an over-eager fashion whilst dancing at a night club, school disco, or wedding reception.

dog track *n.* The song (usually *Lady in Red*) played at ten to two in a nightclub, that precipitates a last-attempt mad dash onto the dancefloor by all remaining *hounds*. A *desperate dance*.

dog with two dicks *sim.* Descriptive of a *tomcat with three balls*. To be incredibly pleased with oneself. *'That's one small step for man, one giant leap for mankind. I'm on the Moon and I'm as happy as a dog with two dicks, me.'* (Neil Armstrong, July 1969).

dog's arse *adj.* To be troubled with wind. *'Excuse my wife. I'm afraid she's got a dog's arse today, Your Holiness.'*

dog's back *n.* See *Bilbo Baggins' foot*.

dog's bollocks *n.* Bee's knees, *donkey's knob, monkey's nuts, cat's knackers etc*.

dog's legs *n. medic.* Temporary weakness in the male thighs following a spot of *back-scuttling* with a *dirty lady*.

dog's lipstick *n.* A shimmery pink retractable cosmetic favoured by magicians' assistants.

dog's marriage *n.* A twenty-minute *al fresco back scuttle* that ends when the neighbours throw a bucket of water over you.

dog's match *n.* A sexual encounter in a public place, *eg.* in a bush, doorway, taxi queue or hospital casualty cubicle.

dole pole *n.* A walking stick used as a prop by an enterprising able-bodied person whilst attempting to claim extra social security benefits. See also *social sticks. 'Eeh. Look at the time. I'll have to run or I'll be late for my appointment at the DSS.' 'Don't forget your dole pole.'*

doley's blackout *n.* A mid-afternoon session of *self-abuse* snatched during a lull in daytime television. Achieved by shutting the curtains after *Quincy* for a quick *tug.*

dolly dagger *n.* A *bob, dildo.*

dollymop *n.* An amateur or inexperienced prostitute.

dolmio day *n.* The first seventh of *rag week.*

dolphin skin *n. medic.* The epidermis of the *herman gelmet.*

Don King in a headlock *sim.* Descriptive of a foreign lady's armpits.

donald *rhym. slang. Fuck.* From Donald Duck.

donger *n. Whanger, pork sword, dill.*

donkey kisser *n.* An inexperienced osculatrix. A lady who *snogs* like a donkey chewing an apple.

donkey punch *n.* Of *bum games*, to knock your partner out cold with a blow to the back of the head whilst in the *vinegar strokes*. Has the same aphrodisiacal effect as slamming a goose's neck in a drawer whilst committing bestiality. Results in inceased orgasmic intensity and a custodial sentence.

donkey rigged *adj.* Of a man, blessed with a sizeable penis.

donkey's earhole *n.* A particularly large, flappy, twitching vagina. A *hippo's mouth*, a *clown's pocket.*

Donkey style, do it *v.* To copulate in the *wrong 'un.* ie, in the *ass.*

donkified *adj.* To have a *horse's handbrake*, to be in a state of *tumescence*. To be *on the bonk.*

donner *n.* An unattractive woman, a *ten pinter.* ie, someone one wouldn't fancy too much when sober.

donny burns *n.* The tan achieved when standing in the away end at Doncaster Rovers on a hot day, when only half of your body is exposed to the rays of the scorching South Yorkshire sun.

donor *n.* One who believes it is better to give than to receive. See *benefactor.*

don't tear it, I'll take the whole piece *exclam.* Ancient, humorous, rag trade-based phrase used in response to an extremely dry, raspy *trouser cough. See also anybody injured?; well struck Sir!*

doofa *n.* A *ten-to-two-er.* From the phrase "She'll do for me".

doomsday book *n. Toilet literature* perused between sobs whilst suffering an apocalyptic rectal breakdown. Usually the *Autotrader.*

doonicans *n.* Assorted *claps,* NSUs and *doses.* From the initials of the bejumpered Irish rocking chair croonster Val.

doorbell *n.* A small button above the *snail's doorstep* that is so difficult to find, that it is often easier to use the *knockers.* The *clematis.* Also *devil's doorbell.*

doorman, have a word with the *v.* To butter up the *bald headed bouncer* in order to be allowed into the premises he is guarding. To *cumulously nimbate* the *clematis.*

doormat basher *1. n.* One who whacks their partner's *fanny* on the back yard wall to get the dust off it, whatever that means. *2. n.* A *lesbo.*

doos *n. Tits.*

dopper n. A *dork.*

doppleganger dick *n.* A *hard on* of such intensity, that one's own face is seen reflected in the shiny head, affording it the appearance of a miniature double. A *mini me.*

doritoes *n.* Exceptionally cheesy feet.

dork *n.* A *dopper.*

Dorothy Perkins *n.* DP, double penetration. Of a lady, to simultaneously have *gentlemen callers* in her front and back pockets. Also a *man at C&A,* a *double decker. 'In the cinema, one so-called film featured a man using disgusting sexual language. Another showed a lady baring her bosoms in the most provocative manner. A third film showed two well-hung men giving a woman a right Dorothy Perkins whilst she repeatedly took the Lord's name in vain. I was so disgusted that I vomited into my handbag. I think Mr Muggeridge next to me felt ill too, as he was groaning and rummaging frantically in his trouser pockets for a handkerchief.'* (Mary Whitehouse's report on a fact-finding trip to Amsterdam's Red Light District, 1968).

dorsal fin *n.* The sharp ridge or crest, consisting of raw cornflakes, which painfully slices lengthways down the *clackervalve* during a *sit down visit* to the water closet.

do the decent thing *v.* Of a lady who is *up on blocks,* to dutifully empty her husband's *bins* by means of an act of *horatio.*

double adapter *euph. AC/DC* man equipped with a *one pin plug* at the front but also having the benefit of a fully-functioning *single pin socket* at the back. A *switch hitter.*

double Barker *n.* A woman blessed with the body of Sue, but cursed with the face of Ronnie. A *bobfoc.*

double bassing *v.* To have sex from behind, fiddling with the lady's left nipple with your left hand and twanging away at her *clematis* with your right - a position similar to the one adopted when playing the upright bass, although the sound is completely different. To perform *charlimingus.*

double booked *adj.* Of a lady, to be romantically entertaining two gentlemen at the same time. A *man at C & A.*

double bouncers *n.* Value for money *tits* that resonate at twice the frequency of the woman's gait. *ie.* two bounces per step taken.

double cuffs *n.* The excessively-large *chinstraps* on a *bear trapper's hat.*

double dipper *1. n.* One who, unable to decide between *rice and chips,* has half a portion of each. A *switch hitter,* a *happy shopper.* A bisexual. *2. n.* One who does a bit of *double dipping.*

double dipping *1. n.* The social faux pas of returning a previously bitten tortilla chip, for instance, into a communal bowl for a second portion of sauce, as seen in the *Seinfeld* episode *The Implant. 2. n.* The social faux pas of tramping your *naughty boot* through all the *muck* in your ladyfriend's *back yard* before waltzing in through her *front door* and leaving *shit* on the *snail's doorstep.*

double doors *n. Beef curtains, cat flaps.*

double dragback *1. n.* An impressive football trick as perfected by the likes of David Ginola. *2. n.* A painful *wanking* accident whereby an inexperienced masturbatrix loses rhythm, resulting in one downward stroke being immediately followed by another, thus causing severe *one string banjo* trauma. An ineptly-syncopated *Barclay's.*

double fare *n.* One whose fat *arse* takes up two seats on a train or bus. A *salad dodger, barge-arse, fat fuck.*

double glazing *n.* Something that the late Ted Moult would almost certainly not have approved of or, indeed, endorsed in a long-running television advertising campaign. Two blokes *blowing their beans* over one *bird* at the same time.

double header *n.* Of *grumble flick cliterati,* the intriguing act of performing simultaneous *horatio* on two *gut sticks.*

double the melt *v.* To give a lady not one, but two portions of hot stringy cheese in her *hambuger.* To squirt a second portion of filling into a *vertical bacon sandwich* with one's *cheddar apple.*

double velvet *n.* A particularly keen *ginger beer, ie.* someone who "loves your bum".

double yolker *n.* A pornographic actor blessed with the elusive ability to fire off two consecutive *pop shots* without pausing for a sit down and a cup of tea in between. It is not known whether this happens in civilian life.

Dougal *1. n.* The agitated, easily-animated cylindrical dog from The *Magic Roundabout. 2. n.* A hairy *fanny* that has really been left to overgrow.

doughnut puncher *n.* A *dinner masher.*

doughy hood *1. n.* Character in *The Archers* played by Arnold Ridley, better known as Private Godfrey in *Dad's Army. 2. n.* A *women's thing* that can probably be fixed with a tub of natural yoghurt.

dowel *1. n.* In carpentry, a piece of wood that fits exactly into a hole. *2. n.* In sex, a piece of *wood* that fits exactly into a hole.

Dow Jones *n.* A fellow who is expert in the art of *footsie.*

downhill skier *n.* See *skiing position.* A *crane operator.*

downtime *n.* The period which elapses between ejaculation and rearousal. In most men, downtime is around 20 minutes, though in the case of Cliff Richard it is now 41 years and counting.

down to the viscounts *euph.* Descriptive of a chap who is bereft of *spangle* and thus scraping the bottom of his *biscuit barrels.* A reference to the apparently unpopular foil-wrapped minty confections which are only eaten when all other snack options have been exhausted. *'Quick Horace, shoot it on my belly.' 'I can't, love, sorry. I'm down to the viscounts.'*

dowsing rod *n.* A piece of *wood* that involuntarily twitches when approaching an area of great wetness.

doxy *n. arch.* Whore, *slag.*

D'Oyly *rhym. slang.* From D'Oyly Carte = heart to heart.

DP *acronym.* Double Penetration. Especially *one up the arse, one up the fanny.* Often leads to a *Newton's cradle.*

Dracula's tea bags *n.* Used *dangermice.*

dragging a wardrobe up a concrete

ramp, like *sim.* A phrase descriptive of a particularly cavernous and rasping act of flatulation.

dragging like a seal's ringpiece *sim.* Descriptive of something that seems to last forever, *eg.* being held captive in Beirut, waiting for a Pink Floyd song to reach the tune, watching an *Only Fools and Horses* Christmas Special.

dragon food *n.* Chocolates bought for *her indoors* when one is in the *cunt book. 'Shit, I've been out on the piss for three days. I'd better stop by the garage and pick up some dragon food before I get home.'*

dragon's nostril *n.* The state of the ringpiece after a hot *Ruby Murray. 'If you fancy giving yourself a dragon's nostril, then korma along to the Curry Capital, Bigg Market, Newcastle upon Tyne.'* (Press release from Abdul Latif, Lord of Harpole).

dragon's snout *n.* A particularly grotesque *turtle's head* which is accompanied by blasts of fiery breath, and may cause maidens to swoon.

drain your spuds *v.* To micturate. To have a *gypsy's kiss, slash.*

drat strap *n.* A G-string worn underneath the sheer garmentry of a young, nubile bit of *crackling.* Named after the cry of frustration and disappointment it elicits from the intending pervert.

draw an ace *v.* On wiping one's *arse* thoroughly, to eventually have an unsoiled piece of paper which indicates that the process has been successfully completed.

draw mud from the well *v.* To *follow through. 'I've just drawn mud from the well, so it's back to Jeremy in the studio.' 'Thank-you Kirsty.'*

drawn-on durex *n.* A biro line drawn around the base of the penile shaft which fools a drunken lady into thinking one has taken sensible precautions.

drayhorse's bottom lip *sim.* A big, floppy *snatch.* Full of carrots.

dread logs *n. Winnets* you could use to batter down a door.

down to one's last bead *adj.* Having an empty *sack, balls like bats' wings.* Bereft of *men's spendings, wankrupt.*

dreadnought *n.* Even bigger than a *dead otter.*

dream topping *n.* Night *spongle,* whipped up in the *farmer's hat* during pornographic REM sleep.

dress-messer *n.* A gentleman with a *hair trigger.*

drink from both taps *v.* To be bisexual, to *bend both ways.* See *double adapter.*

drink my kids *exclam.* Informal variant of *"suck my penis"*, usually used in a declamatory sense, rather than a genuinely sexual one.

drink on a stick *n.* A *nosh.*

drinks under the dartboard, looks like she *sim.* Of a lady who possesses a face that does not conform to classical standards of beauty.

drips in the tap, a few more *phr.* Excuse given by a gentleman who is returning from the pub bogs with a *wet penny in his pocket. 'Look at that. I put it away too early when there was still a few more drips in the tap. Anyway, where was I? Oh yes, your grandad's operation. Well, I'm afraid there were complications during surgery. I think you should prepare yourselves for* *some bad news.'*

drip tray *n.* The often crusty sump in a pair of lady's *dunghampers.*

dripping like a fucked fridge *sim.* Of a lady, to be sexually aroused. *'I'm in the mood for love / Simply because you're near me / and whenever you're near me / I drip like a fucked fridge.'* (Song lyric, *The Mood for Love* by Cole Porter).

dripping like a George Foreman grill *sim.* Descriptive of a *bird* who is *fizzing at the bunghole* or *dripping like a fucked fridge.*

drive from the ladies' tee *v.* Of a man, to sit down in order to have a *slash.*

drive stick *v. US.* To be a lady in uncomfortable shoes, to not *like tennis.* To be a non-*lezza*.

drive the porcelain bus *v.* To pay a kneel-down visit to the lavatory during which one holds the rim like a Routemaster steering wheel and does some *psychedelic yodelling.*

driving on the cats' eyes *v.* To emit a long, low, rumbling *fart* that sounds like it's going to damage one's suspension.

driving range *n.* The perineum. Where one hits one's *balls* when practising with one's *wood.*

drop a clot *v. medic.* To menstruate. *'It was D'Arcy who spoke first. 'Your disdain takes me somewhat aback, Miss Bennet. I fear I might have acted in some way inappropriately to cause you such offence.' 'No, Mr D'Arcy, your behaviour has been impeccable, and the fault lies with me. I am dropping clots at the moment and find myself in the foulest of humours,' she replied.'* (from *Pride and Prejudice* by Jane Austen).

drop a deuce *euph. Lay a cable,* do a *number two, do a duty*, defecate. Phrase popularised in the US comedy show *My Name is Earl.*

drop a gut *v.* To *step on a duck.*

drop a pebble *v.* To erroneously emit a *rabbit tod* whilst attempting to *shoot a bunny*. See also *follow through*.

drop a tadpole in her beer *v. Aus.* To make a lady pregnant. *'Her Majesty the Queen is pleased to announce that after several years of trying, HRH Prince Edward, the Duke of Wessex has finally succeeded in dropping a tadpole in the Rt Hon Sophie, Countess of Wessex's beer.'* (Official notice, Buckingham Palace Gates, May 2003).

drop anchor in bum bay *v.* To arrive at the *rear admiral's* favourite port of call. To wash up on *spice island.*

drop fudge *v.* To *pinch a loaf, crimp one off.*

drop her yoghurt *v.* Of a lady, to have an orgasm in her *parts* for whatever reason.

drop one *v. Let off, drop your hat, step on a duck, float an air biscuit.*

drop one's back *v.* To enflatulise the atmosphere around one's *gammon ring.*

drop one's revels *v.* To suffer an unfortunate chocolate-based *follow through* experience whilst *clearing one's nether throat. 'It's no good. I can't finish this Olympic Marathon, I've dropped me Revels.'*

drop one's yop *v.* To ejaculate messily in a manner reminiscent of a bottle of the popular drinkable yoghurt being dropped onto the tiled floor of a petrol station.

'What's the matter, Cliff?' 'I just dropped my yop, Sue. Best get the Vax out.'

dropout *n.* Underpant condition whereby a *knacker* protrudes from the bottom of the *shreddies*, or famously in Peter Beardsley's case, football shorts.

dropped pie, face like a *sim.* To resemble one who has been bobbing for chips in a deep fat fryer.

dropping the shopping *euph.* See *drop the kids off at the pool.*

drop the kids off at the pool *euph.* To defecate out of your bottom into the toilet.

drop your guts *v.* To break wind. *"Fossilised fish hooks,' croaked Venables. 'Which one of you beanfeasters has dropped his guts?"* (from *Jennings Makes a Daisy Chain* by Anthony Buckeridge).

drop your hat *v.* To *fart.* Also *drop a bomb, drop your handbag, drop a gut.*

drop your hat forwards *v.* To *fanny fart, muff chuff, queef.* To play the *Lawley kazoo,* blow a *Harry Ramsden's raspberry. 'Just as I was donning the beard, she dropped her hat forwards'.*

drown a copper *v.* To sink a *dreadnought*, give birth to a *dead otter.*

drown a duck *v.* To float an *air biscuit* whilst in the shower. Descriptive of the noise produced by a quivering *ringpiece* in the presence of flowing water.

drown some kittens *n.* To pass a litter of small stools which nobody wants to give a home to. Then throw them off a canal bridge in a sack.

drown the chocolate slugs *v.* Alternative to *lighting a bum cigar* for those anticipating a looser stool.

drug smuggler's wait *n.* An interminable period of lavatorial pandiculation which involves sitting on the *bog* waiting for one of them *shits* that take ages to come down, like when you've ate too much meat.

drugs bust *n.* Simultaneous entry of two *bobbies' truncheons* through the front and back doors. Also *police raid, SVSA.*

druncle *n.* A male relative who generally stinks of *refreshment. 'Do something, dear. Your Druncle George has just dropped the baby onto the barbecue again.'*

drunk's piss, as clear as *sim.* Descriptive of something which is perfectly transparent. From the fact that a *heavily-refreshed* fellow's urinary emissions are often so dilute that he can get away without rinsing the sink clean after he's done a spot of *Bradford dishwashing.*

dry bob *1. n.* A public schoolboy who doesn't row. *2. v.* Fully-clothed sex, leading to *milmed kex. 3. n.* A bankrupt *money shot*, a *spaffless stack blow.*

dry docked *adj.* Lack of lubrication situation where a low tide of *blip* prevents the *skin boat* sailing smoothly into *tuna town.*

dry run *n.* A trip to the toilet cubicle, complete with a fifteen minute sit-down with the trousers and *grundies* round the ankles, taken with no intention whatsoever of *laying a cable.* A half holiday enjoyed during the working day which has all the benefits of a lavatory break with none of the *nipsy*-based aggravation that usually accompanies such a visit.

DSB *abbrev.* Dangerous Sperm

Build-up. To have two tins of *Fussell's Milk. 'I'm sorry, Sir Cliff, but you are suffering from DSB. As your doctor, the only course of treatment I can prescribe is an ADW.'*

DSL *abbrev*. Dick Sucking Lips.

dub *n.* Duck in Flowerpot Men language. See *flub*.

duck bread *n.* A girl who is past her prime.

duck butter *n. Aus.* Assorted smegmalogical effluviums accumulating under the *fiveskins* of the unclean.

ducking *n.* Aquatic version of the popular erotic hobby known as *dogging,* which takes place not in a car park, but in a boatyard, harbour or along a quayside. A practice which presumably involves a scandal-ridden Premiership footballer in a raincoat walking along the side of a river accompanied by a duck on a lead, waiting for the opportunity to watch a pair of tabloid newspaper reporters pretending to *have it off* in a cabin cruiser whilst he *tosses himself off* inside his trousers for the benefit of a nearby photographer with a long lens.

duck sandwich *n.* Prominent *pudenders* visible through the tight leggings of fat-thighed ladies. *Knicker sausages.*

duck sausage *n.* A filling gourmet meal which is best eaten in a crouched position. *'I'm glad you got to meet Val Doonican after the concert, nan.' 'Aye, but I had to have three portions of duck sausage off the roadies to get backstage.'*

duck's breakfast *1. n. Welsh.* Early morning *sausage* and *split kippers.* Accompanied by gentle quacking and a flurry of feathers. 2. n. Phrase used to describe how poor people, for example students, start their day. That is to say "a drink of water and a shit."

duck smuggler *n.* A *Glen Miller,* one who produces a *string of pearls*, as if trying to smuggle a duck past customs by hiding it up his *arse*. One who lets out a sequence of quacks whilst walking.

duck soup *n.* The products of a *follow through.* The sixth Marx Brother, *Skiddo.*

duckwalk *1. n.* A unique dance pioneered by virtuoso guitarist Chuck Berry. *2. n.* In *farting,* the process of letting out little pockets of gas in time with each step. An *ugly duckling,* a *string of pearls.*

duel fuel *n. Fighting water.*

duel with the pink Darth Vader *n.* A *Hand Solo*.

duelling banjos *1. n.* A female dormitory *wank race. 2. n.* The vigorous *Scruggs-style* double-tug motion of a *meat vid crane operator.*

duff *1. n. Bum, arse. 2. n. Fadge, minge, twat, clopper.*

duffy's bridge *n.* The *biffin bridge, tinter, taint, barse.* The perineum of either gender.

DUFTO *acronym*. Any old *bird* at a film premier with a whiff of mothballs around her, *eg. Carry On Breathing* star Barbara Windsor. Dug Up For The Occasion.

duggle *v.* To receive or perform an act of oral *horatio* whilst *crimping off a loaf.* To take part in a *blumpkin*.

dugs *n. Baps, paps.* Olde worlde version of *jugs,* still in use amongst yokel folk.

Duke of giblets *n.* A *salad dodger.*

dukes *rhym. slang.* Haemorrhoids. From Duke of Argyles = piles.

dump *1. n.* A 40-minute reading session in the *dunny*. *2. v.* To *curl one off*.

dump and burn *1. v. milit.* RAF term for the act of jettisoning fuel behind engines on afterburn, resulting in a spectacular display of rumbling noise and flames. *2. n.* Going for a *tom tit* after consuming unhealthy levels of spicy food, resulting in rumbling noise and flames.

dumpling *1. n.* A solitary, suety *turd* floating in a pan of *bum stew*. *2. n.* A woman who is blessed with such a *lovely personality* that you would have to roll her in flour to find her wet bits.

dumplings *1. n.* Baby *dumps*. *2. n.* Particularly filling breasts that go well with *meat and two veg*.

dump station *n.* The *chod bin*.

dump valve *1. n.* A thing that a reader of *Max Power* might somehow fasten to his car engine. *2. n.* The *nipsy*.

duncan *n.* A *floater*. From buoyant former Olympic sportsman Duncan Goodhew.

dunce's hats *n.* Them conical pointed *tits* found underneath woollen sweaters in 1950's America. *Twin peaks*.

dung dreadlocks *n.* Haile Selassie's *beaded curtains*. Laid-back *tagnuts*.

dung funnel *n. medic. Fudge tunnel.*

dunghampers *n. Undercrackers, trolleys, bills.*

dung lung *n. medic.* Descriptive of one who has been *necking turds*. A halitosis sufferer.

dung puncher *n.* A gentleman homosexualist. A *doughnut puncher* or *spud fumbler*.

dunk *1. n.* To dip a biscuit in a cup of tea. *2. n.* To dip one's *wick* into a *billposter's bucket*.

dunky *n.* Protective sheath to prevent the penis going soggy and falling off into the *hairy goblet* during dunking.

dunny *n. Aus.* Toilet, *netty, cludgy, shite house*.

dunny budgie *n. Aus.* A fly buzzing round an Australian *bog*.

dusk tusk *n.* Twilight counterpart of *dawn horn,* a cause of insomnia which can usually be remedied by loosening off one's *nuts* with a suitably-sized *wanking spanner*.

dustette *n.* Obsolete hand-held Hoover vacuum cleaner which proved very popular with bachelors who needed to suck the dust off sausages.

dustman's library *n.* An archive of vintage, recycled *niff mags* usually found in the cabins of dustcarts, or the portacabin at the local civic amenity site.

dust the duvet *v.* To *hitchhike under the big top*, to *starch the sheets*.

dusty klatt *1. n. prop.* Young Canadian motorcycle racer. *2. n.* A lady's *parts of shame* that have never done anything to be ashamed of. A *furry hoop* that has seen less use than Jeffrey Archer's honesty box. *3. n.* A redundant *fanny* that won the West 125cc Motorcycle Championship in 2005.

Dutch *n. Sausage sandwich, tit wank, diddy ride.* Also *Dutch fuck*.

Dutch Alps *n.* Small breasts, *fried eggs, stits, patsies, bee stings.* Also *Lincolnshire Cairngorms.* As scaled by a *Dutch mountaineer.*

Dutch arrow *n.* A *woody shaft* shot

up the *bonus tunnel.*

Dutch bellows *n.* A *blanket ripper.*

Dutch blast *n.* Bellows effect achieved at the open end of the duvet when one wants to sample or indeed share the fragrant fruits of a bedtime solo on the *botty bugle.*

Dutch blindfold *n.* In the *69* position, with the woman underneath and the gentleman's *clockweights* fitting nicely in her eye sockets.

Dutch boy *n.* A lady in *comfortable shoes,* a *tennis fan,* a lesbian, *ie.* one who always has their finger in a *dyke.*

Dutch Breakfast *n.* Something you have after *awakening the bacon* that will set you up for the day.

Dutch brylcreem *n.* A glutinous product that you don't particularly want in your hair. *Gunk, heir gel.*

Dutch cap *n.* An extremely tight fitting rubber hat worn in Holland.

Dutch conclave *n.* A particularly impressive form of *Dutch oven* in which a foul-smelling smoke is emitted from the end of the quilt, reminiscent of the moment when the College of Cardinals announces the election of a new Pope by farting up the Vatican chimney.

Dutch door *n.* A *bird* who *swings both ways.*

Dutch floor polish *n. Spunk.*

Dutch hand grenade *n.* A *beefy eggo,* caught in the hand and then detonated under an unsuspecting person's nose. A *cupcake.*

Dutch Marathon *n.* The hasty, yet seemingly never-ending walk home after purchasing a new selection of *fleshmags* from a specialist newsagent.

Dutch miracle *n.* The magical appearance of *art pamphlets* under a mattress or on top of a wardrobe in a hotel bedroom.

Dutch oven *n.* The act of cooking one's partner's head beneath the bedclothes using *cabbage gas.*

Dutch oyster *n.* An exotic mouthful of the contents of one's own *winkle.* One probable consequence of a *Swiss kiss.*

Dutch salute *n. Irish toothache.* An erection.

Dutch satay *n.* The epilogue of a *stick vid* where the starlet sucks on the leading man's rapidly softening phallus after she's been *front* and *back fucked* with it, and had it smear *spunk* all over her *tits.*

Dutch sauna *n. Drowning a duck* whilst sharing a hot shower cubicle with one's spouse. An aquatic *Dutch oven.*

Dutch souvenir *n.* A little something brought back in the urethra to surprise the wife and help you remember Amsterdam.

Dutch strawberry *n.* The *herman gelmet.* With all pips stuck on it.

Dutch teabreak *n.* The act of *relaxing in a gentleman's way* whilst at work. Taking a *monkey's fag break.*

Dutch tug *n.* A no-nonsense paid-for *hand-job.* Do not pay more than £10.

Dutch welcome mat *n.* A stain on the carpet which indicates where a *feeshus* has been inefficiently expunged from the weft at some point in the past.

Dutch wink *n.* The flashing of the *bacon rasher* when crossing and uncrossing the legs. *'The film has action, drama, suspense and a superb Dutch wink from Sharon Stone.'* (Barry Norman, reviewing *Basic Instinct*).

DVDA *abbrev.* Double Vaginal, Double Anal. The Holy Grail of *bongo video* acts, presumably involving four India-rubber men and one uncomfortable woman.

dyke *n.* Lesbian, *tuppence licker, carpet muncher, three wheeler*, a *woman on the other bus*. See also *diesel dyke, bulldyke.*

dyke differential *n.* The notable discrepancy between the attractiveness of the sort of lesbians depicted in *grumble vids, seed catalogues etc.*, and the sort actually encountered in real life.

Dylan *n.* A tangled, matted, unkempt mess of a *bush*, resembling the hairstyle of grizzled singer-songwriter Bob. A *Terry Waite's allotment.*

dyson *n.* A *bird* with a right good suck on her.

dysparpsia *n. medic.* A gastric dysfunction that manifests itself in a series of strident anal announcements. *'Listen to that. there must be a circus in the next field. I can hear a troupe of performing seals tuning up their car-horns whilst the brass band practises clown music on a selection of trombones, euphoniums and sousaphones.' 'No, that's me. I'm suffering from a spot of dysparpsia.'*

Ec

ear chafers *n.* Ladies' stocking tops.

ear pie *n.* A right *bollocking* a woman gives a man when he stays too long in the pub, forgets her birthday, *fucks* her sisters, *etc*.

earlids *n.* Invisible, soundproof flaps of skin which descend over a gentleman's ears when he is conversing with his lady wife.

early day motion *n.* A *turd* break taken as soon as one arrives at work.

early morning dip *n.* To make love to a woman whilst she is still asleep. A romantic act that can carry a 15-year prison sentence.

earn brownie points *v.* Of a gentleman, to perform selfless acts of kindness, like doing the dishes or a spot of ironing in the hope that one's partner will express her gratitude with a game of *mud darts*.

Eartha Kitts *rhym. slang. Shits*, diarrhoea. Also *Brads*.

earthing cable *n.* An elongated *copper bolt* that touches down safely in the *chod bin* water before it has fully exited the *nipsy*. A *bridger* or *bottom log*.

Easter Island statue with an arse full of razor blades *sim. Aus.* A permanently grave, sour expression. A phrase that describes Jimmy Nail to a T.

Easyjet seat pocket, fanny like a *sim.* A *wizard's sleeve*. From the fact that the seats of the older models of jet departing from Luton have huge, overstretched pockets on the back of them, from years of accommodating all manner of bulky goods.

eat breakfast backwards *v.* To *drive the porcelain bus, yoff, barf*.

eat cockroaches *v. 18thC.* To engage in the filthy, disgusting act of *self-pollution*.

eat fancy cakes *v.* Of a gentleman, to have a tendency towards the craftier end of *butchery*. To *jump puddles*, to be a *ginger beer*. *'Popstar Stephen Gately shocked Boyzone fans today when he announced at an awards ceremony that he eats fancy cakes.'* (Trevor McDonald, *News at Ten* headline story, June 2000).

eat humble cock *v.* Of a lady who has been involved in a disagreement with a gentleman friend, to acknowledge in the time-honoured manner that she may not have been right after all.

eating sushi off a barbershop floor *sim.* Performing *cumulonimbus*.

eat one's greens *v.* To do something one would really rather not do just to earn *brownie points* from a female partner, *eg*. listen to her go on about her day, putting some shelves up.

eat out *v.* To *lap fanny*, to *dive muff*, to *cumulonimbulate*. To *lick out*, *dine at the Y*.

eau de colon *n. Rusty water, fizzy gravy*.

ebdon slide *1. n.* In snooker, the careful positioning of the fingers on the table whilst cueing. *2. n.* In sex, the careful positioning of the fingers on the lady's *bits* in order to expose the *clematis*.

EC flag *n.* Nipple.

Eccles cake *n.* A casually discarded *Eartha*. Named after local newspaper hack (name removed following legal advice) of the *Sussex Express* who, after a night on the strong cider, *shat* himself in the pub and shook it out of his trousers before ordering another pint of Biddenden's 9-percenter.

eccles snake *n.* A penis with warts.

eclipse girl *n.* A female lady in a pornographic film or magazine who, if you stare at her for too long, will make you go blind.

econnoisseur *n.* A budget-conscious erotic epicurean, who appreciates the benefits of the Freeman's catalogue bra pages and Smartprice tissues.

ecosser *n.* A patriotic Scottish person who proudly displays his national identity by affixing a sticker to the back of his Japanese car. In French.

eddie *n.* See *stobart.*

Edinburgh *rhym. slang.* A deep-fried *fur burger*. From Edinburgh Fringe = minge.

editing suite *n.* The part of a man's brain that is able to instantly store and arrange stock sexual imagery for future use. *'Look at the jugs on that filly, Hudson.' 'Yes Sir, that's certainly one for the editing suite.'*

e-dophile *n.* A world wide web chat room *nonce.* An internet *diddler.*

Edward II *euph.* A fiery *ringpiece,* combined with severe stomach cramps, internal haemorrhaging and ice cold sweats. From the similar post-curry experience of the famous historical king, who was *bummed* with a red-hot poker by his wife's boyfriend, a situation which led, not long thereafter, to his demise.

Edward Woodward *onomat.* A bathtime *fart.* A *bottle of olives, tottle.*

Edwina *n.* A curry that is a real pain in the *arse.*

eel out of a welly, like shaking an *sim.* Phrase which can be used to describe the experience of having a *shit* that takes very little effort. *'How was it, Mother Teresa?' 'Like shaking an eel out of a welly, your Holiness.'*

e-gasm *n.* A *web-grumble*-assisted *stack blow.*

egg-bound *adj.* Blocked of *dung-funnel*, constipated.

egg in the nest *n.* A bald *noggin* which is still surrounded by a halo of hair, *eg.* the hemispherical pate of comedy scientist Professor Heinz Wolff.

egg Mcwhiff *n.* A particularly sulphurous mid-morning *air buffet* produced after breakfasting at a fast food restaurant.

egg white canon *n.* A 4-inch *blue-veined blunderbuss* loaded with two *balls.*

eggy soldier *n.* The result of taking a *dip* whilst the *red flag is flying.*

e-gret *adj.* A feeling of self-reproach experienced following any ill-considered internet transaction. *'E-grets, I've had a few.'* (Pete Townshend, song lyric).

e-gypsy *n.* One who can't make up their mind which ISP to use, resulting in one's e-mails to them always being returned. A nomad on the information superhighway.

Egyptian PT *1. n. milit.* Sleep. *2. n.* Masturbation.

Eiffel Tower, do the *v.* Of a pair of professional footballers engaged in a *spitroast* with a lucky young lady, to make eye contact and exchange a high five, thus creating the characteristic outline of the famous Parisian pylon.

eighteen spoker *n.* A particularly hairy woman's *arsehole* resembling a tiny bicycle wheel, hopefully without a derailleur gear in the middle.

eighteen wheeler *n.* A *turd* of such

length that it runs a significant risk of jack-knifing in the *pan*. A *stobart*.

elbow bender *n*. A *bar fly*, a *boozer*.

electric chair *1. n*. A device used to keep the number of educationally subnormal black men in Texas at a manageable level. *2. n*. The last resort seat in a pub next to the most crashing bore in the establishment.

electric lemonade *n*. A hallucinogenic, West-country scrumpy cider. Also known locally as *Tone Vale Tonic*, after the former mental institute that housed many of its devotees.

electric spaghetti *n*. *Spunky string*.

electric twitch *n*. Involuntary jerk of the head displayed by *grumble flick* starlets upon receiving a faceful of *jitler*. Named after the similar reflexive spasm which can be achieved by stroking the bars of an electric fire.

elepants *n*. Jumbo-sized ladies' trunks.

elephant man's hat *sim*. Descriptive of a very spacious *fanny*. A *clown's pocket*, a *hippo's yawn*.

elephant nudging a tree, like an *sim*. Phrase used to describe the act of doggedly persisting with sexual relations despite suffering from *brewer's droop*.

elephants *adj*. *rhym. slang*. Drunk. From elephant's trunk.

elephant's ears *n*. Enormous, grey, flappy flaps. Huge *Keith Burtons*.

elephant, the *n*. Penile puppetry diversion. An amusing and charming simulacrum of the popular grey-skinned, gampstand-footed pachyderm achieved using a chap's generative member and his pocket linings pulled inside out. A great way to break the ice at parties or, indeed, to get yourself placed on the sex offenders' register.

eleven-pointer *n*. An altogether successful date. Red, pink, brown (mouth, *fanny*, *freckle*).

Ellen MacNomates *n. prop*. Female version of *Billy no mates*, a girl without any friends. Named after popular lone round-the-world yachtsperson Dame Ellen MacNomates.

Elton John with a fanny, he's like *sim*. Descriptive of someone who obviously doesn't know what they are doing. *'Have you seen that Savo Milosovic trying to play football at Aston Villa? He's like Elton John with a fanny.'*

Elvis *n*. A *shit* that requires so much effort to force out that one almost has a stroke. The oppposite of a *life affirmer*. *'Are you okay? You look terrible, Your Majesty.' 'I'll be fine, Bishop. That Boxing Day Elvis just took it out of me, though.'*

Elvis's leg *n*. The onset of the *vinegar strokes* whilst *fucking* upright in a doorway, bus shelter or taxi queue. Often accompanied by an "Uh-huh-huh" vocalisation and involuntary curling of the lip.

embalmer, the *n*. Specialised wrestling move whereby one's good lady's stomach gets covered with *sex wee*.

Embassy No. 2 *1. n*. A cigarette/excrement combination performed in workplace toilets up and down the country. *'Keep an eye on runway six for me, will you? I'm just nipping out for an Embassy No. 2.'* 2 *n*. An urgent *shit*, usually prompted by the first puff one takes on the first cigarette of the day.

emergency stop *1. n.* In a driving test, the moment when the candidate is required to bring his vehicle to a sudden halt whilst maintaining full control at all times. *2. n.* The act of suddenly pressing the *dead man's handle* upon hearing the missus entering the lounge whilst watching a *noddy film.* It would be a good idea to pull your trousers up too, if sufficient time is available.

emergency strop *n.* An unexpected fit of menstrual temper. A *tammy huff, tamtrum* or *blobstrop. 'Jesus, Dave, how did you get your black eyes, broken nose, missing teeth, stitches and whiplash?' 'The missus done an emergency strop when I wasn't expecting it.'*

emissionary position *n.* A coital arrangement which is guaranteed to bring things to some sort of conclusion when all else has failed and both participants are starting to get bored. *'It's no good, June, me spigot's starting to go soft again. And I think me back's about to give out.' 'Okay Terry. My old lobster pot's had enough too. Let's just switch to the good old emissionary position so you can tip your filthy concrete and we can get off to sleep.'*

Emmas *rhym. slang. Nobbies, farmers, ceramics, lever arches.* From Emma Freud, Clement's chimp-eared daughter, who's got terrible haemorrhoids.

empty one's back *v.* To *crimp off a tail,* to *lay Al Jolson to rest.*

empty one's beer sack *v.* To go for a *piss* in a pub.

empty the bins *v.* To ejaculate. *'The Holy Father condemns as anathema all artificial forms of contraception. The only means of birth control allowable within the Roman church is the practice of ejaculation extra-vagio. That is, to whip the charlie out at the vinegar strokes and empty the bins onto the gunt.'* (Papal Edict, 1988).

empty the caboose *v.* To excrete, pass motions, *drop the kids off at the pool etc.*

empty threat *n.* A terrifyingly loud *fart* that mysteriously fails to assault one's nasal passages. The opposite of an *SBD.*

Ena Sharples' mouth *n.* A disapproving, puckered *rusty bullet hole.* Commonly seen on *grumble mag* models bending over a snooker table. Also *Dot Cotton's mouth,* the *tea towel holder.*

enamel bucket *n.* A big, dry, cold, rattly *fanny.*

end of terrace *n.* A less-than-partial *panhandle.* An erection that shares many of the attributes of a *semi,* but lacks some of its credibility.

end of that bottle of HP, well that's the *exclam.* Phrase to be used following the production of an exceptionally squirty-sounding *Heart to Heart,* that may or may not have resulted in a *follow through.* So called from its audible resemblance to the noises made by the final dregs of a heavily-depleted sauce bottle being squeezed over a *cholesterol special.*

end of the Morning Fresh, sounds like the *1. exclam.* Phrase used when running out of the eponymous cheapo washing up liquid, as one squeezes the final dregs of nasty yellow stuff through the nozzle. *2. euph.* Phrase used typically following a visit to Newcastle's world-famous Curry Capital restaurant, as one forces the last drops of nasty yellow liquid through one's *nozzle*. Unlikely to be accompanied by a wholesome aroma of lemony freshness.

enemy at the gate *n.* A particularly insistent *copper bolt* which makes its presence felt at a particularly inconvenient time. *'Do you, Diana Frances take Charles Philip Arthur George as your lawfully wedded husband, to have and to hold from this day forward, for better, for worse, in sickness and in health, to love and to cherish, till suspicious death do you part in about sixteen years or so?' 'Sorry bish, got to dash. I've got an enemy at the gate.'*

Engelberts *rhym. slang. Eartha Kitts, squirts.*

English batsman *n. Aus.* Someone who doesn't spend very long at the *crease*. A *two push Charlie*, a *two stroke joke*, a *one pump chump*.

English disease, the *n.* Homosexuality, as defined by the French.

English lit *n. rhym. slang.* A *shit*. *'I'm off for an English.'*

English overcoat *n.* The French equivalent of the English *French letter.* A *Coney Island whitefish, cheesepipe clingfilm.*

engorgement ring *n.* A mythical item of *betrothal jewellery* promised to a lady in return for getting one's *nuts* emptied.

Enochs *rhym. slang.* The guts, hopefully not suffering from rivers of blood. From the infamous Tory MP Enoch Bowel.

enormity of the situation *euph.* A *pan handle. 'Come on, love. Why can't you grasp the enormity of the situation?'*

'Enry's 'ammer *n.* A *diamond-cutting* erection of such proportions that it deprives the brain of blood and leaves the owner in a semi-comatose state, as if he had been hit around the head by OAP boxing champ Henry Cooper's trademark left hook. About forty years ago.

ENT *1. abbrev.* Hospital department specialising in audiometry, tympanonometry, electronystamography, mastoid disease treatments and sinus problems. *2. n.* A *shit* or *fart* that attacks the ears, nose and throat.

Enterprise transporter accident *euph.* A nice looking *bird* with lousy *knockers* accompanied by a ugly *bird* with great *knockers*.

entertainment system *n.* One's ladyfriend's *tits, arse* and *fanny*. *'What's that in your bag, Dr Von Hagens?' 'Just an entertainment system. I'm taking it home for the weekend.'*

epilog *n.* Just when you think you've finished *dropping the kids off the pool* and cleaned up after them, then another one emerges as if from nowhere: that's the *epilog*.

equipment *n.* Either a lady's *headlamps* or a gentleman's *unmentionables,* and occasionally both. *'Would it be it alright if I stuck my equipment between your equipment, love?' 'No you can't stick your equipment between my equipment. Now, you've already got your eight favourite records, the Bible and the complete works of Shakespeare. Which other book are you going to take to your Desert Island?'*

erection section *n.* The top shelf of a newsagents.

Erector Scale *n.* Scientific system for the measurement and classification of the intensity of male arousal. Similar to the Richter scale but with *bone ons* instead of earthquakes. *'And finally, an appearance by that Lily Allen on How to Look Good Naked could only manage five on the Erector Scale.'* (Trevor McDonald, ITV *News at Ten*).

Eric *n.* Schoolboy alternative to a *Jake.*

Eros *n.* The pose that must be struck when *pissing* in a toilet with no lock on the door, precariously balancing on one leg with the other holding the door shut.

escape from alcotramp *v.* To suddenly spot something fascinating in a shop window across the street when approaching an animated *Harold Ramp.*

escape sub *n.* A technologically advanced brown, sea-going vessel in which an evil hangover makes its getaway. An *alcopoop.*

ESD *abbrev.* Eat Shitty Dick. To *smoke a pink cigar* fresh from *kak canyon. Hot karl.*

eskimo's glove *n.* Warm, furry mitten that smells of fish and can accommodate one's whole hand. Not unlike a large vagina.

Essex tartan *n.* Burberry.

estimate the bith girth *v.* To perform the first act of coitus following childbirth. *Stirring the paint with a toothpick,* post-natal *last hotdog in the tin.*

etch-a-sketch *v.* To attempt to draw a smile on a woman's face by simultaneously twiddling both of her nipples. *Finding Radio Luxembourg, come in Tokyo.*

eternity leave *n.* The sack. *'My boss caught me photocopying a woman's arse on the office xerox machine, and sent me on eternity leave. What's more, he says he's going to make sure I never get a job in a mortuary ever again.'*

Ethel *n. rhym. slng.* An act of *self abuse.* From Ethel Merman = Sherman tank = wank. *'Where is he? He's due on the balcony to bless the crowds in thirty seconds.' 'Don't worry, Cardinal. He's just went in the bog for a quick Ethel over the letters in the Daily Sport.'*

Ethelbrown the Ready *n.* A pretender to the *porcelain throne.* A *King Richard* in waiting.

ethics girl *n.* The kind of girl who doesn't *fuck* on a first date, won't do it in a car or shop doorway and wouldn't *swallow* even if one could get her to suck it in the first place. The antithesis of an Essex girl.

eticlit *n.* The observance of rules of correct decorum when *dining at the Captain's table.*

Eton leapfrog *n. Bottery.*

euphemersity *n.* An educational institution which has been promoted beyond its abilities, *eg.* The University of Glamorgan which, let's face it, is really Treforest Tech.

everlasting gobstoppers *n.* Something that your *bird* could easily choke to death on. The *clockweights, knackers.*

everything but the girl *1. n.* Hull-based 90s duo featuring a woman with a face like a Nicholas Lyndhurst who's been hit with pan. 2. *n.* A sophisticated *wank* incorporating low lights, soft music and a bottle of wine.

excalibur *n.* A magic *turd* of legendary proportions that rises eerily out of the water in a mist-shrouded toilet.

excalibut *n.* Gentleman's Mach 3 razor clogged up with his girlfriend's *trouser twiglets.*

Exchange & Mart *1. rhym. slang.* To *drop a gut. 2. rhym. slang.* A *dropped gut.*

excremation marks *n.* The tell-tale *skidmata* left on one's gusset following a spot of extra-*grundular moonraking.*

ex files *n.* A *wank bank* folder containing the most filthy memories of sexual depravities enjoyed with previous partners.

exhaust pipe engineer *n.* One who tinkers with *exhaust pipes.*

exhaust pipe *n.* The *Bumhole, fudge tunnel, back box.* Also *tailpipe.*

exhibition position *n.* Variation on *doggy-style* sex. The man takes the kneeling position from behind, places one hand on the lady's back and the other jauntily on his hip. Then turns and smiles at an imaginary audience, pretending to be a moustachioed German *Frankie Vaughan* star.

exit wound *n.* The state of the *freckle* after a particularly fierce *Ruby Murray.*

exorcist *n.* One who is gifted with the power to rid a place of spirits, especially the top shelf behind the bar.

expecting a harsh winter *euph.* Of a *bird,* to be putting on weight or over-eating. *'She's stuffing her face with eclairs. She must be expecting a harsh winter.'*

expresso bongo *1. n.* A *crap* film from the 60s starring Sir Cliff Richard. *2. n.* The fast forwarding through the uninteresting bits of films which almost certainly do not star Sir Cliff Richard.

extras *n.* Something one tentatively asks for whilst winking at a masseuse or osteopath. The *tugging* as opposed to the *rubbing* in a *rub-a-tug shop.*

eyeburns *n.* Where the eyebrow on an hirsute chap continues seamlessly into his sideburn. Also *side-brows.*

eye cabbage *n.* The opposite of *eye candy.* An ugly girl you avoid looking at.

eye magnets *n.* Lovely *tits* at which any red-blooded man could not resist the temptation to *sneak a peek.*

eye of Sauron *1. n.* In JRR Tolkein's *Lord of the Rings,* a "lidless eye wreathed with flame" with which the Lord Sauron watched over Middle Earth, and thus *2. n.* A lidless eye wreathed in flame which is the inevitable consequence of dining at the Curry Capital, Newcastle upon Tyne. A *Johnny Cash, Japanese flag, Wigan rosette.*

eyes like a shithouse rat sim. Descriptive of one with extraordinary visual acuity. *'Check my collar for lipstick will you, Edwina. Only Norma's got eyes like a fucking shithouse rat.'*

eyes like sheep's cunts *n. medic.* Self-explanatory symptom of an extremely bad hangover. See *feel Welsh.*

Ff

F1 finish *euph.* Fitting climax to a piece of cinematographic *grumble.* Three sweating guys shaking their *bottles* and spraying frothy liquid all over each other after a long hard afternoon.

FAB *1. n.* Expression meaning "yes" made famous in the string-heavy children's series *Thunderbirds. 2. acronym.* Standardised weighting order for assessing the quality of a piece of crumpet, *viz.* Face; Arse; Baps. *3. acronym.* The unpleasant olfactory combination of Feet, Arse and Balls encountered when entering a young man's bedroom, a prison cell or a monastery. *'This room smells FAB, Brother Dominic.' 'Yeah, sorry about that. I haven't washed my feet, arse or balls for a month.'*

Faberge egg *n.* A large oval *dump* which comes out encrusted in red jewels as a result of *famers* or a ripped *nipsy.* A *limited edition.*

face fannies *n. Bugger's grips*, sideburns. As sported by the singer out of Supergrass and Anne Robinson.

face, front and forks *euph. milit.* A *whore's bath,* taken when there's no time, opportunity or inclination for a shower. Flannelling the face, chest, groin and armpits. *'You're due on set in five minutes, Miss Collins.' 'Right you are. I'm just doing me face, front and forks.'*

face grating *n.* Performing the act of *cumulonimbus* upon a woman with advanced *five o'clock fanny.*

face painting *v.* To adorn one's spouse with *jelly jewellery*.

face the fast bowlers *v.* To increase the strength of your drinks in order to attain your target of getting *pissed* more quickly.

face the spinners *v.* To turn to a more ladylike-strength drink in an attempt to stop getting *pissed* quite so quickly.

factory AIDS *n.* The miscellany of invisible, yet ever present, bits of dirt, snot, *spunk* and *turd* which is present on all new culinary purchases. *'Trevor, can you pass me one of those new lunchboxes so I can pack the kids' turkey twizzlers?' 'Hang on, luv. I'm just washing the factory AIDS off them.'*

fadge *n.* A cross between a *fanny* and a vagina.

FADS *acronym.* From the motor trade, descriptive of something worthless, *eg.* the trade-in value of any Citroen over 3-months old. Fuck All Divided by Six.

faecal position *n.* The delicate, round-shouldered and slightly curled posture adopted by someone who has been caught short some distance from lavatory facilities.

faecal touch *n.* Opposite of the Midas touch, *ie.* everything this person touches turns to *shit*, *eg.* Clive Sinclair.

FAFCAM *acronym.* Fit As Fuck, Common As Muck, *eg.* Denise Van Outen, Suzanne out of Hear'Say.

faff *1. n.* A lady's *front bottom. 2. v.* To *fart about.*

FAFTAF *acronym.* A woman who is extremely attractive but who unfortunately failed her rocket science exams. Fit As Fuck, Thick As Fuck.

fag *1. n.* An 8-year-old boy at a public school who has to fetch tea, fetch toast and *fetch off* a prefect. *2. n. Tab, ciggie,* a *cancer stick. 3. n. US.* One who is *good with colours.*

fag fireworks *n.* The brief, but

nonetheless impressive night-time pyrotechnic display given to motorists following behind vans.

fag hag *n.* A wizened old woman who prefers the company of homosexuals.

fagnet *n.* A man who, when out clubbing, only manages to attract *botters.*

fagnolia *adj.* The yellowy-creamy-brown colour which used to be found on the interior walls of betting shops and pubs but is now restricted to the houses of chain smokers.

fagnostic *n.* One who either doesn't know or hasn't quite made his mind up which way he wants to swing.

fagriculture *n. Uphill gardening* and its associated lifestyle.

fail one's driving test *1. v.* To prove unable to reach a required level of ability when driving a motor vehicle. *2. v.* To prove unable to steer a *fart* around a *brown obstacle.* To *gamble and lose, follow through.*

faint on *n. medic.* A devastating condition affecting certain males who are *hung like rogue elephants*. When a *fat is cracked*, the shaft drains the body of its blood, causing the patient to become light- headed.

fairy goblet *n.* Bronzed chalice favoured by the more *style conscious* gentleman about town. *Spice island.*

fairy hammock *n.* A *tart's dung-hampers.*

fairy liquid *n. Tart fuel.* Drinks such as WKD and Bacardi Breezers for homos and girls.

fairy wings *n.* The gossamer tracery of *arse* sweat left on the seat when a lardy chap gets up off the *bog* on a warm day.

fall at Beecher's *v.* To *come off* before reaching the finishing post. To suffer from premature ejaculation.

fallen off her bike *euph*. A monthly *cycle accident* leaving a woman bleeding from the *saddle area.*

fallen to the communists *euph.* Of a woman, to have *fallen off her bike. 'Any luck last night?' 'No. She's fallen to the communists.'*

falling down juice *n.* Beer. Also *fighting water, dizzyade.*

fall of soot *n.* The messy result of a failed *driving test.* A *follow through*, a *lost gamble.*

family jewels *n.* Priceless heirloom *knackers.*

fancy wank *v.* To use an ugly *bird's blurtch* to save wear and tear on your wrist. *Hands free.*

fandruff *n. Fanny* dandruff. *Muff-druff, Scurf 'n' turf.*

fanjita *n.* A *tuppence.*

fannanigans *n.* Women's things. From fanny + shenanigans.

fannicure *n.* A pampering of the *bush.* A *quim-trim, eg.* a *Hitler tash.*

fanny *1. n. UK. Snatch, snapper, quim, cunt, puh-seh.* Female genitals, ladies' *pudenders. 2. n. US. Arse, backside. 3. n.* Fictitious Great Aunt.

Fanny Adams, sweet *phr. Fuck all.*

fanny apple *n.* A neonate. A new born baby. *'Births: Smith. At the Portland Hospital. To Evadne and Captain George Everard, a boy, Spartacus, brother to Troy and Elgin. Mother and fanny apple doing well. Deo Gracias.'* (*The Times* Feb 12th 2004).

fannyarse *n.* A *crafty butcher* whose *dirtstar* has been *lubbocked* to the extent that it resembles a lady's *quim.*

fanny badger *n.* See *Blackbeard's ghost.*

fanny batter *n.* The substance which leaves one's chin greasy after a *fish supper. Sloom.*

fanny battering ram *n.* A stout length of *wood* used to burst *Mary Hinges*. A *crowbar.*

fanny bib *n.* A sanitary towel.

fanny bomb *n.* The female organism. *'How was it for you, pet? Did the old fanny bomb go off?'*

fanny by gaslight *1. n.* Post-discotheque, back-alley coitus, *chinook*. A *fork lift truck*, if you will. *2. n.* Title of a 1944 Gainsborough Studios melodrama starring Phyllis Calvert as the daughter of a Cabinet Minister who is unknowingly employed by her father, Lord Manderstoke (James Mason), as a servant, and gets *fucked* in a back alley by Harry Somerford (Stewart Grainger) shortly after chucking out time.

fanny famine *n.* A period of time when a chap leaves his genitals fallow. *Fanny famines* of varying durations are typically experienced by divorcees, catholic clergymen and Peter Pans of pop.

fanny farm *n.* A *knocking shop*. A brothel, *trollbooth.*

fanny filter *n.* The "safe content" option on an internet search engine which prevents teenage boys and office workers locating pictures of the one thing they would like to find on the worldwide information superhighway.

fanny fit *n.* A *bird's* unnecessary histrionic episode. A *tammy huff, blob strop* or *showing off.*

fanny flange *n.* The vaginal escutcheon.

fanny fright *n. medic.* Nervous condition affecting some macho men who suddenly find themselves unable to have *a bit* when presented with an opportunity. *Lack of composure in front of goal.*

fanny full *euph.* A building site term used to describe a small quantity of something, for example casting plaster mixed up in a margarine tub to fill the gaps between sections of coving. *'How much plaster do you want, dad?' 'Just a fanny full.'*

fanny gallops *n.* In a lady, the early rumblings of sexual excitement at the sight of a Calvin Klein Y-fronts poster. The *hots.*

fanny hammer *n.* A *bob.*

fanny hockle *n.* The product of a post-coital *fadge cough.*

fanny hopper *1. n.* A 2-foot diameter inflatable orange vagina with handles at the top. *2. n.* A gentleman who hops from one *fanny* to another. A *stickman*, a *skippy, eg.* Darren Day, Mick Jagger, John Prescott.

fanny licker *n.* A small dog, such as a Yorkshire Terrier or Pekingese, which is best-suited to sitting on a lady's lap. *"Oh God. Tricky-Woo's got worms,' wailed Tristram as he put down the phone. 'Tricky-Woo?' I said. 'Who, or indeed what, is Tricky-Woo?' 'My dear James, it's Mrs Pomfrey's fanny licker,' laughed Siegfried, as he stuck his arm up yet another cow's arse."* (from *Some Vets Do 'Ave 'Em* by James Herriot).

fanny magnate *n.* A commercial purveyor of ladies' favours. A *pimp, fanny farmer.*

fanny magnet *n.* Something or someone to which top drawer *blart* is inexplicably drawn, *eg.* A

Ferrari, Rolex watch, Mick Hucknall.

fanny mechanic *n. medic.* One who performs *MOTT tests*, a *box doc, a snatch quack, a scrape doctor*. A gynaecologist.

fanny nanny *n.* A feminine napkin, fanny bib.

fanny nosher *n.* A *woman in comfortable shoes* who takes the *other bus* to *dine at the Y*. A *tennis fan*, a *lady golfer, a carpet muncher*.

fanny paddy *n.* A *muff huff*, a *blob strop*. A *monty*.

fanny rat *n.* A sexually promiscuous male. A *skippy, a bed hopper. 'Today's birthdays: David Mellor QC, former Conservative politician and fanny rat, 58.'*

fanny swill *n.* The frothy, post-coital substance exuded by a lady after a good session.

fannytastic *1. adj.* Anything wonderful to do with the female genitals. *2. adj.* Descriptive of a thing which is so excellent that it can only be compared with a *fanny*. 'Have you been watching the *Big Brother* this year?' *'No, and it's been fannytastic.'*

fanny tax *n.* Surcharge paid on drinks in a bar staffed by top class *blart*.

fanny turd *n.* A child. *'Births: Chocmonockly-Ffeatherstone-haugh. On February 17th, at the Portland Hospital. To Rupert and Rowenta (nee Ponfrit-Cake), a 6lb 8oz fanny turd, Parkinson Cowan. A brother for Tefal. Deo Gracias.'* (from *The Times*, Feb 12th 2004).

fannyversary *n.* The single once-a-year *fuck* off his missus to which a husband is legally entitled.

fanoir *n. Fr.* French insult. *'Vous etes une fucking grand fanoir, M. D'Artagnan.'* (from *The Three Musketeers* by Alexander Dumas).

FANTA *acronym.* A one night stand. Fuck And Never Touch Again.

fanta pants *n.* A light-hearted term used to describe a woman with an orange *bush*. *'The Red Shoes (UK, 1948) Ground-breaking expressionist fantasy directed by Michael Powell and Emeric Pressburger, starring fanta pants ballerina Moira Shearer.'* (from *Halliwell's Film Guide 2001*).

fan your arse *v.* To perform a male courtship display; masculine showing off. *'Well you can tell by the way I fan my arse / I'm a woman's man, with a sweaty barse.'* (Song lyric, *Stayin' Alive* by The Bee Gees).

farce *n.* The *snot*.

farm bent *adj.* Descriptive of a fellow who finds himself inclined to quadruped romance as a consequence of enforced rural remoteness. *'GRAMS: Wine bar. Int. Day. FX: Door opens. EDDIE GRUNDY: Nelson! Come quickly! There's trouble in 5 Acre field! NELSON GABRIEL: What on earth? EDDIE GRUNDY: It's your dad, Nelson. He's gone farm bent. NELSON GABRIEL: Oh no, not again. GRAMS: Dissolve to ext. day. FX: Distressed cow. WALTER GABRIEL: Ooh, yeah. Take that Daisy. You know you want it right up you, you dirty bitch. FX: Particularly loud moo.'* (from *The Archers,* BBC Radio 4, October 2nd 1983).

farmers *rhym. slang. Emmas*. From Farmer Giles.

farmer sutra *n.* The ancient Dutch treatise on the art of erotic *barn-*

yard love. With a comedy soundtrack.

farmer's breakfast *n.* A *shit* and a drink of water.

farmer's broth *n. Spiff, spodge, sprangle etc.*

farmer's protest *n.* An outbreak of chronic diarrhoea which pebbledashes the *chod bin* bowl with semi-liquid *shit.* From the universal habit of agricultural types who register their objections to unfair bank service charges by spraying thousands of gallons of cow *crap* all over the front of their local branch.

farn't *n.* An *air biscuit* that, no matter how hard one tries, cannot be *floated.* A *fart* that can't.

FARO *acronym.* A gentleman's post-coital afterplay. Fart And Roll Over.

fart *1. n.* A *bottom burp*, an expulsion of foul air from the *chamber of horrors* that causes the *clappers* to vibrate musically like a tuning fork. A *beefy eggo,* a *poot*, an *air biscuit. 2. v.* To *drop* one of the above, *step on a duck.*

fart about *v.* See *faff.*

fartacus *n. prop.* A hero who takes responsibility for a *duck* they didn't *step on*. From the Roman slave Spartacus who was crucified on the Appian way for *letting off* in the presence of Julius Caesar.

fart blanche *n. Fr.* The opportunity to freely *drop a Tommy Squeaker* without fear of detection, *eg*. in a noisy ham-packing factory, in the pits at a stock car race, or when nursing one's great uncle back to health from a near-death diarrhoea mishap.

fartbreak ridge *n.* The rugged, windswept anatomical scarp that runs from the *anus* to the *nutsack* or *fanny,* upon which *farts* sometimes break. The *biffin bridge.*

fart buffer *n.* The methane safety cushion which presages the *turd* and allows one a little extra time to reach the lavatory. The *turtle's breath. 'I'm afraid I must dash, Your Majesty. I've used up my fart buffer and I'm touching cloth.'*

fart catcher *1. n.* Male homeosexualist. *2. n.* Derogatory term for one who waits on another person, *eg.* a valet or footman. 3. n. A BBC News "royal correspondent".

farter *n.* Aus. *milit.* A sleeping bag. *'Tuesday, December 18th, 1912. Ate last of the pemmican in the night. Heavy snow again. Found Bowers dead in his farter. There is no hope for us now.'* (from *The Journal of Captain Scott*).

fartex *n.* Trade name of that tasteless swirly material with lumpy bits which is loudly pebbledashed by the *tradesman's* round the inside of one's lavatory, and which can adversely affect the value of one's property. *Fartex* is applied by means of a portable high-pressure spray system and is available in a wide range of brown shades. Or black if you've been eating liquorice or have intestinal bleeding. Also *arsetex.*

fart funnel *n.* The *arse.*

fart higher than your arse *euph.* To have an inflated opinion of oneself. To think one all that when one ain't, *eg.* talentless fat *fuck* Chris Moyles.

farticles *n.* The crumbs of an *air biscuit,* often found in the sheets after *breakfast in bed.*

farting against thunder *met. meteorog.* Descriptive of a hopeless task that will inevitably end in failure, *eg*. attempting to pay by cheque in McDonald's, saying "no" to a Pennine Windows telesales person, trying to get Jack Straw MP to give you a straight answer to a question, *etc*. *Pissing into the wind*.

farting bracket *n*. A device to the left of the brake pedal found in luxury motor vehicles equipped with automatic transmission, which enables the driver to lift one buttock and *let one go* without taking his attention off the road. *'Once again, the Mercedes E Class has an extensive range of dealer-fit options. But at this price range, things like air conditioning, farting bracket and CD autochanger really should come as standard.'* (Jeremy Clarkson, *Sunday Times* July 2003).

farting clappers *n. medic*. Small, fragile, castanet-like bones up one's *nick* that resonate at particular frequencies, producing an unexpectedly loud "braaap!" sound in polite company.

farting crackers *n*. Trousers. *'When invited to a black tie function, the correct mode of attire for gentlemen would be; white dress shirt and collar, cummerbund, black shoes, black dinner jacket and corresponding farting crackers.'* (from *Debrett's Guide to Etiquette* by Buckridge Pottinger).

farting sideways *v*. To have a bad case of piles. *"Do please sit down, Mr Willoughby,' Lady Marchmaine invited. 'Thank you, madam,' he replied, 'but if it is all the same with you, I shall remain standing. I rode a fox to earth over three counties yesterday and I fear I am farting sideways."* (from *Sense and Sensibility* by Jane Austen).

farting strings *n. medic*. Tendons or ligaments in the *lisks* which are prone to snapping during periods of excessive mirth. *'In a landmark court case, a Birmingham pensioner with an IQ of 6 is suing the BBC after snapping her farting strings laughing at the sitcom My Family.'*

fart juggler *n*. One gifted with the ability to hold and queue *dropped hats* when in a potentially embarrassing situation, *eg*. in a lift, and then fire off a *repeater* when at a safe distance. An *air traffic controller, stacker*.

fart knocker *1. n. Bum bandit, fudge nudger. 2. n*. One who criticises another's *air biscuits*.

fartleberries *n. Dangleberries, winnets, chocolate raisins*.

fart on one's weetabix *euph*. To spoil one's chances. A less vulgar version of *piss on one's chips*.

fartoodeetoo *n*. An amusing, burbling, polyphonic *gut drop* that sounds not unlike the indecipherable burblings of the *Star Wars* Dusty-Bin-a-like droid.

fart sack *n*. The bed. *'Malaria was powerless to resist. His eyes burned into hers like Swarovski crystals. His strong arms enfolded her body as she felt herself being swept away on a monsoon of passion. Roughly, Pablo took her by her heaving shoulders, pushed her down and did her on his king-sized fart sack.'* (from *The Countess and the Matador* by Barbara Cartland).

fart sauce *n*. A *raspberry coulis* that is served with *arse cress*. The rancid juice accompanying a wet *poot*.

fart sucker *n.* A sycophantic *arse licker* or *shirt fly, eg.* any member of Steve Wright's fucking "afternoon posse" on Radio 2.

fart to a shit fight, bring a *v.* In a competitive situation, to be seriously overmatched.

fart wire *n.* The rear string of a thong which bisects the buttocks and, like a cheese-wire cutting through cheddar, will effortlessly cut through the densest *trouser cough. Officer's laces. 'Smile over here for the Daily Star, Miss Goody! Hang on... fuck me... hold the front page. I can see her fart wire!'*

farty winks *n.* A flatulent and refreshing post-prandial nap usually taken on a Sunday afternoon in order to let one's guts settle after a big dinner. *'Jesus. Is the dog ill?' 'No, it's your dad. He's just having farty winks in front of the Grand Prix.'*

fast roping *n.* Unlikely-sounding masturbation technique which involves poking your *arse* with your left thumb whilst *tugging yourself off* with the other hand. So named as it is evidently not dissimilar to the method employed by the military for getting down a crag quickly. *Abseiling.*

fasturbation *n.* Emergency, hurried *self abuse.*

fat bird's shoe, full as a *sim.* Descriptive of a something or someone which is stuffed to bursting point, *eg.* a former glam-rock star's hard disk, a postman's wardrobe, Jim Davidson's skin. *'More spooge, Marc?' 'No thanks, lads. I'm as full as a fat bird's shoe.'*

fat hat *n. Blubber beret.*

fat lass sarnie *n.* A shameful, yet hugely satisfying sandwich that must be consumed out of the view of one's mates on account of its embarrassing nature, *eg.* a crisp, mayonnaise and tomato ketchup bap.

fat lollies *n.* The sort of high denomination seventies-style *thrupenny bits* often to be seen on a cockney criminal's *bird* when he is being arrested mid-*shag* on *the Sweeney. Fat lollies* were also the default *jug* setting on negligee-clad women who typically answered the door to milkman/plumber/mobile gynaecologist Robin Askwith in the *Confessions* films.

fat rascals *n.* Playful *titties.*

fat rash *n. medic.* An area of inner thigh soreness on a *salad dodger,* caused by the severe chafing which occurs when running to the pie shop as closing time approaches.

fattitude *n.* That which is used by *big-boned* ladies in Halifax Yates's when turning down the mock advances of groups of twenty-something males on Fridays.

fattle *n.* Collective term for women whose glands are well versed in lettuce avoidance techniques.

fatty *n.* Something that causes much hilarity in the school showers. An erection. Unless it's the PE teacher's.

fatty clappers *n.* Good old-fashioned no-nonsense *knockers.* The sort of *devil's dumplings* that would make Kenneth Connor have a sort of minor epileptic fit.

faunacation *n.* Sinful acts of congress with members of the animal kingdom.

faux-caine *n.* Particularly poor quality *marching powder,* of the sort that a cash-strapped local television personality might snort up his or her nose through a rolled scratchcard or bus ticket.

faux-pwa *n.* A slip of lap-dancing club etiquette. To *milm* one's *kex* when fishing for a tenner to stuff in a bored dancer's *dunghampers*.

fawn *v.* To *come*, to *reach the Billy Mill Roundabout*. *'The Russian Queen was powerless to resist. Rasputin's eyes burned into hers like sapphires. His muscular arms enfolded her body as she felt herself being swept away in a whirlwind of passion. Then he whipped out his charlie and fawned all down her dress.'* (from *The Lady and the Cossack* by Barbara Cartland).

feasting with panthers *n.* Doing a bit of *the love that dare not speak its name*. See *zorba*.

feather spitter *n.* An over-enthusiastic *pillow biter*.

feck *1. exclam. Ir. Fuck*. Popularised by Fathers Ted and Jack. *2. n.* That quality which a feckless person is lacking.

fecorations *n.* Useful conflation of "fucking" and "decorations" which can be muttered by one not wholly imbued with a spirit of seasonal goodwill when venturing into the attic in early December in search of a damp box of tangled green wire, broken glass and spiders.

feeders' wives *n.* The specialist section of a *bongo mag* which is devoted to amateur photographs of *pillow-smuggling* beauties.

feeding me rabbits *euph.* Having a *wank*. From the character Lucien in Liverpudlian sitcom *The Liver Birds*, who would stay home alone all day and answer the door looking dishevelled, explaining *'I was just feeding me rabbits'*.

feed it a bun *phr.* Term used to emphasise the enormousness of a male member. *'I didn't know whether to suck it or feed it a bun.'*

feed the beavers *v.* To *drop a log* into the *yellow river*.

feed the ducks *v.* To *wank*. From an apparent similarity in hand movements to a man on a park bench *wanking*.

feed the fish *v. nav.* To vomit over the side of a ship, *bury one's biscuits* at sea. A nautical *honk*.

feed the pony *v.* To *frig* a lady's *front bottom*.

feel like Andy Warhol looks, to *v.* To *feel Welsh*.

feel Welsh *v.* To be hungover, to feel none too chipper. To have *eyes like sheep's cunts*.

feeshus *n.* Excrement. *'Who's left a feeshus in the pan?'*

felch *v.* The tender act whereby a gentleman orally retrieves his *spoff* from his partner's *arsehole*. Also *feltch*. *'Birds do it / Bees do it / Even educated fleas do it / Let's do it / Let's felch some spunk.'* (Song lyric *Let's Do It* by Cole Porter).

felchmeister *n. Ger.* A man in lederhosen with a shaving brush in his hat who is particularly adept at *felching*.

felmet *n. medic.* The point where the *fiveskin* is connected to the *bell end*. The *bobby's chinstrap*, the *banjo*.

felt tip *n.* A marker pen *stool* that protrudes from the *nipsy* and keeps drawing lines on one's *bumwad*.

fem *n.* A highly photogenic species of lesbian. Commonly found sitting in pairs on the sofa on TV porn channels. Also *femme*.

femtex *n.* Hormone-based explosive which becomes dangerously unstable once a month.

fenchested *adj.* Of a lady, to be sadly lacking where it counts. To have *Dutch Alps*. Named after the horribly flat fenland area of eastern England.

fent *n.* The erotic perfume of a woman's *clout*. If a worn pair of ladies' pants is draped over a steaming kettle, the room will be filled with the alluring aroma of *fent*.

fent-a-ghost *n.* The strange aroma of *fent* left in your duvet, which lingers no matter how many times you change the bedding, normally experienced after *shafting* a regular *pie eater*. Humorously named after the utterly *shit* 1970s children's television programme *Rent-A-Ghost*, starring Mrs Claypole from *Coronation Street* who is Gail Tilsley's gold-digging mum who used to be married to Alf Roberts who fell off the car park in *Get Carter*.

fentilator *n.* A pair of *birds'* used *grundies* worn on the head whilst *boxing the Jesuit*. A *musk mask*.

fernougle *n. Scots.* A Scotsman's *heated handrail* of humungous proportions. A *sporran splasher*. *'Just got in from the Isle of Skye / My fernougle's lang but my kilt's cut high / The ladies shout as I go by / 'Donald where's yer troosers?''* (Sir Harry Lauder, traditional Scottish song).

fertle *v.* To *feed a lady's pony* through her *bills*.

festival flange *n.* Extra premium strength *minge*. *Disco fanny* that has been baked in the sun and hasn't been washed for two days. The Special Brew of *twats*.

festival hot dog *n.* A hand-held *pap baffle*. As used by the artists Gilbert & George in the preparation of their shitty pictures.

festival knickers *1. n.* The undergarmentry effected by young ladies at open air pop concerts, *ie.* crispy *shreddies* with a long weekend's worth of excitement evident in the gusset. *2. n.* The undergarmentry effected by young ladies at open air pop concerts, *ie.* none at all.

fetching off *n.* The gentle art of *tipping your concrete* into a lady's knicker drawer whilst she's out of the room. *'Hurry up fetching yourselves off, you lot. Carol Decker out of T'Pau's just finishing her encore and she'll be back any moment.'*

fetch the shovel, Mildred! *exclam.* Cry of mock panic upon rising from the *chod bin* and being confronted with the horrors one's *nipsy* has wrought. Also *go get the mongoose!, alert the coastguard!*

FFTBBB *abbrev.* The inevitable converse of a *bobfoc*. A girl who possesses a face pretty enough to be rendered by a Renaissance great, but who has a body resembling a medieval vision of Hell. Face From Titian, Body By Bosch.

fiddler crab *1. n.* In the world of human *relaxation*, a gentleman who has *relaxed* so much that one forearm is the size of Popeye's whilst the other has practically withered away. *2. n.* In the world of marine biology, the South eastern Atlantic crustacean *Uca pugnax*, *Uca pugilator* or *Uca minax*, distinguished by the fact that one of its arm nipper things is much larger than the other, possibly as a result of too much *wanking*.

fiery surprise *n.* To receive a brand spanking new electric fire that one never knew about.

fifth Marx brother *n.* Faecal residue left on the gusset of the *undercrackers* as a result of insufficient wiping. From Ginger Marx. *Skiddo Marx.*

fifty-fifty, go *1. v.* On a popular television quiz programme, to have the computer "randomly" and unerringly remove the two less likely answers, leaving the contestant puzzling over the same pair of possibilities they originally suspected may have been correct. *2. v.* To risk releasing a *Bakewell tart* into one's trolleys, despite the fact that there is a very real possibility that it will be accompanied by half a cup of tea and a chocolate eclair.

fig *n.* A lady's pudendum.

fight a turkey *v. Choke a chicken.*

fighter pilot's thumbs *n. Chapel hat pegs, pygmies' cocks.*

fighting dog's ear, fanny like a *sim.* A phrase that could be used in polite company when referring to the state of a female's *bits* after a right good *hammering.* *'Arachnaphobia was powerless to resist. His eyes burned into hers like hot toast. His muscular arms enfolded her body as she felt herself being swept away in a dual cyclone of passion which reached every nook and crevice of her being and which seemed to last for hours. When he had finished doing her, he rolled off, dropped his guts and lit a Woodbine. 'How was it for you, darling?' he whispered. 'Did the earth move for you?' 'Not half,' she replied. 'You've left me with a fanny like a fighting dog's ear here."* (from *The Egyptian Concubine and the Cheesemonger* by Barbara Cartland).

fighting water *n. Falling down juice, wreck the hoose juice,* Spesh.

filf *n. acronym.* The object of a *chubby chaser's* affections, a *bird* that gives a gentleman *Victoria wood.* Fatty I'd Love to Fuck.

filfy *adj. 'That Fern Britton's well filfy.'*

fill your boots *v.* To make the most of a sexual opportunity. Often prefaced "go on son".

fillet-o-fish *n.* A *haddock pastie* that is on the menu, but for which one has to wait four minutes whilst it is prepared.

film four *n.* The act of having to stay awake till four in the morning in order to *enjoy* a meaningful French art film on the obscure *wankers'* movie channel.

filth machine *n.* An old computer which is kept purely for the purpose of surfing porn.

filthy Ned *n. Dirty Sanchez's* brother.

final whistle *n.* A *fart* that comes in three loud, controlled blasts, causing half the assembled crowd to jump up and cheer.

finding a peanut in a kebab *euph.* Descriptive of the difficulty encountered when a gentleman attempts to locate the *wail switch* during foreplay.

finding nemo *n.* The performing of an act of oral *cumulonimbus. Dining at the Y, licking out.*

finger blessing *v. Firkyfoodling* sans *dunghampers.*

finger food *n.* Something small and delightful you pick up at a party, but which leaves your fingers smelling of fish.

finger of fudge *n.* The consequences of *breaching the hull.* A *taxi driver's tan.*

finger pie *n.* A *handful of sprats,* a *pony feeding session.*

fingers *n.* Sucessfully gaining digital access to one's *bird's snatch.* *"Smell them!', cried Jennings 'Pwoar!' sniffed Darbishire. 'What an ozard ronk. What have you been up to?' Jennings grinned conspiratorily. 'I just got my fingers off Venables' sister in the prep room and I'm never going to wash my hand again."* (from *Jennings and the Strange Urges* by Anthony Buckeridge).

fingersmith *1. n.* A disgusting *self-polluter* of either gender. *2. n. Piss-poor* BBC costume drama about Victorian *carpet-munching,* which disappointed thousands of sofa-bound *fingersmiths* across the country.

fingertip grip *1. n.* In the world of snooker, holding the butt of one's cue with the very ends of one's digits in order to better control a tricky shot. *2. n.* In the world of somewhat desperate late-night-television-fuelled *gentleman's relaxation,* to *chalk your naughty cue* at the sight of BBC snooker presenter Hazel Irvine. Presumably whilst hoping against hope that the whole sordid, dismal transaction will be successfully completed before John Virgo appears on the screen and sets you back a good ten minutes.

finisher *n.* The favourite page of an *art pamphlet* saved for the climax of a *cat stabbing* session.

finishing the dishes *1. n.* That deflating experience when you discover that the fucking dishwasher has not cleaned its contents properly so you have to complete the fucking job yourself, wondering all the while what was the fucking point of getting the fucking bastard thing in the first place. *2. n.* Resorting, following a disappointing or regrettable act of coitus, to a dispiriting act of *monomanual labour. 'When the Lord saw what Onan had wrought He was sore displeased and great was His anger, and he spake unto Onan in a loud voice saying Onan, you did lie in your tent with your wife Tamar and yet while she slept did you then take yourself in your hand and thus did spill your precious seed all upon the ground and everywhere which was exceedingly sinful in mine eyes. And Onan waxed sorrowful for he saw that he had indeed sinned before the Lord, begging forgiveness from Him saying, O Lord, I am sorely repentant for my wickedness but yea, I was only finishing the dishes.'* (from *The Book of Mike and the Mechanics*).

Finnegan's wake *n.* Descriptive of one's face upon waking in the morning after a heavy session *on the turps* and a poor night's sleep. Characterised by grey pallor and puffyness around the eyes.

Finsbury bridge *n.* The *barse.*

fire cover *1. n.* What an heroic soldier requests from his comrades prior to single-handedly storming an enemy machine gun nest. *2. n.* A request made to the wife when on holiday and staying in a tiny hotel room, after you have consumed a dodgy paella and a plethora of *pedro's piss. 'My guts* *are rotten, love. I've got to go to the bog. Put the telly on, will you? Give me some fire cover.'*

fire down below *exclam.* An announcement used by a gentleman signifying the discovery of a genuine redhead.

fireman's blanket *n.* A precautionary *turd*-catching mat of *shit rag* laid on the *bog* water surface, with the intention of preventing noise and/or *splashback.*

fire one across the bows *v.* A *navel engagement* whereby the *pirate of men's pants* withdraws from the battlezone just before the *egg white cannon* shoots its payload into *cod cove.*

fire snakes *n.* Venomous post-curry or post-chilli stools that rattle out the *arse* at a fair old lick.

fire, throw a log on the *v.* To *shit* oneself whilst attempting to light a *fart.*

firing blanks *v.* Post-*snip spoffing. 'You can put the ticklers away love, I'm firing blanks.'*

firing the one o'clock gun *1. n.* Act performed every day around thirteen hundred hours from the parapets of Edinburgh Castle in order to make all the American tourists in Auld Reekie *shit* their tartan troosers. *2. n.* Act performed by a man upon returning home during a lunch-break whilst his flat-mates, kids *etc.* are out. *'Well, that's all the lunchtime news from me Martyn Lewis. I'll be back with the main headlines at six, but meanwhile I'm nipping off home to fire the one o'clock gun.'*

firkin *1. n. arch.* A measure of ale capacity, equal to nine gallons or half a kilderkin. *2. n.* The *fuck-witted* epithet for half the pubs in Britain.

firkyfoodling *n. arch.* Tudor foreplay. *'Dearest Maid Miriam. Until lately did my husband Henry be a most wonderful and caring lover. But forsooth I am most sad to relate that of recent times he wanteth naught but most hasty coupling with me. He spendeth no time on the firkyfoodling. Yea I fear that my tastes for the courses of love hath declined as a consequence. And now he hath vouchsafed to cut my head from my shoulders. Five wives hath he taken already before me, and of two hath he separated their heads from their shoulders. What am I to do? Pray, pray, pray help me. C. Parr, London.'* (Letter to *Daily Mirror*, 1545).

first impressions *n.* Breasts. *Competitive advantages.*

first load *n.* That which is flushed down the *chod pan* prior to that second round of lower intestinal grumbling which heralds the arrival of a bonus *drop of shopping.*

first mud *n.* The *popping* of a *brown cherry.*

first on the dancefloor *euph.* Of a gentleman, being *good with colours, sensitive,* prone to suprapuddular aerobatics and what-have-you. *Queer as a nine bob note.*

first two inches are cold, the *exclam.* A cry to indicate the urgency with which one requires a lavatory. *'I answered the urgent hammering on the door. It was Holmes, in the guise of a Greek Admiral, and possessed of a wild expression the likes of which I had never seen before. 'What is it, Holmes?' I expostulated. 'Why,* *it's three in the morning.' 'There is no time for explanations, Watson,' he gasped as he pushed past me towards my water closet, 'the first two inches are cold.'* (from *The Case of the Great Big Shit* by Sir Arthur Conan Doyle).

firtle *v.* To cut a hole in a poster of one's favourite pop star or film actress, and *fuck* it.

fish *1. n. prop.* Former lead singer out of "Happy Shopper Genesis" pop band Marillion. *2. adj.* Not very good. *Crap, swiss, pants, mouse, fucking rubbish. 'That lead singer out of Marillion is fish'*

fish box *n.* A lady's *twat. Billingsgate box, fish mitten.*

fish drowner *n.* A *clown's pie.*

fisherman's jumper *n.* A damp, overly-hairy *clopper*, smelling not too dissimilar to a deep sea trawler captain's wool sweater after hauling in a net full of haddock. *'Having been accustomed all my life to ideals of a feminine nakedness gleaned from classical antiquities, I was somewhat taken aback on my wedding night to find that my young bride had a right old fisherman's jumper between her legs.'* (from *The Memoirs of John Ruskin*, 1819-1900).

fisherman's sock, pull her on like a *sim.* No-nonsense method of sexual intercourse. *'Concertina was powerless to resist. His eyes burned into hers like zirconium. His muscular arms enfolded her body as she felt herself being swept away on a tsunami of passion. They stood before each other naked, until he could wait no longer. Roughly, he grasped her by the waist and pulled her on like a fisherman's sock.'* (from *The Lady and the Independent Financial Adviser*, by Barbara Cartland).

fisherman's swig *n.* A well deserved sup from the *hairy goblet.*

fish from the other bank *v.* To be *on the other bus,* to *jump puddles,* to be *good with colours.*

fish fryer's cuff *sim.* Descriptive of a pair of well-worn knickers with a heavily-*battered* gusset.

fish-hook shit *n.* A *turd* containing a sharp object that snags the *nipsy, eg.* a peanut, a filling, the wife's *clit ring.*

fish mitten *n.* A *muff* that keeps the fingers and thumb of one hand warm.

fishmitten's bark *n.* An audible release of *clam gas.* A *queef.* A *fanny fart, hail mary.*

fish supper *euph. 1. n.* A Friday night feast with the tang of the sea and plenty of batter. *2. n.* Fish and chips.

Fishwick *1. n. prop.* A small Scottish village 4 miles west of Berwick upon Tweed. *2. n.* The bit of braided string that hangs out of a *kipper* that has *fallen to the communists.* A *mouse's tail.*

fist *1. v.* Of boxers, to punch someone in the ring. *2. n.* Of *puddle jumpers*, to punch someone in the *ring. 3. n.* Of heterosexuals, to punch someone in the *quim.*

fist magnet *n.* Someone who attracts punches to his face, *eg.* Jimmy Carr.

fist of fury *n.* Of a gentleman with a restricted *wank window,* for example whilst his missus has just nipped next door for a cup of sugar, a mindlessly violent act of *self abuse* carried out in a sort of masturbatory red mist. An *armbreaker, bishop rage, power wank.*

fist rape *n.* Taking advantage of your clenched hand after inviting it back to your place for a coffee and a flick through a *meat mag. Knuckle glazing.*

fit *adj.* Attractive, worthy of *one.*

fitbin *interj.* The rudest word in the English language, so rude that its meaning has been encased in 500 tons of concrete and dumped in the Irish Sea.

five against one *n.* A very one-sided but nonetheless enjoyable game of wrestling in which *Madam Palm and her five sisters* attempt to *strangle Kojak.* The game ends when someone *makes the bald man cry.*

five day test *n.* A pointless *Ethel* that never really gets going and typically has no prospect of a satisfactory conclusion. *Strangling the coach.*

five finger spread *n.* Counter-productive attempt to suppress *a yoff* with the hand. A *chuckspreader, yawn sprinkler.*

five knuckle shuffle *n. One-handed workout* to a Geri Halliwell yoga video.

five o'clock fanny *n.* A stubbly *ladygarden.* A *Flintstone fanny,* a *face grater.*

five pee fifty pee *sim.* Anal/numismatical comparison descriptive of the rapidly-alternating diameter of one's rectal sphincter at moments of extreme nervousness. *Bin lid penny. 'Did you see the match last night?' 'Yeah, the last ten minutes were proper five pee fifty pee.'*

five-pinter *n.* A very ugly woman who one would only happily chat up after five pints of *dizzyade.* A *St. Ivel lass.*

five pint facelift *n.* A subjective improvement in one's partner's appearance brought about by the consumption of 62.5% of a gallon of booze.

fives *n.* A traditional Etonian game played with four fingers, a thumb and a *cock.*

fiveskin *n. Fourskin.*

five-to-two-er *n.* A *bird* who is desperate minutes uglier than a *ten-to-two-er.*

fizzing at the bung hole *adj.* Descriptive of effervescent sexual arousal in a woman. *Dripping like a fucked fridge, frothing like bottled Bass.*

fizzle *n.* A gentle or quiet *arse firework.*

fizzy gravy *n.* Diarrhoea, *rusty water.* Always on the menu at the Curry Capital, Bigg Market, Newcastle upon Tyne.

fizzyjizz *n.* Aerated semen caused by over-enthusiastic *cat stabbing. Bubblecum.*

fizzy knickers *n.* A *wide on.*

flaccid flashback *n.* A ghastly, inappropriate, unerotic memory, *eg.* nan burping after eating too much stuffing, topless uncle mowing the lawn, Olive off *On The Buses,* that pops into one's head during sex, causing one to deflate like one of Richard Branson's balloons.

flackets *n. medic. Beef curtains.*

fladge and padge *abbrev.* Of *rub-a-tug shop* services, getting a bit of *Mr Whippy* off a whore in a nurse's outfit. From flageantry and pageantry. *'Bit of fladge and padge today, I think.' 'That'll be fifty pounds, Lord Archer.'*

flag bravo *n. nav.* A large red pennant unfurled atop a ship's masty thing to warn others of any dangerous activity which may be taking place. *2. euph. nav.* A term used by female members of the Royal Navy to describe their monthly period of confinement. *'Ooh, admiral. I wouldn't go munching on me oggie if I was you. I've got me flag bravo hauled up.'*

flags are out *exclam. Wet paint* warning when the fixture list shows *Arsenal are playing at home.*

FLAME *abbrev.* Fanny Like A Mouse's Ear. An expression typically accompanied by a workmanlike rubbing together of the hands and a Mike Reid-style Jack the lad neck-thrust.

Flamingoland *n.* A watering hole with a high density of *Yorkshire flamingos.*

flamingo up *n.* Like a *cock up,* only much, much bigger.

Flanders poppy *sim.* A *ringpiece* that has been through the wars, *ie.* one that is bright red and shot to pieces.

flange *1. n.* A *fish mitten. Muff, beaver, minge. 2. n. coll.* Not a word to describe a group of baboons. The correct term for a group of baboons is "troop" or "congress". So there. *3. n. coll. Fanny, blart, tush, buffage.*

flangepiece *n.* Slang term used when referring to someone as a dolt or buffoon. *'Oi, Menuhin, put your fucking bow down. This movement's supposed to be fucking pizzicato, you fucking flangepiece.'* (Sir Edward Elgar, 1927).

flangina *1. n. medic.* Any form of physical or emotional pain caused to a man by the nagging of his female partner. *'I know I said I'd be back by ten and now it's Tuesday, but for fuck's sake give it a rest will you, woman. You're bringing on my flangina.' 2. n. medic.* Women's things.

flannelled *adj.* The state of one's face after *going down* on a *fish drowner.*

flap a herring *v.* To *fart* in a wet and audible manner, such that the *cheeks* of the buttocks clap together.

flap dabbling *n.* In the world of *masturbating* ladies, to *gusset type* in a disinterested fashion. From flap + dabbling.

flap-flops *1. n.* The shoes commonly worn by old ladies in naturist resorts. *2. n.* The *tits* commonly worn by old ladies in naturist resorts.

flapjack *1. n.* A dense, syrupy cake that has pretentions to healthiness. *2. n. medic.* A *quim quack's* tool for jacking *flaps* apart. A speculum. *3. n.* A device, usually in the form of a small gift, given by a suitor to his intended in the hope that it will help him *get some cabbage* off her.

flapjacking *n.* Two tasty ladies having a nibble at each other's *sticky bits. 'Come and look at this, your holiness. there's a new flapjacking vid on YouTube.'*

flapmates *n.* A pair of *curtain twitchers. Tennis fans.*

flapmonger *n.* One who mongs *flaps.* A *tart farmer,* fanny farmer, *pimp.*

flappetite *n.* A healthy appetite for flaps. From flap + appetite.

flappocks *n.* The confusing yet strangely intriguing in-between-style genitalia of a *trolley dolly* who is half way through a programme of gender reassignment surgery, in either direction.

flap snack *n.* A quick *fish burger* or

bacon sandwich. Elevenses at *the Y*. Token *cumulonimbus*.

flapsnapper *n. medic.* In the world of gynaecology and obstetrics, a firstborn infant which weighs in at more than 9lbs in the old money. *'Births: Haystacks. On March 9th at Halifax Maternity Hospital. To Mavis and Horace, a bouncing 38lb flapsnapper, Giant.'* (from *The Yorkshire Post*, March 11th 1946).

flap snot *n. medic.* A *fannular discharge. Lizzie dripping, clam jam. Gleet.*

flaptulence *n.* The *dropping forwards* of a *lady's hat. Queefage, fanny farting.*

flash *v.* To treat a lucky lady to a surprise private viewing of one's *fruitbowl.*

flasher *n.* A gentleman who frequents parks wearing a mac, beret, little round glasses and trouser bottoms tied round the knees with string.

flash in the pan *1. n.* A *spooge*-free male orgasm. A cashless *money shot. 2. n.* The act for which George Michael was arrested in a Beverly Hills public lavatory on April 7th 1998.

flash the ash *exclam.* A gentle reminder of a person's social responsibility to share his cigarettes with others in his peer group. *'Oi, fuck face! Flash the ash, you tight-fisted cunt.'*

flash the upright grin *v.* To expose the female genitals, *flash the gash.*

flat as a kipper's dick *adj.* Descriptive of unleavened *baps.*

flative *adj.* Of food, that which induces flatulence, *eg.* cabbage, sprouts, *musical vegetables.*

flatliner *n.* A burst of numerous, regularly-spaced *air biscuits* of equal length and volume, followed by one long, sustained release of *brown air.* From this act's rhythmic similarity to the sound made by TV hospital drama heart monitors just before a fashionably-stubbled surgeon reluctantly stops pumping the patient's chest, looks at the clock, then pulls off his rubber gloves and flings them away.

flat Stanley *n.* A sexual encounter involving a very large lady.

flat, straighten up the *v.* Of a closet *puddle-jumping* couple, to hang a *Hollyoaks* calendar on their wall in order to disguise the *whiff of lavender* in the air.

flatty, crack a *v.* To suffer an unfortunate erectile dysfunction in the *trouser department.*

flatulence *n.* The whole kit and kiboodle of *farting.* From the Latin *flatus* = to start & *lentus* = a cold tractor.

flavour of the month *n.* The savoury tang of *moon juice.* The *twaste* left in the mouth following a *scrapheap challenge.*

fleemail *n.* A rapidly-scribbled note of thanks, including a false name and address, left on the pillow of a *munter* by a long gone *fanny hopper* who woke up without his *beer goggles* on.

flembrandt *n.* A distinctive piece of pavement art seen adorning much of London's walkways. *Lung paint.*

fleshbombs *n.* Two large wads of *jubbly gelignite* packed in a woman's *tit pants.*

flesh lettuce *n.* Crinkly downstairs lady bits.

flesh wallet *n.* The *hairy cheque*

book, pubic purse. Somewhere to put one's *money shots.*

fleshy flugelhorn *n.* Tuneful variation on the *bed flute, pink oboe, spunk trumpet, beef bassoon.*

flex, to have a *v.* To *bust off.*

flick finger *n. medic.* The finger with which a woman *flicks herself off.*

flies' dinner gong *n.* A entemologically pavlovian *custard tart.*

flik *n.* Dried up *spoff* found on curtains, furniture, foreheads, shrouds *etc. 'I felt so betrayed when the President denied we had had a relationship. Then my friend Linda Tripp reminded me that I still had the dress with his flik all over it in the cupboard.'* (Monika Lewinsky, Statement to the US Senate Impeachment Committee, 1999).

flinge *n. coll. Blart, tussage, flap.* From flange + minge. *'Come on. Let's go and find some flinge.'*

flingel *rhym. slang. Cunt.* From the instrumental hit *The Rise and Fall of Flingel Bunt* by The Shadows.

flinging in the rain *n.* The act of masturbating in the shower.

fling string *v.* To *jizz* via air mail. To *lob ropes.*

flip flop *1. n.* A poor quality shoe substitute worn by people who can't afford heels. *2. n.* A *tug* administered whilst one is so unenthusiastic about life that one can't even muster up a *semi-on.* A *flap.*

flipper *n.* A Taiwanese *ladyboy* that fools the gagging punter to the extent that he thinks: "Fuck it. I've paid me money, I'll just flip her over".

Flipper's beak *n.* A *shaven haven,* often to be seen poking out of the water and making a clicking sound before wrestling a pistol out of a bank robber's hand.

flipping pancakes *n.* The practice of loosening up one's *batter* prior to sending it arcing up into the sky. On a Tuesday.

float an air biscuit *v.* To release a *tree monkey* from captivity.

floater *1. n.* A *turd* in the pan which will not flush away. *2. n.* A member of the crap 70s soul band, *eg.* Larry (Cancer), who likes a woman that loves everything and everybody.

flock of pigeons *n.* The sound of a loose bowel movement.

flog pocket *n.* The front flap of a pair of Y-fronts, useful when a fellow needs rapid access to his *old chap* for whatever reason.

flogging on *v.* Accessing the internet in search of *left-handed websites.*

flog the log *v.* To *whup one's wood, spank the plank.*

floor chimes *n.* The collection of empty cans and bottles under the driver's seat of a car which roll together, producing a soothing jingle-jangle sound when it goes round a corner, up a kerb or over a bicycle.

floordrobe *n.* The clothing receptacle most used by students, teenagers and men home from the pub.

flop out *n.* Condition whereby the flaccid penis protrudes through the bottom of the underpants, this often occurring during the transfer from a sitting to a standing position.

floppy red cup *n.* The *Hairy goblet.*

flop to pop *n.* A standard interval used to measure the quality of *horatio* techniques. The time taken to ejaculate from a flaccid start. *'Egbert was powerless to resist. Her eyes burned into his like sapphires. Her ladylike arms en-*

folded his masculine body as he felt himself being swept away in a whirlwind of passion. Then she knelt down in front of him and took him from flop to pop in three minutes flat.' (from *The Officer and the Gypsy* by Barbara Cartland).

Florida fartbox *n. US.* An *abnormal load. Orlando dirtbox.*

florins *ryhm. slang.* The *shits.* From the pre-decimal coins known as *two bob bits.*

flossing the squirrel *v.* Of a lady, to be sporting a thong-styled underpant.

flub *1. onomat.* The sound of a *fanny fart. 2. v. Fuck* in Flowerpot Men language. See *dub.*

fluff *n. nav.* A maritime *blow off.*

fluffer *n.* In a *bongo vid* studio, a professional *fellatrix* employed between takes to ensure the tumescence of the male actors.

fluffit *n.* The sweetest name in common use for the *cunt.*

flum *n. Ladygarden, snatch thatch, pubes.*

flump *1. n.* A cylindrical marshmallow sweet. *2. n.* An offensive and hurtful term used by sexist women to describe the flaccid penis of a man who, for all they know, may be suffering from serious medical problems. *3. v.* To thumb in a less than tumescent member when attempting sexual congress whilst completely *hammered.*

flunkey *1. n.* A Royal slave, one who fawns on a *nob, eg.* Nicholas Witchell. *2. n.* A *dunky.*

flush hour *n.* In a workplace, the period of time after morning coffee during which there is even a queue for the gents' *shitter.*

flush puppies *n.* Dalmatian-spotted suede shoes that have been standing too close to a urinal.

flushstration *n.* The sense of increasing annoyance felt when a *faecee* one has just excreted refuses to disappear down the U-bend, despite repeated cranks on the handle.

flute player's lips *n.* Descriptive of the *ringpiece* ejecting last night's curry and beer.

flutter *n.* Of a lady, to urinate charmingly, *viz.* without dropping a loud gut halfway through.

flux capacitor *1. n.* The invention that allows a 35-year-old Michael J Fox to play a teenager in the *Back to the Future* trilogy. *2. n.* The Y-shaped vein on the shaft of the *tallywhacker.*

fly feast *n.* An *al fresco* act of *cable laying,* usually up an alleyway or behind some bushes.

fly sheet *n.* A *fiveskin.*

flying pastie *n.* Excrement wrapped in newspaper and thrown into a neighbour's yard for whatever reason. See *pyropastie.*

flying scotsman *n.* A highly complicated sex act that doesn't sound like it's worth the bother.

flying squirrel *n.* Genital manipulation amusement. *Farmyard* animal impression involving the stretching of one's scrotal leather almost to breaking point, in the style of the wing-like membranes on the popular airborne rats of the genus *Pteromys.*

fly's eyes *n.* A gentleman's party trick whereby the shorts or bathers are pulled tight between the legs so that the *clockweights* bulge out on either side of the *gusset. 'August 6th. We all go down to Cliveden for the weekend. Gerty*

(Laurence) and Fanny (Brice) were there as usual. Ivor (Novello) entertained us all by singing King's Rhapsody by the pool, and followed it by doing fly's eyes. How we all shrieked. Benjamin (Britten) laughed so much he shat himself, poor dear.' (from *The Diaries of Noel Coward,* 1938).

fly's graveyard *n.* The *nutsack* netherworld situated on the dorsal side of the *chicken skin handbag* which to this day remains unseen by human eyes.

fly the flag *v. NZ.* To *zuffle.*

fly tipping *n.* The act of rewarding a fly for excellent service in a soup restaurant.

fnarr! fnarr! *exclam.* Suppressed childish exclamation of amusement uttered after a double entendre. Also *k-yak! k-yak!*

foaming at the bunghole *adj. Frothing at the gash. Glistening.*

foffof *acronym.* Fair Of Figure, Foul Of Face. *Bobfoc.*

FOG *abbrev.* The sort of stare that one gives to a senior citizen at a bus stop in order to avert the possibility of them attempting to strike up a conversation about the weather, the paucity of the old age pension or the size of these new five pence pieces. From Fuck Off Granny.

foggles *1. n. R.A.F.* Wrap-around glasses used in pilot instrument training, which are frosted except for a section at the bottom, so as to restrict the pilot's view to his instrument panel only. *2. n.* A phenomenon whereby, on meeting a lady, one's attention is focused on the lower features to the exclusion of anything above shoulder level. *'She was a blonde, or perhaps a brunette. She might have been ginger. I can't remember, officer. I had my foggles on.'*

fog up *adj.* Of *train pulling,* to be the driver, as opposed to the *porridge stirrer* in the *guard's van. 'Bagsy me fog up. I don't want any of you lot's sloppy seconds again.'*

folder *n.* One whose good breeding, manners and culture have instilled in them the proper way of preparing toilet paper for smudging the *chocolate starfish.*

follow through *v.* To accidentally soil one's *undercrackers* whilst attempting to release a bubble of *carbon dibaxide.* To create *russet gusset, drop a pebble.*

fomp *v. US.* To engage in sexual foreplay, to *firkyfoodle.*

fond of shopping *euph. Good with his hands.*

fond of walking holidays *euph.* A *woman in comfortable shoes,* a *tennis fan,* a *tuppence licker.*

fondleberries *n.* Testicles.

food in the beard *euph.* A symptom of insufficient wiping after a *tom tit.* To have *winnets* in the *crackers.*

food's ghost *n.* An invisible, eerie presence accompanied by a low humming sound and the stench of death. A *McArthur Park.*

foop *n. onomat.* The sound of a penis being removed from an anal passage, presumably a bit like when you blow across the top of an empty milk bottle.

footballer's tie-knot, wide as a *sim.* An expression that describes something that is wider that it ought to be. *'Thank you, Your Holiness, but I'd rather not sit down. I had a cack this morning and the bas-*

tard was as wide as a footballer's tie knot, believe me.'

footstool *n. Pavement toffee, barkers' eggs* and the like, when trodden on.

footwell flavour *n.* The soul-destroying aroma of *footstool* that appears three minutes after turning on the car heater.

Forbsy drop, the *n.* The act of taking a full pint to the pub toilet and returning with it empty in an attempt to look like a hardened drinker. Named after a lawyer from St Albans who can't take his beer. *'Heavily made-up Prime Minister Tony Blair today visited the Labour Club at his Sedgefield constituency, and performed several Forbsy drops for the benefit of television news cameras, before announcing his intention to resign.'*

force field *n.* A thick *fart* that clings to the warp and weft of one's *duds,* preventing anyone from coming within six feet for a good ten minutes. A *Velcro guff.*

FORD *abbrev. medic.* Casualty doctors' notes terminology. Found On Road Drunk.

foregasm *n.* A *stack* which is *blown* whilst still trying to *light the fire.* When a gentleman *spends his money* before he's even got *into the shop.* Going *up and over like a pan of milk* before the niceties of *frigmarole* have been satisfactorily completed. A *Pope-shot.*

foreploy *n.* Any gambit used to get a woman into bed, *eg.* claiming to be an airline pilot, member of the SAS, employee of the month at McDonald's *etc.*

foreporn *n.* The token, exaggerated, wooden acting preceding the *spaff candy* of a *grumble vid.* Usually viewed on fast forward.

foreskinzola *n.* A pungent, unappetising, mature *knobcheese.*

forget-me-mott *n.* An unkempt bed of *gorilla salad,* which could do with a bit of judicious pruning.

forget-me-nots *n.* The final notes in a *Chinese singing lesson.* Droplets which form a tiny but embarrassing wet patch on your trousers. *Dicksplash.*

forgetiquette *n.* To inadvertently forget one's manners, *eg.* when taking a mobile phone call during Earl Spencer's speech at Lady Di's funeral, scratching one's *arse* and sniffing your fingers just prior to shaking the Queen's hand backstage at the Royal Variety Performance.

fork lift truck *n.* An exotic sexual position performed in back alleys and shop doorways, whereby the female participant is hoisted clear of the ground by the thighs in order to keep her *arse* clear of *piss,* vomit, broken glass and spent *jubbers.* A *chinook.*

form *1. n.* Means of judging horses by statistics, before *pissing your money up the wall* at the bookies. *2. n.* Means of judging *birds* by statistics. *Fitness, fuckability, prodworthiness.*

Forsyth *1. n.* A rug worn across the lap to preserve one's modesty whilst vigorously *enjoying* art films in the presence of others. *2. v.* To play the *generation game*; to have romantic liaisons with both mother and daughter. To *play one's cards right,* going "higher" (mother) and "lower" (daughter), if you will.

fort knockers *n.* Highly reinforced

and practically impenetrable bras of the sort that nuns, librarians and Ann Widdecombe might wear.

Forth bridger *n.* An irritable and cantankerous woman who seems to *have the painters in* all year round, *eg.* Germaine Greer, Bonnie Greer, any woman called Greer.

forty wanks *n.* An impromptu and refreshing *shuffle.*

Fosbury plop *n.* An *arse baby* of such proportions that the delivery method involves arching the back in the style of the revolutionary 1960s Olympic high-jumper.

fough *n.* An inadvertent *dropping of the guts* when clearing one's throat. Derivation unknown. Possibly from Frank + Bough.

foul papers *1. n.* In the world of Shakespearean scholarship, manuscripts bearing abandoned drafts of the bard's work. *2. n.* In the world of *arse-wipe* studies, soiled *bumwad.*

foul Paulo *n.* An Italian *Dirty Sanchez.* A faecal moustache.

four-man bob *n.* A large, speedily-ejected *turd.* Possibly rocking backwards and forwards 2 or 3 times before coming out.

four minutes *rhym. slang.* Haemorrhoids. From four minute miles = piles.

fourth base *1. n. US.* Something to do with baseball or American football or something. *2. n.* The *anus.*

fourth party *adj.* The type of motor insurance favoured by the council *estate car* driver, *ie.* none. *'It's alright, mate. That'll just polish out. Anyway, I've got full fourth party insurance. I'll just get back in my car to write down my details.'*

fox licking shit off a wire brush, face like a *sim.* Phrase which is useful when one is referring to someone of a notably miserable mien. *'Did you see John fucking Prescott on the stand at the Labour Party Conference? He looked like a fucking fox licking shit off a wire brush.' 'Thank-you, Martha. And now back to Jeremy in the Newsnight studio.'*

foxymoron *n.* A lady whose incredible physical attractiveness is matched only by her marked lack of intellect. *'Famous people born on November 23rd: John Wallis, influential English mathematician, 1616; Franklin Pierce, 14th President of the United States, 1804; Manuel de Falla, greatest Spanish composer of the last century, 1876; Kelly Brook, wonky-titted foxymoron, 1979.'* (from *'Schott's Oh Fuck Oh Fuck Oh Fuck the Deadline's Tomorrow Book, 2005'*).

Foyston Gap *n.* The space at the top of a woman's thighs, a term peculiar to Greatfield, Kingston upon Hull, East Yorkshire. The *Toblerone tunnel.*

Frampton *1. n. prop.* An overrated 1970s singer with a voice like Steven Hawking. *2. n.* A *fanny fart.*

Francis *n. US.* A lady's *arse.*

franger *n. Dunky, English overcoat, blob, jubber ray.* A gentleman's prophylactic sheath.

Frankenstein's feet *sim.* The illusion of having someone else's feet stiched onto one's legs caused by the serrated indentations left by tight socks on one's ankles.

frankentits *n. Knockers* which exhibit scarring from their implant operations, leaving them looking like something knocked up by Peter Cushing in his laboratory.

Beverly hills are usually revealed as *frankentits* when viewed from underneath.

frankfurter water *1. n.* Salty, meat-flavoured fluid in which a slippery sausage has been steeped. *2. n.* Salty, meat-flavoured fluid which has just come out the end of a *slippery sausage.*

Frankie *rhym. slang. Grumble, scud* material. From Frankie Vaughanography = pornography.

frap *v. onomat.* To *break company* through the *snippit valve.*

freckle maggots *n.* Rolled-up pieces of 3-ply *shit ticket* which congregate around the *tea towel holder* after it has been given a right good wipe.

freckle *n. Aus. Arse, brown eye, chocolate starfish, dot.*

Fred *n. rhym. slang.* Sperm. From the famous golfer Fred Funk, whose name rhymes with *spunk.*

freemason's handshake, fanny like a sim. A tight vagina, particularly one which applies unusual pressure to the second knuckle of one's right hand.

free the Middleton two *v.* To drive over speed bumps at an excessive velocity in the hope of getting one's ladyfriend's *gert stonkers* to bounce right out of her low-cut top. Named after the Leeds area which is richly-blessed with both traffic-calming street furniture and *big-titted* single mothers.

free the tadpoles *v.* To liberate the residents of one's *wank tanks.* To have a *tug.*

fred Leicester *n.* Pungent cheese cultivated in the *brim* of the *farmer's hat.*

French *n.* Popular coital position whereby the man sits astride a bicycle selling onions while the woman perches on the handlebars and inflates his testicles.

French accordian player *n.* A gentleman inexperienced in the art of romancing a lady, who believes the best way to go about things is to press and squeeze everything he can find as quickly as possible. A *clamateur* musician.

french horn *1. n.* Brass orchestral instrument, distinguished by its rotary valves, narrow conical bore and large, flared bell. *2. n.* Sexual position in which the female sits on the male's lap and he gets a mouthful of *tit* and four fingers in her *letterbox. 3. n.* A *bone on.*

French letter *n.* A *durex.*

French palm *n.* Sexual technique which quite possibly explains why our Gallic cousins are widely regarded as the world's greatest lovers. Not to put too fine a point on it, the use of a cupped hand on a lady's *front bottom,* rather in the style of those coarse youths at swimming pools who make *farting* noises under their armpits.

French polish, to *v.* To *buff up one's wood* till you can see your face in it. And all *spadge* comes out the end. To have a *Tom Hank.*

French safe *n.* A secure *box* that can be cracked open by fiddling with a little button at the top. Usually found behind a hinged oil painting on the front of a woman's *trolleys.*

French sickness *n.* Any *cock rot* caught from prostitutes advertising their services in phone boxes for £20 or less.

French snuff *n.* The pungent particles of *shit* which are inhaled from the end of the index finger after it has just scratched the *rusty bullet* *hole.*

French wank n. A *posh wank.*

French week *n.* A long and demanding day at work which is probably equal to the amount of effort expended by our gallic cousins from Monday to Friday. *'How was work today?' 'Crazy, I put in a French week.'*

frenchy *n.* Rubber carrying case for a *French horn.*

Freudian slip *n.* An inadvertent slip of the tongue revealing subconscious sexual desires. Named after crack-headed, *motherfucking* psychoanalyst Sigmund. *'Would you like a piece of my two foot black cock up your arse, Vicar? Oh, I'm sorry, I meant a piece of my home-made sponge cake.'*

friar's chin *n.* To tuck one's vest/shirt/jumper under one's chin to keep it out of harm's way whilst *pulling the Pope's cap off* over a *Tijuana bible.* See *bishop's waltz.*

friar's weeds *n.* A holy unkempt garden of *13 amp fusewire.*

Friar Tuck *rhym. slang.* An act of coition. A *Donald Duck.*

friction bairns *n.* The offspring of a homosexual. So called because the *lavender* father shoots his load solely as a result of friction. *'Ere, did you know that Julian Clary's missus has just had twins?' 'Friction bairns, them.'*

Friday foal *n.* One who, late on a Friday evening, proceeds to take on the ambulatory characteristics of a new-born baby deer. A *beer Bambi.*

Friday night gamble *n.* Rejecting the advances of a perfectly acceptable bit of *tussage* on the chance that one might pull something better later on in the evening. *Twisting.*

fridge magnet *n.* A man whose successive girlfriends' sexual appetites are a source of disappointment. *'Trish won't take it fudge-ways either. What am I, a fridge magnet?'*

fried eggs *n.* Small *baps, titterlings, stits.*

friend of Dorothy *n.* Politically correct terminology for a chap on whom *nature has played a cruel trick.*

friendly fire *1. n. milit.* The actions of US armed forces against journalists, ambulances, wedding parties and anyone who fights alongside them. 2. *n.* An unexpectedly powerful *jizz bolt* that overshoots the belly and hits a *self-abuser* in the face. *3. n.* Of a gentleman *jazz flick* actor, to be caught in the line of fire of a fellow thespian's *pop shot. 4. n.* Small residue of urine ejected from the penis when one is trying to put it back into one's flies following a *scoot.* Usually when wearing light-coloured trousers.

frig *v.* To *frotter, wank,* esp. a lady's *squidge.*

friggonometry *n.* The precise science involved in selecting and arranging one's fingers at the correct angle whilst *diddling* a rude lady's *devil's doorbell.* The *Ebdon slide.*

frightened skydivers *sim.* Descriptive of stools that are reluctant to exit the *bomb bay doors. 'I think I'm going to have to try All Bran. My turds are like frightened skydivers.'*

frigmata *n.* Sanguinous marks on the hands of one who has been *flicking the bean* of a woman when *Aunt Flo is visiting.*

frigment of one's imagination *n.* A

subject conjured up in the mind to oil the wheels of *self abuse*.

frigmarole *n.* Unnecessarily time-consuming foreplay performed on a missus. *Choreplay.*

frigor mortis *n. medic.* State of stiffness in one's *old chap.*

frigspawn *n. Cock eggs* in the bath.

fringe-parter *n.* A gusty *fanny fart* during a session of *cumulonimbus*. A *lip rattler.*

fritter *1. n. NZ.* A hot, *batter-coated morsel. 2. n.* An item of food cooked in a frying pan.

frock *n.* Cosmetic husband in a *lavender marriage*. The male equivalent of a *beard.*

Frodo *n.* An annoying little *turd* that clings to the *ring*. A *geetle* that forces one to *tap the ash.*

frog, catching the *n.* The act following a successful *peel and polish,* whereby a lady cups her hands to collect her manfriend's expelled *baby gravy.*

froggy style *n.* Type of sexual congress performed in the style of the popular boggle-eyed green amphibians, *ie. doing* a lass from behind, then pulling out at the last moment and *spunking* up her back.

frog's chin *n.* The saggy *bag of tripe* that hangs over and obscures the *furry bike stand* of an unacceptably curvaceous lady. The *gunt, bunt, poond, fupa.*

frombie *n.* A lady who is blessed with such a *lovely personality* that the only way a gentleman could bring himself to do her would be "from behind".

fromunder *n.* Type of pungent cheese cultivated by the less hygiene-conscious elements of male society. Also *helmetdale, brimula, knacker barrel.*

frontal forelimb *n.* A prehensile *dobber*. A *middle stump, third leg.*

front bottom *n.* Ladies' *parts of shame.*

front bummer *n.* A woman in *comfortable shoes* who is *fond of walking holidays.*

front loaded date *n.* A social engagement where the male party's sophisticated and gallant veneer gradually slips away, until by the end of the evening he is revealed in all his boorish glory.

frostitute *n.* A lady of the night who gives her clients a service without a smile.

frothing at the gash *adj.* See *frothing at the south.*

frothing at the south *n.* Of a lady, being in a state of preternatural sexual excitement. Also *fizzing at the bung hole, gagging for it, frothing like bottled bass, dripping like a fucked fridge.*

frott *v.* To *frotter.*

frottage *v.* The act of deriving pleasure by rubbing one's clothed genitals on any convenient surface, *eg.* a door jamb, fridge, woman's *arse* on a crowded tube train.

frottage cheese *n.* The sticky end product of a successful act of *frottage.*

frotterer *n.* One who indulges in *frottage, ie.* one who *frotts.*

frube *v.* After an act of *self harm,* to squeeze the remaining drops of *spodge* out the end of one's *giggle stick,* as one would the fromage frais from one of those yoghurt-filled tubes.

fruit bowl *n.* Two plums and a banana. The collective term for a gentleman's *wedding tackle.* The *orbs and sceptre.*

fruit feeler *n.* A gentleman who is

light on his feet, and who tends to *fumble spuds.*

fruit fly *n. Fag hag.*

fruit salad *n.* A small lady blessed with a big *top bum, ie.* a small *peach* with a large *pair.*

fruit up *v.* To *toss* someone else *off,* in a public school dormitory for example. *"What's going on in here?' thundered Mr Wilkins as he burst into the showers. 'Please, Sir,' announced Venables, 'I gave Jennings a ten shilling postal order to fruit me up. Now he says he's sprained his wrist during Latin prep, and he won't give it back."* (from *Suck THIS, Jennings* by Anthony Buckeridge).

frum *v.* To *frig* a *bum.*

frump *v.* To sniff your girlfriend's younger sister's *bills. 'Not going away with the bird's family, mate?' 'No, I'm looking after the house for them. Wouldn't miss out on all that frumping for a big clock.'*

fruttocks *n.* The cheeks of the spare *arse* that certain *salad dodging* ladies possess around the front. The *bilge tanks,* front *buttocks.*

frying chips *n.* The sound a lady makes when she is seated on a *thunderbox, splitting her whiskers* and *putting out a fire.*

FTSE *1. abbrev.* Financial Times Stock Exchange. An index of the performance of the top 100 companies that allows people with pension funds to work out how much they have lost that day. *2. abbrev.* A *pappering of the kex.* Follow Through, Shit Everywhere.

fubes *n.* 13 amp, usually ginger, *pubes.* Contraction of fusewire + pubes.

fuck *1. n.* An act of copulation. A *bang. 2. v.* To *have it off, poke,* fornicate up a lady's *fadge. 3. v.* To beat someone in fisticuffs, esp. a member of the constabulary. *'Come on, let's fuck a copper!' 4. v.* To break or damage something beyond repair. *'Fucking hell. You've fucking fucked the fucking fucker'. 5. v.* To dismiss something with contempt, esp. for a game of soldiers. *6. interj.* Exclamation of surprise or disappointment. *'Oh, fuck!' 7. exclam. interrog.* Slightly stronger version of "on earth" when used in a question. *'What the fuck happened here?' 8. exclam. rhet.* A forceable refutation. *'Did you fuck my wife?' 'Did I fuck!'. 9. n.* That which is given by a person who cares. *'Isn't it dreadful about the Queen Mum dying?' 'No. I couldn't give a fuck'. 10. n* That flying thing which one who doesn't care could not give to a rolling doughnut.

fuckabulary *n.* Those twenty words which, skilfully combined and recombined, make up the entire dialogue of all the porn movies ever made. Also *cockabulary.*

fuckadillo *n.* A quirk or peccadillo in a person's sexual life. *'She always liked to do it with a Bourbon cream gripped between her knees. It was just a fuckadillo of hers.'* (Arthur Marshall being interviewed about the late Duchess of Argyll on the *Russell Harty Show,* LWT 1978).

fuck all n. Nowt. 'Did you fuck her last night at all?' 'Did I fuck. I got fuck all all night.'

fuck all in a five-year plan *adj. Can.* An attempt to justify an extravagant purchase. *'I know strictly speaking we don't need a sub-*

woofer on the stereo, but 800 quid is fuck all in a five-year plan. Now put them scissors down, love.'

fuck an air fanny *v.* To *relax in a gentleman's way.* To *have it off* with a *ghost rider.*

fuckanory *exclam.* An extension of the word *fuck,* used to express extreme shock, disappointment or annoyance.

fuckard *n. arch.* Someone who was no rocket scientist a full five hundred years before rockets were invented. A 15th century *Johnny No-Stars.* A *dolt,* a *fuckwit.*

fuck butter *n.* KY jelly.

fucker *1. n.* A disagreeable, person, often prefixed "big fat". *2. n.* Anything at all. *'Fucking hell, look at the size of that fucker!'* (Sir Christopher Wren on seeing the dome of Saint Peter's in Rome).

fucking the night *sim.* Copulating with a *yeti's welly*. *'How was it for you, Andrew, darling?' 'It was like sticking my cock out the window and fucking the night, Sarah.'*

fuck juice *n. Jitler.*

fuck me shoes *n.* Footwear worn by a *boot.*

fuck off *1. exclam.* A request for someone to leave. *2. adj.* Of a price, quote or estimate for goods or services, an over-inflated figure intended to put the customer off when the supplier doesn't want the business. *'He wants me to clean his gutters out, but I'm not going up there. I'll give him a fuck off price, £250.' 3. adj.* Descriptive of anything that is exceptionally large or intimidating. *'He came to clean me gutters out, and turned up with a big fuck off ladder. And he only charged £250. Well you wouldn't catch me going up there for that money.'*

fuck 'n' chuck *n.* A lady with whom a gentleman has had a *whirlwind one-night romance,* who does the decent thing by leaving you alone afterwards. The opposite of a *bunny boiler*. A *hump 'n' dump.*

fuckpond *n.* A little post-coital pool that forms in a depression on the bottom sheet, usually full of tadpoles. A *fuckpuddle.*

fuckpouch *n.* The overhanging lump of *ladyflesh* which casts a shadow over the main event. The *poond, blubber beret, fat hat.*

fuckshitfuckshitfuckshit *exclam.* Phrase uttered when driving a car through a particularly tight space at too high a speed.

fucksock *n.* The sort of condom one's granny would knit.

fuck stick *n.* A short, stout piece of *wood* used for *fucking* something. A penis.

fucksticks *exclam.* An expression of mild impatience. *'Fucksticks. I've left the communion wafers in the vestry.'*

fuckstrated *adj. US.* To have a severe case of *DSB.*

fuckstruck *adj. Cuntstruck.*

fuck the dog *1. v. Can.* To do absolutely nothing. *'Busy day at the office, dear?' 'Not really. Made a few calls in the morning, went to the pub at dinnertime, fucked the dog in the afternoon.' 2. v.* How the English Arts & Crafts sculptor, typeface designer and printmaker Eric Gill (1882-1940) occupied his spare time when he wasn't sculpting, designing typefaces or making prints. Well, you had to make your own entertainment in them days.

fuck trophy *n.* A baby. Usually applied to the progeny of ugly couples who need proof of their ability to achieve congress.

fuck truck *1. n.* A "UK Amateurs" film production that is unlikely to win the Best Cinematography prize at this year's Academy Awards. *2. n.* A filthy van with a mattress in the back, used for location filming in *1.*

fuckwit *n.* A simpleton, a fool, one of little intelligence, a *bollock brain, Johnny No-Stars.*

fud *n. Scot. Berkeley Hunt.* A *flingel.*

fud slush *n.* Scottish *fanny batter*, usually smeared on the face whilst eating a *haddock pastie*.

fudge *v.* To lie in the spoons position with one's partner, and *fart* so that it vibrates onto their person.

fudge factor *n.* Scientific assessment of how much a chap is *au fait with Doris Day.*

fudge packer *n.* One who packs fudge for a living, for example in the despatch department of a fudge factory.

fudge tunnel *1. n.* A tunnel made out of, or for the underground transportation of, fudge. *2. n.* The *arsehole.*

fudgeways *euph. Up the council.*

fuggit *exclam.* Ancient Egyptian curse uttered when denied a British passport.

fugly *adj.* Fucking ugly.

FUKT *acronym.* Post Office acronym for any parcel marked "fragile", which has come open as a result of being kicked around by bored sorting office staff playing football. Failed Under Kinetic Testing.

Fulham handshake *n.* A friendly greeting exchanged between two gentlemen in a public lavatory cubicle. A *WC Handy.*

fullbeams *n.* Ladies' *headlamps* which really ought to be dipped in order to avoid dazzling oncoming males.

full Belgian *n.* the opposite of a full *Brazilian.* A large, untidy *muff.* A *Judith* or *Terry Waite's allotment.*

full cuntal lobotomy *n.* A loss of reason found in men when presented with open *pissflaps.* The nervous system shuts down and all actions are controlled by the *hairy brain.*

full English *n.* A particularly greasy early morning *bang*, often followed by a big *shit* and a cup of tea.

full English breakfast *n.* A very untidy vagina that is frankly too much to face just after you get up. A big plateful of *knicker sausages, bacon strips*, fried mushrooms and baked beans.

full frontal prudity *n.* A marked reluctance to appear *in the rik* in the bedroom or locker room. Common amongst *plumpers* and *needle dicks.*

full Nelson *n.* When *wrestling oneself,* a hold involving one hand, one eye, and a funny-shaped hat.

full throttle for take off *exclam.* The only way of having a *gypsy's kiss* when in possession of a *diamond cutter.*

fumble bags *n.* Good value *knockers.*

fumbling with your change *n.* Surreptitious act of *self pollution* achieved through the pockets of your trousers.

fun bags *n.* Breasts, *knockers, thru'pennies.*

funbagtastic *exclam.* Upon seeing a glorious pair of *fleshbombs*, one might utter: *'Funbagtastic!'*

fun boy three *1. n.* Novelty pop act

of the early 1980s. *2. n.* The *fruit bowl* of the male. The *meat and two veg, fishing tackle.*

funburn *n. medic.* Painful reddening on the skin around the elbows, knees and buttocks, after *having it off* on a cheap nylon carpet.

funch *n.* Sex during your lunch hour, from fuck + lunch. A *nooner.*

fun cushions *n. Dirty pillows.*

funderwear *n.* Erotic but impractical lingerie. Purchased at great psychological expense by red-faced husbands, only to be returned to the shop the next day by thunder-faced wives. *Gash garnish,* any clothing bought from Ann Summers.

fun extractor *n.* A sour-faced woman sitting in the corner of a room, sucking all the enjoyment out of the atmosphere. *'Jesus, we went round to Tez's but he had the fun extractor turned on and it was a shit night.'*

fun junction *n. medic.* The area in a young lady's *soft undercarriage* between the *front* and *rear bottoms.* Upon arrival, a fellow might exclaim: *'Which way along the fun junction today?'*

funky hammer juice *n.* The *clam bisque* which, it is rumoured, sometimes sprays from a *dirty lady's clopper* whilst she is being *nimbed* on her *cumulus. Oyster juice.*

funky spingers n. Spooneristic *knuckle glitter.*

funny girl *n.* A *trolley dolly* who has that little bit extra. Often found in Thailand and unreliable anecdotes about a friend of a friend who went on holiday to Thailand. A *tiptop.*

fun size *n.* A very small *turd.* But bigger than a *miniature hero.*

funt *n.* The kind of advertising executive that came up with the recent "Do You Speak Micra" campaign.

funtan *n.* A short-lived, healthy glow in the face of a gentleman following a spot of *self-discipline.*

FUPA *abbrev.* Fat Upper Pussy Area. The bloated lower belly of a woman. See *gunt.*

fur burger *n. Minge, hairy pie, vertical bacon sandwich.*

furgle *1. n. prop.* Christian name of the lead singer of the Undertones. *2. v.* To copulate rudely, crudely or noisily.

furry bicycle stand *n.* A *hoop* set into concrete outside the library.

furry letterbox *n.* An eight inch wide, spring-loaded horizontal *clapping fish.* That traps the postman's fingers.

fusewire *n.* A ginger person's *thirteen amp gorilla salad. Fire down below.*

Fussell's Milk *1. n.* A thick, sweet condensed milk. *2. n.* The contents of the male *churns* after prolonged abstinence from sexual activity. *'A sackcloth shirt in place of silk / My nads like tins of Fussell's Milk.'* (from *The Ballad of Ford Open Prison* by Jonathan Aitken).

futtering *n.* A *trip to Hairyfordshire.* A bout of *front door work.*

futurehead *1. n.* In popular music, any member of the eponymous Sunderland-based 4-piece beat combo. *2. n.* The tungsten-tipped head of a *Thora* which announces its impending arrival by burrowing through the *nipsy.*

futz *n. US.* The vagina.

fuzzbox *1. n.* A guitar effects unit popular in the late seventies. A *big muff.* 2. *n.* A *minge.*

fyst *n. arch.* A 15th century foul-smelling *fart.*

fysticuffs *n. arch.* Getting punched by one's beneficiaries after *scaring the cat.*

Gg

Gabrielle *n.* A semi-successful *Velma.* A *King Harold.* Occluding one of your ladyfriend's eyes with a well-aimed *jizzbolt.* A *spoff monocle.*

gag *1. n.* A pre-*spew* spasm, often cause by a blockage in the throat - what Mama Cass did on a sandwich but Linda Lovelace didn't do on a *cock.* *2. v.* What women are doing *for it* when they want it up 'em.

gak *n. Springle, sprongle, sprungle.*

gallagher *n.* The stylised *horatio* technique employed by one who is too vertically challenged to reach the *giggle stick* using conventional methods. Named after the distinctive stance taken by eponymous Oasis frontman Liam, whereby he tilts his head back and mouths upwards into the microphone.

gallon girl *n.* An imperial-quantity-specific *gifwid.* An *eight-pinter.*

galloping knob rot *n. medic.* VD, any painful social disease resulting in the production of *gleet* and the *pissing* of razor blades.

gallop the lizard *v.* To *relax* in a *gentlemanly manner.*

gam *1. n. US.* Lady's leg. *'Hot Diggety! Check out the gams on that broad, Bub.'* *2. v. abbrev. Gamahuche.*

gamahuche *v.* To *cumulate* one's partner's *nimbus.*

gamble and lose *v. US.* The secret vice of a *man of the cloth.* To *fart* and *follow through.*

gammon and pineapple *n. Ham-on-ham.*

gammon flaps *1. n.* Hole in a farmhouse door through which pigs are able to come and go at will. *2. n. Beef curtains, gammon goalposts.* The saloon doors on a *bird's blurtch.*

gammon ring *n.* The *nipsy.*

gander's neck *n.* An extremely long, thick *gut stick* which hisses menacingly if one gets too close.

gang bang *1. n.* A *shit* song by Black Lace. *2. n.* A sexual free-for-all in a tastelessly decorated living room.

gap lapper *n.* A lesbian. Or possibly one who runs repeated circuits around a clothes shop.

gaping gill *n.* The state of an unfortunate *grumble flick* actress's *ringpiece* just after the male lead has withdrawn his *slag hammer.* Named after the famous North Yorkshire pot hole, that is 50m across and 200m deep. But not full of *spunk.* Also *granny without her teeth in, gaper.*

garbonzas *n. Gazungas.*

garboon *n.* One who *barumphs. A snufty, snurglar.*

Gardener's Question Time *1. n.* Achingly dull Radio 4 programme on which middle-aged women from Harrogate ask Eric Robson whether their compost needs pruning if there's going to be a late frost or something. *2. n.* A series of discreet enquiries made of a certain type of street gentleman by a herb enthusiast in the hope of purchasing a certain type of home-grown foliage which is a popular filling for roll-up cigarettes.

garfunkel *1. v.* To cover a public lavatory seat with paper in order to avoid contamination of one's posterior. The late *Carry On* star Kenneth Williams was by all accounts a keen *garfunkellist* when forced to evacuate his troublesome bowels in a toilet other than his own. To *scump.* *2. n.* Any *ad hoc* protective paper structure created in or on a municipal *chod bin*, "like a bridge over troubled water".

garlogies *n. Bell end* bogies.

Garrity dance *n.* The action of moving straight to the landing, knees together, after taking a *Brad* and finding nothing to wipe your *balloon knot* with. Named after the stupid dance popularised by the now deceased lead singer of Freddy and the Dreamers, who was always running out of *shitscrape.*

Gary Glitter *rhym. slang. Shitter, anus.*

gaseous clay *n.* A bowel movement in which the sufferer passes flatulence-assisted stools which look like something from a school pottery lesson and which, upon hitting the pan, '"float like a butterfly". However, because of their high exit velocity, they also "sting like a bee".

gash *1. n. Hairy axe wound* between a woman's *lisks.* The vulva. *2. n. coll. Totty, blit, bush, talent, blart.*

gash and Gary *n.* Of *jazz periodicals,* a comprehensive *below stairs* photograph of a lady in which both her *front* and *back doors* are on display. *Close-up pink.*

gash back *n.* Reward points earned by buying flowers, chocolates *etc.*, which can be redeemed at the *fish counter.* As opposed to *brownie points,* which can be cashed in *up the arse.*

gash baron *n.* A merchant trading in women of questionable repute. A *tart farmer,* a pimp.

gash card *n.* A female only method of payment for goods and services. Accepted by taxi drivers, milkmen and pizza delivery boys. *Hairy cheques.*

gash crash *n.* A motor accident, usually in early spring, caused when drivers are distracted by appealingly-attired females. *Rear ender.*

gash feathers *n.* The plumage on a *bird's nest.* Female pubic hair.

gash mark six *n.* A state of arousal in ladies. *'A lady's hairy oven must be heated to gash mark six before the gentleman slams in his lamb.'* (from *Bedroom Management* by Mrs Beeton).

gash matter *n.* Remnants of a *fish supper* on the chins of *diners at the Y.* An *11 o'clock shadow,* dried *sloom.*

gash pastie *n.* A particularly flaky vagina. *'She was so dry down there it looked like a gash pastie.'*

gashpatcho *n.* Soup which is on the menu once a month. *Moon juice, egg nog.*

gash splash *n.* The feminine equivalent of a *gentleman's wash. 'Bloody hell, Barbara. I just popped next door to borrow Jerry's watering can and I caught Margot having a gash splash in the kitchen sink.'*

gash plaster *n.* A feminine napkin, a *jam rag, dangermouse.*

gashtray *n.* The *gusset* of a lady's *farting crackers.*

gashtronome *n.* A connoisseur of *haddock pasties. Fish supper* gourmand.

gas man *n.* In a *grumble flick* production, an actor whose responsibility is to look for potential leaks in an actress being *spit-roasted* and to plug them up, rendering the said lucky lady *gastight.*

gastight *adj.* Of a *stick vid* actress, to be simultaneously bunged up in all available orifices.

gay *1. adj.* Limp of wrist, tending to ask others to shut doors, critical of the "dust in here". *2. adj.* Of retired colonels who write to the *Daily Telegraph*, a perfectly good word for happy or brightly-coloured. *3. adj.* Synonym for bad, as used by gay disc jockey Chris Moyles.

gay by *n.* A road-side area where *fruit-feelers* can congregate to *look for badgers.*

gaydar *n.* A remote imaging process developed during the war at Bletchley Park which is able to detect leather caps and Judy Garland records at substantial distances.

gaylord *n.* A good-natured term of homophobic abuse used by schoolboys to refer to anyone who is not gifted at sport or who wears glasses.

gazoo *n. Arse, bum.*

gazungas *n. Gert Stonkers.*

gearbox *n.* The *anus. 'Molly was powerless to resist. His eyes burned into hers like anthracites. His strong arms enfolded her body as she felt herself being swept away on a squall of passion. Then, in a single move Buzz pulled down her clouts, bent her over the ironing board and stuck his charlie up her gearbox.'* (From *The Cornish Milkmaid and the Astronaut* by Barbara Cartland).

geek *n.* Someone who knows too much about a subject that it isn't worth knowing anything about, *eg.* computers, PlayStation cheat codes. A *human rhubarb.*

geetle *n.* The little pointed bit of *shit* that hangs outside one's *nipsy* after one has had a *Gladys*. A *bumbob.*

geeze bag *n. Wind bag, fartpants*. A prolific *pump* artist.

geezerbird *n. Gadgy wife, half-a-gadge.* A butch-looking woman.

Geldof *v.* To impose a fairly woeful performance on an unwilling audience who feel it would be impolite not to indulge you. *'Go and find your grandad's mouth organ. He's allowed to Geldof on Christmas Day.'*

gender bender *n.* An effeminate, flowery male of indeterminate or obscure sexual orientation, *eg.* Boy George.

gender blender *n.* A person whose physical and facial appearance offer no clue as to which sex they belong to, *eg.* the man/woman who drove the 47 bus into Nottingham in the early 1980s.

genie rub *n.* Buffing up a *skin lantern* until you are granted three sticky wishes.

genital floss *n.* A skimpy bikini bottom. *Arse floss*. A thong.

genitalia failure *n.* Marshmallowing of the *cock*. The *droop.* Something inexplicable that has never happened before, usually.

genitalman *n.* A chap who lets his *hanging brain* do his thinking for him. *'Today's birthdays: Sir Anthony Hopkins, Oscar-winning actor, 68; Sir Ben Kingsley, Oscar-winning actor, 62; Paul Ross, low-rent gameshow genitalman, 49.'*

gentleman's excuse me *1. n.* A popular *meat flick* scenario in which several blokes take it in turns to *push a lady's guts in. 2. n.* The gallant post-nightclub practice of assisting a *plumper* with whom one has inadertently *copped off* into a taxi, gallantly shutting the door for her and then running like *fuck.*

grass art *n.* The Tony Hart-like placing of garden seats, picnic tables *etc.* on the lawn, so that by the end of the Summer one has created a humorous image in the turf, such as a pair of rudimentary *tits,* a *meat and two veg* or simple expletive.

gentleman's gel *n.* A soothing facial/breast cream for ladies which doubles as a hair styling product. *Heir gel.*

gentleman's machinery *n.* Polite phraseology for a fellow's *rude mechanicals.*

gentleman's reading room *n.* The one room of the house where one may comfortably relax and peruse the *Autotrader* from cover to cover. The *shitter.*

gentleman's relish *n.* A polite term for *jizz,* such as what might be used by society folk at a Buckingham Palace Garden Party.

gentleman's toe pump *n.* The frantic but pleasurable wiggling of the toes, about 15 seconds after the *jester's shoes,* that helps out the last drops of *jitler.*

gentleman's wash *n.* A hurried washing of the male genitals (usually in a pub toilet sink) in anticipation of some forthcoming sex action.

George Best undercoat *n.* The pint of milk drunk "to line the stomach" prior to going out on a drinking binge lasting several days. *'I can't be over the limit, officer. I may have necked 10 pints, but I had a George Best undercoat before I came out.'*

George *v. US.* To *roger.*

German *n.* A sexy romp involving *shitting* on each other like pigs.

German ambassador *n.* A *pastry chef.* From the amusing fact that the German word for an ambassador is Botschafter.

German cornflake *n.* A herpes scab on one's *herman gelmet.*

German eyebath *n.* A *spoff monocle.* A *Gabrielle.*

German rigger *n.* Theatrical term for one who prefers his *rigging* done in the German fashion.

German's eye *n. Jap.* How the *Jap's eye* is referred to in Japan. So called because "it never smiles".

German wings *n.* The peer-reviewed honour bestowed on one has just had their debut *scat* experience. Not the bollocks Cleo Laine-style jazz singing kind, neither.

gerotica *n.* What one gets indelibly burned into one's hard disk the moment one logs onto www.hornygrannies.com. *'Honestly officer, it's just a little bit of harmless gerotica. Someone must have downloaded it onto my laptop as a joke.'*

gertie *1. n. Fanny, minge. 2. n. coll.* Women, *blart.*

Gert Stonkers *n. Gonzagas.*

get *n. Bastard, twat.* Often applied to children, prefixed "You cheeky little..." and accompanied by a swipe to the back of the head.

get a click *v.* To *score, pull, tap off,* with a view to *getting boots.*

get boots *v. US.* To *get it on, get your end away.*

get it on *v. To get off, get it up* and/or *get your oats.*

get it up *v.* A significant part of *getting your end away* after *getting off.*

get off *v.* Of teenagers, to *get a click,* take the first step towards *getting your oats.*

get off at Edge Hill *v.* To do a *coitus*

interruptus, to withdraw before *spangling*. From Edge Hill, which is the last railway station before Liverpool Lime Street. Also *Haymarket* (Edinburgh), *Gateshead* (Newcastle), *Marsh Lane* (Leeds) *etc*.

get on at Baker Street without a ticket *euph*. To do a spot of *caboose work* without first obtaining the necessary authority. From the fact that Baker Street is the main station on the brown Bakerloo line on the *shit-hole* London Underground.

get one's sovereigns on *v.* Whilst preparing for a *pagga,* to adorn one's hands with cheap *clink,* thereby creating a budget knuckle duster effect.

get some blood in it *v.* To have the early stages of a *bonk-on, half a teacake*.

get up them stairs *exclam*. A gentleman's instruction to his wife which indicates that he has finished eating, drinking and watching football, and now wishes to retire to the bedroom to make an ungainly and flatulent attempt at sexual intercourse.

get wood *v.* To attain a state of tumescence, *get string*. *'Quick, Heinz! Roll the camera. Gunther's got wood.'*

get your end away *v.* To *get it on*.

get your oats *v.* To *get your end away*.

get your own back *v.* To sup at the *furry cup* after leaving some *hot fish yoghurt* inside the *snail's doorstep*.

GFS *abbrev. medic*. Doctor's notes terminology used to indicate that the patient may be talking out of their *arse*. Gesticulating From Sacrum.

Ghandi's flip flops *1. adj*. Descriptive of the dryness of a nun's *cunt*. *2. n. Spaniel's ears*.

ghee whizz *n*. A buttery, sludgy *piss* taken by a chap stricken with a urinary tract infection.

ghost jizz *n*. The non-existent result of a *flash in the pan*. A *map of Atlantis*.

ghost rider *n*. The beautiful, fictitious and weightless young lady that a prostrate young man imagines to be astride him during a bout of *self delight*. A *frigment* of a *tugster's* imagination.

ghost shit *n*. Stool or *dump* of which there is no trace when one stands up and turns to admire it. A *poogitive*.

gib *1. v.* To *bullshit*. *2. v.* To gatecrash. *3. v.* To stick your *old man* up a goose's *arse* and slam its head in a drawer.

gibbon gristle *n*. A funky penis.

giblets *n*. A *club sandwich*, a *ragman's coat*.

gick *n. Ir. Shit*.

gift to womankind *n*. Early morning *tent pole* in the *fart sack*.

gifwid *acronym*. A plain lass who becomes the object of a gentleman's affections when he has taken an elegant sufficiency of booze on board. Girl I Fancy When I'm Drunk.

gigglebiscuit *n*. Name given to the sort of irritatingly shallow woman who uses the pursuit of chocolate as the basis for her humour, *viz*. *'Shall I have another chocolate biscuit? Oooh, shouldn't. Naughty! Giggle, giggle'*.

gigglers *n*. Suspender belt. *Giggle band*. 'Get past there and you're laughing'.

giggle stick *n.* The *twig, giggling pin.*

giggling pin *n. Mr Happy.*

gilbo *n.* The kind of phlegm eructated during a cold, or after drinking cream soda. *Gold watch, dockers' omelette, greb.*

GILF *acronym.* Granny I'd Like to Fuck. A sexually-alluring older woman, *eg.* Marie Helvin, Kathleen Turner, Blanche off *Corrie.*

gilgai *1. n. Geol.* In the world of earth science, micro-relief characterised by small hummocks separated by shallow troughs, and hence *2. n.* A *diddy ride* on *Miss Lincolnshire.*

gillespie *n.* A diminutive male generative member. From the well-known graffito on the toilet wall in Wirral Grammar school depicting a small penis with the caption "Gillespie's dick x 4".

gimp *n.* A giant, masked *bummer* kept in a box in the basement of a gun shop.

ginger beer *rhym. slang.* A *pinch of snuff.*

gingle *adj.* The forlorn state of being ginger and single.

gink *n. Geek.* A short-sighted Colonel in a checked suit and bowler hat.

ginster *n.* A young lady who, at first sight, appears rather appetising but who leaves you feeling unsatisfied, disappointed, slightly nauseous and with a strange taste in your mouth. Derivation unknown.

Ginster's finest *n.* A *twat* that looks, smells and tastes like an out-of-date Cornish pastie. Often eaten by long distance lorry drivers.

ginvalid *n.* One who has tragically lost the use of their legs following a long battle with the Gordon's.

gip *n.* The sensation at the back of the throat heralding the arrival of *Hughie and Ralph.*

gipper *1. n.* Legless American footballer played by former late US president Ronald Reagan (now deceased) in the inspirational film *Bedtime for Bonzo. 2. n.* A *bird* who is as filthy as the bait bucket on a fishing boat.

gipsy week *n.* A *bird's* time of the month. *'DON JOHN: Marry, Borachio. How fared thee last night behind the tavern with thy wanton wench Margaret? Did'st thou fill thy boots? BORACHIO: I'faith, I did not the dirty deed. For by my troth, 'twas gipsy week. DON JOHN: Gipsy week, sayest thou? Wherefore is it called thus, sirra? BORACHIO: I'll vouchsafe you for wherefore 'tis called thus, my liege, for when I didst put my hand down her pants, I didst get my palm red.'* (from *Much Ado About Wanking* by William Shakespeare).

giraffe piss *n.* The standard method of urination when in possession of a *panhandle, ie.* to stand with one's legs wide apart and angle the *tent pole* down towards the bowl in the manner of a long-necked cameleopard drinking at a water hole. *Full throttle for take-off.*

giraffe shit *n.* Any stool passed, which causes one to stretch one's neck to get away from the smell.

giraffiti *n.* Vandalism which is spray-painted very, very high.

girlpop *n. Moip, blip, fanny batter.* Secretions of the *Bartholin's* gland.

girly goatee *n.* A lady's pubic effusion, which can be rubbed and tugged at thoughtfully during moments of contemplation.

girobics *n.* The regular fortnightly exercise a long term jobseeker gets every other Thursday when he lifts his lazy fat *arse* off the sofa and ventures forth to collect his *beer tokens*.

giro jolly *adj.* Subject to the euphoric mental state attained by the unemployed on Thursdays.

giroscope *n.* A satellite dish. *Debtors' dish.*

gisp *n. medic.* A term used by doctors in North Wales to describe the bit between the *balls* and the *arsehole. The barse, tintis, great, ABC.*

give Ronaldo a rub down *v.* Celebrity slaphead *wanking* terminology. *Strangle Kojak, take Captain Picard to warp speed, polish Telly Savalas up and down until spunk comes out of his head.*

give the dog a bone *v.* To sexually satisfy a female before one goes rolling home.

Gladys *rhym. slang.* To defecate. From Gladys Knight = shite.

gland grenades *n.* Hairy, wrinkled *spunk* bombs that have a tendency to *go off* in one's hand if they are not *tossed* far enough.

glandlord *n.* The owner of a property who prefers his tenants to pay the rent with their *hairy chequebook*.

gland of hope and glory *n.* A magnificent *custard cannon* which, at the rousing climax to a performance, would bring the crowd to its feet at the Royal Albert Hall, just before you were bundled off the stage, sectioned under the Mental Health Act and put on the Sex Offenders Register.

glandscape *n.* The breathtaking *panhandloramic whacknicolour* vista that opens up before a chap's *hog's eye* whilst he is enjoying a *crescent wank*.

glandstand *n.* A Saturday afternoon erection, starting 5 minutes before *World of Spurt*.

glandular fervor *n. medic.* A disease affecting men which causes them to masturbate like nobody's business.

glarsefibre *n.* The bad-matted yet rust-proof *shite/arsecress* matting effect achieved on a catastrophically ineptly-wiped *freckle*. From the resultant disaster area's resemblance to a crudely-repaired body panel on a crashed vehicle.

Glasgow postman *n.* A thief. After the remarkable frequency with which birthday cards, parcels and giros go missing in the Glasgow postal system.

Glasgow salad *n.* Chips.

Glasgow shower *n.* A quick swipe of underarm deodorant used as an alternative to washing when in a hurry or Glaswegian.

glassback *n.* A person with a poor health record at work. One whose constant illnesses keep them from work, but don't prevent them going to the pub at night or refereeing Premiership football matches at the weekend.

glassblower's pinch *n.* Final and desperate act of urine retention. Last ditch effort before turning your pantaloons into *tramp's trousers*.

Glastonbury main stage *euph.* The state of the *chod bin* following a harrowing post-Curry Capital visit, when it is left looking like the torrential-rain-soaked muddy fields of the popular alternative culture festival. Also *Ray Mears's dinner.*

Glastonbury tailback *n.* The uncanny ability of some people, usually women, to *squeeze their fig* for five days when lavatorial conditions are not quite to their liking.

Glaswegian siesta *n.* A night in a police cell.

glaze a knuckle *v.* To *wank.*

glebe end *n. Lincs.* A quaint colloquial expression for the *herman gelmet,* the origins of which are lost in the mists of time.

glee *n. Spoff, spadge, spunk. 'Blimey, when that Konnie from Blue Peter comes on telly, I can hardly contain my glee.'*

gleet *n. medic.* Unpleasant mucopurulent discharge caused by *cock rot.*

Glenshane pass *n. rhym. slang.* Alternative to the *Khyber*, up which a *bumsex*-fixated Northern Ireland resident could take his missus. *'Don't take me up the Glenshane Pass tonight, Ian. It's giving me terrible piles.'*

gliffet *n.* The scrotal *oxter.* That warm, moist channel between a gentleman's *nadsack* and his inner thigh, where a particularly piquant variety of sweaty cheese matures in the dark.

Glist *1. n.* Julie Walters's favourite dishwasher tablet. *2. n. Ball glaze.*

glistening for it *adj.* Of a lady, sexually aroused, *fizzing at the bung hole. "And we know for a fact, that Lady Marchmaine could not have killed the Bishop,' added Miss Marple waspishly. 'She had ridden from Barnchester to the Manor House in twenty minutes. When she arrived she was glistening for it and spent the afternoon with Brigadier Lewerthwaite in his quarters. So YOU, Nurse Hatpin, must be the murderer!"* (from *Ten Pairs of Knickers* by Agatha Christie).

glitterati *n. coll.* Celebrity paedophiles.

glitter ball *n.* An under 16s' disco.

glob *v.* To emit a viscous fluid slowly and rhythmically out the end of the *giggling pin.*

globes *n.* Hanging objects of joy.

gloke *n.* A woman who exhibits pseudo-blokish behaviour such as watching football, drinking beer, farting *etc*, in the mistaken belief that this will result in her being regarded as one of the lads, *eg.* Sara Cox. A *ladette.*

glorious goodwood *1. n.* Horse-racing meeting. *2. n.* A truly magnificent erection that impresses the passing populace with its magnitude, girth and lovely mane.

glory hole *n. US.* In a *cottage*, that hole made by *bosching,* through which the Bishop of Durham could touch a farmer's *cock* nearly 40 years ago.

glory wipe *n.* The token single sheet polish required after passing the rare but pleasant stool which slips out *like an otter off the bank*, leaving no trace of *Sir Douglas* on or around the *balloon knot.*

gloy *n. Mess,* semen. From the paper glue used in schools. *'Oops! I think I've just trod on the gloy bottle.'*

gluebook *n.* A well-read *art pamphlet* that is no longer openable.

glue gun *n.* Tool used to stick the pages of *niff* mags together.

Gnasher's loot *n.* A promiscuous woman's sexual history, *ie.* a long string of *big sausages.*

gnat's cock hair *n.* A standard imperial measure equal to approximately one and a quarter eighty-eighths of a sixteenth of an inch. A phrase often used to describe any small distance. Often shortened to a *gnat's*. Also *bawhair. 'How far do you want this filing cabinet moving?' 'Oh, just a gnat's cock hair towards the wall, that's all.'*

gnome's hat *n.* At the top of a toilet-dwelling heap of excrement, the drooping conical summit which pokes out above the surface of the water.

gnomon *1. n.* Obscure word known only to the likes of Stephen Fry and Robert Robinson, describing the little sticky-up bit which casts a shadow on a sundial. *2. n.* The little sticky-up bit which casts a shadow on an under-endowed man, *eg.* The Rt Hon Jack Straw MP.

gnosh *v.* To suck a penis in an enthusiastic and extremely noisy fashion.

go ahead London *exclam.* A humorous term used to break the ice when tweaking the nipple of a woman one has only just been introduced to. 6 months probation.

go all the way to Cockfosters *v.* To have a *full portion of greens* with plenty of *summer cabbage. 'I thought I'd have to go home via the Billy Mill roundabout, but she took me all the way to Cockfosters.'*

goal hanger *n.* An annoying, predatory male friend who allows you to work your midfield magic on a girl in a nightclub before stealing your glory by nipping *in the box* for a simple tap in.

goalmouth scramble *n.* A hugely exciting writhing mass of arms and legs which includes lots of intimate contact, but doesn't end up with anyone actually *scoring*. Frantic *heavy petting*.

gob *1. n.* The *North and South. 2. v.* To spit, *hockle. 3. n.* A body of *lung butter* so propelled. A *greb*, a *greenie*.

gob job *n.* A *chewie*, a *sucking off*.

gobbie *n.* See *gob job*.

gobble *n.* Noise made by turkeys.

gobbler *n.* An eager *fellator/fellatrix*. One who frequents a particular Gulch on Hampstead Heath.

gobbler's cough *n. medic.* Condition arising from the build up of genital detritus in the throats of over eager *noshers. White owl pellets.*

gobshite *n.* Someone who talks *crap*. *eg.* any contributor to *Thought for the Day*.

gock *n.* The male version of the *gunt*. Unsightly lower abdominal protuberance filled with residual beer and pies. From gut + cock. *'What's that on the top of your head, Gillian?' 'It's your gock, Geoff.'*

go commando *v.* To *freeball*. To go out *undercrackerless*.

go cunt up *adj. Arse over tit.* Pear-shaped, badly awry. *'Houston, Houston, we have a problem. There's blowback in Challenger's solid rocket boosters. It looks like things could go cunt-up.'* (Silus T Oysterburger, Mission Controller, KSC Florida).

God goggles *n.* The imaginary optical accessories created by decades of religiously-inspired celibacy, which cause a priest to get a raging diamond cutter when he sees a sixty-year-old nun with a moustache.

Godzilla *n.* A ferocious burp, accompanied by clawing motions with the hands.

go faster stripe *n.* A *fanny bush* shaved into a more aerodynamic design. *Pires's chin.*

go for poke *v.* To commit all one's available resources towards the sole aim of achieving some sort of sexual congress.

going down *1. v.* Doing the oral sex on someone, *giving head. 2. exclam.* Expression often used to describe the imminent movement of a lift.

going for a McShit *v.* Visiting the bogs in fast food restaurants when one has no intention of buying the food. If challenged by a suspicious manager, the assurance of a food purchase after the toilet visit is known as a *McShit with lies.*

going for a thong *n.* The act of habitually manoeuvering oneself behind women who are sitting down and leaning forward such that there is a gap between their trousers and their underwear, in the vain hope of catching a glimpse of the tops of their *officers' laces.*

going live *1. n.* A former Saturday morning children's TV programme starring prostitute dungeon visitor Jamie Theakston. *2. n.* Sex performed without a prophylactic appliance. *Riding bareback,* a *bath without wellies, skinnydipping.*

going to the judges *euph.* An indeterminate end to a bout of drunken sex.

go interactive *v.* To *tickle* a lady's *bean.* From the BBC teletext instruction to "press the red button".

gold watch *n.* A small clock or chronometer, made of precious metal which leaps from the throat after a cough. A *docker's omelette, greb, sheckle, prairie oyster.*

golden bogey *n.* A nose-stud.

golden deceiver *n.* A blonde *piece* who looks gorgeous from behind, but is actually a right *dog* from the front. A *backstabber,* a *back beauty.*

golden goal *1. n.* Highly popular innovation in football matches whereby, during extra time, the team that scores first immediately wins the match, thus leaving the opposition gutted. *2. n.* The act of *scoring* in extra time at the end of a night *on the razz,* thereby leaving your mates sick as parrots. After drawing a blank at the club and/or pub, pulling a stunner on the bus home or at the kebab shop.

golden handshake *n.* A rather sloppy *gypsy's kiss.*

golden rivet *n. naval.* The *freckle,* the *dot,* the apple of the *captain's* eye for *rear admirals* who *swab the poop deck. Spice island, bottery bay.*

golden shower *n.* To be *pissed* on by a big German for a saucy treat. *Water sports.*

golden slumbers *1. n.* Title of a ballad written by the 16th/17th century English poet and dramatist Thomas Dekker. *2. n.* Song penned by Paul McCartney, using copyright-free lyrics from *1.*, featured as part of the sixteen-minute medley which ends side two of the Beatles *Abbey Road* album. *3. n.* Nocturnal micturition. *Pissing* the bed.

golden ticket *1. n.* In Roald Dahl's *Charlie and the Chocolate Factory*, the magical token which allowed Charlie Bucket and his aged grandfather to visit Willie Wonka's fantastic confectionary works, and thus *2. n.* In a sexual relationship, permission to enter the wife's mysterious and exciting *chocolate factory,* though preferably without an elderly relative in tow.

goldfrapp *n.* A *Jonathan* executed whilst wearing a *jubber ray.* A *posh wank, French wank, boil in the bag.* A *birthday bash.*

golf ball *n.* An oversized, pock-marked *clit* discovered lying in an area of rough.

golf ball arse *n. medic.* Condition of the *buttocks* after sitting for too long on a beaded car seat.

golf tees *n. Bruce Lees.*

golfer's divot *n.* A shapeless clump of *pubage* flying through the air.

gonad glue *n. Gloy, gunk.*

gonga *n.* A *docker's omelette* that occasionally has to be swallowed rather than served up on the pavement.

gonk *1. n.* A *shit* fairground prize, made out of stolen cats, that looks like a miniature cross between Gail Tilsley and Don King. *2. n.* A *rub-a-tug shop* punter.

gonzagas *n. Guns of Navarone.*

Gonzo's nose *sim.* Descriptive of a gentleman's sorry-looking, unresponsive *trouser truncheon.* Named after the *Muppet Show* character. *'I'd love to give you one, darling, but I've had ten pints and I've got a cock like Gonzo's nose.'*

gonzo vid *n.* Low budget, unscripted pornography where the cast wait until the cameras start rolling before going to the toilet. An acquired taste.

goober *n. Aus.* Antipodean term for *cock venom. 'Strewth, Rolf, what the billabong have you been doing? My underwear drawer's full of goober.'*

gooch *n.* The *barse, tintis, Finsbury bridge, great.*

good Charlotte *n.* The powerful early morning sexual frisson experienced when listening to sultry-voiced Radio 4 newsreader Charlotte Green on the Today programme. A *good Charlotte* can occasionally be somewhat disturbing; for example when she is reading out the death toll in some terrible disaster or the subtly-veiled details of the bizarre erotic adventures of a disgraced Liberal Democrat leadership candidate.

good cop, bad cop *n.* Of two gentlemen, to be faced with the classic *cruiser and tug* combination at the bar; they must chat up both, knowing one will achieve a good "cop", the other a bad one.

good listener *n.* A man who is *good with colours, light on his feet.* One who *likes shopping.*

goods to declare, have *v.* To take the *red channel at customs.*

good time *n.* Street prostitute parlance for a fucking awful time.

good with colours *adj.* Of a gentleman, to be adept at *jumping over puddles.*

gooey in the fork *n.* Of a lady, to be not far short of *dripping like fucked fridge.*

go off *v.* Of women, to pass their "best before" date. *'I tell you what, I wouldn't mind nobbing that Charlotte Church.' 'You'd best get your finger out and do her before she goes off, then.'*

Goofy's ears *n.* Dangling labia, particularly pendulous *gammon flaps.*

goo gargle *n.* A hot protein mouthwash, which is spat out as opposed to being swallowed.

google *n.* *Spunk* produced as a result of internet porn.

googlewhack *v.* To type a bit of *crumpet*'s name into the popular internet search engine with the specific intention of *relaxing in a gentleman's way* over the resulting "hits".

goo gun *n.* A *pocket paste dispenser, jizz stick.*

goolies *n.* The colloquialism for testicles least likely to offend a grandparent. *'Oi nan. Get your glasses on and I'll show you me shaved goolies.'*

goose *n.* A light-hearted sexual assault, often taken in bad spirit by po-faced lesbians.

goose, shit like a *v.* To suffer from a loose motion in the *back body. 'Don't drink that cloudy pint, Kirsty, or you'll be running off to shit like a goose all the way through Newsnight Late Review.'*

gooze *v.* Of a *bongo vid* actress, to make a big show of pretending to swallow her leading man's *milm* after a facial *money shot. 'That bint ain't swallowin', she's just goozin'.'*

gorblimey *adj.* A type of trouser popular among council tenants in the 1950s.

gordon and tony *euph.* Amusingly satirical way of referring to a lady's *pleasure holes* (until mid-2007 anyway), because it's a *cunt* next door to an *arsehole.*

gorilla autopsy *n.* A large, untidy and hairy *clout,* such as the one on Lindsey from the Tartan Arms, Lloret de Mar, circa 2002.

gorilla salad *n.* Ladies' pubic hair. *Twat thatch.*

gorilla's armpit *n.* A *fanny* which would daunt all but David Attenborough.

gorilla's breakfast *1. n.* A *shit* that smells good enough to turn around and eat again right out of the *pan,* as gorillas do in the wild on winter mornings. *2. n.* An affectionate name for an early morning *pan cracker.*

gorillas in the mist *n.* *Boilers* who, through an alcoholic fog, take on siren-like qualities. Can lead to *dances with wolves.*

go through the gears *v.* To perform a *fart* of continuous melody, going up in pitch every few seconds, making a sound like a London bus pulling away.

got mice *adj.* Of a lady, to be *visited by Aunt Flo.* To be *up on blocks.*

go to Barnsley *v.* To *do* the *tradesman's entrance* of a lady. Named after the famous South Yorkshire *shit hole.*

gouch *n.* The *biffin bridge, chin rest, taint, tinter, notcher.*

go ugly early *v.* A nightclub or party gambit. To settle for a keen *swamp donkey* rather than chasing something better and risking ending up with nothing. To *stick at 15. 'Good piss up last week, Gaz. I saw you went ugly early.'*

Govan tumbleweed *n.* Those blue and white-striped bags made of the thinnest imaginable plastic, available from corner shops, cheap off-licences and vendors of deep fried foods, that end up blowing around the streets of the self-styled Glasgow borough of "exceptional opportunity". Govan tumbleweed that ends up stuck in a tree is known as *Govan bunting.*

GPMG *abbrev. milit.* A lady who

looks attractive at a distance but is not quite so alluring when viewed from nearby. Named after the army's General Purpose Machine Gun, which is "good at range but unbelievably messy close up".

grace period *n.* The few precious hours after a hot *cuzza* during which one can *tread on a duck* without the fear of *following through. 'I tried Abdul Latif's Curry Hell, reputedly the hottest curry in the world. Upon the first taste, my eyes melted and my throat burst into flames, and with a grace period of just forty-five seconds I was straight off to the lavvy. On my 2-mile journey home I had to stop the car on 173 occasions, each time not knowing which end to point at the gutter.'* (Restaurant Review by Jonathan Meades, *The Times Magazine*).

Graham Norton's hair *n.* Descriptive of one's *barnet* after being *seagulled* by a gentleman, or after walking under Status Quo's hotel room balcony.

granbies *rhym. slang.* Term widely used in Leicestershire to describe the male testicles or *clockweights*. From the now-defunct concert venue Granby Halls = orchestras. *'He'll be alright in a couple of minutes, your Holiness. He's just had a kick in the granbies, that's all.'*

Grand Old Duke of York *n.* An unconvincing erection, a mix of duty and apathy, one that is "neither up nor down". A *lard on*, a *dobber, half a teacake.*

grandad erector *n.* A sight so sexually stimulating that it could raise the dead.

grandalf *n.* An old *bird* with a *wizard's sleeve.*

grandchav *n.* One who is blessed with grandchildren whilst still young enough to fully enjoy the experience. A *Cardiff grandmother. 'Mum. Could you help me with my homework, please?' 'Go and ask your grandchav, I've not finished mine yet.' 'But she's still doing hers too.'*

Grandma *rhym. slang.* An act of defecation. From the dimly-remembered children's television character Grandma Flump = dump.

grandma's party *n.* A bout of masturbation. Wearing a bowler hat. See *reggae like it used to be.*

grandma's perfume *n.* The smell of *piss. Eau de toilette publique.*

grandma's Wolsley *n.* The greying *minnie-moo* of an old dear which hasn't given anyone a *ride* since the 60s. Something with a pool on the floor under it, that smells of leather, petrol and perished rubber.

gran flakes *n.* The contents of a nursing home Hoover bag.

granny batter *n.* KY jelly.

granny magnet *n.* A male who, having had no luck finding a ladyfriend of his own age, is forced to *cop off* with a right old *slapper, eg.* the *blotto* one with the incontinent laugh being held up by her mates in the kebab shop.

granny's attic *euph.* An unattractive lady, *ie.* one of whose cobwebby *clopper* it could humorously be said, "nobody's been up there in years".

granny's elbow *n.* An unpleasantly-elongated *ball sack.* A *rantallion.*

granny's hat, muff like your *sim.* Descriptive of a particularly hairy *otter's pocket,* possibly smelling strongly of mothballs and damp.

granny's kiss *n.* From a gentleman's perspective, the experience of performing *cumulonimbus* on a badly-maintained *clopper.* Not unlike receiving a smacker from one's sloppy, pucker-lipped grandmother sporting a *Magnum PI* moustache and tasting like she's just eaten a gammon butty.

granny's mouth *n.* A saggy, loose-lipped, whiskery *cunker.*

granny's oysters *n.* Elderly female genitalia.

granny's purse *n.* The condition of one's *clappers* after a comprehensive bowel evacuation, *ie.* firmly snapped shut.

grape smugglers *n.* Tight gentlemen's briefs, as worn by *grumble flick* stars in the 1970s. *Noodle benders.*

grappling hooks *n.* The unyielding fasteners on a lady's *tit pants.*

grassy knoll *1. n.* Site where the second gunman stood during the assassination of JF Kennedy. *2. n.* A *ladygarden*.

grated carrot *n.* Coarse, ginger-coloured *gorilla salad,* suitable for a *vagetarian* diet. Rusty *fusewire.*

grating the cheddar *n. medic.* To accidentally scrape one's *lid* along the zip of one's *flies. "I say, Jeeves. Could you take these trousers to my tailor and have him replace the zip fastenings with good old buttons,' I croaked. 'I only bought them last week and I've grated the cheddar four times. My poor cock end is ripped to pip, don't you know."* (from *Swallow it All, Jeeves* by PG Wodehouse).

grattan *1. adj.* Descriptive of a state of ill-health. *'Shut the curtains will you, love? I must have had a bad pint last night and I feel right grattan.' 2. v.* To masturbate over desperate material in the absence of anything better to masturbate over. See *grattanification.*

grattanification *n.* A young man's use of the bra pages of his mum's catalogue in order to fuel his single-handed progress towards an *argosm*.

grave-sniffer *n.* A senior citizen. A *coffin-dodger, oxygen thief.*

greasebox *n.* A *quim*.

greasy waistcoat pocket *n.* A shallow, well oiled *fanny* large enough for a thumb to be inserted. Or a gold watch.

great escape *n.* A *breakout* that is planned well in advance and released surreptitiously over a period of time. And probably shaken nonchalantly from the bottom of the trouser legs whilst whistling.

greatest hits *rhym. slang.* The *shits. 'Bloody hell, Egon. You're a shadow of your former self. What happened?' I went for a delicious eight-course slap-up banquet at the Curry Capital, Bigg Market, Newcastle upon Tyne three weeks ago and I've had the greatest hits ever since. I tell you, I've a good mind to dock them a star in my next Good Food Guide.'*

great, the *n.* That bit of the male anatomy which is between the back of the *gooch* and the front of the *barking spider.* The *barse, tintis, notcher* or, more crudely, the p*rineum. So-called because any time one's missus goes anywhere near it, one exclaims: "Ooh, that's great!"

Great Yarmouth gnomes *n.* Washing machines, broken tellies and *pissed* mattresses used as garden ornaments in the *shit* Norfolk town.

greb *n. Hockle.*

Greek *n.* Any sex games in which the *rusty bullet hole* is centrally involved. *Swedish.*

Greek sauna *n. A Dutch oven.*

Greek tip *n.* A stray pubic hair adhering to coinage that is handed over in shops, restaurants, *etc. Copper wire.*

green goddess *1. n.* A middle-aged woman doing star jumps and running on the spot on breakfast telly in the 80s. *2. n.* One of those laughably ancient-looking emergency tenders which were brought out of mothballs regularly during the 80s to take the place of proper fire engines during strikes. *3. n.* A vintage, dumpy-looking *bird* who will *do the job* in the absence of a flashier, modern-looking model.

green wings *n.* An unwanted accolade. Sex with a *clappy slapper.*

Greggs dummy *n.* A chicken and mushroom-filled pacifier used by teenaged mums to soothe their teething infants.

Greggs revenge *n.* Descriptive of the delightfully rich aroma produced when one *steps on a duck* after consuming a Greggs Steak Bake.

grey flannel *n.* A pensioner's *opera curtains. Granny's oysters, biltong.*

greyhound *1. n.* A very short skirt, *ie.* one that is only one inch from the "hare". *2. n.* An hilarious heterosexual changing room impression involving an erect *chopper* and a champagne wire.

grey wings *n.* The honour awarded to someone who has indulged in a *rumpular pumpular* act with a ladyfriend of more mature aspect. A medal for a chap who has bravely faced up to a spot of *gash in the attic.*

grimble *n.* Glossy, American marshmallow-hard pornography, usually shown on Bravo on Friday nights.

grime bubble *n. A fart, air biscuit.*

grimsby *n.* A mingsome *minge.*

Grimsby meal *n.* An unpleasant northern *fish supper.*

grimquims *n.* A collection of unsightly *butchers' dustbins, stamped bats, ripped sofas, ragman's coats* and *badly-packed kebabs. 'Did you see last month's Razzle stack? What a bunch of grimquims.'*

grimshits *n.* A portmanteau term for faeces distinctly lacking in cohesion. *Fizzy gravy, bubblepoo* and *bicycle chains* are all *grimshits.*

grind *v.* To have sex with all the fervour of an old bus going up a steep hill in Lancashire. ie, if you stopped, you would be unable to start again.

gripper *n.* More light-hearted heterosexual changing room horseplay, this time where somebody grabs hold of one's *arse cress* and gives it a great big yank. *2. n.* Unusual christian name of a bully who featured in early series of the gritty school-based kids' soap *Grange Hill. 3. n.* Midlands term for one who partakes of solitary hand-based pleasures.

gripping the lather *n.* The precise moment when a spot of innocently pleasurable bath-night self-soaping becomes an undeniable act of filthy beastliness. Again.

gristle thistle *n.* Persistent purple-headed weed, commonly occurring in *moss cottage* gardens.

grizzly bear pit *n.* The *pan* of a

blocked *chod bin*, viewed from above.

groaner *n.* A *Thora* that is so big that it cannot be expelled without vocal assistance. A *U-blocker.*

grogan *n. Scot.* A *log,* a *Douglas.*

groinery *n.* The craft of *morning woodwork*, in which only one *handtool* is used.

groin grease *n.* The sweat that builds up around the inner thighs and *knackers* of a *salad dodger* on a hot day. *Arse feta.*

grolsch *n.* An under-lubricated *snatch, ie.* one that is "not ready yet" and needs another minute's brisk rubbing.

grommet *n.* 1950s *Totty.*

gronk *n. RAF.* To have a *shit*. *"Bandits at three O'clock!' ejaculated Algy. 'Great!' replied Biggles. 'I've got half an hour to have a big smelly gronk!"* (from *Biggles Drops his Fudge* by Capt. WE Johns).

gronk board *n. milit.* A panel where photographs of the ugliest women *banged* by sailors are displayed for the amusement of the entire ship's crew.

groodies *n.* How *charms* are referred to in the film *A Clockwork Orange.*

groovy legs *n. med.* Post prolonged *doggy-style* sex wobbly numbness in the lower limbs. *'I wasn't sure how long I was back scuttling her, but it must have been ages, because when I stopped I had my groovy legs on.'*

G-rope *n.* A *G-string* for the fatter lass.

grope fruits *n. Shirt potatoes, fat rascals.*

grotdog *n.* A lower-grade hotdog, of the sort which might be purchased at Walthamstow Dog Stadium, to pick a location entirely at random.

grot slot *n.* The married man's 30-minute long internet pornography download window which occurs whilst his wife is at the shops.

grotter *n.* The *snatch.*

groundhog lay *n.* A depressingly familiar intercourse routine between a man and his long term girlfriend.

groundhog wank *1. n.* A dismal attempt at *self abuse* which repeatedly peters out, leaving the *wanksmith* with no choice but to start again. *2. n.* The overly-familiar *tug* sequence of a *pornogamist* who only owns one *art pamphlet.*

ground zero *n.* The *freckle* the morning after an evening of heavy *refreshment.*

Grove Hill decking *n. Al fresco* horizontal timber structures typically adorning the front and rear gardens of homes in one of the less affluent estates in Middlesbrough. Pallets.

grow a tail *v.* To defecate, *build a log cabin. Snip a length of spine.*

growl at the badger *v. Scot.* To noisily *nosh* a *beaver*. To loudly *nod at a stoat.* To *gnosh.*

growler *1. n.* The sort of meat and potato pie sold from one of the various catering outlets inside the ground at Gigg Lane, Bury, in the mid-1980s. So-called because within 30 minutes of eating the pie, one's stomach would begin to growl. A *Cornish nasty. 2. n.* The *shithouse. 3. n.* A semi-submerged *dreadnought,* nine tenths of which lies hidden below the surface.

grown-up book *n. Self-help pamphlet, jazz mag, niff mag, noddy book.*

grub *n. Barse cheese.*

grubscrew *1. n.* An act of intercourse performed at work during a lunchbreak, perhaps in a store room or on a photocopier. *2. n.* A tiny, shrivelled *yang*, found on Egyptian mummies, Siberian nudists, Bobby Davro and the Rt Hon Jack Straw MP.

gruffle bag *n.* That strangely satisfying feeling of having *airy pillows* in your *undercrackers,* experienced just after you *cleave off* an *anal announcement.*

grumbelows *n.* A retail purveyor of *seed catalogues.* A *bongo store.*

grumbilical cord *n.* The sturdy wire that links one's satellite dish to one's Sky box, allowing ladies' *grotters* to appear on one's television screen.

grumble *1. rhym. slang.* The vagina, *quaynt, placket, Berkeley.* From grumble and grunt = cunt. *2. n.* Any form of *Frankie Vaughan* featuring *tits, arses and grumbles.*

grumble bee *n.* A *tugster* who is unable to select a favourite *art pamphlet,* and so flits from one to another.

grumbled *1. adj.* Of *tescosexual* gentlemen, the state of being caught mid-way through an act of *jazz*-fuelled onanism, when their spouse returns unexpectedly early from a shopping expedition. *2. adj.* The unfortunate situation when one's mother/wife/cleaning lady stumbles across one's stash of *art pamphletry.* Caught in possession of pornography. *'Mr Baddiel, I was cleaning your room, and I found 56 tons of hard core anal pornography on top of the wardrobe.' 'Oh, no! I've been grumbled!'*

grumblehound *n.* A creature whose nose, upon entering the newsagent, can be seen twitching in the direction of the top shelf.

grumble in the jungle *n. Rhythmic cliterature* found whilst taking the dog for a walk in the woods. That which is found under the *bongo bush. Grummer.*

grumbleweed *1. n.* A Syd Little lookalike, usually the director's brother, who manages to poke a selection of *cliterati,* who would normally not even wipe their *arse* with him. *2. n.* A miraculous patch of undergrowth where discarded pornography can reliably be located. *3. n.* One who has masturbated so many times in one session that he can no longer muster the strength to lift the pages of his *scud mag.* One who has *wanked* himself into enfeeblement. *4. n.* A token *fluff tuft* on an otherwise clean-shaven porn starlet's *snatch.* A *clitler. 5. n.* Any member of the West Yorkshire-based comedy combo, specialising in gasmask-related songs and disturbingly accurate impressions of Sir Jimmy Savile.

grumbleweeds *n.* The matted, sticky mess of *friar's weeds* which one is left with after surprising oneself with a startlingly copious payload of *spoo,* and which will require a good few yards of *shit scrape* to mop up.

grummer *n. abbrev. Biff mags, art pamphlets.*

grump on *n.* Reluctant *wood.* An erection that has to be cajoled to tumescence. Prevalent amongst *jazz* actors, *slag night* strippers and men married to Janet Street-Porter.

grundle *n. US.* The *barse.*

grunter *n.* A much loved and well

respected senior citizen who fought in two world wars *etc*., but who now cannot get off the sofa without grunting.

grunties *n. Jobbies*, faeces, *poo*.

grunts *n*. The type of *fugly boots* whose blurred Polaroid pictures appear on the readers' wives pages of *tijuana bibles*.

guard dogs *n*. A pack of fierce hounds that accompany their attractive friend, preventing any bloke from trying his luck.

guardsman's hat, fanny like a *sim*. Descriptive of an enormous black, hairy *snatch* that could, if one wasn't careful, slip down over one's eyes. Also, *busby berkeley*.

guard's parcel *n*. A present that turns out to be a disappointment. Derived from the advice given to those who live near a railway line frequented by freight trains, *ie*. never pick up what looks like a discarded package near the tracks, it may contain the guard's excrement if he's been taken short. *'Pulling up Beattock, the guard needs a shite / But there's no bogs till Glasgow, much later tonight. / In time-honoured fashion he empties his arsehole / Into brown paper to make a guard's parcel.'* (from *The Shite Train* by WH Auden).

guard's van *n*. When *pulling a train*, the least desirable position in the queue. *'Bagsy I'm not in the guard's van fellas.'* The last *pink carriage* into *fanny* station.

Guatemalan taco *n*. A sexual act which makes a *Cleveland steamer* seem positively salubrious.

gubbed *adj. Trousered, wankered, shitfaced, arseholed*.

gubbs *n. Thru'penny bits*.

guck *n. Muck, spod, gunk, mess, filthy concrete*.

guff *v*. To *let one go, step on a frog*.

guff cloud *n*. The noxious, green vapour produced by *dropping one's hat*. *Carbon dibaxide*.

guided muscle *n*. The *veiny bang stick*.

Guinness rope *n*. A length of stout, dense *cable* which blocks the *pan* after a heavy feed of the black stuff. It takes 119 seconds to lay the perfect length of *Guinness rope*.

guinnets *n*. Jet black *dangleberries* that cling to the *arse* after a night drinking the famed stout. *Buoys from the black stuff*.

gums around me plums, get your *exclam*. An irresistible romantic overture made by a male to a female.

guns of Navarone *n. Whoppers, tits, fleshbombs, milky swingers*.

gunt *n. Can. Bunt*.

gurgler *n*. The toilet, *shite pipe*, drain. *'Have you got a coat hanger? Only I was spewin' up last night an' I coughed me fuckin' falsies down the gurgler.'*

gurk *1. v*. To burp. *2. v. Aus*. To *guff*.

gurkha's sword *n*. A *hard on* which has to be used before it can be put away. From the not necessarily true belief that a member of the tough Nepalese regiment must draw blood with his kukri before he is allowed to return it to its sheath.

gurning chimp *n*. A particularly expressive *fanny*.

gurniture *n*. Orthodontic bracery.

gurnturd *n*. A troublesome and stubborn *digestive transit*, the successful passing of which necessitates the pulling of a Popeye-style grimace. From the comedy facial gymnastics practised by toothless

West Cumbrian drunks sticking their heads through horsecollars during patronising "local colour" pieces on *Nationwide*.

guru Palm and the five pillars of wisdom *n. Madam Palm and her five lovely daughters.* A *wanking spanner.*

gusset *1. n.* The bottom of the *hoggers* area of a woman, the *fairy hammock's drip tray. 2. n. coll. Flange, totty, fanny, blart.*

gusset graze *n. medic.* The friction burn on the side of one's *old man* incurred when administering *a bit of the other* to a young lady whilst tenderly riving her nethergarmentry to one side.

gusset icing *n.* The decorative crust which has fallen off a *bird's clown's pie,* giving her a *gusset like a fish fryer's cuff. Fanny batter.*

gusset nuzzler *n.* A *fanny nosher*, a *lady golfer*, a *lesbian*.

gusset pianist *n. Invisible banjo* player. *'I've heard she plays the gusset piano.'*

gusset shot *n.* The thrilling glimpse of a young lady's *drip tray* with which an observant fellow is occasionally rewarded when watching *birds* dismounting from their bicycles. Perhaps whilst hiding in the bushes outside the nurses' home or a hall of residence. A *sneaky peek.*

gusset sugar *n.* Tooth-rotting *muff-druff. Batter bits.*

gusset typist *n.* A *bean flicker*, female *merchant, gusset piano virtuoso, touch typist.*

gustatory athlete *n.* One who sprints past the salad. Coined by the commentators on nightmarish US TV show *Gluttonbowl* to describe the parade of disgusting, big-boned inbreds taking part in their vile, yet extremely entertaining, eating competition.

gustbin *n.* A rather charming term used to describe the nether regions of a rather large lady.

gut grunt *n.* A burbulent rumbling in the viscera, or any subsequent anal emission.

gutted hamster *n. Gutted possum, gutted rabbit, giblets, roadkill.*

gutters *n.* An unattractive female. *'Have you seen the bird on page 3 today? Jesus Christ, what a fucking gutters.'* (*Daily Mirror* editor Piers Morgan reviewing the papers on BBC News 24, 2002).

gutter's shed *1. n.* A dockside building where fish are filleted. *2. n.* A particularly mingsome *minge.*

guttocks *n.* The rolls of fat that obese women get on their stomachs which, when turned through 90°, look remarkably like their *arse. Fruttocks.*

guyrope *n.* The flap of skin connecting the *flysheet* to the *tentpole*. The *banjo, Tarzan cord.*

guzunda *n.* A potty or *pisspot.*

gwank *n.* A girlie *wank.* A bout of *auditioning the finger puppets.*

gwibble *n.* A dribbly, underpowered ejaculation, opposite of a *pwa*.

gymbo *n.* Those conniving, make-up-encrusted, marriage-wrecking *boilers* who are apparently frequently to be found lurking in posh health and racquet clubs, where they do little or no training in case the perspiration ruins their *warpaint.* From gym + bimbo.

gym buddah *n.* An overweight woman in sportswear, with *overblaaters* and a huge *gunt.*

gymsniff *n. prop.* A gentleman who attends the gym and who prefers to use the apparatus directly after sweaty *birds* in order to sniff the seat.

gynaecolumnist *n.* Any female journalist who uses her newspaper to bang on about *women's things, eg.* Julie Burchill.

gypsy clit *n.* A nomadic *clematis.* One which, despite a fellow's best efforts to find it, never seems to be in the same place two nights running. A *Flying Dutchman,* a *Scarlet Pimpernel.*

gypsy's curse *n.* The loss of *wood* before insertion, as a result of failing to buy some pegs at some point in the past 20 years.

gypsy's dog, like a *sim.* Descriptive of someone who looks like he could do with a square meal. *'Feargal Sharky? He's like a gypsy's dog, him. All ribs and bollocks.'*

gypsy's eyelash *n.* The rogue *clockspring* in the *Jap's eye* that causes the *piss* to go everywhere but in the *bog.* Common cause of *pan smile* or *Queen Mum's grin.*

gypsy's kiss *rhym. slang. Piss.* Usually abbreviated to gypsy's. *'Keep a look out for icebergs, will you? I'm just off below decks for a gypsy's.'*

Hh

Hackney bunting *n.* Police crime scene cordon tape, which is commonly used to decorate the streets of the delightful London borough.

hack off a lump *v.* To *crimp off a length.* To defecate.

haddock pastie *n. Hairy pie,* a *Grimsby meal.*

Hadley job *n.* An act of *horatio* during which the *noshatrix* handles your *tassel* in the foppish, effete manner that the lead singer of *Spandau Ballet* used to handle his microphone.

had the dick *adj.* Descriptive of something which is broken beyond repair. "*What-ho, Jeeves,' I exclaimed. 'Fetch the Frazer-Nash round to the front door, there's a good chap. I feel like taking a spin.' 'I'm afraid that may not be possible, Sir,' he replied. 'Your Aunt Millicent drove it to Ascot and back with the handbrake on, and I fear it has had the dick.*" (from *For Fuck's Sake, Jeeves!* by PG Wodehouse).

haemogobbling *n. Dining at the Y* when the house wine is *moon juice.*

haemogoblin *n.* A gentleman who has a fish supper at the *all-night sushi bar,* despite the fact that it is closed for redecoration.

hag *n.*An ugly woman, *boiler, boot, steg, swamp donkey, ditch pig.*

haggis *1. n.* Unappetising object consisting of meat and oats stuffed into a veiny skin bag. *2. n.* Unappetising object consisting of meat and oats stuffed into a veiny skin bag.

haggis rag *n.* A small piece of fabric, esp. towelling, used for wiping clean or drying the *haggis* after a bout of exercise.

hail damage *n.* The vile, unsightly, dimpled skin found on the thighs of middle-aged celebrity women and brought to the world's attention by gleeful paparazzi. Cellulite.

hairache *n.* The mother of all hangovers. *'I can't go on, Richard. You'll have to do the programme on your own. I've got hairache.'*

hair trousers, to be wearing *v.* To be naked from the waist down.

hairy axe wound *n.* Vertical *gash.* The *mingepiece, quim, cock socket.*

hairy beanbags *n.* Pink 1970s style seating provided within the underpants for the exclusive use of the *bald man, Spurt Reynolds, Kojak, Captain Picard, etc.* Testicles.

hairy brain *n. medic.* The small wrinkled organ, about the size of two plums, that governs a gentleman's thought processes. Also *hanging brain.*

hairy cheque book *n. Gash card, furry purse.*

hairy conkers *n. Knackers, clockweights.*

hairy cornflake *1. n.* An affectionate name for *shit* DJ Dave Lee Travis, coined and used exclusively by himself. *2. n.* Affectionate name for a small, dried crust of *poo* stuck firmly to the *arsecress. 2. n.* An hirsute breakfast cereal that was expensively launched by Kellog's in 1976, but inexplicably failed to find favour with the public.

hairy cup *n. Hairy goblet, furry hoop.*

hairy doughnut *n.* An occasionally jam-filled confection, often dusted with *gusset sugar.*

hairy goblet *n. Hairy cup, front bottom, bodily treasure, parts of shame.*

hairy handshake *n.* A firm five-fingered greeting that costs £10 from a woman behind a skip, after which there are no hard feelings.

hairy knickers *n.* Descriptive of that situation when a lady removes her *farting crackers* and her unruly *minge* makes it appear that she has yet to do so. An extremely well-carpeted *barber's floor,* a *Terry Waite's allotment*. An extreme *biffer.*

hairy mits *rhym. slang. Tits. 'Look at the hairy mits on that! I could do her through a hedge backwards.'*

hair of the dogging *n.* Any attempt to relieve residual feelings of guilt felt by an habitual car park *perv* who assuages his angst by habitually going out and doing it again the next day. *'Where are you off to, Stan?' 'Just popping out for some hair of the dogging, love.'*

hairy pants *n.* See *hairy knickers.*

hairy pie *n. Haddock pastie.*

hairy pint *n.* An unsuspecting person's alcoholic beverage that has been discreetly spiked for the amusement of onlookers with a small quantity of *pubes.*

hairy raisins *n. Hunchback spiders.*

hairy saddlebags *1. n. Knackers 2. n. Pissflaps.*

hairy scallops *n.* The furry shellfish eaten when *bearded clams* are out of season.

hairy swingers *n.* Hirsute *mansacks* containing the *hairy conkers.*

hairy toffee *n. Dangleberries, klingons.*

hairy window *n.* That semi-translucent panel in the front portion of a pair of ladies' *scads*, through which it is just possible to make out her *gorilla salad,* though not her *curtains.*

half a crown thru'penny bit *sim.* Pre-decimal version of *five pee fifty pee,* used to describe the rapid flexing of the *nipsy* during moments of severe anxiety. *Bin lid penny.*

half a jaffa *n.* That which may be glimpsed in the crotch area of a young lady wearing tight jeans. *Twix lips.*

half a lemon *n.* A paradoxical form of lesbian who only fancies women who look like blokes.

half a nasty *n.* A *podge-on, dobber, grump on.*

half a teacake *n.* Not quite a *fatty,* the beginings of an erection. The state you would like your *fruitbowl* to be in when a new woman sees it for the first time.

half babies *n. Spuff, spingler, sprodd, spoddle, heir gel.*

half blood prince *1. n.* A chap's *member* after he's *had it off* with a woman during *rag week.* A *barber's pole. 2. n.* A *cock* that is so floppy it would struggle to get into a *wizard's sleeve.*

half caff *n.* The strength of a fellow's *spooch* immediately post-vasectomy, *ie.* before he's *crashed his yoghurt truck* the requisite twenty times to ensure he's completely *decaff.*

half Elvis, to do a *v.* To fall asleep whilst having a *shit* on the toilet. Usually done by one in an advanced state of *refreshment.*

half leapfrog *n.* Having sex in the *doggie position, setting the video.*

Halfords hero *n.* Motorist behind the wheel of a *noughtomobile,* who has kitted out his bottom-of-the-range hatchback with several hundredweight of expensive tat, including alloy wheels, ludicrous spoilers, an extremely loud stereo and an exhaust pipe like a fucking coal scuttle.

half rice half chips *adj.* Descriptive of a *switch hitter* or *happy shopper*; one who *drinks from both taps/ bowls from both ends. AC/DC.*

half time talk *n.* In a *spitroast grumble flick*, the token dialogue which occurs between the two leading men whilst they change ends, eat orange segments *etc.*

hamburger *n.* Of the female anatomy, that which can be seen in a *hamburger shot*. Something that really ought to have a *dill* stuck into it.

hamburger hill *n.* The large tor that frequently casts *stoat valley* into shadow on ladies of advancing years. A *gunt, fupa.*

hamburger shot *n.* A rear view in a *scud mag* displaying a *vertical bacon sandwich*. A *reverse peach.*

ham fisted *euph. Mid-wank. 'My mum came in and caught me ham fisted the other night. I didn't know where to look.'*

ham howitzer *n.* A *lamb cannon, beef blunderbuss, spam magnum,* any sort of meat + any sort of firearm.

Hamish blue *n.* Ripe, azure-tinted *knobcheese,* found north of the border and south of the sporran.

hamlet *n.* A half-hearted grade of erection, which can be found somewhere mid-way between a *flop on* and a *diamond cutter* on the universal scale of penile harditude. "2B or not 2B".

hammock *n.* Panty liner, *jam rag, sanitary towel, fanny napkin.*

Hammond's hat *n.* A *helmet* covered in *skidmarks.*

ham-on-ham *n.* Descriptive of the delightful sight of two ladies going at it *hammer and tongues.*

Hampton *rhym. slang. Dick.* From Hampton Weenis, a village in Essex with all wiggly blue veins up the side.

ham shank *rhym. slang.* A *Barclay's, J Arthur, Max Planck.*

hamshank redemption *n.* A discreet bout of *male pleasure* enjoyed whilst desperately trying not to waken up one's cellmate.

handbrake *n.* An unwanted and inexplicable thought or image that pops into a fellow's mind, bringing a sudden stop to an act of *self pollution, eg.* his late grandmother looking at him and tutting, his dead budgie lying on the bottom of its cage, the bit of the Zapruder footage where Kennedy's brains fall out the side of his head and his cranium goes skidding across the top of his car's boot, Germaine Greer's *Oz* magazine *hamburger shot etc.*

hand Chandon *n.* A high class *hand shandy* off a posh *bird,* who *pops your cork* with her thumbs under the *brim* of your *lid.*

hand cock's half hour *n.* "Thirty minutes? That's very nearly an armful."

handful of sprats *n. 1950s.* A fistful of *fish fingers, finger food.*

hand job *n.* Manual relief, one of the cheaper *extras* available at the *rub-a-tug shop*, or in the pub car park.

hand love *n.* The sordid act of *self-pollution.*

hand pump *n. milit. Wanker, nut juggler etc. 'Oi! Windsor, you fucking hand pump. Get them* *fucking boots back on, Your Royal Highness.'*

handruff *n.* Flaky deposits consisting of an amalgam of dried *potato fat, perseverance soup* and *helmetdale* found on the palms, thighs and soft furnishings of bachelors who have been watching a few episodes too many of *Desperate Housewives* without occasionally pausing to give the inside of the *farmer's hat* a wash.

hands free wank *n.* See *fancy wank.*

hands like cows' tits *sim.* Descriptive of one who is dextrously inept. An alternative to "butterfingers". *'I'm terribly sorry, Mrs Johnson, but I accidentally cut through a major blood vessel near your husband's heart and he didn't survive the surgery. I'm afraid I was on the pop last night and I've got hands like cows' tits this morning. The nurse will show you out. Good day.'*

hand shandy *n.* A frothy one, pulled *off the wrist.*

hand solo *n.* A solitary interlude of *self improvement.*

hand to gland combat *n.* A three-minute, one-man gladiatorial combat bout involving a *spam javelin.*

handycrap *n.* A *shit* taken by an able-bodied person who goes into *arse labour* only to discover that all the other toilets are occupied, out of order or blocked with *bangers and mash,* and is forced to avail himself in the disabled facilities.

handy pandy *n.* A high risk *sherman,* taken over a particularly fetching children's TV presenter.

hang a rat *v.* To go to the lavatory for a *number two. 'Where is he? He's supposed to be on the balcony blessing the multitude.' 'Keep your fucking hair on. He's just went to the khazi to hang a rat.'*

hanging bacon *n.* A *club sandwich* which hopefully isn't held together with a cocktail stick.

hanging baskets *1. n.* Dangling areas of foliage which can look nice when properly tended but attract flies if allowed to run to seed. *2. n.* Blooming marvellous *tits* which sway in the breeze and look like they've been assiduously cultivated.

hanging brain *n.* A *coffin dodger's clockweights,* dangling out the leg of his shorts.

hanging chod *n.* A semi-detached *turd.*

hanging out the back of *v.* Doggy-style sex. *"What am I to do, Jeeves?' I blustered. 'I've got myself engaged to Agatha AND Marjorie. This really is the the worst pickle of my entire puff.' 'Don't worry, Sir,' soothed the sage retainer. 'I shall arrange for it that Miss Wegg-Prosser walks in and finds you hanging out the back of Miss Lola la Titz from the Prince of Wales Theatre's burlesque production 'Woof! Woof!'"* (from *Gott In Himmel, Jeeves!* by PG Wodehouse).

hanging salad *n. Wedding tackle, fruit bowl, family jewels.*

hang in the balance *v.* Of a fellow's *chap,* to float at the exact midpoint between a *lazy* and a *full lob.*

hangman's noose *n.* A large vagina, big enough to push your head into. A *wizard's sleeve,* a *clown's pocket.*

hang ten *1. v.* In surfing slang, to

stand on the front of the board with all of one's toes curling over the edge. *2. v.* To be *masturbatricized* by one's partner using her feet rather than the more traditional *wanking spanners. 'Riding waves is really sweet / Catching tubes a real good treat / But best of all is hanging ten / With me knob between the missus's feet.'* (from *Wankin' USA* by the Beach Boys).

hang your hole *v.* To *moon*.

hanky panky *n. Slap and tickle, a bit of the other, nookie, how's your father*. Light-hearted *fucking*.

Hannibal Lecter's breakfast *n.* The feast which awaits a man performing *cumulonimbus* on *Billy Connolly's beard,* and the ensuing *pasata grin* it leaves on his face.

ha'penny *n.* Vagina. A *tuppence.*

happy camper *n.* One on whom *nature has played a cruel trick*, yet treats their predicament lightheartedly, *eg.* Graham Norton, Duncan Norvelle, Peter Tatchell.

happy Christmas Heather *euph.* The sinister half-grimace, half-smile worn on the face of one whose prolonged bout of constipation has just reached an agonising, *ring*-bursting climax. Named after the even more pained half-grimace, half-smile allegedly worn by Stella McCartney when she is forced to greet her unidextrous soon-to-be-ex-wicked-stepmother at family events.

happy Harry *n.* A semi-erect penis. A *dobber,* a *lard on, half a teacake.*

happy Havana *n.* A firm, rectilinear *bum cigar* of such pleasing proportions that it could almost have been rolled on the thigh of a sultry temptress, and requires little or no wiping to boot.

happy lamp *n.* The *sixth gear stick. 'I'm horny. Think I'll give my happy lamp a quick genie rub.'*

happy paper *n.* Beer tokens, folding money.

happyrash *n. medic.* A light-hearted dose of the *pox.* Any non-fatal *STD.*

happy sack *n.* The scrotum, clackerbag, *hairy saddlebags.*

Happy Shopper *1. n. prop.* A cheap 'n' cheerless grocery brand. *2. n.* A bisexual - one who *shops on both sides of the street. A half rice half chips person.*

Happy Shopper knockers *n.* No-frills *jugs.* Like proper *tits,* but with less filling. *Skimmed milkers.*

harbour master *n.* A man who has piloted the course of a few *tugboats* in his time, he can tell you. A *stickman, fanny hopper.*

hardbore *n. Grumble* that promises to be a real *meat vid* on the box, but when you get it home you find it's got Robin Askwith, Bill Maynard and Doris Hare in it. And Tony Blair's father-in-law.

hard hat *n.* A *stiffy,* or erection of the male parts. *'Fancy a spot of potholing under the bridge?' 'Not until I've got my hard hat on, love.'*

hard off *n.* Something of a disappointment. *'After all the excitement of our last-gasp comebacks in the quarter and semi-final stages, I've got to admit that our four-nil defeat to Seville in the UEFA cup final in Eindhoven was something of a hard off, Adrian.'* (Then Middlesbrough manager Steve McClaren speaking on BBC Radio 5, May 10th 2006).

hard on *n. Wood,* a *bone on,* a *bonk-*

on. A fully-tumescent gentleman's part.

hariolae *n.* The hairs that foreign ladies cultivate around their *hunchback spiders*.

Harlem shuffle *n.* The facial gurning and involuntary neck spasms that beset a gentleman during the *vinegar strokes,* making him look like septuagenarian *harbour master* Sir Mick Jagger strutting about on stage. *'Quick, camera two, a close up of Gunther's cock. He's doing the Harlem shuffle.'*

harlet *n.* A young *slapper.*

Harley Davidson *n.* An act of lavatoryless defecation, in which the dumper is forced to cling to trees or railings in order to steady himself, thus adopting a position similar to that used when riding an impractical American motorcycle. A *fatboy, soft-tail.*

harlot *n.* A scarlet woman, a wicked lady.

Harlow pub quiz *n.* Entertainment regularly held at the Essex town's popular nightspots. The quizmaster usually asks one of two questions: "What the fuck are you looking at?" or "Do you fucking want some?", to which all the possible answers are wrong.

Harmison loosener *n.* An explosive delivery first thing in the morning which ends up anywhere but near to its intended target. *'Last night's chicken jalfrezi resulted in Derek sending down a ferocious Harmison loosener.'*

Harry *1. rhym. slang. Jizz.* From Harry Monk = spunk. *2. rhym. slang.* Hobo. From Harry Ramp = tramp *3. rhym. slang.* Cigarette. From Harry Rag = fag. *4. rhym. slang.* Cheese sandwich. From Harry Rees-Bandwich.

Harry Rampsdens *n.* Discarded fish and chips, as feasted upon by cheery gentlemen of the road. *Tramps' truffles.*

Harry Ramsden's raspberry *n.* The combination of smell and sound to be endured during a dirty girl's *fanny fart.*

Harry Redknapp's eyelids *sim.* Descriptive of particularly hang-dog *beef curtains.*

Harry's challenge *n.* A daunting *fish supper* that is too much for one man. A big *kipper.* From the menu at the Yardley branch of Harry Ramsden's which offered a meal of that name, and where one was granted a certificate if the portion was finished.

Harvest Festival *n.* Domestic state of play for the bachelor gentleman when, following a fortnight *on the lash*, he is reduced to living on out-of-date tinned food from the back of the cupboard.

harvest festivals *1. n.* One-night stands, *ie.* ploughing the field before scattering. *2. n.* A pair of well-fitting but comfortable underpants where "all is safely gathered in".

hatchback *n.* A woman with prominent buttocks. *'Jesus. Look at the arse on that that Mother Superior over there by Guercini's altarpiece of the Burial of St Petronilla, your Holiness. What a hatchback. You could stand your pint on her parcel shelf.'*

hatch eggs *v.* To remain seated on the *chod bin* long after the last *turd* has been dropped. *'What are you doing in there? I've got the turtle's breath and a new Autotrader.' 'I'm hatching eggs.'*

hat rack *n.* Someone who's head

is only of any use for the storage of hats. A *Johnny No-Stars*, a *shit-for-brains. eg.* Bez out of The Happy Mondays.

hatstand *adj.* Descriptive of one who has mental health issues.

hatties *rhym. slang.* Delirium tremens. A *turps nudger*'s shakes. From *big-boned Carry On* actress Hattie Jelirium-Tremens.

have a go at oneself *v.* To *stab the cat, feed the ducks, stab the ducks, feed the cat.*

have it off *v.* To get *a bit*, have a *portion*, *give* somebody *one.* To get one's *leg over.*

have one's arse in one's hand *euph.* To be in a bad mood, to have a strop on. *'Arnie's BACK!... and this time he's got his arse in his hand!'* (Advertising poster for *Terminator* 3).

Havers, on the *adj.* Descriptive of the way certain blokes smarm up to members of the opposite sex in an overly charming way, *eg.* kissing their hands, listening to them *etc.*, in the style of middle-aged charmer Nigel Havers.

have the painters in *v.* To menstruate, be *on the blob. To fall to the communists.*

Hawaiian muscle fuck *n.* The act of *bagpiping.*

Hawaiian sunrise *n.* A glorious and uncomfortable orange, red, blue and purple aurora, which can be seen around one's *ringpiece* early in the morning after consuming spicy foodstuffs, for example a Vindaloo Special Tandoori Chingiri from the Curry Capital, Bigg Market, Newcastle upon Tyne.

Hawaiian waft *n.* To disperse the aroma after *stepping on a duck,* using an exotic hula-hula motion.

Hawick *onomat.* To *puke*. After the Scottish border town. *'I think I'm going to Hawick.'*

he-dam *n. Knobcheese, helmetdale, purple Leicester, brimula, Lymeswold etc.*

head *n.* Something which is given by women to men, and is afterwards described as "good" by the recipient when talking to friends. A *chewie, nosh, gobbie.*

head for the hills *exclam.* To be forced to hide your *soldier* in the *Dutch alps,* because the *redcoats are in the valley.*

head in one's top pocket, to have *v.* To be so copiously-*refreshed* that one's head cannot balance on one's neck any more and seems to be falling into the top pocket of one's shirt. An extreme form of *nodding.*

headlamps *n. Bristols, jugs, charlies, assets. 'Phewf! I wouldn't mind giving her headlamps a rub.'*

head off a nun, like trying to get *met.* Descriptive of something very difficult to achieve. *Finding a pube in an afro. 'And I fully intend to bring in legislation on asylum that will make getting British citizenship like getting head off a nun before the next parliament.'* (David Blunkett addressing the Labour Party Conference, 2003).

headwind *n. Trouser cough* emitted right under the nose of a fellatrix. *Devil's kiss, Hell's mouth.*

heavage *n.* A *Bristol Channel* that is only there thanks to cleverly engineered *tit pants.*

heave *v.* To vomit, *make a pavement pizza*, release a loud *technicolour yawn.*

heave a Havana *v. Grow a tail*, take

a dump, light a bum cigar, cast Churchill's reflection.

heave-ho *1. n.* The *arse. 'She threw me out on my heave-ho.' 2. n.* The *Spanish archer. 'She gave me the heave-ho on my arse.'*

heavy dick *n.* The very first stirrings of erectivation. The beginnings of a *semi-on. 'Hey, I don't like admitting it, boys, but that tranny off There's Something About Miriam has given me a bit of a heavy dick.'*

heavy shooter *n.* One whose *money shots* tend to be *pwas* rather than *gwibbles*.

hedge coke *n.* Plastic bottles filled with fluid too pale to be true cola, discarded on roadside verges by lorry drivers in order to tempt thirsty runners or cyclists in need of refreshment. *Trucker's tizer, kidney cider, Scania scotch.*

hedgehog *n.* A *ladygarden that was mowed* five days ago. A *face grater.*

hee *1. n. Thai. Minge, hairy cheque book. 2. interj.* A noise made by laughing gnomes/laughing policemen.

hefty-clefty *n.* A *welly top*, a *horse's collar*, a *melted welly*. A very wide *mary*.

Heinz jacuzzi *n.* The luxurious, self-indulgent pleasure to be had in any bath, courtesy of an earlier consumption of baked beans. *'I'd give it ten minutes if I was you, dear. I've just had a Heinz jacuzzi. And probably best not to light any tea-lights in there for a few hours, neither.'*

heirbags *n.* The containers where *liquid kids* are stored, and which handily prevent injury to the *barse* when you are kicked between the legs. The *testicles*.

heir gel *n.* See *heir spray.*

heir spray *n.* A man's *baby juice. Spooge, spoff, spaff, spiff, jitler. Merry monk.*

Helena Bonham *euph.* The *anus.* From the charming English rose actress Helena Bonham-Farter

helicopters, attack of the *n.* Drunken spinning of the head, a sudden reminder that you need to make an urgent call on the *great white telephone*. The *whirlies, wall of death.*

hello Cleveland *exclam.* Phrase uttered by a gentleman who is *doing* a lady from behind and inadvertently *pots the brown* rather than the *pink*. From the scene in *Spinal Tap* when the band find themselves in the wrong tunnel.

helmet *1. n.* The *bell end, glans, bishop's mitre, purple pearler. 2. n.* A quantity of *fellatio.* An amount of *blow jobs. 'My nan wanted to meet Roger Whitaker, and she had to give the roadies some helmet to get backstage.'*

helmetdale *n.* A strong-smelling, mature *knob cheese*.

helmet mag *n.* A *stroke periodical, art pamphlet, noddy book.*

helmet pelmet *n.* The *fiveskin, Kojak's roll-neck.*

helmetscale *n.* Fully-ossified *Lymeswold* that has to be chipped off the *Pope's cap* using a toothpick. Found only on the most determined opponents of genital hygiene.

helmet, to give it some *v.* To engage in an activity with some gusto. To give it *rice*, give it *welly*, give it *sixnowt, go at it three cocks to the cunt. 'It may be necessary to apply a considerable amount of torque* *in order to loosen the wheel studs. Indeed, you may have to give the wheel brace quite a bit of helmet before they begin to yield.'* (from the *Austin Maxi Haynes Manual*, 1978).

hemingway sphinx *n.* A breed of hairless cat.

Hendrix on the high notes *sim.* Descriptive of the facial contortions of a gentleman in the final throes of coitus, reminiscent of the late plank-spanker in full axe frenzy. The *vinegar strokes*.

Henman *n.* An impotent fellow. Named after the former British tennis sensation Tim, who never managed to make it past the *semi* stage.

Henrietta Street *1. n.* An old, narrow, twisty thoroughfare in Whitby and thus *2. n.* An ageing, serpentine *clunge* with a strong aroma of kippers and haddock.

Henry Moore *1. n.* A large pile of *shit* in a public place. *2. n.* A large reclining dog *turd* on the pavement.

he-nut butter *n.* Put crudely, the viscid liquid which contains spermatazoa, the male gametes or germ cells. In more scientific terms, *spaff, jitler, chalaza, baby batter etc*.

herbert pocket *n.* The pocket that the *herbert* slips into. The *arsehole.* From the name of the character in *Great Expectations*, played in the film by Sir Alec Guinness, and given to police upon his arrest for *cottaging.*

Herbie's bonnet *n.* The *beetle bonnet, camel's lips*.

Hershey highway *n. US.* Transatlantic *Bourneville boulevard, Cadbury alley*.

Hershey highwayman *n. US.* An *ass bandit.*

Heskey *n.* A girl who *goes down* at the slightest touch.

hettython *n.* The act of taking the day off work, closing the curtains and watching all five series of *Hetty Wainthrop Investigates.*

hibernating grizzly *n.* A big hairy brown *shit* asleep in the *claypit* that one would be foolish to rouse from its slumbers.

hickies *n. Slapper*-speak for love bites, *shag tags*.

hickory dick *n.* A *cock* so hard it would bend any nails one attempted to drive into it.

hide the salami *n.* A bedtime game for two players, one *sausage* and a *hairy pie*. Also *sink the salami, bury the bratwurst, conceal the Cumberland.*

hiding policemen's helmets *adj.* Of a lady, to be *nipping out, smuggling peanuts.*

high miler *n.* An *old banger* who looks like she's been round the clock a few times, but is still running, *eg*. Joan Collins, Shirley Bassey.

high pressure vein cane *n.* Short for the penis, *prick, tallywhacker, Hector the meat injector*.

high speed rinse *n.* An act of *self pollution* committed in the shower. *Flinging in the rain.*

high velocity trifle *n.* A soft *feeshus* fired from the *chocolate starfish* at great speed, which is instantly aerated into a smooth, frothy confection when it meets the outer atmosphere. The resultant fluffy material is ideal for pebble-dashing porcelain and has powerful adhesive properties when brought into contact with blankets, sleeping bags and quilts.

Hilary *n. rhym. slang.* A *five knuckle shuffle.* From US actress Hilary Swank. *'I just seen that Carol Vorderman flogging loans on the satellite and I knocked out a quick Hilary there and then.'*

hillbilly's hat *n.* A particularly dishevelled *cock socket.* A *clampett.*

hill start *n.* The painstaking task of pleasuring oneself after a heavy drinking session, when reaching *biting point* can take hours.

Hilton breakfast *n.* A product or service which combines substandard quality with a premium price, facts which become apparent only when it is too late to change your mind and run away. Examples of *Hilton breakfasts* include poncy salon haircuts, Galloway pony treks and early morning meals at certain international hotel chains which will remain nameless for legal reasons.

Himalayas *n.* Gentlemen who *till the soil* on very steep inclines.

himbledon *n.* Fortnight long festival of *men's singles* enjoyed by sofa-bound bachelors whilst watching the famous All-England women's tennis tournament on television. With the curtains pulled tightly shut.

hindsight *n.* The reflex action of a man turning swiftly in order to track an outstanding *arse* as it makes its way across the room or along the pavement. Hindsight is estimated to be the cause of 95% of low-speed rear-end collisions on British high streets, and up to 99% of accidents involving straw-hatted vicars riding their bicycles into hedges.

hingoot *n. Scot.* A lady of easy virtue, a *slapper*, a *prossie*, a *good time girl.* Literally, a woman who has enjoyed so much *cock* that her fanny is "hinging oot".

hippo's ear *n.* A *hippo's mouth.* A *donkey's yawn.* A *fanny* like a *bucket.*

hippo's mouth *n.* Another large, unsightly, gaping vagina.

hippo's saddle *n.* Something big, grey and leathery in a lady's *knickers.*

hippocrocapig *n.* Ann Widdecombe if you set her head on fire and put it out with a shovel. A *rhinocerpig.*

hipposuction *n.* Optimistic cosmetic surgical procedure carried out on the larger lady.

hipsies *n.* Tree-hugging new-age travellers who, despite being in love with the planet, nevertheless contrive to leave a big pile of dog *crap, johnnies* and *shit*-filled carrier bags behind when they tow their clapped-out, smoke-churning Transit vans off the site.

hip tits *n.* The large pair of flabby rolls of stomach blubber that hang down around the waists of those unbelievably fat Americans you see waddling around Disneyland. *Bilge tanks, jerry cans.*

hissing Sid *n.* One's *one-eyed trouser snake.*

hit and miss *rhym. slang. Piss.*

hit and run *v.* To indulge in sexual intercourse with a *boiler* despite one's better judgement, then leg it before she wakes up.

hitch-hiking under the big top *n.* Early morning *blanket drill, starching the sheets, polishing the tent pole.*

hitching to heaven *n.* More thumb-based *hand to gland* combat.

Hitler piss *n.* A braced, Nazi salute position from which to have a drunken *Chinese singing lesson* at the pub toilet trough.

Hitler tash *n.* A *clitler*, a *Lamborghini.*

Hitler wank *n.* An act of *self-pollution* performed in a shower with the left arm lodged firmly against the cubicle wall to prevent loss of balance.

HMP *abbrev.* A lady for whom only the finest things in life will do. High Maintenance Pussy.

hobbit *n.* A small hairy thing.

hobbit dick *n.* A *penis* that is wider than it is long. A *tuna can cock, Welshman's cock, choad, chooza.*

hobgoblin *n.* A *bumgoblin.*

hobnail boots, that one wore *exclam.* A phrase shouted loudly in order to make the most of a volubly-*dropped gut.* *'In polite company, following another's audible act of flatulence, it is permissible to offer a comment. If the wind breaker was the wife of a Governor General, one might say 'One-nil to you, Your Excellency'. If the younger son of a Duke has farted, a comment such as 'Fuck me, that one wore hobnail boots, My Lord, would be perfectly acceptable.'* (from *Debrett's Etiquette*, 1928).

hobnob *n.* A big, dirty *ringpiece,* barnacled with such an excess of *winnetry* that it takes on the appearance of the much-loved family biscuit.

hockmagandy *n.* The one day of the year when Scotsmen *fuck* their wives. *Fannyversary.*

hoeing the HP *v.* *Uphill gardening* on the *brown sauce allotment.*

HOFNAR *1. n.* prop. A mid-nineties Seattle-based college band. *2. acron. US.* Hard On For No Apparent Reason.

hog's eye *n.* The serving hatch through which *perseverance soup* arrives.

hog's eye hairpiece *n. Aus.* That long, piss-combed tuft of hair that seems to grow out the end of a dog's *unit.* Like on the top of Woody Woodpecker's head.

hogans *n. US. Heroic charlies, Gert Stonkers, Norma Snockers.*

hole *1. n.* Anything you can stick something up. *2. n.* The next category of sexual attainment up the scale after *cloth tit, tops* and *fingers.*

hole in one *n.* Successful penile intromission without using the hand for guidance.

holiday money *n.* Male genitalia, the *family jewels, meat and two veg,* the *fruit bowl.*

Hollyoats *n.* A leisurely Sunday afternoon bout of *personal pollution* enjoyed whilst watching the omnibus edition of the blonde-heavy Chester-based soap. Careful control is required to avoid emptying one's *saddlebags* as Mr Cunningham appears on screen, or when it cuts back to Vernon in the *T4* studio.

Hollywood wax *n.* A completely depilated *mingepiece.* A *Barthez.*

Hollywood ending *1. n.* A satisfying cinematic denouement in which good triumphs over evil and everyone goes home happy. *2. n.* A *tom tit* that requires no wiping.

Hollywood loaf *n.* A *podge-on, half a teacake.* So named because of its popularity with male actors called upon to perform in the nude.

holmaphobe *n.* A person with an entirely rational hatred of fat *fuck*

Eamonn Holmes.

holy trinity *n.* To engage in anal, oral and vaginal sex in one session.

homburger *n.* A vegetarian fast food option for *good listeners*.

home brew *n.* Laser-print quality *grumble mags* made from *cyber scud.*

hominous *adj.* Of events, about to turn gay with tragic consequences. *'I've just been invited back to a swimming pool party at the home of a popular comedian, all-round entertainer and quiz-show host.' 'That sounds hominous.'*

hommage *n.* Act of devotion performed in a kneeling position.

homnambulist *n.* Chap who gets an inexplicable urge to go walking about on Hampstead Heath in the wee small hours.

homoclaustrophobia *n.* Mainly irrational fear of being trapped in an enclosed space with a *bummer.*

homosexual *n.* A man or woman who is attracted to members of his or her own gender. Often at bus stops. From the Greek homos = lifter, sexualos = togas.

homversation *n.* Of males, the discussion of anything at all except cars and football, but particularly *Coronation Street*, clothes, hair and cottaging anecdotes.

honesty box bargain *n.* A *five fingered discount* available to the value-conscious shopper at railway station newsagents. Named after the express counter thoughtfully provided for the use of passengers who are in a hurry not to pay.

honey altar *n.* The sunken treasure that the *muff diver* goes in search of.

honeypot *n.* A waxy *fanny* surrounded by bees.

Hong Kong Pooey *n.* A process of deduction undertaken whilst ensconced on the *throne* with a bad dose of the *Brads,* whereby the previous day's meals are pondered over in the style of the cheaply-animated *shite* 1970s martial arts/janitor/dog/crimefighter cartoon series *Hong Kong Phooey.* "Was it the binding four-egg omelette for breakfast? No. Was it the cheese pastie and Scotch egg lunch? No. Was it the gallon of Guinness and chicken Madras supper? Could be!"

honkies *n.* Big *muckspreader* round back.

honk up *n. Hoy up, bowk.*

honour the crowd *v.* To *let rip* with such an evil smell that innocent bystanders are forced to stand and applaud. *'And Henman honours the crowd as he bends down to pick up his kit for his annual Wimbledon early exit, and gracious me, judging by the stains on his shorts, the poor fellow must have followed through.'* (Dan Maskell (deceased) BBC TV commentary).

hooberstank *n.* The first, and usually biggest, *fart* of the morning. *Morning thunder, reveille, dawn chorus.* A *breakfast maker.*

hoobs *1. n.* A bizarre set of aliens which appear on Channel 4 in the mornings. *2. n.* A particularly impressive set of *funbags.* From huge + boobs.

hoodwink *1. v.* To deceive, or mislead by falsehood, *eg.* when selling endowment mortgages or pension schemes. *2. v.* The act of squeezing the *fiveskin* over the *Dutch strawberry* in order to encourage the last few drops of *piss* to exit the *blow hole.*

hooker *1. n. US.* A *ho'*, a *pro. 2. n.* A bloke in a rugby scrum who performs sexual favours in return for money.

hooker's toothpaste *n. Slag hammer yoghurt.*

hooking fish *v. Feeding the ducks, stabbing the cat.*

hoop *n.* That aperture into which a man might slam a *dunky.*

hoopage *n.* A spot of the old *bum sex. 'The lotus floats upon the lake in the moonlight / Knickers off love and bend over / I fancy a bit of hoopage for a change.'* (from *Up the Bum No Babies - a Haiku Collection* by Matsunaga Teitoku).

hoop flogger *n.* A lady who is *on the batter.*

hoop, furry *n. Sweep's brush.*

hoop stretcher *n.* A *crafty butcher* who hides his *salami* in a *tea towel holder.*

hootchie *n. US. Totty, blit, muff.*

hootchie cootchie *n. Hanky panky, how's your father.*

hooter *n.* Conk, *neb, sneck.* Nose. Not the singular of *hooters.*

hootermammy *n.* A former *Miss Lincolnshire* who receives a visit from the *titty fairy* during pregnancy. One who has *collected the baby bonus, eg.* Kerry out of Atomic Kitten.

hooters *n. Bazookas, baps, headlamps.* Not the plural of *hooter.*

hoover up *v.* To try, usually unsuccessfully, to "sniff up" the smell of a recently dropped *fart* when one sees an attractive woman approaching.

HOP *acronym.* Hang Over Poo. Giant, exceedingly loose stool, the noisy passing of which is a significant milestone in the recovery from a hang over. An *alcopoop,* an *escape sub. 'Ahh! I feel much better after that hop. Anyone fancy a pint?'*

hop into the horse's collar *v.* Nip to the *municipal cock wash.*

hopper arse *n.* A *forty guts, salad dodger.* A *big-boned* person, with really fat *glands.*

hoptical illusion *n.* A ropey *piece* who appears beautiful when viewed through *beer goggles.*

horatio *n.* Posh Latin term used by doctors, lawyers and police to describe a *chewie.*

horizontal jogging *n.* Hilarious euphemism for sexual intercourse, esp. "a bit of the old...".

horizontally accessible *adj.* Desribing a young lady with *yoyo knickers.*

horn chorus *n.* A very loud early morning wakeup call from an adjacent hotel or halls of residence room, usually at around three am or, failing that, about half an hour after the local nightclubs kick out. The *horn chorus* is typically accompanied by the sound of squeaking bedsprings and/or a rhythmic thumping noise on the connecting wall.

hornbag *1. n.* A bag for keeping horns in. *2. n.* An extremely attractive woman, *ie.* one who gives you the *horn.*

horndog *n.* An extremely unattractive woman, *ie.* one who loses you the *horn.* A *derection.*

horn, the *n.* Ceremonial symbol of a man's affection for a woman, paradoxically given by the woman to the man.

horny *1. adj.* The state of a man

whilst in possession of *the horn*, or indeed a woman who fancies a shot on it. *2. adj.* Descriptive of a woman who gives a man *the horn*. *'Hey, that Kate Silverton on BBC News 24 is well horny.'*

horse eating oats *sim. Feeding the pony. 'And David went unto the house of Bathsheba and she had not known her husband Naboth for ages. And David did put his hand down her knickers and lo, it was like a horse eating oats.'* (*Deuteronomy 6:23*).

horse's collar *1. n.* Vagina. *2. sim.* Comparison implying generous *farmyard* proportions. *Cathedral, clown's pocket, hippo's mouth. 'I wouldn't say my wife's got a tight minge, ladies and gentlemen. That's because she's got a fanny like a horse's collar.'*

horse's doofers *n.* Superlative *mutt's nuts, dog's bollocks*, bee's knees. The *donkey's knob*.

horse's handbrake *n.* A *diamond cutter*, a *concrete donkey*, a raging *bone on* wrought from *pink steel*.

horse's head, sitting on a *n.* Of people queueing for the *dunny*, to be suffering from a more extreme case of the *turtle's head*. *'Hurry up will you, I'm sitting on a horse's head out here.'*

horse's nose *n.* The early stages of a *Beverley Craven* being allowed to grow out. Noticeable when *feeding the pony*.

hosebag *n.* Woman of loose morals. She with a *twat* like a *paper hanger's bucket*. *A boot, slapper.*

hose job *n. Blow job, chewie, horatio.*

hose monster *n.* An ugly woman who cannot get enough hosepipes.

hospital button *n.* A particularly unhealthy looking *gold watch*. *'Call 999 love. I've just howked up a hospital button.'*

hot *adj.* Condition which, in conjunction with *horny*, is often used to describe ugly, fat, bored women eating crisps and doing the *Take a Break* crossword on the end of expensive telephone sex lines, *eg. 'Hot and horny bitches thirsty for your love seed. £1.80/min.'*

HOTBOT *acronym.* The expression of one's desire for a *dog's marriage*. Hang Out The Back Of That.

hot cross bunning *n.* The act of *icing* one's ladyfriend's face in two perpendicular sweeps, with the intention of creating a physiognomical effect eerily remniscent of the popular glazed Easter-time confectionery sweetmeat.

hot cup of tea with two lumps *n.* The practice of *teabagging*, but this time with the lady's mouth full of hot water. *Warming the pod, PG lips, dick brew.*

hot dog *1. n.* An egg delicacy famously enjoyed by the cult actor Divine in the film *Pink Flamingoes* (Children's Film Foundation, 1977). *2. v.* To eat said morsel, freshly laid by a poodle. *3. v.* To slap one's *sausage* into a lady's *buns*, with plenty of onions.

hot-dog end *n.* The *turtle's head*. From the similarity to how a hot-dog sausage looks when poking out of the end of a bread roll. *'Hurry up in the shit house, gran. I've got a hot dog end here.'*

hotel toast *euph.* Descriptive of a girl who's not as *hot* as she once was.

hot fish yoghurt *n.* Cream sauce filling for a *hairy pie*.

hot hello *n.* The warm trickle down her leg that reminds a lady of the deposit that was recently made into her *special bank*.

hot karl *n.* Post-anal sex *horatio*.

hot lunch *n.* See *Cleveland steamer*. Or better still, don't.

hot meat injection *n.* An inoculation with the *spam syringe*.

hot monocle *n.* Half a *Velma*. A facial ejaculation which reduces one's *bird's* ability to see by fifty percent. Also *Gabrielle, King Harold*.

hots, the *n.* What *birds* get for Spanish waiters.

hotty *n. US. Totty, blart.*

hot water bottle *n.* An unattactive woman who is taken into a bloke's bed purely in order to keep it warm. *'I don't know what he sees in her.' 'She's a hot water bottle. He'll chuck her in the Spring.'*

hound *n.* Offensively sexist term for a *dog, steg, boiler*.

hound cable *n. Barker's rope, footstool. Dog shite.*

housewarming gift, leave a *v.* To make a deposit in the toilet of a friend's house, but not pull the chain.

hovis *n.* A particularly tight *snapper.* A *butler's cuff*. From the bread advertising slogan "White with all the goodness of brown."

howard *n.* When an altruistic chap has *blown his beans* up his lady-friend, but takes advantage of his last few seconds of penile hardness to generously give her a couple of extra pushes for good luck. A "little Xtra", named after bespectacled building society mouthpiece Howard off of the Halifax adverts. If the pushes are administered up the *bird's dirtbox*, it is called a *howard brown,* thus using the poor fellow's full name for a cheap comic effect.

Howard's Way *rhym. slang. Colwyn Bay*. From the shit BBC TV drama of the same name. *'Mum, Dad, I've got something to tell you. I'm Howard's Way.'*

how much? *exclam.* Amusing mock-shocked utterance from one who has just *broken wind. Don't tear it, I'll take the whole piece; that's working, now try your lights.*

how's your father *n.* Sex. Often prefixed "Fancy a quick bit of... ahem...?"

hoy *v.* To throw, lob, chuck, esp. beer down one's neck.

hoy up *v.* To *spew up, barf,* esp. beer up one's neck.

HPS *abbrev.* Horizontal Payment Scheme. Female method of remuneration favoured by taxi drivers, traffic wardens and drug dealers. Also *hairy cheque book, gash card.*

HP sauce *n.* Viscous fluid found in the *dunghampers* of excitable *birds*. A savoury condiment product of the *haddock pastie.*

huby *n.* A semi-erect penis, a *dobber, half a teacake*, a lazy *lob on*.

huffle *v.* To *bagpipe*. To take part in an *Hawaiian muscle-fuck*.

Hughie Green *n.* A swift *wank* taken when "opportunity knocks". *'Mr Pickwick closed the door behind Mrs Fezzyfelt, sat down behind his old oak desk, and took the turnip watch from his waistcoat pocket. 'Odds bodkins,' he shouted. 'Five minutes until Mr Sticklebrick arrives. Time enough for a swift Hughie Green.*" (from *The Pickwick Papers* by Charles

Dickens).

Hugo Boss *n.* The act of holding the wife's or girlfriend's head under one's quilt after *farting.* A *Dutch oven.* From the male perfume advertising slogan "Your fragrance. Your rules".

hulk spunk *n.* Snot.

hum *1. v.* To *ming,* stink. *2. v.* To sing with the lips closed, or as near to closed as possible during a *hum job. 3. n.* A Bad smell.

hum job *n.* Vegetarian oral sex involving no meat, just *two veg.* accompanied by simultaneous humming of the musical variety.

Humber Bridge *1. n.* Suspended estuary crossing which connects Grimsby to Hull and thus *2. n.* The thing on a lady which links the *fishy bit* to the *shitty bit.* The *taint, tinter, carse.*

humble grumble *n.* Poor man's porn, *eg.* Women's Health Week leaflets pressed into service as *monomanual literature. Paupernography.*

humdinger *n.* A *fart* which makes the wallpaper peel.

hummer *1. n.* A large, butch military vehicle favoured by Californian hairdressers and Arnold Schwarzenegger. *2. n. Arse, bum. 3. n.* A *humdinger.*

hummersexual *n.* One who finds himself so deficient in the *trouser department* that neither a sports car nor a vast Harley Davidson motorbike can furnish sufficient compensation, and so he is forced to climb behind the wheel of an absurdly large and comically butch 4x4 vehicle. *'Born on This Day in History: Honzhi, Emperor of China, 1470; Henry Ford, Motor Industry Pioneer, 1863; Emily Bronte, Novelist, 1818; Vladimir Zworykin, Russian Physicist, 1889; Arnold Schwarzenegger, Hummersexual Actor, 1947.'*

hummingbird, hung like a *adj.* Having a *cock* like a *Chinese mouse.*

hummingbird's wing *sim.* Descriptive of the speed of a naughy lady's fingers whilst interfering with her *bodily treasure. 'I come home from the pub last night and caught the missus playing her banjo to an Enrique Iglesias video. Her fingers were going like a fucking hummingbird's wing, I can tell you.'*

hump *1. v.* To *shag,* have sex in the style of an old Labrador with its *lipstick* out. *2. v.* To carry heavy amplification equipment to and from a live music venue whilst one's *arse* sticks out the back of one's jeans.

humpty *n.* The act of *humping.*

hunchback spiders *n.* Ladies' hairy nipples.

hunchie *n.* A particularly difficult *mudchild,* that leaves one contorted like a constipated labrador in the park.

hungry arse *n.* Condition afflicting women whereby their *bills* disappear up the *crack* of their *hummer* as they walk.

hungry hippos *1. n.* Frantic and quickly-broken 1970s board game for children. 2. *euph.* Affectionate collective epithet for a herd of salivating, *salad dodging* lasses in the queue for one's local *kebabulance* after a night on the *tart fuel.*

hunt for brown October *n.* The act of seeking out and destroying a *U-bend U-boat.* With a bog brush, stick or barbecue utensil.

hurl *1. v.* To *hoy. 2. v.* To *hoy up.*

hurt yourself *v.* To vigorously *relax in a gentleman's way. 'Thanks for that new porn, mate. I'm going to go home now and hurt myself.'*

hush puppies *n. Blouse puppies* so impressive that all red-blooded men are rendered speechless in their presence.

hussy *n.* A shameless woman, a drunk and an unfit mother.

hymen climbin' *n.* The act of being the first felow to plant his *flagpole* up *Mount Venus*. Plucking a *bird's virgin string.*

hypnotits *n.* Export strength *hush puppies.*

I bet that holds some shit! *exclam.* A compliment proffered to a *bird* with a big *arse.*

Ibiza itch *n. medic.* Any *happyrash* caught by one's *downstairs unmentionables* whilst holidaying on the popular nsu-kissed Mediterranean island. *'He's the man, the man with the Midas...Sorry Mr Broccoli, I've got to go and put some ointment on me clopper. I've got Ibiza itch something rotten.' 'I know, love. We could hear you scratching at it over the French horns.'*

IBM *1. n. prop.* A large computer company. *2. abbrev.* Itty Bitty Meat. A small penis. *3. abbrev.* Inches Below Muff. The units in which a *greyhound skirt* is measured.

I can't believe it's not batter *n.* KY Jelly, *granny batter.*

I can't believe it's nut butter *exclam. 'Oi, waiter. What's this funny-tasting stuff spread on my bread rolls?' 'It's I can't believe it's nut butter, Mr Winner. And all the chefs have wanked into your soup too, you fat cunt.'*

ICBM *acronym.* Of modern day state-of-the-art trouser weaponry, an Inter Cuntinental Ballistic Missile.

iced fingers *n.* Bakers' confectionery-speak for the results of *glazing the knuckle.*

ice the cake *v.* To decorate a *tart* with *cream.* Often seen in European *grumble flicks. 'Gunther! There's only thirty seconds of tape left in the camera. Quick, ice that cake!'*

ice the log *n.* An environmentally-sound toilet visit where one has a *wank* after a *shit,* thereby saving water on the flush and halting global warming.

Iggy popshot *n. Whacking off* on a *TV's ass.*

Ikea bulb *n.* A lady that *blows* first time one *turns her on.*

Imperial barge *n.* The male member. A particularly majestic *skin boat. 'You should have seen how Mrs Eisenhower's eyes lit up when my nine-inch imperial barge heaved into view.'* (from *The Memoirs of Winston Churchill*).

impersonate Stalin *v.* To perform oral sex on a woman, *don the beard, eat hairy pie. 'Hold tight up there love, I'm just gonna do a quick impersonation of Stalin.'*

incapability brown *n.* A *shit* in the garden, left by a passing drunkard.

Indian mustard *n.* Diarrhoea.

Indian rope trick *n.* An impressive erection attained under seemingly impossible circumstances, *eg.* after twelve pints and/or six *wanks.*

indoor fishing *v.* A coarse form of *angling for tadpoles.*

indoor hobo *n.* One who lives inside, but looks like they should be living in a doorway, *eg.* Johnny Vegas, Ricky Tomlinson, Tracey Emin. A *tramp's mate.*

indoor sports *n.* Exercise; specifically a workout for the right arm and wrist.

Ingrid *rhym. slang.* An act of anal excretion. Named after the luscious "tits out" *Hammer Horror* actress Ingrid Pitt.

inheritance *n.* A miasmatic bequest bequeathed to a toilet-goer by the previous occupant.

injury time *1. n.* The dying seconds of a football match where the losing side throw caution to the wind and take a shot at anything in a desperate attempt to score. *2. n.* The last song of the evening in a nightclub.

Inman's twitch *n.* The brisk, staccato, buttock-clenched walk to the toilet when one is attempting to prevent *turtle* egress. From the gait adopted by late 1970s sitcom actor John Inman.

in receivership *adj.* Involved in a toilet situation which necessitates a sudden complete *clearout of stock.* A *dump* where "everything must go". *'I'm afraid Sir Clive can't come to the phone right now as he is in receivership. If you're phoning to complain about the shitty rubber keys on your ZX81 computer, please press one. If you're phoning because your C5 has run out of battery power after less than a hundred yards, please press two. For all other enquiries, please press three.'*

inside burns *n. Thighbrows, judge's eyebrows, Rhodes Boysons.* Effusive lateral *pubage* out the sides of a young lady's *dunghampers. 'I'm with you all the way on burning your bra and everything, Germaine. But could you do something about your inside burns? They're putting me off my stroke.'*

inside job *n.* A game of *pocket billiards.* Vigorously and rhythmically looking for change in your front pockets at a sophisticated lapdancing establishment. An *IPW.*

installing Windows *n.* Excuse given to the missus when one intends to lock oneself in the spare room and *wank* one's *plums* flatter than Tara Palmer-Tompkinson's chest over a series of hardcore internet *grumble* websites. *'What are you doing in there, Jerry? Tom and Barbara are waiting downstairs with a birthday cake for you.' 'Nothing Margot, just installing Windows. Could you push some more tissues under the door, please?'*

interior decorating *n.* Slapping a bit of white emulsion about the womb using the *naughty paintbrush.*

international breeding programme *1. n.* Zoological project whereby examples of endangered species are paired with overseas counterparts in order to maintain a healthy gene pool. *2. n.* A cheap holiday in Tenerife.

internet ready *adj.* Descriptive of one who already *paddles the skin canoe* with their left hand.

internetty *n.* A lavatory cubicle which is within laptop wireless network range, allowing a computer literate toilet-user to browse the worldwide web for antiquarian books, to pick an example at random, whilst he is seated on the *thunder box* masturbating furiously.

interrogate the prisoner *v.* To *box the Jesuit, strangle the parson, choke the chicken, bash the bishop, pull the Pope's cap off, have a five knuckle shuffle, pull your pud, spank the monkey etc.* To interfere with oneself in the *farmyard area. 'Richard, come down and get your tea.' 'I'll be right down, Judy. I'm just interrogating the prisoner. Into your shoe.'*

in the club *adj. Up the duff,* pregnant, preggers. From *in the pudding club.*

in the hockey team *adj.* Descriptive of a lesbidaceous woman. Or *lady golfer.*

in through the out door *1. n.* Title of Led Zeppelin's not very good final album. *2. n.* How Robert "Percy"

Plant might refer to a spot of *back door action.*

in vino fertilisation *n.* The usual manner in which babies are conceived.

ipod earphones *n.* Particular type of *jelly jewellery* furnished simultaneously by two generous gentlemen engaged in an act of *double glazing.* Stereophonic streams of *jitler* dribbling down from a lady's ears. *Shot by both sides.*

Ipswich smile *n.* A *pasata grin.*

iPud *n.* A portable, self-contained source of cheap entertainment which can be accessed via the trouser pockets and which keeps commuters smiling on crowded tube trains.

IPW *acronym.* The act of rummaging for change in one's trousers whilst in a lap-dancing establishment. In-Pocket Wank, an *inside job.*

Irish *1. n.* Heterosexual anal sex, supposedly as a means of contraception. *UTBNB. 2. rhym. slang.* Hairpiece. From Irish coupe = toupee.

Irish alarm clock *n.* Ten pints of Guinness. From the fact that a night on the black stuff more often than not leads to horrific, involuntary bowel movements which cause one to wake early the next morning. *'I hope you don't sleep in tomorrow. You're piloting a Space Shuttle up to the International Space Station, remember?' 'Don't worry, dear. I've set my Irish alarm clock.'*

Irish bhaji *n.* The sort of black, spicy, onion-smelling *Thora* which emerges from the *back body* the morning after one takes on board an excessive amount of stout.

irish luggage *n.* Politically incorrect phrase used to describe the life's accumulations of a *paraffin,* traditionally carted about in a picturesque knotted hankerchief on the end of a stick slung over his shoulder, but more usually in an old supermarket trolley filled with *shitty* bundles of carrier bags.

Irish shave *n.* A *dump.*

Irish toothache *1. n.* An erection, *bone on. 'Is that a gun in your pocket, or have you just got Irish toothache?'* 2. *n. Pregnancy. 'Is that a spacehopper in your smock, or have you just got Irish toothache?'*

iron *rhym. slang.* A *crafty butcher.* From Iron hoof = poof.

IRS *1. abbrev. US.* The yankee taxman. *2. abbrev.* Itchy Ring Syndrome. Irritating anal affliction caused by insufficient wiping of the *chocolate starfish,* or by inflammation of the *farmers.*

I say! *interj.* Caddish expression of delight upon seeing a pair of *dunces' hats.*

Isle of Wight *1. n.* A UK holiday destination made popular by Queen Victoria. *2. rhym. slang.* A load of rubbish. From Isle of Wight = pile of shite. *'That holiday we had on the Isle of Wight last summer was a complete Isle of Wight. We're going to Wales this year.'*

i-shuffle *n.* The self-harming behaviour of a fellow watching a *pudcast* on his ipod.

isnae *n. Scot.* The *taint, tintis, ABC, scruttock.*

Italian chipper *n.* A filthy dirty masturbating woman. From the fact that the Italian word for a deep-fat fryer is apparently *friggatrice.*

itch *n.* The feeling of mild sexual attraction towards his wife which a married man gets on average once every 7 years.

Itchypoo Park *n.* The area around *spice island* during a bout of *IRS.*

it's a buoy! *exclam.* Useful expression which can be employed following the delivery of a sizeable, floating *Meatloaf's daughter.*

it's a knockout *n.* An amusing pub game where an individual with *legs like snapped candles* has to attempt to carry three brim-full pint glasses through a jostling, crowded hostelry from bar to table without spilling any.

it's his stag *exclam.* Phrase shouted by a merry fellow's intoxicated friends as he is roughly half-nelsoned into the back of a police van the night before his wedding. Possibly not acknowledged as a plea of mitigation in a court of law.

I've lost R2 *exclam.* Said following a particularly vigorous expulsion of faecal matter, which leaves the *shitter* traumatised by a wave of aftershocks. Taken from the destruction of the Death Star scene in the little known 1977 film *Star Wars.*

I've loved in it *exclam.* Humorous staff version of the popular fast food advertising jingle, usually sung whilst preparing or serving *McDonald's special sauce* on the minimum wage.

ivory tower *n.* A night-time erectitivation of the *membrum virile.* A *dreaming spire,* a somnolent *dusk tusk.*

Jj

jackage *n. coll.* Any materials used by a fellow for the purposes of *jacking off to, at, on* or *over. Jazz, grumble, grummer, Frankie Vaughan etc.*

Jack Douglas *1. n. prop.* British film and television performer notable for wearing dungarees and a cap, whose Alf Ippatitimuss character was prone to sudden, spasmodic physical tics and hence *2. n.* Any violent, involuntary recoil from something, *eg.* a pint of milk which has gone off, a blocked train lavatory swimming in urine and faeces, or Shane McGowan's breath.

jacked up *1. adj.* To be celibate whilst suffering from a *dose*. *2. adj.* Of a woman, to be *up on axle stands.*

jack off *v.* To *whack off, choke the chicken, jerk the gherkin.*

jack roll *1. n. SA. A gang bang. 2. n. US.* A mugging.

jack shit *n. Bugger all, sweet FA,* zero, *zilch.* Nowt.

jacksie *n.* Polite word for *arse*, especially in the recepticular context. *'You can stick your fucking knighthood up your jacksie, mate. I paid for a peerage.'*

jacksie rabbit *n. Muddy funster.*

jacksydent *n.* A trouser mishap, a *follow through.* From jacksie + accident. *'Paula Radcliffe has pulled out of the 10,000 metres final, after suffering a nasty jacksydent during the marathon.'*

jack the beanstalk *v.* To attempt to pull up the *purple-headed gristle thistle* by the roots.

Jack the ripper *n.* A hard, thick, bloodthirsty *turd* that does its evil work in one's *back passage.* A *ring splitter.*

Jacky Danny *rhym. slang. James Hunt.*

jacobs *rhym. slang.* Testicles. From Jacobs crackers = bollocks. Generally kept close to the cheese.

jade *v.* To enter into something with great overconfidence, only to emerge at the end completely *fucked. 'In an off-the-cuff remark during an informal press briefing today, Tony Blair admitted that he had really jaded the latest war against Iraq.'* (BBC News 24).

jaded *adj.* Unable to perform in any form of marathon event, of either a drinking or a sexual nature, due to prior over-indulgence at the kebab shop. Derived from uncouth former *Big Brother* contestant-turned-vacuous *Celebrity Big Brother former* racist pariah millionairess Jade Goody's hilarious failure to complete a recent London 26-mile road race because she was too fat.

Jade yawning, a fanny like *sim.* A *clown's pocket,* an extreme *hippo's mouth.*

Jafaican *n.* The sort of ludicrous artificial Caribbean accent effected by middle class youths.

jaff *v.* To *wank.* In Norfolk. *'Ooh, I just jaffed behind the slaughterhouse. It was boodiful, really boodiful.'*

jaffas *n.* The *nuts* of the *fruit bowl. Family jewels.*

jail bait *n.* Worms dug up by tunnelling prisoners and later, after their escape, used for fishing.

jailbird *1. n.* An habitual criminal, who accepts arrest as an occupational hazard, and presumably accepts imprisonment in the same casual manner, *eg.* "Lord" Jeffrey Archer. *2. n.* An unattractive lady of whom it might be said: "Christ. I'd rather do time than do her." *eg.* That grim *pro* with whom "Lord" Jeffrey Archer *had it off* before giving her two grand in a brown envelope.

jake *1. n.* A columnar monument erected in memory of a nice pair of *jamboree bags* one once saw, or a notable scene from a *meat vid.* *2. n. Scot.* An ugly woman, *horndog, lumberjill.*

jamboree bags *n. Funbags, fat rascals.*

jambush *n.* A *blobstrop* that comes out of nowhere.

James *rhym. slang.* A *twat* in the pejorative rather than the gynaecological sense. From the inexplicably popular helium-voiced singer/songwriter James Blunt = fucking cunt.

James Browns *n.* The deeply upsetting noises which emanate from a row of office toilet cubicles during the daily 10.00am works *turd off.* From their similarity to the rambling squeals, incoherent grunts and random vocalisations which passed for lyrics in the songs of the hardest working corpse in showbiz.

James Cameron's camera *euph.* A subaquatic *Thora* which, despite repeated flushing, continues to inhabit the haunting depths of one's U-bend. Named after the deep-sea video equipment submersible that was used to provide footage of the sunken RMS Titanic and which, every time it landed on the wreck or sea-bed, caused a cloud of brown rust particles to swirl about. An *Alvin.*

James Hunt *rhym. slang. Jacky Danny.*

jammer *n. Carib.* A *pud.* See also *windjammer.*

jammet *n. Carib.* A West Indian term for a *slapper.*

jamming device *1. n.* James Bond-style Cold War espionage contraption, which is designed to prevent radio signals from reaching the enemy. *2. n.* Something rarely if ever encountered by agent 007; a feminine hygiene requisite. Also colloquially known as a *blobstopper, fanny mouse* or *Dracula's teabag.*

jammy dodger *n.* A lady who uses the fact that the *tomato boat has docked* to avoid performing her wifely duty.

jammy todger *n.* Something you wouldn't get off a *jammy dodger.* A *barber's pole.*

jampax *n.* A *clot mop, cotton pony.*

jam rag *n.* A tampon, *fanny mouse, chuftie plug.*

jam raid *n. Crimson tidal* movement which leaves *tuna town* inaccessible by *skin boat* at certain times of the month.

jam sandwich *1. n.* A tomato saucy threesome featuring two strong-stomached men and a lady who is *reading Cosmo.* *2. n.* A *rag week snatch, ie.* one with two layers of crust and a sticky red filling. *3. n.* Unamusing CB-lingo for a police car, used by lorry drivers who think they are behind the wheel of a chrome-laden eighteen-wheeler running moonshine in *Smokey and the Bandit,* but are in fact driving a grimy 1988 Foden along the A515 between Sudbury and Yoxall looking for a *fat-titted* hitch-hiker to grope and possibly murder.

jam session *n.* An improvised ragtime duet.

jane *1. n.* A ladies' lavatory. *2. n.* A *mary.*

jang *n. Dong. 'Fuckanory. I've caught me jang in me zip. Court is adjourned.'*

janitorial pleat *n.* An unexpected *stiffy* or *tent pole,* named after the unique and unusually-positioned design feature found only in the work trousers supplied to lecherous old school caretakers.

Japanese flag *n.* Appearance of the *arsehole* when blighted by *ring sting. Arse of the rising sun, Hawaiian sunrise.*

Japanese teardrop *n.* An unexpected single drop of *merry monk* that turns up ten minutes after the *bolt* has been shot, regardless of how thoroughly one mops the *herman.* The *missing fish.*

Jap's eye *n.* Politically incorrect male urethral opening, *hog's eye, chap's eye.*

jarred *adj. Pissed, sloshed, wankered.*

J Arthur *rhym. slang. Wank.* From the erstwhile British film distributor J Arthur Rasturbation.

jaywank *v.* To cross the *Billy Mill Roundabout* without due care and attention. To *change up into sixth gear* without regard to the sticky consequences.

jazz *1. n.* Improvised music characterised by syncopated rhythms. *2. n.* The *fadge, mott. 3. n.* Sex, intercourse, *the other. 4. n. Frankie Vaughanography.*

jazz drummer, go at it like a *sim.* To hunch over one's plate and shovel food into one's mouth at an unseemly speed, in a style reminiscent of Gene Krupa or Buddy Rich going at it *three cocks to the cunt.*

jazz egg *n.* A little *spodge* of *spadge.* A *spoff* of *spuff, jot* of *jit.*

jazz festival *n.* The purchase of two or more *Noddy books* at one time.

jazz fusion *n.* The process by which the pages of a *scud mag* are cemented together.

jazz mag *n.* A published pamphlet of artistic material, a gentleman's interest journal. Printed in *whacknicolour.*

jazz magnate *1. n.* A porn millionaire, one who who has benefited from a series of wristy investments. *2. n.* A short, blind, hairy-palmed lunatic who owns a substantial stash of *scud mags.*

jazz oyster *n.* A *bongo book snapper,* prised open to reveal the *clematis* within.

jazz potatoes *n.* Spuds which have been *salted* at the kitchen staff's discretion. *Winner's dinners.*

jazz stash *n.* A fellow's library of monomanual reference works. Usually kept on top of a wardrobe, but in Frank Skinner's case kept in several large warehouses on an industrial estate.

jazz talc *n. Bolivian marching powder, showbiz sherbet, Keith Richards' dandruff.*

jazz trumpeter's cheeks *sim.* Descriptive of a lady's well-rounded *arse.* Dizzy Gillespie's-face-style buttocks.

jazz vocalist *n.* One who encourages himself with erotic one-sided conversations ("ooh, baby, yeah!" *etc.*) with the girls in his *biff mags* whilst practising *self-pollution.*

JB *n.* See *Jodrell.*

j-cloth *n.* A teenager's phenomenally-absorbent underbed sock, used for cleaning up adolescent spillages.

jebbs *1. n.* Manufacturer of crash helmets and hence *2. n.* Big round *knockers* which carry a BSI kitemark and comply with BS 6658.

Jedi *rhym. slang.* A *turd.* From Jedi Knight = shite.

Jehovah's stiffness *n.* An unwelcome erection which arrives at the most inconvenient times and then refuses to leave. A *tiffter, Jake, Eric.*

Jehovah's wetness *n.* In ladies, autonomic dampness *under the bridge* experienced at inopportune moments.

jelly bag *n.* The wrinkled retainer where a gentleman keeps his *Egyptian Halls.* The scrotum. *'How's that, DPM?' 'Sorry, Tracey, nowt's happening yet. Try tickling me jelly bag for a bit. And make it snappy, will you. I'm speaking at a memorial service for the dead of two world wars in twenty minutes.'*

jelly hammock *n. Drip tray.*

jelly jewellery *n.* The earrings, nose studs, fancy spectacles and other facial adornments a lady sometimes receives when she was expecting her partner to give her a *pearl necklace.*

jelly roll *1. n. US. Snatch, muff, totty.* 2. *n.* Getting *fucked* by a jazz pianist who died in 1941.

jelly water mangos *n.* Large *knockers, gazunkas.*

Jenny *n. US. Boris, minge.*

Jeremy Beadle's thumb, hung like *sim.* An unacceptably tasteless and offensive way of referring to a fellow who is somewhat under-endowed *down there. Hung like a Chinese mouse.*

jerk *n.* A stupid, dim or dull person.

jerkin' the gherkin *n.* Jiggling a small cucumber round on the end of a string.

jerk off *1. v. Jack off. 2. n. US.* A *goddam dicksplash, asswipe.*

jerkolator *n.* An extremely noisy *blow job*, performed by someone who comes back for coffee.

jerkwad *n. US. Tosser, fuckwit, wankipants.* A person to whom one might show the elevated second finger of one's right hand before rhetorically inviting them to swivel thereupon.

jerry in the trench *euph.* Phrase used when describing an itchy *ringpiece* when one is in polite company. Useful when one finds oneself suffering from an attack of *arse wasps* or *wire spiders* at Glyndebourne, the Hay-on-Wye Literary Festival or the Queen Mother's funeral, for example.

Jersey Royals *euph.* Smallish, but pert and firm, *shirt potatoes* which are particularly good boiled with a bit of butter on. *Sara Cox's orange pippins.*

jester's shoes *n. medic.* The involuntary upward curling movements of the toes that herald the onset of the *vinegar strokes*, whilst lying on one's back *wanking. 'Zoom in on Gunther for the money shot, camera two. He's got the jester's shoes.'*

jeweller *n.* A gifted manufacturer of *jelly jewellery* and *pearl necklaces.*

jewels *n. Family jewels.*

jibble *n.* The final, sad, leaking tears of *spangle* which drip out of one's *hog's eye* in those *wangst-*

ridden moments of spiralling despair and self-loathing which apparently follow a bout of *self help*. From jizz + dribble.

jig-a-jig *n. It, how's your father*.

jigger *n. 18thC*. That tool with which a man commits *jiggery pokery*. The *fuck stick*.

jiggered *1. adj*. In a state of fatigue. *Buggered, knackered, shagged out*. *2. adj*. Something that a surprised person is confident that they will be.

jiggery pokery *n. Shenanigans*, assorted sexual goings on. *'I'll have no jiggery pokery going on under my roof.'*

jiggle ring *n*. The larger lady's *muffin top* lifebelt, shaken to attract the attention of prospective partners. *'Don't look now, but that munter at the bar is offering you her jiggle ring.'*

jiggle show *n*. A titillating, but *chest tuner*-free early evening television show, *eg*. *Baywatch, Charlie's Angels*.

jiggle the jewellery *v*. To *box the jesuit, rough up the suspect*.

jigglypuff *n*. A man who watches female television programmes, such as *EastEnders* and *Emmerdale*, of his own free will.

jill off *v*. Female equivalent of *jack off*, to *paddle the pink canoe*. Until it leaks.

jimmy hat *1. n*. A latex prophylactic device designed to keep the head of the penis dry during intercourse. *2. n*. A piece of headwear designed for or worn by someone called Jimmy.

Jimmy Edwards *n*. Tufts of *pubage* protruding either side of a bikini bottom, resembling the handlebar moustache of the late *Whacko!* star. *Thighbrows*.

Jimmy Riddle *rhym. slang*. Vicar-friendly term for *turning your bike around*. *'I'm just going for a Jimmy Riddle, vicar.' 'Well don't forget to shake the end of your cock to get the last few drops off it.'*

jimmy sack *n*. School lavatory high jinks. During an act of urination, the *fiveskin* is pinched shut, creating a high-pressure bag of *piss* at the end of the penis. This can be used to chase people as, when released, a *jimmy sack* can be explosive.

Jimmy Savile *1. n*. Yorkshire-born ex-coal miner, who went on to become a founding Radio 1 DJ, and hosted the first edition of *Top of the Pops* as well as *Jim'll Fix It*. (The rest of this definition has been cut in anticipation of a substantial amount of legal advice.) *2. n*. A *bum cigar* of such humungous proportions that it forces involuntary high-pitched warbling noises to issue from its begetter's mouth, in the style made popular by the erstwhile ennobled *Jim'll Fix It* presenter when fixing it for his young guests to mow the lawn in the *Blue Peter* garden, or some other such bit of low-budget BBC tomfoolery.

Jimmy White's brother *n*. The most boring member of any group of lads who turns up every night at the pub to sit in abject, oppressive silence. From the urban legend that when Jimmy White's brother died, his friends broke into the undertakers to take the corpse out for one last *piss-up*.

Jimmy Wonkle *n*. The gentleman's *widdle tap*.

Jim Royle's beard *n.* A *Dylan.*

jism *n.* Semen. Also *gism, jissom, jizz, jizzom.*

jitbag *n.* A *dunky, jubber ray.*

jit gel *n. US.* The contents of a used *jitbag* once it has floated across the Atlantic.

jit gel rag *n. US.* Any available object upon which you wipe your *cock* after sex, *eg.* tissues, underpants, curtains, tramp's beard.

jitlag *n.* The slimy, post-coital *jazz egg* that drops out the end of one's *charlie* about 20 minutes after *stack blow.* The *post bolt,* the *missing fish.*

jitler *n. Spunk.*

jizlas *n.* Thin sheets of paper used to mop up *tugwax.*

jizz *1. n. Jism. 2. v.* To *shoot one's load, lose one's mess.*

jizzaster *n.* The leaving of incriminating masturbatory evidence behind. *'That wad of spunk on the carpet was a fucking jizzaster. Not to mention the Fuck Truck tape in the video, or the circle of open wank mags on the living room floor. Or me lying unconscious in the middle of it all with my trousers round my ankles and my red-raw cock in my hand.'*

jizzbags *n.* The scrotum, *John Wayne's hairy saddlebags.*

jizz bib *n.* A sacrificial T-shirt placed over the stomach and chest to prevent seminal claggage of the chest hair during a horizontal *wank.*

jizz bib *n.* A *shirtlifter*'s goatee beard.

jizz bolt *n.* A glob of ejaculate that leaves the *hog's eye* with enough force to put the television screen through. A *golden shot, Bernie the bolt.*

jizzbolt jury *n.* Any group of men watching and discussing the merits of a *stick vid.*

jizz drive *n.* An external storage medium for *left-handed website* downloads.

jizziotherapy *n.* A three-minute, one-handed massage that relieves stiffness for up to half an hour.

jizz jar *n.* Girlfriend. Probably considered derogatory, although one would think they'd take it as a compliment.

jizz juggler *1. n.* An enthusiastic *wankatrix. 2. n.* One of the less successful variety acts to audition for *Britain's Got Talent.*

jizzle *n.* A drizzle of *jizz.* Derivation unknown.

jizzmopper *n.* A member of the honourable profession of peep show *wank booth* hygienist.

jizzmopper's cloth *1. n.* An absorbent rag used by a *jizzmopper* in the performance of their daily duties. *2. sim.* Descriptive of a *cockoholic*'s knickers.

jizzn't *n.* The *spunk* of a man who's either had a vasectomy or whose *tadpoles* aren't very good at swimming. *'I'm sorry, Mr Dawson. I've had a look at your sample under the microscope and I'm afraid it's jizzn't.'*

jizz off a porn queen's face *sim.* A hardcore version of "water off a duck's back". *'Frankly, Clare Short's criticisms of Tony Blair's presidential style of government are like jizz off a porn queen's face to the Prime Minister.'* (Andrew Marr, Radio 4 *Today* programme, May 2003).

jizzard *n.* A swirling blizzard of the wrong sort of *snow,* sufficient to stop a *train being pulled* in a *grumble flick.*

J-lower *n.* A girl blessed with a substantially bigger and even more gravitationally-challenged *council gritter* than Miss Lopez. See also *Sharon sixteen stone.*

J-No *n. prop.* A self-deluded *bird* with a horrible fat *arse* who believes she looks good in tight jeans or hipsters.

Joan Collins' knickers See *tart's window box*.

job *n.* A *feeshus*.

jobby, a big *n. Scot.* A *dreadnought*. That which is wheeked.

jobby engine *n.* The lavatory or water closet. The *shit pot, bum sink.*

jobby jouster *n.* A Knight of *King Richard the Third.*

jocaine *n. Showbiz sherbet* that's been mixed with baking powder or talc, and thus fails to come up with the goods when snorted through a rolled ten pound note in a lavatory by a sweating children's television presenter. *Salted sniff.*

jockeys *rhym. slang.* Nipples. From jockeys' whips = nips.

jockey's coffin *n.* An exceptionally small and snug-fitting *fluffit*. A *mouse's ear,* a *paper cut.* *'And so it was that Mary was pure and had not known a man and had a snatch like a jockey's coffin, yet she was great with child.'* (*Luke* 1:4).

jockey's starting position *n.* The well-braced *arse*-in-the-air stance adopted by one who is shortly anticipating a *shot from the starter's gun.*

Jodrell *rhym. slang.* A J Arthur. From the UMIST radio telescope Jodrell Wank.

joff *v.* To *milm* one's *grundies* without even being *tumescent.* Derived from Jizz On Flop. *'I joffed when I found my dad's bootleg Night in Paris vid behind some tins of paint in the garage.'*

jogging behind a gritter *sim.* Descriptive of the face of a woman with a less than peach-like complexion, *eg.* Susan Tully, Frances de la Tour, Kate O'Mara. *'Jesus Christ! She's got a face like she's been jogging behind a gritter. Where did you find her?' 'She was jogging behind a gritter.'*

John *1. n. Percy, Willie, John Thomas*. A *cock*. *2. n.* A *pro's* client, a *Hillman Hunter.* *3. n. US.* A *crapper*.

John Craven *1. rhym. slang.* A *shaven haven.* *2. n.* The act of drinking five pints of beer or lager without going to the toilet for a *piss* until the third pint is finished. Derivation unknown, but possibly a reference to a "spoof" article about newsreaders' drinking capacity in issue 28 of the downmarket magazine *Viz* which enjoyed a brief vogue in the last century. A three pint total is known as a Jan Leeming, from the same supposedly "humorous" article.

John Holmes *n.* A massive marijuana cigarette, named after the legendary saucy actor of the same name who reputedly had a large *tassel.* (Not to be confused with a *Luke Jackson* - a rather small and unsatisfying marijuana cigarette named after Luke Jackson from Sutton Coldfield).

John Lees *rhym. slang. Scots. Tits.* From noted dead blues groaner John Lee Hooker = sooker.

John Merrick's cap *n.* A vast, out of shape *fanny.*

johnny *n.* A *dunky*, a *jubber ray.* *'Eurgh! I just found a johnny in my Big Mac.'*

Johnny Cash *1. n.* £2 for 3. *2. n.* A *Wigan rosette*. A *burning ring of fire*.

johnny jibber *n.* To lose *wood* upon opening the *flunkey*. Premature ejaculation and *johnny jibber* are thought to affect 1 in 4 males at some time in their life.

Johnny no-stars *n.* A *dolt*. From the "star rating" system on the badges displayed by staff at McDonald's. One who occupies a place on the lower end of the evolutionary fast food chain.

John Sargent *1. n.* A *fry-up face.* Refers to anyone with features resembling the former BBC Chief Political Correspondent. *2. n.* A great British fried breakfast of which, before commencing, one might say "Now over to BBC Chief Political Correspondent John Sargent".

John the Baptist *1. n.* prop. Biblical character, a sort of Happy Shopper Jesus who got his head cut off at the request of some New Testament pole dancer or other. *2. n.* A pungently prophetic *air biscuit*; one that speaks of a greater one to come (probably in solid form).

John Thomas *n.* How gamekeeper David Mellors referred to his *slag hammer* in the controversial novel *Lady Chatterley's Lover.*

John Wayne's hairy saddle bags *1. n. Jizzbags. 2. n. Saloon doors.*

John Wayne's safety catch, more time off than *sim.* In an office or workplace, descriptive of employees who are constantly ill. *Glassbacks.*

John Waynes *n.* Walking like Mrs Thatcher, George Bush or Tony Blair when he was visiting George Bush, *ie.* that gait adopted after *giving birth to Meatloaf's daughter*. Makes the walker look like they've been sitting on a horse for three days.

joiner's bag *n.* A battered, capacious *blurtch* with all hammers and spirit levels falling out of it.

join giblets *v.* To do *thingy* with a bare lady.

jollies *1. n. Police.* In constabulary terms, trips to scenes of crimes. *2. n.* Women's breasts. *'Look at the jollies on that nun, Your Holiness.'*

jollup *n.* A dollop of *jizz.* From Greek jollopus = dollop of jizz.

jollyrancher *n. US.* One blessed with the cat-like ability to *cannonball, ie.* a man who never leaves the house but orders in a lot of breath-fresheners.

Jonathan *rhym. slang.* A *Sherman tank*, a *Barclay's,* from the masturbating TV presenter Jonathan Ross OBE = toss OBE.

joombye *n. Scot. Jism, jizz, McSpunk,* deep-fried *vitamin S.*

Jordan's toppers *1. n.* Wholesome breakfast bars, full of natural ingredients. *2. n.* The ludicrously-proportioned *chestular assets* of Mrs Andre, full of artificial ingredients, E-numbers and synthetic additives.

Joseph's balls *n. medic. Nuts* that have not been evacuated for a long time. From the supernaturally cuckolded biblical carpenter's testicles. *'How's tricks, Cliff?' 'To tell you the truth, Hank, I've not had any since the late fifties, and it feels like I've got Joseph's balls in my pants.'*

joskin *n.* A country bumpkin, a rustic dolt, a *sheep shagger.*

josser *n. 19thC. Fuckwit* or parasite. The ideal name for someone who is both.

jostle the chosen one *v.* To *pull the Pope's cap off,* to *box the Jesuit.*

jotter *n.* The *teatowel holder, loon pipe, council gritter, gazoo, balloon knot, raisin, chocolate starfish, Gary, rusty sheriff's badge, freckle, clacker valve, kakpipe, corn dot, ringpiece, crapper, aris, quoit, poop chute, panda's eye etc.* The *arsehole. 'Palmolive was powerless to resist. His eyes burnt into hers like malachites. His muscular arms enfolded her body as she felt herself being swept away in a mistral of passion. "I love you, Alfonso,' she gasped. 'Take me now, I'm yours.' 'Drop your grundies and bend over then, love,' said Alfonso, unzipping his heaving slacks. 'I'll slip you a quick length up the jotter."* (from *The Lady and the Travel Rep* by Barbara Cartland).

joy division *1. n.* Seminal indie band whose lead singer hanged himself in Macclesfield after listening to an Iggy Pop album, and you can see his point. *2. n.* The *notcher, carse, barse, Humber Bridge, tinter, taint, tisnae, tissent etc. 3. n. medic. Banjo* trauma, that is to say the unthinkable consequences of an accident wherein "love has torn us apart".

joy plug *n.* The congealed remnant of a successful *wank* that causes a slight pause at the start of a *hit and miss.*

joyrider's moustache *n.* The light growth of fluffy top lip *bum fluff* popular with teenage delinquents.

joystick *n.* Of *choppers*, the cockpit instrument or *knob,* which gets throttled. *Trouser toy, pant plaything.*

joy valve *n.* A lady's *bodily treasure.*

J-pig *n.* An internet *porn monster.*

jubblies *n.* Lovely breasts, *funbags, milky swingers, fat rascals.*

jubnuts *n. Bead curtains, dangleberries, dags.*

judges' eyebrows *n. Spiders' legs.*

Judi Dench *n. rhym. slang.* A stench.

Judith *n.* A very dense, dark *fadge,* as sported by the character Judith in *Monty Python's Life of Brian. 'Bloody hell, love, you've got a right Judith on you. It looks like you've been hit between the legs with a bag of soot.'*

juggage *n.* Collective term for a lady's assets. *'Phwooar. Your missus carries a lot of juggage, don't she.'*

jugged-mare *n.* An aesthetically-challenged woman who is nevertheless worth a go due to her large *tits.* A *bapdog.*

jugged up *1. adj.* Of a happy fellow, to find himself well catered for in the *headlamps* department. *'Dave doesn't come out much since he met Double-D Denise. He's jugged up.' 2. adj.* Of a lady, to be generously endowed in terms of chestular glandage. *'Blimey, she's jugged up. She must have been re-racked, surely.'*

juggernorks *n.* A huge pair of *Gert Stonkers* that come bearing down on you well ahead of their owner. *Stobarts, mammoets, norberts.*

jumble grumble *n.* Car boot sale-quality *self-help* material, *eg.*

Razzle, Nuts, the bra pages of the Freemans catalogue. *Poornography, paupernography*.

juggery pokery *n.* An act of penile love performed amongst a woman's secondary sexual characteristics. A well-sprung *tit fuck,* if you will.

juggler's doughnuts *1. n. prop.* A popular themed fast food store at Alton Towers. *2. n. Shirt potatoes* when handled in the style of a circus performer tossing balls from hand to hand.

juggstaposition *n.* The visual mismatch of two contrastingly-sized pairs of *oomlaters* in close proximity, Trinny Woodall standing next to former Foreign Secretary Baron Owen of the City of Plymouth, for example.

jug jousting *v.* A *bunny rub*.

jugly *adj.* Ugly, but with big *knockers, eg.* Anna Ryder Richardson, Erica Rowe, Lord Owen.

jugs *n.* A lady's *top bum*.

juice of hazard *n.* Any over-strong, export strength alcoholic beverage, *eg.* methylated spirits, metal polish, Carlsberg Special Brew *etc.*, the prolonged consumption of which may lead to unruly and erratic driving, especially when attempting to outrun the police.

juicy flute *n.* A chewy, salty snack for the ladies. The *gut stick*.

JULF *acronym.* Jumped Up Little Fucker, a pushy *twat*.

jullet *n. medic.* The phenomenon of the breasts, upper chest and chins of a *salad-dodging* lady all being merged into the same wobbling mass of flesh. The antipode of the *gunt*. From jugs + gullet

jump *v.* To have sex with someone's bones off the top of a wardrobe.

jump on the grenade *v.* Of a man, to perform the noble and selfless act whereby he *cops off* with an ugly *bird* solely to enable his friend to *pull* her fit mate. From the slightly less impressive story from World War I where a Private threw himself on a grenade to protect his comrades from the blast.

junction nine *n.* A ribald term for a folically-challenged fellow. From the similarly named interchange on the M25, which *goes to Leatherhead. 'Famous people who were born on February 22nd: George Washington, first president of the United States of America, 1732; Lord Robert Stephenson Smythe Baden-Powell, hero of the siege of Mafeking and founder of the Boy Scout movement, 1857; Kenneth Williams, raconteur, diarist and film, stage, television and radio actor, 1926; Bruce Forsyth, chinny junction nine, 1928.'* (from *Schott's Oh Fuck it, That'll Have to Do, I'm Off Down the Pub Book, 2006*).

jungle juice *n. Blip, moip, fanny batter.*

jungle VIP *n.* A woman with pendulous breasts. From the apposite lines of the song performed by Louis, the orang-utan "King of the swingers" in Disney's *Jungle Book*.

junior *n. US.* Penis, usually used in reference to one's own.

junior scrabble, easier than *sim.* Phrase which can be used when referring to an accommodating lady who is quite prepared to allow gentlemen to have penetrative sexual intercourse up her without requiring the poor sods to jump through hoops first.

junk *1. n. coll.* The contents of the *fruitbowl. "I say, Jeeves. Drat these new fangled flies in my plus-fours,' I blustered. 'Haven't I just caught all my junk in the bally zipper mechanism."* (from *Ooh, Yes! Just There! Don't Stop, Jeeves* by PG Wodehouse). *2. n.* The *ejaculate* that lobs out the end of the *cock* part of the *junk*. "Launder these plus fours, Jeeves, there's a fellow,' I said. *'I'm meeting Aunt Agatha for tea, and there's dried junk down the front from where Dulcie Wegg-Prosser gave my old chap a strop in the back of the Lagonda."* (from *Fetch Some Tissues, Jeeves* by PG Wodehouse).

jurassic parp *n.* A bubble of fossilized *carbon dibaxide* from the *tar pit* that could bring tears to the eye of a brontosaurus.

Kk

kakatoa *n.* An earth-shattering anal explosion that can be heard half way round the world and which causes tidal waves and *poonamis* to sweep through the *chod bin,* devastating everything that lies in their path. Also *crackatoa.*

kahoonas *n.* Large wobbly bosoms, *golden bodangers, kermungers, Gert Stonkers.*

kak *n. Keech, kaka, shite.* Feculant matter, to put it crudely. *'These ads with Esther fucking Rantzen in are the final straw. Fetch a jiffy bag, dear, I'm going to send her a kak in the post.'*

kak klaxon *n.* The *rectal hooter* from which loud anal honks are emitted, together with the occasional *bonus ball.*

kakpipe cosmonaut *n.* He who prefers to *dock* his *command module* in the *rear unloading bay.*

kama slutra *n.* Exotic repertoire of sexual positions practised in cars, in shop doorways and behind skips *etc.* on Saturday nights.

kangaroo pouch *n.* A large *granny fanny,* big enough to fit your head in. A *horse's collar.*

kangaroo shagging a spacehopper *sim.* Descriptive of the way a *shit house* door blows in the wind.

Kaplinsky, suffer a *v.* To fail to hear some important information as one's attention is entirely focused upon the thighs or cleavage of the person speaking. Named after Natasha Kaplinsky, whose thighs and cleavage drown out the news on BBC TV's Breakfast Programme.

kazoo *1. n.* A tissue paper-covered aperture which *hums* tunelessly. *2. n.* A completely unmusical musical instrument. A *swannee whistle.*

KD lady *n.* A *lezza.* Named after comfortably-shod Canadian chanteuse KD Lang, who has yet to find the right young man.

Keats *n.* A bout of *self abuse* that one embarks upon, despite being physically debilitated. Named after the romantic poet John Keats who, struck down in his early years with galloping consumption, still managed a couple of *tugs* a day.

kebabble *n.* The incoherent mumblings and inept attempts at ordering food endured by the staff of greasy takeaway outlets after the pubs have closed.

kebabe *n.* A woman who looks incredibly tasty when one is *pissed* at two in the morning, but the thought of whom turns one's stomach in the sober light of day.

kebabulance *n.* Late night emergency vehicle, such as the one parked on Christchurch Road, Reading or Link Road, Sawston.

keck cackler *n.* One with an easily amused *kazoo.* Person who exhibits *canned laughter.*

keck cougher *n.* He who *burps backwards,* or emits *under thunder.*

kecks *n.* See *kegs.*

keech *n. Crap, kak, kaka, keek.*

keel haul *v.* To drag one's tongue underneath a woman from *lip* to *ring.*

keema naan *n.* A shaved *fanny* with the very tip of the *bacon* sticking out.

keeping it on the clutch *v.* To skillfully work a *wank* just below boiling point to see one through the adverts on Bravo. *Treading water,* holding it at *the biting point.*

keep one's powder dry *v.* To feign disinterest in a bout of sex with the wife to ensure one can give it to the girlfriend with both barrels in a later engagement.

keeps his coins in his wallet, he *euph.* Phrase which can be used when referring to a fellow who is *good with colours, sensitive, good with his hands, stylish, a good listener etc. 'See that chap in the bushes with the big moustache?' 'Who, the one bumming the bloke in the leather chaps whilst listening to Judy Garland records on his walkman?' 'Aye. well him, right. Keep it under your hat, but I have it on very good authority that he keeps his coins in his wallet.'*

keep shouting Sir, we'll find you *exclam. milit.* Humorous phrase uttered after someone has *dropped* a particularly loud *gut.* See also *how much?; taxi for Brown.*

keep the change *v.* Of a lady, to imbibe the issue of an act of *horatio*, as opposed to expectorating it. To *swallow.*

keepy-uppy *1. n.* A marathon ball control game practised by schoolboys in the park. 2. *n.* A marathon ball control game practised by Sting in his wife. Tantric sex.

kegs *n.* See *kex.*

keister *n. Nipsy.*

Keith Burtons *n.* Spooneristic *beef curtains.*

Keith Harris, do a *v.* To get your hand so far up a *bird's hole* you could make her mouth move. From the formerly popular flightless duck ventriloquist. Also *do a Rod Hull, give it some Orville.*

Kelly Brooks *n.* An ill-matched pair of wonky *jugs.*

Kemal *n.* A sexual act performed in a sordid or dirty location. Named after the *Big Brother 6* contestant who confessed on camera to *sucking someone off* in a skip. Not even behind a skip. IN a skip, for fuck's sake.

Ken Dodd *v.* To masturbate into your partner's hair whilst they are asleep, such that they awaken next morning with a hairstyle similar to that of the scouse comic.

Ken Dodd's hairbrush *n.* A particularly unkempt lady's *clunge.* From the fact that the erstwhile dentally-challenged taxophobe gagsmith's hairbrush probably looks like a scraggy *twat,* with all bits of unusually-coloured hair stuck out of it at funny angles. *Terry Waite's allotment.*

Kennedy *n.* A sexual session which incorporates penetration in all orifices except the ears and nose. From the sex-mad American president John F. Kennedy who once said "you haven't finished with a woman until you've had her three ways".

Kennedys, the *n. prop.* The male genitalia; the *fruit bowl, meat and two veg, the boys.* Named after the famous US political dynasty, *ie.* Jack and Bobby, and Ted in the middle with his big head.

kennel maid *n.* The hostess of an inexpensive massage parlour.

Kent quake *n.* A gentle rumble followed by the release of an unimpressive amount of *arse gas* through one's *fissure.* A flatulent event which is low on the *sphincter scale,* but which could nevertheless cause a small amount of structural damage.

Keown surgery *n.* A piece of maxillo-facial reconstruction (commonly a broken nose) performed by a no-nonsense centre-half during a Sunday League football match.

kerbside quiche *n.* A *pavement*

pizza.

Kermits, the *n.* Of a gentleman, the unwelcome situation of being constantly stalked and chatted up by a *pig* he would never wish to *fuck* in a million years.

kerrangatang *n.* A large, hairy, heavy metal enthusiast.

Kestrel manoeuvres in the dark *n.* The wayward shuffle of a *Harold Ramp* who has spent the whole day on the *wifebeater.*

kettling *1. adj.* Descriptive of the state of being in dire, immediate need of a *shit.* From the fact that a metal lid placed over one's *clackervalve* in such circumstances would rattle urgently, and possibly emit a high-pitched whistle to boot. *2. adj.* Of a sexually excited woman's *mingepiece*, *frothing* so vigorously that one could, if one were sufficiently ingenious and in possession of a length of suitable pressure hose, use it to power a "Mamod" traction engine across the bedroom floor or a small steam launch across Lake Windermere.

kex *1. n. Shreddies, trolleys,* underpants. *2. n. Round-the-houses, kegs.*

kexorcism *n.* The act of driving out an evil, demonic *food's ghost* from one's *chamber of horrors.*

kexpresso *n.* A type of diarrhoea produced by one who needed a *crappuccino,* but couldn't get to the toilet on time.

key dropper *n.* A *bottee.*

keyboard hero *n.* One who is bravely prepared to engage in prodigious acts of personal courage that would normally entail the risk of a thorough kicking if he were not protected by the anonymity of an internet message board.

keyhole surgery *n.* The act of having a vigorous and satisfying dig around a particularly itchy *teatowel holder.*

KFC *1. abbrev.* Something quick, spicy and filling involving a bit of greasy old *cock* and a *bucket of batter.* Knob Filled Cunt. *'I thought we'd stay in tonight, love. Fancy a KFC?' 2. n.* A girl who will cheaply provide a bit of breast, a bit of leg and a *box* to put your *bone* in.

khazi *n. Shitter, bog, cludgie. NB.* For best effect, this word should be spoken in the style of Wilfred Brambell.

khaki buttonhole *n.* The *chocolate starfish, rusty bullet hole.*

Khyber *rhym. slang. Arse.* From Khyber Parse.

kick start the motorbike *v.* To lift one's leg prior to popping an anal wheelie.

kick the knackers out of *v.* To complete the majority of a piece of work. *'By the February of 1498, and after two full years of work in the refectory of St Maria delle Grazie in Milan, Leonardo had just about kicked the knackers out of his Last Supper fresco. Accordingly, in March of that year he embarked for Florence in order to start inventing the helicopter.'* (from Vasari's *Lives of the Painters*).

kick with the left foot *v.* What players who arrive on the *other bus* tend to do, a football equivalent of *bowling from the pavillion end.*

kid juice *n. Baby gravy, heir spray.*

kid's piss *n.* A nightclub toilet act of urination whereby the *kex* and *bills* are lowered onto the shoes at the urinal by someone too *pissed* to attempt a penile extraction through the flies.

kidney cider *n.* A discarded drinks container at the side of the road containing lorry driver's urine. *Trucker's tizer, Scania scotch.*

kidney fizzer *n.* Uncomfortably biological hangover after a particularly heavy night of binge *refreshment,* characterised by bubbling sensations in the lower back. *Alcoseltzer.*

kidney prodder *n.* During an act of sexual congress, a particularly impressive thrust.

kidneys, shit one's *v.* To experience a traumatic *digestive transit* as a result of severe alarm or a particularly hot *Ruby Murray. 'Come for a meal at the Curry Capital, Bigg Market, Newcastle upon Tyne, and if you don't shit your kidneys, I'll give you your money back'.* (Abdul Latif, Lord of Harpole, short-lived Tyne Tees Television advertising campaign, 1996).

kidney wiper *n. Slat rattler.* See also *purple headed womb broom.*

kid with an ice-cream, like a *sim.* Descriptive of the face of a lucky *grumble flick* starlet after a series of well-aimed *pop shots.* Descriptive of a *plasterer's radio.*

kife *1. n. coll. Blart, totty, tussage, buffage. 2. n. The other.*

kilt *1. n. coll. Skirt. 2. n. coll. Scot.* Blokes.

kilt lifter *n.* A Scottish fellow who is *good with colours,* a *McQueen,* a *gay Gordon.*

King Alfred's cakes *n.* Severely over-cooked products of the *dirt bakery.*

kingbast *n.* A sweary term that can be shouted in front of grannies, vicars, nuns *etc.* without causing offence. Contraction of *fucking bastard.*

King Canute *n.* An enormous *Richard the Third* that blocks the bend and holds back the tide of the flush, causing the toilet to overflow.

King for a day *euph.* To have a bad case of the *Brads, ie.* to spend all day on the *throne.*

King Kong's finger *n.* A *turd* large enough to flatten a car. An *Elvis killer.*

King of the elephants *exclam.* An affectionate chorus, sung humorously in the street whilst pointing at someone with *big bones.*

king of the mountains *1. n.* In bicycle racing, the competitor who is the best at riding his bike up hills. In the Tour de France, the king of the mountains can be recognised by the fact that he wears a distinctive polka-dot jersey. *2. n.* A smug gentleman whose ladyfriend is blessed in the *headlamp* department. Can be recognised by the fact that he's usually to be seen on the front of *OK!* magazine, getting married, renewing his vows, having a christening, releasing a *shit* record, lounging in a swimming pool, recovering from a critical illness *etc.*

kipper *1. n.* The *Billingsgate box, minge, captain's pie. 2. n.* That useful bit of skin that keeps the *plums* safely out of the *arse's* reach. The *barse, tintis, notcher. Perry Como's lip.*

kipper basting *v. Shagging.*

kipper carriage *n.* Any battery-powered contrivance employed by *old trouts* who are bent on terrorising pedestrians and sneering at children who dare to cycle on the footpath between their home and the cat-food shop.

kipper for breakfast *n.* To rise early and go for a *horizontal jog*, an ideal cure for *dawn horn.*

kipper's cunt *n.* Even more pungent than an *anchovy's fanny.* The *ne plus ultra* of fish-smellyness.

kiss for granny *n.* The hermetically-sealed, tightly-pursed peck one gives one's girlfriend after *crashing the yoghurt truck* in her gob. A *nun's kiss.*

kissing tackle *n.* The north and south, *cakehole.*

kissing the tortoise *n.* Some sort of activity that doesn't bear thinking about, as performed by Ian McCulloch out of Echo and the Bunnymen, and subsequently sung about in that band's song *Seven Seas* on the 1987 album *Ocean Rain.*

kiss the Amish *v.* To perform oral sex upon a particularly *Dave Narey* pair of *catflaps.* To *lick out* a *bear trapper's hat, eat sushi off a barbershop floor.*

kiss the frog *v.* Of a lady, to perform *horatio.*

kiss the porcelain god *v.* To *talk on the great white telephone, drive the porcelain bus.*

Kit-Kat *v.* To stimulate a lady with four fingers at once, using a swift, forward thrusting, karate chop-type motion.

Kit-Kat shuffler *n. A masturbatress, weasel buffer, gusset typist.*

kitten eyes *n.* Of a lucky lady who has just received a hefty load of hot *fish yoghurt* in her face, to have difficulty peeling her eyelids apart, in a manner reminiscent of a three-day-old baby cat opening its *minces* for the first time. *'Aw bless. She's got kitten eyes, look.' 'Quick. Freeze the frame, your Holiness. I'm nearly there.'*

kitten hammer *n.* A penis. From the scientific fact well known amongst twelve-year-olds that every time they masturbate, a kitten dies.

kitten hammock *n. Tit pants.*

kitten purse *n.* Charming, feminine term for a lady's *cludge.*

kittens' noses *n. Puppies' noses, jockeys.* Nipples.

kiwi fruit *n.* A particularly hirsute *nadsack.* Named after the Chinese gooseberry, a fruit which exhibits a marked similarity to a hairy scrotum in both appearance and indeed flavour.

klatch *n. Drip tray* flotsam, *jelly hammock* jetsam. *Gusset effluvium.*

kleeneczema *n. medic.* The skin condition contracted when tissue sticks to a *wedding-milky* hand.

kling-ons *1. n.* One of numerous races of *Star Trek* alien with Cornish pastie foreheads. *2. n. Winnets, dangleberries,* assorted anal hangers-on.

klutz *n.* A thickhead. From the German *for fuckwit.*

knack *1. v.* To break. *2. v.* To hit. *3. v.* To hurt. *'He knacked me with a baseball bat and knacked my shin. It fucking knacks, doctor.'*

knackatoa *n.* An unpredictable eruption of sticky magma from a fissure set above hot *rocks.*

knacker *1. n.* A single testicle. *2. n.* A *knobhead. 3. v.* To tire out. *4. v.* To break.

knacker barrel *n.* Attractively-packaged *smegma.*

knackernits *n. medic.* Crabs, *pissnits, mechanical dandruff.*

knackers *n. Balls, nuts,* plural testicles. *'Mmmm. Just taste that reformed mixture of gristle, seagull shit and ground-up turkey knack-*

ers. Boodiful, really boodiful.'

knackrobatics *n.* The vigorous and often spectacular manoeuvring of a gentleman's *John Thomas* during a bout of *bedroom gymnastics,* usually attempted after being inspired whilst watching an educational *bongo vid* such as *Lovers' Guide 1, Lovers' Guide 2, Lovers' Guide 3* or *Anal Assault 7.*

knee shooters *n.* Large breasts with downward-pointing *jockeys.*

knee trembler *n.* Frightening intercourse while both parties are standing up. Often in a shop doorway.

knicker bacon *n.* Labial rashers.

knicker bandit *n.* A raider of washing lines, *Daz back doorstep challenger.*

knicker oil *n.* Alcopops, *tart fuel.*

knicker sausages *n.* Large *fanny lips.* Often found in *frying pants.*

knickers like Jack the Ripper's hankie *sim.* Descriptive of the *dunghampers* of a lady who failed to pad up properly during *cricket week.*

knickertine stains *n. Skid marks* off an *arse* that is a *heavy smoker.*

knight *v.* To reward a lady with one's *pork sword* in recognition of her outstanding service in the kitchen. To *put to the sword*, to *fuck.*

knob *1. n.* The penis, *prick, John Thomas. 2. v.* To engage in the romantic courses of physical love. *'I knobbed the arse off her.'*

knobbysox *n.* Relaxing and absorbent items of hosiery suited to accommodating the more sensitive portions of the male anatomy.

knob cheese *n. Smegma. Foreskin feta* found underneath *Kojak's roll-neck* and around the *banjo* or *cheese ridge.* Also *knob Stilton, knob yoghurt, Helmetdale, bell end brie, Lymeswold, brimula, fromunder.*

knob chopper *n.* Precariously-balanced lavatory seat which falls down while one is having a *piss* and therefore must be held up manually. A *penis fly trap.*

knobelisk *n.* A square-sectioned genital column that is thick at the base and tapers towards the top. *Cleopatra's needle.*

knob end *1. n.* The *herman gelmet. 2. n.* The extremity of a door handle. *3. n.* A *knobhead, jerk wad.*

knob fodder *n. Blart, flange, tussage, fanny.*

knobhead *n. A fuckwit,* thickhead, oaf.

knob hinge *n. anat.* The point on the male anatomy where the lower abdomen meets the top of the *giggling pin;* the fulcrum point of a *bone on,* if you will.

knob jockey *n.* Someone who sits on a door handle whilst the door is in motion for sexual gratification.

knob of butter *n. medic.* Softness in the *trouser department. Brewer's droop. Pele's cock.* Impotence.

knob scoffer *n.* Pejorative epithet implying that an individual likes to *smoke the white owl.*

knob shiner *n.* Someone who is always prepared to polish a *pink oboe.*

knob snot *n. Cock hockle.*

knob socket *n.* Any orifice that a penis could be put into, *eg.* the neck of an oven ready chicken, a hole in a tree, a Hoover dustette, the wife's *fanny, etc.*

knobstacle course *n.* Attempting sex with a *bird* whilst in a drunken stupor. See *labiarinth, Hampton Maze.*

knob throb *n.* The pulsating surge of blood to the genital region which heralds the onset of a raging *diamond cutter.*

knobtical illusion *n.* An excuse given by a man for the apparently pitiful size of his *manhood. 'It only looks small because of the way the bathwater's bending the light. It's a knobtical illusion. It's making the ruler you're holding next to it look bigger too. That proves it.'*

knob toffee *n.* Sperm.

knobwebs *n.* Symptoms of a prolonged period of sexual abstinence, when fluff, dust and spider webs gather around a chap's *cock. 'He said son, you are a bachelor boy / And that's the way to stay / Dusting the knobwebs off your old man / Until your dying day.'* (Song lyric by Cliff Richard, 1962).

knocker hoppers *n. Tit pants, rascal sacks.*

knocker jockey *n.* A small woman with very big *tits.* A *midget gem.*

knocker nest *n.* Bra. See also *over the shoulder boulder holder, kitten hammock.*

knockers *1. n.* Devices for banging on doors. *2. n.* Breasts. *'What a lovely pair of knockers, Lord Owen.' 3. n.* Of football punditry, those who have criticised a player in the past. *'Well Brian, the lad has certainly had his fair share of knockers.'*

knocking shop *1. n.* Brothel, *rub-a-tug parlour. 2. n.* A pub or club where women go to be picked up. A *meat mart.*

knock off the bobby's helmet *v.* To engage in a fistfight with one's *little Kojak.*

knock one in *v.* The female version of *knock one out.* To *play the invisible banjo.*

knock one on *v.* To have it off. *'I've got five minutes before the wife picks me up, love. Do you fancy nipping into the stationery cupboard and knocking one on?'*

knock one out *v.* To have *one off the wrist. 'I've got five minutes before the wife picks me up, love. Do you fancy keeping lookout while I nip into the stationery cupbaord and knock one out?'*

knock the back out of her *v.* Of a man, to have a very energetic *romp* up a lady.

knock the lid off the ark *v.* To release an *arse banshee* of biblical proportions that causes everyone in the room to disintegrate. From the climatic scene of the first *Indiana Jones* movie.

knot splitter *n.* A *toilet baby* of impressive, *nipsy*-challenging girth. *'Gerry (alarmed): What was that scream, Margot? Are you alright in there? (Flush sounds. Toilet door opens. Margot appears, holding doorframe to steady herself) Margot: Get me a gin and tonic, Gerry, and make it a large one. Gerry (pouring drink): What's happened? Margot: That's the last time I eat a slice of Tom and Barbara's Broad Bean Flan. I've just done a knot splitter in there that's probably blocked the drains from Surbiton to Thames Ditton. (Tom appears at the French windows in wellingtons.) Tom: Have you just started the extractor fan in your bathroom, Margot? Margot: Yes. Why? Tom: Well, three of my pigs have just fainted. FX: 10 seconds of canned laughter.*

Cue theme music and end titles.' (Extract from script of *The Good Life Christmas Special*, BBC TV 1978).

know, in the Biblical sense *v.* To have *carnival knowledge* of or to *bang* someone. *'Last year at Club 18-30 I knew about forty birds in the Biblical sense, in eight days! And another six sucked me off.'*

Knowle facelift *n.* Budget cosmetic surgery, whereby bags under the eyes, wrinkles and even eyelids are flattened by the over-enthusiastic application of hair scrunchies.

knuckle glitter *n. Funky spingers.*

knuckle nightcap *n.* A late-night *Sherman* which aids restful sleep. *Forty wanks.*

knuckles, as blurry as a wanker's *sim.* Descriptive of something that is very out of focus. *'Despite intensive, round-the-clock investigations, police been unable to identify any suspects. Unfortunately, although the build up to the murder, the hit itself and the gunman's escape through Fulham in a speeding car were all captured on numerous CCTV cameras, all the footage turned out to be as blurry as a wanker's knuckles.'* (Nick Ross, *Crimewatch UK*, 1998).

koala bear's ears *1. n.* Tufts of female *puberage* sticking out the sides of *dunghampers. Judges' eyebrows, thighbrows. 2. n. Aus.* The *man flaps* that protrude round the sides of over-tight *noodle benders.*

Kojak's moneybox *n.* The *herman gelmet.*

Kojak's roll-neck *n. Foreskin.* Based on the slap-headed lolly-sucking 1970s TV detective who always wore a cheesy-necked pullover.

KOKO *acronym.* An exclamation coined by the Central Office of Information during World War II for the use of armed services personnel. Knickers Off, Knockers Out.

konz *n.* How a native Cornish speaker would refer to a *cunt. 'Oi, fetch us some more clotted cream and jam for my fucking cream tea, you konz.'*

kosher dill *n.* A circumcised *gherkin.*

Kronenberg *n.* A lady who appears from behind to be about "16", but reveals herself to be about "64" when she turns round. From the famous "Young Bird Old Bag" lager made by the Kronenberg brewery.

Kruger *n.* A scary *hand job* from a woman with extremely long fingernails. A *Freddy.*

kumikaze attack *n.* A ruthless close-range facial assault waged by the *Jap's eye. Cum bombing.*

kung food *n.* Chinese comestibles.

Kursk *n.* A giant *dreadnought* mouldering at the bottom of the *pan.*

Kuwaiti tanker *rhym. slang.* A *merchant banker.*

kweef *n. US.* A *pump* from the *front bottom*, a *drop of the hat, forwards*, a *Lawley kazoo.*

KY jelly *n.* Your pudding after a *fish supper* at *granny's oyster bar.*

LI

labia lard *n. Fanny batter, blip, beef dripping.*

labia majorca *n. medic.* A cheap and popular destination for lads on holiday. *Mutton shutters.*

labia minorca *n. medic.* A slightly smaller holiday destination, though just as popular.

labiarinth *n.* A term describing the unnecessarily complex design of a woman's *Hampton Maze.*

labiathan *n.* A dauntingly large and unwieldy *fanny.*

lab kebab *n.* Ladies' donner labiums. The *vertical bacon sandwich, fur burger.* Looks quite appetising when you've had a *skinful.*

labrador lipstick *n.* A dayglo pink *stalk on.*

lab technician *n.* Someone with a workmanlike attitude to handling *knicker bacon.*

lace curtain *1. n.* An exceptionally long *fiveskin, Serge Gainsbourg's mouth. 2. n.* A delicate gossamer fretwork of *helmetdale.*

lack of composure in front of goal *1. n.* Syndrome suffered by footballers who fail to score when presented with a gilt-edged opportunity. *2. n.* A sudden lack of penile composure whereby one's *midfield playmaker* fails to rise to the occasion. *Falling at the final hurdle. 'Pele there, suffering from a rare lack of composure in front of goal, Brian.'*

ladyboy *n. ornith.* A confusing species of *cock bird* with female plumage and *tits.* A *chickboy.* Native to Bangkok and Iggy Pop's hotel room. A *shim, tiptop, trolley dolly, bobby dazzler.*

Lady Chalk of Billingsgate *n.* Thrush, a yeast infection of the vagina. *'I regret to announce that Lady Chalk of Billingsgate is visiting at this present time, Bishop. Could you pass the yoghurt?'*

ladygarden *n.* The fertile patch where a *downhill gardener* plants his seeds.

lady golfer *n.* A *wearer of comfortable shoes.* A *carpet muncher, tennis fan, KD lady.*

lady in waiting *1. n.* Actress in a *meat movie* threesome who, temporarily, has nothing to do. A *grumble gooseberry,* a *ballflower. 2. n.* A reclining *grumble flick* actress anticipating the imminent arrival of several short flights from the *Greek Island of Testos. 3 n.* The lady in a *flesh mag,* who is sure to "do the job", but is held in reserve until the rest of the publication has been thoroughly investigated. A *finisher.*

lady killer *n.* A penis of such extreme length of girth that it could prove fatal. A *cunt buster,* a *kipper ripper, kidney wiper.*

lady marmalade *n.* Patti Labelle's *labia lard. Fanny batter* with bits of orange peel in it.

Lady Penelope's minge *n.* A *snatch* that is *boiling beetroots,* ie. one with "a string attached".

lady's low toupee *n.* A *merkin,* a *cunt rug.* An all-weather *ladygarden.*

lady-tramp *n.* A woman of deceptively sophisticated appearance who lets herself down the moment she opens her mouth, *eg.* Denise Van Outen, Hilda Baker.

lager bomb *n.* A strong-smelling *becksfart,* a symptom of *brewer's flu.*

lairy-focals *n.* Aids to double vision which make a bloke feel hard as nails whilst rendering all the ugly women he sees beauty queens. Particularly fighty *beer glasses*.

Lake Wendouree *n. Aus*. Ejaculation. From the very, very small, sticky lake at *Ballarat*, Australia.

lamb cannon *n*. A high calibre arms development dating somewhere between the *mutton musket* and the *bacon bazooka*.

lamb hangings *n*. A none-too- appetising *butcher's window* display. *Mutton shutters, beef curtains, gammon goalposts, steak drapes, bacon strips, flackets*. A lady's *labia majorcas*.

Lamborghini *n*. A *cunt 'tache*. A small, pointless tufty outcrop of pubage remaining on a *shaven haven*. A *jazz fanny*. A *clitler*.

lamp a champion *v*. To squeeze out a much larger *shit* than you thought possible. To *punch way over your weight* in the lavatory.

Lance Harmstrong *n*. Nickname given to a *scratter* who acts dead hard despite riding round on a toddler's mountain bicycle, tucking his tracky bottoms into girl's white socks and wearing an *Essex tartan* hat.

landing *n*. The area between the bedroom and the lavatory, or between the *shitter* and the *sack*. The *barse*, *ABC*, the perineum. A place where it's probably best to leave the light off, all things considered.

landlady's forearm *n. medic*. Ailment closely linked to *bingo wings*, suffered by fat, dumpy women, *eg*. Star Psychic Sally Morgan, her off *Wife Swap* and all dinnerladies.

landmine *n*. A fresh *dog's egg* hidden in a suburban lawn, which is often detonated by a lawnmower leading to untold misery.

langball *n*. Type of *dangleberry* which attaches itself to *John Wayne's hairy saddlebags*.

langer *n*. Penis.

langered *adj*. *Wankered*. *Refreshed*.

lapdog *n*. A Spearmint Rhino dancer with a *lovely personality*.

lapos *acronym*. A *knob* sported by the less generously endowed gentleman. Like A Penis Only Smaller. *'STRAW, Jack, Lab., Blackburn (1979) b. 3 Aug. 1946. Ed. Brentwood Sch.; Leeds Univ.: Inns of Court Sch. of Law. Parliamentary Career: Contested Tonbridge and Malling 1974, succeeded Barbara Castle in this seat, Foreign Secretary (2001 - 2006)*, presently Lord High Chancellor of Great Britain and Secretary of State for Justice (2007 -). *Chairman All Party Lapos Group (1979 -).'* (from *Who's Who With a Really Really Small Cock*).

lapper *n*. *Hairy pie* eater, *bacon sandwich* connoisseur.

lap poodle *n*. A gently-bouffanted *minge*, much in fashion in the 1970s. A *Judith, Jackson, muffro*.

laptop *n*. A light, compact, perfectly-formed piece of kit that can be booted up on your lap or table as desired. A *throwabout*.

larder lout *n*. A person *with a lovely personality* who can't stop grazing. Fridge clearances a speciality.

lardigan *n*. A woollen outer garment worn knotted around the waist by larger ladies in a futile attempt to hide their big, fat *arses*.

lardi gras *n*. A Lizzie Duke-heavy festival of *cracksuit-wearing, bigboned scratters* which takes place every Saturday afternoon outside the golden arches at a precinct near you.

lard of the manor *n.* The *piabetic* bloke who lives on your estate. A *Duke of Giblets.*

lard on *1.n.* A porn star's perfunctory *hard on* which does the job, but only just. A *satiscraptory bonk on. 2. n.* The state of non-sexual excitement felt by a *bigger-boned* gentleman when approaching a Ginster's display. *3. n.* The sort of small erection experienced when looking at a *plumper.*

lard wimple *n.* A *pelican's beak, chin airbag.*

larse *n. medic.* The lateral point of the upper thigh where the leg becomes the *arse.* The bit seen in *jazz mags* that remains white even though the model has spent many hours on a sunbed. *'...the femoral vein ascends behind the semi-tendinosus, where it joins the great saphenous vein just behind the larse and continues on to meet inferior vena cava half way between the tits and the fanny...'* (from *Andy Gray's Anatomy*).

lashing strap *1. n.* In the haulage industry, a 3-inch-wide strap and buckle arrangement with a breaking strain of 5 tons, used by lorry drivers to tie down heavy loads onto the backs of their trucks. *2. n.* The choice of thong or *tit pants* strap for the fatter lass, *eg.* Michelle MacManus off *Pop Idol.*

lash on, get a bit *v.* To find some female company. *'Howay, let's gan oot an' get a bit lash on.'*

last hotdog in the tin *sim.* Descriptive of penetrative sex with a lady possessed of a *wizard's sleeve. Wall of death,* dipping a worm in a bucket.

last meat supper *n.* Final fling before marriage. It's all *fish suppers* thereafter.

last minute bookings *n.* The desperate and desperately unattractive *blart* that one is free to pull at 1.59 am after the *ugly lights* come up in a nightclub. *Floor sweepings, sediment.*

last night's pizza *n.* A woman that was hot when you picked her up, but doesn't seem quite so hot the next morning. *Hotel toast.*

last orders *n.* The ring of an *arse bell* that causes a stampede of similar magnitude to that experienced at 10.50 pm in pubs up and down the land. *'Stand back, your holiness. I had three scotch eggs and a pint of Bass for lunch, and I've just called last orders.'*

last orders at the pink bar *euph.* Announcements heralding the onset of the *vinegar strokes. 'Are you on the pill, love, 'cos it's last orders at the pink bar?'* (Wilfred Hyde-White quoted in the *Memoirs of Joyce Grenfell*).

last pint in the barrel *n.* A particularly wet, sticky and unsatisfactory *shite.*

last post *n.* Ceremonial act of taking down one's *bird's knickers* last thing at night.

last resort *n.* A light-hearted pet name for the wife, *ie.* that which one reluctantly returns to after a failed night *on the pull.*

last turkey in the shop *n.* Yet another bit of *ad hoc* genital vaudeville that never fails to impress the ladies, although it typically finds somewhat less favour with one's probation officer. See *the elephant.*

last week's lettuce *n.* An unappetising lady's *cludge,* from its similarity to an out-of-date salad, *ie.* brown, limp, sweaty, and sticking to the side of the bag. *'Fancy a lick of last week's lettuce, Charlie?' 'No thanks, Camilla.'*

last whoreders *n.* The chaotic rush for *rashgash* in a meat market at ten to two. *The witching hour, two o'clock binrake.*

last year's hanging basket *n.* An untidy, straggly *mott. Terry Waite's allotment.*

latch lifter *n.* A borrowed fiver which enables one to enter a public house. *'Lend us a latch lifter till I get my giro,* will you?'

lathered *adj. Pissed, plastered, langered.*

laugh at the carpet *v.* To *park a tiger.* To vomit.

laugh at the grass *v. Aus.* An *al fresco* liquid guffaw at a particularly amusing bit of floor. *'Where's Bruce, Bruce?' 'He's outside laughing at the grass, Bruce.'*

launch your lunch *v.* To *hurl one's biscuits.*

lava lamp *1. n.* A kitsch electrical appliance that was all the rage in the 1960s and again now, especially in the Gadget Shop. *2. n.* The appearance of the bath after one has *waxed the dolphin* in it.

lava lamp, guts like a *sim.* The unpleasant sensation that big, glowing, waxy bubbles of gas are backing up one's large intestine. Possibly following a night on the pop or a delicious curry from the Curry Capital, Bigg Market, Newcastle upon Tyne.

lavatory *n.* The smallest room, little house, *loo,* water closet, convenience, place of easement, *shithouse, crapper, privy, bog,* latrine, *cackatorium, temple of cloacina,* toilet, *khazi, thunder box, comfort station, meditation room, library, gentleman's reading room,* shitter.

lav child *n.* A *turd.* Arse baby.

lavender *adj.* Pertaining to *good listeners.*

lavender marriage *n.* Any matrimonial coupling about which there is a whiff of *lavender.*

lavitation *n.* The yogic exercise performed when hovering over a public lavatory seat so as to avoid direct contact when having a *shit.*

lav train *n.* The swarm of ladies that all go to the toilet together in pubs.

Lawley kazoo *n.* A *hat dropped forwards. Harry Secombe's last raspberry.* A *kweef.* Derivation known, but subject to legal restrictions.

lawn monkey *n.* The possible consequences of a *split jubber ray.* Also *yard ape, turf chimp, fanny turd.*

lawn sausages *n. Park links, dog's eggs, dog toffee, hound cable.*

lay *1. n.* Prospective or past sexual partner. *'I knew your wife many years ago. She was a terrific lay.' 2. v.* To *fuck* a woman with a small amount of cement and a trowel.

lay a cable *v.* To *build a log cabin, grow a tail, drop a copper bolt.*

lay a cuckoo's egg *1. v.* A party trick where a foreign *bogie* is introduced into an unconscious reveller's nostril for the amusement of the other guests. *2. v.* To get someone else's missus *up the duff. 'Have you seen him? Nowt like his brother or his dad. He's fucking ginger. Somebody's laid a cuckoo's egg there, if you ask me?'* (*Nigel Dempster's Diary,* 1984).

lay-and-display *n.* A type of European lavatory where the *twinkie* lands on a dry porcelain surface for inspection prior to being flushed away.

lazy lob on *n.* A semi-erect penis, a *dobber, half a teacake.*

lazy man's wee *n.* A gentleman's sit-down *piss,* usually taken in the middle of the night when his aim cannot be trusted. A *she-pee.*

lead in your pencil, to have *v.* To be *on the stonk.* Not like one of those floppy, leadless pencils.

lead the children of Israel to safety *v.* To commit an act of *rag week cumulonimbus.* To *part the red sea.*

lead the llama to the lift shaft *v.* To point *Percy* at the vagina.

leap of filth *n.* The feeling of blind trust needed when buying *grumble* online. 'He told us: *'I feel badly let down. I made a twenty quid leap of filth and you can't even see it going in.' Cyril...' 'Thank-you Esther.'*

leap round *n.* A round of drinks purchased by the slower drinker in the group, in which he does not buy a drink for himself, to prevent himself falling behind. Similar in concept to a leap year, only with a pint less rather than a day more.

learn *v.* Of a man, to make love to his sweetheart. *'Get on that bed. I'll fucking learn you, you dirty bitch.'*

leather on willow, like the sound of *sim.* A very pleasing *crack. 'Was her topiary in good order?' 'Leather on willow, mate. Leather on willow.'*

leave her on charge *v.* To deliberately keep the missus in a state of sexual anticipation. *'Me and the wife are going away for a lovely weekend without the kids tomorrow, so I'm not sure whether to give her a good seeing-to tonight or to just leave her on charge. What do the panel think?' 'Bob Flowerdew?'*

lecher's nightmare *n.* A grisly underwear display given by stilton-thighed elderly ladies when they sit in deck chairs. *Next month's washing.*

left footer *n.* A gay or Catholic person, but ideally one who is both.

left-handed batsman *n.* Someone who prefers his balls delivered from the *pavilion end.*

left-handed web site *n.* An internet website specialising in *cyberscud,* causing visitors to use the mouse with the wrong hand.

left legger *n.* A lady who particularly enjoys being *sorted out* on the front passenger seat of a car. Derived from the technique of hanging her left leg out the window, thus affording the driver unhindered access to her *cunker.*

left luggage *n.* Traces of *feeshus* left in the toilet bowl even after flushing.

left the lid off the gluepot? who's *interrog.* Rhetorical device implying that someone smells of *merry monk. 'Jesus, Your Majesty! Who's left the lid off the gluepot?'*

leg bye *n.* When a *Harmison loosener* trickles down leg-side for some unexpected *runs.*

leg elvising *n.* The frantic *Ed Sullivan Show*-style gyrations performed whilst trying to shake a bit of *follow through* out the bottom of one's trouser leg.

leg iron shuffle *n.* The gait adopted by one with the *turtle's head,* trying to make it to the *crapper* without *signing his bills.*

leg lifter *n. Benefactor.* Somebody

who *breaks company*.

leg man *n.* One who prefers ladies' *gams* to their *tits* or *arses*.

leg necklace *n.* An act of *cumulonimbus.*

lego hand *n. medic.* A tertiary form of *wanker's cramp.* A condition afflicting the hand of one who has overindulged in *self-pollution.* From the similarity to the rigid empty grasp of the Danish toy figures.

leg over *n.* A *sausage and doughnut situation. 'Did you get your leg over?' 'No, but I got tops and three fingers.'*

leg tensing *n.* The act of tensing one's leg when having a *toss. 'This wank is going nowhere. I'd better get a bit of leg tensing in.'*

leg warmer *n.* The *fiveskin* or *peparami wrapper.*

leisure facilities *n. medic.* Breasts, *competitive advantages.*

leisure trove *n.* A veritable Aladdin's cave of *relaxation-oriented literature,* such as might be discovered in the study of a recently-deceased vicar by his startled family.

Lemsip and a wank *n.* A cure for whatever ails you. A p*anhandleacea.* After listening to one's tale of woe, divorce, sacking *etc.*, a mate might reply, *'Have a Lemsip and a wank and you'll soon feel better.'*

Lemmy's warts *n.* Off-puttingly big nipples.

lend *v.* To give, in the *sausage* sense. *'Phwoar! Your mum's a bit of alright. I wouldn't mind lending her one'.'*

length *n.* An imperial saucy postcard unit of *the other*, as *slipped* to a woman by a man who works in a lino factory.

Lenny, do a *v.* To exhibit the symptoms of a *morning glory, ie.* to be "up at the crack of dawn". An amusing reference to the popular light entertainer Lenny Henry, whose penis has often been erect near the vaginal entrance of his wife, the actress Dawn French.

Leonardo *n.* An annoying little piece of *shit* that refuses to go down the *pan* after the main *dreadnought* has sunk. Named after the little actor who annoyingly floated around, refusing to die quickly at the end of *Titanic.*

Leo Sayer *rhym. slang.* All dayer. *Bender*, a prolonged drinking session, all day party.

lesbiany *adj.* Appertaining to lesbianism. In a *rub-a-tug shop* one might enquire: *'Any chance of you and your mate doing something lesbiany?'*

lesbionage *n.* The furtive act of watching a couple of *carpet munchers* as they *munch* each others's *carpets,* perhaps whilst up a ladder and wearing infra-red night vision goggles.

lesbo *n.* A *tuppence licker, bean flicker, carpet muncher, lickalotopus, dyke.*

lesbology *n.* The scientific study of lesbian activity. A branch of feminism studied almost exclusively by males which involves much scrutiny of video footage.

Leslie gash *n.* A luscious-lipped pouting *fanny.* After the Ivy Tilsley-gobbed former Homebase ad star.

let off *v.* To *let rip, blow off, launch an air biscuit.*

let one go *v.* To *let off.*

let Percy in the playpen *n.* Of a woman, to consent to intercourse.

let rip *v. Let one go.*

let the dog out *v.* To nip home at lunchtime and *feed the ducks* after a frustrating morning surrounded by *office beaver. Fire the one o'clock gun. 'Hold all my calls, Miss Jones. I'm just nipping home to let the dog out.'*

let the twins out *euph.* Of a lady, to remove her brassiere.

lettuce *n.* The crinkly leaves underneath the *gorilla salad*. The *piss flaps*.

lettuce licker *n.* A *lezza*.

lever arches *rhym. slang.* Haemorrhoids. From lever arch files = Chalfonts.

lezza *n.* A woman who is *fond of walking holidays*.

lezzo boots *n*. Any clumpy, unfeminine footwear worn by women. The opposite of *fuck me shoes. Fuck off slippers.*

libratory *n.* A *crapper* which is well stocked with *shiterature.* From library + lavatory.

lick a bus battery *v.* To commit *cumulonimbus* on a lady who is 2.66 times skankier than a *nine- volter.*

lickalotopus *n*. Scientific name for an experienced *carpet muncher*.

lick both sides of the stamp *v.* To be *AC/DC*, a *happy shopper*, a switch hitter, *half rice half chips.*

licker licence *n.* Permission to have a drink from the *hairy goblet.*

licking a nine-volter *n.* The act of *cumulonimbus* on a particularly skanky *snatch,* the eye-watering effect being the same as placing your tongue across the terminals of a PP3 battery.

lick of paint *n. Mexican lipstick. Pasata grin*. Consequence of a late *licker licence.*

lick one's arse and call it chocolate *phr.* Expression used to bring a deludedly optimistic person down to earth. *'Mr Speaker, my Right Honourable friend the Chancellor has told the house that thanks to his prudent fiscal policies the economy is in a stronger position now than ever. He is entitled to take that view, of course, and he is likewise entitled, should he wish, to lick his arse and call it chocolate.'* (Miss Widdecombe (Conservative) *Hansard* report, October 2001).

lick out *1. v.* That which is done by a small child to a bowl of cake mix. *2. v.* That which is done by a moustachioed porn star to a *haddock pastie*.

lick-twat *n. prop.* One who has the gift of tongues. A *cumulonimbalist*.

lid *n*. The bit above the *brim*. The *herman gelmet.*

Lidled *adj.* Descriptive of a town or district that is in decline, evidenced by the opening of a branch of Lidls. Also *Nettoed, Aldied. 'Dover, once the gateway to Europe, home of the White Cliffs, now sadly Lidled.'*

life affirmer *n. Shit* taken during the worst depths of a hangover or other depression which is of such magnitude that it restores one's vital signs. A *crap* which would make the late Fred Astaire dance down the street, occasionally bouncing his silver-topped cane off the kerb.

lifting the cheek n. The sly behaviour of a *cushion creeper*.

lighthouse cat, rank as a *sim.* Descriptive of a gentleman who has experienced an excessively long period without getting his hands on a *bird. 'Giz a shot on your clopper, Una. I feel as rank as a lighthouse cat.'*

lightning in a bottle *n.* A photographic *art study* which captures the moment a gentleman *expels his custard* in a shot arcing majestically towards the face of a beautiful young lady. Named after the equally tricky task of photographing a lightning bolt.

lilies on the pond *n.* The artistic practice popularised by impressionist painter Claude Monet of laying sheets of toilet tissue on the water surface before giving birth to *Meatloaf's daughter.* A *pap baffle.*

lils 1. *n.* 1950s/60s *Tits.* 2. n. Stits. From Liliputians.

lime water *n. Semen, spunk, spooge, spangle, tweedle.*

lineman's pastie *n.* A very full disposable nappy thrown from a train window at loafing, orange-clad track workers.

lingam *n.* Hindu. Penis. From ancient *grumble book The Karma Sutra.*

links effect, the *euph.* The aromatic toilet visit which is enjoyed the morning after a night on the beer and *Ruby Murray,* when one's *arse* resembles a sausage machine as operated by a cack-handed contestant on *The Generation Game.*

lino munching *n.* The correct term for *rug munching* when the munchee's *pile* has been waxed off.

lion tamer's corpse *sim.* Descriptive of the sorry state of one's *chap* after a *rag week romp. Barber's pole.*

lippie *v.* Of a dog, to *frotter* on one's leg with its *lipstick* out. *"Aw. He must like you, Dr Watson,' expostulated the great detective, sucking on his pipe thoughtfully and adjusting the brim of his deerstalker with the handle of his magnifying glass whilst playing his violin. 'He's trying to lippie your leg, look."* (from *The Hound of the Baskervilles* by Arthur Conan Doyle).

lip reading *n.* Observing women in tight pants who have the *camel's foot. 'If she bends over any more I'll be able to read her lips from here.'*

lip ring *n.* A lipstick line around the circumference of one's *sword* which enables one to gauge how far it has been *swallowed* whilst one's wife is in the next room being sick.

lip ripper *n.* A magnificently girthsome *charlie.*

lip service *n.* A lacklustre act of *horatio* performed by a timid or blocked-nosed *nosher.*

lip sink *n.* The wash basin in the ladies' toilet of a pub in which *birds* have the female equivalent of a *gentleman's was*h when they have *pulled.*

lipstick *n.* A dog's *cock,* available in a variety of shimmery colours.

lipstick lesbian *n.* Glamorous, feminine female homosexual, commonly found on the Adult Channel but rarely down the pub.

lip stretcher *n.* A particularly girthsome *choad.* A *Pringle tube.* A challenge to a pair of *DSLs.*

liquid bookmark *n.* A homemade means of recording one's place in the pages of a gentlemen's *art pamphlet.*

liquid gold *n.* A cup of tea in Betty's tearooms.

liquid kids *n. Spooge, spunk*, heir gel, baby gravy.

liquid laughter *n. Puke, psychedelic yodelling.*

liquid rage *n. Fred.*

liquorice allsort *n.* A dark haired woman who frequents both the tanning salon and the tooth-whitening clinic. From her resemblance to the popular Bertie Bassett confectionery homunculus.

liquor portal *n.* The hole in the space/time continuum found outside pubs which transports the inebriated to the safety of their hallways in the blink of an eye. A science fiction *beer scooter.*

little & large show *1. n.* Early evening BBC1 series featuring the eponymous contrastingly-sized double act, which unaccountably ran from 1978 to 1991. *2. n.* A pair of *Kelly Brooks* in a low-cut top or bikini.

Little Ben *n.* A small *Big Ben*.

little death *n. Fr.* In a male, the post-coital feeling of *shagged outity* which is symptomised by the opposite of rigor mortis.

liver lapels *n. Beef curtains, labia majorcas*, especially when used on Ed Gein's home-made suit.

live rounds in a training exercise, use *v.* To fire potentially dangerous *spammunition* into the field of battle when it might have been more sensible to keep your *bacon bazooka* safely muzzled, *eg.* whilst having a final *bang* with a departing ex or whilst enjoying a drunken penetrative *romp* up a chubby waitress with big *tits*. *'Why the long face, Boris?' 'Ich bin caught auf using live rounds in ein training exercise, Des.'*

liver sock 1. *n.* The *fanny.* 2. n. A *butcher's favourite.*

Livingstone daisies *1. n. Bot.* Attractive flowers that come out when the sun shines. *2. n.* Attractive *knockers* that come out when the sun shines, causing taxi drivers to mount the pavement, milkmen to fall down manholes and straw-hatted vicars to ride their bicycles into fruit barrows.

lizard rag *n. Aus.* A scaly piece of bedside cloth used for wiping excess *spoff* and *moip* from one's *bloodstick* after *popping the turkey in the oven.*

lizard's lick *n.* A feeble ejaculation that barely clears the *hog's eye,* the unimpressive result of excessive *beauty shivering.* A bankrupt *money shot.* A *gwibble.*

Llewellyn-Bowen's cuff *n.* An over-elaborate vagina. A foppish *ragman's coat.*

load *1. n.* 1996 Metallica album. *2. n.* The quantity of *cock hockle* blown, chucked or shot at the point of orgasm. *3. n.* That which is shed by a lorry driver, whilst *wanking* in a layby.

loaded *adj. Aus.* To be in need of a great big *shit*. To be *touching cloth. "Curiouser and curiouser' thought Alice, as the white rabbit came scampering past. 'I wonder where he's going in such a hurry.' 'Oh, my dear paws!' he cried. 'Oh my fur and whiskers, I'm loaded. If I don't reach the lavatory soon I shall surely papper my grundies."* (from *Alice's Adventures in Wonderland*, by Lewis Carroll).

loaded for bear *1. adj.* Hunting term, indicating that one is packing particularly impressive ammunition. *2. adj. Fucking* term, indicating that one is packing particularly impressive ammunition.

loading the mag *euph. milit. Thumbing in a slacky.* The act of easing a *lard-on* into a *fanny* in a porn film.

load of old shoes falling out a loft, like a *sim.* Descriptive of a heavy bout of loose, lively diarrhoea. A *flock of pigeons.*

load rage *n.* A violent confrontation in which a purple-faced *bald man* is struck viciously with a *wanking spanner.*

lobcock *n.* A large, flaccid penis such as could be *lobbed* onto a pub table by its drunken owner the way that Michael Elphick hits the fish on the bar in *Withnail and I.*

lob on, lazy *n. Half a teacake.*

lobotomy bay *n.* Semi-mythical destination of any serious drinking binge.

lob ropes *v.* To *jizz* onto something through thin air, *eg.* a face, some hair, some *tits etc.*

locked out, Mrs Brown is *euph.* Having *followed through. 'Apologies, Your Excellency, but I really must be excused. I've just opened the back doors and it appears Mrs Brown is locked out again.'*

locksmith *n.* A girl who has an impressive working knowledge of *knobs* and their operation.

log *n. Bum cigar, brown trout.*

logarhythm *n.* The shaking of one's *arse* in an attempt to break the neck of a dangling *turtle.* The working out of a *simple harmonic motion.*

log cabin *n.* A wendy house for *Meatloaf's daughter.*

log fire *n.* The pain experienced in the *back body* the morning after eating a particularly spicy *Ruby Murray. Ring sting, Johnny Cash.*

log flume *1. n.* Simultaneously defecating and urinating down the same leg of one's kex. *2. n.* A *turd* in a pub *pissing* trough. *3. n.* A *Thora* splashing down into the pan.

lollipop lady *n.* A woman who is partial to the occasional *slice of cheesecake.*

lolly bag *n.* Scrotum.

lolly stick *n.* Anything pointlessly, but intentionally added to a pile of *shite.* A *turd's barnacle. 'Has anyone seen that Big Brother's Little Brother? What a fucking lolly stick that is.'*

long ball game *1. n.* In football, a series of aimless pokes in the direction of the box in the hope of scoring. *2. n.* In bed, a series of aimless *pokes* in the direction of the *box* in the hope of *scoring.*

long distance Clara *1. n.* Wholesome female lorry driver in BBC children's series *Pigeon Street. 2. n.* A *lorry driver's lunchbreak, ie.* having a *crap* in a lay-by. *'Come in Steady Eddie. When are you expected back at the depot?' 'Control, this is Steady Eddie. I'm currently on the A66 but I had a wick Ginsters for breakfast at Abingdon Services, so I'm going to need ten minutes for a long distance Clara in the Barnard Castle lay-by.'*

longshanks *n.* One who is blessed/cursed with a very low-swinging *chicken skin handbag.* A *rantallion.*

lonk *v. German.* To *shit* oneself on orgasm.

look at *v.* Euphemism for masturbation. *'Did you look at that porn film I lent you yesterday?' 'Yeah, I had a quick look.'*

look for badgers *v.* To cruise for gay sex. Also *stretch one's legs.*

looking for Beadle *n.* Desperate behaviour of one who is mired in terrible circumstances. The over-optimistic hope that the tidy-bearded television prankster has had a hand in one's present woes, and will shortly appear dressed as a policeman or something, so that everything will be alright. *'I tell you what, Mark, after all that stuff in the papers about shares and ministerial rules I was looking for Beadle when I left Downing Street for Portcullis House, where I was due to appear before the Work and Pensions Committee.'* (David Blunkett, speaking on BBC's *Football Focus* programme).

loon pipe *n. Anus.*

looniform *n.* Characteristic garb of one who favours screaming at the traffic as an occupation, usually consisting of a 1970s jacket and trousers that clear the ankles by a good three inches.

loop the loop *v.* To order a *vertical bacon sandwich* to *eat out* and a *drink on a stick* for the lady, *No.69* on the menu.

loose at the hilt *adj.* Having diarrhoea, *the Brads.*

loose clacker *n. coll.* A herd of *ten-to-twoers.* Ropey *cabbage.* The group of girls remaining unspoken for at night club chucking out time.

loose fries in the bag *euph.* Descriptive of a feeling of serendipitous sexual jubilation on discovering the *bird* one is *copping off* with has hidden extras, *eg.* has a shaved *snatch*, is wearing stockings, is a *swallower.* From the joyous feeling experienced when, on finishing one's McDonald's, one finds extra chips in the bottom of the bag.

loose lips *adj.* Affectionate description of a woman who has been *cocked* more times than Davy Crockett's rifle.

loose, on the *adj.* Of a *dirty lady, frothing like bottled Bass.* Having a *wide on.*

loose sausage meat *n.* A flaccid penis which cannot be funnelled into a condom. *Stuffing the marshmallow. 'Sorry love, my sausage meat seems a bit loose.'*

loose shunting *n.* A *dog's marriage* with a *clown's pocket.*

Lord Foulbowel *n.* One whose lower chamber is a rich source of *brownhouse gases, eg.* a Coventry City fan who spends 72 hours farting in a car accompanied by 4 friends as they attempt to visit all 92 football league grounds to raise money for charity.

Lord of the Pies *n.* A *salad dodger*, a *double sucker.* One whose *big bones* and *glands* are always dragging him into bakeries.

Lord Winston's moustache *n.* A particularly hairy and poorly-trimmed *biffer,* named after the exuberant face fungus of the popular ennobled telly boffin, test-tube *fanny apple* pioneer and former leading *twat mechanic* Dr Robert Winston. Also *Rhodes Boysons, whack-os.*

lorry driver's breakfast, fanny like a *sim.* Descriptive of a *clopper* which is cheap, greasy and requires plenty of sauce before consumption.

lorry driver's lunchbreak *n.* A *crap* in a layby, a *long distance Clara.*

lose some weight *v.* To perform a *digestive transit. 'Sorry, Your Majesty. I need to lose some weight. Could you point me at the nearest* *shitter, love?'*

lose the marathon *v.* To take a long time to complete an act of *axcreeshus*. Derivation unknown. *'That crap took me so long I would've lost the marathon.'*

lose your manners *v.* To *shoot a bunny* whilst in polite company.

lose your mess *v.* To ejaculate, *shoot your load*.

losing ten seconds *adj.* Descriptive of one who has a *mole at the counter.* From Paula Radcliffe's 2005 London marathon run, during which she experienced controversial *traffic calming measure* difficulties that slowed her down by the specified time interval whenever a "violent stomach cramp" wracked her scrawny frame.

lotties *n. Lils, dugs.*

loudmouth soup *n.* Beer.

Louis *v.* To force out a stubborn *turd* with such strain that one pulls a face like Satchmo going for a top E.

love bat *n.* During a game of sexual intercourse, the short, stout implement with which the man strikes his wife's *cunker.* See also *slag bat.*

love beads *n. milit.* Road surface farm animal containment provision which provides exceedingly fleeting and intermittent sexual stimulation for squaddies in the backs of "rumpety-pumpety" army trucks. A cattle grid.

love bumps *n. Funbags, guns of Navarone.*

love cough *n.* The *dropping forwards* of a *lady's hat.* A *queef*, a *Lawley kazoo*, a *frampton.* A *fanny fart.*

love juice *n.* That liquid produced in the *Billingsgate box* upon which the *skin boat* sails. Often referred to as *luv jooz* in illiterate 1970s *scud literature. Blip, moip.*

love lane *euph.* Poetic euphemism for a *bird's clopper.*

love palace *n.* Coarse version of *cunt.*

love puff *n.* Gentle, romantic *air biscuit* launched in the direction of one's partner in bed, often the morning after a *Ruby,* in an attempt to cement the intimacy of the moment.

love sausage *n.* Big pink *banger* served with *hairy love spuds*.

love socket *n*. Vagina, entry point for the *main cable.* Also *rocket socket, serpent socket, spam socket.*

love spuds *n*. Starch-filled root vegetables found in the *shreddies.*

love torpedo *n. Rumpleforeskin.*

love tripe *n.* The savoury folds of tender flesh around a *bird's goalmouth.* The *labia majorcas* and *minorcas.*

love truncheon *n. Copper's torch.*

love tunnel *n.* That place in which *Percy* the small pink engine shunts his *load.* For about three minutes before he *blows his stack* and his *back wheels come off.*

lower decking *n.* The act of deliberately not flushing away a *dreadnought* in one's work toilets, then hiding in the adjoining cubicle to savour the next occupant's reaction.

low hanging fruit *1. n. polit.* Funding which can be cut back easily during a belt-tightening budget. *2. n. Nads* that hang out of badly-designed shorts.

low loaders *n.* Saggy breasts with a small amount of ground clearance. *Ulrikas.*

LRF *abbrev.* Low Resolution Fox -

a female who appears to be attractive from a long distance, but is in fact unbelievably ugly close up.

lucky dip *n.* The fortunate, final wipe of one's *ring* which reveals a hidden *clod,* thus preventing *pappered pants* and an *autographed gusset.*

lucky Pierre *n.* In *botting* circles, the busiest *botting* link in a three man *bum chain*; the filling in a *shirt lifter* sandwich. A *botter* who is simultaneously a *bottee.*

lullage *n.* The overhanging flab seen on fat lasses wearing trousers they fully intend slimming into. A *gunt,* a *poond,* a *muffin top.*

lulu *n.* A lady who is getting on a bit, but is still worthy of *lengthage*. A *gilf.*

lumber *1. n.* A raft of tightly-packed *turds* occluding the toilet water surface in a *chod bin* after an afternoon testing the "all you can eat" buffet at an Aberdeen Steak House. *2. n.* A unspecified quantity of erect peni.

lumberjill *n.* A hatchet-faced woman that fells one's *mighty redwood.*

lunchbox lancer *n. arch.* Medieval term for a *cocoa shunter*. *'Fear not the French, for their knights are without heart, and their King without wisdom. But keep thine backs as to the wall, for amongst their number thou shalt find more than a few lunchbox lancers, I can tell thou.'* (from *Henry V part III* by William Shakespeare).

lunchbox *n.* In British tabloid journalism, that conspicuous bulge in athlete Linford Christie's shorts, where he used to keep his sandwiches, a carton of Ribena, a Twix and an apple.

lunchboxing *n.* Unbelievably perverse sexual practice which makes a *Cleveland Steamer* sound about as rude as getting a peck on the cheek off Julie Andrews.

lunching at the Lazy Y *v. Dining out* cowboy style, on *hairy pie*, beans and coffee.

lung butter *n.* Phlegm, *green smoking oysters*.

lungry *adj.* Having an appetite for cigarettes. *'Giz a drag on that, your Excellency. I gave up for new year and now I'm proper fucking lungry.'*

lung warts *n. Stits, fried eggs. Parisian breasts*.

lurpy *n. Can.* Heterosexual *horatio.*

lush puppies *n.* Those grey slip-on brogues or loafers worn with white socks by middle-aged, *turps-nudging* "oldest swinger in town" types. *'Oi, Ho-Chi Minh or whatever your fucking name is. Where've you put me lush puppies?'*

Luton, a *n.* Pubic hairstyle named after the popular Bedfordshire airport. An amateurish attempt at a *landing strip,* but with patches of different length *bush* everywhere.

lychees *n.* A sweeter, more exotic *knacker*-speak alternative to *plums*.

Lymeswold *n.* Mild, blue, soft *knobcheese. Full fat fromunder, knacker barrel.*

Mm

Mabel syrup *n.* Old *bird's flange juice.*

macbeth *n.* Whilst sitting on the *bog* straining, the release of an apparently ferocious *Exchange & Mart* that comes to naught. A *dropped gut* that is "full of sound and fury, signifying nothing", as William Shakespeare had it in his Scottish Play. Macbeth, that is.

mac in the bath, I wouldn't wear my *exclam.* Expression of a gentleman's unwillingness to don a prophylactic sheath on his *cock end.* Also *'I wouldn't wear my wellies on the beach.'*

mack *n.* Penis, *tadger.*

mackerel *1. n.* Pimp, controller of prostitutes. A *tart farmer. 2. n.* The *tarts* he farms. *3. n. coll. Cabbage.*

mackerel microphone *n.* The bit of a lady that a fellow presses his lower face against, horse-racing-commentator-style, whilst carefully adjusting the settings on her *Bruce Lees* when he is attempting to *call Radio Tokyo.* The *cleft, quacker* or *furry hoop.*

mad cow disease *1. n.* Viral disease caught off cheap pies. *2. n. medic.* A monthly hormonal condition causing distress to men's ears. *Rag rage, tammy huff, blob strop.*

Madam Palm and her five sisters *n.* A hand when used for five minutes of harmless fun that will certainly result in its owner being cast into a lake of fire by our infinitely merciful God. A *wanking spanner.* Also *Palmela Handerson. 'I'm nipping off to bed with Madam Palm and her five sisters.'*

madam's apple *n.* A warning sign that the stunning Thai temptress you have picked up in a Bangkok bar may turn out to be equipped with *plums* and a *tummy banana* as well as a *large pear.*

Madam Twoswords *n.* A multitasking actress in a *stick vid* or *art pamphlet* who has a gentleman's waxy *charlie* in each hand. A *crane operator,* a *downhill skier.*

mad as a lorry *adj.* About as *radge* as it is possible to be.

Madeley *n.* A bloke who feels comfortable talking about relationships, star signs, *Sex and the City, Ally McBeal* and *shit* like that.

mad woman's shit, all over like *sim.* Descriptive of something extremely disorganised and chaotic. *"I really must apologise for the most dreadfully untidy state of my study, Mrs Fezzypeg,' said Mr Pickwick as he anxiously cleared a bundle of papers off the chair nearest the fire, motioning at his visitor to be seated. 'Only my Tax Return's supposed to be in tomorrow and as usual, my bank statements are all over the room like mad woman's shit."* (from *The Pickwick Papers* by Charles Dickens).

magic circle *1. n.* A group of conjurors who never reveal their secrets. *2. n.* Paul Daniels's *nipsy.*

magician *euph.* A pal who is good with colours. From the fact that, on a night out, he will often "disappear with a poof".

magician's hankie *1. n.* A *shite* that just keeps on going and going, like the endless knotted cloths pulled out of conjurors' hats. *2. n.* A *botty burp* which, to the surprise of the assembled audience, continues to emerge over an astounding length of time, and in several audibly discrete segments.

magician's knickers *n.* Pants that keep disappearing up one's *arse.*

magicking the beans *v.* The late Gareth Hunt's *wanking* action.

magic sheet *n.* An enchanted blanket, often seen in American TV movies which clings to an actress through some invisible force, covering her *fissions.*

magnificent seven *n.* The frankly unlikely scenario of getting the opportunity to unload one's *weapon* in every available orifice on a woman.

magnificent six *n.* The same act as above, but performed on Daniella Westbrook.

magnify *v.* Of a gentleman, to trim back his pubic foliage in order to create the illusion that his *endowment* is more substantial than it actually is. *'Did you see the chopper on that stripper tonight, Ada?' 'Aye I did, Dolly. But don't be too impressed - it was tied off and magnified.'*

mahogany chair leg *n.* An unusually wide, closely grained and uncomfortable *stool,* which appears to have been turned on a lathe by a Victorian craftsman in the days when things were built to last.

mailed and sent *rhym. slang.* On *the other bus.*

main cable *n.* One's live AC feed into the *love socket.*

make a bald man cry *v.* To masturbate. *'Have you seen Kylie's arse on the front page of the FT today? It's enough to make a bald man cry.'*

make a clog *v.* At the climax to an act of onanistic *self delight,* to fire one's *custard rifle* into a sock. From the fact that, after being left for a few days, said item of hosiery becomes as hard as a piece of traditional Dutch wooden footwear. *'What are you doing in the shed, Ruud?' 'Making a clog, dear.'*

make babies *v.* To go *bone jumping,* to fornicate with the object of *dropping a tadpole in a young lady's beer.*

make like a Chinese helicopter pilot *v.* To masturbate, *grin like a wanking Jap* whilst *polishing the joystick.*

make the rounds *v.* To have a final grope of all one's ladyfriend's *treasures* before falling asleep.

make the weigh-in *v.* To enter the toilet as a middleweight and come out half an hour later as a welterweight. To have a really big *shit.*

make your shit hang sideways *v.* To be annoying. *'That Matthew Kelly really makes my shit hang sideways.'* (Bernard Levin, TV Review in *The Times*).

making nylon *v.* An experiment in the bath resulting in the creation of viscous, stringy threads that stick to the hairs of one's legs.

malapriapism *n.* A mistaken penile intrusion into an orifice which is close by, but not the same as, another one, leading to an unintentionally amusing effect. A *cock up.*

male varnish *n.* Viscous fluid which is worn all over the hand, across the chest, and on one's ladyfriend's face. Like nail varnish, but harder to remove from clothing. *Vitamin S.*

mambas *n.* Mammaries, *mumbas.*

Mambo number five *1. n.* An annoyingly catchy novelty hit record which contains an instrumental line that sounds like a repetitive *fart. 2. n.* A repetitive *fart* that has all the makings of an instrumental line in an annoyingly catchy novelty hit record. A *Rotterdam Ter-*

mination Source.

mamfest *1. n.* The stirring sight of a lot of ladies' breasts *en masse, eg.* at the beach, in a nightclub, through a hole drilled in the wall of a ladies' changing room. Contraction of mammary festival. *2. n.* A particularly fine and well presented pair of *bangers.*

mammaries *n.* Mammary glands, *tits, swinging pink milk churns, knockers.*

mammary dandruff *n.* Morning-after residue from a *sausage sandwich*, the remnants of a *pearl necklace*.

mammogram *n.* An item of mail containing a few saucy snaps of his missus's bare *norks,* which is hopefully sent to a member of Her Majesty's armed forces by his good lady and not the milkman.

mamnesia *n. medic.* A highly specific form of male memory loss. Upon seeing a fantastic pair of *norks,* the sufferer forgets key facts about himself, *eg.* that he is married, that he has four children, or that he is the presenter of a topical quiz show. Also *penile dementia.*

manaesthetic *n.* Dextrous manual self-manipulation of a fellow's nether regions that brings on a state of pain-free slumber at the end of each day.

managlypta *n.* Peculiar raised relief effect observed on the walls of a gentleman who is prone to acts of *self harm,* but who cannot be *arsed* to find a tissue, sock, pet *etc.* on which to deposit his *erotic spendings. Managlypta* is most commonly found decorating the surfaces immediately adjacent to a long term bachelor's computer desk.

manbag *1. n.* A practical and fashionable portmanteau which can be slung across the shoulders, an accoutrement typically favoured by Europeans and creative media types. Not in any sense a handbag, despite all appearances to the contrary. *2. n.* The *sack* in which a chap retains his *two veg.* The scrotum.

manberries *n.* Coarse term for the *clockweights, John Wayne's hairy saddlebags, knackers etc.* Testicles, *yongles.*

manberry sauce *n. Gentleman's spendings.*

mancy *n.* A very girly fellow. One who is as *good with colours* as a nine bob note.

mandruff *n.* Flakes of dried *love-piss* found on one's wife's head and shoulders.

manker *n.* A *wanker* from Manchester, *eg.* Liam Gallagher.

M & S turd *euph.* A *shite* which is worthy of special attention due to its exceptional quality. "This is not just a turd, this is a five-day matured, chicken vindaloo with garlic naan and eight bottles of Cobra turd."

man eggs *n.* Sperms.

man fanny *1. n.* A changing room entertainment whereby a bare gentleman impersonates a bare lady. A *cockafanny. 2. n.* A risible goatee beard sported by polytechnic lecturers and 45-year-olds who have just bought a motor bike.

manfat *n.* Semen. Also *man milk.*

manflaps *n.* The tiny flaps surrounding the *Jap's eye,* usually only visible when taking a much needed high pressure *piss.* The *hog's eyelids.*

Manfred *rhym. slang. Jitler, jism,*

spaff. From the not-particularly-famous-amongst-cockneys German philosopher Manfred Bunk = spunk.

mange *n.* See *mangina.*

mangina 1. *n.* The badly-sewn Cornish pastie-like seam running along the underside of the scrotum that stops one's *clockweights* falling out and rolling under the fridge. 2. *n.* The *nipsy* of one who is *good with colours*. 3. *n.* The hilarious men's locker room jape of sticking one's *meat and two veg* back between one's legs to create a convincing simulacrum of a lady's *clout*. 3. *n. Old Greg's* downstairs mix-up.

manging *adj. Minging.*

mangos *n.* See *jelly water mangos.*

man handle *n.* The *bone on* that a store detective gets upon apprehending a female shop lifter in anticipation that she may offer to *talk to the judge* in the stock room.

manhood *n.* In British tabloid journalism, the penis.

man in the iron mask *n.* An extremely hirsute *snatch* trapped inside a pair of knickers. From the classic tale by Alexandre Dumas.

manjack *n.* A *poo* which is so rigid that it starts lifting you off the *bog* seat when it hits the bottom of the *pan.*

man mastic *n.* Sticky white substance used for sealing ladies' eyelids *etc*.

man mayonnaise *n. Gentleman's relish, hanging salad cream, semen mayo.*

man meringue *n.* A light, crumbly nest of dried *milm* found on the inside of a gentleman's well-worn *Bill Grundies.*

mannequim *n.* A *sailor's favourite* or similar ersatz *spouse.*

mannery glands *n.* A portly gentleman's dugs. *Bitch tits, moobs, moomlaaters.*

manny *n.* The convincing illusion of womanhood achieved when a gentleman tucks his *giggling stick* and *knackers* back behind his legs. A *cockafanny*. A contraction of man + fanny. See *man fanny, mangina.*

man of the cloth *n.* Our *farter*, who, despite fervent prayer, finds that he has besoiled his raiments. A *through-follower.*

man on the inside *euph.* The stage of a *digestive transit* just before the *turtle's head. 'Why's Colin walking so funny?' 'He's got a man on the inside.'*

manopause *n.* Male mid-life crisis, characterised by the acquisition of a sports car, a motorbike and/or a girlfriend young enough to be one's daughter.

man overboard *n.* A *bald man in a boat* whom you fear has become detatched from his mooring, but who turns out to be a pellet of compressed *shit scrape.*

man pop *n. Spooge, jitler, baby gravy.*

mam sandwich *n.* Two amply-proportioned *milkers* with the head of a happy gentleman wedged snugly between them.

manshake *n.* A vigorous three-minute greeting for one's best friend.

manshee *n.* One who could conceivably be a man or a woman.

man's makeup *n.* The light brown stripe left on a light-coloured bath towel by a chap's vigorous drying of his *potty slot.* Often blamed on his missus's foundation or bronzer.

'Terry, you dirty bastard. Why can't you wipe your arse properly? You've left man's makeup all over the towel again.' ' I've not done that, June, you fucking cow. It was you taking your slap off when you were pissed last night.'

manties *n.* Women's underwear worn by a bloke who is firmly in denial about his true proclivities. *'Nah, I'm not wearing a G-string, they're manties. There is a difference.'*

man trap *n.* The female genitals, the *hairy love pit.*

mantrum *n.* A hissy fit thrown by a man. For example, the bit off that Elton John fly-on-the-wall thing when he was in the south of France and the woman went "yoo-hoo" at him when he was playing tennis, remember, and he ran back up to his hotel suite and started packing his suitcase? That was a mantrum.

manwich *n.* The lucky chap filling pressed between two slices of ladies.

man with nice nails *n.* One who is *good with colours.*

mapatasi *n. Aus. Minge.* From "Map of Tasmania", the small hairy island that smells of fish off the south east coast of Australia.

map of Africa *n.* The cartographical stain left on the bed sheet and often the mattress below after an exchange of bodily fluids. A splodge of *splooge.* Also *map of Ireland, map of Hawaii.*

marabou stork *n.* A *fixed bayonet, the old Adam.* An erection.

maracas *n. Knackers, clackers,* those things that swing beneath *tallywhackers* making a rattling sound.

marge *n.* A loose woman. From margarine, which "spreads easily". Also *Flora.*

margold *n.* The common male ability to do five *pop shots* in two hours. To do a margold. After a boast by *grumble* thespian Bill Margold on Channel 4's *After Dark* programme many years ago.

Marianas trench *1. n.* The deepest recorded sub-marinal depression on Earth, found in the Pacific ocean and reaching a depth of 35,839 feet below sea level. *2. n.* A *fanny* like a fucking bucket.

marks of Mecca *n.* Carpet burns on the knees caused by excessive worship at the *hairy temple.*

marks out of two? *interrog.* From one ogling male to another, to cue the reply "I'd give her one."

mark your territory *v.* To *drop your guts* and walk away.

Marley arse *n.* Accumulated *winnetage,* leading to *anal dreadlocks. Tagnuts* that have gone to pot.

Marley's chains *euph.* Breasts that, despite having gone south in a big way, must still be carried about by their owner. From the chain-dragging ghost of his former business partner that visits Scrooge in Charles Dickens's *A Christmas Carol.* Also *Ulrikas.*

marmalade madam *n. 17thC. Tom, doxy, flapper, laced mutton.* A *ho'.*

Marmite driller *n.* One who jumps over puddles on the *marmite motorway.*

Marmite kofte *n.* The sort of viscous black *shite* that, instead of dropping into the *chod bin* pan in the traditional manner, chooses to smear itself around the *nipsy* like so much axle grease. The resulting Augean Stables-style cleaning session only ever happens when one is in a hurry to catch a plane, train, last orders or read the closing headlines at the end of the *BBC Six O'Clock News*.

Marmite motorway *n. Anus, arse, back passage.*

Marmite pot, arse like a *sim.* A *ringpiece* which, after a particularly sticky *Brad Pitt,* seems to have a never ending supply of *shit* and the wiping of which will never *draw an ace.*

Marmite stripe *n.* Brown stain or *skidmark* found on unwashed *shreddies. Russet gusset.*

Mars bar *1. n.* A caramel, nougat and chocolate confection, which when eaten daily is a proven aid to work, rest and recreation. *2. n.* A substantial and impressive *burnout.*

mars bra *n.* The common practice (in Germany anyway) of *dropping a length of dirty spine* onto your ladyfriend's *dirty pillows.*

Martin! Martin! Martin! *exclam.* Phrase which can be shouted when standing next to someone whose repeated *gut dropping* implies that they may imminently *curl one off* all over the floor. From the zookeeper on *Blue Peter* who persistently called the name of his off-screen helper when Lulu the elephant tried to *shite* all over John Noakes' left foot.

Marty Feldmans *n.* On certain ladies, the lop-sided *tits*, where the nipples point up, down and all around. Named after the late comedian Marty Feldman, whose distinctive nipples pointed in different directions.

mary *1. n. Sponge, pillow biter, angel. 2. n. Bean flicker, carpet muncher. 3. n.* A *liver sock.*

Mary Chipperfield *n.* A *wank ie.* a *monkey spamking* session. From the famous circus chimp dominatrix of the same name.

Mary Hinge *n.* Spooneristic *biffer.*

Mary Poppins' bag *n.* A surprisingly roomy *fanny*. A *clown's pocket.*

mash *v.* To fondle a lady's *shirt potatoes* as if testing them to destruction.

massage parlour wank *1. sim.* Something that is performed quickly and efficiently. *'And the wheel change and refuelling was performed like a massage parlour wank by the Ferrari mechanics and Schumacher should exit the pit lane still in the lead.'* (Murray Walker). *2. sim.* Something that is expensive and over too quickly, *eg.* the Pepsi Max ride at Blackpool.

master of ceremonies *1. n.* In this modern "hippy-hoppy" style of so-called music, a fellow in an ill-adjusted baseball cap who shouts about how super he is into a microphone. *2. n.* A red-faced, tail-coated man at a formal dinner who hits a wine glass with a spoon to get everyone's attention, before introducing some mercenary *cunt* like Jimmy Carr who then gets up and makes a few lame cracks about the managing director's golf handicap in return for several thousand pounds and a free tea. *3. n.* One's *knob, todger, old man etc.* The male penis.

masturmentary *n.* TV programme with a high *tit* and *fanny* count with a token bit of information thrown in to justify its showing, *eg.* a behind the scenes look at the porn film industry. The staple fare of late night satellite telly.

matelot's matress *n. nav.* A thick piece of bedding material provided to keep *Jack Tars* jolly in their bunks. A Wren.

Mather & Platt *rhym. Lancs. Manc.* A lady's *bodily treasure.* Named after an old established Mancunian engineering company. *'I wouldn't mind getting me hands on her Mather & Platt, our Liam.'*

mathsturbate *v.* To have a vowel and three consonants whilst thinking about Carol Vorderman. To practise one's *six-nowt times table.*

mating call *n.* The activation of pub toilet hand-driers as a deliberate attempt to impress any *birds* within earshot.

mayor's hat *n.* A *howzat* often eaten by goats.

McArthur park *1. n.* A 1970's maudlin ballad by Richard Harris. *2. n.* A particularly evil *dropped gut* that gives the impression that "something inside has died".

McDonald's farmyard *n.* The restaurant area of a high street fast food outlet, filled with sundry dullards, *scratters* and fatties grazing on burgers and fries whilst snorting appreciatively.

McEwan's Exports *n.* Fiercely nationalistic Scottish people who take every opportunity to proudly declaim their love for their homeland, despite choosing to live in America. Or Australia. Or Spain. Or anywhere except Scotland, *eg.* veteran syrupped former milkman turned spy Sir Sean Connery.

mckeith *n.* A textbook *dump.* Named after excrement-obsessed TV gerbil Gillian McKeith.

McKeith's handbag, smells like *sim.* Anything that *ronks* of *shit,* as one imagines the previously-mentioned comedy PhD-ed *turd-tamperer's* accessories must. Also *Oaten's briefcase.*

McSplurry *n.* The type of *grimshit* one experiences after dining for a week solely at a fast food restaurant. *Bubblepoo.*

McSquirter twins *n.* A gentleman's *clockweights.* Named after the sadly-demised, unconscionably right-wing pair of blazered *Record Breakers* co-hosts. The *gonk-faced Mother Teresa sisters.*

McSuck *n.* An *horatio* delivered with a force equivalent to that required to drink a newly poured McDonald's Thick Shake.

MDF *abbrev.* A *dobber.* Medium Density Flop-on. Not quite *wood.*

me *n.* Personal pronoun used at the end of a sentence to emphasise preference. *'For all these wenches are beauteous fair, and I doth admire them all, me.'* (from *Romeo and Juliet* by William Shakespeare).

meat and two vag *n.* A *threesome* involving two ladies and a smiling man who keeps pinching himself.

meat and two veg *n.* A gentleman's *undercarriage.* A *pork sausage* and a couple of *love spuds.*

meat balloons *n.* Older boys' playthings, which do not stick to the wall even after protracted rubbing on a jumper. *Mumbas, large tits.*

meat flower *n.* Delightful, poetic term for a lady's *bodily treasure.*

meat flute *n. Pink oboe.*

meat harp *n.* A vaguely fan-shaped instrument that a lady may choose to strum angelically from time to time. A *bird's fly-trap.*

meat injection *n.* An inoculation against virginity.

Meatloaf's daughter *n.* A big boned

mudchild. A *dreadnought*.

meat market *n*. Bar or club where *birds* with short skirts and blotchy legs dance round their handbags, waiting for a *pull*. A *meat rack, buttock hall*.

meat moth *n*. A *spam butterfly* commonly attracted to the bright lights of a *grot mag* photographer's flashgun.

meat movie *n*. A *grumble flick*.

meat paste *1. n*. Something your mum puts on your sandwiches at school. *2. n*. Something disgruntled chefs put on the burgers at McDonald's.

meat petite *n*. Descriptive of a Little Richard.

meat platter *1. n*. An unappetizing raffle prize on offer in a working men's club. *2. n*. An unappetizing *clopper* on offer behind a skip a working men's club car park.

meat tie *n*. Formal pink neckwear for topless ladies. Tied with a shiny purple knot. With all *spunk* coming out the end. The sausage in a *sausage sandwich*.

meatus *n. medic*. The proper name for the *hog's eye*, apparently. *'Hello? This is Mr J Brown from Notting Hill. I'd like a confidential word about my meatus, doctor. I stuck a propelling pencil lead down it for an experiment and I think it's snapped.' 'I'm terribly sorry, you must have dialled the wrong number. This is Midday Money on Good Morning with Philip and Fern. You're live on air.'*

mechanic's bulge *n*. Arm muscle unavoidably cultivated by a chap who lies on his back *tightening bolts* all day.

mechanic's nails *n*. Finger-end condition cause by *bumwad push-through*. *Taxi-driver's tan*.

mechanical dandruff *n*. Royal Air Force *crabs*.

medieval fireplace *sim*. A vast, gothic vagina with a big piece of pork slowly revolving in it.

medophile *n*. One who has become so accustomed to participating in *saucy mesomes* that it has become his preferred form of sexual activity. One who is no longer *master of his own domain*.

meeting with the big man *n*. A session of *self-indulgence* whilst at work. *'Coming to the cancer verandah, Dave?' 'No can do. I've got a meeting with the big man.'*

megraine *n*. Intermittent illness afflicting ladies and footballers when they realise they are no longer the centre of attention.

Mekon *1. n. prop*. The chief villain and leader of the Treens featured in Dan Dare's *Eagle* adventures of the 1950s, distinguished by his enormous cranium and little body, and hence *2. n*. A badly-poured pint which is "all head and fuck all else".

melanied *adj*. Drunk, battered, *blatted*. From the surname of All Saints popsie Melanie Blatt. *'I'm sorry Moira, but I can't let you go on air and read the news in that state. You're absolutely melanied.'*

Melbourne *n*. A soft *cock*.

melching *v. Minge felching*.

melon farmer *exclam*. The BBC-authorised, poorly-dubbed version of *motherfucker* used in films such as *Die Hard* and the entire *Beverly Hills Cop* series. Also *ever-loving, muddy funster*.

melons *n*. Female breasts. A large "pear".

melted welly *n*. A poetic term describing a lady's *bodily treasure. 'Spatula was powerless to resist. His eyes burnt into hers like mamellated chalcedony. His muscular arms enfolded her body as she felt herself being swept away on a noctilucent cloud of passion. 'Am I the first?' whispered Dartanyan. 'Sort of,' she vouchsafed in return, her voice quivering with unrequited passion. 'I've not let the other two have a shot on me melted welly yet."* (from *The Lady & the 3 Musketeers* by Barbara Cartland).

melvin *v.* To grab by the *balls.*

Melvyn *1. rhym. slang.* A cigarette. From Melvyn Bragg = fag. *2. rhym slang.* Sexual intercourse. From Melvyn Bragg = shag. *'Me and the missus always light up a nice Melvyn after we've had a quick Melvyn.'*

menage à moi *n. Fr.* A three-in-a-bed romp where the two ladies fail to turn up. A *wank.*

menage à une *n. Fr.* A saucy *mesome.*

men in the rigging *n. naval.* Small *tagnuts* trapped in the hairs of sailors' *arses. 'Six months since leaving Tahiti and no sign of land. We ate the last of the breadfruit weeks ago. Water and toilet paper strictly rationed. Crew growing restless, complaining of scrofula, scurvy and men in the rigging. Lord help us.'* (from *The Diary of Fletcher Christian*, 1789).

men's spendings *n. arch.* Withdrawals from the *clackerbag.*

men-stool cycle *n.* The happy period of a man's life when his *shit* appears at the same time every day.

menstrual arithmetic *n.* The reliably accurate calculations performed by a clued-up *left-footer* to decide whether it is safe to *shoot his load* up his missus, who is also the mother of his eighteen children.

menstrual cycle display team *n.* Any group of *birds* consisting of a moody one, a happy one, a normal one and a randy one.

merchant *rhym. slang. Kuwaiti tanker.*

merkin *n.* Man-made *mapatasi,* a *stoat syrup, pubic Irish.*

mermaid *1. n.* A fat *bird* with a pretty face, but nothing worth bothering with below the *tits. 2. n.* A woman who is good to look at, but just won't open her legs.

mermaid's flannel, wet as a *sim.* Descriptive of a very, very, very wet *fanny.* Also *otter's pocket, clown's pie, fish drowner.*

merry monk *rhym. slang.* The happy result of *pulling the Pope's cap off.*

Mersey trout *n.* A sweetcorn-eyed brown scouse fish.

Merthyr socialite *n.* A South Wales man-about-town who is often spotted in a giddy social whirl flitting between William Hills, The Windham and The DSS offices.

mesome *n.* A *one-in-a-bed romp.* A wank. *'I'm off upstairs for a mesome.'*

mertis *n.* Gereral term for any unpleasant substance, such as an accumulation of white residue at the corners of an overweight cruise liner chef's mouth, something your dog lies in on a vet's back room floor whilst recovering from a general anaesthetic, or that sticky sediment you get between the fingers of a sweaty man who moves filing cabinets up and down fire escapes for a living. *'Montellimar supreme. A frothy concoction of delicious* *milk chocolate, with a tempting vanilla praline mertis filling, topped off with chopped hazelnuts and a dead bluebottle which must of fell in the machine at the factory.'* (Description from *Netto Chocolates Belgian Assortment*).

MESS *acronym. Spunk.* Named after the chef's secret ingredient in McDonald's Extra Special Sauce.

mess *n.* Semen, *gunk, cock hockle.* That which is lost when one *chucks one's muck.*

Messerschmitt knickers *n.* An easy lady's *scads, ie.* ones which "come down without much of a fight".

Metal Mickey/Minnie *n.* One who wears an inordinate amount of cheap *bling* in the forlorn hope that it will somehow help them look classy.

metime *n.* The temporal period which a *gentlewoman* puts aside for the purpose of *relaxation.*

Mexican aftershave *n.* The acrid tang of chilli and garlic left in the *bog* after a rather nasty night of beer and spicy food.

Mexican picnic *n. SVSA,* a *drugs bust.*

Mexican barbecue *n. SVSASO.* A *Mexican pinic* with a *cock* in the mouth for good measure.

Mexican lipstick *n.* The embarrassing *Thompson's tide marks* often found after *eating out* with a lady who was *up on blocks.* A *pasata grin.*

Mexican screamers *n. medic.* A gastroenterological disorder characterised by fiery liquid excrement. *Tijuana brass-eye, Mexican shat dance.*

Mexican suicide *n.* To die peacefully in one's sleep. *'It is announced with deep regret and sadness that Her Royal Highness Princess Margaret committed Mexican suicide at 6.32 this morning at St George's Hospital.'*

mezoomas *n. Pink velvet cushions* on which the *family jeweller* prefers to display a *pearl necklace.*

Michael Owen's knee, a dick like *sim.* Something that goes pop within a minute.

Michaels *rhym. slang.* Piles. From the 1970s TV game show host Michael Miles. *'These nylon trolleys don't half chafe me Michaels.'*

Mickey 1. *n. Irish. Dick.* 2. *adj. Mouse. 'Sarah was a bit Mickey this morning. I think she was pissed again.'*

Mick Jagger smoking a cigar, like *sim.* A mid-way point during the launch of a *bum torpedo,* when it is neither in the tube nor heading for the beach, but is somewhere in between. *Casting Churchill's reflection. 'If I leaned forward now, Jeeves, it would look like Mick Jagger smoking a cigar.'*

middle leg *n.* The penis. Also *middle stump, third leg.*

middle order collapse *1. n.* All too typical performance of the England cricket team when faced with the prospect of a victory or a draw in a test match. Or even just the slight possibility of not losing by an innings and six hundred runs for once. *2. n.* A sudden want of tumescence halfway through a bout of penetrative affection.

Middlesbrough accent *n. medic.* A severe cough. *'The patient typically presents complaining of headache, high temperature, a productive Middlesbrough accent and nausea. Treatment - 200mg Amoxyl, three times a day'* (Tu-

berculosis - a Guide for Doctors - Health Department leaflet).

midfield playmaker *1. n.* In football, an overpaid, prancing, centrally-positioned player, *eg.* a *knob* like Glenn Hoddle. *2. n.* A *knob.*

midge's bawhair *n.* A metric division of length that can only be measured using an electron microscope and a magnifying glass at the same time. A hundred times smaller than a *bee's dick. 'Fuck me, Henri. You'd better let me drive for a bit. I've had less than you and we were a midge's bawhair from hitting that white Fiat Uno, you know.'*

midget gems *n.* Small, petite but perfectly-formed *teats,* such as the delights found on Keira Knightley or Amanda Holden.

midget porn *1. n. Grumble* thoughtfully provided by publishers for keen masturbators who are, ironically as a result of their hobby, too vertically challenged to reach the newsagent's top shelf. Examples of midget porn include *Ice, Nuts* and *Front. 2. n. Art pamphletry,* videographic *grumblery* and interwebular erotica featuring the saucy carryings-on of little people, and usually featuring a coked-up woman dressed in a distinctly half-arsed Snow White costume, one would imagine.

midget's surfboard *n.* A bachelor/teenager/priest's *spongle*-hardened sock which has become petrified by a plethora of *emissions* and which is on the Home Office's list of approved weapons which can be used against household intruders. Also *Womble's toboggan, Mother Shipton's sock, bachelor's boomerang.*

mid-loaf crisis *n.* Anything that spoils the enjoyment of a good *tom tit, eg.* a doorbell or telephone ringing, a dawning realisation that there is no *bumwad*, or a policeman approaching the shop doorway.

midnight mouth organ *n.* A high-cholesterol instrument played with relish around kicking out time in town centres across the land. A kebab.

midruff *n.* The exposed area of torso between a young lady's cropped top and her low-cut jeans which may have been toned, tanned and firm a couple of years ago, but which now hangs over her waistband like so much uncooked bread dough. Mutton tops.

midstool *v.* Act of a chap who is so hopelessly lost in love that he would happily kiss the *clackervalve* of the object of his desire whilst they are half way through *dropping anchor* at *bum bay. 'FREDDY: You know what, Professor Higgins? Miss Doolittle's the girl for me. I'm head over heels in love with the gel and I don't care who knows it. Dash it, old man, I think I'd even midstool Eliza if she asked.'* (from *Pygmalion* by George Bernard Shaw).

mighty Wurlitzer *1. n.* An enormous organ. *2. n.* Reginald Dixon's *cock.*

mild astegmatism *n. medic.* Bizarre ophthalmological phenomenon whereby the subjective attractiveness of a young lady decreases at a rate proportional to the amount of light ale one has imbibed. Like *beer goggles*, but in reverse.

mile 'I' club *n.* Similar to the Mile High Club, but for the solitary traveller. *Spinning one's own pro-*

pellor in an aeroplane toilet.

MILF *acronym*. Mums I'd Like to Fuck. *Yummy mummies*.

milf float *n*. A pretend sports car, such as the Peugeot 206CC, driven by an attractive young mother in an effort to recapture the carefree spirit of her lost youth.

milf grand prix *n*. The impressive grid line-up of gleaming four-wheel-drive sports utility vehicles which takes place on the pavements outside the gates of every posh secondary school in the country at 3.30pm.

milkers *n*. *Dairy bags*.

milking the thistle *n*. *Scots*. *Wanking*.

milkman *n*. That whistling chap who comes, bringing *yoghurt* in the early morning.

milkman's bonus *n*. An unexpected gift after delivering the *cream* to Mrs Brown. A *winnet on a stick*, *shitty dick*.

milkman's gait *n*. The walk adopted by someone who has *overshagged*.

milk of human kindness *n*. See *liquid rage*.

milk race *1. n*. Adolescent *wanking* game for two or more public school children. *2. n*. A barrack room *toss-up* to decide who eats the last cream cracker.

milk shake *1. n*. The uncontrollable quaking caused by imminent *stack blow*. *Elvis's leg*, *Cecil Parkinson's disease*. *2. n*. The combination of wobbles, undulations and simple harmonic motions that a middle-aged woman's *bits* perform while she's riding her bloke. *3. n*. A dance favoured by *birds* who are past the first flush of youth, involving an excess of alcohol and much swaying of the hips.

milk shower *n*. A form of soft-core dairy-based *watersports* that may be engaged in by a man and his lactating missus whilst she is enjoying a ride on his *solicitor general*.

milk the cow with one udder *v*. To be the only hand in the *farmyard area*.

milk the snake *v*. To practise *self abuse*.

millennium domes *n*. The contents of a Wonderbra, *ie*. very impressive when viewed from the outside, but there's actually *fuck all* in there worth seeing. Disappointing *tits*. See *heavage*.

millennium falcon *n*. Epithet used when referring to a dodgy *bird* which your mate has been *banging*. From the *Star Wars* film dialogue referring to Han Solo's spaceship; "You came in that thing? Wow, you're braver than I thought."

Mills & Bone *n*. Erotic literature with plot pretensions for the red-blooded bachelor.

milm *v*. To cover something in *jism*. *'Oy, mum, I've milmed me kex.'*

mimsy *1. adj*. Descriptive of the state of the borogroves. *2. n*. A *clopper*.

minotaur *1. n*. In Greek mythology, a monster with a man's body and a bull's head. *2. n*. In nightclubs, a monster with a woman's body and a face like a cow's *arse*.

mince medallions *n*. *Dangleberries*, *kling-ons*.

mince morsel *n*. An exceptionally pungent *Exchange & Mart* released in a confined area by an anonymous assailant.

mincident *n*. An unplanned and unnerving encounter with a gentleman adept at *jumping over pud-*

dles, eg. whilst bending over for the soap in a communal shower, failing to stand with one's back to the wall as a Gay Pride march comes past or when inadvertently sticking one's *cock* through a hole in a public lavatory cubicle wall.

miner's face, as filthy as a *sim.* Descriptive of a very accommodating lady who is eager to please in the bedroom. Right dirty.

miner's snot *n.* The liquid, stringy black *lav children* that can result from a night spent *sniffing the barmaid's apron.*

miner's sock *n.* A perspiring, debris-laden *clopper* after a hard day's graft.

ming *1. v. Scot.* To emit a foul smell, to *hum. 'Hoots mon, it's minging in here!'* 2. *n.* A foulsome miasma. *'Gaw, blimey! What's that blooming ming?' 'I'm afraid Jocky Wilson has done a shit in your shoe, Mr Bristow.'* 3. *v.* To exude ugliness. *'That Jade Goody is minging.'* 4. *n.* The bill, the *scuffers,* the *bizzies.* 5. *n.* A new marijuana cigarette made up from discarded ends. A tramp's *spliff.* 6. *n. prop.* The evil Emperor in *Flash Gordon.* 7. *n. coll.* A quantity of ugly women. *'Don't bother going to Simbas tonight. The place is heaving with fucking ming.'*

Ming the merciless *n.* An exceptionally foul-smelling *horse and cart.*

minge *n. Snatch, cludge, clopper, blurtch, quim.*

minge benefits *n.* The *snatch*-related rewards received by a man as a result of a selfless act performed for a loved one, *eg.* cooking dinner, buying flowers or sitting through *EastEnders* without complaining.

minge binge *n.* The frantic fish-eating spree of the *gash gannet.*

minge hinge *n. medic.* The female child-bearing pelvic area. *'This is the tale of Dora Duckett / Who had a minge hinge like a bucket / Her hubbie swore it was so wide / His charlie never touched the side / Despite her Albert Hall-like muff / He somehow got her up the duff / One night she cried out "Wake up Sid! / I think I'm going to have the kid!" / "Don't panic dear," her husband said / "I'll call the doctor from his bed" / The quack said "How d'you do" to Dora / And slipped his hand in to explore 'er / He stuck his arm right up her clout / As anxiously he felt about / "What's up?" Mr Duckett said / "Can you feel the baby's head?" / "Fuck the sprog," the doctor cried / "There's room for octuplets inside! / I've got my hand up your wife's crotch / Because I've lost my fucking watch."'* (from *Odd Odes* by Cyril Fletcher).

mingelicious *adj.* A *front bottom* alternative to the more *fat arse*-centric term of approbation *bootylicious. 'That Kylie Minogue is right mingelicious isn't she, Cardinal?'*

minge mat *n. Mapatasi, velcro triangle.*

mingeneering *n.* The science of *fanny mechanics. Snatch patching,* gynaecology.

mingerling *n.* To move and socialise amongst the less obviously attractive ladies in a nightclub after resigning oneself to the fact that one isn't going to pull a *looker. 'Well, looks like all the class blart has been snaffled. Better start mingerling, I suppose.'*

minge winker *1. n.* A striptease artiste. *2. n.* She who flashes her *gash, eg.* whilst folding her legs. *'Today's birthdays - Sharon Stone, minge winker, 49'.*

minglewank *n.* A surreptitious *tug* performed through the trouser pocket in a crowded place, *eg.* on a tube train, in a supermarket, at a funeral.

miniature heroes *1. n.* Small *fudge nuggets* which, even in the face of vigorous wiping, cling tenaciously to the *arse cress. 2. n.* Tiny *arse bars.*

minihughie *n.* A mouthful of *spew* that can be discreetly swallowed back down. The *vurp's* slightly bigger brother.

mini series *1. n.* A troublesome *log* that requires several flushes to see it off. *2. n.* A pile of *shite* starring Jane Seymour.

minjury *n.* An accident that occurs to a lady's *foofoo. 'Careful with that champagne bottle, Fatty, you'll do someone a minjury.'*

mink *n.* A more up-market name for the wife's *beaver.*

minkle *n.* Hampshire term for a lady's *front pocket. 'Fuck me, vicar. You can see her minkle.' Can also be used as a friendly greeting. 'Hallo vicar, you fucking minkle.'*

mink's minge, soft as a *sim.* Descriptive of something which is very soft, *eg.* fine velvet, silk pyjamas or Keith Flint out of The Prodigy. *'New Andrex Ultra. 50% longer, 50% stronger, but still as soft as a mink's minge.'* (Ad Campaign, Bartle Bogle Heggarty BBD DDP Needham Buggery Bollocks).

minky *1. n.* A French monkey. *2. n.* A species of whale. *3. n.* A *hornbag.* An attractive female.

minnie moo *n. Foofoo.*

minute man *n. medic.* One afflicted with the hilarious and shameful condition of premature ejaculation. A *two push Charlie,* a *point and squirt merchant.*

miserbation *n.* The practice of *wanking* over free underwear catalogues, travel brochures and other sundry *humble grumble,* as indulged in by parsimonious bachelors who consider shelling out good money on a copy of *Razzle* to be a frivolous waste of money. *Ebenezer spooging.*

miser's shite *n.* A miraculous bowel movement, the wiping of which causes no soiling of the first sheet.

Miss Hastings *n.* An ugly woman who is in fact the least ugly woman in one's environs. From the heavily be-uglywomanned Sussex seaside town.

missionary impossible *n.* A lady with a *lovely personality* who can only be *poked* in the *doggy position.* A *lumberjill,* a *bobfoc,* a *frombie.*

Miss Lincolnshire *n.* Any woman with *spaniel's ears. 'And this year's Miss Lincolnshire is Patsy Kensit.'*

Miss Pwllheli *n.* The ugliest female in any locale who could, should she wish, move to the north Wales town and win its annual beauty pageant by default.

Miss Selfridge shuffle *n.* The embarrassed, self-conscious little dance performed by a man left waiting in the lingerie department of a department store whilst his wife is in the changing rooms.

missus button *n.* The control on the front of a PC (often labelled "reset") which can be hit to remove all the vile, hardcore *grumble* from the screen when one's wife or partner returns home unexpectedly.

Mitchells *n.* Huge pairs of *tits*. Termed after their resemblance to the bald heads of *EastEnders* hard boys Phil and Grant. *'Dear Miriam, I found a lump in my left Mitchell and I'm scared to go to my doctor in case she gives me bad news.'* (Problem page, *Daily Mirror*, June 2002).

Mobe *n.* Abbreviation of Moby Dick. An epic *turd*, longer than a *mini series*, which may require harpooning with the lavatory brush to see it off.

mobile throne *n.* A portable *shit house* that everyone avoids at pop festivals because the floor is two inches deep in *mocking birds*.

mocking birds *rhym. slang. Douglas Hurds.*

mock turtle *1. n.* A character in *Alice in Wonderland* by antique kiddie diddler Lewis Carroll. *2. n.* Something that feels like a *shit*, but turns out to be a *fart*.

model T fart *n.* A *wind breakage* that sounds like one is about to be run over by Laurel and Hardy.

mod's parka *n.* A young lady's *clopper* of a particularly unattractive mien, resembling a sort of floppy funnel with a bit of flea-bitten fur stuck round the collar. Possibly encountered on Brighton beach whilst a youth in a leather jacket strikes it repeatedly using a length of metal pipe.

mofo *n. abbrev.* Abbreviation for *monkey feather*.

mohair knickers *n.* Large, unruly *minnie moo*; one with *spider's legs*. A *biffer*.

moip *n.* Female genital lubrication. *Froth, fanny grease, vagoline, beef dripping.*

moip mop *n.* A gentleman's beard used to soak up *sloom*, in the same way one would use a slice of bread to soak up gravy. *'Short back and sides, please. And could you trim the stray bits off my moip mop.'*

moist and meaty *adj.* Alliterating adjectives used extensively to describe the female and male genitals respectively, as well as dog food.

mole at the counter *euph.* A mammalian *turtle's head*. *"From the imprint of his shoes, Watson, I deduce that our quarry is a left-handed doctor of unusually short stature, who has known prosperity but has lately fallen on hard times. And by the short, irregular length of his stride, it is apparent that he has a mole at the counter,' said Holmes.'* (from *The Case of the Speckled Bowl* by Sir Arthur Conan Doyle).

mole in the back garden *n.* Small, brown animal that pops its head out for a second, leaving an unpleasant mound of soft dirt around the edge of its burrow.

mole's eye *n.* A *fanny* which makes a *mouse's ear* look like a *horse's collar*. *'Consignia was powerless to resist. His eyes burnt into hers like ambers. His muscular arms enfolded her body as she felt herself being swept away on tradewind of passion. "Now, Fernando,' she gasped. 'Take me now. All these years in the convent I've been saving myself for the right man, and now I've found you.' 'Fucking get in," breathed Fernando. 'You must have a snatch like a mole's eye."* (from *The Nun and the Windowcleaner* by Barbara Cartland).

molten brown *euph.* An unpleasant, morning-after-Vindaloo-style *digestive transit,* which melts the *balloon knot.* Named in direct contrast to the rather pleasant bathroom cosmetics manufacturer. A *rogan splosh, dump and burn.*

moment of clarity *n.* The instant following *stackblow,* when a *self-polluter* is assailed by intense feelings of disgust and self-loathing, and vows never to touch himself *down there* again. Just like he did an hour ago. *Wangst, wanguish.*

moobs *n. Man boobs.* From man + boobs.

moomlaaters *n.* Traffic-stopping *moobs.*

moneymoon *n.* The magical, but all too short period of financial stability which one enjoys after paying one's wages in or taking out a purple loan.

money shot *n.* The moment in a *bongo flick* where the leading man makes a small deposit from *Kojak's money box,* usually into the leading lady's face. A *pop shot.*

money tits *n.* The sort of smashing *Davy Jones's lockers* any man worth his salt would happily hand over his hard-earned wages to see unfettered, *eg.* the *fat rascals* fastened to the chest of leek-chomping warbler Charlotte Church.

mongrel *n.* A *dobber,* a *semi, half a teacake.* A *cock* in a state of semi-turgidity that is neither one thing nor the other. A *knob* which is *on the bounce.*

monkey *n.* Vagina. A *toothless gibbon. 'Does the monkey want a banana?'*

monkeybagging *n.* Man's means of heightening his pleasure whilst an act of oral *horatio* is being performed on his *tummy banana. Monkeybagging* involves the simple act of tugging one's partner's ears away from, and perpendicular to their head, thus modifying the shape of their mouth and lips.

monkey bath *n.* A bath so hot, that when lowering yourself in, you go: "Oo! Oo! Oo! Aa! Aa! Aa!"

monkey cum *n.* Any cream-based *tart fuel, eg.* Bailey's.

monkey feather *exclam.* Bizarre substitute for *m******f****** dubbed into Eddie Murphy films on BBC1 to avoid offending some stupid old cunt. Also *mother father, money farmer, melon farmer, muddy funster.*

monkey pie *1. n.* A chip shop delicacy heated to the temperature of the earth's core which, upon taking the first *Bee Gees bite,* causes its purchaser to cry out in a series of inarticulate, high-pitched simian shrieks. *2. n.* A hairy, ill-mannered *clopper* that keeps blowing raspberries.

monkey run *n.* The awkward act of half-sprinting, half-hobbling from the computer to the bathroom, performed by a web *grumble* enthusiast with the *jester's shoes* who has realised too late that all the socks are in the wash. A gait which brings to mind that of Clint Eastwood's ginger simian sidekick Clyde in the *Every Which Way but Loose* movie series. A *wounded soldier's walk, bishop's waltz.*

monkey's chin *n. Twix lips, beetle bonnet,* a prominent *mound of Venus.*

monkey's fag break *n.* Like slipping out for five minutes for a fag, but for a *ham shank* instead of a *Harry Rag.* A *wank* at work.

monkey's fist *n.* A small, brown *Richard the Third.* Found by a cockney vicar on the pavement.

monkey's forehead *1. n. velcro triangle, mapatasi.*

monkey's kneecap *n.* A scabby *quim* one could spend all day picking the fleas out of.

monkey's tail *n.* A small lick of *turd* on the rear of the seat caused by sitting too far back whilst *dropping the kids off at the pool.*

monkey's toe *1. n.* A nipple big enough to peel a banana. A *Westminster Abbey hatpeg. 2. n.* The *turtle's head.*

monkey wank *n.* To masturbate oneself or another person using the feet. Whilst swinging in a tyre.

Monkhouse's Syndrome *n. medic.* To vomit into the mouth and swallow with a tortoise-like gulp and hand gesture, reminiscent of the late Bob Monkhouse introducing a punchline. *Bob's Full Mouth.*

monk's chain *n. eccles.* A circle or line of friars, public schoolboys or BBC football commentors interfering with each other's *parts of shame.* A *daisy chain,* a *circle jerk.*

monk's chunks *n.* The excess *smeg* build-up of a man who has given up caring any more.

monk's cowl *n.* A *wizard's sleeve.*

monk's hood *n.* A voluminous *Jacky Danny.* A *wizard's sleeve,* a *hippo's mouth, Jade yawning.*

monks' trunks *n.* Underpants that are crunchy with dried *spunk.*

monster munch *n. Cunnimingus.* From the comparable olfactory experience of sticking one's face in a bag of the popular pickled onion snack and breathing deeply.

Montezuma's revenge *n. medic. Mexican screamers,* the *shits. Tijuana cha-cha.*

monthly wrench *n.* The variably-sized *tool* which a chap employs in order to *tighten his nuts* whilst his *ride* is *up on blocks. Wanking spanner.*

Monty *n.* A *blopstrop, tammy huff.* From the mood swings of Ryder Cup winner and perennial *moanarse* Colin Montgomerie.

moo *n.* A name to call the wife when one thinks the word "cow" is too offensive. *'Where's me bladdy tea, eh? You fucking stupid old moo.'*

moobs *n.* Flabby breast-like structures sported by non-sporting gentlemen whose only form of daily exercise is to jog past the salad in the works canteen. From man + boobs. *Man breasts, mannery glands, bitch tits.*

mooey *n.* A *sausage wallet, minnie moo.*

moomph *1. v. Aus.* To sniff a lady's bicycle seat. *Barumph, snurgle. 2. n. Aus.* One who *moomphs. A garboon, snufty, snurglar.*

moon *v.* A rugby move, where the prop forward sprints around the defending back four to the rear of the bus and presses his naked *arse* up to the back window.

moonie *1. n. prop.* A follower of the Rev Ying Tong Yiddel-I Moon. *2. n.* An act of *mooning. Hanging your hole.*

moon juice *n.* The liquid product of a lady's monthly discomfort. The cargo of the *tomato boat. Lunar mess, fanny jam.*

moonraker *1. n.* One who is prone to the vigorous and blatant scratching of their *ringpiece. 2. n.* Space-based James Bond film in which, for the purposes of a particularly off-colour Christmas afternoon pun, a weightless Roger Moore apparently attempts to *thumb in a slacky* after already losing his *mess* up a scientist who is named to imply that she is a talented *fellatrix*.

moonwalk *n.* The optical illusion of walking without moving achieved by someone trying to wipe a *dog's egg* off their shoes onto the grass.

moose *n. Boiler, steg.* Often a feminist who's got *Don King in a headlock*.

moose knuckles *n. Can. Camel's foot, Ninja's toe.*

moosetrap *n.* The protracted, often expensive, and frankly unnecessary efforts expended when attempting to seduce a right *boot* of a lass when, in reality, a simple "Fancy a bang?" would probably achieve the same outcome. Inspired by the popular charity shop 1970s children's boardgame *Mousetrap*, which featured an overly complicated contrivance for the purpose of entrapping a small plastic rodent that was frankly going nowhere.

moped *n.* A fat woman. Fun to *ride*, but you wouldn't want your mates to know.

more Ginster than gangster *adj.* Descriptive of the sort of portly *twat* with a shaved head, tracky pants, white polo shirt, lots of expensively cheap jewellery, and who has to use the roof of his ageing BMW in order to haul himself out onto the pavement before strutting off like an overweight Al Capone. *'The guy thought he was some kind of toughnut, but actually he was more Ginster than gangster.'* (from *The Pram in the Lake* by Raymond Chandler).

more tea vicar? *phr.* Faux-farcical attempt to distract a clergyman after the launch of an *air biscuit*, now widely used to diffuse post-*fart* tension. See also *keep shouting Sir, we'll find you; speak up caller, you're through.*

morgan *rhym slang. Arse.* From Morgan Stanley Dean Witter = shitter.

morgue cheater *n.* A senior citizen. A *coffin dodger*, an *oxygen thief*.

mornflakes *n.* Residue found in one's *pubes* after carelessly *relaxing in a gentleman's way* several times the previous evening.

morning glory *n.* The appearance of a *tent pole* first thing in the morning. A *dawn horn*.

morning level crossing *euph.* The first *piss* of the day. From the fact that you have to wait for the barrier to go down before you can proceed. Even though, on a real level crossing, you have to wait for the barrier to go up before you can proceed, obviously. Unless you're a train driver.

morning line, the *1. n.* Channel 4 horse-racing programme hosted by Happy Shopper Steve Rider Derek Thompson and celebrity nose-picker John McCririck. *2. n.* The results left in one of them back to front German *shitters* when one *releases the chocolate hostage* after a breakfast of schnitzels, boiled cabbage and lager.

morning thickness *n.* A post-slumber state of erectivitation. Also *morning wood, morning glory.*

morning thunder *n.* The first, usually very powerful *fart* of the day.

morning wood *n.* Ante-meridian tumescence.

Morrissey's stag night, like *sim.* Descriptive of a public house peopled entirely by broken men of indeterminate age staring silently at their half-empty pint glasses. *'Shall we go to Yates's instead? It's like Morrissey's stag night in here.'*

mortal *adj. Refreshed* within an inch of one's life.

Moses effect *n.* What a seatbelt or bag strap does to a lady's *baps, ie.* causing them to part like the Red Sea.

mosquito's tear *n.* An unimpressive quantity of ejaculate produced by a young man or bachelor at the conclusion of his ninth *pull* of the day, when the amount of *spuzz* issuing from his *hog's eye* is roughly equivalent to the quantity of liquid which drips onto the cheek of an insect of the family *culicidae* during the final scenes of *Love Story,* when Ali McGraw pegs it.

Moss Bros hire trousers, more cocks in her than a pair of *sim.* Descriptive of a loose-moralled lady who boasts an impressively extensive sexual back catalogue. *'I tell you what, I wouldn't say she's easy, ladies and gentlemen, but she's had more cocks in her than a pair of Moss Bros hire trousers. So in conclusion, can we all raise our glasses and toast the bride and groom?' 'Thank-you, vicar. And now it's time for the best man's speech.'*

moss cottage *n.* The ideal home for *John Thomas.*

mosstril *n.* A single nasal aperture of the sort sported by celebrity types (*eg.* Daniella Westbrook) who find *Keith Richard's dandruff* a bit moreish.

mothball diver *n.* One who savours *granny's oysters. A biddy fiddler.*

moth boy *n.* The member of a drinking party who, upon entering a pub, proceeds directly to the bandits, attracted by the flashing lights. *Fruit fly.*

motherfucker *n.* In films directed by Quentin Tarrantino, an unpopular gentleman. A polite term which can be used in the place of obscene terms such as *melon farmer, monkey feather, money farmer etc.*

Mother Hubbard's dog *sim.* Descriptive of an underused *minge, ie,* drooling and *gagging for a bone. 'It's noo a score and seven years since her beloved Bonny Prince Albert passed awa'. Today, whilst oot aside the loch, Her Majesty confided in me that she missed his big wullie affy bad, and that most o' the time, her wee royal badger was akin tae Mother Hubbard's dog.'*

mother's love *n.* The quality which alows one to re-enter the *cludgie* after *laying a cable* when others have deemed the *ming* too evil to tolerate.

motion sickness *n.* Nausea caused by doing a *dump* so foul that it makes one gag.

motion thickness *n. Travel fat.*

motorboat, the *n.* The act of placing one's face between a lady's *baps* and pushing them together from either side whilst making the noise of an outboard motor. A woman can thus be described as *motorboatable* if she possesses sufficient *motorboatability.* A *two-stroke man sandwich.*

motorcycle kick stand *n.* The morning erection that manifests itself whilst one is asleep on one's side, preventing one from rolling over onto one's stomach.

motorhead *1. n.* A famous heavily metallic popular music combo, famous for their jaunty songs, including *Ace of Spades* and *Killed by Death*. *2. n.* An urgent *blowjob* delivered at breakneck speed behind a sleazy burger bar, cinema or skip.

mott *1. n.* A lady from Cumbria. *2. n.* Part of a Norman fort from GCSE history. *3. n.* A *minge, mapatasi.*

mottzerella *n.* A stringy, warm substance with the appearance of melted cheese, found on a *smeesh* which has been somewhat neglected in hygiene terms. *Voodoo butter, chodder.*

mound of Venus *n.* The craggy outcrop above *salmon canyon* usually hidden by a dense covering of *bush*. A *beetle bonnet, monkey's forehead, grassy knoll.*

mount *v.* To *hop on* for *a bit*.

mountbattens *n.* Small fragments of shattered *turds* found floating in the toilet.

Mount Fujis *n.* Uncannily conical tits as seen in 1950s American B films. *Twin peaks, sweatermeat, dunce's hats.*

mouse *adj.* Descriptive of someone who is poor at what they do. *Swiss. 'That Eamonn Holmes is a bit fucking mouse, isn't he?'*

mouse meat *n.* Cheese.

mouse's ear, fanny like a *sim.* Descriptive of a tight *minnie moo,* a *butler's cuff.*

mouse's tongue *sim.* Descriptive of a very small penis. With cheese on the end.

mousetrap *1. n.* Agatha Christie play which performs a sort of Care in the Community role for bad actors. *2. n.* A bin found in the ladies' restrooms where women may discreetly dispose of their feminine hygiene products, such as *jamrags, fanny nannies,* and *chuftie plugs*. *3. n.* One's wife's *minge* for the week or so each month when she is *dropping clots.*

moustaka *n.* A female lady's pubic hair which has been neatly parted down the centre in the style of a Wild West saloon bartender's moustache.

mouth muff *n.* A goatee beard normally sported by someone who mans an IT help desk and likes T'Pau. A *cocksucker's doormat.*

mouth-to-muff *n.* Lesbotic resuscitation technique. Also *quimlich manoeuvre.*

moving Blackbeard's eyepatch *n.* The time-saving practice of riving the gusset of a lady's *applecatchers* to one side in order to gain a swift entry to her *James Blunt*. Also *using the catflap, playing the violin. 'Lift your legs up, love. I can't get your knickers off.' 'Aw bloody hell. I'm really tired. can't you just move Blackbeard's eyepatch while I catch forty winks?'*

moy *1. n.* Helmet cheese. *Smegma.* *2. adj.* Shit. esp. *dog's moy*. *'Waterworld (1995. Dir. Kevin Costner) starring Kevin Costner and Dennis Hopper. A visually-striking, futuristic pile of high budget dog's moy.'* (*Halliwell's Film Guide*).

Mr Benn, to do a *v.* To get so *mullered* that one goes into a toilet in a pub, and the next thing one remembers is exiting the toilet of another pub, suspecting one has had a little adventure inbetween.

Mr Blobby *1. n.* Tidy-bearded annoying *cunt* Noel Edmonds's rubber-suited annoying *cunt* side kick. *2. n.* A gentleman during the one week in four when he has to do without, due to his wife being *Mrs. Blobby.*

Mr Bond *n.* A particularly buoyant *turd* that returns to the surface of the water even after flushing. *'Ah, so we meet again, Mr Bond.'*

Mr Brown is at the window *euph.* To have the *turtle's head*. First used by Queen Victoria. *'Pray forgive us, Mr Gladstone, but we cannot receive you at the moment. Mr Brown is at the window, and we fear we may papper our kex.'*

Mr Flitcroft's woes *n.* Constant reminders that one's relationship is on the rocks, *eg.* a piece of music, a photograph, a fifty-thousand strong jeering crowd.

Mr Happy's business suit *n.* An *English overcoat.*

Mr Hyde *1. n.* The uncontrollable, throbbing, dribbling, twitching, hairy beast into which Dr Jekyll transforms in the famous book and Russ Abbott sketch by Robert Louis Stevenson. *2. n.* The uncontrollable, throbbing, dribbling, twitching, hairy beast into which one's *knob* transforms when a particularly *fit bird* walks past.

Mr Jones *1. n. 19thC.* Penis. *2. n.* A butcher who frequently purports that "they don't like it up 'em".

Mr Sausage *n.* The excitable trouser man. Title of a *Mr Men* book that was hastily withdrawn from sale within an hour of going on sale in 1976.

Mr Trebus's yard *sim.* Descriptive of a much-neglected, unhygienic and rat-infested *clopper.* With a couple of mopeds buried in it. From the late *Life of Grime* star's shit-filled garden.

Mr Whippy *1. n.* Semi-viscous ice-cream that comes out of a tap in a van. From 60p. *2. n.* Flagellation, corporal punishment dished out at *rub-a-tug shops*. From £25.

Mr Whippy's in town *exclam.* Declaration that all is not well in the *chamber of horrors.*

M32 *n.* A *tit fuck, ie.* the most direct route for *coming* into the *Bristol* area.

muck *1. n. Mess, baby bouillon, load, bolt*. That which is *shot. 2. n. 'Have a look on Bravo, vicar. There's usually a bit of muck on there at this time of night.'*

mucksavage *n.* A *bumpkin*, a *buffle*, a *cabbagehead*. A *joskin*.

muck spreader *n. Arse, bum.*

muck truck *n.* A late night emergency food vehicle parked at the side of the road near a pub or club at chucking out time, where the cuisine is often somewhat less than haute, but looks smashing after a gallon or so of *pop. A kebabulance.*

muck trumpet *n.* A tunefully farty *brass eye.*

mucky dip *n.* A *scuttling* up the *coal hole.*

mucky *n.* Any item of a pornographic nature, book, video, *etc*. *'Have you got any mucky I can borrow?' 'Yes, but don't get any spragg on it this time.'*

mud *1. n.* Excrement. *2. n.* Excrement 1970s pop group.

mud button *n. Winnet, dangleberry, tagnut, clinker, etc.*

mudchild *n.* A *sweaty morph*. Also *mud child.*

mud darts *n. Anal love. Bum sex.*

mudeye *n. Arse, ringpiece*, one's

old-fashioned *fifties tea towel holder*.

muddy funster *1. n.* A *botter*. *2. n.* A *melon farmer*.

muddy welly *n.* A soiled prophylactic sheath which is best left by the *back door*.

Mudgee mailbags *sim.* Great big *norks*. Named after the remote Australian outback town of Mudgee, which gets its post delivered twice a year, apparently receiving it in large *tit*-shaped sacks. *'Christ, you've got knockers like Mudgee mailbags, Your Majesty.'*

mud hole *n.* That *hole* from which one *blows mud*. The *crop sprayer, cable layer*.

mudlark *1. n.* A horse which enjoys heavy ground. A *mudder*. *2. n.* The sort of goings-on enjoyed by foreign sex perverts on the internet.

mud oven *n.* The rectum of the *anus*. *'Mitochondria was powerless to resist. His eyes burned into hers like haematites. His muscular arms enfolded her body as she felt herself being swept away in a pyroclastic flow of passion. Then he said those words of which she had dreamed so long, yet never dared hope to hear. 'How much to give you one in the mud oven, then love?'* (from *The Aged Prostitute and the Scouse Football Star who Got Signed by Manchester United for Twenty-Eight Million Quid* by Barbara Cartland).

mudpussy *n.* The *arse,* when used by heathens for purposes for which the Lord did not intend it.

mud valve mechanic *n.* A *brown pipe engineer, exhaust fitter*.

mudwife *n.* One who assists another during the delivery of a particularly large, or breech, *Meatloaf's daughter*. *'Bobby Brown admitted on television last night that he has had occasion to act as a mudwife to his constipated missus Whitney Houston.'*

mud wrestling *n.* A long and messy battle on the toilet, involving much grunting and groaning, which usually ends in either a fall or a submission.

muff *1. n. Minge, fanny*. *2. v.* To *shag,* have intercourse with. *3. v.* To fluff, miss an easy goal-scoring opportunity. *'Oh fuck! Emile Heskey has muffed it.'*

muff diva *n.* A histrionic lady of sapphic inclination.

muff diver *n.* A footballer who misses an easy goal scoring opportunity, then falls over in an attempt to win a penalty kick.

muff diver's dental floss *n.* Female pubic hair.

muff huff *n.* Menstruational moodiness or PMT. A *period drama*, a *blob strop*.

muffia *n.* A collection of criminal women, or women married to criminals.

muffin *1. n.* Flour-based bakery product. *2. n.* 1960s TV mule whose name remains a source of perpetual hilarity among the elderly and infirm.

muffin tops *n.* The pastry-like midriff overhang achieved by lasses wearing tight, low-slung *kex*.

muffle *v.* The female equivalent of *zuffle*.

mufflinks *n.* Female genital jewellery. Pierced fanular silversmithery. *Curtain rings*.

muff nudge *n*. The light brushing of a female hairdresser's *beetle bonnet* against one's elbows when she leans forward to cut one's hair.

muffocation *n.* Inability to breathe when a *dirty lady* is sitting on your face.

muff riders *n. Birds' crabs.*

muffro *n.* Female pubic coiffure that resembles nothing so much as the popular hairdo which was famously sported by Jermaine Jackson in the seventies. On his head, of course, not his *cunt.*

mufftash *n.* The stylish, Kevin Webster-style furry residue which adorns the upper lips of those who have but recently been *licking out* a lady's *mimsy.* A *Barnsley moustache.*

muff trumpet *n.* A *fanny fart* that would have a troop of soldiers standing by their beds.

mug stains *n.* Large, dark, flat *jockeys* that often appear during pregnancy.

Mugabe *n.* The frankly silly postage stamp-sized tuft of *muff turf* left above the *wuwus* of certain porn actresses and *jazz mag* models. *A muffgabe, clitler.*

mule's lip *n.* A large foreskin.

mullered *adj. Langered.*

muller love *n.* The temporary amorous feelings one has towards a right *pig* as a result of being *mullered.* Finding someone attractive when looking at them through *beer goggles.*

mullet *n.* Inbreds' haircut favoured by country and western singers, the verminous guests on the *Jerry Springer* show and 1980s footballers.

mulligan *n. Aus.* Penis.

mumbas *onomat.* Breasts. If *oomlaaters* made a noise, they would say "mumbas" in a deep, fruity baritone.

mumble in the jungle *n. Cunnibungalus.*

mumblers *n.* Tight women's bicycle shorts through which you "see the lips move but can't understand a word".

mummy returns *n.* A *brown zombie* that comes back wrapped in *shit tickets.*

mumph *onamat.* See *flub.*

Mumrah's cock *n.* The tissue wrappings placed around *Pharaoh's flute* to prevent any spillages of *kid juice* onto ceremonial robes *etc.* Particularly handy whilst re-enacting the ancient Egyptian creation myth of Atum, who had a swift *one off the wrist* on the Primordial Mound in the Void of Nu, and was surprised to discover that the first *wad* of supernatural *jitler* out of his *hog's eye* contained both the god Shu and the goddess Tefnut, who became the parents of all the other elements of the world. From the bandage-wrapped mummy in *Thundercats*™.

mumrar *n.* The act of sneaking up behind your mother and shouting "RAR!"

munch bunch *n.* A gang of *dykes* in a carpet warehouse.

mung *1. n.* Type of bean which is popular with *Guardian* readers. *2. n.* A particularly runny type of *arse feta. 3. n.* That smell which emanates from within the fleshsome rolls of a *Duke of giblets. 'Rik – I like what you did with the song, but I'm not sure that your interlude of vigorous breakdancing during the middle eight was such a good idea. There was a right fucking mung in here by the time you reached the last chorus. Dr Fox has had to open the window.'*

mungos *n.* Great big sideburns as worn by Jerry Dorsey, lead singer of Mungo Jerry. *Bugger's grips, face fannies.*

municipal cockwash *n. Town bike, box of assorted creams, buttered bun.*

munter gatherer *n.* A fellow who appreciates the company of women with *lovely personalities.*

munts *n.* Particularly butch, though not necessarily *lesbotic* ladies, often found amongst the sailing community. From men + cunts.

murray walker *n.* One who enjoys an *al fresco Ruby* whilst meandering back from the pub. Named after the excitable Formula 1 motor-racing commentator Martin Brundle.

muscle mary *n.* An extremely well-built *ginger beer.* A *canny hard puff.*

mush in the bush *n.* The kind of sex act that Dick Van Dyke might perform on Julie Andrews. *Cockney cumulonimbus.*

musical vegetables *n.* Baked beans, as eaten by cowboys and *trouser trumpeteers.*

musical wank *n.* A *strum* undertaken to the rhythm of some music.

musk mask *n.* To wear a lady's *undercrackers* as a balaclava whilst having a right good *wank.*

mustang *n.* Of *shitty arses,* that stubborn *dangleberry* which cannot be shaken off.

mute button *n.* In a public lavatory, for example, the invisible remote control that you apparently operate upon entering, which renders any *trap* occupant completely silent until they have heard you wash your hands and leave the room.

Mutley chunter *n.* The act of voicing disapproval under one's breath when forced to perform an act under duress, in the style of Dick Dastardly's dog. Usually involves muttering "ratting, dratting," *etc.* through tightly-clenched teeth.

mutton dressed as kebab *sim.* Ugly women who doll themselves up and make themselves look even worse, *eg.* Julie Goodyear. Also *mutton dressed as spam.*

mutton musket *n.* A smaller, more portable field weapon than the *lamb cannon.* Also *mutton bayonet, mutton dagger.*

mutton tugger *n.* In a slaughterhouse, one whose job it is to pull the meat off the bones of old sheep.

mutt's nuts *adj.* Descriptive of something which is very good. The *dog's bollocks, the vicar's cock.*

mycoxafloppin *n. medic.* The principal active ingredient in Viagra.

Myleene *rhym. slang.* The *anus.* From the fat-titted former Hear'Say songstress Myleene Klarsehole.

mystic smeg *n. Erectoplasm.*

mystic steg *n.* A malevolently *fugly* presence which haunts you, asking you what your fucking star sign is.

Nn

nadbag *n*. The *nut sack, pod pouch, scrot sling, chicken skin handbag.*

nadger *n*. A testicle which has been battered black and blue. *'I tell you what, she loves it rough. She's left me with a right pair of nadgers, Mother Superior.'*

nadgina *n*. A *cockney's pod purse,* which has been refashioned into a *cludge* at the skilled hands of a dextrous surgeon. *'Day forty-four in the house, and Nadia's giving her nadgina a quick rinse in the sink.'*

nad nogg *n*. *Splod.*

nadpoles *n*. *Jizzbag taddies. Spunks,* spermatozoan humunculi.

nads *n*. *Knackers,* testicles, *plums.*

Nagasaki tan *n*. A sunbed induced glow of such ferocity that it appears that one was present an the detonation of an atom bomb, *eg.* one sported by Judith Chalmers, Des O'Connor, Jodie Marsh, Dale Winton.

NAKED!!!!! *adj*. Not in any real sense naked. A variation on the original word, used on the cover of lads' mags in order to hype up pictures of some *bird* who is either not naked at all or is strategically covering up her bits, so you can't see them and she may as well be wearing a big jumper. Also NUDE!!!!!, STARKERS!!!!!, WE ALREADY RAN THESE PICTURES SIX MONTHS AGO & WE HOPE YOU DON'T NOTICE!!!!!

name that tune *exclam*. A humorous exclamation called out to draw attention to an amusing breaking of wind at a middle class dinner party.

nana Kournikova *n*. A *bird* who appears to be fit from the back, but who on turning round is revealed to be a pensioner. A *Kronenberg,* a *Toyah.*

nan bread *n*. *Bingo wings, dinner ladies' arms, arm tits.*

nan's grin *n*. A toothless *Beverley Craven.*

nan's mattress, as pissed as your *sim*. To be in an extreme state of *refreshment. 'Ladies and gentlemen, welcome aboard flight BA103 from Oslo. We would advise you to keep your safety belts fastened throughout the flight as it looks like it could be quite a bumpy ride. We're not expecting any turbulence, it's just that the captain is as pissed as your nan's mattress.'*

Narnia, so far in the closet he's in *euph*. Of a man, to be in denial over how chromatically adept he is.

nastonbury *n*. *Festival fanny.* The ripe *fent* coming off a *clout* that hasn't been cleaned for four days.

national grottery, win the *v*. To be the lucky discoverer of a massive deposit of porn hidden under a *bongo bush*, in a skip or a recently-deceased vicar's study.

nature's make-up *n*. A range of black and blue eye cosmetics favoured by the wives of certain British sportsmen and ex-James Bond actors.

naughty Nazi salute *n*. A *herman gelmet* standing to attention.

nauticals *rhym. slang*. Piles. From nautical miles.

navigator of the windward pass *n*. A *rear admiral.*

Navy cake *n. milit.* Army and Air Force term for the *arse.*

NBR *abbrev.* No Beers Required. A good-looking woman. Opposite of a *five pinter.*

NCP yoghurt *n*. The viscous off-white fluid spilled onto their *grot mags* by car park attendants *relaxing* in their booths. *'Excuse me, mate. Have you got any change for the ticket machine...? Eurgh. What's all that stuff on your hands, trousers and splashed across the open pages of your bongo book?' 'It's NCP yoghurt, that's all. And no, I don't have any change for the machine. Fuck off.'*

NDL *abbrev.* Nipples Don't Lie. Body language phenomenon that gives anthropologists an insight into how they are getting on when chatting up *birds* in the pub.

Neapolitan knickers *n.* The disgusting state of a proper old *slapper's gusset.* Vanilla, strawberry, chocolate, the lot.

neckbreaker *n.* A *log* of such length, rigidity and tensile strength that it lifts the *shitter* vertically off the *pot*, crushing his or her neck against the ceiling. It is a little-known fact that Queen Victoria's death certificate gives her cause of death as "a neckbreaker occasioned by eating a plethora of black pudding, fruitcake and milk stout for her tea the day before."

necking turds *v.* Accusation made against one suffering from halitosis. *'Excuse me, madam, I don't wish to appear rude, but have you been necking turds?'*

neck tripe *n.* The unappetizing hanging flesh that adorns the throats of ageing ladies.

ned *n.* A Glaswegian *scratter.*

neddies *n. Nellies.*

needle dick *n.* Light-hearted, affectionate term of locker room abuse/ridicule describing a fellow with a small penis. *'Oi, we're one man short for the five-a-side here. Where's needle dick?' 'Didn't you hear? He's killed himself.'*

nellies *n. Knockers, tits, neddies, melbas.*

Nelson Mandela *rhym. slang. Wreck the hoose juice, wifebeater.* Stella.

nelson's column, a *n.* A profound tumescence. Something that is tall, hard as rock, has one eye at the top, and attracts filthy *birds.* And Japanese tourists with cameras.

Neptune's kiss *n.* A cold, wet smacker on the *tea towel holder* caused by *splashback.*

Nescafe handshake *n.* An act of masturbation. A reference to the adverts where coffee granules used to appear in deceased *New Avengers* star Gareth Hunt's hand after he pretended to have a *wank*. Also *magicking the beans.*

net curtains *n.* Old ladies' *drapes,* which tend to twitch over to one side when the neighbours come out.

nether eye *n.* That single *unseeing eye*, situated in the *nether region*, which cries brown, lumpy tears.

nether throat *n.* In *farting*, the *poot chute*, *botty bugle*. *'Pardon me while I clear my nether throat.'*

nettie *n.* Outside loo, *clart cabin, shite house. Dunny, cludgie, growler, khazi.*

Netto fabulous *adj.* Descriptive of one who eschews posh jewellers such as Tiffany's and Asprey's in favour of down market *blingmongers* like Price-drop.TV and Argos.

Netto ghetto *n.* A shopping arcade consisting entirely of discount stores, *eg.* the Loreburn Centre, Dumfries.

new age traveller's cheque *n.* A giro.

Newcastle cup run *euph.* Descriptive of that wistful feeling experienced by gentlemen looking down at their own erections and wishing they could *suck* themselves *off.* From the fact that they know "it's within reach, but it's never going to happen".

new sheriff in town, there's a *exclam.* Phrase used when someone visiting one's home delivers an *air biscuit* which achieves hitherto unprecedented levels of pungency.

Newton effect *n.* When struggling to pass a three *breather ring dreadnought*, the pleasing sensation as the force of gravity takes over.

Newton's cradle *1. n.* A still fashionable, chromed executive toy which, by means of colliding, suspended balls demonstrates Newton's third law of motion. *2. n.* The off-putting and often *timber-felling* image of two *grumble flick* actors banging their *knackers* together as they perform a *DP.*

Newton's revenge *n.* The cruel effect of gravity upon aged *tits.*

next sale *n.* Twice-yearly incident where one is awoken at some ungodly hour to clear out a pile of unwanted *shit.*

NFF FFN *abbrev. Nice From Far, Far From Nice.* Descriptive of a lady who looks alright from a distance, but is a right *steg* close up. A *Thora bird,* a *golden deciever.*

NGTs *abbrev.* National Geographic Tits. Flat, pendulous breasts as sported by old tribeswomen in the aforesaid school library *jazz mag. Spaniel's ears.*

niags *rhym. slang. Nuts.* From Niagra Festicles = testicles.

nicely poised *adj.* Of a gentleman, to be prone to *jumping puddles.* To be *good with colours, on the other bus.*

nice piece of glass *n.* Comestible ordered by humorous males at the bar. *'I'll have a nice piece of glass in a Stella sauce, please.'*

nichter scale *n.* Tabulated rating system used to articulate how much one would prefer not to *do* someone. *'Have a look at the fucking state of that. Christ on a fucking bike. She must register at least 9.5 on the nichter scale.'* (Sir Terry Wogan, introducing the Serbian entry to the 2007 Eurovision Song Contest).

nick bent *adj.* Temporarily travelling on the *other bus* whilst staying at Her Majesty's pleasure.

nickles and dimes *1. n.* Low denomination US currency. *2. n.* A low denomination *grumble vid money shot.* A *stick flick lizard's lick. 'Goddammit, Gunther. That was goddamn nickles and dimes.' 'What do you expect? It's the fifth popshot I've done in two hours.'*

nick one to the wicketkeeper *v.* To fail to avoid the *follow-on* whilst wearing white trousers.

niff mag *n. Bongo comic.*

niftkin's bridge *n.* Female equivalent of the *biffin bridge* or *barse.*

Nigella shites *n.* The aftermath of eating upper class fodder.

night bus *1. n.* A cheap ride home after a night *on the sauce.* Usually stinks of fags and puke, and costs about two quid. *2. n.* A cheap *ride* at home after a night on the sauce. Usually stinks of fags and puke, and costs a Bacardi Breezer.

nightclub bouncers *n.* Pairs of burly *knockers* that are exposed to the public on Friday and Saturday nights. *'Fancy your chances with* *those nightclub bouncers, Dave?' 'Not really. To tell you the truth I think I'd rather get my head kicked in by those two big doormen instead.'*

night watchman *n.* A *copper bolt* that has failed to flush away and is discovered the next morning.

nikey pikey *n.* A white-baseball-capped, Saxo-driving, Reebok Classic-wearing self-unemployed gentleman, as found on the Central Avenue area of Hayes, Middlesex.

nillionaires' row *n.* Name given to any run down street in one of the country's less salubrious residential areas.

NIN *acronym. medic.* Normal in Norfolk. Doctor's shorthand implying that your physical and mental characteristics indicate that your mother is possibly also your sister, cousin, aunt and perhaps even your father.

nine-bob-note, as bent as a *sim. Colwyn Bay.*

nine dart leg *1. n.* The successful completion of a game of darts using the minimum number of throws possible, a feat achieved notably on TV by Phil "The Power" Taylor during the 2002 World Matchplay Championship. *2. n.* The successful completion of a sexual encounter in the shortest possible time, usually achieved by a *two push Charlie.*

ninety-sixing *n.* A spot of *sixty-nining* that goes a bit wrong. For example, when one's partner farts directly up one's nose, spoiling everything for ever.

ninja's toe *n.* A *camel's foot.*

ninth finger *n.* The *cock.*

nip and tuck *n.* The act of *nipping off* one of *Bungle's fingers* at the knuckle, with the result that the stump is retracted cleanly into the *bomb bay*. The correct response to a *mid-loaf crisis.*

nip 'n' roll *n.* The dextrous art of relieving an itch in *John Wayne's hairy saddlebags. Sorting out the boys.*

nipnosis *n.* Trance-like state induced by concentrating one's gaze on a pair of bobbing *milkers.* Often only ends when the *nipnotised* subject drives through a red light and broadsides a police car. *Titnosis.*

nipping Christian *n.* A cutpurse, a thief.

nipping the turtle *n. Crimping off a length, shutting the bomb bay doors.*

nipplecakes *n.* Appetising breasts that one wouldn't mind *icing. Baps.*

nippodrome *n.* Any place where a chap can go to enjoy a lively display of *milkers, eg.* a lap-dancing establishment, a nudist beach, the male squash court changing rooms at Newcastle Polytechnic where there used to be a *Carry On Camping*/Sex Offenders Register-style hole drilled through into the ladies', apparently.

nip on *n.* A nippular erectivation. A nipple *hard on.*

nipotism *n.* In the world of business, the discriminatory practice of hiring and promoting ladies on the basis of *first impressions,* to the detriment of the careers of their more flat-chested counterparts.

nipsy *n. medic.* The pincer-like muscle just around *Ena Sharples' mouth* that cuts one's *Bungle's finger* to length when contracted. The blade of the *cigar cutter.*

nip/tuck *euph.* A lady who is not only blessed with *nipples like pygmies' cocks,* but also has a *front tuck like a camel's hoof.*

nitby *n.* Semi-acronymous term describing a chav baby. Corruption of "Not in the Baby Book", from the unusual names given to *Greggs dummy*-sucking nippers, *eg.* Tiaamiii, Chardonnay, Beyonce, Scratchcard *etc.*

Noah's arse *n.* In the world of adult videography, a delightfully erotic scene involving double anal penetration. From the fact that in the flood/boat fairy story detailed in the biblical book Genesis, the animals "went in two by two".

nob *1. n.* A hay clarse, hoity-toity person. A toff. *2. n.* A small piece of butter. *3. v.* To *fuck,* to penetrate with the *knob.*

Nobbies *rhym. slang.* Haemorrhoids. From 1966 toothless footballer Sir Norbert Staemorrhoids.

nobgoblins *n.* Those mythical creatures that make one's *meat and two veg* itch the second one is in polite company.

nob snog *n.* A genteel term for an act of *horatio.*

nob Tarzans *n. medic. Genital guests* who swing from *pube* to *pube* through one's underpant jungle. *Crabs.*

nob turban *n.* A crest of Kleenex adorning one's post-*wank helmet. Mumrah's cock.*

nocturnal emission *n. medic.* The end result of a *wet dream.*

noddies *n.* The bikini overflow of an unwaxed lady, from its similarity to the effusive *bugger's grips* worn by 1970s rock legend Noddy Holder. *'Cor, look at the noddies on that Bulgarian lass.'*

nodding donkey *1. n.* A type of mechanical hacksaw used in metalwork. *2. n.* An ugly *bird,* usually with big teeth and ears, who doesn't often turn down the chance to *chew on a carrot.*

noddy *n.* Condom, *French letter, a cock "holder".*

noddy book *n. Bongo mag.*

Noddy Holder's sideburns *sim.* Descriptive of a particularly luxuriant ginger *bush,* the kind that Charlie Dimmock probably has.

nodge *v.* To observe the sexual activity of others. To *voy,* to *dog.*

nodger *n.* A *peeping Tom, voyeur.* A *merchant* who prefers "live" *grumble* rather than the recorded variety.

noely *1. n.* Affectionate self-coined nickname for TV and radio unpersonality Noel Edmonds. *2. n.* A *cunt* which is so small and tight that no-one can get any enjoyment out of it. Derivation unknown.

no glans land *n.* The nether regions of a lady's nether regions. The *carse, taint, tinter, notcher, twitter, snarse* or whatever.

noinkers *n. Jubblies, kahunas, shirt potatoes, boobs, sweater fruit, knockers, cab man's rests, baps, funbags, bumpies, neddies, chichis, mambas, dirty pillows, chebs, charlies, diddies, doos, cajooblies, jugs, bubbies, zeps, bazongers, headlamps, whammies, norks, bangers, tits, dumplings, hogans, thrupennies, assets, churns, whammers, yoinkahs, begonias, mumbas, pink pillows, top bollocks, melons, oomlaaters, nellies, choozies, chubblies, chumbawumbas, blimps, charms, baby's dinners, fun cushions, paps, bojangles, garbonzas,* *airbags, Gert Stonkers, puppies, Bristols.* A lady's b*soms.

no job *n.* Being *sucked off* by a lady whilst so *pissed* one can hardly feel it. See also *bland job.*

nolita *n.* A woman who looks to be in her mid-teens from the back, but who turns out to be in her mid-50s from the front. A *Kronenberg* or *back beauty.*

nollies *n.* Word used by posh southern ladies when referring to a gentleman's testicles. From nuts + bollocks + goolies. *'The Archbishop of Canterbury's shoes were so shiny that when he lifted his arms up to crown me Queen of Great Britain and all her Commonwealth Dominions, I could see his big hairy nollies reflected in them.'* (HM the Queen, interviewed by Matthew Wright on *The Wright Stuff*, Channel 5).

nollocks *exclam.* A curse which can be used in polite company without causing offence. *'Don't talk fucking nollocks, vicar. Of course you want another cup of tea.'*

nonebrity *n.* A pointless media figure who would love to rise up high enough to scrape onto the bottom end of the D-list. For example, that bloke off that thing with her who used to be in *Big Brother*, him who always seems to appear in those things with her off *Celebrity Love Island*, you know, that one who's living with her with the big *tits* off the adverts who used to go out with him out of Boyzone or was it Westlife.

noodle benders *n. Aus.* Close-fitting Speedo-style swimming trunks. Also *dick stickers, meat hangers.*

nookie *1. n.* Sex, only a *bit* of which it is advisable to have at any one time. *2. n. prop.* A humorous name for a ventriloquist's bear.

nooner *n.* See *funch.*

Norfolk *n.* A man-sized measure of vodka, *ie.* six fingers. From the flat area of England where the folks keep themselves to themselves, if you know what they mean.

norkelling *v.* When on holiday, the act of wandering along the beach to examine the wares on display. Preferably from behind a pair of *perv windows.*

nork hammock *n.* Of female fashions, a halter neck top.

norkolepsy *n. medic.* A trance-like state in men caught in the beam of a fantastic pair of *headlamps, eg.* in the office, swimming pool, night club, church *etc. Titnotism.*

norks *n. Knockers.* Also *norkers, norgs, norgers.*

norks and mingey *euph.* The feminine triumvirate. A pointlessly laboured pun on the title of hyperactive lycanthropic funnyman Robin Williams's 1978-1982 US sitcom *Mork and Mindy.*

Norman Cook *n.* A measure of alcohol which after being drunk can make a *Fat Bird Slim.* Approximately two *St. Ivels.*

Norma Snockers *n.* Wieldy *bojangles.* See also *Gert Stonkers.*

norris *rhym. slang.* One of these dirty women who says she can ejaculate. From the late right wing *Record Breakers* presenter Norris McWhirter = squirter.

north face *n.* Mountain climber's euphemism for the more difficult route up a lady. *'Gladys had the painters in the South Col, so Alf decided to attempt the tricky north face.'*

norton *n.* A *bearded clam.*

Norwegian's lunchbox *sim.* Descriptive of a *clopper* that smells like half a stone of whale blubber marinated in roll-mop herrings and sour milk.

Norwegian wood *1. n.* An erection achieved in a sauna. *2. n.* Title of a Beatles song, which John Lennon wrote after getting an erection in a sauna.

NORWICH *acronym. milit.* Cipher used on military correspondence - Knickers Off Ready When I Come Home. First used during World War I, when Norwich was known as Korwich.

no score drawers *n.* Unflattering ladies' undergarments worn when the *pools panel is sitting* and the dividend forecast is low.

nosebleed *n.* A *fart* that is *fuck off* strong. An *air onion.*

nose, blow one's *v.* To wipe away the post-ejaculation *sprongle* from one's *hog's eye. 'I had to blow my nose on the back of her dress before pulling my pants back up.'*

nose fruit *n.* Bogies.

nose jizz n. Snot.

nosh n. An act of oral affection which, according to Bill Clinton but perhaps not his wife, does not constitute sexual relations.

noshferatu *n.* The sort of chap who dosn't mind *dining at the Y* whilst *the painters are in.* One who likes his *tuna* with plenty of *tomato sauce.*

nosh off *v.* To perform *cumulonimbus* on a man.

nosh out *v.* To perform *philately* on a woman. To *lick out.*

noshtalgia *n.* Fond remembrance of particularly good tunes played on one's *pink oboe* in days gone by.

notcher *n. Biffin bridge.* The area of skin between the *clockweights* and the *starfish*, so called because it's "notcher" *bollocks* and it's "notcher" *arse. The great.*

not the marrying kind *adj.* Descriptive of a fellow who is *nicely poised* or *good with colours. 'Has your Cedric found himself a nice girl and settled down yet?' 'No, well you know my Cedric. He's not the marrying kind.' 'Still a male prostitute then?' 'Yes.'*

not now, Cato *exclam.* Phrase made popular in the Peter Sellers *'Pink Panther'* films, which can be used by a gentleman who is affected by an unwanted bout of priapism, *eg.* on a bus, whilst looking at the frozen foods in the Heaton, Newcastle branch of Safeway's in about 1990, or whilst blessing the masses from an open-topped Range Rover.

nought and a one, a *euph.* Obsolete beardy-weirdy computer operator slang for a *gypsy's kiss.* From the fact that when operating an old fashioned ICL card-punching machine, pressing the nought and the one buttons at the same time encoded a *slash. 'Where are you going, Mr Babbage?' 'I'm just off for a nought and a one whilst my difference engine reboots.'*

noughtomobile *n.* A vehicle that occupies the lowest possible position on the *fanny-magnetism* scale, *eg.* a souped-up Daewoo Matiz with *Max Power* stickers.

nought to sixty *1. n.* Measure of acceleration time by which men in pubs judge the relative merits of various Lamborghinis, Ferraris and Aston Martins which they have never even seen, let alone driven. *2. euph.* An incredibly rapid erection which takes everyone around it by surprise. A *viagra sunrise.*

now back to Davina *exclam.* A humorous interjection or quip, to be made immediately prior to *letting off.*

NTL *n.* An excessively long stay on the toilet reading the paper, philosophising *etc*. After the telecommunications company who spend months *laying* just one *cable.*

nubility, the *n.* A clique of high class young ladies that give a bit of *blue blood* to anyone driving past.

nudger *1. n.* A *Colwyn Bay* male. *2. n.* What a *fudge nudger* uses to *nudge fudge*.

nuggets *1. n.* Testicles. *2. n.* Any inedible part of a chicken or turkey, when coated in batter or breadcrumbs. *eg.* Its *nuggets*.

number one *euph.* A *penny, tinkle*.

number threes *n.* Vomit.

number two *euph.* A *sit down, tuppence*, a *duty.*

nummghh *exclam.* The insulting noise made by pushing the tongue into the lower lip, usually directed at a person of low sense, or one who has inadvertently asked a foolish question. Regionally accentuated by either loose wristed hand waggles or transverse elbow-crested ear slaps.

nunga munching *v.* The ganneting of *hairy pie, licking out* a lady's *clunker* with relish.

nunnery *n.* Elizabethan name for a *rub-a-tug shop* from an age when nuns were widely believed to wear *yo-yo knickers*.

nun's fanny *1. sim.* Descriptive of something that is extremely dry, *eg.* the Sahara desert, Amy Winehouse's throat. *2. euph.* Anything that is particularly tight, *eg.* any space a lady attempts to park a car in, the glove that OJ Simpson didn't wear when he wasn't murdering his wife.

nun's rug *euph.* A vintage item which is nevertheless in absolutely mint, unused condition. *'For sale. L-registered Morris Marina in magnificent muconium beige livery with mouseback vinyl roof. This car has covered just 6 miles since new and has been kept in a dry, heated garage for the last thirty-two years, only being taken out once by its careful lady owner for a short run to the shops and back in 1973, after which it broke down and refused to restart. It still bears the original polythene seat-covers and has not even been run in yet. A real nun's rug of a classic which can only appreciate in value in the coming years. £18,500 ono.'*

nun's tits, pale as a *sim.* Descriptive of skin that doesn't get much exposure to sunlight. *'After answering his latest set of drugs charges, crack-guzzling Babyshambles frontman Pete Doherty stumbled down the courtroom steps looking pale as a nun's tits.'* (Report, BBC Radio 6Music News, every fucking half hour).

nun's tits, useful as a *sim.* Phrase used in reference to something, or someone, of no obvious utility whatsoever. *'Have you seen that (insert name of a newly-signed expensive football player here)? he's about as useful as a nun's tits.'*

Nurembergs *rhym. slang.* Haemorrhoids. From Nuremberg Trials = piles. Also *Seig Heils, four minute miles.*

nurfing *n. Barumphing, snurgling, moomphing, quumfing.*

nut butter *n.* A lightly-salted dairy product served hot from the male *churns* onto *baps*.

nut chokers *n.* Gentlemen's tight *shreddies, budgie smugglers, noodle benders*.

nutcrackers *n.* Unfeasibly tight "spray-on" *round the houses* sported by *rock poodles* such as Justin Hawkins out of comedy band The Darkness.

nut custard *n. Banana yoghurt.*

nut fangle *n.* Pre-*wank* prep work.

Nutkin *n.* Of a man, the worst hairstyle it is possible to have, *eg.* those worn by Phil Harding (*Time Team* yokel archaeologist), Bill Bailey (troll-like comedian) and Terry Mancini (has-been QPR footballer). Named after TV animal trainer and former sealion's dinner Terry Nutkin.

nutmegs *n. Balls* that hang down right between a footballer's legs.

nuts *1. n.* A fellow's *pods*. *2. n.* Things your missus only eats as a special treat at Christmas. That'll be your *pods* again, then. 3. *adj.* Mental. *'You should meet my brother, he's absolutely nuts. Seriously, he made a skin suit from his landlady and got sectioned under the 1971 Mental Health Act.'*

nut sack *n.* The scrotum, *nadbag.*

nymph *1. n.* The caterpillar of a dragonfly. *2. n.* A sexy young *bird.*

nympho *n.* Sex-crazed *bird* that's *gagging* for it 24 hours a day, 7 days a week. The sort who would *shag* a pneumatic drill and blow up the generator. Usually works on a premium-rate telephone *wank* line.

nymphomaniac *n.* One who can't get enough of premium-rate telephone *wank* lines. A short, blind, insane man living in a sleeping bag on a shop doorstep.

NYPD blue *n.* A *poke,* where the *pokee* assumes the position of someone being frisked by New York's finest, against the wall or across the bonnet of a car. A *dog's marriage.*

Oo

OAP-dophile *1. n.* A *biddy fiddler* or *granny magnet. 2. n.* A young woman who is inexplicably attracted to a (usually extremely wealthy) elderly man, *eg*. (Long list of names deleted on legal advice).

Oaten's briefcase, it smells like *sim.* Descriptive of a particularly unpleasant misama. Derivation unknown. *'Did you have second helpings of that twenty-two bean casserole last night? It smells like Oaten's briefcase in here this morning.'*

oats *n*. A *portion* of that which one gets during sex with a Quaker. *Tiffin, crumpet.*

OBE *1 abbrev.* A memorable token of one's evening out, awarded by a nightclub bouncer as one is ejected from his establishment. One Behind the Ear. *2. abbrev.* Order of the Brown Entrance. An honour bestowed on a gentlemen for services to his *bird's shitter. Brown wings.*

Obi-Wan's cape *euph.* Phrase used to describe the unfortunate occurence of extreme flaccidity inside a chap's *grundies* (for example following immersion in cold water) to the extent that his *old man* completely vanishes, leaving in its stead an empty crumpled, pile of skin resembling nothing so much as a small, pink walnut whip. With the wrinkly nuts dangling underneath it rather than perched on the top. *Shrinkage.* From the scene in *Star Wars* where erstwhile Jedi Knight Sir Alec Guinness gets whacked with a neon tube by the Green Cross Man. *'Not tonight, Josephine, I've just got out of the swimming pool and I've got Obi-Wan's cape.'*

occupy the crease *1. v.* In cricket, to build a long innings without worrying unduly about anyone else's best interests. *'Boycott is a selfish cricketer, regularly occupying the crease with scant consideration for the needs of his team.' 2. v.* To pleasure one's missus orally. *'Boycott is a selfish lover, seldom occupying the crease and showing scant consideration for the needs of his ladyfriend.'*

offer a Jaffa cake *v.* To instigate a homosexual courting ritual involving the popular orange-flavoured biscuit/cake confection. If any male accepts another's offer of a Jaffa cake, then they are tacitly agreeing to partake in an act of anal romance.

office meerkats *n.* Groups of infantile male workers who repeatedly stand up and sit down between the hours of 11.00am and 1.00pm, in order to peer throught their windows at attractive females going on their lunch.

officers' laces *n.* Ladies' string-like thongs buffed brown between their *arse cheeks.*

off-piste *euph.* Sexual term whereby a gentleman ventures away from the officially-sanctioned area into more rugged and challenging terrain. *'Come on, love. I've cooked dinner and even helped with the washing up. How many more brownie points do I need before I can go off-piste?'*

off the meaten track *euph.* Descriptive of a woman who is *off solids* or *on the turn.* In the early stages of *lesbitis.*

off the team *adj.* To be forbidden from playing on the *furry turf.* To be in your missus's *cunt book.*

off your face *adj. Ripped to the tits* on the demon drink.

off your trolley *adj. Hatstand, nuts,* mental.

oil of goolay *n.* A white, sticky-type foundation cream which reduces the signs of ageing when applied to ladies' faces out the end of one's *cock.*

oil spill *n.* An *Eartha* that constitutes a health threat to marine life.

oil tanker *rhym. slang.* An *onanist, merchant.*

oil the bat *v.* To *polish the pork sword, wax the dolphin.*

oil the truncheon *v.* To buff up the *bobby's helmet, collect kindling, wank.*

oily loaf *n.* A well-baked *turd.*

oily rags *n. rhym. slang.* Cigarettes.

OJ's glove *1. n.* The state of the hand after *finger banging* a lady during *ragweek. 2. n.* An extremely tight-fitting *liver sock.*

okra *1. n.* Tropical plant of the mallow family, *Hibiscus esculentus,* colloquially called lady's fingers, and hence *2. n.* A dirty woman's act of *self pollution.*

old Adam *n.* Onan's partner in crime.

Old Bailey bird *n.* An embarrassingly unattractive ladyfriend who you would ideally like to smuggle into the house under a blanket, in a style reminiscent of the way that the police bundle particularly unpopular murderers into court buildings on the news.

old dog's nose, dry as an *sim.* Descriptive of a *pink wafer.* A *moipless muff. 'What's up love? I've been tickling your wotsit for three minutes and you're still as dry as an old dog's nose.'*

olden doubloons *n.* The *dunghampers* of a young lady who eschews *clackerfloss* preferring instead *bills* of a more matronly cut. *Elepants.*

oldest toad in the pond *n.* A particularly low, vociferous, grumbling *mariner's chart,* usually after eight pints of stout and a bar of Bourneville.

old faithful *1. n.* A spectacular eruption of hot steam from a hole in the ground in Yellowstone National Park, USA. *2. n.* A spectacular eruption of hot *spooge* from the mouth of an inexperienced *cock nosher,* particularly one lying on her back.

old holborn *n.* The frayed edges of the *velcro triangle,* a *pant moustache. Spiders' legs.*

oldie horn *n.* See *prunetang.*

Old Leigh oyster *n.* A particularly viscous phlegm delicacy which requires a sight more chewing than its bivalve namesake. A *docker's omelette.*

old man *n.* Penis. Also *old fella. 'The old man's been out of work for six months. Most days we play pocket billiards to keep him occupied.'*

Old McDonald's combover *n.* Stray *pubage* agonisingly trapped under the brim of the *farmer's hat. Bobby Charltons.*

old shocker, the *n.* To surprise one's sexual partner by poking a cheeky *pinkie* up their *chuff* during intercourse. *"I say, Bertie. You'll never guess what,' gasped Piggy excitedly. 'I've just been in a clinch with Marjorie in the rose garden. Just as I got to the vinegar strokes, she popped me the old shocker. Quite took me aback, don't you know."* (from *Now Start Humming, Jeeves* by PG Wodehouse).

Oliver *rhym. slang.* Inebriated. From Oliver Twist = pissed. *'Please Sir, can I have some more?' 'Fuck off, you're Oliver.'*

Olympic village *n.* Any urban area with a disproportionate number of fat, unhealthy inhabitants wearing shitty, polyester-based sportswear.

omelette maker *n.* A lesbian, *lady golfer*.

onanism *1. n.* Incomplete sexual intercourse. *Vatican roulette. 2. n.* What the biblical *wanker* Onan the Barbarian did when he *spilled his seed* on the wainscotting. *Cuffing the dummy.*

one *n.* A *poking*. The SI unit of sex, given to a woman by a man and measured from the moment it *goes in* to to moment it *goes off*. Equivalent to six tenths of a *portion*, 180% of *some*, and 2.36 *bits of the other*.

one cartridge, ignition off, clear out the cylinder *exclam.* Phrase used when performing a particular sort of explosive, underpant-wrecking *Exchange & Mart*. From the scene in the classic Sunday tea-time film *Flight of the Phoenix*, when pilot James Stewart uses up a precious ignition cartridge to clear engine debris, much to the annoyance of kraut modelmaker Hardy Kruger.

one cheek sneak *n.* The stealthy approach to *shooting bunnies*. From a sitting position, lifting one *buttock* in order to slide out an aurally-undetectable *air biscuit*. A *cushion creeper, leg lifter.*

one-eared spacehopper *n.* Cliff Richard's genitals. A *panhandle* on someone with *DSB*.

one-eyed pant python *n.* A *cock* that could crush a pig to death.

one-eyed trouser snake *n.* A *spitting cobra.*

one-eyed Willie *n. Pirate of men's pants.*

one-eyed Willie's eye patch *n.* A condom, *English sou'wester and full-length kagoule.*

one-eyed zipper fish *n.* A *Cyclops, trouser trout.*

one four seven *1. n.* In snooker, a complete clearance in which the player empties the table in a single visit, scoring maximum points in the process. *2. n.* In toiletry, a complete clearance in which the toiletee empties his *Camillas* in a single sitting, finishing with a black. *'Watch my pint, boys. I'm going for a one four seven.'*

one-handed mag *n. Jazz magazine, rhythm read, art pamphlet, a grumbular* periodical.

one-holed flute *n.* A *pink oboe*, a *blue-veined piccolo*, a *purple headed* (insert name of vaguely-cylindrical woodwind instrument here).

one in the pump, to have *1. v.* To have the *hots* for a female. *'Phoar! I've got one in the pump for her, I can tell you.' 2. n.* Drinking parlance for a pint paid for but not yet poured.

one o'er the thumb *n.* A *five knuckle shuffle. 'Quite satisfied, Scrooge closed the door and locked himself in; double-locked himself in, which was his custom on these occasions. Thus secured against surprise, he took off his cravat; put on his dressing-gown and slippers, and his nightcap; and sat down before the fire with a copy of Razzle for a quick one o'er the thumb.'* (from *A Christmas Carol* by Charles Dickens).

one oar in the water *n.* Descriptive

of someone unlikely to forge a successful career in rocket science, but who may find gainful employment chasing trolleys round Sainsbury's carpark. *'Doctors feared that after his near fatal quadbike accident, Mayall could have been left with one oar in the water. Amazingly, he made a full recovery, although he will remain on fit pills for the rest of his life.'* (Profile of Rik Mayall, *The Guardian,* Sept. 2001).

one off the crossbar *n.* To be just not quick enough in dropping one's *scads* after being caught short by an unexpected visit from *Mr Whippy.* To *beskid* the waistband of your *shreddies.*

one off the wrist *n. Five knuckle shuffle, wank, hand shandy.*

one point five *n.* A toiletry visit product that falls somewhere between a *number one* and a *number two.* A runny *shit.* Or more rarely a lumpy *piss.* A *bicycle chain.*

one pump chump *n.* One who *goes off* on the first push. Twice as fast as a *two push Charlie.*

one-man orgy *n.* A long-lasting and elaborate *cat stabbing* session involving assorted stimuli, speeds and positions. *Everything but the girl.*

one string banjo *n.* A skin-covered instrument upon which a man might strum to his heart's content.

one-stroke cylinder engine *n.* A *Bakewell* released whilst walking that lasts for several paces. A *string of pearls, duckwalk.*

onepack *n.* A *beergut, party seven.*

oneplay *n.* Pre-masturbatory arousal techniques.

oner *n.* The line of condensed *arse cleft* perspiration left on a plastic seat after it has been sat on in the summer months. Upon exiting a taxi and preparing to pay, one might point to the seat and say, *'There's a oner, keep the change.'*

oneymoon *n.* A romantic week's break from the missus which affords the married gentleman a welcome opportunity to enjoy an uninterrupted seven day period of luxurious *self abuse.*

oneymoon suite *n.* In an hotel, a room set aside for unaccompanied commercial travellers who do not wish to be disturbed; must include at least two *Frankie Vaughan* channels and a copious supply of quilted toilet tissue.

on her dabs *adj.* Of a lady, to be menstruiferous. Boiling *beetroots, serving strawberry jam for tea.*

onk, on the *adj.* Of the male generative member, up and fighting. *'I popped a bluey, and half an hour later I was on the onk for the first time in twenty years.'*

only shit with the arse you've got *phr.* Civil engineering expression bemoaning the provision of substandard tools and/or materials. *'Fuck knows if we'll ever get the 2012 Olympic complex finished. Then again, you can only shit with the arse you've got.'*

on the batter *adj.* Of a lady, to be involved in the practice of showing successive gentlemen good times behind a skip for £5.

on the bench *adj.* After being *off the team,* to be optimistic that you may be given a late chance to *score.* To be in your missus's slightly better books. *'After the shameful episode with the exotic dancer I have alas been off the team these last six weeks. Today I bought my darling Victoria a bunch of flowers from* *the all-night garage, and I think I am on the bench.'* (from *The Journal of Prince Albert*).

on the blob *adj. Riding the menstrual cycle, up on blocks, fallen to the communists.*

on the bonk *adj. Sergeant Sausage* when saluting.

on the bus to Hebden Bridge *adj.* Descriptive of a *woman in comfortable shoes,* or *tennis fan.* From the unusually large amount of *lesbitious* women living in the Yorkshire mill town.

on the hoy *adj. On the piss, on the razz, hoying* it down one's neck, and then back up again onto one's shoes.

on the job *adj. At it.* Busying oneself with one's partner's plumbing.

on the mop *adj.* Of a lady, to be suffering from *women's things.*

on the musical side *adj. Light on one's feet.*

on the nest *adj.* To be treating your *bird* to a big juicy *worm.*

on the other bus *adj.* Homosexual, *bowling from the Pavilion end.*

on the pull *adj.* Fishing for *kipper, on the salmon, on the sniff.*

on the slipway *adj.* Of stools and stool movement, having the *turtle's head. 'Get out of that fucking bathroom will you, I've got a dreadnought on the slipway.'*

on the sniff *adj. On the pull, on the tap, getting a bit lash on.*

on tow *adj.* Of a woman, to be *up on blocks.* From the visible rope.

ooglewhack *v.* To have a much-needed *whack,* after having *oogled* an attractive lady.

oomlaaters *n.* Very large *chumbawumbas, mumbas.*

oomph! *n.* Sex appeal. *'By crikey, that Norma Major, she hasn't half got some oomph!'*

oor wullie *n. Scots.* A double-ended *neck massager* kept in a drawer at the but 'n' ben.

oot on the tap *adj. NE.* Out *on the pull,* as opposed to *on the hoy.*

OPE *abbrev.* A dazed and otherworldly sensation brought on by a visit to a mechanic, dentist, solicitor *etc.* Out-of-Pocket Experience.

open a packet of ham *v.* To let off a *beefy eggo.* From the practice of ham production line workers who *fart* into the packages of ham before sealing them. *'Who's opened a packet of ham?'*

open clam shots *n. Full-on oysters, close-up pink.* Artistic/medical *adult* camera work.

open Dracula's coffin *v.* An act involving a protracted creaking noise, accompanied by an ungodly stench. To *drop a McArthur Park.*

Openshaw rush-hour *n.* Weekdays between noon and 1pm, when all the *tax dodgers* finally get their fat *arses* out of bed, jump into their people carriers and go into town to spend their benefits at Primark.

open the bloodgates *v.* Of a woman, to shed the first tears that herald the commencement of *rag week.*

open the hangar doors *v.* Of an experienced lady, to prepare herself for sexual intercourse. *'Wisteria was powerless to resist. His eyes burned into hers like amethysts. His muscular arms enfolded her body as she felt herself being swept away in a hurricane of passion. Gently, Renaldo laid her down on the silken ottoman in front of the roaring fire. Then, as he pulled her knickers off, she lifted her legs and opened the hangar doors.'* (from *The Lady and the South*

American Footballer by Barbara Cartland).

open your lunchbox *v.* To float an *air biscuit* reminiscent in aroma of yesterday's egg sandwiches.

opera house *n.* A large vagina with heavy pink safety curtains.

operate the spangle pump *v.* To express oneself onanistically. *'Oh bugger. The plumber's operated the spangle pump into my knicker drawer again.'*

orangina *1. n.* Refreshing continental citrus beverage, made with real orange pieces. *2. n.* A particularly untidy ginger *clopper,* which wouldn't look out of place between the legs of Clint Eastwood's monkey's missus.

Orang Utan salad *n.* Ginger *gorilla salad. Fusewire.*

orchestras *rhym. slang.* The testicles. From orchestra stollocks = bollocks.

oreo *n.* An inverse *chocolate sandwich*.

organzola *n. Helmetdale.*

orgasm *1. n.* A *fanny bomb*, a *stack blow. 2. v.* To *ring the bell*, *shoot one's load*, *chuck one's muck*.

Oscar *n. US. Dick,* penis.

Oscars night *n.* An unpredicted bout of heavy *women's things,* which leaves a red carpet from the front door to the *crapper.*

osteopornosis *n.* medic. Degenerate condition symptomised by skeletal atrophy, progressive hypermetropia, early-onset pre-senile dementia and hairy palms.

other, a bit of the *n. Some.*

otter *1. n.* An aquatic mammal. *2. n.* A bald male gentleman who isn't interested in *beavers.*

otter's nose *n.* When getting *tops and fingers*, that which is felt by the latter. Something wet *under the bridge. 'I got a result last night. I touched the otter's nose.'*

otter off the bank, like an *sim.* Phrase used to describe a *turd* of particularly fine composition, which slips from one's *bumhole* with a certain amount of panache.

out of botty experience *n.* A *dump.*

out to the wing *exclam.* Comment typically made by older gentlemen before they *break wind.* So used because of the characteristic noise made by an old leather football when it was hoofed with a sturdy boot. *'Out to the wing.' 'Indeed your holiness. Shall I get a nun to open the window?'*

overblaaters *n.* Pendulous *oomlaaters* which rest on a big round gut.

overclubbed *1. adj.* In golf, descriptive of an approach shot chipped towards the green which misses its intended target and tangles itself in the rough, eliciting groans from disappointed spectators. *2. adj.* In a *meat flick,* descriptive of a *pop shot* loosed off towards an actress's face which misses its intended target and instead tangles itself in her hair, eliciting groans from disappointed spectators.

over the lines, colour in *v.* To spray a lady with semen after withdrawing from an orifice. To *crash the yoghurt truck* outside the delivery bay.

over the shoulder boulder holder *n.* Industrial bra, heavy lifting apparatus for *jelly water mangos.*

owner operator *n.* A lorry driver who *sheds his load* wherever the fancy takes him.

own goal *n.* A blast from the *kazoo* which is so obnoxious that even he who dealt it cannot stay in its presence.

own up *v.* In a *breaking company* situation, to identify oneself as the *benefactor*. *Read the will.*

Oxford john *n.* A slow-braised *lamb shank.*

oxygen thief *n.* A senior citizen, a *coffin dodger.*

oyster *n.* A *bushman's hankie.*

oyster catcher *n.* A lady of *lesbitious* tendencies. From the fact that she is, like her ornithological namesake *Haematopus palliatus*, a *bird* which spends a great deal of time in pursuit of *bearded clams.*

oyster shot *n.* In the world of glamour photography, a carefully composed, lit and framed shot of a model's *clam* as she bends over, viewed from behind.

Ozzy ramble *n.* The shuffling, confused gait adopted by a man with a *horse's handbrake* and his trousers round his ankles, as he tries to manoeuvre around the sofa in order to secure a better angle to gain entrance to his good lady's *coconut husk*. From the shuffling, confused gait characteristic of shuffling, confused heavy metal pipistrelle gourmand Ozzy Osbourne.

Pp

pace car *n.* When paying a *sit down visit,* the slow, unaerodynamic leading *turd* that once out of the way, allows the fast, souped-up *botrods* behind it to put their foot down into the first bend.

packet *n.* The contents of the *kecks* visible in relief at the front of the *trolleys*. Male equivalent of the *camel's foot. Darcy Bussell's foot-rest,* the *lunchbox.*

paddle one's own canoe *v.* To enjoy a leisurely punt using a short pink pole. With all veins up the side. *'Dysphagia was powerless to resist. His eyes burnt into hers like soldering irons. His muscular arms enfolded her naked body as she felt herself being whisked away on a meringue of passion. 'Ravish me now,' she gasped. 'Take me here on the chaise longue, I'm all yours.' 'Sorry ma cherie, I'd love to oblige,' replied Toulouse-Lautrec as he adjusted his top hat and pince nez. 'But I've just spent all afternoon paddling my own canoe in sniffer's row at the Moulin Rouge, and now my clockweights are flat as a crepe suzette."* (from *The Artist's Model and the Short-arsed Post-Impressionist Painter* by Barbara Cartland).

paddle the pink canoe *v.* To *friggify*. Weekend recreational pursuit of the *gusset typist*.

paddling pool *n.* Male showertime entertainment whereby the *five-skin* is pulled apart and the *charlie* is aimed up at the showerhead, causing it to fill up with water to the satisfaction of the *pool attendant.*

Paddy's hankie *n.* The hand.

Paddy McGinty's goat *1. n.* Hilarious song made famous by twinkle-toothed sweater-wearing crooner Val Doonican. *2. n.* Pungent, hairy *snatch* that could eat a mayor's hat. Also *Delaney's donkey.*

padlocks *n. Tits* that would be better off in socks than in bras.

paedophile's door *euph.* Anyone who combines a low income with constant high expenditure. *'MRS ALLONBY: They say, Lady Hunstanton, that Lord Illingworth finds himself perpetually penurious. Indeed, in that respect he is not dissimilar to a paedophile's door. LADY HUNSTANTON: Indeed Mrs Allonby? And why, pray tell, would that be? MRS ALLONBY: Because, Lady Hunstanton, he is always broke.'* (from *The Importance of Being Bummed by Jockeys* by Oscar Wilde).

paedo pellets *n.* Werther's originals.

paedorinal *n.* In a public lavatory, the urinal which is situated alongside the shorter, small boys' version.

paedoscopes *n.* Those thick-rimmed National Health Service spectacles exclusively worn by trainspotters, scout masters and other assorted sex cases. *Paedospecs.*

paedosmile *n.* A particularly sinister grin, the type a kiddie fiddler might have.

PAFO *acron. medic.* Term used by consultants in Accident and Emergency departments to explain random cuts and bruises. Pissed And Fell Over.

page three Stannah *n.* A scantily-clad lady of advancing years, who nevertheless provides one with a bit of a lift.

pagga *n.* A free-for-all combat between anyone who wants to join in.

pagga starter *n.* A strong beer which breaks the ice at fights. *Supermarket smack, spesh.*

painting the ceiling *v.* Having a go with the *naughty paintbrush* whilst in a supine position.

paint the baby's bedroom *v.* To slap a bit of *managlypta* around the vaginal walls.

paint the back door *v.* To drop a wet *fart, follow through.*

paint the town beige *v.* To indulge in an unambitious, lacklustre night out with one's mates.

paisley removal *n.* Pointing *Percy* directly at an area of *pebble dashing* in order to amuse oneself during a *Chinese singing lesson*. See also *piss polo*.

palace gates *n. Fanny lips, beef curtains*.

palma sutra *n.* The mystical art of *cranking one off* in a number of improbable positions, *eg*. the swan, the swooping dove, the *sticky belly flap cock.*

Palmela and her five sisters *n. prop.* The right *cunt scratcher.*

Palmela Handerson *n.* One's dream date to go out for a cruise in the *wanking chariot.*

palmesan *n.* The result of *pulling the Pope's hat off* repeatedly and excessively without pausing to perform the occasional spot of basic genital maintenance in between. Particularly rife amongst those presently seeking gainful employment. Also *dolecelatte.*

palm fruit *n.* A lady's *chestular* offerings. A couple of *handfuls.*

palmistry *n.* A mystic art involving the flat of the hand and the *cock.* The skilled *palmist* is able to look a few minutes into the future and foresee a period of mopping up *jizz.*

palmouflage *n.* Any form of *grumbular* disguise utilized when approaching the tills at the newsagent, *eg*. A copy of the *Spectator* wrapped round *Razzle* or a copy of *Razzle* wrapped round *New Cunts 85*. Or a copy of *New Cunts 85* wrapped round *Viz.*

palmorama *n.* A late night "investigative" report into the American porn industry or similar, eagerly watched by single men who have a penchant for hard news. A *masturmentary, rudimentary, sockumentary.*

palm Sunday *n.* A relaxing *day of wrist* spent in one's own company in the absence of other weekend commitments.

palm ticklers *n.* Small, flat *lils* with protruding nipples. *Empire biscuits.*

palpootations *n.* Involuntary and unnerving contractions of the *nipsy* which make the heart beat faster the morning after a night *on the pop.*

panaconda *n.* A South American *dirt snake* of enormous length, that suffocates its victims if they get too close.

panda's eye *n.* A *ringpiece.*

pander *1. v.* To act as a go-between in an act of sexual intrigue, *eg*. to go and buy a hamster and some parcel tape for that odd couple in the flat below. *2. n.* A large, impotent, bamboo-eating mammal.

panderer *n.* One who *panders.*

P and O *euph.* A quick, perfunctory act of intercourse. A *roll on, roll off.*

panhandle *n.* An erect penis, *wood, stalk*, a *bonk on.*

panhandle pipes *n.* A Peruvian

sex act, whereby a woman blows across the top of several men's *cocks* of differing length side by side. Presumably in a shopping precinct.

panjammer *n.* A stool that laughs in the face of the flush. A *U-blocker,* a *plumber's bonus,* a *crowd pleaser.*

pankled *adj.* Having one's pants pulled down to one's ankles. Derivation unknown.

pan of burnt chips *n. orthodont.* Descriptive of dentition that leaves a lot to be desired. *'So in she comes with another fucking fishbone stuck in her craw. So she opens her mouth and it's like a pan of burnt chips in there. I know she's 102, but for Christ's sake, she should have had them out years ago.'* (from *The Memoirs of Doctor Gladstone Gamble, Balmoral GP in Residence*).

pan pipes *n.* A simple wind instrument that plays haunting music in the *shit house.*

pan scourer *n.* A vagina covered in a coarser grade of *muff swarf. Brillo fanny.*

pan smile *n.* The crescent-shaped *piss*-bleached patch of carpet that grins yellowly around the base of the toilet. The *Queen Mum's smile.*

pantballing *n.* An involuntary, messy but exciting sport, usually played on Saturday and Sunday mornings by men who were copiously *refreshed* on dark beers and a *Ruby Murray* the previous evening.

pant hamster *n.* Natural prey of the *one-eyed trouser snake.*

pantilever *n.* The *piss handle.*

pant moustache *n.* Effect achieved when the *mapatasi* extends symmetrically beyond either side of the *shreddies. Thigh brows, whackos, Rhoydes Boysons.*

pants *1. interj.* Exclamation of dismay. *2. adj & n.* Rubbish, *shit, pig's arse, bollocks. 'You're talking pants!'*

pant stripper *n.* Any fancy alcoholic drink that more or less guarantees free access to the *hairy pie. Knicker oil, WD69.*

pantymonium *n.* A flatulent charivari. A loud volley of *farts* causing havoc in the *undercrackers.*

pap baffle *n.* The scrunched-up piece of *shit scrape* placed in the *pan* which makes the person in the next cubicle genuinely believe that your *crap* doesn't make a "plop" when it hits the water.

paperchase *1. n.* The athletic pursuit of *bumwad* from cubicle to cubicle with trousers and *grundies* around one's ankles. *2. n.* The manic sprint around the house trying to pick up all the incriminating soiled tissues and *grot mags* one has strewn about before the wife returns from her shopping expedition.

paper cut *n.* Opposite of a *wizard's sleeve.* A *fanny* tighter than an *OJ's glove.*

paper hanger's bucket *n.* A big sloppy *twat* full of wallpaper paste.

paper over the cacks *v.* To discreetly drape an unflushable, floating *Richard the Third* with toilet tissue in a vain attempt to mask its identity.

paper saver *n.* A bowel movement that leaves the paper clean straight off the tee.

Papillon's purse *euph.* The rectal orifice when used as a repository for valuables, *eg.* when in a prison, boarding school or whilst negotiating the "Nothing to Declare" channel of a Turkish airport. From the film starring Steve McQueen in which the convicts stashed their cash up the pipe.

pappalonia *exclam.* Outburst of appreciation for a woman with a massive set of *gazongers*.

papper *v.* To *shit*. *'Oh no, I think I just pappered me trolleys. So it's over to John Kettley for the weather whilst I have a look.'*

paps *1. n.* Celebrity-hungry photographers who murdered our Princess of Hearts. *2. n. arch.* Olde Worlde *Tittes*.

papsack *n.* A pair of *tit pants*, a *knocker hopper*. A *brassiere*.

parade ground poo *n.* A *turd* of such magnitude that the only fitting response is to hang a *bumrag* flag on it and salute as it passes out of the *chod-bin*.

paradise pie *1. n.* A very succulent pudding served in restaurants. *2. n.* A *puh-seh* that is mouth-watering to the eye.

paraffin *n. rhym. slang.* A gentleman of the road. A hobo. From paraffin lamp = Harold Ramp.

paraffinalia *n.* The tools of the trade accumulated by a professional *hobo, eg.* dozens of bags containing rubbish, an old pram, a greasy anorak and a family-size plastic bottle of white cider.

parallel parked *adj.* In bed together, having sex. *'Were you parallel parked with her last night?' 'Not half! I was in up to the bumper mate.'*

paralytically incorrect *n.* A consequence of heavy intoxication where one's easy-going, tolerant views are discarded in favour of a rather more robust manifesto.

parfume de plop *n.* Acrid odour which accompanies a *twin tone* and heralds the arrival in the *bomb bay* of a *Peter O'Toole*.

Paris-chute *euph.* Something that rarely fails to open, as sported by the well known hotel-named socialite, chihuahua enthusiast and scrawny twilit internet *grumble* star.

Parisian breasts *n.* See *lung warts*.

park and ride *1. n.* Scheme run by one's local council. *2. n.* Scheme run by one's local prostitutes. *3. n.* Hurried intercourse in the back seat of a stationary car. A *rear-end shunt*.

park the custard *v.* To *laugh at the carpet*.

park the fudge *v.* To *shit*, pass a stool, *crimp off a length*.

park the pink bus v. To *slip* a lady a *length*. *'Time for bed. Come on, let's park the pink bus in the furry garage.' 'Okay. Then we can have a fuck.'*

park the tiger *v.* To puke, *yodel*, let out a *technicolour yawn*.

park your breakfast *v.* Light a *bum cigar*, *lay a cable*.

parlour *n.* Place where one is only allowed on special occasions. The *bonus tunnel*.

parp *1. onomat.* A romantic foreplay technique whereby one squeezes a breast in the same way that a clown would honk a car horn. *2. n. onomat.* A *fart*.

parson's sack *n.* The swollen state of a *scrotbag* which is as *full as a fat bird's shoe* following an enforced period of celibacy and/or masturbatory abstinence. *'Testicular pressure. The greatest internal pressure sustained in a pair* *of testicles is one of 65 atmospheres (995lb/ sq.in) or approximately 49,400mm of mercury at sea level, in the parson's sack of the pop singer Sir Cliff Richard (GB), following a 45-year build up of seminal fluid'*. (from *The Viz Sexist Book of Records*, Boxtree £4.99 or 3 copies for 10p at car boot sales).

particulars *n.* Of low budget British sex comedies involving police officers, ladies' *bills,* knickers. *'Excuse me, madam, but I may need to take down your particulars. And have a look at your snatch.'*

parts of shame *n.* A God botherer's genitals.

party popper *n.* When a chap's wife or mistress struts around the house naked with the tail of her *fanny mouse* hanging out of her *skirting board,* and he feels the urge to pull it and see if her *arse* flies off. See *time bomb fuse.*

pasata grin *n. Mexican lipstick, clown's smile.*

passion cosh *n.* A stout, six-inch, hand-held weapon. With all veins up the side. A *love truncheon.*

passion fingers *n. Aus. milit.* An Australian army term for a clumsy fellow, *ie.* everything he touches he *fucks.*

passion flaps *n.* A more romantic alternative to *piss flaps.*

passion pit *n.* Bed, *fart sack, scratcher, wanking chariot.*

passion wagon *n.* Clapped-out van, usually a Ford Transit, with blacked-out windows and a *piss*-stained mattress and several empty beer cans in the back. Also *shaggin' wagon, spambulance, fuck truck.*

pass the hat round *1. v.* To collect money for the driver on a coach trip. *2. n.* To take part in a *gang bang. 'On their tour bus going from gig to gig, the members of Motley Crue like to pass the hat around.'*

pass the mic *1. n.* A section from the woeful TV show *The Hitman and Her*, where a couple of *slappers* took it in turns to wail into a microphone. *2. v.* A scene in all decent *grumble flicks* where a couple of *slappers* take it in turns to suck the leading man's *charlie.*

pastie baby *n.* An ear-ringed neonate sucking on a *Greggs dummy.*

pastietute *n.* A *good time girl* whose idea of a good time involves a couple of Steak Bakes and a custard slice. A prostitute who is a good deal heavier than her *slagboard postcard* picture might suggest.

pathfinder *1. n. milit.* A lone soldier who is sent ahead of his platoon in search of enemy activity or pockets of resistance. *2. n.* The first, brave finger to venture into the gusset region of a young lady's *dunghampers* in order to check whether the *Russians have invaded. 3. n.* An *air biscuit* that lets one know in no uncertain terms that it's time for a *tom tit.*

Patrick, pull a *v.* Of a man who is about to *tip his filthy concrete,* to contort his face such that it resembles that of the famous astrologer, comedy glockenspiel player and *Sky at Night* presenter Patrick Moore, with one eye half open and the other scrunched shut. *'Gunther, we're running out of tape here. Just pull a Patrick so we can all go home, will you.'*

patty *n.* A posh lady's *snatch, ie.* what HM the Queen calls her *cunt.*

Paul Daniels' hankie *sim.* Descriptive of a flaccid *member* being manually encouraged into a lady's opening. From the "hankie in the fist" trick performed by the eponymous suddenly-bald magician. *Playing snooker with a piece of string, pushing marshmallows into a moneybox.*

Paula, have a *v. 1. v.* To relieve oneself in a public place. From Olympic marathon live TV *shitter* and London marathon live TV *pisser* Paula Radcliffe. Also *do a Radcliffe.* 2. v. To interrupt an important task in order to have a "wee". *'Dr Barnard, we're ready for you to put in the new heart.' 'Hang on a tick. I'm just off for a quick Paula.'*

Pauline *rhym. slang.* A *minge.* From former *EastEnders* misery-guts Pauline Fowler = growler.

Paulsgrove street party *n.* A lively all day *al fresco* celebration which involves looting, drug runners, prostitutes, police armed response units, surveillance helicopters and general rioting. Named after one of the popular *shit hole* estates in Portsmouth.

pavement pizza *n.* The contents of your stomach as they appear after *barfing* in the street. A *parked tiger*.

pavement skating *n.* Sliding, Torville & Dean-style, on a moist *barker's egg* whilst running for a bus.

Pavlov's log *n. medic.* Conditioned reflex action causing one's *bomb bay doors* to start opening upon seeing a toilet. From the famous experiments of Russian psychologist Professor Ernst Pavlov, who rang a bell every time his dog done a *shit.*

pay in installments *v.* To be forced to make multiple lavatory visits to relieve the *Camillas* after a night of *Ruby Murray* and brown ales.

peach stone *n.* A hibernal scrotum, clenched tightly like a Scotsman's fist round his change.

peanut brittle *n. medic.* Condition of a hardened drinker whose only solid intake for some days has been items available at the bar. Symptoms include mental fragility and uncontrolled shaking. *'Harry froze as they spotted an unshaven Mr Snape slumped at the bar of the Black Cauldron. 'We're done for now', he cried. 'No we're not,' replied Hermione. 'He's been drinking all weekend and he's completely peanut brittle.''* (from *Harry Potter and the Wizard's Sleeve* by JK Rowling).

Pearl & Dean necklace *n.* A frankly unlikely sexual scenario, where one *jizzes* onto one's girlfriend in the pictures, presumably whilst shouting: "Pa-paa...pa-paa...pa-paa-paa... pa-pa-pa...paaaaow!"

pearl divers' lungs *sim.* Descriptive of the impressive ability of a man to *go down* for prolonged periods without the need to come up for fresh air.

pearl grey tea *n.* Effeminate beverage which is customarily sipped in the afternoon with the little finger cocked elegantly. The taste, smell and texture of *pearl grey tea* are the subject of much heated debate; some people guzzle it down hungrily whilst others prefer to spit it out. *Spunk, spooge, spaff, spoff, springle.*

Pearl Harbour *n. prop.* A place where one's *Jap's eye* commits atrocities.

pearl necklace *n.* Those globular consequences of having a *sausage sandwich* at the *Billy Mill Roundabout* that so delight the ladies.

pearly gates *1. n.* What you knock on when you die. *2. n.* The sloppy *cat flaps* of a woman with multiple piercings in the *farmyard area.*

pebbledash *v.* To *crop spray* the toilet bowl with *clarts.*

pecker *1. n. US.* Penis. *2. n. UK.* Nose.

pecker wreckers *n.* A *bird*'s corrective orthodontical scaffolding.

pecking *v.* The head-nodding motion exhibited by one in such a *state of refreshment* that they can hardly keep awake.

pedal *rhym. slang.* To commit an act of *self-pollution.* From pedal and crank = Jodrell Bank.

pedalophile *n.* One who hires an item of holiday boating equipment, the better to practise a spot of ocean-bound *hornithology* whilst *cleaning his glasses.* A very specific epithet which you don't really get the opportunity to drop casually into the conversation very often, to be frank.

pedigree chum *n.* Unpleasantly sexist term describing the *salad-dodging ditch pig* one you always seem to get in the middle of a bunch of *fit birds.*

pedro's piss *n.* Bland Spanish lager such as San Miguel, served lukewarm in plastic cups on the Costa del Sol. *'Eggo and chippos, please mate, plenty-o ketchup and another pint of pedro's piss, por favor.'*

pee *1. v.* To *piss. 2. n.* Some *piss.*

peel *1. v* . To strip, pose nude. *2. v.* When so doing, to draw back the *beef curtains. 'Crikey, have you seen Razzle? I never knew Joanne Guest was a peeler.'*

peel and polish *n.* A swiftly-administered, no frills *blow job. 'Ten quid for full sex, fifteen for anal, three quid for a quick peel and polish.'*

peeling the carrot *v. Spanking the monkey.*

peel the furry prawn *v.* To manually attend to the *pudenders* of a young lady who is disinclined to wash.

peemale *n.* A man who urinates sitting down, possibly as a means of expressing solidarity with women, but more likely through alcoholic exhaustion. One who *drives from the ladies' tee.*

peep over the garden fence *v.* To attempt to conceal an unwanted erection by flattening it upwards against the stomach and tucking the *helmet* behind the waistband of the underpants. A *Kilroy*, a *Chad.*

peg *v.* Of a lady, to do a gentleman up the *council gritter* with a *strap-on.*

PEGOOMHS *abbrev.* The sudden psychological condition which manifests itself upon completion of coitus. Post Ejaculatory Get Out Of My House Syndrome.

Pele's cock *n. medic.* An inability to attain an erection, with reference to the Brazilian goal ace's *cock drop* ads. Male sexual impotence.

pelican's beak *n.* A flappy double chin that is unpleasant to look at, *eg.* that of the late Thora Hird, or Hugh Lloyd.

pelican's yawn *sim.* A *fanny* big enough to hold 50lb of fish. A *hippo's mouth.*

pelt lapper *n.* A lady in *comfortable shoes*, a *tennis fan, a lady golfer.*

penalty pox *n.* A *clap* contracted from a bout of adulterous *futtery.*

Penfold has drowned *exclam.* A witty warning made to one's housemates that there is a mole-like substance floating in the *shit pan.* From 1970s cartoon vermin Dangermouse's annoying *turd* of a sidekick.

penguin *1. v.* Act performed by a prostitute whereby, upon receiving payment but before providing service, she pulls the gentleman's trousers around his ankles and runs off down the alley. From the resemblance of the client's gait to that of the flightless arctic bird as he attempts to give chase, much to the amusement of onlookers. *2. n.* The trouser-ankled, cheeks apart waddle adopted by one who has been surprised after *dropping the kids off at the pool* by a lack of *bumwad*.

penile dementia *n. medic.* The effect a *panhandle* has on its owner in the company of a *hornbag*, causing him to temporarily forget about his wife and children.

penis *n.* A man's *old man*, a chap's *chap*, a gentleman's *gentleman*. The *veiny bang stick, slag hammer.*

penis fly trap *n.* A precariously balanced toilet seat which stays vertical for a few moments before dropping upon unsuspecting *helmets* in its path. A *knob chopper.*

penny dreadful *1. n.* A cheap, third-rate novel picked up when nothing else is available. *2. n.* A cheap, third-rate woman picked up when nothing else is available.

penny farthing *1. n.* An enormous bike, which is somewhat difficult to mount due to its enormous size, though surprisingly easy to ride once you get going. *2. n.* An enormous *bike,* who is somewhat difficult to *mount* due to her enormous size, though surprisingly easy to *ride* once you get going.

penny farthings *n. Kelly Brooks.* A comically mismatched set of breasts. With a man in a top hat bouncing up and down on top of them.

penny stamp *n. rhym. slang.* A happy-go-lucky, nomadic gentleman of the road, who answers to no-one as he takes his carefree pleasures where he may, merrily wandering the highways and byways of the land. *'Aw bloody Nora. A penny stamp's been and left a great big Thora Hird on the fucking steps again.' 'Can't you just step over it, Your Majesty?'*

pensioner falling downstairs *sim.* Descriptive of the noises made by a series of solid motions hitting the water in quick succession. A *load of old shoes falling out of a loft.*

pensioner's banquet *n.* Free food samples in supermarkets, *eg.* bits of cheese *etc*.

pensioner's leg *n.* A thin, pale, knobbly, varicose-veiny penis.

pensioner's tits, as low as a *sim.* Descriptive of something that is lower than one would reasonably expect. *'The ball pitched on middle and off and stayed as low as a pensioner's tits all the way to the stumps. A terrific delivery.'* (Bob Willis commentating on England v Zimbabwe, BBC Radio *Test Match Special*, Summer 2003).

peperami wrapper *n.* The *fiveskin* or *leg warmer.*

Percy *1. n. UK.* Penis, especially

Robert Plant's penis. *'I'm just off to point Percy at the porcelain.'* *2. n.* A small green 0-6-0 saddle tank steam train named after the late Rev W Awdrey's small, green penis.

Percy Thrower's lawn *n.* A *muff* that has been allowed to go to seed. A hairy, unkempt *fanny. Terry Waite's allotment.*

perform Alkan's trois etudes op. 76 *1. v.* In the world of classical piano music, to play the three studies written by Charles Valentin Alkan in which the first movement is designated for the left hand alone, the second for the right hand alone, and the climactic finale is achieved with both hands working together. *2. v.* A virtuoso *Sherman* using first the left hand, then the right hand and finally both hands at once.

period drama *n.* Moody and erratic behaviour of women at times of menstruation. A *blobstrop, tammy huff, showing off.*

period features *1. n.* Blocked fireplaces, draughty sash windows, warped panelled doors, paint-encrusted decorative mouldings and other sundry desirable architectural bits and pieces which allow thieving estate agents to bump up the prices of houses. *2. n.* In women, short temper, sore nipples, irrational behaviour and the propensity to throw sharp objects violently across the room.

period pain *n. medic.* A dull, cramping ache in the ears and brain of an adult man which recurrs regularly every twenty-eight days when the missus is *on the blob.*

perousal *n.* The frisson of sexual arousal attained whilst flicking through a prospective purchase in *Grumbelows.*

perpetual motion *n.* A seemingly endless *shit.*

Perry Como *rhym. slang.* An easy listening *crafty butcher.*

perseverance soup *n.* The tiny tears from the *hog's eye* which precede ejaculation. The clear secretion which lubricates the glans. That which comes out of the kitchen before the main course. *Dew on the lily, ball glaze.*

Persian shampoo *n.* The act of ejaculating into your partner's hair and rubbing it in. Then rinse and repeat.

persil *n.* A gentleman homosexualist of the *Colwyn Bay* persuasion. One who is *good with colours.*

personalities *n.* Tabloid euphemism for breasts. *Charms, assets, terrible arthritis. 'My, you've got a lovely pair of personalities. What are they, double-Ds?'*

Peruvian num-nums *n.* The involuntary chewing noises emitted whilst turning over in one's sleep during the early hours of the morning.

perv windows *n.* Sunglasses.

petal dick *n.* A gentleman drinker who requires the toilet before his fifth pint. A *shandy pants, shandy pandy.*

Pete feet *n.* Name given to a *bird* who arouses suspicion because of her abnormally proportioned lower pedal extremities. Named after *Celebrity Big Brother* contestant, Colobos-monkey-coat-wearing, comedy-rubber-lipped, scouse *trolley dolly* and former Dead or Alive front-person Pete Burns. *'I only realised she was a Pete feet after I'd handed me cash over. After you with the anusol, there mate.'*

Peter O'Toole *rhym. slang.* A *Thora Hird.*

Peter two pumps *n.* An inexperienced *swordsman.* A *two push Charlie, two pump chump.*

petit filou *n.* A *hairy yoghurt pot* so small that the *naughty spoon* has trouble getting in. A *mouse's ear.*

pezzle *n.* How a Cornish farmer probably refers to his *slag hammer.*

phalitosis *n. medic.* Post-*horatio* breath.

phallucy *n.* Any statement made by a man about the size of his *third leg, eg.* in the readers' letters page of a *grumble book* or a small ad in a *greet & meat* mag.

phantom farter *n.* An anonymous *benefactor.*

phantom of the opera *n.* Appearance of a *stick flick* actress after her co-star has *crashed his yoghurt truck* copiously down the side of her face.

pharoah's tomb *1. sim.* Descriptive of a post-argument atmosphere. *2. rhym. slang.* The spare room.

phat *adj.* A modern "street" term used to denote excellence. Also *bad, badass, kickass. 'Shnizzle my pizzle, vicar, this new Flemish double manual harpsichord of yours is really phat.'*

philosopher's stone *n.* A *turd* that emerges after a couple of hours' intense concentration.

phlegm brûlée *n.* A particularly creamy *docker's omelette* with a hard crust. Usually hocked up during a hangover.

photo finish *1. n.* A session of *horizontal jogging* in which both contestants break the tape at the same time. Also *dead heat. 2. n.* The frantic action of trying to leaf through your *jazz mag* to find your *finisher* when you're at the *point of no return.*

photon torpedo *n. Star Trek* convention terminology for a *tom tit* expelled with such force that it completely destroys any *klingons* in the area.

phuq *n. & v.* Ingenious alternative to the word *fuck* which, whilst perfectly understandable, is able to evade the attentions of over-solicitous business e-mail censoring systems.

phwoarberries *n.* Big, ripe, juicy *tits.* With cream all over them. Breasts which, even when covered up elicit a strangulated cry of "phwoar!" in the style of Kenneth Connor spotting Joan Sims in the shower in *Carry On Up the Jungle.*

piabetic *n.* A larger-boned fellow who risks falling into a coma if not kept regularly supplied with pastry-based products.

Picasso arse *n.* A lady's *chuff* in knickers so tight that she appears to have four buttocks.

Picasso face *n.* Descriptive of a *bird* who is certainly no oil painting.

picket line copper *n.* The front man in a *bum chain.* From the way he is jostled about from behind, one would imagine.

pick it up and run with it *1. exclam.* Desperate expression commonly used by ex-public school *rugger buggers* who have screwed up their lives by becoming media sales managers. *2. v.* To *cop off* with a *right howler* and get her out of the nightclub before any of your mates see her.

picture but no sound *euph.* Descriptive of the wife's mood when one rolls in from the pub as *refreshed* *as a newt* with one's *earlids* pulled firmly down.

piddle *1. v.* To *pee. 2. n.* Some *pee.*

piddle paddle *n.* An unconvincing and unathletic "quick dip in the ocean" taken whilst at the seaside, where one ventures in only waist deep and emerges shortly thereafter with a refreshingly empty bladder. A *seawee.*

pie blight *n. Muff druff.*

pie chart *1. n.* A circular diagram divided into sectors, the various sizes of which represent different quantities or amounts of pie. 2. n. The centrefold pages of a gentleman's *artistic periodical.*

pie curious *adj.* Descriptive of a person who, whilst not a full blown *Duke of Giblets,* is nevertheless not averse to a spot of sly *salad-dodging* from time to time.

pie-hider *n.* A *gunt, bilge tank, muff pelmet.* The kind of overhanging gut that allows a lady to strip from the waist down whilst still retaining her modesty.

pie-liner *n.* A femidom.

pie shifter *n.* A *big-boned* person who can single-handedly clear the Ginster's display in their local petrol station. *'Famous people who have died on 11th February: Pietro Cataldi, mathematician, in Bologna, Italy, 1626; Rene Descartes, mathematician, in Stockholm, Sweden, 1650; Willhelm Killing, mathematician, in Munster, Germany, 1923; Egbert van Kampen, mathematician, in Baltimore, Maryland, 1942; Vladimir Smirnov, mathematician, Leningrad, USSR, 1974; William Conrad, pie shifter, in Hollywood, California, 1994.'* (from *Schott's Increasingly Desperate Christmas Gift Book,* 2004).

piece of piss *n.* An easy thing. *'Hey, this show jumping thing is a piece of piss.'* (Christopher Reeve), *'Hey, adjusting television aerials is a piece of piss.'* (Rod Hull).

pieceps *n.* Bulging stomach muscles made famous by former Everton goalkeeper Neville Southall.

pieman's wig *1. n.* An artificial hairpiece worn by a purveyor of pastry-enveloped foodstuffs. 2. *n.* An untidy *cunt-rug.*

pig at a tatty, going at it like a *sim. Yorks.* To engage in an act of oral pleasure with uninhibited gusto in Yorkshire. *"Eeh, by gum, Cathy lass. Slow tha' sen down a bit', said Heathcliffe. 'Appen tha's going at it like a pig at a tatty."* (from *Wuthering Heights* by Charlotte Bronte).

pig at the gate *euph.* A *mole at the counter, Mr Brown at the window.*

pig bite *n.* A poetic term for the vagina. *'A daughter of the Gods, divinely tall / And with a pig bite like a horse's collar.'* (from *A Dream of Fair Women* by Alfred Lord Tennyson).

pigboard *n.* The rear wall of a metropolitan phonebox.

pigbox *n.* A Nissan Micra full of rough women, driving round a provincial town playing Destiny's Child and hunting for *cock.*

pigeon's breakfast *n.* Some sick. A *pavement pizza.*

pigeon's chest *n.* The female swimsuit *lunchbox.* The *beetle bonnet, shark's fin.*

pig fart *n.* The erotic sound a lady's intimate parts may occasionally make whilst she is in the process of getting a good *stuffing.* A *queef.*

pigpenning *n.* Sitting surrounded

by, and stewing In, your own filthy, foetid smells because you simply can't be *arsed* to get up and move to safety. Named after the character in the long-running *Peanuts* cartoon strip who was constantly enveloped in a cloud of his own scribbled flatus.

pig's tits *rhym. slang.* The *shits. 'After you've been to the rub a dub, climb the apples and pears to the Curry Capital, Bigg Market, Newcastle upon Tyne, for a Ruby Murray that will give you the pig's tits, or your money back.'* (Advert in *Country Life* magazine).

pig's toe *n. The pig's trotter.*

pig's trotter, the *euph.* Prominent and well-defined labial *moundage* which is visible through a lady's leggings. A phenomenon also sometimes referred to as a *camel's foot, twix lips* or *knicker sausages. 'You'd best sit behind the desk to read the news tonight, Kirsty. You've got a right pig's trotter in them kecks.'*

PIK *acronym.* Pig In Knickers. An extremely unattractive, fleshy woman.

pikea *n.* Open air broken furniture showroom. Usually set up in Essex laybys after the travellers have moved on.

pikey bollards *n.* Large rocks and boulders placed along roadsides in areas where the local inhabitants already have plenty of pegs.

pikey sauna *n.* A lingeringly warm *dirty cough* that hangs around in the trousers, making one's *bollocks* sweat.

pikey's banquet *n.* The sort of dodgy-looking and hideously-overpriced burgers and hotdogs which are sold at fairgrounds and festivals.

pikey's bonus *n.* A *grumble flick* found inside a stolen video recorder. A *scouser's jackpot.*

pikey's pit stop *n.* A visit to a garage forecourt to refuel one's car when one has neither the means nor inclination to pay. A *splash 'n' dash.*

pikeys' wedding *n.* A *pagga,* a fierce fight. *'January 18th, 1915. This morning some of the chaps went over the top. The German guns were merciless, cutting them down like wheat stalks before the scythe. I have never witnessed such a pikeys' wedding and I'm sure it will haunt me for the rest of my days.'* (from *The Diary of Rupert Brooke*).

pile high club *1. n.* The notional society of fellows who have distinguished themselves by *papering their trolleys* whilst seated. *2. n.* Exclusive brotherhood of those who have earned their *brown wings.*

pile of dead fannies, smells like a *sim.* Descriptive of something which gives off a foul, fishy odour. *'Bloody hell, Dr Von Hagens. What have you got in your garage? It smells like a pile of dead fannies.' 'It's a pile of dead fannies, mein dear chap.'*

pilgrim's pocket *n.* A particularly dry *clout. 'Edwina was powerless to resist. John's eyes burned into hers like semi-precious lapis lazulis. His strong arms enfolded her body as she felt herself being swept away on a mistral of passion. She gasped as she felt his powerful, but gentle fingers teasing at the moist flower of her secret sanctum. 'Fuck me, your* *minge is sopping,' he exclaimed. 'Norma's twat's always dry as a pilgrim's pocket."* (from *The Junior Health Minister and The Chief Whip,* by Barbara Cartland).

pillicock *n. arch.* A *tummy banana.* From the pig's *pizzle* used in an early form of badminton.

pillock *n.* Tame, TV sitcom-friendly insult. Possibly derived from *pillicock.*

pillow biter *n.* One who bites their pillow, often in a moment of steeply-raked horticultural delight. Also *mattress muncher, feather spitter.*

pillow mint *1. n.* Small, inexpensive chocolate treat left on a guest's bed in better hotels in order to create the illusion that customer satisfaction is of the slightest importance to the management. *2. n.* A hefty *feeshus* left in the *pan* with the express intention of offending the next occupant of the *shithouse.*

pills *n. Pods, knackers, niags.*

pilot light *n.* An ex-socialite now restrained by the *pink handcuffs, ie.* one who "never goes out".

pimp my ride *1. n.* Television programme in which knackered old *bangers* are given a new lease of life. *'Please, MTV, pimp my ride.' 2. v.* Surgical programme in which knackered old bangers are given a new lease of life. *'Please, doctor, pimp my ride. Paying special attention to her saggy tits, triple chin, beergut and flabby arse.'*

pinballing *v.* To make progress home from the boozer by a series of ricochets from one item of street furniture to the next. Accompanied by the ringing of bells and clunking noises.

pinch a loaf *v.* To *curl one off.*

pinch of snuff *rhym. slang.* A *crafty butcher.*

Pinder's tits *euph.* Descriptive of something that you are not really bothered about any more. From the fact that glamour model Lucy Pinder is never going to get her *nips* out and what's more, after waiting this long, no-one particularly cares. *'You going to get Kate Bush's new album, then?' 'No. It's Pinder's tits, that.'*

pineapple *rhym. slang.* Semen. From pineapple chunk = spunk.

pinhole *n.* A *Mary* that makes a *mouse's ear* look like a *hippo's mouth.*

pink *v.* Of a lady, to make a *fanny slug* on a window for the amusement and edification of passers by.

pink, the *n.* A really good eyeful of the female genitals, esp. in a *meat mag.*

pink bat's face *n.* A nocturnal, high-pitched *meat moth.*

pink berets *n.* Large, flat breasts with stiff *nips.*

pink breathalyser *n.* The alternative drink-driving test offered to inebriated lady motorists by the more resourceful *scuffer.*

pink cigar n. Penis. Not to be confused with *bum cigar,* except in Germany. *'Tell me madam, do you perchance smoke the pink cigar?'*

pink Darth Vader *n. Knob.* From the *Star Wars* character with a *bell end* helmet.

Pink Floyd *euph.* The act of entering the dark side of a lady's *moon. 'Fedora was powerless to resist. His eyes burned into hers like diamonites. His strong arms enfolded her body as she felt herself being swept away on a 930 millibar sea surge of passion. Suddenly, she* *felt Jalfrezi's hot breath on her cheek as he whispered in her ear. 'Can I put Pink Floyd on tonight, love?' he asked. 'Alright then,' she replied. 'But only if you promise not to play any of your shit prog rock records while your cock's up my arse.''* (from *The Woman Named After a Type of Hat and the Man Named After a Chicken Dish* by Barbara Cartland).

pink oboe *n. Bed flute. 'Tell me madam, do you perchance play the pink oboe?'*

pink pillows *n.* Ladies' *love cushions*, bosoms.

pink shit, have a *v.* The end of a romantic evening of *back door work.* The termination of the process of anal intercourse.

pinksmith *n.* One who is expert in *fannycraft.* A *crumpeteer.*

pink steel *n.* Even harder than *wood.* Material used to forge *diamond cutters.*

pink ticket *n.* Imaginary *vadge* visa issued to a husband when he spends the night apart from his wife. *'Eureka! I've got my pink ticket for the conference on Tuesday.'*

pink velvet sausage wallet *n.* Short for *quim.*

pink wafer *n.* A *blurtch* which resolutely refuses to exude *fanny batter* even after being lovingly coerced for several minutes.

pinot grigio pashmina *n.* Like a *bacardigan,* but for posh *birds* in Wilmslow or Alderley Edge; a warm yet invisible shawl consisting of several glasses of white wine.

pint glass figure *n.* Like an hourglass figure, but with very little narrowing in the middle, *eg.* Vanessa Feltz, Fern Britton.

pintle *n.* Olde Worlde Chopper. *Pipe cleaner, pizzle.*

pip *n.* An upper class *hat* of the kind one might imagine Penelope Keith *dropping.*

pipe *1. n. Fr.* An act of oral love. A *nosh, chewie, blow-job. 2. n. Cock.*

pipe bomb *n.* An explosive *shit* that goes off without warning in the *pan,* causing massive collateral damage.

pipecleaner *1. n.* Furry wire used by children to make models in playschool. *2. n.* The first *piss* taken after committing an act of *self-pollution. 3. n.* A *blood sausage.*

piper at the gates of dawn *1. n.* An early Pink Floyd album. *2. n.* An early morning *turtle's head. Cock-a-doodle-poo.*

pipe smoker *1. n. US. Botter . 2. n.* A person who smokes a pipe.

pirate *n.* A *breastitute* lady, *ie.* one with a sunken chest.

pirate of men's pants *n.* Swashbuckling term for your *jolly rogerer, cock, one-eyed willie.*

pirate's piss *n.* The *piss* you have with one eye shut to improve targetting after a long night *on the pop.*

Pires penalty *n.* An unsatisfying and embarrassing *dribble* instead of a *shot* which hits the *back of the net.* A *money shot* that's down to its last couple of coppers; a *gwibble.*

piss *1. v.* To micturate. *2. n.* Some micturition. *3. adv.* Extremely. *'That driving test was piss easy'. 'Your three-point turn was piss poor.'*

pissabled *adj.* A state of drunken infirmity whereby one is unable to walk upstairs, park one's car properly *etc*. Also *shandycapped.*

piss bliss *n.* The moment just before a long-awaited *scoot,* when a gentleman keeps it in for a couple of seconds longer, primarily for a cheap thrill.

piss chase *1. n.* Excuse for an *ad hoc* pub crawl, especially during cold weather. A game of *piss chase* involves going into a pub for a much needed *wazz,* and whilst there feeling morally obliged to have a pint. This results in one again being in urgent need of the lavatory a quarter of a mile further down the high street, and so on and so forth until closing time. Or indeed until death from old age, now that the pubs never shut. *2. n.* Popular playground game in Germany.

pissed *1. adj. UK. Soused, potted, refreshed. 2 adj. US.* Annoyed. *'That cotton-pickin' Osama Bin Laden has gotten me real pissed, bub.'*

pissed as a tramp *adj.* To be so *refreshed* as to not care where one sleeps.

pissed up *adj.* Descriptive of a fellow who is comprehensively *wankered.*

piss factory *n. Vict.* A public house.

piss flaps *1. n. Labia, beef curtains. 2. interj.* Exclamation of disappointment. *'Oh piss flaps! I never win the Lottery!'*

piss-fork *n.* A post-coital bidirectional urine flow. *Twin-jets.*

pisshead's labourer *n.* A barman.

pissing in the wind *v.* Wasting one's time, attempting the impossible.

pissing tic-tacs *n.* The peculiar sensation of urinating whilst suffering from a nasty dose of *knob rot.* Not quite as bad as *pissing razor blades.*

piss it up the wall *v.* To fritter away something, *eg.* money, talent, urine.

piss it *v.* To do something *piss* simple, *piss* easily.

piss kitten *n.* The completely redundant spare woman who follows her friend to the toilet, for no other reason than to increase the length of the queue.

piss like an American fighter pilot *v.* When extremely *Brahms,* to micturate in a haphazard and inaccurate fashion, *ie.* spraying urine all over the floor, seat, shoes, John Simpson, *etc.*

piss mist *n.* The fine mist that forms around a urinal trough at shin level when having a *gypsy's kiss.* Only noticeable when wearing shorts. *Wee fret.*

piss off *1. exclam.* A polite form of *fuck off. 2. v.* To annoy. *'The graphics on the BBC news really piss me off.'*

piss on your chips *v.* To put yourself at a long-term disadvantage through a foolhardy short-term action. *Fart on your Weetabix*

piss, piece of *n.* A portion of easiness. *'Hey, flying this Concorde out of Charles De Gaulle Airport is a piece of piss.'*

pisspint *n.* A drink purchased "because it's only fair, isn't it", when calling in at a public house for the sole purpose of making use of the *bogs.*

piss polo *1. n.* Game of skill whereby disinfectant tablets are pointlessly manoeuvred in a urinal trough by the participants' *wazz* streams. *2. n.* A very unsuccessful flavour of sweet.

piss porch *n.* The skin awning

which protects a lady's *bald man in a boat* from the weather.

piss pot *1. n.* Lavatory bowl. *2. n.* Idiot, fool. *3. n.* Old-fashioned motorcyclist's helmet.

pisspotical *adj.* A state of confusion, disarray or disharmony, *ie.* that which apparently exists at Houghton-le-Spring Housing Benefit Office.

piss proud *adj.* To be the owner of a *dawn horn*, a *morning glory, motorcycle kick stand.*

piss rusty water *v.* To pass liquid *feeshus.*

piss sauna *n.* The all-enveloping fog of urine steam in an outside pub lavatory on a cold winter's evening.

piss up *n.* An ale soirée; a social gathering of boozing companions.

piss whip *n.* The effect created by drunkenly waving one's *pezzle* up and down whilst having a *gypsy's kiss.*

piss whistle *n.* A *bed flute, a pink oboe.*

piss with the lid down *v.* To do something very foolish, to make a schoolboy error. *"Mr Paravicini's murderer is in this very room, and I'm afraid it is you, Brigadier Lewerthwaite!' cried Miss Marple. The room fell silent. 'After murdering him, you dressed him in his pyjamas and carefully put his cufflinks on the dressing table to give the impression that the crime had been committed after bedtime, when you were playing bridge with myself and the Bishop. However, I'm afraid you pissed with the lid down, Brigadier,' she said. 'What the deuce do you mean?' Lewerthwaite blustered. 'Simply this,' she continued. 'You placed the cufflinks on the right hand side of the dressing table when the position of the inkwell on his Davenport clearly showed him to have been left handed.'* (from *Ten Little Black and White Minstrels,* by Agatha Christie).

piss wicks *n.* One's shoelaces in a urine-soaked pub toilet.

pissy fit *n.* The kind of foul-tempered strop that can only be achieved when one is *blind refreshed.*

pisticuffs *n.* A comical, drunken attempt at combat.

pisto *n.* Nasally-abusive miasma prevalent in tower block lifts, multi-storey car park stairs or around gentlemen of the road. "Ah, pisto."

pistorectomy *n. medic.* The act of vomiting up one's own internal organs whilst life-threateningly *merry.*

pit bull *n.* A stocky, tenacious *Thora,* usually the final one of a visit, that hangs onto the *ringpiece* like grim death. An *angry monkey,* a *Harold Lloyd.*

pit cat *euph.* A little-used *clopper.* A *pussy* that never sees the light of day.

pitch a tent *v.* To get *wood* either beneath the bed linen, or conspicuously in your trousers.

pitch inspection *n.* The checking of one's *bills* for any sign of a *bonus ball* after a risky *Exchange & Mart.*

pitch invasion *1. n.* Entertaining 1970s football match behaviour in which the crowd unexpectedly leaves the stands and makes its way onto the field of play. *2. n.* Entertaining *farty-arse* behaviour in which a quantity of *feeshus* unexpectedly leaves the *arse* and makes its way onto the *gusset* of the *trol-*

leys. A *follow through*.

pit clit *n. coll.* Gorgeous lycra-clad *blart* that stand around holding umbrellas on the starting grid of F1 races.

pit fillers *n.* Massive *thru'penny bits* which emigrate towards a *bird's* oxters when she's lying on her back.

pit prop *n.* Strategic structural member found in a *passion pit*. A *tent pole*, a *dawn horn*.

pizzle *n. medic.* A sorry-looking *penis*, like one would imagine the Pope has. *Gonzo's nose*.

placket *n. arch.* A Medieval maiden's *cunt*.

plamff *n. Scot.* One who, apparently bored of sniffing bicycle seats, opts to cut out the middle man and sniffs the gussets of ladies' soiled *bills* instead, *eg*. Jonathan Ross OBE.

plank *n.* A planned *wank*. From planned + wank. A useful entry in a stressed executive's diary for when his wife or girlfriend is absent which, during any subsequent inquisition into his scheduled assignations, can be explained away as a highly improbable trip to a local timber merchants to peruse their selection of stout battens.

Planter's hum *n.* The nauseating smell of *air croutons*. From the aroma of a freshly-opened bag of dry-roasted peanuts.

plap *1. n. onomat.* The sound a *digestive transit* makes when it hits the *chod pan* water, particularly if it's one of them ones with the consistency of warm plasticine. *2. n. onomat.* An alternative to a *Peruvian num-num*.

plasterer's radio *sim.* Descriptive of a lucky lady who is heavily adorned with *jelly jewellery*. Frequently found on Japanese and American cyber-scud.

plastic cockney *n.* A *mockney*. A posh person who affects to be an Eastender, *eg*. Ben Elton, Nigel Kennedy, Shane MacGowan.

plasticine hammer, knocking a nail in with a *sim.* Descriptive of the difficulty experienced when trying to *bang* a young lady who has signally failed to provoke a sufficient level of tumescence in one's *chap*. *Playing snooker with a piece of string*.

plastic paddy *n.* A posh person who affects to be Irish, *eg*. Shane MacGowan.

plate *1. n. Arch. Horatio. 2. n. Arch. Cumulonimbus.* A general purpose term for oral/genital shenanigans performed behind a Victorian skip. *'How much, love?' 'Twenty bob for full, ten for hand or fifteen for plate.'*

play a tune on the devil's clarinet *1. v.* To masturbate. *2. v.* To borrow a woodwind instrument from the Lord of Hades, before knocking out a jazz standard on it.

playaway *n.* Masturbatory technique of chaps not overly-endowed in the trouser department, *eg*. Pygmies, Jamie Theakston, the Rt Hon Jack Straw MP. From the song lyrics: "One finger, one thumb, keep moving".

play dough *n.* Disposable income, *beer tokens*.

play good cock/bad cock *v.* A popular method of *self-interrogation* in which alternate violent and gentle strokes are employed to get the suspect to *spill his guts*.

playing Buckaroo with Muhammad Ali, like *sim.* Descriptive of a situation where one cannot lose, *eg*. racing Eddie Large up Mount Snowdon, running a premium rate phone-in competition on GMTV, or standing for election against John Redwood.

playing chopsticks *v.* A beginners' duet. Mutual masturbating.

playing snooker with a piece of string *sim.* Trying to *sink a pink* with a *marshmallow cue.*

playing the accordian *v.* To alternately pull apart and squeeze together the cheeks of one's *arse* when perched on the *choddy hopper* in an effort to encourage the last bit of *shit* to drop off before polishing one's *nipsy.*

playing the bone-a-phone *v. Wanking,* pulling oneself a *hand shandy.*

playing the invisible banjo *v.* George Formby-style female masturbation technique. *Scruggs style.*

playing the upside-down piano *sim.* The overture to the second movement of *hiding the sausage. Firky-foodling.*

play statues *v.* To stop suddenly in the street with a pensive look upon one's face as one tries to determine whether one has just done a *guff* or a *poo.*

playsturbation *n.* Portmanteau term describing the activities of a single gentleman or temporarily home-alone husband who spends his time alternately playing console games and *pulling himself off.*

play the Atari *v.* To waggle one's *joystick* furiously, whilst poking one's tongue out with concentration and excitement, in the style of an 80s computer console gamer having a *wank.*

play the B-side *v.* To swap from the Missionary position to the *doggie* position. *'I got fed up with looking at her face while I was giving her one, so I flipped her over and played the B-side.'*

play the back nine v. *Irish golf*. To use one's *wood* to play into the bunker, *get the dog in the bathtub*.

play the bacon kazoo *v.* To *nosh* noisily on a *lab kebab.*

play the pink oboe *v.* To perform oral sex on a man, presumably with a thin reed sticking out of his *hog's eye*. Often used to denote homosexuality. *'I didn't know Michael Barrymore played the pink oboe.'*

play the violin *v.* To scrape your *bow* against a lady's *G-string*. To make sweet music with a lady after merely pushing the *jelly hammock* of her *dunghampers* to one side.

play the whale *v.* To *spew.*

play your arse right *n.* Game which can be played by two men sitting outside a health club or swimming pool, for example policemen in their patrol car, plumbers in a van or emeritus professors of moral philosophy sitting in the window of a teashop. Based on the formerly popular Bruce Forsyth TV vehicle *Play Your Cards Right*; in this variant contestants have to predict whether the *muck spreader* of the next lady who emerges through the front door will be bigger or smaller than the last.

pleasure *v*. Tabloidese, to *suck* or *wank off*. To perform a lewd act on oneself or on someone else.

pleasure trove *n.* A dazzling collection of *niff mags* found under a hedge or on top of an older brother's wardrobe.

plinth *v.* Of males *on the job*, to manoeuvre oneself into a comfortable position for penetration.

plonker *1. n.* Penis. *2. n. Crap* put-down line from Britain's favourite tedious TV sitcom.

plop corn *n.* Thrill-seeking undigested yellow foodstuff which rides one's *log flume.*

ploughing the sand *1. v.* A seemingly never ending and unrewarding job, *eg.* painting the Forth Rail Bridge, working as BBC Radio 6Music's Pete Doherty or Amy Winehouse news correspondent. *2. n.* Being *on the job* whilst far too *inebriated* to *shoot one's stack.*

ploughman's *n.* The *barse, taint, notcher etc. 'Mr Kneivel's motorbike hit the last bus at an approximate speed of 120mph, before careering into several fruit machines and a tuppenny waterfall. He suffered severe internal injuries including fractured ribs, two broken legs and a fractured skull. He also ripped his ploughman's wide open on the petrol tank.'* (Doctor's report, Las Vegas County General Hospital, 1978).

ploughman's lunch *euph.* A dirty *bird's all day breakfast,* from the fact that it looks like beef, smells like cheese and tastes like pickled onion.

pluke *n.* A facial spot. A zit.

plumbago *n. medic.* Painful ache in the *Gladstones* caused by over-revving the *spunk* engines without releasing the *horse's handbrake. Lover's nuts, blue balls.*

plumber's bonus *n.* A *U-blocker* of such proportions that it has to be dealt with by someone who has served an apprenticeship. A *windfall.*

plumber's lung *n.* A violent *arse bark.*

plumber's mate *n.* A bored housewife who entertains herself during the day by watching repeats of *Flog It* and *sucking off* sundry tradesmen who have called to fix the washing machine.

plumber's privilege *n.* The ancient right granted to plumbers, which entitles them to relieve themselves into whichever appliance they have just installed, *eg.* sink, bath, dishwasher *etc.*

plumber's toolbag *n. Furry bicycle stand, mott.*

plumber's wipe *n.* The art of shoving one's hand into a lady's *driptray,* and rubbing backwards and forwards, in the same way that a plumber would wipe a recently-soldered joint.

plum duff *rhym. slang.* A homosexualist.

plumpa-lumpa *n.* A short fat *bird* with a bright orange face.

plumper *n.* A *Buffet slayer.* A lady of ample proportions.

plums *n. Knackers, balls,* testicles.

plum sauce *n.* Ejaculate.

plums to prunes *euph.* The before and after states of a chap's *hairy saddlebags. 'Jonathan was powerless to resist. His eyes burned into the centrefold's minge like quartzes. His hairy hand enfolded his battered charlie as he felt himself once again being swept away on an onanistic whirlwind of passion. Then, all too soon it was over and he felt his ardour subsiding. 'Bloody hell, that was fast,' he panted as he wiped his hand on the curtains. 'I went from plums to prunes in less than a minute.'* (from *The Film 2005 Presenter and the Japanese Jazz*

Mag by Barbara Cartland).

plum tomatoes *n.* The state of a chap's *knackers* after he's done it with a lady who's *on the blob.*

plunker *n. US. Johnny,* a *spunk*-proof jumpsuit for a *plonker.* A *Trojan, jubber.*

Plymouth Argyles *rhym. slang. Piles.*

poacher's folly *1. n.* In traditional countryside parlance, the act of shooting at rabbits and thereby scaring away the big game. *2. n.* In nightclub parlance, the act of chatting up the first rough *bird* one sees in a club and thereby scaring away the decent *tussage. Going ugly early.*

poacher's pocket *1. n.* A fashion accessory favoured by illicit hunters and shoplifting television celebrities. *2. n.* A very large *fanny.*

Pob lips *n.* The state of the *ring-piece* during an acute bout of diarrhoea. From the low budget spitting Welsh children's TV puppet of the same name.

pobolycwm *n. Welsh.* Literally "People who like quim".

pocket battleship *1. n.* A compact, heavily-armed warship, such as The Graff Spee. *2. n.* A short, yet aggressive *hard on.* A Bob Hoskins amongst erections. 3. *n.* An ugly, short *bint, eg.* that fucking nightmare off *Wife Swap.*

pocket billiards *n.* A game for one player, two *balls,* and a *cock.*

pocket bonk-on *n.* Like pocket chess and pocket Scrabble, a genital erection that is for some reason smaller than usual, but still perfectly functional. Ideal for caravan holidays.

pocket fisherman *n.* He who plays with his *tackle* through his trouser pockets.

pocket frog *n.* A *fart, botty burp, anal announcement.*

pocket pinball *n.* A game where the testicles are fired up into the chest, where they ricochet from organ to organ whilst bells ring and one's eyes spin round.

pocket rocket *1. n* A small, but powerful motorbike. *2. n.* A small, but powerful *knob.*

podcast *1. n.* A broadcast of digital content played back on one's personal entertainment device. *2. n.* A broadcast of the contents of the *pods* caused by using the digits to play with one's *personal entertainment device.* 3. *n.* A metric unit of *spaff* equal to approximately one fortieth of an *almond.*

podge-on *n.* A small *semi on* which presents one's *old man* in a more favourable light than it deserves. *Half a teacake, dobber.*

pod purse *n.* Where the loose change for a *money shot* is kept.

pod race *n.* To *crack one off* in a high-pressure situation where time is of the essence, *eg.* while the missus is out making a cup of tea or choking on a boiled sweet.

poe *n.* The *fadge.* From the Gothic author Edgar Allen Minge.

poe slap *n.* A *fanny nanny, danger-mouse.*

POETS day *acronym.* Friday. From Piss Off Early, Tomorrow's Saturday.

poffle *v.* To *shart. Gamble and lose.*

pog *n. Scratter.*

pogie *n. US.* Where American *plonkers* go dressed in their *plunkers.*

pogue mahone *exclam. Gael.* Original name of the Pogues. An anglicisation of the Irish "pog mo thoin", meaning "kiss my arse". A reasonable request, given the state of Shane MacGowan's mouth.

pointer sisters *n.* A slightly perkier version of the *Winslet twins*.

point Percy at the porcelain *v.* To take Robert Plant to the toilet for a *wee wee.*

poke *v.* What *plonkers* do to *pogies*.

poke holes in a cheap door *phr.* Property of a *diamond cutter. 'When Elizabeth was near, D'Arcy's heart raced, and he got a panhandle that could poke holes in a cheap door.'* (from *Pride and Prejudice* by Jane Austen).

pokelore *n.* Mythical yarns of exciting sexual adventures spun to mates down the pub.

poker hand *n.* A morning spent on the lavatory evacuating one's *Camillas.* A *running straight* followed by a flush; then a *full house* followed by a royal flush.

poke the spider's eye *v.* To dig at one's *claypit* through one's *farting crackers.*

pokey bott wank *n.* A two-handed act of *self gratification* which combines wanking with one hand whilst sticking a finger from the other one up your own *arse. Abseiling. 'Are you coming up to bed, Tony?' 'In a minute, Cherie. I'm just having a pokey bott wank.'*

pokies *1. n.* Gambling machines, or one-armed bandits if you will. *2. n.* Ladies' *nips* when visible through their clothing. Ringo Starr's sister-in-law Daisy Duke out of *The Dukes of Hazzard* was well known for her *pokies*. By a spooky coincidence, the pilot episode of *The Dukes of Hazzard* was entitled *One-Armed Bandits. Chapel hat pegs, pygmies' cocks, blind cobblers' thumbs etc.*

polestruck *adj.* A shallow lady who is erotically fascinated by firemen and their equipment.

pole tax *n.* A pecuniary sum or duty levied upon the patrons of *gentleman's entertainment* venues before the next performer deigns to appear on stage. Usually in the form of putting a quid in a pint glass, or a hat.

pole vault *n.* Vagina, *stench trench*, strong room where the *spam sceptre* can be safely housed. For a couple of minutes.

police horse fart *n.* A *change of heart* capable of dispersing an unruly mob.

policeman *n.* An amusing way of *dropping one's bait,* specifically the act of placing both hands behind the back and bending the knees out in a comical fashion as a prelude to the release of flatus. Can be accompanied by the words "'ello 'ello 'ello" or indeed "evenin' all", in the style of Dixon of Dock Green, according to personal preference.

policeman's dinner *n. US.* An *arsehole.*

policewoman's treat *n.* A bobby's *bob.*

polish a turd *met.* To fruitlessly attempt to dress up something *shite*, *eg.* the relaunch of the Morris Marina as the Ital, or putting a baseball cap on William Hague.

polish one's spectacles *v.* To surreptitiously *masturbate* one's penis through one's pockets, *eg.* when looking for change in a strip club or when sexually aroused on a tube train.

polish the lighthouse *v.* To *throttle Captain Birdseye* in the bath.

POLO *acronym. milit.* Code used on military correspondence prior to coming home from a posting abroad. Pants Off, Legs Open. See also *NORWICH.*

polony party *n.* A social gathering of two or more consenting adults where party games include *hide the sausage, park the salami* and *split the kipper*. And one's party bag would contain a slice of cake and a dose of the *clap*. An orgy.

pommel horse, an army surplus *sim.* Descriptive of a woman who is slack in both the moral and vaginal senses. *'Or will lucky Benedict choose number three, the vivacious Mother Superior who loves to party and has had more jumps than an army surplus pommel horse?'*

Pompey pineapple *n.* The high tension raked-back hairstyle favoured by *bingo clink*-clad southern slappers.

pompom *n. Jam.* A furry thing waved by cheerleaders to entertain a crowd.

ponce *1. n.* A *pimp*. *2. n.* Brian Sewell soundalike. *3. v.* To borrow something with no intention of giving it back, *eg*. cigarettes, garden tools, the Elgin Marbles.

pong *n.* The smell of a *poot*.

pony *rhym. slang. Shit.* From pony and trap = crap.

poo *1. exclam.* A word spoken with fingers on nostrils to describe an unpleasant odour. *2. n. Shit. 3. v.* To do a *duty*.

pooaplegic *n. medic.* One who, having sat on the toilet for too long, has lost all feeling below the waist. A *crapple.*

pooch coning *n.* A decidedly risky sexual pursuit which involves smothering *nut butter* over your privates, it says here, and then getting your next door neighbour's dog to lick it off. Nice to know that it's got a name at last.

Poocomknockerphilication *n. Cleveland steaming*, as performed by Ken Dodd.

poodini *n.* One of those rare *turds* that magically escapes through the U-bend without any assistance whatsoever, even if you'd got a policeman to chain it up in a canvas bag first. A *ghost shit.*

poof *n.* A man who doesn't want another pint.

poo fairy *n.* Magical entity which regularly visits the female half of the population, resulting in the male half being under the handy illusion that ladies never need to *lay a cable.*

poof dust *n.* Phrase used by schoolboys to describe talcum powder in the days before there was such a thing as diversity training.

poof's pizza *n.* Quiche. Also *puff's pizza.*

poofter *n. Aus.* An Australian man who doesn't want another ten pints.

poogina *n.* A lady's back *front bottom.*

poo horn *n.* The kitchen utensil kept by the *chod bin* for easing *pan-blocker*s round tight-fitting U-bends, *eg*. bread knife, scissors, egg whisk. *'Nip upstairs and fetch the poo horn down, will you love? The kids want an omelette.'*

poomerang *n.* A *turd* which is able to return from the U-bend with twice the force with which it was flushed away in the first place.

poon *n. Fanny, crumpet, toosh. 'I guess, this means my poon days* *are over.'* (Abraham Lincoln after his inauguration in May 1776). *'Knickers off, this is poon city!'* (Bill Clinton after his inauguration in June 1993).

poond *n.* A *gunt,* a *fupa*. From the Geordie "a poond o' tripe".

pooning *n.* The act of sniffing ladies' bicycle seats.

poontang *1. n.* A *clopper. 2. n.* Some *clopper.*

poo packer *n.* A *stylish* chap.

poop catchers *n. Knickers, dunghampers, bills.*

poop chute *n. The bumhole, arse,* up which parking tickets can be rammed.

pooping cough *n. medic.* A highly debilitating smoker's condition which, when coughing severely whilst *heavily refreshed,* causes one to *soil* one's own *rompers. 2. n.* Clearing one's throat melodramatically whilst ensconced in a public lavatory cubicle, in order to disguise the shameful fact that one is having a *shit.*

poo preview *n.* An *air buffet*, an *mariner's chart.*

poornography *n. Grumble* of a core which is somewhat less than tumescent. The sort of soft-focus cotton wool-strength *grot* broadcast on Bravo, Men & Motors, or on Channel 5 in the old days before they started doing primetime *farmyard pig wanking.* (From poor + nography).

poor sense of direction, have a *v.* Of a man, to be *good with colours.*

poosex *n.* A charming word for *brown love.*

poosticks *n.* Game whereby lolly sticks are inserted into *barkers'* eggs by curious children. *"What are you doing?' squeaked Piglet excitedly. 'I'm pushing a lolly stick into a dog shit,' replied Christopher Robin.'* (from *When we Were Alive* by AA Milne).

poot *1. v.* To sound one's *botty bugle*, often after eating *musical vegetables. 2. n.* A *flies' dinner gong.*

poo tea *n.* An unrefreshing brown infusion made by allowing *logs* to brew in the pot for a long time. *PG shits.*

poot flute *n. Trouser trumpet, singing ring, cornhole cornet, swannee whistle.*

pooter *n.* The *bum* bellows with which you *poot*. The *poot flute.*

poove *n.* A *crafty butcher.*

poovert *n.* A poo pervert or *scat man.* A *crothers.* Usually a German, if truth be told. From poo + pervert.

poovery *n. Bottery* and everything associated therewith. *Bumcraft.*

POP *acronym.* Post Orgasmic Piss. *'Thanks for the fuck, Your Majesty. I'm just nipping to the lavvy for a pop.'*

pop a knocker *v.* Of a lady, to overreact to a situation in a melodramatic fashion. *'Christ, love, it was only a chewie off your sister. There's no need to pop a knocker.'*

popazogalou *n.* A *chewie*, a *gobble*, a *blow job*. From the name of the landlord in the film *Personal Services* who accepted payment in kind.

popemobile *n.* Sexual position favoured by members of the *dogging* community. With the front seats folded fully flat, the man lies on his back and the woman sits atop him in the *reverse cowboy* position. Through the steamed-up National Health spectacles of the casual passer-by *wanking* in his trousers, her erotic gyrations resemble nothing so much as the pontiff waving to the adoring crowds from behind the two-inch-thick bulletproof glass of his trademark automobile.

Popeye eating spinach *sim.* To engage in enthusiastic *cumulonimbus*. With a pipe in one's mouth. *'And the husband of Bathsheba did venture forth for Regal Super Kings that numbered two score and did leave Bathsheba alone in the tent. And David did enter the tent and did know Bathsheba. And David did kneel before Bathsheba, and lo, he did go at it like Popeye eating spinach.'* (from *The Book of Clive* 6:3-5).

Popeye wipe *n.* The first, agonising attempt at a spot of *ringpiece* polishing after one has *dropped* a quantity of unruly, *screaming Mexican kids off at the pool.* From the resulting adoption of a facial expression resembling that of the popular spinach-chomping, one-eyed cartoon schizophrenic.

pop her cork *v.* To give a lady an organism. Presumably by shaking her up and down for twenty seconds and then pushing her *clit* up with your thumbs.

poppycock *exclam.* Nonsense, bollocks. *'I just seen Amy Winehouse at the bar buying a soft drink.' 'Poppycock.'*

pop shot *n.* Scene in a *grumble flick* in which a male actor is required to splash his *population paste* for the camera, after being suitably prepared by the *fluffer*. A *money shot.*

pop the turkey in the oven *v.* To pluck the feathers from one's penis and put it in a vagina at gas mark six, prior to getting one's father-in-law to cut it into slices. To *fuck.*

population paste *n. Joy gloy,* semen, *spunk, Aphrodite's evostick, jazz glue, prick stick.*

pop-up book *n.* A special type of reading matter where things magically spring into three dimensions as one leafs through the pages. A *bongo mag, art pamphlet, DIY manual.*

pop-up box *1. n.* Something utterly *shit* which cannot be avoided on the internet. *2. n.* Something utterly smashing which can be seen on the internet. A prominent ladies' pubular mound. Also known as a *proud mary*, *beetle bonnet or pigeon's chest.*

pop-up panic *n.* The bowel-loosening fear that comes from having to hurridly close down internet *grumble* sites one has been ogling due to the impending approach of a boss, spouse or parent, only to be suddenly assaulted by a barrage of obscene pop-ups that multiply the more one tries to delete them.

pop your cherry *v.* Lose your virginity, *break your duck.*

porcelain tingle *n.* The cold shock that occurs when one's *bell end* touches the lavatory pan when sitting on the *throne*. A *harprick.*

pork *1. v. Aus.* To *fuck*. *'I couldn't pork her because she had the painters in.' 2. n. Aus.* The *spam javelin.*

pork 'n' stalk *n.* A lady with whom one has had a whirlwind one-night romance, who continues to bomard one with texts, phone calls and cooked pets. A *bunny boiler.*

pork and beans *adj.* A term to describe a *happy shopper,* or *Betty*

Both. One who *bowls from both the pavilion and the members' end. Half rice, half chips. 'Birthdays: David Bowie, formerly pork and beans, now just beans, singer, 56 today.'* (*The Times* Jan 8th, 2003).

pork pills *n. pharm. Cock drops, blueys.* Viagras, *Bongo Bill's banjo pills.*

pork prescription *1. n.* A *bacon bazooka*, to be swallowed twice a day instead of meals. *2. n.* Doctor's authorisation for a *meat injection.*

pork scratchings *n. medic.* Irritation of the *old chap* as a result of a misguided liaison with a promiscuous lady. A *dose. 'Excuse me, barman. But have you got pork scratchings?' 'Yes. I got them when I fucked your missus under the pier last week'.* (Bamforth's *Seaside Chuckles* postcard by Donald McGill, 1926).

pork stork *n. 'Dad, where do babies come from?' 'The pork stork, son.'*

pork sword *n.* Penis, *tallywhacker, lamb cannon.*

pornbroker *n.* The man at work who can be relied upon to lend you a bit of *mucky* to see you through hard times. A *pornmeister,* a *jazz magnate.*

porn buddy *n.* A *cliterary executor.* A single fellow's best friend who, in the event of his untimely death, is charged with the important task of removing and disposing of his stash of *grumble* before his grieving parents arrive to search through his effects for touching mementoes and stuff to put on eBay. If former Poet Laureate and lifelong jazz enthusiast Philip Larkin's *porn buddy* had managed to carry out the Hull University librarian's final wishes, it is estimated that the resulting bonfire of hardcore *art pamphlets* would have been visible from the Moon.

porn cocktail *1. n.* In certain "niche" areas of saucy film making, a beverage concocted from the mingled *tadpoles* and *man mayonnaise* of a number of male performers which is ingested with a limited amount of relish by the female lead. *2. n.* Residue found on the bedsheets of frustrated teenagers.

porn flakes *n.* The crusty bits found on the sofa/sheets the morning after a late night *scruff video* session.

porn flour *n.* Any powdery substance used for the purpose of locating the wet parts on a larger lady. *'I'm off out with big Janice from accounts tonight.' 'Good luck, mate. Don't forget to take a bag of porn flour.'*

porn fuzz *n.* Characteristic picture quality of an 18th generation *bongo vid. Readybrek glow.*

porn glare *n.* The cruel, frustrating shaft of light which partially obscures the spreadeagled *bird* on the double page spread of an *art pamphlet* as the victim strives for *vinegar. Razzle dazzle.*

pornhography *n. Grumblular* entertainment featuring female participants of notably poor quality.

porn horn *n.* A three-quarters-hard erection regularly seen being fed into the models in *scud films.* An *Indian rope prick.*

pornithologist *n.* One who enjoys looking at pictures of *birds* rather than going out and looking at them in the flesh. A *cock twitcher.*

pornithology *n.* The scientific study of two *birds at it like fucking knives. Lesbology.*

porn mauve *n.* Distinctive colour assumed by all male genitalia in *grumble vids,* although rarely if ever seen in real life.

porn mirage *n.* A cruel trick of the light, whereby a *tug*-hungry adolescent spots some *grummer* under a hedge, which on closer inspection turns out to be an Argos catalogue or the *Sunday Mirror* TV guide.

pornogamy *n.* Amongst impoverished gentlemen, the practice of remaining continuously faithful to the same dog-eared *seed catalogue* for all their sexual and emotional needs.

pornoisseur *n.* A gentleman who appreciates only the finest things in one-handed life.

porno mouth *n.* A young lady whose coital utterances closely resemble the dialogue from *grumble flicks, eg.* "split me in two with your big cock" *etc.*

porn on the fourth of July *sim.* Temporary Tom Cruise-style male lower body paralysis that occurs when attempting to stand up to turn off the video after loosing off several rounds from the *mutton musket.*

pornorama *n.* A magnificent, breathtaking array of *meat mags,* arranged in a vista to provide variety and spectacle whilst having a *tug.* A *wank crescent, glandscape.*

porn penguin *n.* A brisk, comical waddle across the living room in order to pause, rewind or fast forward through the plot-related bits of a *tug film* when the batteries have failed in your remote.

porn sacrifice *n.* A poorly-hidden stash of low-quality *grumble* designed to put your missus off the scent of the *export strength* stuff. A *blue herring, stalking horse.*

porn trauma *n.* Upon reaching the *vinegar strokes* whilst watching an *art film* and finding the screen suddenly filled by a big, sweaty bloke with large sideburns, being too late to stop, and *gwibbling* to a disappointing finish. See *vinegar Joe.*

pornucopia *n.* A seemingly endless supply of *jazz, eg.* the top shelf of the magazine rack at Barton Park lorry services on the A1.

porn vortex *n.* A whirling fifth dimension where time has no meaning, encountered when browsing the worldwide web for *left-handed websites.* One could fall into a *porn vortex* and emerge ten minutes later to discover that three days have elapsed.

porridge gun n. Tool for distributing *population paste* quickly and efficiently.

PORT *abbv.* A politically correct term for a *bird* with small *tits.* Person Of Restricted Tittage, *eg.* Jilly Goulden.

port and starboard scran spanners *n. naval.* Knife and fork.

portion *n.* A large but nonspecific quantity of *the other.* See also *one, a length, a bit. 'I'd give her a portion, and no mistake.'*

Portuguese breakfast *n.* A hearty bowl-full to start the day. A watery, clotted *shit* that resembles the sort of thing they'd probably eat over there.

Portuguese man o' war *1. n.* Name given to a buoyant jelly-fish, *Physalia atlantica,* characterised by the presence of one or more large air-sacs, by means of which it drifts about on the surface of the ocean. *2. n.* Swimming shorts so inflated with *carbon dibaxide* that they float above the surface of the pool, causing alarm to fellow swimmers.

posharean *n. medic.* In obstetrics, a Caesarean section performed for no other reason than to keep the mother's *twat* nice and tight.

posh wank *n.* A *mess*-free masturbatory manoeuvre undertaken whilst wearing a *jubber ray*.

postman's arse *n. medic.* Condition caused by chronic chaffing of the *bum cheeks* and thus characterised by a painful red ring around the *tea towel holder* which afflicts those whose working day involves much walking and sweating.

potato fat *n.* The starchy gloop that issues from a gentleman's *spuds* when he mashes them a bit. *Spunk, tattie watta, spud juice.*

pot brown *v.* To sink a long *pink* into the *herbert pocket.*

potch *v. Wales.* To partake of an extra-marital affair in the valleys. *'See that Jones the song? Well he's been potching for years, isn't it, Look you, boyo, bach?'*

potholer *n.* An adventurous *mud child,* one end of which is connected to your *chuff* whilst the other has made its way round the U-bend, where its head pokes out through the meniscus in the trap, like a small, blind Loch Ness Monster. Also known as a *bumbilical.*

Pot Noodle horn *n. Brewer's droop.* A *cock like a wet noodle.*

pot pink *v.* To moor the *skin boat* in *cod cove*.

Potsdamer Platz *1. n. prop.* Area of no-man's land between dour, communist east and capitalist fun-loving west Berlin. *2. n.* The area of *no-man's land* between a lady's dour, communist *arse* and capitalist fun-loving *minge.* The *butfer, carse, tinter, taint, notcher, snarse, biffin bridge, Humber Bridge, niftkin's bridge etc. Checkpoint Charlie.*

potter's wheel *1. n.* A thick, convoluted *blurtch,* sagging under its own weight such that it resembles a trouser-suited *joskin*'s attempt to throw a clay pot on the *Generation Game*. *2 n.* Situation where a man carefully attempts to nurture a relationship with a lady over a period of time, only to ruin all his hard work by *copping a feel* too early. The *baker's impatience.*

potty-mouth *n.* US. Some sweary *cunt* who merely shows up their *fucking* lack of vocabulary.

potty slot *n.* The *bum crack.*

pouch *n.* An ageing, saggy *mott* that hangs between the legs like a sporran.

pound the pork *v.* Of *pinksmiths*, to pummel a hot *pork sword* into shape. *Pound the pudding*.

pouring Pot Noodle *adj.* Producing an unappetizing, runny *poo,* though not quite unappetizing and runny enough to be described as Cup-a-Soup.

power ballad *n.* An *Elvis killer* of such colossal girth that, as it is passed, the victim raises his clenched fist into the air and pulls a face which calls to mind that of the lead singer of Boston during the chorus of *More than a Feeling.* A *Meatloaf's daughter.*

power cake *n.* A turbo-charged *cupcake* which is unleashed in front of an electric fan.

powerwank *n.* A brisk, efficient *tug* slotted into a busy work schedule. Often performed by politicians, captains of industry and de Vere Hotels bar staff on a fag break.

pox *n.* Venereal disease, specifically syphilis. *Cock rot, clap.*

prairie dogging *v.* Of an *arse*, to have a stool poking in and out like an inquisitive gopher. A moving *turtle's head*.

prairie wind *1. n.* 2005 album by warblesome country rocker Neil Young; a moving song cycle of dreams, memories, family ties and the passage of time, if you will. *2. n.* A gently sulphurous zephyr that softly rustles the *arse cress* as it wafts across the barren *flies' graveyard.*

pram face *n.* A famous woman, perhaps a pop star or TV presenter, whose face would more suitably adorn a young mother pushing a pram around a council estate, for example misunderstood *Celebrity Big Brother* multiculturalist Jo O'Meara.

pram fat *n. Plum sauce, heir gel, baby gravy.*

pramland *1. n.* Shop on Hull's Holderness Road that sells baby paraphenalia. *2. n.* Hull's David Lister School, whose pupils are allegedly amongst *1*'s biggest customers.

pranny *n.* Fool, *arsehole, twat.* A form of insult popular amongst The Troggs pop group during recording sessions in the 1960s. Also *prannet*.

prat *1. n.* The *buttocks* of the *fundament* of the *arse*. *2. n.* A *pranny, fuckwit, arsehole.* A doltish sort.

prawn *n.* A girl with a fit body, but an ugly face. From the edible crustacean, where the body is tasty, but the head is thrown away. A *bobfoc.*

prawn crackers *n.* The crispy tissues found beneath the bed. *Popshottadoms.*

prawn penknife *n.* A more diminutive version of a *pork sword*, possibly incorporating a small tool for removing stones from seahorses' hooves.

prebound *n.* Realising your current relationship is doomed, the act of beginning another one before finishing your old one, the better to facilitate a smooth changeover of services.

pre-cum *n.* Substance often referred to in the letters pages of *jazz mags* but rarely mentioned elsewhere. Certainly not on *You and Yours* on Radio 4. *Perseverance soup, dew on the lily, ball glaze.*

pre-emptive strike *n.* The act of emptying one's *shot pouch* a couple of hours before going into action so as to make the ensuing battle last a bit longer.

predator's face *n.* A somewhat unsettling vagina, which you would nevertheless not mind swinging a length of *wood* into.

preek *n. medic.* That fluid which is secreted from the *bishop's mitre* before *spoffage,* to lubricate the *gut stick. Ball glaze, tatty watter.* A contraction of *pre-cum.*

prefer one's peas minted *euph.* To be a *pastry chef.* Alluding to one who participates in the *burgling of turds.*

pregnot *adj.* Of a lady, to look like she's *up the duff* when she is, in fact, just *big-boned.* Particularly the stomach bone.

prehab *n.* That extended period of

being *heavily refreshed* which typically precedes a stopover in the Priory.

premature pinch *n.* The snipping off of an unsmoked *bum cigar* when disturbed in the act, by an important telephone call for example, or a fucking Jehovah's Witness knocking on the fucking door.

prepare for the wurst *exclam.* A romantic imprecation uttered to a lady by a gentleman just before he *slams in the lamb.*

prepare yesterday's lunch *v.* To go for a *shit.*

pressed ham *n.* The effect achieved by pushing one's naked *buttocks* onto the photocopier at the office Christmas party.

pressing matter *n.* An urgent *tom tit. 'No time to open the new parliamentary session today, I'm afraid, Lord Chancellor. I've got a pressing matter to attend to. By the way, you haven't seen this week's Autotrader anywhere, have you?'*

press the devil's doorbell *v.* To *flick the bean.*

presuptual agreement *n.* Legally binding drinking itinerary agreed at the beginning of an evening, eg. "Right, so we start at the red Lion, go on to the White Horse and finish at the Miner's Arms before having a magnificent Ruby Murray at the Curry Capital." As is the case with its ante-matrimonial contract counterpart, a presuptual agreement typically ends in a vicious fight and a costly court appearance.

prick *1. n.* A penis. *2. n.* A *twat, fuckwit*, fool. *3. n.* A life-threatening finger injury often suffered by fairy tale princesses. *4. n.* A small doctor with a hypodermic syringe.

prick-stick *n.* A white DIY glue in a handy tubular dispenser used solely to stick the pages of an *art pamphlet* together. *Man mastic.*

prick tease *n.* A woman who goads one's *penis* by calling it names.

priest's hole *1. n.* A cramped hiding place, usually behind the fireplace or under the floor in a large 17th century house, where fugitive Catholic clergymen could be concealed from the authorities. 2. n. A choirboy's *nipsy. 3. n.* A *minge* that's a tight squeeze. A *paper cut, pinhole, mouse's ear.*

pudcast *n.* A spot of *Frankie Vaughan* downloaded onto a video iPod.

pringle *1. n.* Yet another word for one who sniffs bicycle seats. A *snufty, snurglar, barumpher. 2. v.* To reach the point, when drinking, when one knows, realises and accepts that one is going to continue drinking until becoming unconscious. From the famous eponymous saddle-shaped crisp advertising slogan, *viz.* "once you pop, you just can't stop". *'We're on air in five minutes. Where's Moira?' 'I saw her in the bar at lunchtime, but she was already pringling then. Best see if you can find Huw instead, he's only had a couple.'*

prison pussy *n.* The *anus, mud pussy.*

prison vision *n. medic.* A condition brought on by prolonged abstinence from female company, which causes the sufferer to lower his standards considerably, finding almost any woman attractive. *Porridge goggles, Camp X-ray specs. 'When I came out after 27 years* *of predominantly solitary confinement, I was suffering from terrible prison vision. Shortly after my release, I remember being entertained by Her Majesty the Queen at Buckingham Palace, and getting a bit of a chirp-on when her mum bent over to pat a corgi. Truly, incarceration is a terrible thing.'* (from *The Long Walk to Freedom* by Nelson Mandela).

private fur *n.* A lady's *secret squirrel.*

privates *1. n.* Inoffensive unisex term for genitalia invented by the Women's Institute in 1904. At the opposite end of the rudeness scale to *fuckstick, bollocks* and *cunt. 2. n.* A double entendre enabling *Carry On* scriptwriters to confuse low-ranking soldiers with their *meat and two veg.*

probe and drogue *n. RAF.* Repeated attempts, whilst drunk, to achieve penetration. Named after the mechanism used for in-flight refueling.

probo *n.* One who makes a very comfortable living from vagrancy. A professional *Harold Ramp* with a mobile phone and a Rolls Royce parked round the corner, of the sort only ever encountered by the puce-faced letter-writers in the *Daily Mail.*

procrasturbation *n.* The act of repeated, and often pleasureless *self-love* brought on by the need to stave off more weighty tasks. *'For heaven's sake, Lester, stop procrasturbating and get your tax return filled in.'*

prodworthy *1. adj.* Of a fortunate young lady, deemed suitable for sexual relations by a man. *2. n. prop.* Ironic surname of the feminist Councillor played by June Whitfield in the film *Carry On Girls.*

profanigram *n.* The sort of selection of consonants and vowels which it would be nice to see Carol Vorderman pull out during the letters round of *Countdown, eg.* ssipflasp, rowneyeb *etc.*

professional outdoorsman *n.* A Ray Mears-type who drinks metal polish. A *Harold Ramp.*

Professor Pissflaps *n. prop.* An epithet given to a female who thinks she is more intelligent than the average bloke, *eg.* any *bird* who turns up on *Newsnight Late Review. 'Alright, Professor Pissflaps, you've had your say. Let some fucker else get a word in edgeways.'* (David Dimbleby to Germaine Greer, *BBC Question Time,* March 2002).

Professor Plum *1. n.* the purple-bodied player in a game of *Cluedo. 2. n.* The purple-headed player in a variety of bedroom games.

proles' royce *n.* A stretch limousine with a screeching gaggle of drunken teenage girls hanging out of the window.

prolog *n.* The *turtle's head.*

promance *n.* The sort of semi-regular relationship enjoyed with a specific *lady of the night.*

promise to oneself, on a *euph.* Of a gentleman, to be anticipating a spot of *rhythmic relaxation. 'Where are you off to, Otis? I thought we were going badger baiting.' 'Sorry lads, but I'm on a promise to myself.'*

promosexual *n.* One who is unnecessarily forward in promoting his homosexuality. Characterized by an unwelcome excess of exaggeratedly camp behavior. One who is forever banging on about being *good with colours.*

proof of purchase *n.* The sort of expensive, showy jewellery and expensive, showy vehicles bought for nubile blonde pieces by professional footballers.

prostitrout *n.* A good time girl who needs a bloody good wash.

protein shake *1. n.* Thickly-textured sports drink, freshly-prepared to help young men build muscle mass, and thus *2. n.* Gloopy *splod,* made from *plums* and thus rich in *vitamin S.*

proud mary *1. n.* A large Mississippi river boat. *2. n.* A lady's pronounced pubic mound. The *mons veneris, grassy knoll. 3. n.* A *bird's bits* that *keep on burnin'.* A *clapped-up clapping fish.*

prune juice *1. n.* Anal seepage. *2. n. Mabel syrup.*

prunetang *n.* A lady of considerably advanced years who has, by some unearthly means or other, managed to remain a bit of a looker, *eg.* Catherine Deneuve, Ginger Spice, Margaret Beckett. A *gilf*. A witty corruption of *poontang*, an American word for *blart.*

pruning the roses *euph.* To have *hairache*. Once used by the late Brian Clough as an excuse for non-attendance at Nottingham Forest matches in the 1980s/90s.

psychedelic yodelling *n.* Vocal projection of your *biscuits* out your *gob*.

pube dude *n.* Schoolboy phrase used to describe the kid in the playground who had a hairy chest and 4 o'clock shadow by the age of twelve. *'Oi, Venables. Stop drawing on that desk at once or I'll send you to the headmaster's office, you little pube dude.'*

pube farmer *n.* An unemployed person. A *doley.*

pube in an afro, looking for a *sim.* A crude variation on "looking for a needle in a haystack". Also, *looking for a baw hair in an afro (Scot)*.

pube lunch *n.* A tasty *bacon sandwich* with a token garnish of *gorilla salad*, served all day in a friendly atmosphere. *Cunch, fish dinner.*

pubic library *n.* An array of *flesh books* kept on top of a wardrobe for easy reference.

pubiquity *n.* The uncanny ability of stray strands of *gorilla salad* to turn up anywhere and everywhere, *eg*. on a bar of soap, between one's teeth, in the back of one's throat in the middle of the night, in McDonald's burgers, Mc-Donald's chicken nuggets, McDonald's thick shakes *etc*.

pub scarecrow *n.* The inhabitant of one's boozer who has the uncanny ability to frighten away the *birds.*

pub singer *n.* A solo performer, grunting and yodelling in a cubicle whilst *laying a cable.*

pub terrier *n.* A breed of small, yappy, unpredictable, aggressive though not necessarily dangerous, man whose presence makes one feel oddly uneasy. Found in most public houses in Britain.

PUD *acronym.* Post Urinal Drip. A *wet penny in the pocket.*

pud *1. n.* The *willy.* That which was always *pulled* by Ivor Biggun (aka Doc Cox of *That's Life* rude vegetable fame), in his *Wanking Song. 2. n.* An economically-drawn three-line graffito of the male genitalia.

pudding burner *n.* Slatternly lady who frequents pubs on a Sunday lunchtime when she should really be at home cooking a hearty traditional meal for her husband.

puddle, dropped in a *euph.* The state of a *bongo periodical* which has been subject to heavy and/or prolonged use. *'Christ. I wouldn't have lent you my Razzle if I'd have known it would come back in this state, George.' 'Yeah, I know. Sorry. I dropped it in a puddle.'*

puddle jumper *n.* A *fruit feeler, spud fumbler.*

pudendum *n.* Genital area. From Latin pudes = meat pie & dendum = two potatoes.

pud-whapper *n. US. Wanker*, jerkwad, an obnoxious person.

puff *1. v.* To exhale cigarette smoke. *2. n. prop.* Magic dragon that lived by the sea. *3. n.* A consumer *of fancy cakes.*

puff fluff *n.* An insufficiently-malodorous *dropped hat,* which calls the *farter's* sexual orientation into question. A *gaseous gay, botter burp.*

pugwash *n. Aus.* Cleaning of the teeth using *tapioca toothpaste* and a *naughty paintbrush*. A *blow job.*

puh-seh *n. US.* A *grumble flick* vagina. Something that a more-or-less tumescent *meat vid* thespian is generally keen to stick his *hampton* up.

puke *v.* To *spew.*

pull *1. v.* To *tap,* pick up members of the opposite sex. *'I pulled last night.'* 2. *n.* A spot of *self improvement. 'I didn't pull, so I went home, watched the free ten minutes of the Fantasy Channel and had a bit of a pull.'*

pull a pint on the piss pump *v.* To pour oneself a 5ml *hand shandy*.

pullaby *n.* Something which, when accompanied by a rhythmical rocking motion, soon brings on a state of contented slumber.

pull a train *v.* To take turns at *stirring the porridge*, to participate in a *gang bang*.

pulled the ripcord *euph.* Descriptive of a once svelte lady who has sadly ballooned like an inflatable raft and turned into a *bed breaker.*

pulletariat *n.* That class of society principally engaged in *monomanual labour.* The plebian social stratum that lives alone and watches *sockumentaries* whilst awaiting news of gainful employment. *Doleys, pube farmers.*

pullfilment *n.* The tired yet satisfied feeling a chap has after spending an evening perusing *seed catalogues* or watching *socktator sports*.

pulling power *n.* The strength of one's *fanny magnetism*.

pull off *1. v.* To manoeuvre a car away from the kerb. *2. v.* To drag a drunken friend away from a fight in which he has the upper hand, usually whilst shouting "It's not worth it" or "Leave it, he's had enough". *3. v.* To masturbate. *'I picked up a hitchhiker in and she offered to pull me off in my cab. I was so disgusted that I pulled over, strangled her and rolled her up in some carpet. Then I pulled myself off.'*

pull out and pray *n.* A method of contraception that is also a test of faith. Birth control as used by people with dozens of children. *Vatican roulette.*

pullseye *exclam.* Humorous ejaculation spoken by a fellow who has just successfully reduced his *bird's* field of vision by a factor of fifty percent.

pull the Pope's cap off *v.* To *bash the Bishop, box the Jesuit.*

pull the turkey's neck *v. Choke the chicken.* See *throttle the turkey.*

pull up to the bumper *v.* To *do* Grace Jones *up the shitter,* but only after she's asked you nicely.

pull your pud *1. v.* To *wank. 2. v.* To drag a dessert along in some sort of trailer.

pullympics *n.* Televised female sporting events that leave a certain type of male viewer in a somewhat more exhausted state than the participants, *eg.* beach volleyball, ladies' tennis, nude mud wrestling on the Playboy channel.

PUMA *acronym.* Pants Up My Arse. A specific reference to *cleftal* discomfort. *Hungry arse.*

pump *v.* To *fart, poot, pass wind, shoot bunnies, drop a rose petal.*

pump action mottgun *n.* An advanced, rapid-fire development of the *mutton musket. twelve bore popshotgun.*

pumper's lump *n. medic.* The condition of enhanced right forearm muscle due to excessive *wanking. Arnie's arms, hairy pieceps.*

pumping up the tyres *v.* Involuntary movement of the leg during the *vinegar strokes. Elvis's leg, Elvis tremble.*

pump up the jam *v.* To take a *cranberry dip.* To *stir the paint.*

punami *n.* In a bar, a tidal wave of binge-drinking *flange* out on a *slag night.* From punani + tsunami.

punani n. A lady's bits and bobs.

punani granny *n.* A significantly older woman who is none the less still worth one. A *gilf, lulu.*

punch above one's weight *1. v.* In boxing, to come out on top in a bout with a superior fighter. *2. v.* Of a gentleman, to succesfully *woo* a young lady whom he might ordinarily consider to be out of his class, *eg.* Les Dennis *pulling* Amanda Holden, anyone at all *pulling* Charlotte Church, Shane MacGowan *pulling* anyone at all. To *curl one in.*

punch its head in *v.* What a gentleman does to his *gentleman* when *relaxing in a gentleman's way.*

punch the clown *v.* To make *custard* shoot out the top of *Charlie Cairoli's hat.* To *wank.*

punch up the whiskers *n.* A *knee trembler* or similar romantic encounter in a train lavatory, taxi queue, Radio 5 lift or Building Society doorway.

punish *v.* To put one's ladyfriend *to the sword* in an enthusiastic manner. To administer a few strokes of the *old walking stick* to a *bird* who wants it really.

punk cock n. A *hampton* with multifarious piercings. A *knob* which is upsettingly bejewelled with chains, rings and pop rivets.

punks *rhym. slang.* Breasts. From punk rockers = knockers. *'Gonorrhoea was powerless to resist. His eyes burned into hers like topazzes. His strong arms enfolded her softly yielding body as she felt herself being swept away in a solar wind of passion. Before she had a chance to protest, he had whipped off her tit pants and started mucking about with her punks.'* (from *The Lady and the Powdered Egg Salesman* by Barbara Cartland).

puppies *n. Bubbies.* Affectionate euphemism for *thru'penny bits.*

Also *two puppies fighting in a bag*.

puppies' noses *n.* Little cold, wet nipples.

purple-headed womb broom *n.* See *purple-headed yoghurt warrior*.

purple-headed yoghurt warrior *n.* See *purple-headed womb broom*.

purple helmet *1. n. Pink Darth Vader*'s headgear, *bobby's helmet, German helmet, Roman helmet, bell end. 2. n.* Any member of the former Rover Aerobatic display team.

purple pearler *n.* An extendable icing tool for decorating pink blancmanges.

purse *n.* A *snapper*

push gas *v.* To *poot, let rip*.

push her guts in v. To have sex with a lady. *'Oh Joan Hunter Dunn / With your strong legs in shorts / Your boyish good looks / Your excelling at sports / Your long golden hair / Your ruby red lips / Let me push in your guts / Twixt the council dump skips.' (Joan Hunter Dunn* by John Betjeman).

pushing sauce *v.* The stage of coitus immediately after the *vinegar strokes, ie.* when the *yoghurt truck* has *crashed* and is in the act of *tipping out its filthy concrete.* Ejaculation. *'Bond and Fanny Akimbo made love on the silken sheets of the mini-sub's bed. Suddenly, the videophone crackled into life and the face of M appeared, seated at his familiar Whitehall desk. 'Ah, there you are 007. We've had reports that Blofeld is planning to blow up China with a big ray gun,' he said excitedly. 'I'm afraid I have my hands rather full at the moment, Sir,' replied Bond, raising a quizzical eyebrow. 'Call me back in about 10 minutes after I've pushed me sauce and zuffled me charlie."* (from *Goldtops and Goldfingers* by Ian Fleming).

push the envelope *1. v.* In test pilot circles, to test the aeronautical capabilities of a prototype aircraft. 2. *n.* In *pant shitting* circles, to *shit* one's *pants*.

push through *n.* the consequence of buying "Economy Brand" *bumwad. "Would you care for another scone, Father Brown', asked Lady Chelmshurst. 'Bless you, but thank you no,' replied the small priest, blinking owlishly and proffering a smelly digit towards his hostess's nose. 'I've just been to lay a cable and I fear I had a push through."* (from *Father Brown Points the Finger* by GK Chesterton).

pussy *1. n.* Of erswhile British TV sitcoms set in quiet, overstaffed department stores, a much-stroked pet cat frequently referred to by Mrs Slocombe. *2. n.* Molly Sugden's *cunt*.

pussy pelmet *n.* A short mini skirt, a *greyhound skirt*.

pussy poof *n.* A *todger dodger,* a *three wheeler,* a *tennis fan.* A lady who is *fond of walking holidays* in preference to having a penis pushed up her vagina.

put the baby to sleep *v.* To administer the rocking action which is often required to get a restless *baby's arm* to settle down at night. Or at lunchtime. Or halfway through the afternoon, and again twice before tea-time for that matter.

put one's mind to other things *euph.* To *give it six nowt* on one's *old walking stick.* To masturbate. *'Once settled in my cell, and in* *some comfort, I put my mind to other things. Into a sock.'* (from *Borstal Boy* by Brendan Behan).

put the handbrake on *v.* To *hide your pride* during an act of *self pollution* when rudely interrupted by an unwanted visitor, *eg.* your mum, your granny, the police *etc*.

put the red lights on *v. naval.* To have a silent *wank* in bed so as not to disturb one's wife. Also *silent running, American beauty.*

putting from the rough *v.* Golfing equivalent of *bowling from the pavilion end.*

putting toothpaste back in the tube *sim.* Descriptive of the difficulties encountered when attempting sexual congress whilst less than fully tumescent. *Thumbing in a slacky, playing snooker with string, pushing a marshmallow in a moneybox.*

put to the sword *v.* To make love to. *'From the Charing Cross Theatre, where I saw Mr Herbert give his Death of Icarus, to tea with the French Ambassador, and thence home to bed whereupon I put Mrs Pepys to the sword before settling down to sleep.'* (from *The Diary of Samuel Pepys*).

putz *n.* A yiddish *prick. Schlong.*

pygmies' cocks *n.* Erect nipples. *'Did you see Sharron Davies on Olympic Grandstand? She had jockeys like pygmies' cocks.'*

pyjama glue *n.* A handy starch-based adhesive, particularly useful for bonding and stiffening cotton fabrics. Also good for sticking together the pages of *tit catalogues,* the wife's eyelids *etc. Prick-stick.*

pyroclastic flow *n.* In curryology, an explosive outburst in which dust, rock, lager, vindaloo and hot, sulphurous gas are ejected from one's *crinkly crater* at high temperature and speed.

pyroflatulate *v.* To light one's *farts.* See also *afterburner, blue streak.*

pyropastie *n.* Excrement wrapped in newspaper, then set alight on next door's doorstep in the hope that the occupant will stamp it out.

Pythagoras piss *n.* Ancient Greek act of trigonometrical urination performed such that one's forehead is propped against the lavatory wall, and one's body consequently forms the hypotenuse of a right-angled triangle.

Pythonesque *1. adj.* Of humour, in the distinctive surrealist style of the groundbreaking programme *Monty Python's Flying Circus. 2. adj.* Of a gentleman's parts, *fucking* massive.

Qq

Q-tits *n. Fun bags* that are not what they appear to be, *ie.* ones that have been artificially enhanced by the use of padded *tit pants,* leading to disappointment after *unwrapping the meat.* Derived from Q-ship, a term used to describe warships disguised as civilian vessels in 20th century naval warfare, so actually the opposite meaning if you think about it.

quack *n. onomat.* A sudden sound emanating from one's *bills* when one *steps on a frog.*

quackamole *n.* A smooth, greenish paste occasionally produced after an over-ambitious clearance of the *nether throat.* Not suitable for dipping nachos into.

quacker *n.* Poetic epithet for a lady's *garden of delight.*

quail *n.* A tasty young *bird* who's game for anything.

Quaker, to bury a *v.* To *lay a cable. 'Do come in, Mr D'Arcy. Miss Bennet has just nipped upstairs to bury a Quaker. Would you care to wait in the drawing room until she has wiped her arse?'* (from *Pride and Prejudice*, by Jane Austen).

quakers *n. Oats.*

qualifications *n.* Breasts, *first impressions, competitive advantages. 'Admittedly her CV looks a bit thin, and her interview responses were somewhat lacklustre, but she has some excellent qualifications.'*

quality control *n.* The release of a small amount of *fart* to see how bad it is before releasing the rest. *Tasting the wine.*

quandong *1. n. Aus.* A difficult *lay*, a hard, as opposed to an easy, woman. One who wears armour-plated *knickers*. *2. n.* A prostitute, *hooker, ho'.*

quarter pounder *1. n.* An unacceptably thin woman. *2. n.* An unacceptably fat *shit.*

quaynte *n.* Chaucerian *placket.*

quaz *n.* An ugly half-human *wanker,* a *bell end* ringer. Abbreviation of Quasimodo.

Quebec Bravos *n.* Metropolitan Police phonetic radio code. QBs = Quality Breasts, used by bored *scuffers* on Saturday night city centre duty. *'Calling all units, calling all units. Quebec Bravos in the High Street. Any units wish to assist? Over.'*

queef *n. Can.* A *Lawley kazoo,* a *hat dropped forward,* a *flap raspberry.* Also *kweef.*

queen n. A person who is raving *good with colours.*

Queen Amidala's lipstick *n. Chod bin* seat *skidmark* named after its resemblance to the *Phantom Menace* character's bizarrely-applied *gob* make-up.

Queen Mum's smile n. A *pan smile.* The staining on the lavatory carpet created by years of *pissing like an American pilot*

Queensway *n.* A regular mammoth rectal stock clearance where *everything must go. Next sale.*

queer *1. adj. pre-1960.* Odd, peculiar. *2. n. post-1960.* A *ginger beer. 3. adj. post-1960. Colwyn Bay.*

queerdo *n.* A strange homosexualist, *eg.* Pete "Dead or Alive" Burns.

quiche *1. n. Taint, notcher, barse,* whatever. *2. n . Puff's pizza.*

quickie *n.* A swift bout of intercourse that one often fancies in the same way that one fancies a cup of tea. A hurried *one. 'Oh, it's half time. Do you fancy a quickie,* *love?' 'Er... go on, then. But stick the kettle on first.'*

quim *n.* Refined word for the *mapatasi* such as a gentleman might use at a hay clarse cocktail party. From the Welsh cwm = valley beneath the 13 amp fuse wire.

quimbecile *n.* A stupid fellow who is also a *cunt, eg.* "Lord" Jeffrey Archer.

quimble *n.* A tremor of excitement in a *bird's snatch.* A *fanny gallop.* From quim + tremble.

quimbledon *euph.* Any ladies' sporting event watched by gentlemen who are paying little attention to the scores. *'Where's me socks, love? Maria Sharapova's playing Serena at Quimbledon.'*

quim bling *n.* Ladies' genital jewelry. *Mufflinks, curtain rings.*

quimby *n.* The middle person in a *threesome,* the filling in a sex sandwich. See also *lucky Pierre.*

quim chin *n. Muff mouth, cunty chops.* A bearded fellow. *'Did you see Noel Edmonds on telly last night? What a stupid fucking quim chin.'*

quiminals *n.* Prison lesbians. *Queen bees.*

quim pro quo *n. Lat.* An ancient Roman *blarter* system where goods and services are exchanged for *gash. Hairy cheque book.*

quimle *v.* To eat *hairy pie.*

quimple *n.* One of them chin dimples that looks quite like a *fanny.* As sported by Martin Kemp, Kirk Douglas and Katie Melua. From Quite like a fanny + Dimple.

quim reaper *n.* A fellow who harvests more than his fair share of *meat harps.*

quimpotent *adj.* Descriptive of a frigid lady who is unable to reach the required level of sexual arousal required by the gentleman.

quim strings *n.* Imaginary internal female organs, resembling *Coronation Street* Deirdre's neck, that tighten in stressful situations. *'Bob Cratchit raised his glass. 'To Mr Scrooge, the founder of the feast', he said cheerily. 'Ha! Founder of the feast indeed,' screeched his wife. 'Why, I'll no sooner drink a toast to him that I would the devil himself, the mean-hearted, penny-pinching, tight-arsed...' 'Now, now, Sara,' interrupted Bob. 'Don't go snapping your quim strings. It's Christmas day, and we shall drink to Mr Scrooge."* (from *A Christmas Carol* by Charles Dickens).

quimwedge *v.* To *do it* with a lady.

quince *1. n. Aus.* A mincing *queen.* *2. n.* Something that owls and pussycats eat with a runcible spoon.

quoit *n. Ring, hoop, rusty sheriff's badge, balloon knot, tea towel holder.* That which gets *tossed* on a ship.

quornography *1. n.* Softcore vegetarian pornography, *ie.* no *meat.* 2. n. Any photographic or video imagery where the principal female subject is gaining pleasure from using a *fanny hammer,* that is to say a "meat substitute".

quumf *v.* To sit in waiting outside a public library and take the opportunity to sniff ladies' bicycle seats as soon as possible after their owner has dismounted and gone inside. To *barumph, snurgle, moomph, scrunge.*

Rr

rabbit *n. Her indoors, giving it this.* Major cause of *GBH of the ear-hole.*

rabbit pie *n.* The *faff.*

rabbit's chops, arse like a *sim.* Descriptive of the unsettling twitching of the *blood orange* when one is in imminent need of an *Eartha.*

rabbit's tail *n.* The split second flash of white cotton gusset caught in one's peripheral vision when a lady crosses her legs at the other side of a waiting room.

rabid dog, fanny like a *sim.* A *clown's pie, cappuccino twat, fish drowner.*

race snails *v.* Of a gentleman and former Conventry City manager, to drive very slowly close to the kerb in order to ask directions from a prostitute after becoming lost in a red light district.

racing dog's bollocks on a frosty morning *sim.* Descriptive of the state of one's eyes the morning after a heavy night *on the turps, eg.* hungover chef Keith Floyd. *Eyes like sheep's cunts.*

rack *n.* Female mammarial display, collectively the *tits, funbags. 'She's got a lovely rack on her. Very well presented. And nips like a fighter pilot's thumbs.'*

rackattack *exclam.* Secret gentlemen-only phrase that can used to surreptitiously alert one's companions to an approaching feast of *eye magnets. 'So, before we move on to the evening dress section, let's see all the lovely contestants in their swimsuits for one last time... Fuck me, rackattack!'* (Michael Aspel, presenting the Miss World Contest, BBC TV, 1973).

Radcliffe *n.* A car that at first sight looks like a good runner, but ends up completely *fucked* at the side of the road after about fifteen miles.

Radcliffe, do a *1. v.* To fail to finish a pint. *2. v.* To give up three quarters of the way through a pub crawl, fall in a gutter, and have a bit of a cry.

radge *1. v.* To become furious, to lose one's *blob. 2. n.* A furious episode that a person "takes" or "throws". *'This little bairn puked on us, so I took a fuckin' radge.'* (Mother Teresa of Calcutta). *3. n. adj.* In a state of *radge.*

radgey *n.* One who is predisposed to taking or throwing *radges.*

radio rental *rhym. slang. Radgy, hatstand,* mental.

RAF *abbrev.* Rough As Fuck. Particularly ugly or unattractive.

rafcam *acronym.* Rough As Fuck, Common As Muck.

rag and bone man *n.* One who doesn't mind getting a *barber's pole* now and again.

rag doll *n.* A tasty-looking *tart* that is temporarily *off the menu.*

ragman's coat *n.* A *turkey's wattle,* a *raggy blart,* a *pound of liver,* a *club sandwich.* An untidy vagina.

ragman's trumpet *n.* A capacious *fanny. Big Daddy's sleeping bag.*

ragtop *1. n.* A convertible motor car. *2. n.* An uncircumcised *charlie, aardvark's nose.*

rag week *1. n.* Seven days during which students get *pissed* and behave like *cunts* in the name of charity. *2. n.* Time of the month when the *flags are out. Blob week.*

railway sleeper *n.* The largest, firmest and most angular *Thora* known to mankind, which makes a *dead otter* look like a minor *follow through.*

rainbow yawn *n. Puke,* a *technicol-*

our laugh, pavement pizza, a *sung rainbow*.

raindance *n.* The Native American-style rhythmical stamping moves made by the feet of one with a full *beer sack* as he tries to get his keys in the front door following a night *on the pop*.

rainman *n.* A woman with phenomenal mental capacity, who can commit to memory every single male misdemeanor committed throughout the duration of a relationship. These are then regurgitated *ad nauseam* during arguments or for guilt trip purposes, emotional blackmail *etc*.

raise 'n' gaze *n.* Charming male quirk. In the newsagents, the unavoidable and instinctive act of lifting one's eyes and checking out the top shelf *jazz periodicals*.

raisin *n.* The *corn dot, freckle*.

raisin bag *n.* The *nut sack, clackerbag, hairy pod purse, John Wayne's hairy saddlebags*.

raisin factory *euph.* An old people's home. From the fact that senior citizens are left there to dry out and wrinkle before being shipped out in a small box.

rake the cage out *v.* To *build a log cabin*, give birth to a *Richard*.

Ralph *onomat.* To vomit. Also *call Huey*.

Rambo'd *adj.* So *pissed* that one believes that one can take on any amount of people in the car park and win.

ram job *n.* Vatican-approved, conventional heterosexual sex, as opposed to a *blow job, hand job or Hawaiian muscle fuck*. A *knob job*.

rammadanny *n.* An enforced monthly *Jacky Danny* fast.

ram raiding on a scooter *adj.* Descriptive of less than attractive women. '*She was a worthy woman, yette sore ugglie, with a face lyke shede been ramme-raidynge onn a scooter.*' (from *The Miller's Tale* by Geoffrey Chaucer).

ram shackled *adj.* Engaged in the act of *botting*.

RAM sleep. *n. abbrev.* The phase prior to deep sleep. Rapid Arm Movement.

randy *n.* Cowboy version of *horny*.

Rangoon ring *n. medic.* Curry-induced blistering of the *nipsy*. A *Wigan rosette, Japanese flag, Johnny Cash, Hawaiian sunrise*.

rantallion *n. 18thC.* One whose *shot pouch* is longer than the barrel of his *fouling piece*.

rascal wrapper *n. French letter, blob, rubber johnny, cheesepipe clingfilm*.

raspberries in syrup *sim.* The consistency of *shit* after a night *on the hoy*. The kind that makes you pull a face like Kenneth Williams going "Ooh, Matron!"

raspberry *rhym. slang.* Break wind. From raspberry tart = fart. '*Did you just drop a raspberry?*' '*Yes. And when I bent down to pick it up, I farted and it fucking stinks.*'

Rasputin *n.* An unkempt vaginal or anal beard.

rat *n.* A lady's *bodily treasure*. The *parts of shame*. '*Excreta was powerless to resist. His eyes burned into hers like sequins. His strong arms enfolded her tender body as she felt herself being swept away in an Aurora Borealis of passion. Then he said the words her heart had ached to hear for so long. 'Giz a quick shot on your rat, love. I* *want to catch last orders.*" (from *The Lady and the Disgraced Former Manchester United and Northern Ireland Footballer* by Barbara Cartland).

rat arsed *adj. Shit faced.*

rat catcher's bait box *n.* An unpleasant tasting *fanny.* A *nine volter, crabby patty.*

rat killer *n.* A foul *turd* capable of exterminating any pipe-dwelling rodent within a mile of the S-bend.

rat's cocks! *exclam.* Expression of extreme disappointment. Drat, confound it, curses, *etc. "My God!' the boatswain cried. 'What has happened to the ship?' 'The Pequod has been stove in by a Leviathan, a Great White Whale!' replied the helmsman, scarce able to comprehend the enormity of his own words. 'Rat's cocks,' yelled Ahab. 'That's fucking torn it!"* (from *Moby Dick* by Herman Melville).

rat's nose *n.* An inquisitive bit of *poo* poking out of the *nipsy* to see if the coast's clear. *'FX: DOOR OPENS, BUCKET CLANKS. Mrs Mopp: There you go, Mr Handley. Your smallest room's as clean as a chinaman's chopsticks. Tommy Handley: Thank Christ for that, Mrs Mopp. I've been stood out here three quarters of a fucking hour with the rat's nose. FX: RUNNING FOOTSTEPS, DOOR OPENS AND CLOSES, ZIP, FOGHORN, SOUND OF LARGE SHIT HITTING WATER. Orchestra: Signature tune to finish.'* (Script of *It's That Man Again*, broadcast on the BBC Home Service, March 1942).

rat stance *n.* Characteristic, hunched standing position adopted by a fellow who is having a spot of *hand to gland combat* in a shower. *'So there I was in the rat stance, I'd got to the jester's shoes and she walked in on the vinegar strokes. Nothing could stop me by then.'*

rattle and hum *1. n.* Title of a 1987 documentary about Bonio and his pop group. *2. n.* A loud and obnoxious-smelling visit to the *cackatorium* when, if it is the weekend and you have had a heavy night and a curry, you may find yourself singing *Sunday Bloody Sunday.*

Ravi Shankar *rhym. slang.* A gentleman who plays a small, pink sitar.

Ray Mears trying to start a fire, going at it like *sim.* Descriptive of a very energetic and vigorous session of tugging and rubbing at one's *twig,* which is reminiscent of the tubby TV nettle-chomper attempting to instigate an *al fresco* conflagration without using matches. *'Oi, mind me bloody banjo string there love. You're going at it like Ray Mears trying to start a fire.'*

razz *v.* To *hoy up, puke.*

Razzle *n. prop.* An unpretentious, no-nonsense *jazz mag.* In its own words "The magazine that makes your cock go big".

Razzle dazzle *1. n. Porn glare. 2. n.* Temporary blindness caused by a particularly nasty *growler shot* in a *self help book.*

Razzle stack *n.* The fondly-remembered, and deeply erotic tabeau in the said *art pamphlet,* featuring six vertically-arranged *quims.* Now sadly banned due to the regular near-suffocation of the lowermost participant.

Razzlet *n.* A slightly overweight,

not too bright female, whose only hope of escaping her humdrum existence is to appear in cheap 'n' cheerful *bongo mags*.

reach around *n*. In *botting*, pouring your partner a *hand shandy* whilst *ram shackled*.

reading Cosmo *euph*. Of a lady, to be absorbed in one of her regular *monthly periodicals*. To be *dropping clots, up on blocks, on her rags etc. 'Fancy a quickie, babe?' 'Nah. I'm reading Cosmo this week,'* or indeed *'I'm getting worried, love. Cosmo hasn't been delivered yet. It's nearly a fortnight late.'*

Reading Hoover *n*. Foot used to clean the carpet by grinding in the dirt until it vanishes. Named after the houseproud Berkshire town. *'Oh no, I've knocked the ashtray over.' 'No problem, love. I'll use the Reading Hoover on it.'*

reading the Financial Times *n*. Performing *cumulonimbus* on a particularly large, loose-lipped, pink *clopper*.

reading the paper *v*. To examine one's used toilet tissue to catch up on the latest news of one's anal health. To peruse the *rusty bulletin*.

readybrek glow *n*. The fuzzy, red outline surrounding everyone on a 6th generation copy of a *stick vid*. *Porn fuzz*.

Ready, Steady, Wank *n*. A game of skill based on the popular, similarly-named cookery show. The competitor has just half an hour and the most unpromising of materials (a month-old copy of *Chat, Murder She Wrote* on the telly *etc*.) to *crack one out*.

reality wank *n*. A *toss* over someone one could *poke* in real life, therefore making it better and more realistic. Likely subjects include one's girlfriend, the local *bike* or Sonya off *EastEnders*.

rear admiral *n*. A sailor who prefers to navigate the *Windward passage*.

rear goggles *n*. Notably unreliable mechanism whereby one fondly imagines the front elevation of a woman merely by assessing her rearward appearance.

rear gunner *n*. In aviation terms, a marksman who shoots one of his own side by firing his *lamb cannon* into their *bomb bay*.

rearotica *n*. *Seed catalogues* for *uphill gardeners*.

rear tits *n*. The fleshy parts of the body that hang over the *titpant lashing straps* of ladies with *nice personalities*. *Gwats*.

receiver of swollen goods *n*. Someone involved in a nefarious transaction with a *bum bandit*.

rectal retort *n*. A witty *fart*.

rectoplasm *n*. A message from the other side which makes everybody's hair stand on end. Something that comes out of your *bum* which is so scary it makes you *shit* yourself. A *McArthur Park*.

rectospect *n*. The realisation that, with hindsight, something was a bit *arse*.

red alert *exclam*. Discreet *sotto voce* warning exchanged between males, advising each other to tread carefully around the lady of the house/office due to her having *women's things*. Also *code red*.

red ring *n*. Inflammation of the *chocolate starfish* as a result of being *skittered*. See *Japanese flag*.

red sock, arse hanging out like a *sim. medic*. Descriptive of a full rectal prolapse. Such as one caused by a deliciously fatal plate of Curry Hell, the hottest curry in the world. Exclusively available at the Curry Capital, Bigg Market, Newcastle upon Tyne, the only restaurant to receive the coveted 5 Prolapses award in the *Viz Good Curry Guide*.

red tie *n.* To finish oneself off with a *sausage sandwich* after having had enough of the *cranberry dip*.

red wings *n.* Dubious honour bestowed upon one who eats *haddock pastie* during *rag week*.

refecate *v.* To fill one's bowels by eating *crap*. *'The missus has had me on a veggie diet all week, so I'm just popping along to Maccy D's to refecate.'*

refreshed *adj. Fucking mortal.*

refusal *1. n.* In show-jumping, when a horse approaches the fence but only briefly puts its nose over the bar instead of jumping. *2. n.* In *shitting*, when a reluctant *Sir Douglas* pokes its nose out of the *ringpiece* for a second before, despite Herculean efforts from the toiletee, returning back to the warmth and safety of the *dirt bakery*.

reggae like it used to be *n.* Masturbation. Wearing a bowler hat.

relax in a gentleman's way *v. euph.* To *interfere with oneself* down there. *'Scrooge pulled up his nightshirt, tucked it under his whiskery old chin and began relaxing in a gentleman's way, trying hard to conjour up a mental picture of Mrs Cratchit in the rik. Suddenly the room was filled with an eerie light, and there before him stood the second spirit, the spirit of Christmas Present.'* (from *A Christmas Carol* by Charles Dickens).

release the chocolate hostage *v.* To liberate *Richard the Third* after his incarceration in one's *chamber of horrors*.

release the handbrake *v.* To *drop a gut* into your hand and then present it into your friend's face for his olfactory delectation. To offer a *cupcake*.

release the hounds *n.* To empty one's *arse*.

remaster the back catalogue *1. v.* In the world of pop music, to re-release an artiste's old records with slightly different covers. *2. v.* To enjoy a romantic interlude up an old flame.

remould *n. Rubber, single finger Marigold glove, blob.*

re-offender *1. n.* In the world of probation officers and their clients, a little shit that keeps appearing over and over again. *2. n.* In the world of going to the toilet, a buoyantly recalcitrant *thirty-three-and-a-third* that re-surfaces repeatedly after flushing.

rerack *1. v.* In snooker, pool or billiards, to use a triangular frame to re-arrange the balls on the table at the start of a game. *2. v.* To surgically improve a woman's *headlamps*. *'No way those bad boys are real, Detective Inspector. She's been reracked for sure.' 'You might be right, doctor. Anyway, let's cover them up and we'll get the husband in to see if he can positively identify her.'*

research a book *v.* To look at *Frankie Vaughan* beamed in from the more *glittery* reaches of cyberspace.

reserve chute *1. n.* In the world of sky-diving, a secondary canopy which can be deployed in the event that the first one fails to open properly. *2. euph.* The *arsehole. 'Woman in hotel bed wearing a corset and bridal veil, and with a 'Just Married' suitcase on the floor: 'Sorry, love. I'm on me rags. You'll have to use the reserve 'chute.' Red-nosed man in a top hat who is removing* his trousers: 'Geronimo!" (postcard by Donald McGill from *Bamforth's Funny Seaside Chuckles Series,* circa 1936).

restoration fund *1. n.* Appeal run by your local vicar who, despite the fact that the Church of England has an investment fund totalling several trillion pounds, has no money to fix a couple of tiles back on his roof. *2. n.* Whatever's left in your wallet after a night *on the pop,* which can be used the next day to buy aspirin, water, a fry-up, the hair of the dog or whatever else is required so you can rejoin the human race. *'I went out with a hundred quid, but there's only sixteen pee in the restoration fund.'*

retain water *v.* Of a *plumper,* to eat lots of cake.

retch *v.* To vomit, but with more noise and less *puke.*

retox *n.* The opposite of a detox, undergone by offshore workers after a two-week alcohol-free shift on the rigs. *'That trip was shit, Dave. I'm hitting the boozer for a retox.'*

retrosexual *n.* One who has sexual intercourse with someone from his or her past, *eg.* a former friend from school, college, prison, chapel of rest *etc.*

return fire *n.* A cold, sniping splash of *chod bin* water that darts straight up one's *wrinkled penny* while *bombing China. Splashback.*

return serve *n.* The reappearance of a *turd* you thought you had seen the last of.

reveille *n.* An early morning *brass eye* fanfare delivered with military precision, that makes your company jump out of bed.

reverse cowgirl *n.* A *cowgirl* who has been bucked through 180 degrees, a sexual position much favoured by *meat vid* cinematographers as one can see it *going in.* A *fucking bronco.*

reverse Doagan *n. NZ.* A *chocolate hostage* released into the *chod bin* whilst sitting the wrong way round, leaving a breathtaking *skidmark vista* for the next unfortunate lady patron of the toilet.

reverse elephant *n.* What happens when one has *flown right past Dresden* without managing to locate a lavatory. A large *Thora* hanging out of one's *bomber aris,* creating the illusion when viewed from the rear of a pink-eared, brown-trunked pachyderm.

reverse peach *n.* A rearward elevation of a lady's *parts of shame,* such that they resemble a ripe and juicy, fuzzy pink fruit.

reverse rucksack *n.* A large *abdominal holdall,* used by the *lard of the manor* for storing all the pies.

reverse thrust *n.* The act of *getting off at Edge Hill.* The *interruptus* of one's *coitus.*

RFHTFH *abbrev.* Phrase applied to eastern European women, or a fat lass in a Sheffield bun shop. Rather Fuck Her Than Fight Her.

rhino horn *n.* A well-matted tarantula among *arse spiders.* Definitely not an aphrodisiac.

rhythm and blues *n.* Viagra-enhanced *art appreciation* for the mature gentleman.

rhythm mag *n. Jazz mag, scud book, art pamphlet,* one-handed reading material.

rhythm section *1. n.* In a pop group, the bass and drums. *2. n.* In a newsagent's, the shelf where they put the *jackage. 3. n.* In a *jazz mag,* the mucky pictures of bare ladies as distinct from the textual padding.

rhythm stick *n.* The late Ian Dury's *cock.* The *sixth gear stick, joy stick, copper stick, giggle stick, blood stick. Slag bat.*

rib *n.* The missus, her indoors. From the children's fairy story *Adam and Eve.*

rib cushions *n. Dirty pillows.* Breasts.

Richard *rhym. slang.* A stool. From Richard the Third = turd. *'I've just given birth to a ten pound Richard. Ooh, my poor ringpiece!'*

Rich Tea quickie *n.* A sexual encounter which is reminiscent of the act of dipping one of the popular biscuits in one's tea, *ie.* a solitary dunk followed swiftly by a disappointing collapse.

Rick Stein's bin *n.* Derogatory phrase implying that a lady's *bodily treasure* smells not unlike the celebrated fish-chef's dustbin. *'No offence, Cilla, but I'm going to have to call it a day. It's like Rick Stein's bin down here.'*

riddle of the sphincter *n.* A mysterious *Bakewell tart* that make your nose fall off.

ride *v.* That which one does to a *bike.*

rider's block *n.* To irretrievably lose *wood* half way through intercourse as a result of a sudden, unexplained nasty sexual image entering the mind, *eg.* Jack Duckworth doing *oral* on his wife Vera while Ivy Tilsley *bobs* him with a *strap-on.*

ride the baloney pony *v. US.* To *wank.*

ride the clutch *1 v.* To teeter on the brink of the *vinegar strokes* in an effort to prolong the act of coitus. *2. v.* To maintain the hovering state between releasing the *pace car* and making *skidmarks* on one's underpants. To rein back the *turtle's head.* To *fight a rearguard action.*

ride the dirtbike *v.* To partake in a bit of *backdoor action.*

ride the great white knuckler *v.* To have *one o'er the thumb.*

ride the porcelain bus *v.* To be suffering from the *Engelberts.*

ride the waves *v.* To poke an amply proportioned lady. See also *moped. 'It's not as bad as you might think, if you just slap the fat and ride the waves.'*

riding sidesaddle *n.* Descriptive of the *mincing* trot much favoured by men who are *good with colours.* The kind of gait adopted by Mr Humphries when he was summoned by Captain Peacock.

right hand cream *n.* Hand and face moisturiser made from a special blend of *nut oils.*

rigid digit *n.* An erect penis, *bone, bonk on.*

rik, the *n.* That which a bare person is in. The *nuddy.*

Rigsby *n.* A no-handed urination of such vigorous release and force that the hands can be safely placed on the hips for its duration.

rim *1. n.* Circumference of the *anus. 2. v.* To *go around the world.* Looking for a shop selling extra strong mints.

rim job *n.* A bout of *bummilingus.*

rim shot *1. n.* That thing the drummer does after David Letterman has read out a joke. *Bahdumb bahdish. 2. n.* When having a *pony and trap,* the deeply regrettable experience of inadvertently directing a stream of urine under the seat, but over the rim of the *chod bin,* soaking one's *hoggers.*

ring *1. n. Hole, jacksie, anus, brown eye, chocolate starfish. 2. n.* Confusingly, also the *fadge.*

ring bandit *n.* A *fruit feeler.*

ringbinder *1. n.* A notebook containing spring-loaded clamps for the purpose of holding loose sheets of paper. *2. n.* An exceptionally tenacious *arse baby* which necessitates repeated wiping before the *freckle* is even vaguely free of *bum chutney.* A *Marmite pot.*

ring burner *n.* An exceptionally hot curry prepared for the entertainment of the waiters and kitchen staff in Indian restaurants.

ringcraft *1. n.* A generic term covering the multitude of techniques, moves and tactics associated with the ancient and noble art of boxing. *2. n.* A generic term covering the multitude of techniques, moves and tactics associated with the ancient and noble art of *giving someone one up the council gritter.*

ringlets *n.* A young lady's anal beard.

ring master *1. n.* The master of ceremonies at a circus. *2. n.* An expert *botter.*

ringmaster's dog *n.* A sexually experimental and enthusiastic lady who shocks even the most seasoned lover with her willingness to perform strange and exotic acts, *ie.* one who "knows more tricks than a ringmaster's dog".

ringpiece *n.* A *Samantha Janus.*

ring pirate *n.* A renegade *rear admiral.*

ring rusty *1. adj.* Descriptive of an ageing pugilist who has not fought for quite some time. *'Prince Naseem Hamed, the ring-rusty boxer, was yesterday jailed for fifteen months by a judge at Sheffield Crown Court.'* (from the *Yorkshire Post,* May 13th 2006). *2. adj.* Descriptive of someone who has abstained from giving or taking it *up the back garden* for a while. *'Prince Naseem Hamed of E-wing is no longer ring-rusty, according to sources close to the former boxer's showering companions.'* (from the gossip column, *Wakefield Prison News,* May 16th 2006). *3. adj.* Descriptive of one who has gone through a prolonged period of constipation.

ringside seats, have *v.* To be *turtling* something rotten. To have a heavyweight *mole at the counter.*

rings of sat-on *n.* The bright red semi-circular marks left imprinted on a man's thighs and buttocks after a long and satisfying session of study in the *bog library.*

ringstinct *n.* A mysterious seventh sense that tells a *farter* to wait until he is safely ensconced on the *chod bin,* thus preventing *follow through* in his *scads.*

ring sting *n. medic. Soreness* of the *seventh planet.*

ring stinger *n.* A *Ruby Murray* that induces *ring sting* and leaves one with an *arse* like *a Japanese flag.*

ring the bell *v. Pop the cork,* detonate the *fanny bomb.*

ring the waterboard *exclam.* A humorous announcement made following the birth of a particularly hefty *toilet baby. 'Oi love. You'd better ring the waterboard and tell them to get the big knives out at the shit farm to chop that one up.'*

ringtone *n.* A *fart.*

ring worm *n.* A *shirtlifter's Jimmy Wonkle.*

rinky dink *1. n.* Stink, that unpleasant odour created by a *fyst, Richard the Third's BO. 2. adj.* Descriptive of the Pink Panther.

rinse the lettuce *v.* To wash the *beef curtains, in situ* as it were. Female equivalent of a *gentleman's wash.*

Rio *n.* A bald *cunt* with wavy lips, often seen in the "Readers' Wives" pages of *bongo mags,* or on the pitch at Old Trafford.

ripped out fireplace *n.* A *butcher's dustbin.*

ripped sofa *n.* A *badly-packed kebab.*

ripped to the tits *adj.* Inebriated using drink and drugs. Also *whipped to the tits.*

ripping up rags *sim.* Descriptive of the sound of a long drawn out *fart.*

rise from the dead *v.* To achieve a *bone on* by looking at erotic pictures of women who have since passed on, *eg.* Marilyn Monroe, Jayne Mansfield or Hattie Jacques, *etc.*

rising main *n.* In pubic plumbing, the *tatty watta* supply pipe usually fed in through the vagina. The *main cable.*

riveting stick *rhym. slang. Dick.* From the jeweller's instrument.

road apples *n.* Horse *shit.*

roadhead *n. US.* Hitch hiker's currency. An act of *horatio* performed in return for a lift.

roadkill *n.* A rather flat, dry, *hedgehog.*

roadkill ruby *n.* A curry containing meat of dubious provenance.

road less travelled, the *1. n.* Title of a poem by Robert Frost, which has been interpreted as a declaration of the importance of personal freedom. *2. euph.* The *back passage.* A tasteful and cultured turn of phrase which can usefully be employed whilst subtly suggesting to one's ladyfriend that she might like to *turn over a new leaf.*

road thrill *n.* An *art pamphlet* which has been discarded in a layby by a trucker.

road to Grimsby *n.* The *farse, tinter, carse etc, etc.* The bit between a lady's *front* and *back bottoms.* So called because there's always a whiff of fish and it's not far from a *shit-hole.*

roast chicken *n.* Any member of a one woman/two premiership footballers configuration who gets cold feet at the last minute.

roast ghost *n.* An *air buffet* that is not suitable for vegetarians.

robbing the date locker *n.* The burgling of *turds.*

Robin Cook's beard *n.* A sparsely-vegetated ginger *minge.* A *grated carrot,* a *council twat.*

robocrap *n.* The ominous feeling in the lower bowel which leaves a fellow in no doubt that he only has "twenty seconds to comply".

rock around the cock *n.* For any number of reasons, a quantity of seaside confectionary strewn about the male genitals.

rock candy *n.* An effeminate, yet intimidating fellow. A *muscle Mary.*

rocket polisher *n.* An over-enthusiastic cleaning of the *pocket rocket* leading to detonation on the launchpad. And *spunk* everywhere.

rocket socket *n*. Vagina.

rocket strap *n*. The waist band of the *undercrackers* when used to tether the *old man* discreetly upwards to allow a be-*travel-fatted* fellow to alight decorously from the bus.

Rockfords *rhym. slang. Arse grapes, Nobbies, Emmas, Michaels, farmers, ceramics, Chalfonts*. From the TV series *The Rockford Piles*.

rock poodle *n*. A lightweight heavy metallurgist, complete with long shaggy hair and puffed-up leather jacket.

rocks *1. n.* Masses of hard, stony matter, esp. an extensive formation of such matter. *2. n.* Big, hairy *bollocks. 3. n.* Those which one "gets off" whilst *on the job*.

Rocky press-ups *n*. The act of *wanking* in the shower, pulling on one's genitalia with one hand whilst using the other one to lean against the wall for balance. The aquatic sinner ends up looking vaguely reminiscent of Mr Balboa doing one of his impressive one-armed, biceps-building exercises.

rod *n. Spam sceptre*.

Rod Hull's roof, as wet as *adj*. Descriptive of a sexually-excited lady; one who is *frothing like bottled Bass. 'Septicaemia was powerless to resist. His eyes burned into hers like 18-carrot diamond-cut Moissanites™. His muscular arms enfolded her body as she felt herself being swept away on an El Niño of passion. She could wait no longer. 'Take me now, Kendo,' she panted. 'Me cunt's as wet as Rod Hull's roof.''* (from *The Lady and the All-In Wrestler* by Barbara Cartland).

Rodney *n. prop. rhym. slang*. Convoluted term for a *shite,* named after the mediocre Australian fast bowler Rodney Hogg, whose name rhymes with *bog. 'Where've you been, Olivia?' 'In the dunny having a Rodney, Cliff.'*

Rod Stewart's disease *n. medic. Rabbit tods*. Named after the gravel-throated veteran crumpeteer's early band the Small Faeces.

rod the drains v. To *back scuttle*.

rod walloper *n*. One who *gives it sixnowt on the old walking stick*.

rodeo sex *n*. A borderline-illegal bedroom game where the couple adopt the *doggy position*. The gentleman then calls out an ex-girlfriend's name and sees how long he can stay on for. Also *bronco sex*.

rogan splosh *n*. An incredibly runny *shit,* accompanied by a fusilade of splattering *farts* the morning after a *roadkill ruby*.

roger *v*. To *fuck*. Often in the past tense. *'I gave her a jolly good rogering.'*

roger ramjet *n*. A *botter*.

Roland Kirk *1. n. prop.* A jazz musician (1936-1977) rightly lauded for his ability to get a tune out of two or more horns simultaneously, and thus *2. euph.* A *jazz actress* rightly lauded for her ability to get a tune out of two or more *horns* simultaneously.

Rolf Harris eating a banana *sim*. Descriptive of the close-up intercourse scenes in a very blurred, 200th generation *scruff video*.

Rolfies *n*. The pseudo-Aboriginal gasps and grunts produced when trying to pass an extremely large *didgeridoo.*

rolling down the hill *euph.* Of a *custard,* to make its way under its own steam down the guts towards the *chuff. 'I'd open a window if I was you, your Holiness. Only I had Chicken Tonight and six pints of homebrew for tea yesterday, and I can feel one rolling down the hill.'*

rolling the dice *n. Feeding the ducks, spanking the monkey.*

rolling thunder *n.* An overlong *air buffet* served up whilst walking past a line of people, such as would be dropped by Her Majesty the Queen backstage at the Royal Variety Performance.

roll in the hay *n.* What everyone wanted to have with Julie Christie in *Far From The Madding Crowd.* And Donald Sutherland did with her in *Don't Look Back.*

roll mop *n.* A mature lady's rolled-up *mackerel flaps.*

roll out the barrel *v.* To introduce your sizeable new girlfriend to your mates.

roll out the carpet *v.* To unpick the end of a fresh *bogroll* in order to impress a visitor.

roll out the red carpet *1. v.* When hosting a ceremonial event, to make someone feel very welcome. 2. *v.* When *hosting the decorators,* to make someone feel very unwelcome.

rollover week *n.* When the *painters are in.*

roll the crevice *v.* To attempt to wipe one's *freckle* with the coarse cardboard tube after exhausting the supply of *bumwad.*

roly-poly *adj.* Tabloid prefix for any celebrity who's half a stone overweight. For example, *'Roly-poly actor Leonardo Di Caprio...'*

romancing the bone *n.* An evening in alone with a meal, a bottle of wine and some soft music, followed by a top shelf *stick vid. Everything but the girl.*

romp *v.* To chase a woman in a corset round and round a bedroom, lifting the knees very high, accompanied by "BOING!" noises when leaping onto the bed.

Ronson *rhym. slang. Arse.* From Ronson lighter = shiter.

rook's nest *n.* An exceptionally untidy *faff. 'Cor! Look at her. I bet she's got a minge like a rook's nest - all shit and sticks.'*

room clearer *n.* Of flatulent emissions, a *fart* which registers one notch higher than *breaking company* on the sphincter scale.

rooneyed *adj.* Descriptive of one demonstrating an advanced case of sunburn, in the fashion of the scouse footballing wunderkind Wayne. *'Bugger the sunscreen, let's just get rooneyed.'*

Rooney ramble *n.* A gentle stroll through a red light district.

Rooney's boot *euph.* An item that is meant to offer protection when worn whilst *shooting* but which fails at an inopportune moment with catastrophic results. *'Frankly, son, you were a mistake. Every time I look into your smiling little upturned face I rue the day I bought them Rooney's boots from the vender in the pub bogs.'*

Rooney's charisma *n.* That mysterious and indefinable quality which allows a fat, potato-ugly, prematurely-balding prostitute visitor to secure a top shelf bit of *cabbage* for himself.

rooster *n.* A lady's *nether-wattle. Half a pound of liver.*
root *v.* To make love to.
rope the pony *v.* To *gallop the lizard.*
roseberry topping *1. n.* Frequently climbed hill offering unrivalled vistas over the magical petrochemical wonderland that is Middlesbrough. *2. n.* Put bluntly, the appearance of a chap's *bald man's hat* following a rampant session of *hide the sausage* whilst *Arsenal are playing at home.*
rose-tinted testicles *n.* Those items through which one looks back fondly on all previous sexual encounters when trapped in a long-term relationship.
rotoplooker *n. US.* Penis, *chopper.*
rotters *n.* Unpleasant looking *lungs.* The sort of saggy *tits* with *knee-shooter nips* normally encountered during amateur style entertainment in the furthest reaches of the satellite television channel menu. *Nasty bags.*
roughage *n.* Unkempt pubic foliage. High-fibre *holefood.*
rough as a three quid handjob *sim.* Used in reference to something or somebody unpleasantly coarse. Popular *tit* model Jordan could accurately be described as being *rough as a three quid handjob,* for example. And often is.
roughing up the suspect *v.* What a vice squad copper tells his superiors he's doing when he's caught *polishing* his *bobby's helmet* in the seized porn store room.
round at Freddie's *adj.* To be *nicely poised, good with colours, light on one's feet. 'That Duncan Norvelle - he's married with three kids, you know.' 'Never. I thought he was round at Freddie's.' 'No. That's just an act.'*
roundhead *n.* A *pink Darth Vader* after the surgical removal of his *Kojak's rollneck,* a *yiddled whanger.*
round the houses *1. rhym. slang.* A cockney fellow's trousers. *'Have you seen my round the houses, love? I need them to go for a piece of chalk down the frog and toad to the rub-a-dub for a kitchen sink and a kids from fame of horse and carts with my dinner plates.' 'Aren't they in the Bobby Moore with your student grants, electric shocks and love really hurts? I'm sure I put them there after I Clarence the cross-eyed lionned them this four-minute warning.'* *2. n.* Prostitutes' argot for all-over erotic stimulation. *'How much for a spot of round the houses in a skip, love?' 'Fifteen quid, Lord Archer. Or ten if I don't have to touch your disgusting spotty back.'*
round up the tadpoles *v.* To *wank, bash the bishop.*
rover's return *1. n.* Name of the fictional public house where every single resident of Coronation Street goes drinking three or four times a day. *2. n.* The act of stepping on a freshly-laid *dog's egg* on the way back from the pub, and dragging it home on the sole of your shoe.
rowlocks *n.* British comedy staples. *'These contrivances on my boat serve as fulcrums for my oars.' 'Rowlocks.' 'No, it's true I tell you.'*
row the boat *v.* A dual *tug* boat, multiple *wanking.* Nautical variation on the *downhill skiing* position.

royal decrees *n. Movements* passed whilst sat on the *throne.*

Royal Marine *n.* A *fanny* with a buzz cut.

Royal premiere *n.* The act of menstruation, *ie. rolling out the red carpet.*

Roy Castle's kettle *n.* The use of a choked down *nipsy* in order to use a forcible *Exchange & Mart* to "scratch" an itchy *ringpiece.* A *Dutch cornet.*

Roy Castle's last blow *n.* A frankly unimpressive *trouser trumpet* that sounds like it's feeling very sorry for itself.

Roy Walker moment *n.* A satisfying but morally dubious sexual encounter, *eg.* with a friend's wife or a woman old enough to be one's mother. Or a friend's mother. From the *Catchphrase* personality-vacuum's TV catchphrase "it's good, but it's not right".

rub-a-tug shop *n.* Brothel, bordello, house of ill repute. Massage parlour supplying a rub down and a *tug off.*

rubber beer *n.* Booze bought with a return ticket. A pint one hasn't seen the last of. *Jesus beer.*

rubber gash *n.* The sailor's favourite. A plastic *fanny* which the manufacturers claim is "better than the real thing". At £8.99, that's got to be the bargain of the century.

rubber johnny *n.* A *blob,* contraceptive, *a jubber ray.* Also *rubber, trojan, dunky.*

rubber kebab *n.* An item of fast food with a high coefficient of restitution which bounces back from the stomach onto the pavement or taxi driver's head.

rubber's rag *n.* A rigid piece of once absorbent fabric kept conveniently close to a bachelor's computer workstation.

rubiks *rhym. slang. Gorilla salad, fusewire.* From Rubik cubic hair = pubic hair.

Ruby Murray *rhym. slang.* A *cuzza.*

ruby Tuesday *1. n.* Rolling Stones song which was the 19th best-selling record of 1967. *2. n.* The day the missus goes *up on blocks.* Especially if it's a Tuesday.

rucksack *n.* A badly-adjusted underpant or thong, hitched up a lady's back. With a tin mug and a frying pan hanging off it.

rudimentary *n.* A late night TV *wanking* opportunity, thinly-disguised as a factual programme, *eg.* a behind-the-scenes looks at the worlds of lap-dancing, the US hardcore porn industry or *tits* and *fannies.* Also *masturmentary, sockumentary. 'Are you coming up to bed?' 'In a minute, dear. I'm just watching a rudimentary. Do you know where there's any tissues?'*

ruffle my lettuce *euph.* What a polite Canadian woman says when she is going to take a *Chinese singing lesson. 'If you would excuse me for a moment, gentlemen, I'm just going to ruffle my lettuce. In fact, fuck it. Whilst I'm on the shitter I may as well snip off a length of dirty spine too.'*

rug hugger *n.* Male version of a *fag hag.* A straight man who seeks out the company of women who enjoy the mastication of carpet *on the bus to Hebden Bridge.*

rug munchers *n. Fanny noshers.*

ruined *adj.* A very attractive woman whose sex appeal has nonetheless been almost entirely nullified by her association with an unsuitable gentleman. *'Christ, that Billie Piper's a horny chimpoid.' 'Yeah, but that ginger twat Chris Evans has been there. That's ruined her for me.'*

rummage *n.* A jumble sale-style act of *self-delight* indulged in by a dirty lady.

rump gully *n.* Viewed from *biffin bridge*, the gradually sloping valley beyond *kak canyon*.

Rumpleforeskin *n.* Penis, *John Thomas, junior*.

rumpo *n. Rumpy pumpy*.

Rumpole suntan *n.* An alcoholic red face as modelled by the late *Rumpole of the Bailey* actor Leo McKern.

rump ranger *n. Chocolate cowboy*. One who takes an unhealthy interest in *rusty sheriff's badges*.

rumpy pumpy *n.* Lightweight sexual shenanigans, slightly more erotic than *how's your father*. US equivalent *hoochie-coochie*.

running behind *euph.* Polite excuse which can be given when one is unable to stop and chat with a friend or colleague as a result of an overdue appointment *dropping a load of semi-viscid kids off at the pool. 'Film actor, director, grand old man of the British stage, tonight, Sir John Geilgud, this is your life.' 'Sorry Eamonn, can't stop. I'm running late.'*

runs, the *1. n.* What English cricketers get when they face fast bowlers. *2. n.* What English cricketers don't get when they face fast bowlers.

run the taps *v.* To take a *leak* following a spot of *bumfoolery*. From the practice of letting the taps run in a house with rusty pipes, in order to let out any unpleasant brown residue which may be present in the water.

runway, taxiing down the *n.* The sensation experienced as you cross the last six feet towards the *crapper*, as your long-delayed stinky *passenger* slips into the *departure lounge* and makes a *break for the border*.

rushin' roulette *n.* A suicidally-dangerous game whereby a gentleman attempts to *knock one off* when there is a fairly good chance that his wife may walk in on him.

Rusholme roulette *n. Farting* in the full knowledge that there is a one in six chance of *shitting* one's *kex*. Named after Rusholme, the district of Manchester famed for its curry houses.

russet gusset *n. Skidmarks* or *dangleberrian* deposits on the *shreddies*. *Marmite stripe*, the *starting grid at Brands Hatch*.

Russian wedding ring *n.* Three different shades of gold. Found on close inspection of the missus's *tea towel holder* after she's had a good curry-night *crap*.

Russian yawn *n.* A *thirty-four-and-a-halfer*, a *cannonball*. A self-service *suck-off*.

rusting copper pipe *n.* A *night watchman*. One of them stubborn *arse sausages* that sit in the *pan*, refusing to be flushed away, and giving off a Readybrek-style brown aurora into the water.

rusty scone cutter *n.* A very unhygienic dough-shaping implement. The *arsehole*.

rusty sheriff's badge *n.* Ride south along *biffin bridge* from *John Wayne's hairy saddlebags* and there it lies, right in the middle of *kak canyon*. Just before you reach *rump gully*. The *anus*.

rusty trumpet, play the *v.* To perform *horatio* very shortly after receiving a *rear admiral's* attention.

rusty water *n.* Liquid *feeshus* which is *pissed* out of the *arse.*

rusty zip *n.* An improperly-wiped buttock cleft, where the *shite* has been spread about and then left to dry out. *Robert Smith's mouth.*

rut *v.* To *tup.* In the style of a deer or billy goat.

Ss

sack artist *n.* A womaniser, gigolo, *fanny rat, fanny hopper. Crumpeteer.*

sacofricosis *n. medic.* A mental condition, the main symptom of which is the desire to cut a hole in one's pocket to facilitate *self-pollution* in public places. *'We've get your test results back, Mr Ross OBE, and it's bad news. You've got advanced sacofricosis.' 'Oh, cwumbs!'*

saddlebags *1. n.* Labia, *piss flaps. 2. n.* Scrotum. *3. n.* Leathery receptacles on bicycles where testicles are stored.

safety dance *1. n.* Song by Men Without Hats that reached some position or other in the charts in a particular year in the previous century. *2. n.* The rhythmical *buttocky* shuffle performed whilst trying to find a position on the toilet seat that guarantees a smooth, efficient, smear-free and non-hazardous passage of one's *digestive transit.*

saga lager *1. n.* Sherry or mild, depending on gender. *2. n.* Geriatric *piss. 'I'd visit my granny more often if it wasn't for the smell of saga lager.'*

saga louts *n.* Packs of tea-fuelled pensioners travelling by coach who lay waste to garden centres and stately home gift shops.

sailor's ale *n.* The thick, salty, tangy beverage drunk by *sea bent* mariners whilst on long voyages. *'Adrift upon a glassy sea / No wind upon our sail / We pulled the boatswain's trousers off / And drank his sailor's ale'* (from *The Rime of the Ancient Mariner* by Samuel Taylor Coleridge).

sailor's shot sock, fuller than a *sim.* Descriptive of when something is filled to bursting, *eg.* a post-Christmas binliner, the 4.24pm Newcastle to Prudhoe train, Tom Jones's skin, Cliff Richard's saddlebags.

salad days *n.* Descriptive of the *lettuce-licking* past times of a woman who is now back chomping sausages like a good 'un.

salad dodger *n.* A contumelious epithet for a fat bastard. One who at a buffet sidesteps the lettuce and celery and heads straight for the pork pies. *"Contrarywise', continued Tweedledee, 'if it was so, it might be; and if it were so, it would be; but as it isn't, it ain't. That's logic'. 'That's not logic, that's bollocks, you salad dodger."* (from *Through The Looking Glass* by Lewis Carroll).

salami slapper *n.* He who tolls upon his own *bell end*. A *wanker*.

Salford snail *n.* Common species of mollusc (*Helix aspersalford*) that leaves a distinctive trail of thin horizontal lines scratched into the doors of 4x4s in inner city areas. Evidence of *Salford snail* activity is often found in the vicinity of groups of hooded *scratters*.

Sally bumps *n. Peanuts* in the process of being *smuggled*. Prominent nipples. From the *chapel hatpegs* constantly visible through the clothing of *Coronation Street* character Sally Webster.

Sally Gunnell *n. prop.* A motor trade term to describe a used car, *ie.* "it's not much to look at but it's a fucking good runner".

salmon *1. rhym. slang.* Sexual excitement. From salmon on prawn = the horn. *'I saw Pam Anderson's video on the internet last night. It didn't half give me the salmon,*

I can tell you.' 2. *rhym. slang. HMP*. Tobacco. From salmon and trout = snout. *''Ere, you don't half give me the salmon, Lord Archer. Fancy giving me a blow job for an ounce of salmon?'*

salmon canyon *n*. Piscatorial pass leading to *tuna town*.

salmon handcuffs *n*. *Pink handcuffs*. Invisible restraints that keep a gentleman from seeing any of his friends. The metaphorical restraints with which a *pussy-whipped* gentlemen is shackled. *"This is quite rum do, Jeeves', I exclaimed. 'I've met Piggy for cocktails every Friday for ten years. Where the pip can he be?' 'If I may be so bold,' intoned Jeeves in that way of his, 'he has recently taken up with a soubrette from a London show, and I fear she has slapped the salmon handcuffs on the poor cunt."* (from *What the Fuck, Jeeves?* by PG Wodehouse).

salmon's head *n*. A hatless *one-eyed zipper fish* as viewed from underneath.

saloon doors *n*. A pair of well-used, swinging *fanny flaps* that one's *cock* swaggers into, only to be thrown out three minutes later after a bit of frantic banging. Wild West-style *beef curtains*.

salsa dip *n*. A splash about in the *crimson waves*.

salt *n*. 1960s Mod term for a *bird*.

salt and pepper *n*. Horrible little *tits* where the nipple area is larger and more protruding than the rest of the breast, giving them the appearance of the silver-capped condiment shakers found in cafes.

Samantha *rhym slang*. A *ringpiece*. From Samantha Janus.

Samantha foxhole *n. arch*. A bucolic repository for relaxation-themed literature.

Sam Plank *rhym. slang. Stoke-on-Trent*. An act of *self abuse* named after the popular Radio Stoke disc jockey. *'Did you manage to pull last night?' 'No. I went home for a Pot Noodle and a Sam Plank.'*

Samurai *n*. A fearsome, ceremonial *pork sword*.

sand hole *n*. Of crowded beaches, the hole caused by sunbathing on one's stomach in order to conceal a *Jake*.

S and M *n*. *Rub-a-tug shop* parlance for sado-masochism. *Mr Whippy, fladge and padge*.

Sandy Lyles *rhym. slang*. Haemorrhoids.

Sangatte, do a *v*. Of married men, to make a *bid for the tunnel* in the middle of the night, almost certainly only to be turned back by the wife.

Santa's beard *n*. A festively voluminous example of *jelly jewellery* festooning a lady's chin.

Santa stuck up the chimney *exclam*. A reference to *blobstopper* removal problems, often as a consequence of drunken intercourse.

santorum *n*. Amongst people who are *nicely poised*, the frothy mix of lubricant and faecal matter that is sometimes the by product of their saucy carryings-on. Amusingly named after the anti-gay US senator Rick Santorum. *Sexcrement, shum, toffee yoghurt*.

sarson's nose *adj*. The condition of the *old fella*, post *vinegar strokes*, after leaving a *salty dressing* on the *pink lettuce salad*.

Satan's banquet *n*. An unlikely sounding variation on the *devil's kiss*, whereby a saucy lady delivers a still-warm baguette from her *dirt bakery* into the waiting mouth of a *poovert* friend underneath, by way of a kinky treat.

satiscraptory *adj.* Decriptive of something of a poor, but adequate standard, *eg*. BBC local radio, the Edge's guitar playing, McDonald's food.

sat-nav *1. n.* An in-car electronic device which allows reps to find their way to cheap hotels and massage parlours whilst avoiding areas of traffic congestion. *2. n.* An in-head device which allows *bladdered* gentlemen to find their way home on a Saturday night whilst they are unconscious with the drink.

Saturday night beaver *n.* Dance-floor fauna and, you would imagine, the title of a *grumble film* or two.

sauce *1. n.* Booze, usually when taken in large quantities. *'That Keith Chegwin didn't half hit the sauce, you know.'* *2. v.* To seduce. *3. n.* Cheek. *'He asked to borrow me motor, and then said could I bring it round and make sure the tank was full. What a fucking sauce!'*

saucy *1.adj.* Of British seaside postcards; featuring busty young ladies, fat old ladies, hen-pecked husbands, frigid spinsters, honey-mooning couples, nudist camps, people sticking their cocks through fences and getting them bitten by a goose *etc*. *2. exclam.* Barbara Windsor's inevitable response to a sexual overture, whether intended or accidental.

sausage and doughnut situation *n.* Heterosexual intercourse. *'I did NOT engage in a sausage and doughnut situation with that woman. Miss Lewinsky. She merely sucked me off a bit and stuck my cigar up her cludge. Then I dropped my yop on her frock.'* (President Bill Clinton giving evidence to Special Prosecutor Kenneth Starr).

sausage casserole *n.* The insertion of more than one porky *banger* into a lady's *hotpot* for a warming winter treat. A *top hat.*

sausage fat *n. Jitler.*

sausage grappler *n.* A *salami slapper.*

sausage jockey *n.* Any small Irish man who sits on a sausage and then bounces up and down. A *sausage rider.*

sausage kennel *n.* The *rear quarters* of a *good listener.*

sausage pizza *n.* Closest thing to a *sausage sandwich* that *Miss Lincolnshire* is able to provide. A *diddy ride* on a lady with *stits.*

sausage pot *n.* A lady's privates.

sausage sandwich *n.* A juicy *salami frotted* between two pink *baps*, the end result of which is a *pearl necklace. Dutch*.

sausage supper *n.* Female equivalent of a *fish supper*. A *nosh* on a *cock* sticking out of a pile of mashed potato.

sausage wallet *n.* A wallet for putting sausages in. A *fanny*.

SBD *abbrev.* Of *farts* and *farting,* Silent But Deadly. A subtle release of fatally-pungent *botty gas.*

SBJ *abbrev. medic.* Doctor's notes terminology for a senior citizen or *coffin dodger, low flying angel, estate agent's dream.* Still Breathing, Just.

SBV *abbrev.* Of *farts* and *farting,* Silent But Violent. *Minging fizzle* from the *fart fissure*.

scads *n. Kicksies, dunghampers, thunderbags*.

scallywagon *n.* Boxy white van with blacked-out square windows, the preferred mode of transport for guests of Her Majesty.

Scania scotch *n.* Dark yellow, pungent spirit found in old lemonade bottles at the side of motorways and A-roads, having been discarded there by the hitch-hiker-murdering HGVdrivers who distil it in their kidneys. Also known as *wagon wine* or *trucker's tizer.*

scare the cat *n.* To produce a startlingly loud *trouser cough*.

scarlet emperor *n.* A red, rather bruised, male reproductive organ after an extended session of *self-help*.

scat n. Form of *shite*-fixated *grumble* particularly popular amongst our saucy Germanic cousins.

scatman *1. n.* A jazz singer who improvises nonsense Bill and Ben-style lyrics because they've forgotten the proper words, *eg*. Sammy Davis Jnr., Cleo Laine. *2. n.* A teutonic *poo-game enthusiast*.

schizophrenic face *n.* Of a lady, to have stunningly beautiful eyes, but a nose like Ricky Tomlinson's.

schlong *n. Yiddish.* A large *putz*. A *schlonger.* A *kosher dill*.

schlong shed *n.* Condom, *stopcock, stiffy stocking*.

schmeckie *n.* Opposite of a *schlong.*

scholar's bonus *n.* A rare, but cherished glimpse of a short-skirted young lady's intimate nethergarments as she pedals past in a cycle-heavy city such as Oxford or Cambridge. *Rabbit's tail*.

schoolboy error *n. Shooting one's load* far too early whilst *on the job*. Premature ejaculation.

school dinner *1. n.* A foul, brown mess, served in a large white bowl, the smell of which makes you heave. *2. n.* A toilet full of *shit*.

school play curtain, fanny like a *sim.* A lady's *part* that has so many flaps and folds that it obstructs and frustrates one's progress. From the familiar childhood experience of fumbling about behind a large curtain trying to make your way onto the stage to deliver your lines during a school play. A *labiarinth, hampton maze*.

school run *1. n.* The act of dropping one's kids off at the school at the same time every morning. *2. n.* The act of *dropping one's kids off at the pool* at the same time every morning.

scissor bone *n.* The nipsular guillotine which chops one's *logs* into manageable lengths. The *cigar cutter.*

scissor sack *n. medic.* A non-fatal genital injury in men caused by sitting down awkwardly in overly tight trousers. A *gentleman's discomfort, torsion of the testes*.

scissors, paper, stone *1. n.* A traditional playground game. *2. n.* The hand motion used by German porn stars in *fisting* movies, *ie.* first two fingers, then four, then the full monty. *'Get out of the pool and we'll have a game of scissors, paper, stone.'*

scissorwork *n.* Hot *quim*-to-*quim lezbo* action. *Bumping fur.*

scleg *n.* The sweat-prone yet sensitive area of skin between a fellow's *haggis* and his leg. Not to be confused with the *barse.* From scrotbag + leg. Also *bluck leg*.

scobie *n.* The low-level urinal at the

end of the row, used by children, midgets and Dwight York. From Scobie Breasley, the diminutive jockey of the 1960s and 70s.

scooberty *n.* That period of adolescence when the male voice oscillates wildly and unpredictably between *basso profundo* and *soprano,* and thus resembles that of a popular, cheaply-animated caretaker-hunting cartoon Great Dane.

scoobysnack *n. Oral sex* involving a dog and a very tall sandwich.

scooter *n.* A two-stroke *arse.*

scoots *n. medic.* An affliction characterised by morbid frequency and fluidity of faecal evacuations. The *Brads, Engelberts.*

score from a set piece *v.* To *pull* a *bird* who is a friend of a friend, or one on a blind date, *etc.*

score from open play *v.* To *pull* a *bird* one has never met before by simply bumping into her in a pub, club, chippie, funeral parlour, *etc.* and chatting her up.

scosser *n.* A *wanker* from north of the border. A clever elision of the words Scotch + tosser. *'Have you seen them McDonald brothers on the X Factor? What a pair of fucking scossers.'* (TV Review by AN Wilson in *The International Herald Tribune*).

scotch egg *1. n.* Party foodstuff of absolute last resort. *2. n.* A *turd* which has rolled out of the trouser leg of a *Harold Ramp* who hails from north of the border.

scotchguard shite *n.* A *Brad* which, no matter how messy it feels on exit, leaves one's *brown eye* miraculously unsullied. Named after the 3M product sold to countless paranoid housewives by surly soft furnishing salesmen.

Scotch pancake *n.* A pool of *spew.* A *pavement pizza.*

Scotsman's lounge *1. n.* An historic pub in Cockburn Street, Edinburgh. *2. n.* The gutter. *'That's my 20th pint of the day. I'm just off for a lie down in the Scotsman's lounge.'*

Scottish bedwarmer *n.* A *fart*, anal announcement.

Scottish breakfast *n.* Two paracetamols.

Scottish play *1. euph.* Shakespearean drama (*Macbeth* or *Hamlet* or something), the title of which cannot be spoken by superstitious *chickenshit* actors in case ill fortune befalls them. *2. n.* Anal sex with an otherwise respectable partner.

scouse *v.* To misappropriate opportunistically. *'I say, what a poor show. I left my dressing room unlocked for five minutes and when I came back my gold and diamond cigarette holder had been scoused.' (Terry-Thomas, Liverpool Magistrates Court, 1960).*

scouse honour *exclam.* Merseyside-based variation of Baden-Powell's famous oath of youthful trustworthiness. *'Yeah, no worries. I'll look after the till, mate. Scouse honour.'*

scouser's cashpoint *n.* A fruit machine.

scouser's digit *n. medic.* Affliction, particularly common in the north west of England, preventing the sufferer from keeping his fingers out of the till.

scouser's fingers *sim.* Descriptive of an unkempt *clunge. 'Jesus, woman. Your clout's as sticky as a scouser's fingers.' 'I know. But to be fair, I only came in to have* *my root canal done.'*

scouser's key *n.* A crowbar, hammer, half a brick or anything used to open someone else's back door.

scouser's laptop *n.* A pizza.

scouser's library *n.* A job centre.

scouse slippers *n.* Prison-issue white training shoes.

scouse tax *n.* A cheeky charge levied out of one's pockets by lovably light-fingered Liverpudlians when shopping on Merseyside.

scout movement *n.* A wholesome act of defecation performed in the great outdoors. A *brown owl* or *bear grill.*

scran *1. n.* That bit of a fellow's anatomy which falls between his *hairy swingers* and his clacker-valve. The *barse, tintis, notcher, stinker's bridge.* The *perineum. 2. n.* Dinner, *snap.*

scranus *n.* The fucking *barse* again.

Scrapheap Challenge *1. n.* Channel 4 programme where teams compete to construct contraptions from scrap metal. *2. n.* The prospect of having to perform *cumulonimbus* on a *bird* who is *up on blocks*. So called because of the general messyness, metallic taste and all-pervading odour of dirty blood.

scrapyard dog, going at it it like *sim.* Phrase evocative of a newly-acquired ladyfriend administering a *chewy* in the romantic surroundings of a vandalised playground or other bit of hastily-discovered abandoned wasteland.

scratch *v. Liverpud.* Of a scouse fellow, to sign on. *'I can't fix your roof Thursday. I'm scratching.'*

scratcher *n.* Bed, *fart sack, wanking chariot.*

scrattitude *n.* The cocky self-confidence that members of the lower orders display by stepping off the kerb and causing traffic to slow down or stop while they take their time casually sauntering across the road. Literally the attitude of a *scratter.*

scratter *n.* A person of limited finances and breeding, *eg.* 8 Ace. Also *ronker, pog, ned.*

screamer *n.* A raving *good listener.*

screamin' eagles *n. Stick vid* cinematography term for a scene where a man feeds his *cock* to two or more open-mouthed women who are on their knees, like a parent bird feeding a big purple worm to its hungry chicks. *Baby birding, passing the mic.*

screaming monkey *n.* A bit of female genitalia. Probably the bit which looks the most like a screaming monkey.

scree *1. n. coll.* Shale-like nuggets of *shit.* Approximately the size of a marrowfat pea.

screw *v.* To have sex piggy-style, rotating clockwise due to a corkscrew-shaped *cock.*

screwnicorn *n.* A mythical and somewhat magical sex act whereby a lesbian puts a *strap-on dildo* on her forehead and goes at her partner like a bull at a gate.

scrincter *n.* The bit between the scrotum and the sphincter. The *tintis, scran.*

scrobbing *n. onomat.* The sound made by a dog when licking its own genitalia.

scrogg *1. v.* To partake in in an act of penetrative sexual intercourse up a lady. To *fuck. 2. n.* An act of penetrative sexual intercourse partaken up a lady. A *fuck.*

scrote *n. Knacker, bollock brain.* A

versatile testicular term of abuse.

scrotee *n.* The sort of feeble, adolescent beard which appears to be composed principally of spare *nadbag* fluff.

scrotinise *v.* Of a female friend, to carefully and expertly examine a chap's *clockweights.*

scrotum pole *n.* Old Red Indian erection at the foot of which lie *John Wayne's hairy saddlebags,* and around which *Madam Palm and her five sisters* do ritual dances to precipitate *spunkfall.*

scrotum ticklers *n.* The huge comedy moustaches favoured by the acutely-observed homosexualists who used to populate the cartoons illustrating Richard Littlejohn's columns in *The Sun.*

scrub *n.* An exfoliant facial treatment bestowed upon the *nosher* of a *stubbly bush.*

scrubber *n. Slapper,* vulgar woman, *dollymop.*

scrubbery *n.* Any place where groups of young ladies tend to gather, *eg.* by the tills in a 24-hour garage, round a night bus driver, on a shopping precinct bench, outside an off-licence, in an abortion clinic waiting room *etc.*

scrubbing the cook *n. milit. US. Bashing the bishop, cuffing the suspect, knocking off Patton's tin hat.*

scruburb *n.* A less than desirable area to live.

scruff *n.* Pornography, *muck, grumble. "Look what I've got', said William breathlessly , as he emptied the contents of his jumper at the Outlaws' feet. 'It's a load of scruff. Jumble found it under a hedge."* (from *William's Milk Race* by Richmal Crompton).

Scruggs style *1. n.* In the world of banjo musicianship, a popular approach to bluegrass playing popularised by Earl Scruggs, which gets impressive results from frenetic picking with the thumb, index and middle fingers. *2. n.* In the world of *invisible banjo playing,* to place one's thumb on a lady's *clematis* and one's index and middle fingers up her *blurtch* and *chuff* respectively, before trying to get a tune out of her. 3. n. A lady *practising her fingerwork, perfecting her licks.*

scrumping *1. n. US.* Having sex. *2. n. UK.* Stealing apples.

scruncher *n.* Opposite of a *folder.*

scrunchies *1. n.* Of *slappettes,* the colourful elasticated hairbands captured by rival teenage *slappers* in battle. *2. n.* Excess batter in a chip shop. *Scraps.*

scrunger *n.* Another name for one of those bicycle seat sniffers found lurking around the bicycle racks of convents and women's drop-in centres. A *garboon, snufty, snurglar, nurfer.*

scrunion *n. Aus. medic.* The wrinkly scrotal remnant immediately preceding the perineum. From scrotum + onion.

scrunt *n. coll. Blart, flange, gusset.* A group of attractive women. *'Suddenly, at the age of 25, the Prince was cast as the world's most eligible bachelor. On a Royal tour of New Zealand in 1973, he found himself having to batter off top-end scrunt with a shitty stick.'* (from *HRH The Prince of Wales* by Jim-Bob Dimbleby).

scrut *n.* Hardcore *oyster grumble* that would satisfy the curiosity of even the most ardent amateur gynaecologist. *Close up pink.*

scruttock *n.* The area of skin 'twixt *scrot* and *bot*. The *barse, tintis.*

scuffer *n.* A *cozzer*, a *rozzer*, a *tithead*, a *filth. 'Look out, it's the scuffers!'*

scuffing *n.* Hands-free *self abuse* technique, which involves rubbing one's *cock* against the mattress until the job is done. Presumably the hands are then brought back into service in order to clean up the mess.

scuff it *1. v.* In football, to lose concentration at the critical moment, leading to a disappointing shot. *2. v.* In *fucking*, to lose concentration at the critical moment, leading to a disappointing *shot. To suffer a lack of composure in front of the goal.*

scumbag *n.* The ultimate term of abuse known to British tabloid journalists.

scumble *1. n.* A *shit,* heavily-dated paint effect inflicted on the participants of TV room makeover programmes. *2. n.* A language spoken exclusively by *Harold Ramps.* From Scottish + mumble.

scummertime *n.* The start of the school holidays when a flood of teenage *ronkers* descends upon a town's unwitting shoppers.

scummy mummy *n.* The opposite of a *yummy mummy.* A coarsely plebeian materfamilias, if you will.

scumper *n.* Someone who lays sheets of bog roll on the seat of a public toilet so as his *arse* does not touch the same place as someone else's *arse* has touched. The late *Carry On* star Kenneth Williams was known to *scump.*

scum shovel *n.* Any form of public transport used extensively by the underprivileged, *eg.* the no.11 Torry to Northfield bus in Aberdeen.

scumwad *n. US.* The ultimate term of abuse known to American tabloid journalists.

scungies *n.* Disreputable *scads. 'What's the matter, Carol?' 'While I was onstage, performing a medley of my hits including China in Your Hand, some dirty bastards have been in the dressing room and wanked on my scungies.'*

scuns *n. Scads.*

scunt *n.* Like a *scosser,* but even worse.

scutter *n. Slut, shag bag, scrubber, slapper.* A lady of easy virtue.

scuttle 1. *v.* To *sink the pink*, or *brown*, esp. in a hurried fashion from behind. *2. n.* A swift, frantic act of intercourse. Or something to keep the coal in.

scuttler *n.* A fellow who, for whatever reason, will not *piss* alongside another at a urinal, but instead scuttles off into a cubicle, usually locking the door too.

sea bent *adj.* Descriptive of a matelot whose sexual tastes have been re-oriented due to a prolonged period of enforced maritime abstinence. Of otherwise heterosexual sailors, tempted to have a *ride on the other ferry* whilst at sea. *'Kiss me Hardy, I'm feeling distinctly sea bent.'*

sea biscuit *1. n.* Legendary (not literally) US racehorse, recently immortalised (not literally) in a *shit* (literally) film. *2. n.* Nautical equivalent of an *air biscuit,* delivered whilst in an over-relaxing bath. *3. n.* A *turd* floating in the *briny. 'Observant Admiral (Who has, through his extended telescope, spotted trouble in store for* *the heroic Channel swimmer half way through his heroic natation of "La Manche" 'twixt Dover and Calais, and resolves to vouchsafe this important information "post-haste" to the natatorial half-man half-fish by hailing him at the top of his not inconsiderable voice): 'Look out, Captain Webb. There's a sea biscuit on the top of the next wave.' Captain Webb (With a big turd stuck in his mouth): 'Too late.'* (cartoon by Sir John Tenniel in *Punch*, 1875).

seafood taco *n.* A lady's *clout* that smells like a fishmonger's hands and could lead to an upset stomach.

seagulling *1. n.* The mischievous act of dropping *jizz* onto a passer by from a height, *eg.* a tree, a roof or a Status Quo hotel room balcony. Could lead to *Graham Norton's hair. 2. n.* Amongst the *dogging* community, spattering the windscreen of a vehicle with *spongle,* in the manner of a passing kittiwake with loose *camillas.*

seagulls' wellies *n.* Maritime used *blobs. 'How was your swim, David?' 'Awful. I was only in the water ten minutes and I swallowed a turd and three seagulls' wellies. I'm going to write to the council.'*

seahorse *n.* A man doing a woman's job, *eg.* arranging flowers, designing dresses, pushing a baby about in a pram. From the comedy fish the hippocampus, the male of which species carries its wife's young about like some sort of *puff.*

seal of Hades *n.* The boundary between our world and the *devil's kitchen.* The *ringpiece.*

sea monster *n. Swamp donkey, hippocrocapig.*

seaside shithouse, fuller than a *sim.* Descriptive of something that is replete to bursting point. *'Take that bin bag out will you, Your Highness. It's fuller than a seaside shithouse.'*

season cliff hanger *1. n. US.* In TV drama series, a final show which ends just at the exciting part, encouraging viewers to watch the next series. *2. n.* A large *shit* which cuts off at the exciting part causing one to wait for what feels like an eternity to get the ending.

secaturds *n. medic.* The muscles surrounding the *nipsy* that provide the power to operate the *turtle guillotine.*

second post *n.* A supplementary delivery of *anal parcels* which takes one by surprise half way through the morning.

second sitting *n.* An immediate, unavoidable return visit to the *shitter* after wiping and washing.

secret smile *n.* A *cunt.*

security check *1. n.* Rounds made last thing at night to assure oneself that the front and back doors are definitely locked. *2. n.* Last thing at night grope of the missus to check that her *front* and *back doors* are definitely locked.

sediment *n.* The *totty crud* that remains unsyphoned at chucking out time in a night club.

see a friend to the coast *euph. Drop the kids off at the pool.*

seed *n.* That which was scattered on the stoney croft by Onan, and great was the wrath of the Lord.

seed catalogue *n.* A *flesh mag.*

seeing to *n.* Sexual servicing, a "jolly good" one of which is often said to have been given to a woman by a man.

see you next Tuesday *sort of acronym.* Ingeniously offensive parting pleasantry allowing you the satisfaction of calling someone a *cunt* to their face without them knowing it.

self-catering *n.* See *self discipline.*

self-cleaning oven *1. n.* In the world of kitchen appliances, a cooker which does not in any sense whatsoever clean itself. *2. n.* The *cludge* of a female *ejaculatrix.*

self discipline *n.* Character- building regime engendered in the armed forces and public schools. *Masturbation.*

self help manual *n.* An item of literature that aids *relaxation.* An *art pamphlet,* a *flesh mag,* a *bachelor's newsletter.*

self indulgent *adj.* Prone to treating *junior* to a brisk *rub down* from time to time.

selling Buicks *n. US.* Vomiting. From the similarity of the sounds made by a *chunderer* to the cries of the Buick street vendors of Detroit, *viz.* "Buick! Buick!"

semen *n. Aphrodite's Araldite, joy gloy, gunk, spunk, goo.*

semenal *adj.* A highbrow, intellectual way of referring to something as being *wank.*

semen-olina *n. Spunk* of an especially lumpy nature.

sement *n.* Quick-drying, gloopy substance used for binding *hardcore. Sement* has to be mixed vigorously for a couple of minutes before it is applied. *Jazz glue.*

semi *1. n.* A *lazy lob on,* a *dobber,* a half-erect penis. *2. n.* A house joined to one other house.

semi-demi-on *n.* A *quarter-on, half a lob on.* The first stirrings of *dobberdom.*

semi-on *n.* A partially-tumescent *membrum virile. Half a teacake.*

send a sausage to the seaside *euph. Sink a few U boats.*

senorita beater *n.* Any Spanish lager, such as San Miguel *etc. Pedro's piss.*

separate-us apparatus *n.* A *condom, stiffy stocking. 'Did you remember to bring the separate-us apparatus?' 'Oh, Rat's cocks! I didn't. Perhaps we'd better just play the bagpipes tonight.'*

serpent socket *n.* That hole into which the *one-eyed trouser snake* is plugged.

serpent's tongue *n.* A forked *piss* caused by a *jazz egg* blocking the *hog's eye. Twin jets. 'Jesus! You've pissed on the floor again.' 'Sorry, love, only I had the serpent's tongue this morning.'*

serving it up *v.* Of a gentlemen, to be *having it off* with, or *slipping a length* to, a lady. *'Throughout the early eighties, Prince Charles was plagued by persistent rumours that Major James Hewitt was serving it up to Princess Diana.'* (from *Charles the Biography* by Little Jimmy Dimbleby).

Seth Armstrong in a SARS mask *sim.* An erotically-alluring description of a vaginally hirsute lady wearing thong underpants.

set on fire and put out with a shovel, looks like she's been *sim.* Lighthearted expression which can be used to gently broach the subject of an *eight-pinter*'s appearance. *'I don't fancy yours much, mate. She looks like she's been set on fire and put out with a shovel.'* (Dr Rowan Williams, the Archbishop of Canterbury, whilst officiating at the wedding of His Royal Highness the Prince of Wales and Camilla Parker-Bowels in the function room of the Travelodge, Windsor, on 9th April 2005).

setting the video *v.* Sexual position, in which the lady is on her knees and elbows, with her *arse* in the air, tutting exasperatedly.

seven pint stunner *n.* A *bird* whose inner beauty only struggles to the surface after one has quaffed the best part of a gallon of *Nelson Mandela.*

seven stepper *n.* An extended *Exchange & Mart* which, as its name suggests, lasts for a good few paces as one saunters down the street. A length-specific *string of pearls, duckwalk.*

seven/ten split *1. n.* In ten-pin bowling, a *pair of skittles* so far apart that hitting them both with a single shot is almost impossible. *2. n.* A really wide *fanny* that can only be taken on whilst wearing special shoes.

seventy-one-er *n.* A *sixty-niner,* but with two fingers up the lady's *bonus tunnel* for good measure.

sex *1. n. It, the other, dirties. 2. v.* To pump someone full of semen. *'Babe, I'm gonna sex you up.'* (*Sex You Up* song lyric, George Michael). *3. n.* A lady's *mingepiece. 'I want your sex.' (I Want Your Sex* song lyric, George Michael).

sex act *1. n.* Versatile, vague tabloid term used to describe and denigrate specifically non-specific acts or *shenanigans* which have been "performed". Usually prefixed "vile", "lewd" or "sordid". *2. n.* Vile, lewd and sordid acts performed on a stage at Club Baghdad, Barcelona, to pluck an example out of thin air.

sexcrement *n. medic.* The foul mix of bodily fluids that is passed through the *nipsy* after several sessions of *backdoor love. Santorum.*

sexile *n.* A forlorn, lonely fellow in a bar, constantly checking his watch and desperately trying to make a half last all evening because his flatmate is *getting his end away.*

sex wee *1. n.* An ejaculation of *spongle. 2. n.* The *spongle* that is ejaculated.

Shabba *n.* Multiple *J Arthurs.*

shackled *adj.* The condition of a man searching the house for *arse paper* with his trousers and underpants round his ankles.

shackles, arse like a bag of *sim. naut.* Charming maritime expression used to describe the rear end of a lady who has successfully *dodged* a significant quantity of *salad, ie.* whose *back porch* is reminiscent of half a hundredweight of lumps of steel in a sack. *'Isn't that Vanessa Feltz putting her shopping in her car? Christ on a bike, she's got an arse like a bag of shackles.'*

Shadsworth six-seater *n.* An ambulance, named after the delightful area of Blackburn, where trips home after a night out are customarily taken in just such a conveyance.

shaft *1. v.* To *shag, screw. 2. n.* The mast on the *skin boat. 3. n. prop.* A black private dick that's a sex machine to all the chicks in town.

shafterburn *n.* Painful friction-induced scorching of the *skinclad tube* caused by excessively *relaxing in a gentleman's way.*

shag *1. v.* To copulate, to *fuck.* A

once shocking term, now lame enough to be used by "right on" vicars. *2. n.* A sexual encounter, a *screw*. *3. n. US.* 1950s dance craze. *4. n.* Type of sea bird. *5. n.* Tobacco. *6. n.* Something to do with piles on carpets.

shag bag *n.* Loose woman, *a bike.*

shag dust *n. Fuck powder.* Make-up.

shag factory *n.* Joint which is heaving with *blit, knickerville, blart city*.

shaggability *n.* Measurement of how *prodworthy* a person is on an arbitrary, non-scientific scale.

shaggable *adj. Worth a one.*

shagged out *adj.* Exhausted, *jiggered, buggered, zonked, fucked.*

shaggin' wagon *n.* A *passion wagon*, a *fuck truck*, a *spambulance.*

shagging a bike *sim.* To describe sex with an extremely thin woman. *'These supermodels, nice faces, some of 'em, but get 'em in the fart sack and it's like shagging a bike. I would imagine.'*

shagging a waterbed *sim.*To describe sex with an extremely fat woman. *Slapping the fat and riding the waves.*

shag monster *n.* A not necessarily ugly woman who has a voracious appetite for something to do with carpets. A *nymphomentalist.*

shagnasty *n.* A *shag monster* who is also extremely ugly.

shag slab *n.* The *altar of lurve*, bed, *passion pit, cock block, fart sack, scratcher*.

shag tags *n.* Love bites, *hickies, suckers*.

shake a tit *v.* To defecate spooneristically.

shake hands with the French *v.* To push one's finger through the *bumwad* when wiping the *freckle.* To *breach the hull, push through.* From the similarity to the moment when the two bore drills met in the Channel Tunnel and the English bloke forced his hand through the thin divide to shake the hand of his Gallic counterpart. *'Did you wash your hands before kneading that dough, Nigella?' 'Erm, no, Charles. But it's okay, it's not as if I've shaken hands with the French today.'*

shake hands with the mayor *1. v.* To greet the leading alderman in one's borough, perhaps whilst he is judging a sandcastle, snowman or large vegetable competition in a municipal park. Like they do. *2. v.* To interfere with your own *bits and bobs,* whilst paying scant regard to the medically-documented risks that you run, *viz.* going blind, insane, hairy-handed, bald and/or short.

shake hands with the wife's best friend *v.* To perform an act of *self-pollution*.

shake hands with the Wookie *v.* Of those men blessed with eight-foot-long hairy *cocks* that make growling noises, to *wank*.

shake shifter *n.* The first pint of the day. *'Good morning and welcome aboard flight BA 103 from Oslo. The captain's had a shake shifter, so we'll shortly be proceeding to the runway to commence our take-off.'*

shake the bishop's hand *v.* To have a *piss,* as opposed to sticking your hand through a hole in the lavatory wall *and wanking* him off.

shake the lettuce *v.* Of females, to *pee* and give the *beef curtains* a quick tumble dry afterwards.

shake the snake *v.* Male equivalent of *shake the lettuce,* the object being to dislodge any *forget-me-nots* before returning the *schlong* to the *shreddies.*

shaking hands with the unemployed *n.* Having *one off the wrist.*

shaking like a shitting dog *sim.* A bad attack of the DTs after a night on the *sauce.*

shaking like a flatpack wardrobe *sim.* Descriptive of the female equivalent of the *vinegar strokes.*

shampoo the rug *v.* To lose one's *population paste* on a *mapatasi.* Perhaps when *getting off at Edge Hill.*

sham-rock *n.* Descriptive of a man who, despite talking the talk, couldn't knock the head off a half of shandy. *'Today's Birthdays: Jean Picard, French astronomer, 1620; Ernest Hemingway, Nobel Prize-winning American author, 1899; Isaac Stern, Ukrainian violin virtuoso, 1920; Ross Kemp, balding sham-rock Fruit & Fibre ad actor, 1964.'*

Shamu *n.* An overly-acrobatic *dreadnought* that splashes the spectating testicles. From the performing whale of the same name that lives simultaneously in Florida, California and Texas.

shandy andy *n.* A *jizzmop.*

shandydextrous *adj.* To be blessed with the ability to give one's *monkey* an equally vicious *spanking* with either hand.

shandygram *n.* A luridly-worded SMS message, typically texted to a female acquaintance with the left hand after one has taken onboard a plethora of love potion. In 2004, the *News of the World* published several *shandygrams,* purported to have been sent to Channel 5 pig-*wanker* Rebecca Loos by simpleton billionaire free kick merchant David Beckham.

shandy sunbed *n.* A bench in a park or a precinct. The *tramp grill.*

shandy tan *n.* The ruddy-red complexion sported by *Harold Ramps* after spending too long asleep on the *shandy sunbed.*

shanny *1. n.* A type of fish, specifically the smooth blenny. *2. n.* Appropriately enough, a depilated vagina. From shaved + fanny.

shark *v.* To go on the *pull,* using aggressive, sly or cunning tactics.

shark's fin *n.* The profile of a neighbour's *beetle bonnet* viewed through a tight bikini bottom whilst sunbathing on the beach. *Pigeon's chest.*

shark's mouth n. A somewhat unsettling term for a gentleman's urinal.

shark's nose *n.* A lady's *clematis* when it is in an advanced state of arousal, to the extent that it would scare away all but the bravest *muffdivers.*

sharks sniffing, have the *euph.* Of a lady, to be afflicted with her monthly uncleanliness. *"My darling, at last we are alone,' murmured Heathcliff, as he took Cathy in his arms. 'I cannot wait a moment longer. I must have you now.' 'Sorry, love, I've got the sharks sniffing,' she replied.'* (from *Wuthering Heights* by Tracey Bronte).

Sharon sixteen stone *n.* A *bird* who crosses her legs when she isn't wearing any knickers and you still can't see anything. See also *J-lower.*

shart *v.* To pass wind with an unexpected non-gaseous component.

To *follow through.*

shat nav *n.* The use of cutting-edge automotive GPS technology in order to locate a fast food restaurant where one can *go for a McShit.*

shat on from a height *v.* To be badly exploited, humiliated, let down.

shatin underwear *n.* The amusingly-soiled *undercrackers* found up back alleys, in shop doorways and stuffed through building society letterboxes on Sunday mornings.

shatkins *n.* Rapid, astonishingly-effective diet based on the somewhat controversial theory that the most effective way to lose weight is to acquire a bacterial stomach infection by the intake of meat only, especially 2am burger bar fayre. *'Good grief, you've lost weight since yesterday.' 'Yes, six stones. I've been on the shatkins diet.'*

shat trick *n.* The professional goal of the salaried worker, *ie.* three *Mr Browns* in one working day.

shave a horse *v.* To have a *piss, take a leak, turn your bike around.*

shaven haven *n.* A bald *monkey's forehead, John Craven.*

Shearer's Island *n.* That increasingly isolated patch of hair on the front of a balding gentleman's head. Named after balding former footballer Alan who, if you look, has a distinctly desolate-looking doormat of hair on the front of his head. Viewers of the recent *South Bank Show* about Dusty Springfield will agree that Neil Tennant out of the Pet Shop Boys now has one of the most impressive *Shearer's Islands* in modern day Britain.

shed *n.* A large, promiscuous woman. Somewhere to stick *tools.*

shedded *adj. Trousered, cattled.*

sheep dog trials *rhym. slang. Carpet tiles.*

sheep's heart on a Vim tin *sim. Scot.* Descriptive of a *hard on* to be proud of.

sheep sitting *adj. On the blob, dropping clots.*

sheet music *n.* Aeolian emanations from beneath the covers as two lovers semi-consciously serenade each other with their *wind sections.* Usually performed at the break of day following a night *on the pop.*

sheezer *n.* A woman who exhibits a disproportionate number of male traits in her everyday behaviour, *eg.* drinking, watching football, smoking a pipe, excessive masturbation.

Sheffield hammer *n.* A rolled-up newspaper used to hammer nails into bits of wood, which can be unrolled before the *scuffers* arrive.

Sheila's wheels *n.* The *clockweights* of a trans-gendered antipodean *trolley dolly.*

shejaculate *n.* The *love relish* that some women supposedly fire from their *fur burgers* when they suffer an organism.

shelling *n.* Yet another supremely unlikely-sounding homosexual practice, most probably cooked up in the fevered imagination of a popular tabloid columnist, which involves the removal of a snail from its shell and the insertion of said evicted mollusc into a *puddle jumper's nipsy* in order that he can savour the wriggling sensation. If they do do it, they ought to be bloody well ashamed of themselves.

shenis *n.* What you need in order to make the most of a *mangina.*

Sherman *rhym. slang.* A *tug.* From

Sherman tank = wank.

sherry monocle *n.* Upper class equivalent of *beer goggles.*

she's a bit bang! knock knock *exclam.* Humorous phrase used to describe a lady with a substantial *bow frontage.* Descriptive of a woman caller whose *generous provisions* inevitably make contact with the door before her knuckles do.

Shetland *n.* A tiny *turd.* From the fact that it is, like the miniature horses famously drawn by the late Norman Thelwell, a small *pony.*

Shetland pony's cock, sticks out like a *sim.* Useful expression descriptive of something which is conspicuously obvious. From the fact that the *blood sausages* of the popular miniature horses are noticeably sizeable in comparison to their diminutive stature. *'It's no good, Johnny. We're going to have to lose the syrup. It sticks out like a Shetland pony's cock under the studio lights.'*

Shetland rabbit, hung like a *sim.* To have a *cock* like that of Bobby Davro. Also *hung like a Chinese mouse.*

she-tox *n.* A period when a married gentleman's spouse is away, during which he cleanses his system of her wholesome influences. A welcome relapse into bachelorhood ways of drinking, *wanking* and curry-eating himself daft.

shift *v.* To *bang, poke, screw.*

shifting furniture *euph.* To produce a loud, scraping *horse & cart* which sounds like people moving heavy objects around in the flat upstairs. *'Eat your lunch at the Curry Capital, Bigg Market, Newcastle upon Tyne and I, Lord Abdul Latif of Harpole, personally guarantee that you'll be shifting furniture by teatime.'*

shift, put in a *v.* To have sexual intercourse with a partner when one can't really be *arsed. 'What's up, George? Why the long face?' 'Oh, it's me and the missus's 34th wedding anniversary. She'll be expecting me to go home and put in a shift tonight.'*

shims *n. Ladyboys, flippers.*

Shipman, to do a *v.* From Harold Shipman. To inject a lady much older than oneself. *Granny banging, biddy fiddling.*

shirt fly *n.* A "yes man". One who is always up the gaffer's *arse.* A *fartsucker*, a *brown noser*, a *Penfold.*

shirtful *n.* A well-stocked *rack. 'My, what a shirtful. You've got the job.'*

shirt lifter *n.* A tall man employed in a clothing shop to place stock on high shelves.

shirt potatoes *n. Tits, melons, top bollocks, fat rascals, milky swingers.*

shirt raiser *n.* A mighty zephyr from the *brass eye.* An enormous *Bakewell.*

shit *1. v.* To *shit,* defecate, *sink the Bismarck, build a log cabin, crimp one off, light a bum cigar. 2. n. Crap,* excrement, stools, assorted faecal matter. *3. n. Git, sod, get,* a *shitty* person, usually "little". *4. adj. Crap,* useless. *'Shit weather for this time of year, eh, vicar?' 5. exclam.* Oh dear.

shit a brick *1. interj.* Exclamation of surprise. *2. v.* To be scared, to *papper* one's *trolleys.*

shitboy *n. Northumb.* Term of abuse for one engaged in menial employment. *'How, shitboy! Big Mac and* *chips!'*

shitcloud *n.* A common meteorological phenomenon involving a silent movement of wind and a strong smell of bad eggs.

shit diamonds *v.* The end result when one is desperate for a *number two,* but is nevertheless denied access to the *chod bin,* so that one's *feeshus* get packed tightly into the *bomb-bay. 'Hurry up in there, your Holiness. I'm shitting diamonds out here.'*

shite *n. & v.* See *shit.*

shite alight *n.* A doorstep incendiary *Thora* used as an offensive-smelling weapon against one's neighbour's slippers.

shit-eating grin *n.* Exaggerated, smug, self-satisifed smile as worn by the likes of Noel Edmonds.

shitegeist *n.* Collective consciousness or shared feeling that the world is *crap.*

shite house *1. n.* A poorly-constructed abode. 2. *n.* A well-constructed brick lavatory building. 3. *n.* The smallest room.

shiter *n. Arse, kak cannon.* That which *shites.*

shit-faced *n. Arseholed,* intoxicated, *wankered.*

shit-for-brains *n.* One who is intellectually challenged. A *joskin, fuckwit, dolt.*

shit house *n.* See *shite house.*

shit house shin pad *n. nav.* A concealed *grumble mag* wrapped around a sailor's leg under his sock as he makes his way to the HMS Ark Royal *crappers* for a *wank.*

shitingale *n.* One who breaks into song whilst *dropping a length of dirty spine,* usually in order to shield his audience from the slightly less tuneful sounds being produced by his *turtle guillotine.*

shititch *n. medic. Brass eye* irritation suffered by one who has exited the *cludgy* without wiping properly. An attack of *arse wasps* or *wire spiders.* From shit + itch. *'Mr Glitter, will you please stand still while we take aim?' 'Sorry mate, only I had a dodgy plate of Tai Hea Ngam Chua for my final meal and then when I went off to drop me shopping there was no paper in the crapper. I've got terrible shititch here, I tell you.'*

shit kiss *n.* A small, star-shaped brown mark left on the chin of a none-too-fussy *cumulonimbulist.*

shit limpet *n.* A lady who is hopelessly devoted to her loutish *cunt* of a boyfriend, despite regular beatings and his constant infidelity.

shit locker *n. Arse, bomb bay, chamber of horrors.*

shit machine *n.* A dog. *'I fired three shots, and moments later the hellish, glowing beast, whatever it was, lay dead in the Grimpen Mire. If I had hesitated for a second, or had my aim been less than true, it would most certainly have killed Sir Henry where he stood, as Stapleton had intended. 'My God, Holmes,' I expostulated breathlessly. 'What on earth is it?' The great detective stepped forward and examined the foul creature's still-luminous form through his eyeglass. 'A simple trick, Watson,' he announced presently. 'It is merely a large shit machine which has been coated with phosphorus.''* (from *The Shit Machine of the Baskervilles* by Arthur Conan-Doyle).

shitmus test *n.* Like a litmus test, only instead of indicator paper in a laboratory there's *arse paper* in a lavatory, and instead of an acid/base there's an *anus* that might have let *something slip* whilst *stepping on a duck. 'Crikey, I think there was something in that. I'd better go and take a shitmus test.'*

shit on your own doorstep *euph. Foul the nest, eg. shag* one's mother-in-law whilst totally *pissed. Piss on your chips, fart on your Weetabix.*

shit pump *n.* The television. *'I'm off to bed, love. Don't forget to turn the shit pump off when you come up.'*

shits, the *n.* Of *smallroom dancing*, those up-tempo *trots* which include the *Tijuana cha-cha*, the *sour apple quickstep* and the *Aztec two-step*.

shit scrape *n. Arse wipe,* bathroom tissue.

shit-smuggler's rucksack *sim.* The *ne plus ultra* of halitosis. *'Fuck me, what have you been eating, Your Majesty?' 'I don't know what you mean, Lord St. John.' 'Your breath smells like a shit-smuggler's rucksack, ma'am.'*

shitsophrenia *n. medic.* The condition where the sufferer alternates between having wild *squirts* and normal bowel movements.

shit splitter *n.* A g-string worn so tight on the lady's *heave-ho* as to fillet the *brown trout* in the unlikely event that she *follows through* on a *cheese cracker.*

shit stabber *n.* A *stylish pork swordsman*.

shitstopper *n.* An unexpectedly large household bill, derived from the practice of reading the mail whilst on the toilet. *'And now we move onto the case of Mr Jack Trubshaw of St Neots, who last winter received a right shitstopper from British Gas, even though his central heating is oil-fired.'* (Nicky Campbell, *Watchdog,* BBC TV).

shitter *1. n.* Anus, *kakpipe, council gritter. 2. n.* A sit down lavatory, the *pan.*

shitterati *n. coll.* Collective term for the heroic figures of the age who turn up on programmes such as *I'm a Celebrity, Get me Out of Here, Britain's Worst Celebrity Drivers' Pets from Hell, etc.* The kind of people who would happily fuck a pig if it were to get their face on TV, *eg.* Bubble off *Big Brother*, the coughing major off *Who Wants to be a Millionaire*, The Hamiltons, Jeremy Spake *etc.*

shitter chatter *n.* Long-winded anal babble emitted when a *shit* is expected.

shitter's ridge *n.* The *scranus* etc.

shit tickets *n. Bumwad, arsewipes, turd tokens, brown shield stamps.*

shitting through a sponge *n.* A novel toilet ability gained after a night eating delicious curries at the Curry Capital.

shit trigger *n.* The first cigarette of the day, which has the effect of pulling the pin out of the *chod grenade. 'I Love Phillip Morris king size. It's not just because they're clean and fresh tasting. It's not just because their mellow taste gives me mouth and throat comfort and freedom from cigarette cough. And it's not just because they have a great shit trigger action and give me all day smoking enjoyment. I love them because they're the mildest high tar cigarette on the market.'* (*I Love*

Philip Morris advertisement featuring Lucille Ball, 1953).

shitty shitty gang bang *n.* A particularly messy *arsefest*.

shitty stick *n.* A stick, covered in *shit*, used by men with powerful cars and expensive aftershave to stave off advancing *scrunt*.

shitwreck *n.* The broken-up remnants of a scuttled *dreadnought*, lying in deep water by the S-bend.

shit your pants *v.* To *drop a brick, cake your kecks, papper your trolleys*.

shniffle-piffler *n.* Somebody else who sniffs lady's bicycle seats.

shock to the cistern *euph.* An uncomfortably large *copper bolt* that challenges the swallowing capabilities of the average *chod bin*.

shoebox special *n.* A magnificent *Thora,* exhibiting a length and girth of which one is so proud that one feels tempted to fish it out of the *bum sink,* put it in a shoebox and take it to work to show it off to one's colleagues.

shoe bun *n.* A profiterole of *hound cable,* a *barker's egg custard tart. 'This is one small step for a man, one giant leap for...Fuck me, I've just stepped in a shoe bun.'*

shoelace view *n.* A gentleman's surreptitious glimpse of a *bird's* gusset gained whilst pretending to tie his shoelace.

shooting boots on, to get one's *1. v.* Football commentator's phrase, to describe the actions of a player who has excelled in the "kicking the ball at the goal" part of the game. *'Rooney's certainly got his shooting boots on for Manchester United today, Gary.' 2. v.* Phrase describing the bizarre contortions a gentleman's feet go through in the moments leading up to a *pop shot. 'Rooney's certainly got his shooting boots on up that raddled old prostitute today, Gary.'*

shooting bunnies *n.* Polite euphemism for *letting rip*. Passing wind, *blowing off*. Also *killing the Easter bunny*.

shooting times *n. Self help literature, DIY mags, bachelors' newsletters.* Bongular magazines.

shoot in your boot *euph.* To be so sexually excited as to ejaculate into one's footwear.

shoot your load/bolt/wad/stack *v.* To ejaculate, *lose your mess, discharge the mutton musket.*

shopkeeper *n.* A sudden, movement of *stoolage* into the *bomb bay,* that occurs completely unexpectedly. Named after the fez-wearing fancy dress shopkeeper in *Mr Benn*, who would habitually appear in a similar unnerving manner.

shopping *n.* The underpant aftermath of *follow through. 'Did I detect a twin tone there, your Honour?' 'I'm afraid so. Court adjourned for fifteen minutes whilst I check my trolleys for shopping.'*

shop round the corner *v.* To be *good with colours.*

short arms inspection *n. milit.* Armed services slang for an *under the bridge* medical examination, specifically looking for evidence of *cock rot.*

short-changed *adj.* Descriptive of the situation that obtains when a video clip one has downloaded stops just short of the *money shot,* so you have to phone Barclaycard and get them to cancel the transaction.

shot from the starter's gun *euph.* A *cock* up the *arse.* See *jockey's* *starting position.*

shotgun fart *n.* A sudden ballistic *poot* which peppers pellets of *crapnel* into the toilet bowl or underpants.

shoving paper down a Greek toilet *n.* Attempting to sort out a problem, but only succeeding in making things a whole lot worse. *'I cannot help making the observation that complaints about the Government's policy over Iraq would be more acceptable from those who had opposed this reckless excursion in the first place. My right honourable friend's answers, however, give an impression that is not borne out by events on the ground. The United Nations calculates that 3,000 Iraqi civilians are being killed every month. In those circumstances, how long is the Prime Minister prepared to continue pursuing his current policy of forcible occupation, which is merely shoving paper down a Greek toilet?'* (Sir Mingies Campbell MP, quoted in *Hansard*, June 8th 2007).

show job *1. n.* The making of theatrically appreciative noises by a gentleman who is the recipient of a particularly artless act of oral *horatio. 2. n.* The sort of transparently fake *nosh* typically performed in front of a roaring fire and filmed from behind a lace curtain in one of them glossy, softcore *spam vids* they show on the Sci-fi Channel late at night, where a *bird* moves her head up and down in front of a bloke whilst he pulls a face like he's just shut his *knackers* in the car door.

showroom finish *n.* The effect of rubbing your *naughty polish* into a ladyfriend's *bodywork* and then buffing her *headlamps* till they gleam.

shoulder boulders *n.* Big breasts, *gazungas.*

show off *v.* Of a woman, to exhibit the hystrionic symptoms of premenstrual tension.

shpaddiel *n.* Long-winded comedy anecdotage from David Baddiel which result in a death-like silence.

shramp *v.* To enjoy the incredibly common hobby of sniffing ladies' recently-vacated bicycle seats. To *quumf, snudge, snurgle, snuftify.*

shreddies *n. Undercrackers, kecks, trolleys, scads, scuns.*

shrek *n.* A large, shaven-headed man with bad teeth and protruding ears found on low-brow, daytime moron-bating programmes such as *Trisha* and the *Jeremy Kyle Show.*

shrimp *v.* To suck someone's toes for perverted sexual gratification.

shrink-wrapped gammon *n.* A lady who wears clothing several sizes too small for her *lovely personality.*

shtup *v. Yiddish.* To have sex, *fuck, bang.*

shum *n.* That mixture of excrement and ejaculate which is a by-product of certain practices which are rightfully frowned upon in polite society. *Santorum.* From shit + cum.

shunt *v.* To *shtup.*

shushes *n.* One's early morning preparations for the day ahead. A *shag,* a shave, a *shit,* a shower and a shampoo. *'His Holiness will be out to canonise you in a moment, Mother Teresa. He's just finishing off his shushes.'*

shuttle cock *n.* One who *explodes* on re-entry. Or occasionally *goes off* a few seconds after lift-off.

Siamese quims *n. Scissor sisters. Lezzas* who are constantly *bumping fur. Carpet bumpers.*

sicasso *n.* A colourful bit of pavement art in which can be seen figurative elements of diced carrots, peanuts and crisps. An example of late night abstract expressionism reminiscent of the action paintings of Jackson Pollock.

side winders *n. Spaniel's ears* which appear to be gravitating towards the oxters. *Pit fillers.*

sideburns *n.* The marks left on multi-storey car park walls by women who should either get power steering or trade down to a *witch's broom.*

sidepipe *n.* A semi-erect *cock* visible down one leg of a tight pair of trousers, as sported by *rock poodles* and gentlemen in tightly-packed London Underground carriages.

sidesaddle *1. n.* A demure horse-riding style preferred by ladies so as not to snap their *virgin strings* before their wedding night. *2. n.* Non-conventional *porcelain pony*-riding style favoured by the more capaciously-buttocked defecator.

sidewinder *1. n.* Some sort of snake that is often seen in nature documentaries, scuttling across the desert sand like a scaly brace and bit. 2. *n.* Missile used by the Americans to shoot British reporters. 3. n. The elevation of one's left or right buttock in order to facilitate the surreptitious release of a *Judi Dench.* A *one cheek sneak.*

shot at the title *n.* A do-or-die chance to have a go on a *bird's snatch.*

sign no dockets, tip the load and *euph.* Of a gentleman, to deposit his *filthy concrete* in a place where he wouldn't want anyone to find out about, *eg.* up the *clopper* of a lady who his mates might regard as falling short of their rigorous quality control standards. From the habit of cheeky HGV drivers who, in order to avoid tedious form-filling and ridiculous red tape, prefer to empty skipfuls of rubble, asbestos, toxic clinical waste, dead hitch-hikers *etc.*, in remote lay-bys and under picturesque country hedgerows.

Signora Romero *n.* An apparently beautiful woman who, on closer inspection, is sporting a moustache under her makeup. From the natty facial hair visible in close-ups of Cesar Romero's Joker in the 1960s *Batman* TV series.

sign the visitor's book *v.* To leave a note of appreciation at the bottom of another's *skidpan. Sign the guest book.*

Sigourney Weaver *rhym. slang. Beaver.*

silencer *n.* A *pap-baffle.*

silent movie, watch a *1. v.* To enjoy the slapstick, dialogue-free antics of Buster Keaton, Harold Lloyd, Fatty Arbuckle and friends. *2. v.* To anxiously thrash one's genitals within an inch of their lives whilst watching a *grumble vid* with the sound muted so as not to disturb the wife asleep upstairs.

silicone strap *n.* The strap of a shoulder or handbag which pulls tightly in between the *baps,* enhancing their size and profile without the need for costly cosmetic surgery. A *tit splitter.*

silicone valley *n.* The cleavage

'twixt adjoining *bazongers*. The *Bristol Channel*.

silly string *1. n.* A light-hearted novelty *shit* that squirts out of one's *aeros-hole* in a rapid and erratic manner. Breaks the ice at parties. Occasionally incorporating small solid lumps, when it is known as a *bicycle chain. 2. n.* Sticky substance light-heartedly sprayed in the face of an actress in a slapstick *art film*. Kept in a cannister that requires vigorous shaking.

Simon Cowells *rhym. slang.* Bowels, *ie.* things that can be irritable and are usually full of *shit*.

Sindy's dildo *n.* A particularly under-endowed endowment, that is to say a risibly small penis. *'I seen that Keith Chegwin nude quiz show last night. Fuck me, I thought I had a small cock, but Cheggers's was like Sindy's dildo.'* (HRH Prince Charles, addressing the Royal Institution of British Architects, Mansion House 2002).

sing a rainbow *v.* To *shout soup*.

sing at St. Pauls *v.* To perform *cumulonimbus* on a woman with a *bucket fanny*.

Singer *n.* Sexual athlete, he or she who goes *at it* like a sewing machine.

singing ginger *n. Scot.* Glaswegian slang for any beverage containing alcohol. *'An' gie me a bottle o' yer cheapest singing ginger, Jimmy.'*

singing into the mic *sim. Horatio* performed in the style of a *slag night* karaoke star.

singlie rosettes *n.* The discarded *jizzmops* that adorn the floors of unattached men's rooms. *Poppadoms, wanker's crisps, porn crackers*.

sing sweet violets *v.* Airy version of *building a log cabin*, to *take a dump*.

sink a few U boats *v.* To drop a few *depth charges*.

sink plunger *n.* A *tug* administered by an inexperienced woman where she appears to be attempting to snap your *banjo* and pull your *fiveskin* over your *clockweights;* the action she would use when unblocking a plughole. Opposite of a *squid wank*.

sink the Bismarck *v.* To launch one *fucking* enormous dreadnought, deposit a *U blocker*.

sink the sausage *v.* To get one's *leg over*.

siphon the python *v.* To take a *Chinese singing lesson, see a man about a dog.* To go for a *gypsy's*.

Sir Anthony *rhym. slang.* A proper *charlie.* From Sir Anthony Blunt = cunt.

Sir Cliff's neck *n.* The bit of taut, elongated *scrotum* just above the bit that's got your *knackers* in.

Sir Douglas *rhym. slang. Shit.* From Sir Douglas Turd.

SISO *acronym.* A gentleman who suffers from premature ejaculation. A *two-push Charlie.* From Straight In Straight Out.

site box *1. n.* In the construction industry, a filthy, dented, cold and rattly receptacle that everybody is allowed to chuck their tools in at the end of the day. *2. n.* In a public house, a resident female with a filthy, dented, cold and rattly *box* that everybody is allowed to chuck their *tools* in at the end of the night. A *shed*.

sit on job *n.* Term used in the construction industry referring to the hanging out of a contract. *'You want it finished for the* 2012 Olympics Opening Ceremony? *Up your bollocks, this is a sit on job, mate. We'll get* eight more *turkeys out of this one, don't you worry.'*

sitting on an elephant *adj.* To be highly *burbulent*, to have *brewed a massive one up.*

sitting on the stove *euph.* Of a lady, to have been *scuttled* from behind so hard and so often that she develops twin circular red glowing patches at the back and top of her thighs, as if she has been resting her *arse* on the two front rings of the cooker hob.

sitting on your balls, it's like *sim.* Descriptive of the unpleasant and distinctly sickening feeling experienced when watching the fake jollity and camaraderie between the hosts of BBC's Breakfast Programme.

six-back *n.* The not-overly-attractive rolls of lard on the backs of fat grannies. *Back tits.*

six nowt euph. Descriptive of something performed on the *old walking stick* with gusto and enthusiasm.

six-pack grip *n.* See *tenpin.*

six point niner *n.* A *sixty-niner* which is interrupted by a period, *viz.* "6.9".

sixteen valve *n.* A stunner, a corking *bird*.

sixth gear *n. Wanking*, especially in a parked car. See *stick shifter*.

sixtitty-nine *n.* A sort of splendid lesbian version of *looping-the-loop* which somehow involves four knockers.

sixty grit *1. n.* The coarsest grade of sandpaper available. *2. n.* The coarsest grade of woman available. *'Up betimes, and much perturbed to find a veritable piece of sixty grit alongside me in the fart sack. Resolved never again to mix the port and the stout.'* (from *The Diary of Samuel Pepys*).

sixty-eight *n.* Oral sex undertaken on the understanding that the favour will be returned. *''Ere, give us a sixty-eight and I'll owe you one.'*

sixty-nine *n. Soixante-neuf, loop the loop.* Also *sixty-niner.*

size aero *euph.* The opposite of size zero. The dress size of a lady who has a tendency towards over-indulgence in the popular, eponymous bubble-filled chocolate confection.

size ten *euph.* How girls of sizes fourteen to eighteen describe themselves prior to going on a blind date.

skanky panky *n.* Scoring with a member of the lower orders.

skeet *1. v. US.* To shoot clay pigeons. *2. v.* To *shoot your load*. To come off at the *Billy Mill roundabout.*

skeeze *v. US.* To *shag, shtup*.

Skeggie donkey *euph.* A *bint* who'll let anyone get their *leg over* for a quid. And has all flies round her arse.

skelpit erse *sim. Scot.* Descriptive of a face that looks like a *smacked arse.*

skiddy fiddler *n.* One with an unhealthy interest in soiled undergarments. *'Today's birthdays: 1804 - Alan Clark, pioneering telescope manufacturer; 1841 - Oliver Wendell Holmes Jr., US Supreme Court Justice; 1859 - Kenneth Grahame, author of Wind in the Willows; 1943 - Lynn Redgrave, eminent film and stage actress; 1964 - Mark Oaten MP, skiddy fiddler.'*

skid marks *n.* Severe *russet gusset*,

pebble dashing of the *undercrackers*, the *turtle's brylcreem*.

skidmata *n.* The miraculous brown wounds which manifest themselves on the fingertips of one who is a martyr to thin *bumwad*. Also *taxi driver's tan*, *mechanic's fingernails*.

skiing position *n. Wanking* two men off at the same time while wearing only a h*elmet, goggles and thick mittens. Crane operating.*

ski jump *n.* That challenging first *slash* of the day when one has woken up *piss proud*.

skimmed milk *1. n.* Horribly thin and weedy dairy produce that invariably spoils a perfectly good cup of tea. *2. n. Baby gravy* with all the goodness taken out. *Decaff spaff* that would also, to be fair, spoil a cuppa.

skin boat n. Penis. *'I think I'll sail the old skin boat to tuna town.'*

skin chimney *n.* A flue that requires regular sweeping with a *womb broom*.

skin-clad tube *n.* A *live sausage*, a *girlometer*.

skin flick *n.* A tame *fuck feature*, blue movie, *mamba matinee*.

skin flute *n.* A *fleshy flugelhorn*, *bed flute*, *pink oboe*.

skin grafts *n.* Somewhat unimpressive *tits*.

skinternet *n.* Ceefax, teletext. From skint + internet.

skinny latte *n.* The thin, watery fluid typically released at the climax of a chap's third *glad-handing* of the day when he is *working from home*.

skipper 1. n. A lady's elusive *clematis*, *love button*, *wail switch*. See *bald man in a boat*. *2. v. naut.* In naval parlance, to wipe one's *arse* on a slice of bacon prior to presenting it to the captain in a sandwich.

snurglar's delight *n.* A velocipede which offers double the *quumfing* opportunities for an enterprising *snufty*, *shniffle-piffler* or *shramper.* A tandem.

skipper's tablecloth *n.* Several sheets of *bumwad* laid carefully across a *self indulgent* chap's stomach and legs in order to contain and absorb any spillages which may occur whilst he is *tossing* in his bunk.

skippy *n.* A promiscuous male who jumps about from *bush* to *bush*. A *fanny hopper.*

skirt *n. coll. Fanny, blart, toosh, talent*. *'I've got a pink ticket tonight. Let's get down the bar and pick up a bit of skirt.'*

skirt lifter *n.* The female equivalent of a *shirt lifter*. A *carpet muncher*, a *lezza, Victorian photographer*.

skit *v.* To *shit* diarrhoea.

skittered *adj.* Afflicted with the *skitters*.

skitters, the *n.* The *shits*, the *squirts*, the *Earthas, Alex Wurtz.*

skittling *n. Dining at the Y* during *rag week*. From the popular fruit-flavoured confectionery catchphrase, *ie.* "Taste the rainbow".

skittuin *n.* The product of the *skitters*, especially in dogs, *canine paint stripper,* puddles of brown acidic gunge on the carpet.

Skoda going over a cattle grid, like a *sim.* Phrase used to describe the throes of female ecstasy. *Shaking like a flat-pack wardrobe. 'After some hours tramping across the remote glens beyond Cairnsmore of Fleet, I found myself hungry and tired at the door of a herd's* *cottage set in a nook beside a waterfall. The door swung open as I knocked, and stepping inside the lowly dwelling I was surprised to see the householder, a dour, elderly shepherd, up to his apricots in his wife. He was banging away like a steam-hammer as I entered, and, oblivious to my presence, the lady of the house was shaking like a Skoda going over a cattle grid.'* (from *The Sixty-Nine Steps* by John Buchan).

skull buggery *n. Pugwashing, salami-sucking*. Also *skull-fucking*.

skunk stripe *n.* The characteristic white residue left by dried up *bum sweat* in a pair of ladies' black *grundies*.

skyagra *n.* A quick flick through the satellite TV channels before bedtime, made by a middle-aged gentleman in search of something to boost his flagging sex-drive.

slabberdash *v.* In fighting or romance, to slap one's opponent or lover upon the side of the face with a semi-erect penis. To *chap*.

slack mabbut *n.* A *hippo's mouth*, a *beef wellington*.

slacktivity *n.* Swinging the lead in the workplace, *eg.* idly rating the women who walk past, stealing stationery, masturbating in the toilets.

sladger *n.* A west country term for a lady's *minge*. A *Cornish fanny, konz*.

slag *1. n.* A woman of little virtue, *slapper*. *2. n.* Waste material from a mine. *3. n.* Term of abuse (pronounced "*slaaaaaag*") applied liberally to male criminals and other assorted *toe rags* in *The Sweeney*.

slag off *v.* To deprecate verbally.

slagazine *n.* Ladies' periodical that does not make too many intellectual demands on its readership, *eg. Take a Break, Chat, Hello, OK, Spare Rib etc*.

slagbait *n.* Aftershave.

slag bat *n.* A crude term for the *blood stick*.

slaggle *n. coll.* Collective noun for a group of young ladies who are generous with their affections. From slag + gaggle.

slag hammer *n.* A *tool* a gentleman uses for *banging twats* rather than nails.

slag heap *n.* A run-down pub or nightclub in any northern town.

slag night *n.* High-spirited female binge drinking excursion in a town centre. A *hen night*. Also *slag do*.

slag stamp *n.* A tattoo applied to the small of a *salad dodger's* back in the mistaken belief that it will draw attention away from her enormous *arse*.

slag wellies *n.* Knee-high boots.

slam dumping *n.* A light-hearted jape whereby the prankster *shits* in the cistern rather than the bowl. *Top decking*.

slam hound *n. US. Slapper, slut*.

slam in the lamb *v.* Bayonet manoeuvre involving the *mutton musket*.

slam on the brakes *v.* To stop wiping one's *arse* for some reason, *eg.* the house burning down, with the full knowledge that the process is incomplete, resulting in *skid marks* or *russet gusset*.

slam spunk *v.* To have *it off*.

slap and tickle *n.* A sex act, a bit like *rumpy pumpy*, whereby a man wearing a dress shirt and sock suspenders chases an excited lady round a bed before catching her, playfully slapping her *buttocks*, tickling her ribs and *fucking* her up the *cunt* with his *cock*. A *romp*.

slap and trickle *n.* A perfunctory, routine act of *self abuse* that elicits only a half-hearted return on one's *wristy investment,* possibly as a result of the four *wanks* one has had in the previous couple of hours. A low budget *money shot*.

slaphead *n.* A *chrome dome*, a *baaldie*.

slaphood *n.* A *slapper's* prime of life.

slapper n. A dirty woman. She who has been around a bit. From the Yiddish "schlepper" meaning "I don't fancy yours much".

slapperazzi *n. coll.* The humorous youths who use their mobile telephones to make amusing films of their friends committing acts of grievous bodily harm on innocent bystanders. *Happy slappers*.

slapper trapper *n.* A man who, lacking the wherewithal to trap a *fox*, settles for hunting *swamp hogs* instead. A *pig-sticker.*

slappertite *n.* A hunger for loose women. *'Do you fancy a fuck, Bill?' 'No thanks, Hillary. I don't want to ruin my slappertite.'*

slappette *n.* A betracksuited, *hickied*, bubblegum-chewing, *scrunchie*-wearing fledgling *slattern*.

slapster *n.* One afflicted by male pattern baldness, alopecia or mange.

slapstick *n.* A light-hearted, comical *wank*.

slap the monkey *v.* To *chimp oneself* till one is *blue in the arse*. To do a *Mary Chipperfield.*

slash *n.* A *piss, wee wee, number one*.

slash and burn *1. n.* Impressively-efficient third world deforestation technique. *2. n.* A painful symptom of the *pox* and the *clap*.

slash palace *n.* Public lavatory.

slash point *n.* Sheltered area in a town centre which affords privacy for the purpose of depositing urine. *'Hang on lads, I've just got to nip to the slash point before I flood me Calvins.'*

slate layer's nailbag *sim.* Descriptive of very saggy or battered *labia*.

slats *1. n.* Ribs. *'I'm gonna rattle her slats with me womb broom.' 2. Aus. Beef curtains. 'I'm gonna part her slats with me womb broom.'*

Slaven Bilic *rhym. slang.* Spillage, specifically the emptying of a couple of *nutsworth* onto a game young lady's face. Named after the anvil-faced Croatian footballer.

sledge *n.* A bloke who is constantly *pulled* by *dogs*.

sledging *1. n.* Unsporting cricket match repartee designed to put batsmen off their stroke. *2. n. Aus.* Consenting impolite *rumpy pumpy*. Acts of intercourse during which one or both parties abuse each other with colourful profanities. Foul-mouthed pillow talk. *'August 6th. To the BBC for a recording of Call My Bluff with Frank (Muir), Ian (Ogilvy), Angharad (Rhys), Hannah (Gordon) and Joyce (Grenfell). Joyce afterwards invited me to take tea in her room at the Savoy. One thing led to another and we ended up sledging into the early hours. Gracious, what a potty-mouth she can be.'* (from *Fiddling in the Foliage*, the memoirs of Arthur Marshall).

sleep in a tent *v.* To have a large penis. *'Fancy coming back to my place? You'll not be disappointed.*

I sleep in a tent.'

sleeping beast *n.* Flaccid *cock, marshmallowed main pipe.* A *dead budgie.*

sleeping fruit bat *n.* A vagina with *flaps* which are so big and leathery it appears that the lady has a mammal of the genus *Pteropus* napping between her legs. A *resting pterodactyl.*

sleeping policeman *1. n.* A hump in the road, designed to slow down traffic and remove exhaust pipes from sports cars. *2. n.* An officer of Her Majesty's Constabulary in his pyjamas with his eyes shut. 3. *n.* An *angry* penis, tucked up behind the belt in order to conceal it from family or friends. A *kilroy.*

sleeping pull *n.* When a fellow is unable to sleep, he may have one or two of these to help him nod off.

sleep vaulting *n.* Gentleman's nocturnal discomfort, which involves him growing a massive *tent pole* whilst asleep, only for it to jam into the sheet when he tries to turn over, thus startling him into pained wakefulness. A *motorcycle kickstand* complication.

slice *n.* A portion of *hairy pie.* A vagina.

slice of cheesecake *n.* A *plate* of *horatio. 'Belgravia was powerless to resist. His eyes burned into hers like caborundums. His strong arms enfolded her tender body as she felt herself being swept away in an Aurora Australis of passion. Eagerly she fell to her knees, pulled down his scuds and helped herself to a slice of cheesecake.'* (from *The Lady and the Darts Player* by Barbara Cartland).

Slimbridge, dawn chorus at *sim.* The cacophonous symphony of hooting, quacking, honking and whistling which emanates from a lavatory cubicle occupied by a person *paying in installments* for a particularly virulent and delicious *slip-up* feed. From the aural similarity to the early morning sounds heard at the late Sir Peter Scott's famous duck zoo.

slime *v. Aus.* To ejaculate, *chuck one's muck.* To reach *Lake Wendouree. 'Have you slimed yet Rolf?'*

slip a length *1. v.* To *give a good seeing-to to someone. 'I'd slip her a length any day of the week.' 2. v.* In the world of *saucy* seaside postcards, a conversational misunderstanding involving a landlady with a tenant who works at a linoleum factory.

slip her a crippler *v.* A few notches up from *slip her a length*, to *shtup* someone so hard they can't walk.

slippers, shit in his *v.* To *do the dirty* with a good friend's missus. *'Are you going to poke me then, Eric? I'm absolutely gagging for it.' 'No, I can't Patti. It just wouldn't be cricket to shit in George's slippers like that.'*

slippery as a butcher's cock *sim.* Untrustworthy, sly. From the well known fact that all butchers take carnal advantage of the meat in the back room before selling it.

slit *n. Blit, fanny, vertical bacon sandwich.* See *slot.*

slobberchops *n.* The thin film of translucent *blip* secreted from the *bacon sandwich* that forms a crust in a *bird's dunghampers* after intercourse. *'How dare you accuse me of knocking one out whilst you were on holiday, that's the remnants of your slobber-chops,* *you cheeky cow.'*

slob's oven *sim.* Descriptive of an overused and undercleaned *fanny.* With black, carbonized chips lying round the bottom of it. One that would benefit from a good scrubbing with Mr Muscle and a wire brush.

sloom *n. medic.* The lubricating secretion of the lady's Bartholin's glands. *Blip, moip, chin varnish.*

slop dodger *n.* A prudish or frigid lady who for some reason objects to getting her face *bespunkled* by a gentleman.

slop on *n.* A state of female sexual arousal. A *wide on.*

sloppy seconds *n.* To *stir the porridge.* To stick one's *naughty paintbrush* into a *billposter's bucket.*

slot *n. Slit.*

slot garnish *n.* A frilly bit of nothing which looks nice, but is quickly pushed to one side so one can tuck into the *meaty main course.* Any ladies' *farting crackers* bought from the Ann Summers shop.

slot machine *n.* A battery-powered neck massager, shaped like a big nobbly *cock.* A fruity vibrator.

slow puncture *euph.* One of those days when one seems to be constantly losing gas. *'I don't know what was in that fifteen pints of Younger's Scotch Bitter I had last night, but I seem to have a slow puncture today.'*

slug *n.* A woman who simultaneously combines the twin qualities of sluttishness and ugliness, *eg.* that fucking nightmare off of *Wife Swap* again.

slug on a brillo pad *sim.* Poetic description of the result of *relaxing* rather too often and violently in a *gentleman's way. 'I tell you what, Natasha, I'm going to have to cancel my wank channel subscription. My cock looked like a slug on a brillo pad this morning.' 'Thanks, Dermot. And now over to Everton Fox with the weather.'*

slumberlumber *n. Morning wood.* A timber kickstand for one's wrinkly, pink-wheeled hairy motorcycle. *Dawn horn.*

slut *n.* A woman who doesn't wash her nets often enough and has the milk bottle on the breakfast table.

slybrarianship *n.* A chap's discreet stewardship of his *grumble* stash.

smackanory *n.* The heart-rending tale of woe with which heroin addicts routinely regale passers-by in the hope of relieving them of their small change.

smackdonalds *n.* A residence in a less than salubrious *scruburb* where money is deposited in one window and pharmaceuticals are dispensed at another.

smacket *n.* A drug addict's multi-pocketed coat worn when skulking round shops.

smack generator *n.* A retailer of second hand electrical goods which is used by thieves to convert stolen goods into cash to spend at *smackdonalds.*

smackhead special *n.* A nourishing bus station cafe feast, consisting of pie, chips, peas, two slices of buttered toast and a pot of tea, all for £1.25.

smack oneself about *v.* To *relax in a gentleman's way.*

smackpool illuminations *n.* Extremely premature and gaudy Christmas lights found adorning houses in the country's less exclusive locales.

smacksuit *n.* A set of market-bought athletic clothes of the sort favoured by youngsters on Britain's more vibrant estates.

smack tokens *n.* Items of electronic equipment, *eg.* car radios, laptop computers, videos *etc.*, with the plugs cut off.

smear campaign *1. n.* A series of verbal or written attacks deliberately intended to defame or discredit someone. *2. n.* What happens inadvertently when one has the *turtle's head. Fudging the issue. 'Oh come on, just answer the question, Mr Howard. In your capacity as Home Secretary, did you or did you not threaten to over-rule the head of the Prisons Service Derek Lewis? Yes or no.' 'I'm not going to answer that, Jeremy, but what I will say is this - if I don't pot the brown soon I'm going to embark on a smear campaign.'*

smear test *1. n. medic.* Medical procedure which detects precancerous cells in the cervix. *2. n.* Toilet procedure to determine if one has got all the *shit* off one's *nick.*

smear test pizzas *n.* Budget supermarket pizza on which the toppings have been kept to a minimum for reasons of economy.

smedgie *n. Can.* An hilarious practical joke whereby a lady's *bills* are vigorously yanked up her *clopper.* From smeesh + wedgie.

smeesh *1. n. Can.* Female reproductive *farmyard area.* The *snapper. 2. n. Can.* A collective noun for ladies. *Blart, tussage, cabbage. 3. n. pej. Can.* A doltish fellow. A *fuckwit.*

smeesh hawk *n. Can.* A *clout* with the *gorilla salad* shaved into a mohican.

smeg *1. n.* Pungent *knob cheese. 2. n. prop.* Amusingly-named Swedish manufacturer of white goods. *3. n.* A substitute for *fuck* overused in *Red Dwarf.*

smeg cup *n.* The cupped hand traditionally used by *wankers* as a receptacle to catch their *muck* when *pulling the Pope's cap off* in a standing position. A *wanker's chalice.*

smegma dome *n.* A baby *bell end,* with a waxy, red skin. The *lid, Dutch strawberry.*

smegma *n. Smeg.*

smeg peg *n.* An unwashed penis, with a gamey aroma redolent of cheese, *spunk* and stale *blip.*

smelling mistake *n.* Emitting an unpleasant miasma and/or a comical sound from one's *fundament* at a time when one would be best advised to grit one's teeth and hang on for dear life in an attempt to keep it in, *eg.* at a funeral, whilst exchanging one's wedding vows, when being chased through a spaceship by an alien, whilst hiding in Carol Vorderman's wardrobe at Yorkshire TV *etc., etc.*

smellmet *n.* A smelly *helmet.* From smelly + helmet.

smellody *n.* A *botty bugle* solo of a particularly musical timbre.

smell the toffee, wake up and *exclam.* Useful phrase which a married man can use when a *breakfast maker* has failed to rouse his missus from her slumbers.

smig *n. W. Yorks.* A person of *shit* quality from Huddersfield.

smint shuffle *n.* The practice whereby a gentlemen allows a small breath-freshening mint to dissolve under his *fiveskin* in order to make his *herman gelmet* cool and tingly in preparation for a subsequent *wank*. The technique can also be used by the more considerate *noshee* prior to receiving a *nosh* to mask the aroma of *hedam* and thus make the experience slightly less vile for his *noshatrix*.

Smithfield porter's cap *n*. A *clopper* deprived of its necessary monthly launder.

SMOG *acronym*. Suck Me Off Gob. A lady's mouth which appears capable of drawing a golfball through 200 yards of garden hose, *eg*. Angelina Jolie, Sophie Marceau or any Brazilian *bird* one cares to mention.

smoke *n*. A *chewie*, a *nosh*. A *blow job*. *'Excuse me, Miss Taylforth, this is a no-smoking taxi.'*

smoke a gadgee *v*. To take a few drags on a *pink cheroot*. Though not in a public place.

smoke out the mole *v*. To induce a reluctant *feeshus* by means of lighting up a cigarette.

smoke the bald man *v*. To light up a *salami cigarette*.

smoke the white owl *v*. To commit an act of *horatio*.

smoking bangers *sim*. Descriptive of a woman with a lovely personality, *ie*. a *bird* who looks as though she's been sparking up fireworks.

smoo *n*. *Aus*. A *minge*, a *sportsman's gap*.

smoot *n*. *medic*. A *bird's* private area. *'The babysitter wanted me to go to bed after Big Brother, so I gave her a right kick up the smoot, mum.'*

smuggling a brownie *v*. To have the *turtle's head*. *'He seemed quite anxious to get away, officer. I suspect he was smuggling a brownie.'*

smurfing *v*. *Blue surfing*. Trawling the information superhighway on the lookout for pictures of *tits* , *bums, fannies, the lot*.

smush piece *n*. The *faff*. A lady's *front bottom*, a *clopper*.

smut *n*. Mild *jazz*. *Porn lite* that would make a maiden aunt purse her lips like a dog's *ringpiece*.

snag your jeans on a nail *v*. To emit a high-pitched, rasping *ringtone*.

snail's doorstep *n*. A *clapping fish* that is as *wet as an otter's pocket*.

snail trail *n*. *Smoo juice* in a lassie's well-worn *scuns*.

snake v. To *fuck, poke, bang, futter*.

snake charmer *n*. A girl who has an uplifting effect on your *pant python*, such that it rises up and sways about in her face.

snakeskin *1. n*. The clothing sloughed off in one piece and found at the bottom of the bed after a night *on the piss*. *2. n*. The dried, flaky layer that tends to form overnight on the stomach of an unhygienic male who nods off after commiting an act of *self-pollution*.

snake spit *n*. The clear fluid that precedes the *jizz bolt*. *Pre cum, perseverance soup, ball glaze, preek*.

snap and tickle *n*. Of an *earthing cable*, the phenomenon of it touching the bottom of the *chod bin* before snapping off at the *clackervalve*, and then striking the back of the *chicken skin handbag* as it falls.

snap, crackle, plop *onomat*. The sound made in the bowl during a particularly satisfying session of *parking one's breakfast*.

snapdragon *n*. A normally agreeable female who under certain circumstances, *eg*. when *up on blocks* or full of *tart fuel*, becomes a vicious, fire-breathing monster.

snapped candles *sim.* Descriptive of one's legs after a night *on the lash,* when one is wearing one's *wobbly boots.*

snapper *1. n.* North-east colloquialism for a thin fellow. *2. n. milit.* Royal Naval slang for one who is *nicely poised. 3. n.* A lady's *bodily treasure.*

snap the key off in the lock *v.* To suffer an unsatisfying *shit. 'Good dump, dear?' 'Sadly not, my petal. I'm afraid I've snapped the key off in the lock. I'll have this pine cone in all night now.'*

snart *n.* To sneeze and *fart* at exactly the same moment, resulting in *nose jizz* on the face or *rabbit tods* in the *bills.* Or both.

snatch *n. Quim,* vagina, *liver sock.*

snatch 22 *n.* An aesthetically unconventional woman who would, paradoxically, require so much beer to *fuck* that you couldn't *get it up* anyway.

snatch fence *n.* An invisible, *cock*-proof barricade erected down the centre of a matrimonial bed following a domestic argument. A *gash barrier.*

snatchlings *n.* Up-and-coming *talent.*

snatchment area *n.* The geographical radius from which a drinking establishment draws its female clientele.

Snatchmo *n.* A *fanny* with lips strong enough to play *Basin Street Blues* on an E-flat trumpet.

snatch mouse *n.* A tampon, *cotton pony, Prince Charlie, chuftie plug.*

snatch patch *n.* A feminine hygiene product. A *fanny nanny.*

snatchphrase *n.* A particularly successful chat-up line.

snatch quack *n. medic.* One who has the sexy, enviable job of examining malfunctioning *minges.* A *box doc, fanny mechanic.* A gynaecologist.

snatch rats *n.* Ladies' sanitary products. *Jampaxes, jam rags, etc.*

snatch worms *n.* Tiny pieces of tightly-rolled bog paper that lurk in the labial folds, normally only discovered during particularly expert *cumulonimbus* which dislodges them from their hidey-holes.

sneaky Hitler *n.* The surreptitious slipping of one's index finger under one's nose in order to savour the aroma of one's ladyfriend's *blip.*

snedge *1. n.* Snow. *2. n. Jism.*

snedger *n. Snufty, snurglar, snudger, quumfer.* Another name for a smeller of ladies' bicycle seats.

sniffers' row *n.* In a strip club, the seats that are closest to the stage.

sniff the cork *v.* To check one's finger the morning after going *knuckle deep* up the missus's *bonus tunnel,* to determine whether your hand needs a proper wash with soap or whether a quick wipe on her flannel will suffice.

sniggerette *n.* A drug addict's *tab* containing a quantity of *happy baccy.* A *spliff.*

sniping *n.* Accidentally shooting a jet of *slash* through the gap between the rim of the *chod bin* and the underside of the seat and onto your *kex* whilst sat down having a *tom tit.* A *Wee-Harvey Oswald, rim shot.*

snipper reflex *n. medic.* The counter-productive and inexplicable urge to cut a *cable* before it is fully *laid,* usually resulting in an *arse like a Marmite pot.*

snippit valve *n.* The *anal sphincter.* The *nipsy.*

snitches *n. Two aspirins on an ironing board, stits, fried eggs.*

snob sick *n.* Vomit with plenty of canapes and Chardonnay in it outside a wine bar.

snobtoss *n.* An act of cultured *self-pollution* committed whilst watching a sophisticated, subtitled movie on FilmFour.

snog *v.* To *swap spit, tongue wrestle, play tonsil hockey*.

snogging water *n.* A male grooming lotion that smells like *Joan Collins' knickers. Fanny-magnetic* aftershave, such as Hi Karate or Old Spice.

snoodling *n.* An unlikely-sounding sexual practice reputedly favoured by gents who are *good with colours,* whereby one of them pulls his *fiveskin* over the *herman gelmet* of his chum. Also *docking,* a *clash of heads.*

snookered behind the red *adj.* Unable to *sink the pink* due to the time of month, and faced with a *difficult brown.*

Snoopies *n. Spaniel's ears, Ghandi's flip-flops.*

snoregasm *n.* The culmination of a *wet dream.*

snorkeller's lunch *n.* A wet fish dish which is a particular favourite amongst *muff divers.*

snorkelling *n.* The holding of a gentleman's *nollies* in a lady's mouth whilst she applies a repetitive stroke to his *favourite member.*

snorker *n.* A *sausage, poky banger, Cumberland.*

snot *n.* The perineum of the lady. Because "it's not" *etc. etc.*

snotty hammock *n.* The gusset area of a *bird*'s intimate apparel at the end of a long day. A *toddler's sleeve.*

snoutcasts *n.* Those poor unfortunates who are forced to huddle in pub, factory and office doorways to enjoy their *cancer sticks. Fag lepers.*

snout pout *n.* That haughty uptilt of the nose favoured by *pedigree ratters* with ideas somewhat above their stations, *eg.* Posh Spice, Candice who used to be *in Corrie.*

snowball *v.* To blow *salami cigarette* smoke back into the tobacconist's mouth.

snowdrifts *n.* The extra *fanny lips* that larger ladies have, which are crisp and white due to the fact that they never receive any sunlight.

snowdropper *n.* Underwear fetishist who steals to sniff, usually from washing lines. A *knicker bandit.*

snudge *v.* To sniff a lady's bicycle seat after she leaves it chained to the railings. *To moomph.*

snuffling for truffles *sim.* Descriptive of a loud and somewhat messy performance of *cumulonimbus.* From the act's resemblance to the phenomenon of a large, wet-nosed pig rooting through the topsoil looking for a pungent, yet valuable actinomycete. Though presumably without a large mob of excitable French peasants watching. *Darth vulva.*

snufty *n.* One who *snudges.* A *garboon.*

snurge v. To *snudge, snurgle, barumph.*

snurglar *n. Quumfer, snudger,* bicycle *snufty.*

snurgle *v.* To *snuft, snudge, shramp, quumf, scrunge, pringle, snerge, snedge, snaffle, snarze, snerk, snerdle, shniffle-piffle, nurf, moomph,* *barumph, garboon, poon, snarf, snurdle* or *snurge.* To sniff the recently-vacated bicycle seats of young ladies, a hobby that seems to be named more often than it is performed.

soap dropper *n.* One who is *good with colours.* One who is *light on his feet.* From the prison shower etiquette where, like a Georgian lady dropping her handkerchief in the park to attract the attention of a suitor, a big, hairy *nick-bent* psychopath with an erection drops the soap in the showers to woo a prospective companion. A *botter.*

so solid poo *n.* An extremely troublesome *dump* which feels like passing a handgun wrapped in a sock.

soap-on-a-roper *n.* One who prefers not to bend down in communal showers.

soapy carpenter *n.* A man who is *good with colours.* From the fact that he "lathers at the sight of wood".

soapy tit wank *n.* A *sausage sandwich* served in the bath or shower. *'Take two bottles into the shower? Not me. I just go in there with me bird and she gives me a soapy tit wank.'*

sob stopper *n.* A small present of little value which is acquired on the way home by a thoughtful man who has drunk too much and stayed out too late, in the hope of stopping his missus turning the fucking waterworks on. Examples include cheap chocolates bought from all night garages and bunches of flowers stolen from cemeteries and railings.

social hand grenade *n.* A married man who comes out *on the pop* so infrequently that when he does he is a major liability to those around him.

social sticks *n.* Crutches that are only used when the bearer is going for a medical, signing on, cashing his giros *etc.* See also *dole pole.*

sockbreaker *n.* A *strum* of such vim and vigour that the weft of one's chosen *jitler* receptacle is eroded.

sock jock *n.* One who likes to ride the *baloney pony* harnessed with a trusty item of hosiery.

sock method *n.* To *roll the dice* into a sock in the absence of anything else to *roll the dice* into. See *crunchie.*

sock sucker *n.* A prudish woman who insists on one donning a *dunky* before *noshing* on one's *slag hammer.* A *French puritan.*

socktator sport *n.* Any game played by scantily-clad and copiously-perspiring young ladies which is broadcast to a rhythmically appreciative male audience. Also *pullympics, quimbledon fortnight.*

socktits *n.* Very long, saggily pendulous *chichis. Spaniel's ears.*

sockumentary *n.* A *masturmentary, rudimentary, palmorama.* A TV programme best enjoyed whilst wearing an odd number of socks.

sod *n.* A loose piece of turf in an *uphill garden.*

sodom eyes *n.* The look of love that one gives the missus at bedtime to let her know that there is more than a cuddle on the cards.

sofa spud *n. US.* An enthusiastic televisual autodidact. An American equivalent to the British *couch potato.*

soft on, have a *v.* To be confronted by a less-than-exciting amorous prospect.

soggy moggy *n.* A romantic epithet to describe the *back to front* of a lady who has reached a sufficient state of arousal so that it will *go in* without too much fuss. A *slop on.*

soixante-neuf *n.* Top-to-tail *horatio-cumulonimbus.* French for *sixty-nine. Loop the loop.*

sol *n.* A swift drink at the pub after work, *ie.* "A quick half and then home". A cheeky reference to lumbering footballer Sol Campbell and his recent "personal trouble".

solicitor's office *n.* Something a gentleman enters in a spirit of optimism, only to leave a short time later screwed, shafted and penniless.

solicitor's tie *n. Fr.* A *pearl necklace.* Costing £160 an hour plus disbursements.

someone let him in *exclam.* An amusing remark which can be used immediately after an audible *rectal report* has been filed. See also *more tea vicar; speak on, sweet lips that never told a lie.*

someone's tinkered with Herbie *exclam.* A witty riposte one delivers when one *backfires* unexpectedly. From the lines delivered in *The Love Bug* after the baddy has sabotaged the eponymous VW beetle, causing its engine to cough and splutter. See also someone *let him in; more tea vicar?*

somewhere to park the Harley *euph.* A particularly massive *arse.* From the fact that the buttock cleft on just such an outsized posterior would be the ideal place to lodge the wheel of a 700lb 1340 Softail Fatboy motorcycle in order to prevent it falling over.

sonic bog lock *n.* The random assortment of whistles, coughs, hums and throat clearings that are made by the patron of a public *crapper* cubicle with no lock on the door.

SO19 officer *euph.* Any overly eager gentleman who, whilst in a state of excitement, prematurely pumps several rounds from his *mutton musket.* Into an innocent *Brazilian.*

sooker *n. Scots.* A *tit.*

Sooty and Sweep's frying pan *n.* Capacious women's genitalia.

Soprendos *n.* A series of gentle *farts* which precede a *Thora.* From the catchphrase of Victoria Wood's formerly-obese magical faux-Spaniard ex-husband: "Piff, paff, poof".

soreskin *n.* A sore *foreskin.*

sound the charge *v.* In a row of engaged toilet cubicles where shyness prevents any and all occupants from performing their foul ablutions, to blow the first *botty bugle* blast. *'I was sat in there ages until someone sounded the charge.'*

soup but no croutons *adj. medic.* Descriptive of a low *springle count, spoogeless spaff. Firing blanks, derren.*

soup cooler *n.* A lipless *fart* that has the characteristics of a gourmet gently and silently blowing across a bowl of piping hot lobster bisque in a posh restaurant.

sour apple quickstep *n.* Another diarrhoea dance. The *Tijuana cha-cha. 'Your wife is taking rather a long time in the powder room'. 'Yes, I'm afraid she's dancing the sour apple quickstep tonight.'*

sour mash *n.* A particularly soft morning *shit,* usually sponsored by Jack Daniels or Jim Beam.

south col *n.* Mountain climber's

euphemism for a lady's *front bottom*.

southern sideburns *n. Thighbrows.*

southmouth *n.* The *snatch, fadge, quim.*

Southport *1. n.* The *arsehole. 'Fancy a trip to Southport tonight, love?' 'Yeah, alright then.' 2. n.* Lancashire town at the mouth of the Ribble Estuary. *'Fancy a trip to Southport tonight, love?' 'Eurgh! Certainly not. Don't be disgusting.'*

SOW *1. acronym.* Sexy Older Woman. A lady one wouldn't ask to leave the bed, despite her advanced years, *eg.* Honor Blackman, Nanette Newman, Geri Halliwell. *2. n.* One notch up from "cow" on the female insult scale.

spacers *n.* A pair of breasts which, though large in size, exhibit no cleavage due to their distance apart. *East-westers.*

space shuttle *n.* A *shit* that has a tendency to break up on entry into the *bog bowl.* A *Columbia, six million dollar man.*

SPAD *acronym.* Signal Passed At Danger. To drive your *Interclitty 125* at full pelt into the *tunnel,* despite seeing the red warning signs at the entrance. To stick your *cock* into *Billy Connolly's beard.*

spaddel *n. Spooge, spoff, spaff, spangle, gunk, jitler.*

spadework *n.* The hard graft that must be undertaken before planting one's *seed* in the *ladygarden. Frigmarole, choreplay.*

spadger *n. Aus.* Vagina.

spaff *1. v.* To *spoff* or *spod. 'No, no, no, Gunther! Be professional, spaff on the chest, not in the pussy.'* (from an unidentified grumble flick, circa 1980). *2. n. Splid, splunt, sploffer, sprankle.*

spam alley *n.* The target zone for *spam javelin* throwers.

spambidextrous *adj.* Able to *beat one's truncheon meat* with either *wanking spanner.*

spambulance *n. Shaggin' wagon, fuck truck, stick transit.*

spam butterfly *n.* A finger-assisted *close-up pink* shot in a *bongo mag.* A *peel.*

spam castanets *n.* Percussive *scallops,* a *clapping fish.*

spam danglers *n.* The sloppy, protruding inner flaps of a lady's *hooter.* Generously-proportioned *bacon strips, gammon goalposts.*

spam fritters *n.* Labia. *Dangly ham,* especially when served in *batter.*

spam javelin *n.* An 8-foot long *cock* with a sharpened end.

spam monkey *n.* An ape that is partial to indulging itself with *luncheon meat.*

spamogram *n.* Stylised pictographic representation, or hieroglyph, of a disembodied set of male genitalia, usually seen scrawled on toilet walls, bus shelters, religious textbooks and the backs of photographs of washing machines posted to disc jockey Mike Read. A *three-line pud.*

spamouflage *n.* Copies of *Time, The Economist, London Review of Books etc.*, picked off the lower shelves of newsagents in an effort to give the impression that one's copy of *Hot 'n' Horny* was merely an ironic afterthought. *Palmouflage.*

spam purse *n.* A particularly unsightly *snapper,* usually found in the nether regions of women with *lovely personalities.*

spam sceptre *n.* The ceremonial rod that sits atop the *crown jewels.*

spandrels *n. Men overboard, croutons, tiger nuts.* General vaginal detritus.

spangle *1. n.* A sticky, unpleasant mouthful that is most often spat out. *2. n. Spunk.*

spangle bangle *n.* A hair band kept close to her bed by a keen *fellatrix,* in order to keep her hair out of her eyes as she performs *horatio.*

spangle dangle *n.* A lady's intimate jewellery item, hanging off her pierced *pygmy's thumb,* popular amongst actresses in *self help* films.

spaniel's ears *n.* Sagging, flat *thruppenny bits. Snoopies, Fred Bassets.*

Spanish archer *n.* The push, the "El Bow". *'She caught me in bed with her sister and her mum, and she gave me the old Spanish archer. Tchoh! Women, eh?'*

Spanish cravat *n.* A *pearl necklace.* Also *Dutch cravat, Chinese bow tie.*

Spanish plumbers *n.* Ill-tailored trousers, from their tendency to pinch the base of the urethra and thus "always leave it dripping".

spank banks *n.* A mental reference library of erotic imagery, which can be consulted when *spanking the monkey.* Also *mammary banks.*

spankerchief *n.* A tissue, or square of fabric for mopping up post-*monkey-spanking banana yoghurt.*

spanking *n.* A form of corporal punishment still practised in *rub-a-tug shops.* See *Mr Whippy, fladge and padge.*

spankrupt *adj.* Descriptive of a gentleman who, upon *advancing the manly meat,* finds himself bereft of inspiration.

spank the monkey *v.* To *bash the bishop, burp the worm.*

spank the plank *1. v.* To play the electrical guitar in a "pop" beat combo. *2. v.* To *toss* oneself off.

spanky hanky *n. Jit gel rag, wank sock.* Anything used for clearing up *gunk* after a *tug.* A *spankerchief.*

spanner *1. n.* Not the sharpest tool in the shed; a right *fuckwit. 2. n.* Top *stoat,* one who "tightens one's nuts" A *monkey wench.*

spare *n.* In a *meat market,* that *flap* which is not yet sold.

spare elbow skin *n. John Wayne's hairy saddlebags, chicken skin handbag.* The scrotal sac.

spare room offence *n.* Any minor misdemeanor that upsets a wife or girlfriend, *eg.* coming home drunk, forgetting her birthday, *fucking* her sister *etc.*

sparrowfart *n.* Early morning.

sparrowfuck *n.* A rapid act of *congress* between a man and a woman, reminiscent of the 1-second *spunk up* of the common house sparrow, *Spuggius domesticus.*

spasbo *n.* In modern youth slang, one who has picked up an anti-social behaviour order for a really *wank* reason, such as swearing in the street, dropping litter or having sex with a horse.

spasm chasm *n. Spam alley.*

spastard *n.* A politically incorrect term for one who exhibits the qualities of both a spastic and a *bastard.*

spatchelor *n.* A single fellow who results to *floor-scraping* tactics in order to pick up the crusty bits of *sediment* off the dance floor at chucking out time.

spat out toffee, face like a *sim.* Descriptive of a lady with a physiognomy somewhat reminiscent of a *stripper's clit.*

spawning *v.* The saucy act of masturbating in a public swimming pool.

speaking clock *n.* A fellow afflicted with premature *spoffage.* A *two-push Charlie.* From the fact that he "never gets past the third *stroke*".

speak on, sweet lips that never told a lie *exclam.* Poetic riposte which can be delivered to humorous effect after a *duck* has been audibly *stepped on.* See also *someone's tinkered with Herbie; keep shouting Sir, we'll find you.*

speak up caller, you're through *exclam. Speak up Brown, you're through.*

speak Welsh *v. Shout soup, blow chunks, yoff.*

spearmint wino *n.* A *heavily refreshed* gentleman of no fixed abode who insists on undressing and gyrating in the street.

spear the bearded clam *v.* to perform a trick involving a *spam javelin* and an hirsute bivalve.

spear the blow hole *v.* To have sex with a *BWR.*

speed dating *1. n.* Something people probably do in bloody Richard Curtis films or them fucking Bridget Jones books. *2. n.* The use of the fast forward button whilst watching a *Baywatch* DVD in order to find a suitable lady with which one can enjoy a brief yet torrid relationship. *3. n.* The act of looking out of a train or bus window into the bedroom windows of passing houses in the hope of seeing a nice pair of *milkers.*

speeding ticket *1. n.* Expensive piece of ephemera resulting from a minor motoring misdemeanour. *2. n.* A small *tod* which nevertheless entails a lot of paperwork. A *shit of a thousand wipes.*

speedophile *n.* A suspicious-looking man in a swimming pool who does a lot of watching but very little swimming.

spelky fence *sim.* A *John Craven* that is in the early, stubbly stages of pubular regrowth. A *cuntry file. 'It was like running my hand across a spelky fence.'*

spend a pound in pennies *v.* To play the *tuppenny waterfall,* to *shit the jackpot.* To suffer a *fall of old shoes from the loft.*

spend one's money before one gets to the shop *euph.* Of an over-eager gentleman, to *spongle* his *spaff* before the *glebe end* has entered the *faff.* To suffer the enjoyable, time-saving affliction of premature ejaculation.

spend tuppence in ha'pennies and farthings *v.* To pass loose stools, have diarrhoea. To release a *flock of pigeons.*

spent fuel rod *1. n.* A bar of depleted uranium following its removal from a nuclear reactor. *2. n.* A sadly-depleted and flaccid *giggle stick* following its removal from a *clopper.*

sperm *n. medic.* How doctors refer to *spunk, gism.*

sperm burper *n.* A sensible lady who isn't afraid to guzzle *spadge.*

sperm curdler *1. n.* A Victorian kitchen utensil made from copper. *2. n.* A satanically *fugly woman, eg.* Ann Widdecombe, Kathy Staff, Tracey Emin.

sperm noodle *n.* An airing cupboard-dried sleeping bag which has previously been used by a sexually-overactive male who has inadvertantly impregnated it with a quantity of *dream topping*. Best avoided by ovulating, damp females.

sperm perm *n.* Hair style achieved by the application of three squirts of a glutinous product from a cylindrical container. With all wiggly veins up the side and a couple of hairy *knackers* dangling underneath.

sperm wail *n.* A low grunting noise emitted at the moment one's *moby dick spouts*. An ejaculatory ejaculation. See *spuphemism*.

sperm worm *n.* The penis.

spew *1. v.* To vomit, *park a tiger*, be sick. *2. n.* The sick itself. *'Mum. This soup tastes like fucking tramp's spew.'*

sphinny *n.* The *nipsy*. *'I think we should stop, Rod. Me sphinny isn't what it used to be.'*

Spice island *n. Stinkhole Bay, Dilberry Creek*. A foul-smelling archipelago favoured by sailors on their *trips around the world*. The *arsehole*.

spicy duck *n.* An *Exchange & Mart* that sounds like Donald Duck throwing up, and probably presages a swift trip to Primark to buy some clean *underkecks*.

spiddle *n.* A term for the *piss* a lady takes after intercourse. A mixture of *spunk* and *widdle*.

Spiderman wank *n.* Of a gentleman, an act of *self-pollution* undertaken whilst wearing a pair of lady's *bills* on the head, such that the *gusset* is directly over the nose, leaving eyeholes in the place normally filled by legs. A *musk mask*.

Spiderman, do a *v.* To *spunk up* into one's hand, then attempt to remove it by *flicking ropes* against the wall.

spiders' legs *n.* Of *muffs*, rogue pubic hairs which protrude beyond the knicker line, the hairs of a *pant moustache*.

spill one's beans on the worktop *v.* To *ice* a lady's *buns*. To *lob ropes*.

spill the beenys *v.* Of a bachelor television watcher, to experience the inevitable *yop-dropping* climax to a session of viewing Channel 4's *Property Ladder* programme, hosted by the magnificently-fronted Sarah Beeny.

spill the Brasso *v.* To *drop one's yop, donate to the church fund*. To ejaculate whilst *polishing the coal scuttle*. *'What's all this mess on the carpet?' 'Sorry mum, I spilled the Brasso. What's good for getting spunk out of tufted Wilton?'*

spin cycle *n.* The final, frenzied stages of a *gentleman's act of relaxation*, when the floor starts to vibrate and nearby crockery starts to rattle and fall off shelves *etc*. A *wanker's vinegar strokes*.

spinner *1. n.* Member of that semi-religious, polo-neck wearing folk band without whom no variety programme in the 1970s was complete. *2. n.* A petite lady who can be spun on one's *cock* like the propellor on a beany hat. A *throwabout*, a *cock puppet*.

spinning plates *n.* An old-fashioned novelty act in which the performer attempts to keep both of a lady volunteer's nipples erect at the same time.

spirit level arse *n.* A little bubble of *fart* that lodges between the *arse cheeks* and acts as an indicator of one's inclination.

spirit levelled *adj.* In the ultimate

state of *refreshment*. As *refreshed as a fucking newt*.

spiss *n*. The mixture of sperm and urine produced during a post-coital wee-wee. *Spiddle*. *'That was a truly beautiful lovemaking experience, darling. Now keep toot for the scuffers while I have a spiss in Bradford & Bingley's doorway.'*

spit *v*. What fussy or frigid women do instead of *swallowing*.

spit a nut *v*. To *gamble and lose*. To *follow through*, to *shoot the breeze*.

spit her rag out *v*. Of a lady during *cricket week*, to uncontrollably eject her *jammy dodger* onto the floor whilst undergoing a spontaneous and unnecessary bout of *showing off*. Also *pop a knocker*.

spit roast *n*. Someone simultaneously skewered at both ends by *pork swords*. A *sausage jockey* who plays a *pink oboe* whilst still in the saddle. A *corn on the cob*.

spitwank *n*. A lazy or prudish lady's *horatio* avoidance technique; specifically a saliva-assisted *J Arthur* masquerading as a *blow job*. Normally experienced when the man has recently spent time shifting a heavy filing cabinet up or down a fire escape, imbibed several pints of export strength lager or *EastEnders* is about to start.

spla water *n*. Semen, *gunk*.

splash 'n' dash *1. n*. In motor racing, the act of heading to the pits for a quick fill when short on fuel within the last few laps of the race. *2. n*. In *dumping*, to head to the *crapper* when *touching cloth* whilst late for an important engagement. *'Where's Huw? He's on air in forty-five seconds.' 'Don't worry. He's just gone for a splash'n'dash*. *3. n*. A *squat 'n' squirt*.

splashback *1. n*. An area of tiles behind a sink. *2. n*. Unfortunate tidal effect of a *depth charge* or *belly flopper* within the pan, resulting in splashing of the *arse* and *barse*.

splash diet *n*. A weight loss programe that involves the shedding of pounds of unsightly excrement. A *dump*. *'I can't do these jeans up again. I'd best just go on a splash diet. See you in ten minutes.'*

splashdown *n. milit*. Official Parachute Regiment terminology for a *wetting of one's bed* after a mammoth drinking session.

splash me boots *v*. To have a *piss*, take a *leak*.

splat *n. medic*. *Bollock batter*, *fetch*.

splay *v. US*. To draw back the *beef curtains* and make a grand entrance.

splice *v*. British version of *splay*.

splinge *n*. A particularly lubricious *kipper mitten*. A *bag of slugs*.

split a kipper *v*. To *part the whiskers*, to *have it off*.

splitarse *n*. An offensive, sexist term for a *bird*. *'Birthdays: TV and film actor Tom Selleck, 57. Olympic Gold medalist diver Greg Louganis, 43. Splitarse boffin Germaine Greer, 64.'* (from *The Times*, Jan 29th 2003).

split bag of mince *n*. A *gutted rabbit*, a *butcher's dustbin*.

splitter cable *1. n*. An adaptor from Maplins for plugging two television sets into a single chipped satellite decoder. *2. n*. A *Thora Hird* which is so humungous that it rents one's *Jap's flag* in twain.

split the beard *v*. To *part the whiskers*, again. After 20 minutes or so.

And a fag.

split the winnings *euph.* To halt the *laying of a cable* halfway through. *'And after four days without movement Job took up his toilet and great was his relief. But even as he released his burden there came a voice and it was the Lord. And the Lord spake in a loud voice saying Come unto Me Job. And Job replied saying Oh God, what is it this time, for I have only just sat down. And great was the wrath of the Lord. And He commanded Job to split the winnings and come now unto Him. And great was Job's discomfort.'* (from *The Book of Job*).

splod *1. n. Sprag, spoff. 2. v.* To *sprag, spoff.*

splodge *v.* To masturbate semen over a glossy magazine.

splosh *1. n.* Money. *2. n.* Britain's leading periodical for those interested in genito-spaghetti pursuits.

spluff *1. v.* To *spunk up. 'She took her bra off and I spluffed in my pants.' 2. n. Spunk. 'Nice tits, Mother Superior. By the way, is there anywhere I can put these pants? They're full off spluff.'*

splurry *n. Fizzy gravy*. Diarrhoea.

splutterbeans *n.* The *Eartha Kitts.*

spock *v.* To make a "V" with one's fingers and boldy go where no man has gone before, *ie.* two up the *twat* and two up the *arse.*

spocks *n.* Socks that have been used as a ejaculation receptacle or post-*bust off* clean-up device. From spodge, spadge, spoodge, spaff, spangle, spingle, spongle, *etc.* + socks.

spod *n.* See *spooge.*

spof *n. Spod.*

spoilers *1. n.* Aerodynamic wing modifications that prevent Citroen Saxos from flying into the sky when being driven up and down in Burger King car parks. *2. n Buttocks, mudflaps.*

spoilsports bra *n.* An item of intimate apparel used by women who unaccountably wish to suppress the natural movement of their *bangers.*

spondle *n. Spooge, spluff, spangle, jitler, knob toffee.*

sponge *1. n.* In a *puddle jumping* couple, the one who has feathers stuck in his teeth. *2. n. prop.* A silent character played by Colin Bean in *Dad's Army.*

Spongebob's nose *n.* A distinctly unimpressive, yellow *cock.*

spooge *n. US. Spoff.*

spooge scrooge *n. A trojan*, condom, *rubber policeman.*

spooge stick *n. Gut stick, fuck rod, slag bat*. The penis.

spoot *n. Scot.* A word for *spunk.* Usage limited to Campbeltown on the Mull of Kintyre. If you went into the pub in Machrihanish and said the beer tasted like spoot, they wouldn't know what you were talking about.

sporran catalogue *n.* A *grot mag.* Specialising in ladies with snap-shut, shaggy grey *snatches.*

sport relief *1. n.* Marathon charity event at the end of which one feels compelled to make a £15 donation to the cause. *2. n.* Trampy marathon *self abuse* session at the end of which one feels compelled to make a 15ml donation to the pages of West Bromwich's most dispiriting daily newspaper.

sports bag *n.* A handy *cottaging* accessory in which one partner stands to conceal his feet and avoid detection by lavatory attendants looking under the door. See *bagging*.

sports model *n.* A woman who has had her *tubes* tied and thus provides worry-free sexual fun for caddish males.

spouse *1. n.* One's marital partner. *2. n.* Her *fanny*.

sprag *1. n. Spoff, splod. 2. v.* To *spoff, splod.*

spreader *n.* A variation on a *moonie*, whereby the buttocks are manually pulled apart to reveal the *freckle*.

spreadsheet *n.* Shiny, crinkly toilet paper found in public lavatories which only succeeds in smearing the *shit* around one's *arse* like a plasterer's float.

sprew *n. Spongle, jitler, spragg. Spunk.*

spring a coil *v.* To *lay a cable, drop a copper bolt, build a log cabin, grow a tail, drop your fudge, pinch a loaf, crimp one off, drop the shopping, drown a copper, give birth to a dead otter, light a bum cigar, park your breakfast or drop off a length of dirty spine. 'Anyone seen the new Viz kicking about anywhere? I'm off to spring a coil.'*

spring clean *n.* A gentleman's first morning visit to the *crapper* after a night on the *lash*, where he has a *dump* and a *slash*, blows his nose, picks the sleep from his eyes and generally begins the miraculous process of coming back to life.

spring onion roots *n.* An elderly *tart's* unruly *gorilla salad.* The *welcome mat* of a lady of advanced years.

sprogdrop *n. medic.* Pregnancy. A state of *up-the-duffness*, expecting a *lawn monkey*.

sprouts *n.* Children.

spud fumbler *n.* A *puddle jumper. 'Today's birthdays: Antoni Gaudi, Catalan biomorphic architect, 1852; Alexei Alexeyevich Abrikosov, Nobel Prize-winning Russian physicist, 1928; George Michael, drug-driving spud fumbler, 1963.'*

spud, to *v.* To deliberately mess up a job interview in order not to jeopardize one's benefits. Named after the character in *Trainspotting*.

spuds deep *adj. Up to the maker's nameplate.*

spuffer *n.* An extremely localised Tyne Dock colloquialism describing male ejaculate.

spuffing dust *n.* The plight of a gentleman who is experiencing a *jizzbolt* drought, following a 6-hour *wanking* marathon.

spuncle *n.* A sperm donor. From spondle + uncle.

spunctual *adj.* Of a gentleman *grumble thespian.* To be able to *spoff* on cue or to a pre-arranged schedule.

spuncture *n.* An incidence of latex failure at a critical moment whilst using a *jubber ray.* A leak in a *beef wellington*, a bursted *blob.*

spunk *1. n.* Semen, *seed. 2. n.* Spirit, pluck. *3. n. Aus.* A good-looking man, dish, hunk. *4. n.* Tinder made from fungus. *5. v.* To ejizzulate, to *spooge*, esp. upwards.

spunk-curdling *adj.* Descriptive of a woman who can induce an instantaneous *derection* at a hundred paces. *'Deaths; Andrea Dworkin, spunk-curdling American feminist writer, 58.'*

spunk-drunk *adj.* Delirious nature brought on by over-consumption of *root beer*.

spunk dustbin *n*. A *spooge bucket*, *box of assorted creams*. An exceptionally accommodating young lady, who has a *twat like a paper hanger's bucket*.

spunk gurning *n*. The delightful faces a *grumble flick* actress pulls as she excitedly anticipates the *tipping* of the romantic lead's *cement* onto her face.

spunk juggler *n*. An *onanist* on a unicycle.

spunkled *adj*. Besprinkled with *spunk*.

spunkling *adj*. Sparkling or glistening as a result of being *spunkled*, *eg*. Gillian Taylforth's chin, the hat of a commissionaire at a hotel where Status Quo have booked a room with a balcony.

spunk mail *n*. The lifelong postal monsoon of unsolicited pornographic brochures and catalogues received as a result of foolishly buying a Linzie-Dawn McKenzie video from an ad in the back of the *Sunday Mirror* twelve years ago.

spunk rat *n*. A good looking bloke, as described by females.

spunk run *n*. *RN*. On Her Majesty's warships, the 2-inch gap down the side of a sailor's bunk where he stows *pop-up books,* soiled *grundies* and tissues on which he has *blown his nose.*

spunk shuffle *n*. The walk adopted by one's girlfriend to stop the *congregation* leaving the *cathedral* before she reaches the *bog*.

spunky wrench *n*. A *wanking spanner.* A gentleman's hand.

spuphemism *n*. A humorous *sperm wail*. A jolly shout upon *spoffage, eg*. "There she blows!" "Tim-berrrrr!" or "Yabba Dabba Dooooo!"

Spurt Reynolds *n*. Pet name for the tearful *bald man* who sits on the *hairy beanbags*.

spurtual reality *n*. The act of pausing a *skin flick* before *lobbing ropes* onto the TV screen, in order to create the impression that you are involved in the action; a feeling that, one would imagine, very quickly gives way to a vivid sense of self-loathing, not to mention an urgent need to clean a load of *spunk* off the telly before the missus comes in.

spurt your curd *v*. To spread your *spunk*, to *spunkle* others with your pluck and spirit.

squack *onomat*. The sound of a male ejaculation.

squaddie's delight *n*. A woman in the armed forces who is not *on the bus to Hebden Bridge.* A heterosexual Army, Navy or Air Force lady.

squaddie's mattress *n*. *milit*. Army version of the naval *matelot's mattress.* A lady who *spreads* for soldiers, especially round the back of Cheeks nightclub, Aldershot.

squaddie's sleeping bag *n*. A well-used and crusty *haddock pastie. 'Joan Hunter-Dunn was nothing like the bird in the poem, you know Michael. I licked her out once behind a skip in Camberley and she had a blurtch like a squaddie's sleeping bag, I can tell you.'* (Sir John Betjeman on *Parkinson*, BBC TV, 1975).

squashed spuggy/spoggy/sparrow *n*. An elderly lady's vagina. *Granny's oysters.*

squat 'n' squirt *n*. A manoeuvre often performed up dark alleys by ladies returning from the pub, and filmed by CCTV operators. A *splash 'n' dash.*

squatter *n.* An annoying little *turd* that takes up residence in one's *arse* and refuses to leave, unless threatened by Bermondsey Dave.

squeak the breeze *v. US.* To *fart, talk German, pass wind.*

squeaky toy *n.* A *fart* which sounds, and indeed occasionally smells, not unlike the popular, shrill noise-producing dog amuser.

squeeze the fig *v.* When needing a *tom tit* in a public place, to keep one's *nipsy* firmly clenched to prevent the *turtle's head* poking out.

squeeze the lemon *v.* Of women, to urinate. Possibly onto a pancake.

squeezing the cheese *v. Sausage stretching.*

squench *1. n.* A moist *fart* which feels like one has *gambled and lost. 2. n.* A character in Dickens's *The Old Curiosity Shop* who suffered a *fall of soot* during Little Nell's funeral.

squibble *n.* The second in a triumvirate of gentleman's *popshots,* the first of which is a squirt and the third of which is a dribble.

squidge *n.* A vagina with a *wide on.*

squid legs *n.* The thin, rubbery tentacles found floating on the water after a bath night session of *making nylon.*

squid marks *n.* Fishy *skids* in a lady's *fairy hammock.*

squid wank *n.* The kind of *wank* received from a lady inexperienced in the provision of *wanks*. Derived from the distinctive cuttlefish-like movement of the hand. A *tail of the unexpected, scuttlefish.*

squirrel covers *n.* A lady's *dung-hampers.*

squirter's alley *n. medic.* The *bodily treasure.*

squirting like a badly laid paving slab *sim. medic. Shitting* through the *eye of a needle, pissing rusty water* out of one's *arse,* in the style of an *affpuddle,* as defined in the *Meaning of Liff.*

squirts *n. medic.* In proctology, a series of fiery eruptions from the *chamber of horrors* resulting in a pyroclastic flow from the *farting fissure.* A condition also known as the *skitters*, the *Earthas, the Engelberts.*

squirty dirt *n. Medic.* Faeces of an extremely low viscosity. *'Come to the Curry Capital, Bigg Market, Newcastle upon Tyne - for a curry you won't forget in a hurry.'*

squishpot *n. US.* The area right below the *devil's doorbell.*

squits *n. medic.* Dangerous wet *farts*, constantly bordering on the *follow through.* Junior *squirts.*

STA *abbrev. Grumble* industry code denoting the job prospects of a starlet with less than conventional good looks. Straight To Anal.

St. Bernard's chin *sim.* Descriptive of a *muff* that has had lots of *ropes lobbed* at it. A heavily *bespunkled mingepiece.* Also *bloodhound's jowls.*

St. George *v.* To lance one's old dragon from behind. To take part in a *dog's marriage*.

St. Ivel *n.* An imperial measurement of beer, equal to 2 $^1/_2$ quarts or $^5/_8$ of a gallon. Five pints. *'Mr Barratt appeared unsteady on his feet as he got out of the car. I asked him if he had been drinking and he replied 'Not really. I've only had a St. Ivel.''*

stabbin' cabin *n.* A secondary residence kept for the sole purpose of quick extra-marital encounters, *eg.* a discreet flat in Belgravia, a small cottage in the Cotswolds, or a 12-foot caravan on the cliffs at Scarborough.

stabbing the cat *n. Self discipline.* From the motion of knifing an invisible feline on one's lap. Similar to *feeding the ducks,* but with the emphasis on the downward stroke.

stack blow *n.* A gentleman's *organism.*

stacked *adj.* Overstocked *rack* in the *snork* department. *'I fell in love with my wife at first sight. She is particularly well stacked.'*

stagecoach *n.* A cramped, filthy ride which leaves you in need of a wash. Also *riding shotgun.*

stalagshites *n.* Naturally-occurring, upward-pointing turdiferous deposits which form in porcelain basins.

stale bait *n.* A *bit of stuff* that's gone slightly past its "best before" date.

stalk *n.* Erection, *stiffy*. A *third leg, middle stump. 'Excuse me, if I look like a tripod. I just can't seem to get rid of this stalk. Anyway, let's carry on. Ashes to ashes, dust to dust.'*

stalk fever *n. medic.* Condition affecting men on *big cock day*.

stall shy *adj. medic.* The psychological condition that renders borderline *scuttlers* unable to micturate in public lavatories unless there is vacant stall between them and the next micturater. *Stage fright.*

stamped bat *euph.* One of the most horrific kinds of *ladypart* imaginable; a *bodily treasure* that resembles nothing so much as a flying rodent that has been subjected to a heavy shoeing. A *snatch* that not even Ozzy Osbourne would consider eating. *'Nostalgia was powerless to resist. His eyes bored into hers like zirconium-coated drill bits. His muscular arms enfolded her body as she felt herself being whisked away on a souffle of passion. Gently he lowered her bloomers, and a thrill of forbidden excitement shot through her loins as she felt his hot Latin breath beginning to creep down her crab ladder towards her altar of Venus. But it was not to be. 'Bloody Nora,' shouted Sextus Empiricus from between her legs. 'I'm not licking that out. It looks like a fucking stamped bat.''* (from *The Lady and the 2nd Century Pyrrhonic Skepticist Philosopher* by Barbara Cartland).

stamp on the toothpaste *v.* To ejaculate in an over-excitable manner.

standard eight *1. n.* More-or-less obsolete double-run home movie format which involved opening the side of the camera half-way through the exposure of the film in order to turn the spool over, thus ensuring that the mid-point of any domestic cine presentation in the early 1970s was characterised by flashing psychedelic orange lights. This was followed shortly by the splice, where the two twenty-five foot lengths of longitudinally split 16mm film had been joined together at the processing laboratory, snapping in the projector and the image on the screen melting before one's very eyes like something out of *The War Game* and a bout of swearing whilst your dad tried to re-thread the film through the white-hot gate with his fingers. *2. n.* Crapulent 1950s small family automobile, particularly suitable for the sort of small family that didn't require any boot space or a car that would climb any sort of gradient, and hence 3. *n.* A gentleman equipped with a small, underpowered *trouser engine* which is inclined to conk out mid-journey.

standby on *n. Half a teacake.* A penis in a state of semi-tumescence ready to leap into action if required.

stand on *n.* A *bone on*, a *stalk.*

standing on the fireman's hose *sim.* At the conclusion of the evening's fourth or fifth bout of *Jesuit boxing*, a complete failure to release *jaff.* An *air horn.*

standing ovation *n.* Mark of respect given to a *digestive transit* which is so impressive that one has to get up to have a good look at it.

stand lunch *v.* To provide an *air buffet* which stops anyone in the room feeling hungry any more.

stanky *n.* The glaze that is left on the *shaft* of the *choad* after a bout of *kipper splitting.* May be *zuffled* on curtains or wiped on a *stankychief*.

starboard bow *n. RN.* The *arse.*

starch pill *n.* A Viagra tablet, a *bluey.*

starfish trooper *n.* An *arsetronaut.*

starfucked *adj.* The loss of credibility suffered by a product as a result of its endorsement by a *shit* celebrity. Walkers crisps, Benecol margerine and Homebase DIY have all been *starfucked.*

starter button *n.* The *clematis,* the *wail switch.* The *clit.*

starter leads *n.* Suspenders, *giggle bands.*

starting line at Brands Hatch *1. sim.* Descriptive of severely *beskidmarked undercrackers.* Guaranteed to cause embarrassment the first time they are handed to one's newly-wedded bride for washing. *2. sim.* The *skid pan* of a student house or dysentery hospital *chod bin.*

start the horn mower *v.* To perform the particularly vicious upstroke often demonstrated by the inexperienced female *masturbatrix.*

star trek *n.* Any sexual encounter where one would be going (boldly or otherwise) where no man has gone before, *eg. getting tops and fingers* off Ann Widdecombe or doing Richard Littlejohn up the *shitter.*

Star Wars door *sim.* In *backdoor work,* descriptive of the manner in which the *death star* closes after the *pink Darth Vader* is removed. See *hoob.*

stash dash *n.* The sprint from front room window to *grumble* collection once the front gate is securely fastened behind the wife as she pops out for a pint of milk.

stauner *n. Scot.* A dour, granite-hard *bone on.* An *Old man of Hoy.*

steak drapes *n. Gammon goalposts, beef curtains.*

steakwich *n.* The external genitalia of a lady of a certain age which resembles a traditional British pub snack.

stealth bomber *n.* A subtle *leg lifter.* A mystery *benefactor*, phantom raspberry blower. An anonymous, gaseous altruist.

stealth moose *n.* An *LRF.*

stealth sites *n.* Football, car and DIY websites which can be quickly clicked on after *desktop dusting* in order to fool the more IT-literate missus

steg *n.* A woman resembling a ferocious, spiny, squat, prehistoric dinosaur. Abbrev. of stegosaurus.

stellacide, commit *v.* To purposely down an excessive quantity of *Nelson Mandela* in order that one's sorrows choke on their own vomit.

stellanoia *n.* The state of aggressive paranoia which one attains shortly after imbibing one's tenth pint of *wifebeater.*

stellaporter *n.* A futuristic form of instantaneous transportation which warps the time/space continuum, leaving one outside the front door mere moments after leaving the pub. Often with a wet trouser leg, a shoe full of *piss* and a half-eaten kebab.

stellarisation *n.* Process by which a man is rendered unable to father children. *'Sorry love, I can't do it. I've been stellarised, see.'*

stellavision *n.* Premium strength *beer goggles.*

stelloquence *n.* Term descriptive of a mightily *refreshed* late night kebab shop customer's witty, free-flowing banter and the fluent, well-informed discourse with which he regales his fellow prospective cat-meat snack purchasers.

stemmer *n.* A *chewie* in which the dirty lady is able to swallow the whole shebang. A *deep throat.*

stench trench *n.* The *ha'penny.*

Stephen Hawking's treadmill *sim.* Descriptive of something or someone of little use, *eg.* "personal transport revolution" the Sinclair C5.

step on a duck *v.* To create a quack, *fart. 'Pardon me, Ladies and Gentlemen. Do not adjust your wireless set, Mrs Simpson just stepped on a duck.'* (from The Abdication Broadcast of Edward VIII, 1937).

step on a frog *v.* To *step on a duck.*

step on a rake *v.* To attain a particularly speedy erection.

step on one's dick *v.* To make a mistake or blunder. *'It is with deep regret that I am today leaving the office of Home Secretary, in which capacity it has been my great honour to serve in this administration for the past 16 months. It is a job with an exceptionally wide brief, encompassing as it does many serious issues, not least of which is the treatment of foreign national prisoners who have completed their sentences – a matter for which I have taken overall responsibility and on which I have staked my reputation. The Prime Minister, as is his right and responsibility, has made the judgement that I have stepped on my dick, and therefore my continued occupation of my current position is likely to stand in the way of the continued reforms which remain necessary. I am therefore being relieved of my cabinet post with immediate effect, and returning to the back benches.'* (Rt Hon Charles Clarke MP, statement to the House of Commons, reported in *Hansard,* May 5th 2006).

Steptoe & Son *n.* A drab and depressing sexual position, whereby a solitary, clapped out old nag kneels on the bed, proffering her knackered back end up to her old man, who slowly and disgruntledly *bangs* her whilst gurning and muttering under his breath. And then stops to shovel her steaming dung into a bucket.

Steptoe's face *n.* A saggy non-too-fussy set of *flackets*. *ie.* "they will take in any old rag or bone".

Steve *n.* A Scotsman who *shops around the corner*, *eg.* Jimmy Somerville. From Steve McQueen.

Steven and the twins *euph.* A fellow's *meat and two veg*, often referred to by Ian Beale in *EastEnders*. The *Kennedys*.

Steve Wright *n. rhym. slang.* A *shite* with a contingent of turdy-hangers on. Named after the *crap* Radio 2 presenter. *'I'm just off for a Steve Wright in the afternoon.'*

Stevie Wonders, the *n. medic.* The involuntary wobbling of the head that one exhibits when desperately trying to stay awake, *eg.* a student in a Friday afternoon lecture or a lorry driver on the M6. From the erratic head movements of the Motown star. *'The trial of the Millennium Dome Jewel Robbers was held up today after Judge Michael Coombe was spotted having a severe attack of the Stevie Wonders during the defence council's summing up.'* (Nicholas Witchell, *BBC News*, November 2003).

stick at 15 *v.* From the pontoon playing gambit, to settle for a low quality score; thus to go for the first half decent bit of *blart* who shows interest in a night club. See also *go ugly early*.

sticklebrick *n.* A particularly difficult and uncomfortable *tod.* A *pine cone.*

stickman *n.* A *fanny hopper*, a *skippy*.

stick shifter *n. Wanker.*

sticky belly flap cock *n.* Post *curd-spurting* condition enjoyed by *monkey spankers*.

sticky keys *1. n.* Some sort of annoying computer function on the Windows operating system which is activated by pressing the shift key five times, apparently. *'I was just messing about on the computer and I turned on sticky keys by accident.'* *2. n.* The inevitable result of an overenthusiastic and poorly-aimed session of *one-handed web-surfing*. *'I was just messing about on the computer and I got sticky keys by accident. And spunk all over the mousemat and screen. And printer.'*

sticky toffee pudding *n.* A thick, dense *Thora* that adheres to everything it touches, particularly one's *arse cress*.

sticky wicket *n.* A well used *crease* with all the bounce *fucked* out of it. A *box of assorted creams.*

stiff drink *n.* A warming tot of *vitamin S* quaffed by females and *puddle jumpers*. A *drink on a stick.*

stiff enough for the wife *adj.* Descriptive of something which, while not optimal, is adequate for the job at hand. *'Is that plaster dry yet, Dave?' 'No mate, but I reckon it's stiff enough for the wife. Let's sling the wallpaper up and we can piss off down the pub early.'*

spooch *n. Spooge, spodge, spadge, splang etc. Jism.*

stiff *n.* A corpse. *'Come on jerkwad, let's plant the motherfucking stiff and get out of here.' 'Very well, vicar. I'll tell the organist to miss out the last two verses of the Funeral March.'*

stiff lock *n.* A *piss-proud spooge stick.*

stiffy *n.* A *stalk.*

stiffy stocking *n. Rascal wrapper, cheesepipe clingfilm, Spurt Reynolds's sickbag.*

stig *n.* One who is a little bit *coun-*

cil. One who is *common as shite*. A dump dweller. *'Birthdays: JK Galbraith, economist, 95. Arthur Schlessinger, historian, 86. Mario Puzo, author, 83. Sarah Ferguson, Royal stig, 44.'* (*The Times*, Oct 15th 2003).

still fighting *adj*. Of a curry or spicy meal, to display the same or greater aggression on the way out as it did when it went in. *'Are you all right in there, love?' 'No. It's that chilli I had last night. It's still fighting.'*

stilt on *n*. A long, thin, cheesy erection.

stilton muffle *n*. A pungent and unwashed *fish mitten*. A particularly stenchsome *trench*.

Sting wank *n*. A post-pub act of *self- pollution* which, as a result of the amount of alcohol one has consumed, becomes a turgid marathon lasting many hours. From the former Police frontman's notoriously fruitless attempts to *go off* up his missus.

stink *1. n*. The distinctive odour of well-matured *knob cheese*, eggy *air biscuits*, a *stilton muffle etc*. *2. v*. To emit such a smell, to *ming*. *3. n*. A fuss. *4. n. Aus*. A scrap, fight, *pagga*.

stink sponge *n*. A chair or bus seat which someone has just *dropped a gut* into.

stinky finger *n*. Having ate up the *captain's pie* without a knife and fork. *Stinky pinky*.

stinky Mervin *n*. The *Finsbury bridge, biffin bridge, barse, carse, taint, notcher, etc*.

stir the tanks *v*. To have a *wank* without ejaculating. From the routine procedure on the ill-fated Apollo 13 which inadvertently led to an explosion. See *almosturbate*.

Stirling *rhym. slang*. A *wank*. From Stirling Moss = toss.

stirring the porridge *n*. Having *sloppy seconds*, dipping one's *naughty brush* into a *billposter's bucket*.

stits *n*. Small *tits, bee stings, Dutch Alps*.

stoat *n*. In the world of pant nature, the natural prey of the *one-eyed trouser snake*.

stobart *n*. An articulated *turd* that jack-knifes in the pan.

Stobby doorbell *n*. A handful of gravel directed at the window of an upper floor residence to alert the occupants as to one's presence below. Used extensively in the salubrious Stobwells district of Dundee.

Stockport overcoat *n*. A thick coating of glitter spray which, when combined with a boob tube and miniskirt, keeps the young ladies of the Cheshire town snug and toasty on the bitterest of winter evenings. A *Bigg Market duffle coat, Whitley Bay parka*.

Stoke chamois leather *n*. An orbital sander, used to remove grafitti from the boarded-up windows which are commonplace in the popular Potteries shit hole.

stonads *n*. Testicles which have fossilized due to under-use. *'A lifelong celibate, Sir Isaac got the idea for his popular Newton's Cradle executive toy when his stonads banged together as he was sitting down under an apple tree to invent gravity.'* (from *Connections* by James Burke).

stone *n*. The reason a *sponge* has got feathers stuck in his teeth.

stone cold stunner *1. n*. A wrestling

move, actually a variation on the ace cutter, made popular by redneck grapple fave "Stone Cold" Steve Austin. *2. n.* An actress in a vintage black and white movie who manages to give one the *horn* despite the fact that she is almost certainly six feet under. See *rise from the dead.*

stone of contentment *n.* The excess 14lbs avoirdupois rapidly acquired by a bloke when he moves in with his ladyfriend and starts spending a significant proportion of his spare time sitting on his *arse* watching repeats of *Coronation Street.*

stoner's grocer *n.* An all-night petrol station selling family-sized chocolate bars and biscuits to narcotics enthusiasts at unsociable hours.

stones *n. arch.* Olde Worlde *balls. Bollocks, knackers.*

stonker *n.* Erection, *hard on, stiffy.*

stop at Boots *v.* Phrase expressing optimism about the outcome of a romantic interlude. *'You going to get in Tracey's knickers tonight, then Steve?' 'Well, I'm stopping at Boots, put it that way'.*

store defective *n.* A retail store *fuckard.*

stout trout *n.* The impressively charcoal-hued *Eartha* that transpires following an eighteen-hour sampling of dark ales and burgundy pie.

straightening your hat *n.* Raking one's kex out the crack of one's *arse.*

straighten your tie, let me *exclam.* Phrase used by a woman who is offering to give a man an erection in the *trouser department.* Or just possibly suggesting that she is about to re-arrange his neckwear.

strain the potatoes *v.* To *strain your greens.*

strain your greens *v.* To have a *piss.*

strange *n.* Any woman whom one has not had *carnival knowledge* of. An antidote to a *groundhog lay.'I know she's minging compared to the girlfriend, but you can't beat a bit of strange, can you?'*

stranger, the *n.* The act of sitting on one's hand until it falls asleep before a bout of *bishop rage,* giving the feeling of a *hand job* from someone else.

strangle Kojak *v.* To *make the bald man cry,* to *peel the carrot.*

stranks *n.* The delightful "fridge magnet bunch of grapes"-style *shit* clusters one finds plastered to the porcelain in public convenience *chod bins.*

strapadictomy *n.* Routine operation to strap on a *dildo.*

strawberry Sunday *n.* Of a gentleman, the point when he is so desperate for a *scuttle* that he no longer cares that *rag week* is not yet over.

stray steaks *n.* Outsized flappage. *Beef curtains* of Brobdingnabian proportions.

streaker *1. n.* One who removes their clothes and runs about at sporting events whilst the BBC pretend they are not there, *eg.* that witless *twat* from Liverpool. *2. n.* A *Richard the Third,* slightly smaller than a *U-blocker* and with a slightly pasty consistency, which leaves behind a brown streak as it scuds around the *pan* on being flushed away. A *brown arrow.*

Stretch Armstrong *n.* One gifted with the ability to eat *gorilla salad* whilst simultaneously *finding Radio Luxembourg.* Also *Superman.*

stretched quimosine *n.* An extremely elongated *fanny* that has taken plenty of people for a ride.

strike a damp match *1. v.* To stimulate oneself against an unwitting stranger in a crowd, *eg.* on a tube train, in a queue to see the Pope lying in state. To *frotter. 2. v.* To attempt to have a *wank* with a *soft on.*

strike oil *v.* When doing a *duty* on the lavatory, to eject a *feeshus* with such force that its impact causes a vertical spout of water which hits one squarely in the *jotter.*

strike up the colliery band *euph.* To produce a protracted *trouser cough* from your *brass eye.*

strike while the iron's hot *v.* To have an opportunistic *Barclay's* as a result of spotting something completely *wankworthy* when out and about, *eg.* in the bus station toilets after spotting a cracker on the number 38, or in a department store toilet after encountering a really sexy mannequin in the lingerie department.

string *n. Wood,* tumescence. *'Quick, everybody, Gunther's got string. Fluffer off set, please and roll camera.'*

stringbean *n.* A long, thin, probably green, penis that gets left at the side of your plate.

string of pearls *n.* A series of tiny *botty burps* released in quick succession whilst walking. *Air croutons.*

stripper's clit, face like a *adj.* Of a woman, having a *charming personality.*

stripy laugh *n.* A *parked tiger*, a *Welsh monologue.*

stroke mag *n.* An item of top shelf literature, *art pamphlet, gentleman's interest magazine.*

stroke of midnight *n.* A free *one off the wrist,* courtesy of the Adult Channel. A *discount wank.*

stroker *1. n.* A *wanker, ie.* one who masturbates, *eg.* Jonathan Ross. *2. n.* A *wanker, ie.* one who is a *twat, eg.* Jim Davidson.

stroker's cough *n.* The retching gag reflex of a lucky lady who has bitten off more than she can chew.

stroke the dog through the letterbox *euph.* To slide one's hand down the front of a lady's knickers.

Stromboweli *n.* Somewhat contrived alternative to *Vesuviarse,* describing a fumerole that ejects bursts of hot gas and high velocity debris on a regular basis.

strong favourite *n.* A *fart* that can be forced out as hard as you want with no risk of *following through,* because you have just been and went for a huge *shit.* From the fact that you know for certain that you are not going to *gamble and lose.* A *banker.*

strop *1. n.* A sort of leather thing that old fashioned barbers use to sharpen their razors. *2. n.* A lady's, usually period-propelled temper tantrum. A *wobbly,* a *wendy. 3. n.* That which a bachelor has in order to *relax* whilst reading a *newsletter* or watching a *masturmentary.*

strop sign *n.* A sometimes subtle indication that one's female partner *has the painters in.* If missed, a *strop sign* can lead to painful repercussions. *'Did you get any last night?' 'Nah. When I got back from the pub I went straight through a strop sign and had to sleep in the spare room with a bag of frozen peas on my bollocks.'*

struggle nugget *n.* A troublesome

duty that only comes out after putting up a fight.

strum *v.* A relaxed *tug* on the *one-string banjo.*

strumpet *n. arch.* Olde Worlde *Brass.* Also *strombone.*

strumping *v.* Predatory behaviour by a *bird*, the female equivalent of *sharking*.

strum the hairy harp *v.* Of a disgusting lady, to essay a few arpeggios on her *upside down piano.* To *shuffle the Kit-Kat*, *gusset type.*

student garden *n.* An uncared-for *fritter.* A scrubby area of *cunt turf.* With a fridge in it.

student knob *n. medic.* A *cock* that has been *wanked* black and blue.

stuffing a marshmallow in a piggy bank *v.* Of those unfortunate situations involving *brewer's droop*, to attempt to force one's *loose sausage meat* into the *slot.*

stunt cock *n.* In a *bongo vid*, when the leading thespian is unable to sustain *wood* or provide a *money shot*; cue the *stunt cock*, a fat ugly cameraman with a *concrete donkey* on a *hair trigger*.

stuntman's tyre *sim.* Descriptive of the state of the *council gritter* after spicy food, *ie.* like a tyre that has been doused in petrol and set on fire ready for a daredevil to jump through.

sty at night, the *n.* The last pickings of *salad dodging swamp hogs* hanging round the *swill* van outside a nightclub after the *two am bin rake.*

style conscious *adj.* A euphemistic term describing a fellow who is *good with colours. Stylish. 'Has your youngest lad married yet, Maureen? He was very style conscious, as I recall.' 'No he hasn't. Well, he's not really found the right girl yet, you see. And he's very busy, too, of course. He runs a company manufacturing poppers, gimp masks and butt plugs.'*

succubus *n.* A phantom night-time *cocksucker* once thought to be responsible for *nocturnal emissions.*

suckers *n. Shag tags.*

suck face *v. US.* To kiss. *'Git a goddamn move on an' finish your mother fuckin' popcorn, you sonofabitch. I wanna suck some face.'*

suckhole *n.* In radio studios, one who is employed to scream with laughter at everything Russell Brand says. A *brown noser, toady, arselick, sycophant, fart catcher.*

suckhole's dilemma *n.* Of a *shirt fly,* to be in a situation where they don't know whose *arse* to lick first, *eg.* a salesman in a room full of purchasing managers, or Ben Elton in a palace full of Royals.

sucking a tramp's cock, like *sim.* Descriptive of the consumption of something which is unpleasant, or which leaves a foul taste in the mouth, *eg.* Netto budget fishcakes or Ricky Tomlinson's penis.

suck off *v.* To perform *horatio*, to do a *chewie*, give some *head.*

suck the poison out *v.* Of a young lady, to perform an altruistic act of *horatio* on a man who is suffering from a life-threatening erection. *'She clasped his neck, and for the first time Bertram learnt what an impassioned woman's kisses were like upon the lips of one whom she loved with all her heart and soul, as Tess loved him. 'There - now are you convinced of my true feelings?' she asked, flushed, and wiping her eyes. 'I'm still not* *sure, love,' he replied, undoing his zip and withdrawing eight quivering inches of pink steel. 'But I might believe you if you suck the poison out of this bastard."* (from *Tess of the d'Urbervilles'* by Thomas Hardy).

sudoku wank *n.* Something that takes about ten minutes, gives you a brief feeling of satisfaction when you complete it, but leaves you wondering why you bothered.

sugar-free spongle *n.* The ejaculate of a vasectomised male. *Australian gravy.*

sugared almond *n.* The *clematis.*

sugar walls *n.* Sheena Easton's *slice* sides.

suitcase handle, gusset like a *sim.* Descriptive of the petrified state of a dirty *bird*'s crusty 3-week-old knickers.

summer assessments *n.* The first day in the year when ladies deem it opportune to leave their jumpers at home and venture forth wearing tight tops and loose blouses, so that gentlemen can review their *qualifications. 'Take the table outside the pub, lads, and don your examiners' sunglasses for the summer assessments.'*

summoning Moira *n.* The desperate act of frantically conjuring up a mental picture of cadaverous newsreader Moira Stewart in order to suppress a potentially embarrassing *diamond cutter* just before getting off the bus.

sump *n. medic.* The part between the *front* and *back bottoms* on a lady. The *manifold,* the *rocker box,* the *fire break,* the *kerb.* The *tinter.*

Sunderland's trophy cabinet, a fanny like *sim.* A large, empty void, based on the fact that the eponymous, notoriously unsuccessful football team owns a large, empty trophy cabinet shaped like a *vagina.* A simile which can be varied, depending on one's footballing allegiances and/or geographical prejudices.

sunnies *n. Aus. Tits, baps.*

supermarket smack *n.* Special Brew.

surfboard *1. n.* A flat-chested female, *Miss Lincolnshire. 2. n. Aus.* A piece of equipment used by women to *catch the waves* when the *red flag is flying.* A *fanny nanny* for a heavy *aunt Flo.*

surfing the crimson wave *n. Riding the menstrual cycle.*

surf 'n' turf *1. n.* The act of orally probing a lady's *rusty sheriff's badge* during an act of *cumulonimbus. 2. n.* An 1980s-style meal served at a Berni Inn, consisting of a fish and steak combo that tasted like one was orally probing a lady's *rusty sheriff's badge* during an act of *cumulonimbus.*

supreme champion *1. n.* That pedigree dog which has been raised on a diet of fillet steak and patty de fwa grar that gets paid thousands of pounds to sit by a big silver cup and advertise tinned kangaroo bollocks for a couple of weeks after it wins Cruft's. 2. n. Offensive, sexist terminology describing the *best in show* out of a group of *hounds.*

surprise, sur-fucking-prise! *exclam.* Remark made at a depressingly predictable event, *eg.* England losing on penalties.

survivor *n.* A buoyant *stool* which resists all attempts to *send it to the beach.*

SWAB *acronym.* Young ladies who

respond to a gentleman's attempts at wooing with monosyllabic disinterest. Single Word Answer Bitches.

Swaffham *v.* Of a lady, to practise the gentle art of cramming both a gentleman friend's *clockweights* in her mouth at the same time. Named after the town in Norfolk, where all the womenfolk, without exception, are experts in this procedure.

swagman's hat *n. medic.* Condition of the *anus* when infested with numerous *tagnuts. 'Holmes surveyed the water closet cubicle before announcing, 'The game is afoot, Watson, and our quarry has a bandy-legged gait.' 'How the devil do you know that, man?' I exclaimed. 'Elementary. The Izal toilet paper means he will almost certainly have a ringpiece like a swagman's hat.''* (from *The Red-Ringed League* by Sir Arthur Conan-Doyle).

swallow *v.* What proper women do.

swallow the bear *v.* To perform *cumulonimbus* on a lady with a right old *biffer* on her.

swallow the oysters *exclam.* A phrase of friendly encouragement to a *nosher* who is being a little too fussy about eating all her *porridge* up.

swamp *v. milit.* To *piss*, urinate.

swamp donkey *n.* Female who is not overly endowed with physical beauty. A *tug boat, boiler, sea monster, steg.*

swan *1. n.* Big posh duck that can break a man's arm with one flap of its wing. *2. n.* The wife of a *pavilion end bowler,* whom he marries in order to mask his true sexual orientation. So-called because she's a *queen's bird.* The *beard* in a *lavender marriage.* 3. n. Style of *wanking* that can break a chap's arm.

swank *1. v.* To walk into a room like one was walking onto a yacht. *2. n.* A secretive *five knuckle shuffle* utilizing minimal wrist action which is enjoyed whilst lying next to one's sleeping partner. Normally practised following the rejection of drunken sexual advances. An *American beauty.*

swap spit *v.* To *suck face.*

sweatermeat *n.* Phrase used to alert friends to the presence of a nice pair of *tits.* Usually accompanied by clockface directional information. *'Sweatermeat at 3 o'clock.'*

sweater puppets *n. Fondleberries.* Particularly animated breasts that keep a fellow entertained. *Milky swingers.*

sweats *rhym. slang.* An affectionate term for people of Caledonian extraction. From sweaty socks = jocks.

sweaty bullets *n.* Low calibre *slugs* that appear in a fellow's *grundies* whilst he is undertaking strenuous physical exercise, such as moving a filing cabinet up a fire escape or throwing twenty car batteries into a high skip.

sweaty Morph *n.* A *mudchild,* a *turd.*

swedge *n.* That piece of folded bogroll which a sweating *pie shifter* wedges in his *potty slot* in order to stop his *farting clappers* rubbing together. A *manpon, botcap, toffee rizla. 'Substantial Andrex swedge worn by Bad Manners frontman Buster Bloodvessel (Douglas Trendle) whilst performing Just a Feeling in a deep-sea diver's* *suit on Top of the Pops c. May 1981. Complete with certificate of authenticity. Estimate £3000 - £4000.'* (extract from Christie's Rock Memorabilia Auction Catalogue, August 2004).

Swedish *n. Greek.*

Sweeney! *exclam.* A humorous utterance shouted out in the style of Flying Squad DI Jack Regan by a man who is *kicking a lady's back doors in.*

sweep's brush *n.* A *Judith.*

sweep the yard *v.* To loudly scratch one's pubic area making a sound like sweeping paving slabs with a hard-bristled broom.

sweetbreads *n.* The testicular component of the *family jewels.* The *clockweights,* the *plums,* the *knackers.*

sweetcorn itch *n.* An itchy ringpiece as a result of insufficient wiping. *IRS.*

sweet FA *acronym.* Sweet Fanny Adams, *fuck all,* absolutely nothing. Nowt.

sweet tits *n.* Affectionate male term of endearment for females. *'Goodnight, goodnight! Parting is such sweet sorrow / That I shall say goodnight until it be morrow, sweet tits.'* (from *Romeo and Juliet* by William Shakespeare).

swift *n.* A bit like a *swallow,* only faster. So fast, in fact, that there isn't the option to spit.

swill out the trough *v.* Female equivalent of *cleaning inside the farmer's hat.*

swim against the tide *v.* To take a *dip* whilst the *red flag* is flying. *To surf the crimson wave.*

swing both ways *v.* To be a *switch hitter.*

swingers *1. n.* Sinister, grim-looking couples who have uninhibited sex in suburban houses with other sinister, grim-looking couples. *2. n. Clockweights, knackers, pods, gourds.*

swirly *n.* Bullies' lavatory game whereby the victim's head is pushed into the *crapper* and the flush pulled. *'I say you chaps, look out! Campbell and Milburn are in the bogs and they've just given Clare Short a swirly.'*

Swiss *adj.* Completely useless. *'Did you see Henman play at Wimbledon? He was completely fucking Swiss.'*

Swiss army wife *n.* Rare and amazing lady who can work, bring up the kids, cook, hoover, open beer bottles and polish her husband's *family jewels* all at the same time.

Swiss finger *n.* An erect *todger* with a pink iced topping, upon withdrawal from a lady on the eve of a week's *visit from the painters,* or in the 24 hours following their departure. From the similarity to the doughy confection of the same name to be found in the window of all Ainsley's branches.

Swiss kiss *n.* A *post-horatio spangle*-flavoured snog.

Swiss movement *n.* A *chod* dropped in the *pan* with almost nazi-like precision by a person with disciplined and regular bowel habits.

switchcraft *n.* The magical ability of a woman to make incredible amounts of cash disappear into thin air whilst out shopping.

switch hitter *n. US.* Person who *bats with both hands,* a bisexual, a *happy shopper.* One who approaches the *oyster* and *snail buffet* with a broad plate.

swive *v. 17thC. Fuck. 'Swiving hell. I've had to take six chops at the King's neck and I've still not got his swiving head off.'*

swope *n.* The hairstyle affected by balding men whereby strands of hair on one side of the head are grown long and swept over the dome, giving the impression of a full head of hair, *eg.* Robert Robinson, Bobby Charlton, Desmond Morris.

sword swallower *n.* A circus *fellatrix.*

syllojism *n.* A logical argument about *wanking* that begins: "All men are human".

syrup *n.* Hairpiece. From syrup of fig = Irish jig. *"Q: 'Just look at this, 007.' Bond: 'What is it, Q? Looks like an ordinary syrup to me.' Q: 'Yes, but one tug on the chinstrap and it turns into a miniature helicopter.' Bond: 'Hmm! Hair raising!'" (From Never Say Never Again,* 1983*).*

Tt

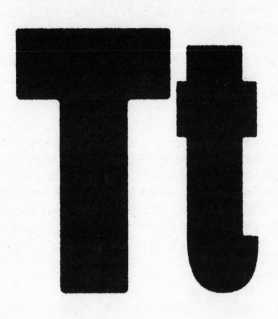

tabby afro *n.* A collection of different-coloured *pubes* found blocking the plug hole of the bath in a shared flat.

tackle *n.* What you catch if you go fishing in your flies.

tacklebags *n.* Underpants, *bills, scads, scuns, dunghampers.*

tackleshack *n. Tacklebags.*

taco tickler *n.* A *gusset typist.*

tactical chunder *n.* Student *refreshment* technique. A deliberate *technicolour yawn* performed to make a bit of extra beer room in the stomach, or to delay the arrival of a *helicopter attack.*

tadger *n.* A thing that tadges. Also *todger.*

tadpole net *n. Blob, rubber johnny, cheesepipe clingfilm.*

tadpole yoghurt *n. Gentleman's relish, man mayonnaise,* dressing for a *sausage sandwich.*

tagnuts *n. Toffee strings, winnets, clinkers, dangleberries, bead curtains. Rectal hangers on, arse cress Tarzans.*

tail *1. n. arch.* That which wags when it sees a pretty lady. The *veiny bang stick. 2. n. Fluff, totty, skirt, talent. 3. n.* Your *bum.*

tail ender *n.* A small dollop of *doings* that one must wait for after the main stool has been expelled, the finial on a *log cabin* roof. *Geetle.*

tail gunner *n.* A *style conscious* fellow.

tailpipe *1. n.* The exhaust of a motor car. 2. *n. US. Corybungo.*

tail shot *n.* A *change of heart.*

tail wind *n. A southern breeze* tending to push one forward.

taint *n. Niftkin's bridge.* Because "'tain't your arse and 'tain't your fanny".

take a packed lunch *v.* To take one's girlfriend on holiday to avoid all the *fucking about* and loss of drinking time that goes with finding a suitable female at one's destination. *'I went to Ibiza last year and wasted the first day and a half sorting myself out with some tart to bang. I'm going to Agya Napa this year, and I'm taking a packed lunch.'*

take an air dump *v.* To *let rip, blow off.*

take Captain Picard to warp speed *v.* To masturbate. To *strangle Kojak, pull Paul Daniels' head off.*

take communion *v.* To kneel before the altar and partake of a portion of *haddock pie* during *rag week. Fish on Friday.*

take one in the company's time *v.* Whilst at work, to hold in a *number two* until one's unpaid break is over, thus ensuring that one gets paid the full hourly rate for having a *shit.*

takeout *n.* A professional escort, whose door-to-door sexual services are ordered from a menu over the phone.

take the cat to the vet *euph.* To knock off work early. See *let the dog out.*

take the crust off *v.* Nautical term describing the precautionary pre-disembarkation *wank* taken by trawlermen before they are reunited with their ladyfriends. *Take the edge off.*

take the edge off *v.* To *relax in a gentleman's way* in order to prolong a putative *scuttle* with one's partner. To *put a wank in the bank. 'Got a big night with the missus planned. I'd better go and take the edge off first.'*

take the goalie off the pitch *v.*

To withdraw contraception in a positive effort to conceive a *turf chimp*.

taking the steps at Goodge Street *euph.* A lonely, last resort act of *self pollution,* only embarked upon to *get the boys out of the tube* in extreme circumstances. From the lonely, last resort means of exiting the eponymous London Underground station, which entails a life-sapping trudge up 136 steps.

talent *n. coll. Crumpet, bush,* attractive females. *Scrunt.*

talent scout *n.* A designated member of a group who looks round the pub door to check that the *blart* inside is worth pushing one's way to the bar for.

talk German *v.* To *fart, blow off,* puff on an imaginary *bum cigar*.

talk on the great white telephone *v.* To be sick in the lavatory. *Drive the porcelain bus.*

talk to the boss *exclam.* A married man's response to his wife's request for some of his hard-earned cash to fritter away on luxuries. An instruction to perform an act of *horatio*. *'It's no good, love. I'm going to have to go shopping. We're right out of baby food and the twins need new shoes.' 'It's not up to me, you'd better talk to the boss.'*

talk to the judge *n.* To *suck a copper's truncheon* by way of avoiding a speeding ticket. *'I know I was doing 75 in a 30 zone, officer, but is there any way we can work this out? Perhaps if I spoke to the judge behind that skip?'*

tallywhacker *n. 18thC.* Penis, *old man.*

tammy dodger *n.* A gentleman forced to go to the pub, chippy, video shop, church, round the world balloon attempt *etc*, to avoid his *blob-stropping* missus.

tammy huff *n.* A monthly feminine mood swing. A *blob strop.*

tampon *1. n.* A small, highly-sophisticated implant which enables women to play tennis. *2. n.* An injury-prone footballer, from the fact that he is "one week in, three weeks out", *eg*. Darren "Sicknote" Anderton, who didn't play for Spurs, Birmingham and England.

tam rag *n. Jampax.*

tamtrum *n.* A monthly exhibition of petulance. From Latin tampus = fanny rags & trum = hissy fit. A *blobstrop,* a *tammy huff, showing off.*

Tamworth *n.* Perjorative term for a ginger person, named after them pigs which have ginger bristles and funny-looking eyes.

tandoori whisper *n.* Silent, yet exquisitely rancid, burst of *wind* following an Indian meal.

tango butter *n. Fanny slobber, sloom.*

tank *v.* To *scuttle, roger*.

tank driver's hat *n.* A particularly hairy *fanny* with flaps that fasten under your chin. A *biffer, bear trapper's hat.*

tanked up *1. adj.* Usefully drunk, sufficient to fight or drive a car very fast. *2. adj. milit.* To be sufficiently equipped with tanks.

tank slapper *1. n.* An exciting incident that happens to a motorcyclist shortly prior to a thrilling ride in an ambulance. *2. n.* An ugly biker's moll.

tanorexia *n. medic.* Psychological disorder common in footballers' wives types who, despite daily *cancer shop* sessions, still believe they are pasty when in fact they have the skin tone of an Oompa-Loompa.

tantric shit *n.* An extremely prolonged visit to the porcelain *chod bin*, where one sits for four hours, *humming*.

tap off *v.* To successfully *tap up*.

tap up *1. v.* Of football managers, to make an illegal approach to a player who is signed to another team. *2. v.* Of Football Association officials, to chat up and attempt to instigate a sexual liaison with a typist in a lift at FA headquarters in Soho Square.

tapioca tash *n.* Facial ornamentation, popular amongst *stick vid* starlets.

tapioca toothpaste *n.* Dental gel for a *trouser leg trombonist*, just the thing when *brushing the au pair's teeth*.

tapping on the high hat *v.* Rhythmic, percussive *jazz* masturbation.

tapping the ash *n.* Refers to the vigorous shaking and pulling apart of the buttocks in an attempt to force out the troublesome *turd* that ends a *shitting* session, but refuses to drop into the *pan*. Akin to tapping the end of a cigarette in order to encourage the ash to drop. *'Are you going to be long in the crapper, Archbishop?' 'Shouldn't be long now, Your Majesty, I'm just tapping the ash.'*

TAPS *acronym. medic.* Technical term used by doctors on medical notes, Thick As Pig Shit.

Tara's tits *euph.* Nothing. Fuck all. From the notorious It-Girl Tara Palmer-Tomkinson's distinct lack of *bikini filler*. *'We have spent three months searching the secret bunkers and military bases of Iraq in search of chemical warheads and weapons of mass destruction, but thus far I must report to the Security Council that we have found Tara's tits.'* (Dr Hans Blix's report, 27th Jan 2003).

Tarantino hangover *n.* The kind of hangover whereby one's memory behaves in the style of *Pulp Fiction*; one's recollections of the night before appear in a seemingly random order and one has to wait until one has seen all of them to finally understand what happened.

tar baby *1. n.* A sticky, black trap that nearly proved the undoing of Brer Rabbit in the *Uncle Remus* stories. *2. n.* A sticky, black *crap* that proves the undoing of anyone who has spent a night quaffing Guinness. Leads to an intractable combination of an *arse like a Marmite pot* and *buoys from the black stuff*.

Tarbucks *n.* A set of *tits* so impressive that the viewer involuntarily shouts "ho-ho!" in the manner of the cheeky, gap-toothed scouser comedian and golf enthusiast Jimmy.

Tardis fanny *n.* A deceptively spacious *snatch*. Opening the saloon doors to find a disappointing *cathedral* when one was expecting a *priest's hole*.

tarmac round the garage *sim.* Descriptive of a slightly grubby *path to the back door*, making *rear entry* an unpleasant prospect.

tarrantless *adj.* Even less talented than Chris Tarrant, *eg.* Steve Penk, Eamonn Holmes, that arsehole mate of Robbie Williams's who used to do *You've Been Framed* for a few weeks before they got Harry Hill in.

tart *n. Slapper, dolly bird,* a nice bit

of *cheesecake.*

tart farmer *n.* A *pimp.*

tart fuel *n.* Any alcoholic drink consumed by young women which gets them going. *Knicker oil. 'She's very light on tart fuel. She'll go all the way to Cockfosters on three bottles of Hooch.'*

tart ink *n.* That which is used to draw a more attractive face onto a plain woman. Make-up, *fuck dust.*

tart's window box, a *n.* What one smells like when one has too much aftershave on. *Joan Collin's knickers.*

tart-throb *n.* A low grade hunk who is unaccountably alluring to ladies from the lower echelons, *eg.* Peter Andre, Robson Green.

Tarzan cord *n.* The narrow lace which attaches *Kojak's roll-neck* to the *bobby's helmet.* The *guy rope,* the *banjo.*

tash *n.* Any one of a wide variety of vaginal topiary arrangements, ranging from Robert Mugabe to Nietzsche.

tassel *n.* Innocent schoolboy term for the penis. *Winkle, willie, winkie-woo, slag hammer.*

taste the rainbow *v.* To have a little taste of everything from the "All You Can Eat" *pant buffet.*

'taters *n. Nads, balls, bollocks.* The testicles. Contraction of potatoes. *'We Englishmen are conscious of our status / Which is why the beastly foreigners all hate us / But it's always seemed to me / that it's simply jealousy / 'Cos they're envious of the size of English 'taters.'* (From *The Stately Genitals of England* by Noel Coward).

ta tas *n. Noinkers, jubblies, cajooblies, jugs, bubbies, charms, baby's dinners, fun cushions, paps, bojangles, thrupennies, assets mambas, dirty pillows, chebs, charlies, diddies, doos, puppies, Bristols, airbags, Gert Stonkers, kahunas, shirt potatoes, boobs, melons, oomlaaters, nellies, choozies, chubblies, chumbawumbas, blimps, sweater fruit, knockers, churns, whammers, yoinkahs, begonias, mumbas, pink pillows, top bollocks, neddies, chichis, cab man's rests, baps, funbags, bumpies, zeps, bazongers, headlamps, whammies, norks, bangers, tits, dumplings, hogans.* That'll be breasts, then.

tatties *n.* Testicles, *love spuds.*

tat twat *n.* A snobbish term used to describe a member of the pond-level social class often to be seen swimming round car boot sales and *Car Booty* on daytime BBC1. *Scratter, ronker.*

tatty watta. *n. Nat. Am.* Red Indian word for *spud juice,* semen. Literally "potato water".

taxi *v.* To *come* late. Or never at all.

taxi driver's minute *n.* Any period of time which is longer than half an hour.

taxi driver's tan *1. n.* An area of sunburn on the right index finger caused by hooking it on the top of the cab whilst driving along. *2. n.* A similar effect caused by *breaching the hull.* A *filter tip, mechanic's nails.*

taxi for Brown *exclam.* A witty riposte to an *anal retort,* such as what Dorothy Parker or Oscar Wilde might have said after they *dropped their guts.*

taxi greyhound *n.* One who bolts out of a cab door like a whippet, leaving his mates to pay the fare.

taxi tiger *n.* A desperate last-chance lunger on the way home.

Taylforth *1. n.* A disastrous *blow-job* in a car. *2. n. medic.* A severe attack of pancreatitis which can only be relieved by being *sucked off* in a layby.

Taz *1. n. prop.* A hairy cartoon beast that dribbles, found in the Antipodes. *2. n.* A hairy *grotter* that dribbles, found in ladies' *dunghampers.*

TBS *abbrev.* Toxic Bott Syndrome. Severe noxious emissions or *brewer's farts. Burning bad powder.*

TCM *abbrev. medic.* Turd Cutting Muscle, *crimper, cigar cutter,* anal sphincter. The *nipsy, secaturds.*

TCS *abbrev.* Traction Control System. When *farting* following a bellyfull of *dizzyade* and/or curry, the precise control of the *nipsy* required to allow one to *squeak one out* without producing any *wheelspin*, thus preventing *laying rubber* in the undies.

teabagging *v.* To make a strong brew with *Fussell's Milk* and two lumps. A last-resort sexual practice whereby the man lowers his *pods* into the lady's mouth.

tea chicken *n.* Game played by severely hungover flatmates, whereby they sit immobile waiting for the first one to bottle it and offer to put the kettle on.

teaching William a lesson *n. Punishing Percy, pulling the Pope's cap off. "What's all this banging and groaning?' bellowed Mr Wilkins as he burst into the dorm. 'Please, Sir,' piped-up Venables. 'It was Darbishire teaching Jennings a lesson."* (from *Jennings and the Mysterious Body Hairs* by Anthony Buckeridge).

tea cosy *n.* A place to hide one's *spout* whilst thinking about the true object of one's affections. *'Deaths: Lady Diana Spencer, shopping enthusiast, landmines campaigner and Prince's tea cosy, 36.'*

tea fairy *n.* Term used to describe a rather poor drinker. *'Come on, George, you big tea fairy. One drink won't hurt you.'*

tea pot *1. n.* A male from the Larry Grayson school of posturing. *2. n. Self harm* position. One hand pulling at the spout and the index finger of the other hand stuck up the nipsy to stimulate the *walnut.* Superficially resembles the "I'm a little teapot" nursery rhyme dance, though with distinctly less innocent overtones.

teapot shuffle *n.* Descriptive of the pose adopted by internet-fuelled *self-polluters ie. pulling themselves off* with the left hand, whilst the right arm is extended to faciltate control of the mouse.

teapot sucker *n.* A *bottom shelf drinker*, a teetotaller.

tear in a coalman's jacket *sim.* A large, raggy *blart.*

tear off a piece *v. US.* To have sex. *Tear one off.*

tearful wank *n.* A light-hearted taunt directed at a newly heart-broken male colleague. It involves sticking the bottom lip out, and doing a masturbating gesture with one hand and a "boo hoo" gesture with the other.

tea strainer *n.* A bowel movement that is forceably withheld during teabreak so that one can have a *tom tit* and get paid for the pleasure. *Time and a turd, taking one on the company's time.*

tea towel holder *n. Anus, ringpiece, freckle.* From the 1950s plastic "finger poke" cat's *arse*-style kitchen accessory.

teat-seeking missile *n.* A man who fails to maintain proper eye contact when talking to women.

technicolour yawn *n.* A *yoff.*

tecwens *n. medic.* An attack of pathetic fake coughing that one effects at work the day before one throws a sickie. From the *Who Wants to be a Millionaire* coughing *knacker* Tecwen Whittock. *'The lads are playing Locomotiv Moscow tomorrow, live on Sky, only the kick off's at two in the afternoon. Cough! Cough! Ooh, dear. I can feel a touch of the Tecwens coming on.'*

ted *n.* The *Teddington.*

Teddington *rhym. slang.* The Penis. From the *Magpie* studio address Teddington Lock = corn on the cob.

teddy's leg *n.* State of stool expulsion somewhere beyond the *turtle's head*, but prior to *touching sock*. Point midway through *smoking a bum cigar. Bungle's finger.*

tee off *v.* To *wank* and/or *fart*. Not necessarily at the same time.

Tees duck *n.* Sky rat, *shitehawk.* A seagull.

teeter meter *n.* Calibration scale assessing the attractiveness of women based on how far from sober one would have to be to *slip them a length. eg.* Kylie Minogue would be 0 on the teeter meter, whereas Gail Tilsley off *Coronation Street* would be 15 pints of Stella with whisky chasers.

Tegel airport *1. n.* Berlin's busiest air transport hub, famous for having two hexagonal terminal buildings. *2. n.* Over-excited planespotter terminology for a lady's twin nether openings.

teggat *n.* A short-necked *turtle's head* which is unable to *touch cloth*, and retreats back into the *bomb bay*. A *Hoskins.*

temazepalm *n. medic.* Hand-induced insomnia relief.

tenapause *n.* The stage in a woman's life-cycle when she loses the ability to control her bladder effectively.

ten minutes' peace and quiet *n.* An offensive term used by sexist men to describe getting a *chewie* off their *bit of fluff. 'Mr Campbell-Bannerman: Yes, Mrs Pankhurst, I agree that the introduction of universal suffrage is a worthy political objective, and I shall endeavour to include it in the King's speech at the beginning of the next parliamentary session...but only if you give me ten minutes peace and quiet. Mrs Pankhurst: Glub! Glub!'.* (Cartoon in *Punch* by Bernard Partridge, 1905).

Tennants poetry *n.* A moving sonnet of threats and expletives, usually *scumbled* by a dishevelled Scotsman while leaning forwards.

Tennants tan *n.* The reddish-purple glow that an ardent lager connoisseur acquires after years of wandering from bar to bar in a *pissed-up* frenzy of unquenchable thirst. Also *tramp's tan.*

tenner lady *1. n.* A female who is *pissed* after just ten quid's worth of *sauce. 2. n.* A cheap, incontinent *prossie. 'Excuse me, are there any tenner ladies in the area? I fancy a cheap, sordid poke with a tart who is the very antithesis of my own, fragrant missus who* *has full control of her bladder.' 'There's one over there by that skip, Lord Archer.'*

they're firing Sir, they're firing! *exclam.* Yet another one of those humorous ripostes to a *rumpet voluntary.* See also *keep shouting Sir, we'll find you; speak up caller, you're through; a bit more choke and she would have started; you'll have to buy that now, you've ripped it; that's working, now try your lights; speak on, sweet lips that never told a lie; well struck Sir.*

throbbin' hood *coll. Notts.* A sore *fiveskin.* A *little john* that as been excessively "made merry on".

tinkle on the ivories *1. v.* To play the piano, usually in a *half-arsed* sort of way, the opposite of going at it *three cocks to the cunt.* You could never accuse Count Basie of *tinkling on the ivories,* for example, whereas it describes Richard *fucking* Clayderman's insipid noodlings to a tee. *2. v.* To participate in a particular sort of *watersport.* To take a *gypsy's* in a ladyfriend's *north and south.*

tiptop *acronym.* A transexual who has yet to go the whole way and is still mid-way through the gender re-alignment process. Tits In Place, Tackle Op Pending.

tennis elbow *n. medic.* A condition of the right arm caused by repeated games of *singles. 'Ooh, that's a nasty case of tennis elbow you've got there, Tim. And Andy.'*

tennis fan *n.* A woman who takes the *other bus* to Wimbledon. A *lady golfer.*

tenpin *v.* To place digits simultaneously in the *tea towel holder* and the *fish mitten.* From the grip used in ten pin bowling. To *spock.*

ten pint princess *n.* A *donner.*

Tenpole Tudor *n.* A *slapper, ie.* one who has had the *swords* of a thousand men.

ten-to-two shuffle *n.* A perfunctory dance that *pissed up* gentlemen engage in with the *floor sweepings* at the end of a long and unspectacular evening *on the pull. 'Any luck last night?' 'No. Ended up doing the ten-to-two shuffle with some dental receptionist. She gave me a bit of duck sausage and got the last bus home.'*

tent pole *n. Stiffy,* erect penis, especially in bed. A *trouser tent, morning glory, dawn horn, dusk tusk.*

ten pounds of shit in a five pound bag *euph.* Useful phrase which can be used when referring to either a deceptively-powerful motor car or a *generously-boned* woman who has shoehorned herself into a dress which is several sizes too small for her. *'How do I look, Andrew?' 'Like ten pounds of shit in a five pound bag, Sarah. But we've got to get going. The Archbishop of Canterbury is waiting.'*

tequila sunrise *n.* The awe-inspiring visual effect produced when a man's bright yellow urine flows into the *pan* where the previous (female) occupant has *blobbed.*

terminal five *n.* The *landing strip* on a very large woman. Named after the biggest runway in the UK, which is at Heathrow Airport.

Terry Funk *1. n. prop.* A popular Discotheque personality in the Midlands, circa 1970. *2. rhym. slang.* Marijuana cigarettes, from Terry Funk = skunk. *3. rhym. slang. Spooge,* from Terry Funk = spunk. *'Waiter. There's some Terry*

Funk in my soup'. 'Yes, Mr Winner. That's because the chef, the entire kitchen and serving staff, and indeed the rest of the customers have masturbated into it.'

Terry Waite's allotment *sim.* Descriptive of a badly-overgrown *ladygarden. 'Marriette was powerless to resist. His eyes burned into hers like emeralds. His muscular arms enfolded her body as she felt herself being swept away in a monsoon of passion. 'Bloody hell! You've got a twat like Terry Waite's allotment!' he cried, as he pulled out the waistband of her bloomers and peered inside.'* (from *The Peasant Girl and the First World War Soldier* by Barbara Cartland).

Tesco finish *n.* In pornographic cinematography, the sort of *pop shot* where the over-enthusiastic gentleman actor vigorously attempts to squeeze every last drop of *spaff* out of his *gut stick.* From the all-conquering town centre-fucking supermarket's well-known advertising slogan; "Because every little helps".

tescosexual *n.* A man whose incidence of sexual activity peaks during his wife's trips to the shops.

test card wank *n.* A *tug* one has, not because one is feeling particularly *fruity,* but simply because there is nothing else to do. A *loose end away*.

test ride *n.* In the executive world, the act of taking the *office bike round the block* before deciding whether or not to dump one's missus for her.

Tewkesbury doorstep, wetter than a *sim.* Descriptive of a lady who is suffering a flash flood *down south. 'I tell you what, Geoff, she can't have had it for a while. Her fanny was wetter than a Tewkesbury doorstep.'*

textbook dog *n.* The recognition of an absolutely perfect *doggy-style* position seen in everyday situations, *eg.* a secretary crawling on the floor to find a contact lens.

Thames trout *n.* A fishy-smelling, rainbow-coloured, *spawn*-filled object with its tickling days now long behind it, typically found floating near one of London's major sewerage outlets. A spent *jubber.* A British variation on the American *Coney Island whitefish.*

Thames whale *n.* A large *turd* which appears in the *pan* without any explanation, and which is reluctant to return to the sea.

thanksgiving dinner *n.* An act of *oral affection* performed on a lady who has *got the painters in. Dinner at the Y* with extra ketchup. *Cranberry dip.*

thatched cottage *n. arch.* A delightfully picturesque half-timbered *cunt* with roses round the *piss-flaps.*

thatch hatch *n.* A chocolate-boxy *box.*

thatch 22 *n.* Sexual dilemma faced by a gentleman considering committing *cumulonimbus* on a lady with an horrendous *clown's pie.*

that one came with a prize *exclam.* Polite phrase acknowledging that an *air biscuit* has been accompanied by a *malteser* or two. *'That one came with a prize, Judy. You run through the star signs while I nip into Fred the weather man's dressing room to scouse a pair of clean grundies.'*

that one jumped the queue *exclam.*

Humorous phrase which can be used when one has inadvertently *dropped* an item of *shopping* whilst *stepping on a duck* in polite company.

that one's got a skin on it *exclam.* Humorous riposte following the release of a *fart* that has been *stewing* a little too long in the *back boiler*. From the similarity to a milky coffee that has been left too long in the cup.

that's working, now try your lights *1. exclam.* Phrase shouted by a motor mechanic following the successful testing of a car's horn. *2. exclam.* Phrase shouted following the successful floating of an *air biscuit.* Also *sew a button on that; catch that one and paint it blue; good health;, pin a tail on that* and *there goes the elephant.*

Theakston's *rhym. slang.* The rear *fundament*. From Theakston's bitter = Gary Glitter. *'Jesus love, no offence, but your breath stinks. Tell you what, I'll do you up the Theakston's tonight, eh?'*

Thelonious *rhym. slang.* Semen. Named after the jazz pianist Thelonious Spunk.

the other *n. It*, the old *how's your father.*

there we are then *exclam. acronym.* A covert way of calling another person a *twat.* See also *see you next Tuesday, can't understand new technology.*

thesbian *n.* A *grumble flick* actress who does *girl on girl* professionally, but is not a *tennis fan* in real life.

the third place *n. Splaystation 2.* The *arse.*

thick as a ghurka's foreskin *sim.* Descriptive of someone who is as *thick as a Welshman's cock.*

thickening up *adj.* To be in the early stages of erectile tumescence. The penile equivalent to that moment when you're stirring a pan of Bisto on the hob and it suddenly starts to look and behave a bit like gravy. *Getting a bit of blood in it. 'You'll have to excuse me sitting down whilst I read this next disgusting continental hardcore scan magazine, Mrs Whitehouse, only I'm definitely thickening up in spite of myself.' 'Feel free, Lord Longford. I'm as horrified as you at these explicit photographs of depraved behaviour, yet I am ashamed to admit that I'm dripping like a fucked fridge.'*

thick repeater *n.* A large bore semi-automatic, single barrel *mutton musket.*

thick spunk *n.* Extremely fertile, high motility *spaff. Jitler* that requires factor 40 contraception. *'I've got eight brothers and six sisters thanks to Pop's thick spunk. Gee whiz, his sperm count is so high, I'll bet mom has to chew before swallowing.'* (Little Jimmy Osmond interviewed in *Look In*, 1972).

thigh ticklers *n. Bugger's grips, face fannies, sideboards. 'Ooh, Dr Rhodes Boyson. What a magnificent set of thigh ticklers.' 'Thankyou, Your Majesty.'*

thighbrows *n.* A profusion of bikini overspill. *Loose baccy.*

think of the money shot *n.* In *bongo videography,* the less than enthusiastic expression on the lead actress's face as Ron Jeremy, Bill Margold or Ben Dover, or possibly all three, empty their *pods* into it.

think outside the box *1. v.* Yet another meaningless corporate buzzword expression commonly used by the sort of desperate utter *arseholes* who appear on programmes like *The Apprentice. 2. v.* The actions of a thoughtful gentleman in bed, *ie.* one who doesn't immediately focus his attentions on his ladyfriend's *cludge,* but considerately mashes her *tits* for a couple of minutes first.

thin lizzy *n.* An undercracker *skidmark.* From the verse in that group's song *Dancing in the Moonlight (It's caught me in its spotlight)* which goes "I should have took that last bus home / But I asked you for a dance / Now we go steady to the pictures / I always get chocolate stains on my pants."

third leg *1. n.* Cricketing position between mid-off and gully. *2. n.* The *middle stump.*

third up, the *euph.* Building site terminology for a mistake. From the fact that in the construction industry there are three "ups", *ie.* muck up, tea up and fuck up.

third way, the *1. n.* New Labour's way of combining traditional socialist and conservative policies, for example by increasing NHS spending whilst closing hospital wards. *2. n.* Anal sex.

thirty-four-and-a-halfer *n.* A hermit blessed with the miraculous ability to perform *horatio* upon himself. A *human cannonballer.*

Thora bird *n.* A *nana Kournikova.*

Thora Hird *1. n. prop.* Pelican-throated actress of stairlift testimonial fame, no longer alive at time of going to press. *2. rhym. slang.* A *turd.*

Thorntons, little bit of *sim.* Euphemism used when attempting to talk the wife into a bit of *backdoor action.* From the famous gift toffee manufacturer's advertising slogan, *ie.* "Skilled in the ways of the chocolatier". *'Roll over, love. I fancy a little bit of Thorntons tonight.'*

thousand island dressing *n.* The sauce which coats one's *naughty spoon* after tossing the *gorilla salad* when *cranberry dip* is on the menu.

thousand mile service *euph.* A woman's *unclean time,* when she is *up on blocks.* An *oil and filter change.*

thrap *v.* To masturbate furiously, to give it *six nowt* on the *Right Honourable Member for Pantchester.* Also *thrape.*

three card trick *rhym slang. Prick. 'She got her jazz bands round me three card trick and started giving it six nowt.'*

three cocks to the cunt *euph. Con gusto.* Doing anything to the extreme, *eg.* driving at 180mph down a country lane, drinking vodka in pint glasses, driving at 180mph down a country lane whilst drinking vodka in pint glasses.*'Ferdinand Hiller remembered Sterndale Bennett's piano playing as "perfect in mechanism, and, while remarkable for an extraordinary delicacy of nuance in the quieter passages of the Mendelssohn Barcarolle, full of soul and fire in the finale, which he always played three cocks to the cunt".'* (Cecil Gaybody, writing in *Classic FM* Magazine).

three coiler *n.* A canine *turd,* the curled and crimped result of not having walked the dog, usually found on a carpet.

three day event *1. n.* A swift half after work on Friday, which lasts all weekend until you return to the office on Monday morning, much to the chagrin of the wife.

three dick gob *n.* A capacious mouth. *'The next record is You're So Vain by Carly Simon, the lady with the three dick gob. And it's for Terry, who is seven today. Lots of love from mummy, daddy, nana and granpa Johnson and nana Robins.'* (Ed "Stewpot" Stewart, *Radio 1 Junior Choice,* 1974).

three-fag omelette *n.* For a non-smoker, the satisfying yet unfamiliar pattie of phlegm coughed up the morning after having drunk enough to *ponce* a few fags off a mate at about ten past eleven.

three for a bob *rhym. slang.* The *corn on the cob.*

three inch soilpipe, fanny like a *sim.* Charming plumber-speak to describe the genital accoutrements of a lady whose *bodily treasure* is at the other end of the tightness scale from a *mouse's ear.*

three-legged race *n.* When *fuck-struck,* to stumble up the stairs with a *bone on.*

three mile island *n.* An extremely noxious rectal meltdown with a half-life of about ten minutes. A *Smellafield.*

three piece suite *n.* That which has to be plumped up and rearranged on a regular basis to ensure seated comfort. The *Meat and two veg, wedding tackle.* The male *undercarriage.*

three wheeler *rhym. slang. Dyke, lesbian.* From three wheeled trike, which is a popular means of transport for *women in comfortable shoes.*

throatmanship *n.* The noble art of gagless *horatio,* as practised by the late actress Linda Lovelace.

throb on *n.* A *wide on, slop on.*

throne *n.* The Queen's *crapper.*

throne bone *n.* The throbbing *bonk on* that sometimes pops up temptingly whilst a young man is *dropping a length of dirty spine.*

throne room *n.* The Queen's *shit palace.*

throng *adj.* Descriptive of a fashionably skimpy item of intimate apparel being worn by someone who really should have known better, *eg.* women with nice personalities, oldies or Jade Goody. From thong + wrong. *'Did you see what Bob's bird was wearing when she bent over?' 'Aye Joe, that's just throng, that.'*

throttle pit *n. Aus.* The *dunny.* Toilet.

throttle the turkey *v.* To masturbate in Norfolk.

througher *n.* A 24-hour drinking session. A *Leo Sayer, MGM.*

throw *v.* To *barf, hoy, chuck.*

throwabout *n.* A petite woman who can be easily and casually "thrown about" from one position to another during sex. A *laptop.*

throwing a Woodbine up Northumberland Street *sim. NE.* Unsatisfying sex with a *bucket-fannied* individual. Also *throwing a sausage up Briggate* (Leeds), *chucking a fag down Parliament Street* (Nottingham). *'Why man, it was like hoyin' a Woodbine up Northumberland Street.'*

throw meat at the problem *v.* Of a couple whose relationship is on the rocks, to engage in an act of penetrative romance.

throw one's cap into the hangar *v.*

milit. To have sex with a lady endowed with a *poacher's pocket.* From the naval act of throwing a rating's hat into the bowels of a through-deck cruiser. Also *throwing a kitbag in a dry dock.*

throw out the garbage *v.* To flush out one's *spooge pipe.*

throw the towel in *1. v.* Of a boxing trainer, to concede defeat when his fighter is getting his *fucking* head kicked in. *2. v.* To give up trying to have a *poke* because the missus has *got the painters and decorators in.* 3. *v.* Of a lady, to casually insert a *mouse.*

throw your bollocks at the clock *exclam.* An exclamation of total exasperation. *'We've been talking about the future of power sharing in Northern Ireland for five weeks now, and they still won't sit in the same bloody room. It's enough to make you want to throw your bollocks at the clock.'* (Senator George Mitchell, Report on the Northern Ireland Peace Process).

thru'penny bits *1. rhym. slang. Tits. 2. rhym. slang.* The *shits.*

thruster *n. medic.* A muscle, somewhere in the neck or jaw, the tensing of which forces out stubborn *shits* and *farts.*

thumb a ride on the rocket *adj.* To *take Captain Picard to warp speed.*

thumb bumming *v. Touching last night's tea.*

thumbing in a slacky *v.* The first act of an optimistic bout of lovemaking for which the gentleman's spirit is willing, but his flesh is weak. *Pushing a marshmallow into a moneybox.*

thumbrise *n.* The time of day at which a fellow in a loving relationship is allowed out of the house by his other half, to go for a quick drink with his mates.

thumbset *n.* The time by which he has to be back in the house with his *pink handcuffs* on.

thumper *1. n.* A big, pounding erection, a *stalk,* a *stiffy. 2. n.* In the Walt Disney film *Bambi,* the annoying rabbit who, if the extracts shown every fucking week on *Screen Test* were anything to go by, spent the entire movie encouraging the lead character to walk out onto a frozen pond.

thumpology *n.* The resolution of disputes by recourse to physical argument. *Closing time counselling, chin music.*

thunder bags *n.* Underpants, *trolleys.*

thunderbirds *n.* Women of ample proportions. *Barge arses, size aeros.*

thunder box *n. arch.* Lavatory, *shitter.* Also *thunder bowl.*

thunderbox shuffle *1. n.* A song by Skiffle king Lonnie Donnegan that reached no. 3 in 1960. *2. n.* The *arse* dance performed whilst sitting on the *chod bin* trying to *get* the *pit bull out of the kennel.*

thundercrack *n.* The kind of *fart* that requires one to check one's *kex* for *bullets.* A *squench.*

thunder mug *n.* Chamber pot, *guzunda.*

thunderslash *n.* A splendidly loud urination delivered *con gusto* directly into the water of the pot. A *dad's piss,* a *round of applause,* a *standing ovation.*

ticket to tottieville *euph.* See *token for the cockwash, pink ticket.*

tickle Fat Ed *v.* Of a fellow, to *pleasure himself* in a leisurely, almost lackadaisical manner. As one would do on a chaise-longue in a gazebo, or in a blazer and straw boater whilst drifting in a punt.

ticklers *n.* Corrugated condoms, amusing *French letters* which are ribbed for your pleasure.

tickle tackle *n. Anteater's nose, cock collar, lace curtains.* The *fiveskin.*

tickle the baby *v.* To engage in a spot of sexual intercourse with a pregnant ladyfriend. *'What was the milkman doing upstairs?' 'Nothing love. He was just tickling the baby.'*

tickle the pickle *v.* See *jerkin' the gherkin.*

tickle your pip *v.* To be aroused sexually by Leslie Philips or Terry-Thomas.

tickling the scampi *v.* A means of getting *fish fingers.* Feminine *monkey spanking.*

tied by the brown rope *adj.* To be confined to the *chod bin* by an intractable *Brad.*

tiffin *n.* An afternoon *fuck* off Sid James in a pith helmet.

tiffter *n.* An unwanted erection, *Jake.*

tiger's back *n.* The decorative striped effect left in the *pan* after a particularly sticky *Meatloaf's daughter* has *gone to the beach.*

tighter than airport security *sim.* Description of a frigid *bird;* one who refuses to take any liquids on board.

tighter than a teenage wanker's curtains *sim.* Descriptive of something which is very secure. *'And as the Queen's carriage glides majestically up to the steps of the Palace of Westminster, security is, of course, tighter than a teenage wanker's curtains.'* (David Dimbleby, commentating on the State Opening of Parliament, 2007).

tightie *n. Scot. medic.* The feeling of discomfort experienced when attempting to peel back the *fiveskin* due to it being stuck to the *helmet* with *cheese.* Possibly something to do with the humid atmosphere found inside a kilt.

Tijuana bible *n.* A *jazz mag.*

Tijuana cha-cha *n.* The *trots.* See *sour apple quickstep, Mexican screamers.*

tile hanger's nailbags *sim.* Sagging, lumpy *charlies. 'She had tits like a tile hanger's nailbags.'*

time and a turd *n.* The art of having a *tom tit* at work whilst being paid overtime by an unwitting employer. *Taking one in the company's time,* an *I'm allright cack.*

timebomb fuse *n.* A length of string emanating from a lady's *bodily treasure,* from which a trained expert can infer that a violent, explosive outburst is imminent. Also known as a *party popper, mouse's tail.*

time dream *n.* Lazy Sunday evening television watcher's pleasant reverie enjoyed whilst broken-pot-obsessed show *Time Team* is on. The dozing, sofa-bound viewer allows his mind to wander, specifically to pondering which of the comely, fresh-faced, trench-dwelling young female archaeology students he would most like to discover his own fossilised *bone,* before rubbing the soil off it with her thumb.

time to water the cactus *euph.* Women's things. From the fact that a lazy man often uses his wife or girlfriend's *thousand mile service* interval as a reminder to perform his regular monthly chores. Also *time to to pay the rent, time to worm the cat, time to feed the ducks.*

Tim Henman *n.* A *penis* which promises great things but fails to achieve anything even vaguely resembling hardness, *ie.* it doesn't even get to the *semi* stage.

Timmy twostroke *n.* A gentleman blessed with the enviable ability to *blow his stack* after a couple of *cock stabs.* A *two-push Charlie.*

tincture *n.* An alcoholic drink taken for medicinal purposes, perhaps at breakfast time or during an early morning walk back from Boozebuster.

tinker's curse *n.* An involuntary and highly ill-timed erection that takes the gloss off social occasions. *'Do you, Charles Philip Arthur George, take Diana Frances... oops, sorry about that. I've got the tinker's curse.'* (Dr Robert Runcie, the Marriage of Prince Charles and Lady Di, 1981).

tinker time *1. n.* On *Scrapheap Challenge*, the extra hour allotted to the teams on the morning after the build, when they are allowed to make minor adjustments to their deathtraptions. *2. n.* Sunday afternoon televisual interlude enjoyed by bachelors when Lisa Rogers is on the screen.

tinny mallet *n.* A perfectly normal bloke, who turns into an utter, utter annoying *cunt* after a couple of cans. A *halfpint Harry* or *two pot screamer.*

tin of Vim with an apple on top *sim.* A fictitious penis measurement.

tinter *1. n.* High class *totty,* top class *talent. 'That Mick Hucknall's a jammy get. A face like his and he still gets all the top tinter.'* *2. n.* A lady's *barse,* because "'tin't 'er arse and 'tin't 'er fanny". The *taint.*

tipping the teapot *n.* Situation which occurs when, owing to a fully or semi-erectivated state, a fellow is unable to aim his *tassel* at the toilet bowl for a *slash* and must therefore bend his whole body to attain the required angle of incidence.

tipping the velvet *n.* Of TV companies, the practice of promising *full-nutted* viewers explicit *lesbo cumulonimbus* in order to boost ratings.

tipple *n.* The very tip of the nipple.

tiptoe through the two lips *euph.* Of a lady, to gently strum her *invisible ukulele.*

tip-toe tottie *n.* The various *wank pamphlets* adorning the top shelves of *Grumbelows,* which would thwart shorter men such as Ronnie Corbett, "diddy" David Hamilton and wee Jimmy Krankie when he grows up.

Tipton uppercut *n.* A knee in the *bollocks.*

tiptop *acronym.* A transexual who has yet to go the whole way and is still mid-way through the gender re-alignment process. Tits In Place, Tackle Op Pending. A *bobby dazzler.*

tip your concrete *v.* A sophisticated term for ejaculation when *cough your filthy yoghurt* seems inappropriately coarse. *'If you could just go into the booth and tip your concrete into this receptacle, Mr Elton.'*

tisnae *n.* A scotch lassie's perineum. The *McSnarse.*

tisn'ts *n.* Very small, practically non-existent breasts. *Knockers* that barely merit the description *tits.*

tissent *n.* The *taint, tinter, tintis.*

tissue chrysanthemum *n.* Once dry, the shape of any piece of *bumwad* in which one has *caught the lads* at the culmination of a *ride on the great white knuckler. Prawn cracker, wanker's poppadom.*

Titanic *n.* A lass who *goes down* first time out. An *Ikea bulb.*

tit fairies *n.* Mythical visitors who magically transform the wife's *fried eggs* into *TNTs* during and after *sprogdrop.* Not that she'll let you on them for the next ten years.

tit for brains *n.* A woman who makes up for her lack of intellectual capacity with a surfeit of *chesty substances. 'Today's birthdays: George Best, thirsty Northern Irish footballer, 1946; Dale Winton, orange television also-ran, 1955, Morrissey, daffodil-arsed miserablist, 1959; Katie Price, tit for brains Grattan Celebrity Mum of the Year and Face of Foxy Bingo, 1978.'*

tit for twat *n.* The act of fondling a woman's breast in the vain hope of getting her sufficiently aroused to permit one to have a shot on her *blurtch.*

titilate *v.* To excite with bosoms.

tit kitten *n.* A diminutive lady who compensates up for her small stature by having superior *leisure facilities.* A *midget gem.*

tit leech *1. n.* A baby. *'Births: Fforbes Hhamilton. 23rd November, at The Portland Hospital. To the Hon Hector and Julia (nee Ffyffe-Lewethwaite-Ffyffe), a 6lb 4oz tit leech, Tarquin Hector Sebastapol, brother for Semolina. Deo Gracias.'* (*The Times*, Dec 2nd 2001). *2. n.* A bloke who enjoys sucking on his wife's *jugs.*

tit man *n.* He who prefers *Bristols* to *arses* or *gams.*

titnotised *adj.* To be involuntarily mesmerised by a smashing pair of *churns. Nipnotised.*

tit pants *n.* A bra.

tit pizzas *n.* Big, round, mottled, crusty aereolae. With garlic bread for starters.

tits *1. n.* Breasts, *knockers. 'What a pair of tits.' 2. n.* Foolish or derisory people. *'What a bunch of tits.' 3. n.* Nerves. *'Christ, that Justin Lee Collins gets on my tits.'*

tits on a fish *n.* Descriptive of a supremely useless thing. *'Did you see (insert name of striker currently having a run of bad form) play on Saturday? He was about as much use as tits on a fish.'*

tits out for the lads, get your *exclam.* A compliment proffered by a large group of aggressively drunken men to any female above the age of puberty.

tit scrap *n.* The fighting motion of the breasts of a very *big-boned* council estate woman who chooses not to wear *tit pants* as she walks to Netto, Boozebuster or bingo.

tits in her handbag, she's got her *euph.* An amusing reference to a lady who has failed to attain a sufficiently impressive level of mammary development. *'I don't fancy that Tara Palmer-Tomkinson much, Dalai Llama. She's got her tits in her handbag, her.'*

tit splitter *n.* A lady's fashion bag worn diagonally across the torso such that it bisects the *headlamps.*

tit tap *n. medic.* A nipple. *'Cam-*

era three. Forget about the crazy paving, zoom in on her tip taps, quick.' (Director's instruction, *Ground Force*, BBC TV).

tittoo *n.* A small piece of body art found in the breastular region. A *tit* tattoo.

tittybollocks *n. medic.* Women's breasts which are no bigger than a man's testicles.

titty fuck *n.* A *sausage sandwich*, a *diddy ride*.

titty mustard *n. Daddy's sauce.*

tit up *v.* To get one's *tops* off a *bird. 'The Man Who Titted Up the Lord Mayor's Mother During the Loyal Toast'.* (Cartoon in *Punch* by HM Bateman, 1926).

tit wank *n.* A *soapy tit wank*, without the soap.

titwicks *n. medic.* Ladies' nipples. *'When it comes to feeding baby, breast really is best. Mother's milk contains the perfect balance of nutrients that your child needs, and although the titwicks may be painful for the first few days, feeding quickly becomes a relaxing and bonding time for both.'*

TNTs *abbrev.* Two Nifty Tits.

toad in the hole *n.* An ugly bloke accompanied by an absolute stunner, *eg.* Rod Stewart and whichever blonde *piece* is letting him *on her nest* this week.

toast a bum crumpet *v.* To *fart. 'Houston, we have a problem. We're down to our last two hours of oxygen and Fred has just toasted one hell of a bum crumpet.'* (Mission Control TX log. Transmission from Jim Lovell, Commander, Apollo 13).

toasted cheese sandwich, like a *sim.* Phrase used to describe a woman's *kitten purse* that hasn't seen any saucy action for an inordinately long time, if at all. *'Right then. Would you shag Ann Widdecombe for a grand?' 'I don't think it'd be possible. It would be like trying to pull apart a toasted cheese sandwich.'*

toaster *n.* A crumb-filled vagina with two slots and a spring mechanism that you have to fish your *cock* out of with a wooden spoon.

toaster sex *euph.* Polite expression describing *backdoor action.* From the fact that, like a slice of bread, "the longer you leave it in, the browner it gets". Also known as *the third way* or *bum craft.*

toast to the Queen *n.* A *fart* that scores highly in all three categories; volume, longevity and stench. Often followed by a round of applause.

Toblerone tunnel *n.* The gap, triangular in cross section, between the tops of a slender woman's thighs and her *skin gusset*, into which the popular confection would slide neatly.

tockley *n. Aus.* The *gut stick. 'Ooyah! I've caught me tockley in me zip.'*

toddlers *n.* Collar bone decorations of the sort worn by *Miss Lincolnshire. Dutch Alps, stits.*

todger *n.* That which todges. The penis. Also *tadger, tockley, tool. 'Ooyah! I've caught me todger in me zip.'*

todger dodger *n.* One who leaps out of the way of an on-coming *male genital.* A lesbian.

toffee apple *n.* The glans of the *gut stick* after it's been dipped in something hot and sticky.

toffee Rizla *n.* An absorbent pad of toilet paper worn in the *arse cleft* of a *double sucker* to absorb moisture and guard against *buttering* of the *cheeks*. A *manpon, swedge*.

toffee strings *n*. See *bead curtains*.

toffee yoghurt *n*. That semi-viscous mixture of mingled bodily fluids which, one fondly imagines, dribbles down the backs of *puddle jumpers'* legs after they have successfully completed one of their randy romps. *Santorum, shum, sexcrement*.

toggle and two *euph. Nav.* A Jack Tar's *meat and two veg*.

toilet duck *n*. An untimely and probably unwanted erection which manifests whilst one is sitting on the *pot*. Named after the well known brand of *chod bin* cleaner which boasts of "reaching under the rim".

toilet snails *n*. Cryptozoological molluscs that slither around the *bog pan* in student houses, leaving brown *skidmarks* that no-one claims responsibility for.

toilet stilt *n*. A particularly long and rigid *stool* which stands on one end and clears the water surface by at least three inches. A *bowl vault*.

toilet suicide *n*. A loud explosion followed by a low groan from a lavatory cubicle.

token for the cockwash *n*. A romantic gift bestowed upon a lady by a man, (*eg*. flowers, chocolates, bottle of *screwtop*) in the hope that it will get him *a bit*. *'I'm just nipping down the off licence to get a token for the cockwash.'*

Tokyo optician *sim*. A light-hearted term of abuse for a *slapper, ie*. one who has seen her fair share of *Japs' eyes*.

tolly ring *n. medic*. Condition prevalent amongst employees in the printing industry, the chief symptom of which is soreness in the anal area. So-called because sufferers believe that inhalation of the aromatic hydrocarbon solvent toluene, which is used as a cleaning agent in their workplace, is what causes their *farts* to burn their nipsies. *'I'm sorry, Mr Caxton. You'll have to finish typesetting the 1475 edition of Recuyell of the Historyes of Troye yourself. I'm off home to put some ointment on me tolly ring.'*

tom *1. n*. Prostitute. *2. v*. To carry out prostitution. *'Are you tomming it?' 3. rhym. slang*. Tomfoolery = joolery.

tomato boat has docked, the *euph*. Phrase used to put hubbie off his stroke when *Arsenal are playing at home*.

tomb raider *n*. A gentleman whose preference in ladies lies at the more mature end of the scale. A *granny fucker, biddy fiddler*.

Tom Hank *rhym. slang*. A *Jonathan Ross*.

Tommy Cooper, to do a *v*. To die on the big stage in mid-performance. To lose *wood*, just like that. *'Sorry, love, we'll have to stop. I've done a Tommy Cooper.'*

Tommy's out *n*. A light-hearted party game where one of the guests secretly lays a cable in the house and shouts "Tommy's Out", whereupon everyone else tries to find it. *'To Aldeborough for the weekend, guest of Benjamin (Britten). What a hoot. Simply everyone was there including Larry (Olivier), Ivor (Novello), Terrence (Rattigan) and Alfie (Bass). Charades in the orangery, then after supper we played a game of Tommy's Out* *which ended at three in the morning when Kit (Hassall) found a dead otter in the piano stool, courtesy of Johnny (Gielgud).'* (From *The Diary of Noel Coward*).

toms *rhym. slang.* The *splatters.* From tom tits = squits. *'Please excuse Peaches Honeyblossom from games today as she's got the toms something rotten. Yours sincerely, Sir B Geldof (dad).'*

Tom Thumb's arsehole, a fanny like *sim.* The kind of *twat* one would imagine Emily Bishop off *Coronation Street* to have. A *mouse's ear.*

tongue and groove *1. n.* Basic carpentry technique. *2. n.* Basic *carpet-munchery* technique.

tongue fu *n.* An over-zealous act of *cumulonimbus* which leaves the victim feeling like her *gammon flaps* have just gone five rounds with Jackie Chan.

tongue job *n.* A lick, as opposed to a *blow job.*

tongue punchbag *n.* A *bald man in a boat,* a *clematis.*

tongue shui *n.* The ancient, mystical art of knowing the best place to stick your tongue to get the best flow of energy through your missus's *snatch.*

tongue wrestling *n. Tonsil hockey.*

tonight Matthew *euph.* A plain, ugly or indeed plain ugly, girl seen at the start of a drinking session, who returns later magically transformed by one's *beer goggles* into a gorgeous celebrity lookalike.

tonk *v. onomat.* To *fuck, poke, sht-up.*

tonsil hockey *n. Snogging, spit swapping.*

Tony Martin *n.* The act of *giving it* to someone from behind with both barrels. A double *back scuttle.*

tookus *n. Totty, scrunt.*

tool *n.* Penis, *manhood.* All the *DIY* enthusiast needs, along with his *wanking spanners* and a couple of suitably-sized *nuts,* to perform a spot of *DIY.*

toosh *n. Totty, blart. 'There's not enough toosh on this oil rig.'*

toot *v.* A child and vicar-friendly term for a *parp.*

toot meat *n.* Penis. From the fictional musical sweet of a similar name. *Bed flute, meat flute, pink oboe.*

toots *acronym.* The toppest sort of *top bollocks* available. Derived from the fact that they could be termed Ten Out Of Tens.

toot toot *1. n.* Risqué BBC parlance for vagina. *2. onomat.* The noise made by the *spunk trumpet* during a *blow job.*

tooth coming through, have a *euph.* To be suffering from *IRS.* To have a *wire spider,* a *sweetcorn itch, pine cone.* To have a very itchy *ring-piece.*

toothless gibbon *n.* A *clapping fish.*

toothless sea lion *sim.* A smelly and unkempt *minge. 'I don't think I'll see her again, Cilla. She had a fanny like a toothless sea lion.'*

top banana *exclam.* Give that man a coconut, whacko-the-diddle-oh. Jolly good.

top bollocks *n.* Breasts, *jubblies.*

top bum *n.* A woman's embonpoint and decolletage.

top deck *v.* Of a house guest, to defecate in one's host's cistern, rather than, more conventionally, in the toilet, for comic effect. *"I say, Jeeves, he was a bit of a rum cove, what? Did you see him* *pass the port from left to right?' 'Indeed I did, Sir,' replied the sage retainer. 'I took the liberty of top decking the servants' bathroom before leaving."* (from *Heil Hitler, Jeeves!* by PG Wodehouse).

top dog *n.* An unattractive woman in a workplace whom one fancies simply because all the others are even worse. The least unattractive of a set of unattractive ladies. Default *blart.*

top dressing *n.* A term used in the catering industry for an *air crouton* dropped next to a table by a disgruntled waiter.

top hat *n.* The implausible achievement of a lady with three blokes up her *wizard's sleeve.* After a dish of the same name in the restaurant on the Stenna Ferry, consisting of three pork sausages in mashed potato sitting in a Yorkshire pudding.

topless hand shandy *1. n.* A lemonade and beer drink, pulled from a pump by a barmaid naked from the waist up. *2. n.* A squirt of something fizzy pulled from a *love pump* by a masseuse who is naked from the waist up. *Topless relief. £15 ono.*

topless relief *n.* The cheapest item on the menu in a *toss parlour.*

toploader *n.* A shared marijuana joint, in which the roller has generously overfilled his own half in order to get himself more *monged* than his sharee.

top of a coconut *n.* Descriptive of a *Hitler tash* which has been neglected.

tops and fingers *adj.* Scale on which sexual achievement is measured by teenage males. See also *cloth tit*. *'Get far last night?' 'Not bad. I got my tops and two fingers.'*

top shelf tornado *n.* A purchaser of *bliff mags,* who rushes into the shop, selects his quarry in the blink of an eye, swiftly secretes it within the covers of a daily newspaper and heads for the till with remarkable haste.

top stealth *n.* The alternative approach of entering a newsagents, grabbing your desired *bongo mag,* paying and leaving with such cunning that no-one bats an eyelid.

tornado alley *1. n.* The area of the USA in which twisters are most frequent, encompassing the lowland areas of Mississippi, Ohio and the lower Missouri River valleys. *2. n.* The low-lying region between the *council gritter* and the *love spuds,* in which unusually fierce spiralling winds run wild. The *taint, tintis, notcher, barse etc.*

toss *1. v.* To *wank,* usually "oneself off". *2. v.* To flip pancakes through 180° during cooking.

tossanova *n.* Any gentleman that is celebrated for his prowess at wrist-intensive, bachelor-orientated pursuits.

tossed salad *n. US.* Anal sex between male prisoners. *'More tossed salad, Lord Archer?' 'No thanks, Mr Big, I'm completely stuffed.'*

Tosser del Mar *1. n.* prop. Principal town on the Spanish Costa Brava. *2. n.* A discreet underwater *wank* at a topless beach, rendered undetectable thanks to the laws of refraction and Mediterranean murk.

tosser's twitch *n.* Nervous affliction suffered by *wankers* during periods of abstinence.

tossing the caber *v.* Having *one off the wrist* with a massive length of *wood.*

toss parlour *n.* A *rub-a-tug shop.*

tosspitality *n.* The thoughtful facilities provided for hotel guests who wish to *relax in a gentlemanly manner, eg. grumble* channels on the telly, box of tissues on the bedside table, curtains *etc.*

toss pot *1. n.* a jar for keeping *toss* in. *2. n.* A person held in low esteem, a *fuckwit.*

tosstalgia *v.* The act of *smacking oneself about* whilst fondly remembering a former ladyfriend.

Tottle *n.* A bath-time *air biscuit.* From the joke with the punchline "But, Sir I distinctly heard you say, 'What about a water bottle, Tottle?'".

totty *n. coll.* Girls, *fanny. 'Hey, this car's a fanny magnet. Since I bought it I've been beating off the totty with a shitty stick.'*

touch *v.* To *fondle,* usually "up", esp. with a paintbrush.

touch and go *euph.* The phenomenon of premature ejaculation, the unfortunate affliction whereby the sufferer can barely *stick it in* before shooting his *population paste. 'HAMLET: What a piece of work is man! How noble in reason! How infinite in faculties! And yet, dear Rosencrantz, with narry a pregnant pause my accursed spongle did spray. Hardly did I tarry within dear Ophelia's sweet clout. ROSENCRANTZ: Verily, my Lord, her ladyship did lament that your congress was an ephemeral joy; a fleeting pleasure, fading afore 'twouldst be prehended. HAMLET: Aye, 'tis true. It was touch and go alright.'* (from *Macbeth* by William Shakespeare).

touch base *1. v.* Nonsensical corporate *twat* buzzword. *2. v.* To make a spatial awareness misjudgement whilst wiping one's *teatowel holder* following a *tom tit,* sometimes resulting in a *taxi driver's tan* or, in extreme cases, *beef palm.* A *masonic handshake.*

touching cloth *adj.* That stooling stage immediately after *turtle's head* when the *Sir Douglas* establishes contact with the *trolleys. 'Is there a bog round here mate? I'm touching cloth.'*

touching socks *adj.* The stage by which time it is too late to look for a toilet, but time to look for a trouser shop.

touching the void *n.* The unsettling sensation of wearing a dressing gown without any clothes on underneath. Also a successful film about falling down a hill.

touch last night's tea *v.* To insert a digit into the *ringpiece* of a lady with loose morals.

touch on *n.* The first stirrings of a *panhandle,* caused by something like the swimwear pages of the Grattan catalogue, or the problem pages of a tabloid newspaper. A *twitch on.*

touching ball *1. n.* In snooker, a situation where one ball is touching another, allowing the participant to shoot in any direction without a penalty. *2. n.* In pornography, exactly the same. *Newton's cradle.*

Tourette's juice *n.* Freshly-squeezed orange juice, of the sort that is so bitter it makes the drinker twitch and swear involuntarily.

tourist's touchpool *1. n.* In a marine wildlife complex, the much-visited but rarely-cleaned, crab-infested section which smells of fish and where members of the public can dip their hands in. *2. n.* A filthy *slut's clout.*

towbar *n.* A bulbous *turtle's head.* With a 12 volt output.

towel hook *n.* A *hard on* that's strong enough to support the weight of a damp bath towel.

tow oneself round the cabin *v. naut.* To indulge in a bout of vigorous *self abuse.*

Toxteth airshow *n.* A low-level aeronautical spectacular performed by police helicopters chasing *twockers,* drug traffickers and other sundry ne'er-do-wells. A *Moss Side airshow.*

TPTs *abbrev. Tara Palmer-Tomkinsons.* See *Braille tits. Small stits, tisn'ts.*

tracer fire *n.* Type of food that passes through the alimentary canal entirely unscathed (*eg.* sweetcorn), and shows up the next day in the toilet.

tractor pull *1. n.* A sophisticated entertainment enjoyed by inbred redneck Americans whereby a large block of concrete is dragged along some mud by a piece of souped-up farm machinery. *2. n.* A romantic Italian lovemaking technique whereby the gentleman sticks his *charlie* up his *bird's shitter* whilst he has his *pods* stuffed up her *clopper.*

tradesmen's entrance *n.*The *back passage.*

trade spit *v.* To osculate.

traff *v.* To *fart, let off. 2. v.* To stifle a *fart,* and sort of swallow it back up one's bottom. *'I was sat next to this cracking bird on the train all the way from Doncaster to Manchester. I must've traffed eighty or ninety times.'*

traffic calming measure *n.* A *turd* in the road that could take your exhaust off. A *Radcliffe's sleeper.*

train horn *n.* A lady's party trick in which she *drops a gut,* and *drops her hat forwards* in quick succession, creating a tuneless, two-toned blast. Also known as a *Robson and Jerome.*

trampagne *n.* A homeless person's celebratory beverage, laid down for special occasions, *eg.* White Lightning, Red Label Thunderbird, Mr Muscle Drain Foamer. *'Break out the trampagne, boys. I've found an Embassy with 10 left on it.'*

trampari *n.* A turpentine substitute aperitif taken as an appetiser before a bin-rifling buffet.

tramp duty *n.* A guilt-based tax levied on one who passes a *Harry Ramp* on a regular basis.

tramp eating a kebab *sim.* An enthusiastic performance of *cumulonimbus.* The male equivalent of a *dog eating hot chips.*

tramp grill *n.* Any city centre area where *Harry Ramps* gather in the summer to soak up the sun. The *shandy sunbed.*

trampon *n.* A *dangermouse* that's been left in the *trap* long after it should have been taken out.

tramp's aftershave *n.* The manly and sexy aroma which wafts out of a pub at eight o'clock in the morning, and drives the bag ladies wild.

tramp sauce *n.* The rancid, sticky substance painted over the tongue and on the corners of the mouth by elves whilst one is asleep following a night *on the piss.*

tramp's breakfast *n.* A *docker's omelette.* A pavement *greb, prairie oyster.*

tramp stamp *n.* Any tattoo on a slatternly *bird's* body, usually around the base of the spine or on the left *qualification*. A *tittoo*.

tramp's delight *n*. Low cost cider.

tramp's housewarming *n*. The act of *pissing* oneself.

tramp's hat *n*. A large, shapeless, sweaty and discoloured *clopper*. With knitted pubes. A *shell hole, John Merrick's cap*.

tramp's jackpot *n*. A perfectly-intact discarded cigarette.

tramp's mate *n*. Someone who looks like they probably stink, *eg*. Jim Royle, Jocky Wilson, Tracey Emin.

tramp's tan *n*. The healthy, ruddy complexion achieved by spending a lot of time in the fresh air. Drinking metal polish. *Shandy sunburn*.

tramp steamer *1. n*. A ship which doesn't have any fixed schedule or published ports of call. *2. n*. A refreshingly *al fresco dreadnought* left for us all to enjoy by a cheery *Harold Ramp*.

tramp's tiara *n*. A bobble hat.

tramps' treacle *n*. *Supermarket smack*. Special Brew.

tramps' truffles *n*. Discarded chips.

trampton *n*. An area frequented by those of no fixed abode where they consume copious amounts of *trampagne* and watch the world go by, generously sharing their profanities with members of the public.

trampy tea *n*. Unsavoury beverage made by someone who, despite having filthy, scabby fingers, insists on squeezing the teabag against the spoon with their thumb. Into your fucking tea.

tramp Vegas *n*. telephone booths, vending machines and parking meters that are regularly checked for rejected coins by *gentlemen of the road*.

tranny *1. n*. An old fashioned radio. *2. n*. Transvestite, transparency or transit van, *eg*. a fetish photographer might say *'Shit. I left that tranny of the tranny in the back of the tranny.'*

transformer *n*. One who, on *coming out*, transforms instantaneously into a being that lives up to every homosexual stereotype, *eg*. purchasing tight T-shirts, adopting a mincing gait, drinking G&T and constantly going on about Judy Garland.

Transit of Venus *1. n*. Small spot crossing the face of the Sun behind thick clouds once every 150 years. *2. n*. A mobile boudoir, *ie*. A van containing a heavily stained mattress and the smell of *spunk*. A *shagging wagon, fuck truck, lust bus, spambulance*.

trap *n*. A toilet cubicle in a line of toilet cubicles.

trapped in the Himalayas *adj*. To be mid-way through a *tit wank*.

trap pirouette *n*. The light-footed, on-a-sixpence-style 180 degrees twirl performed when a fellow walks into an empty public lavatory cubicle only to find that it has been the subject of a *dirty protest*, been *pebbledashed* with *arse-gravy* or is full of *bangers and mash*.

travel fat *n*. Unwanted *stalk* which sprouts on public transport. A *stiffy* generated by sitting on a seat located directly over the axles of a corporation omnibus. Also *travel fat, traveller's marrow, diesel dick, routemaster, Varney teacake*.

travel iron *1. n*. A small, hard thing that puts creases in one's trousers on holiday. *2. n*. A small, hard thing that puts creases in one's trousers on a bus.

Travelling Wilberries *1. n.* Short-lived pensioner supergroup. *2. n.* Time-served *clagnuts.*

trawlerman's wellie, fanny like a *sim.* Descriptive of a commodious *snapper.* With the eye-stinging smell of dead kipper.

trawler's bilge *n.* Festering *moip,* stagnant *blip.*

traxedo *n.* Elegant evening wear sported by the *scratting* classes on a night out, consisting of a fake designer tracksuit purchased from a market stall.

treacle *1. n.* Term of affection used solely by Pete Beale in *EastEnders. 2. rhym. slang.* An *air biscuit.* From treacle tart = Bakewell tart.

treading water *n.* Light *strumming* on the *banjo* in order to keep one's interest up during the dull plot bits in a *grumble flick.* Maintaining a *satiscraptory* level of *wood. 'You're under arrest, Mr Herman.' 'But officer, I wasn't wanking, I was just treading water.'*

tread on a frog *v.* A wetter sounding version of *step on a duck.*

treasure trail *n.* The female equivalent of the *crab ladder.* The hairy line of fluff that joins the navel to what's buried down below.

tree log *n.* A *chocolate shark* whose snout is in the water before its tail leaves one's *arse,* a *Cuban bum cigar,* a *bridger, earthing cable, bottom log.*

tree monkey *n.* A *hand on heart.*

tremble trigger *n.* The male *G-spot,* lurking up the *chocolate starfish,* just behind the *doughnut.*

triage *n.* Mental process of a chap entering a nightclub, whereby he mentally sorts the attending *flap* into three groups; those that deserve attention immediately, those who can wait until after a few pints and those who are beyond help.

trick *n.* Customer in a *rub-a-tug shop,* a *Hillman Hunter,* a *gonk, a John.*

trick or treat *n.* A *tree monkey* that could easily *drop a log.* A possible *follow through.*

triggernobetry *n.* The ability to produce instant ejaculation in a man by prodding his prostrate gland with the finger, practised by pros, nurses and Countess of Wessexes.

trilogy *n.* Also known as *brown Star Wars.* A *turd* of such epic proportions it has to be released in three instalments. The first can stand on its own as a complete adventure. The second links to the first, but has a dark, inconclusive feel generating an air of foreboding and leaving itself wide open for an unknown ending. The final chapter has drama, excitement and moments where you think all is lost. A grand battle is waged where good overcomes evil and peace is restored in your *arse.*

trim *n.* Tidy *bush, talent, totty.*

tripe hound *n.* A *fugly dog.*

tripe stick *1. n.* Evil-smelling piece of chewable gristle which keeps a faithful dog's mouth occupied. *2. n.* A pet food treat.

triple crown *1. n.* The Holy Grail of Rugby Union players; to win matches against the other three home nations. *2. n.* The Holy Grail of Rugby Union players; to *shout soup, piss* and *shit* oneself in the back of a taxi.

triple jump *1. n.* A soft playground sport as practised by grinning sometime God-botherer Jonathan

Edwards. *2. n.* To *have* all three available *holes* in one session.

Trisha fodder *n. coll.* Those *Essex tartan*-clad inhabitants of *nillionaires' row* whose personal tragedies and woes are meat and drink to the producers of plebeian daytime TV talk shows.

Trisha porn *n.* Cheaply-produced *grumble vids* where thick, single mothers get "seduced" and *fucked* by the likes of Ben Dover and Marcus Allen.

Trisha trash *n.* The kind of human vermin that appear on mid-morning riff-raff debates. British *caravan trash.*

tristram hand shandy *1. n.* An amusing, yet rambling and ultimately inconclusive, *wank,* named after the book by Laurence Sterne which nobody has ever finished, and what's more anybody who tells you they have is a liar. A *cock and balls story. 2. n.* An act of *personal pollution* performed by the brother of James Herriott's boss on *All Creatures Great and Small*, probably when he was supposed to be sticking his arm up a cow's *arse* in a barn or drinking a cup of tea and eating a slice of cake whilst Tricky-Woo *pissed* on his shoe or something.

trogg *n.* A simpleton, or *fuckwit.* See also *pranny.*

Trojan *n. US.* An American brand of war-like, Greek *French letters.* A brand name which brings to mind the story of the Trojan horse is, if you think about it for a moment, a strange one for a condom manufacturer to have chosen.

Trojan arse *n.* A toilet bowl invasion that takes one by surprise in the middle of the night and sends one back to bed in a state of sleepy bemusement. A somnambulodefecation.

trolley dash *n.* Of a punter, to chase a prostitute who has stolen his trousers down a back alley, wearing his underpants, shoes and socks.

trolley dolly *1. n.* An air hostess. *2. n.* A *ladyboy, shim, bobby dazzler.*

trolleys *1. n. Kecks 2. n. Underkecks.*

trollop *n.* See *trull.*

trollop snack *n. Helmet cheese, foreskinzola.*

tromboning *v.* A thoroughly impractical sex act in which a woman or *Colwyn Bay* man *rims* his pal's *brass eye* whilst simultaneously reaching round the front to give it some elbow on his *horn*, the action being akin to playing a trombone. A *George Jism.*

troop the colour *v.* To leave a *skidmark* down the right or left hand side of the pan as a result of sitting side-saddle on the *crapper,* like the Queen on parade.

trots, the *n.* The rapid foot movement required to convey a diarrhoea sufferer to the lavatory urgently. See also *Tijuana cha-cha, sour apple quickstep, Turkish two-step.*

trouser arouser *n.* A *fit* lass, good looking *bird.*

trouser bandit *n.* Slightly more polite version of *turd burglar.* A *puddle jumper* who steals trousers.

trouser browser *n.* In a lap-dancing establishment, public park or cinema specialising in continental "art" films, a gentleman engrossed in an increasingly agitated search for loose change in his pockets.

trouser chuff *n.* A Cornish seagull that lives in some trousers.

trouser cough *n.* A clearing of the nether throat.

trouser department *1. n.* Section of a department store dealing with men's legwear. *2. n.* Area of the department store in which middle-aged men experience problems.

trousered *1. adj.* To be wearing trousers. *2. adj. Wasted, arseholed, wankered, shit faced.*

trouser engine *n.* Gentleman's machinery which, when sufficiently fuelled with beer, can be cranked into life and will thenceforth run by itself with a vigorous repetitive action until its *nuts* work loose.

trouser folder *n.* A person who, one would imagine, would have to carefully fold their clothes after taking them off before they could indulge in sexual intercourse, *eg.* Sven Goran Ericsson, Simon Cowell, Bruce Forsyth.

trouser jazz *n.* A session of different-sounding blasts on the *bum trumpet* released in quick succession.

trouser leg trombonist *n.* Popular female musician who plays in the same ensemble as the *skin flautist* and *pink oboe* virtuoso.

trouser Mauser *n.* A small rapid firing *porridge gun*. A *pump action mottgun, mutton musket.*

trouser rain *n.* A small downpour in the *keg* region leading to a few damp patches in the south. A *wet penny in the pocket.*

trouser rake *n.* A stiffer version of the *trouser snake*. Often pops up and hits women in the face when stood on.

trouser rouser *n.* A *brass eye*-opener. A *Bronx cheer.*

trouser snake *n. One-eyed pant python.*

trouser tent *n.* Embarrassing portable erection made from canvas or other trouser material, with a zip up one side, supported by a rigid *wood shaft*. If occurring whilst seated this can easily be concealed with one's bowler hat.

trouser tits *n.* A large pair of prominent *testicles. Man marbles. 'I tell you what, Colin. My trouser tits battered her chin.'*

trouser trout *n.* Something one tickles in one's *trolleys* before taking it out and banging its head against a rock.

trouser trumpet *1. n.* A be-bop solo blown on the *botty bugle*. *2. n.* The E-flat *anus.*

trouser truncheon *n.* The stiff *pole* a bobby takes out in the back of his van on a Saturday night. A *turned-on copper's torch.*

trout *v.* To *pull*. *'I was out trouting last night. Ended up with a right old five-to-twoer. Had to chew me own arm off this morning.'*

trout jelly *n.* Artificial sexual lubricant. *I can't believe it's not batter, Grandma's little helper, granny batter.*

trucker's mate *n.* Someone who looks like he could be a sex case, *eg.* Roy off *Coronation Street.*

trucker's Tizer *n.* Brownish-yellow liquid, thought by many to be the urine of long-distance lorry drivers, often spotted in plastic bottles reposing on the hard shoulders of motorways, disguised as pop.

truffle hunting *v.* Taking a *trip around the world. Rimming.*

truffleshuffle *n.* The characteristic gait of one who has *split the winnings.*

trull *n. 19thC.* A prostitute, a *hooer*. With fat *tits* but not many teeth, as stabbed up by Jack the Ripper in Old London Town.

trump *v.* To *fart* or *pass wind* in a chair-shaking way.

trumpeter's lips *n.* The involuntary pursing of the *tea towel holder* at moments of extreme fear. *'Any man who tells you he is not afraid to go into battle is either a fool or a liar. It is the fear that makes him fight. I personally had the trumpeter's lips throughout the North African campaign.'* (from *The Memoirs of Field Marshal Montgomery*).

truncheon *n.* A solid, one piece *turd* which, if grasped, firmly could be used to stun a miscreant.

truncheon voucher *n.* A *ticket to the policeman's ball*. A constabulary bribe.

trunk *n.* A large *knob* which squirts water over Johnny Morris.

try a little Freddie *v.* To indulge in a spot of light *bummery*, out of curiosity more than anything. *'After Lancing, Evelyn Waugh went up to Oxford, where he read History at Hertford College. During his three years there, he neglected his formal studies and threw himself into a vigorous social scene populated by artists, actors, poets and aesthetes. He later recalled: "Moving in such artistic circles in those heady, hedonistic days between the wars, one was inevitably tempted to try a little Freddie from time to time. I tried it at least twice, but found it most disagreeable as it tended to make my nipsy feel sore."'* (from *Waugh and Peas - The Novelist and his Allotment Produce* by Michael Holroyd and Alan Titchmarsh, Macmillan Books).

trying to get the last pickled onion from the jar *euph.* Deep *gusset typing* whilst biting the tongue.

try on the comedy beard *v.* To perform *cumulonimbus, impersonate Stalin*.

tubby chaser *n.* A man who thinks *thunderbirds* are go, *eg.* Lenny Henry. Also a woman who prefers her *beefcake* to be a *salad dodger*.

TUBER *acronym. medic.* Doctor's shorthand written on the notes of good looking female patients. Totally Unnecessary Breast Examination Required.

tubesteak *n. Beef bayonet on the bone.*

TUBFUF *acronym.* Thumb Up Bum, Finger Up Fanny. All business.

tufty club *n.* A *vertical bacon sandwich* surrounded by scraggy outcrops of *gorilla salad*. Named after the 1960s/70s schools road safety campaign fronted by a threadbare squirrel which was animated in a sub-Ray Harryhausen style repeatedly nearly stepping out in front of motor vehicles.

tug *v.* To *pull*, as in a *pud*. A lighthearted *wank*. *'Dinner's ready, Sidney!' 'Down in a minute, dear. I'm just having a little tug.'*

tug boat *n.* A woman of plain appearance and compact, muscular build. A *swamp donkey*.

tuggernaut *n.* A lorry driver *shedding his load* in his cab at Barton Park Services on the A1.

tug of love *n. Pulling your string,* and putting your heart into it.

tug of phwoar *n.* A spontaneous and urgent *one off the wrist* brought on by a particularly *horny* sight, *eg.* an attractive *bird*, the bra adverts on Underground escalators.

tug of raw *n.* The tenth *Barclay's* of the day for the gentleman who is *working from home.* A *blood wank.*

tug of war *n.* A notably hard and tiring act of *self pollution* undertaken whilst *heavily refreshed.* A *J Arthur* which requires a lot of willpower to bring to a *satiscraptory* solution.

tugpusher *n.* Of schools, workplaces and police stations, the individual who has taken on the responsibility for distributing hardcore *art pamphlets* amongst his colleagues. A *pornbroker,* a *grumblemonger.*

tug pamphlet *n.* A *jazz magazine.*

tugwax *n. Spongle, spadge, jitler.*

tumblepube *n.* A fur ball of *clock springs* and other discarded pubic foliage which wafts around when the *bog* door opens.

tummy banana *n.* A *gut stick.*

tummy Tetris *n.* The strange, yet not unpleasant, sensation whereby one's unborn *change of hearts* slot together satisfyingly in one's alimentary canal, before disappearing with an amusing noise.

tummy truncheon *n. Sixth gear stick, porridge gun,* penis.

tump *n. Welsh.* The *beetle bonnet,* the *monkey's forehead.*

tumwiper *n.* Any unfashionable item of clothing received as a gift from a well-meaning relative or friend that is immediately relegated to the function of wiping *spoof* off one's stomach after *self help.* A *jazz rag.*

tuna taco *n.* A hot dish, not requiring cutlery, served when *dining at the Y.* If eaten with a side order of *cranberry dip,* it could lead to *Mexican lipstick.*

tuna town *n.* The female genitalia, *Billingsgate box.*

tup *1. v.* To have sex, *fuck. 2. v.* Of sheep-to-sheep shagging, red hot *horny* ram on ewe action.

tuppence licker *n.* A *lesbo, bean flicker, carpet muncher, pelt lapper.*

tuppenny all-off *1. n.* A cheap, no-nonsense haircut popular amongst national servicemen in the 1960s. *2. n.* A no-nonsense *fannicure.* A *Brazilian.*

tuppie *n. Scot.* A Dundonian term for a lady's *fluffit. 'There's nae a kitten, moose or puppy / Ha'f sae soft as ma wife's tuppie.'* (from *The Song O' the Dundee Growler* by Robbie Burns).

turbo shit *n.* The high-speed *dump* required to fool a ladyfriend into thinking you had only went for a *gypsy's kiss.* A *greyhound's egg.*

turbot for tea *exclam.* Announcement that the *fish supper* is served. *'Never mind that tug, Sidney. It's turbot for tea.'*

turd *n.* A cylindrical unit of *shit,* longer than a *tod.* A link of *feeshus.*

turd burglar *n.* Stealthy thief who forces entry into the rear of a person's premises via the inside of the *chocolate drainpipe.*

turd clippers *n. US.* Buttocks.

turd degree burns *n. medic.* Post-curry *shitting* injuries. *'A man was taken to hospital last night after being found unconscious on the pavement outside a curry restaurant in Newcastle upon Tyne. He was suffering from shock, alcohol poisoning and had turd degree burns covering 90% of his anus. A spokesman for the restaurant said 'Come to the Curry Capital, Bigg*

Market, Newcastle upon Tyne." (BBC News 24, 1st Jan).

turd eagle *n. Aus.* A large *blowfly.* A *dunny budgie, poobottle.*

turder *n.* The begetter of a *feeshus.*

turd eye *n.* The mystical sixth sense that usually, though not always, enables a pedestrian to avoid tripping over a length of *canine cable.*

turd fairies *n.* Mythological creatures that are thought to be the cause of the mysterious *ghost shit* phenomenon, *ie.* those stools of which there are no trace when one turns round to admire them in the *pan.*

turdis *n.* One of them detached, modern, portable, space-age-looking public conveniences that could well be a phonebox or small internet cafe. A *turd tardis.*

turdsearch *n.* The desperate hunt for reading material one embarks upon when *Mr Brown is at the window.*

turdulence *n.* The area of dirty air affected by a particularly foulsome *trouser trumpet,* usually dispensed by a man walking in front of one in a tightly-packed shopping establishment, *eg.* the make-up section at John Lewis.

turfer's knee, wetter than a *sim.* Descriptive of a lady's *clunge* in a state of preternatural excitement. A phrase that can be usefully employed when referring to a *clown's pie* that is *frothing like bottled Bass* or, indeed, *dripping like a fucked fridge.*

turf out *1. n.* An anal spring clean. A well needed *tom tit. Next sale, Queensway. 2. v.* To excrete.

Turin shroud *1. n.* Famous medieval sheet with a face painted on it. *2. n.* A piece of lavatory tissue draped tastefully over a floating *log* that will not flush away.

turistas *n. Turkish two-step.*

turk *v.* To take someone or something up the *council. 'Sit down please, Lord Archer.' 'If it's all the same with you, Governor, I'd rather stand. I've just been turked in the showers by Jonathan King.'*

turkey *n.* The *cracker* you think you've pulled whilst drunk at the office Christmas party who turns out to be a rough old *bird* who only gets *stuffed* once a year.

turkey moss *n.* Serious *fluff* on a *bird's bodily treasure. Gorilla salad.*

turkey-neck *n.* That which is *throttled* in Norfolk.

turkey twizzler *1. n.* Unappetizing helix of nondescript brown matter of mysterious and sinister provenance, served to schoolchildren in lieu of real food. *2. n.* A thin, spiralling *turd* which retains its corkscrew shape even after it has been dropped into the *pan.*

turkey's wattle *n.* A *ragman's coat,* a *club sandwich.*

Turkish *1. n.* Heterosexual *back door work,* whilst wearing curly slippers. *Irish. 2. rhym. slang.* An excrement. From Turkish delight = shite. *'What's the matter, Eric?' 'Jocky Wilson done a Turkish in me shoe. Again.'*

Turkish bath *n.* A *Glasgow shower.*

Turkish dagger *n.* A curved *Thora.* With a jewel-encrusted handle that one wouldn't, frankly, fancy holding in one's teeth.

Turkish revenge *n.* A *stab* up the *arse.*

Turkish rinse *n.* A quickfire bathing technique popular amongst *soap-dodgers,* consisting of a rudimentary scrub of one's armpits, gusset and *giggle stick*.

Turkish shower *n.* A *Glasgow shower*.

Turkish slippers *n.* The *jester's shoes*.

Turkish two-step *n.* *Smallroom dance* not dissimilar to the *sour apple quick step, Tijuana cha-cha*, or *Aztec twostep*.

turned-out trouser pocket, arsehole like a *sim.* A dropped *clacker valve*, resulting from either an excess of *Turkish*, or a red hot Indian.

turn Japanese *v.* To make like a Chinese helicopter pilot, gripping his *joystick* for grim life and concentrating on keeping his *chopper* up.

turn your bike round *v.* To go to the lavatory. *'Excuse me, I'm just going to turn my bike round. Have you got any arse paper?'*

turpsichord *n.* A public house pianoforte, as played by rubber-fingered drunks.

turps nudger *n.* A *top shelf drinker*. *'Have you seen that bloke who reads the news on Tyne Tees? Jesus, what a fucking turps nudger.'*

turquoise *n.* A lady who allows the *dog in the bathtub*. One who doesn't object to being *turked* up the *bonus tunnel*.

turtle *1. n.* A passive sexual partner, *ie.* "Get her on her back and she's fucked". *2. n. coll. Blit, fanny, fluff, talent. Birds. 3. n.* One of the least sexy *bum games* a flatulent couple can play in the bedroom, the winner being the last one to poke their head out from under the duvet.

turtleberries *n. Winnets, dangleberries, Payne's Poppets.*

turtle bungee *n.* The dangerous sport of releasing and retracting *turds* by clever use of the sphincter muscles just before they *touch cloth*. *Prairie dogging, gophering.*

turtle guillotine *n.* The *nipsy, cigar cutter, clackervalve.*

turtle power *n.* The unstoppable superhero-like strength exhibited by a determined *chod* as it tries to overcome the tightly-clenched *nipsy*.

turtle recall *v.* The brief retraction of the *turtle's head* whilst en route to the *thunderbox*.

turtle's breath *n.* The very final warning *fart* before the turtle pokes its head out to *autograph the gusset*.

turtle's den *n.* The *bomb bay, dirt kitchen*.

turtle's head *n.* The initial protrusion of a stool though the *tea towel holder*, the point at which contracts are exchanged for the building of a *log cabin*. *Touching cloth, the monkey's toe.*

tush *n. US. Bum* (but not a tramp), *ass* (but not a donkey).

tussage *n. Talent*, female *buffage, blart, totty.*

TV *1. abbrev.* A television. *2. abbrev.* A *tranny*.

twanger *n. Whanger.*

twangers *n. onomat.* Generic term for ladies' undercrackers, but more specifically those worn by dirty *scutters*. Named after the sound the gusset makes as it leaves the crotch when pulled hastily down from either side. *'And Lady Diana Spencer looks resplendent as she walks down the aisle, keeping up the age old traditions. She's wearing an old 18th century tiara, a magnificent new wedding dress, a diamond necklace borrowed from* *her friend the Duchess of Argyll, and a pair of blue twangers.'* (Sir Alastair Burnett, Royal Wedding commentary, ITN, 1981).

twang the wire *v.* To pluck out a *jazz rhythm* on the *one-stringed banjo.*

twankunt *n.* Descriptive of someone who is not just a *twat,* but also a *wanker* and a *cunt* to boot. *'Birthdays: Lord Archer - author, politician and twankunt, 62 today.'* (*The Times*, April 15th 2002).

twaste *n.* The taste of a *twat.* From twat + taste, one would imagine. *'Come on, eat it all up.' 'I don't like the twaste.'*

twat *1. n.* A *minge. 2. n.* Stupid person. *3. v.* To hit, beat up.

twatalogue *n.* A magazine of pornotholgical interest. An *art pamphlet.*

twat burger *euph.* A polite euphemism for an *act of oral affection* performed upon a woman's *bodily treasure.* Hopefully without too much ketchup on it.

twat burglar *n.* A man, presumably wearing a mask and stripy jersey, who steals another bloke's missus.

twaterpillars *n.* Female version of *willipedes. Cloppular crabs, mechanical dandruff.*

twatful *1. n.* A good *seeing to* in the sexual sense. *'Just 8 pints tonight, lads. Got to get home to give the rib a twatful.' 2. n.* An imperial measure of *spangle,* equal to 2 *nutsworths* or $^1/_{10}$ of an *Almond. 'Sister Amoeba was powerless to resist. His eyes burned into hers like a sort of stone. His papal arms enfolded her body as she felt herself being swept away in some sort of weather system of passion. Then he lifted his cassock and gave her a twatful.'* (From *The Mother Superior and the Holy Father*, by Barbara Cartland).

twat mag *n. Bongo periodical.*

twatmates *n.* Gentlemen who have both had a portion of the same *haddock pastie, eg.* Bryan Ferry & Mick Jagger, Michael Jackson & Nicholas Cage, and Sir Donald Campbell & Claude Greengrass off *Heartbeat. Custard cousins.*

twat nappy *n.* See *clot mop.*

twat nav *n.* Motoring terminology; the wife with a road atlas.

twatois *n.* The sort of fake Jamaican dialect favoured by middle class youths wishing to enhance their street credibility.

twat pamphlet *1. n.* A *grumble book* or *flesh mag* purchased by people who aspire to having a *wank, eg. Razzle, Knave, Splosh etc. 2. n.* An aspirational lifestyle magazine read by *wankers, eg. Dazed & Confused, Wonderland™, Wallpaper.*

twatplates *n.* Car registration plates where the numbers have been respaced or mutilated in order to make them spell out something that they don't from a distance, *eg.* those on a Fiat Punto where the owner has placed a black screw at the bottom of the two 1s in P11 NTO.

twat rats *n. Cunt mice* for ladies with a heavier flow of *fanny jam.* Industrial strength *dangermice.*

twat rattler *n.* A *plastic cock,* a vibrator, *neck massager, bob.*

twatriot *n.* Someone who waved a Union Jack and shouted "Come on Tim", between every point whilst Tim "Spoilt Bastard" Henman got thrashed at Wimbledon every fucking year. Also, to be found wearing a plastic Union Jack hat and singing *Land of Hope and Glory* at the Last Night of the Proms.

twat seats *n.* The back two rows on the upper tier of a double-decker bus or an EasyJet flight from Newcastle to Alicante, reserved for cap-headed *scratters* who wish to cycle through their ringtones, engage in foul-mouthed, shouted debates and/or light-hearted vandalism and otherwise *act the twat.*

twatslapping *n.* The untraceable slapping noise generated *below the stairs* when a man and a lady are doing *thingy.* A *Blair's ovation.*

twatters *n.* Smashing *churns.* The sort that Nell Gwynn would have sported. *Fat rascals.*

twattoo *n.* A badly-conceived, situated, designed and/or executed piece of body art, *eg.* the word "Brooklyn" written above someone's *arsecrack* in Ye Olde English capital letters.

twatwrapper *n.* A multi-pocketed garment of the sort worn by the sex cases who stand at the end of railway platforms spotting trains. An anorak.

tweedle *1. n. rhym. slang.* Male ejaculate, *jitler* or *Thelonious.* From Tweedledum = cum. *2. n. rhym. slang.* Urine, *wazz* or *piss.* From Tweedledee = wee.

twenty-eighth of Mayhem *n.* The day marking the start of *rag week. Ruby Tuesday.*

twenty-five yard screamer *1. n.* Some sort of long range kick in an association football match. *2. n.* A former ladyfriend whose only means of social interaction with you seems to involve yelling your sexual shortcomings at you from a distance whilst full of *bitch piss.*

twernt *n.* The *tinter.*

twice off the same hard *1. n.* Of a gentleman, the once-in-a-lifetime phenomenon of achieving two orgasms from the same erectivation with no intervening *downtime,* and thus *2. euph.* Any once-in-a-lifetime phenomenon. *'And what is there to look forward to in the night sky next year? Well of course, the big story is the return of Halley's Comet which is only visible every 76 years. So it's a real twice off the same hard for most astronomers.'* (Patrick Moore, *The Sky at Night*, 1985).

twig & giggle berries *n.* The *fruitbowl,* the *meat and two veg.*

twiglet factory *n.* A heaving dancefloor populated by sweaty-*arsed* women wearing G-strings or thongs.

twink *n.* A *fart* so potent that it makes the hairs on your *arse* curl. Named after the home perm solution of the 1970s.

twinkie *1. n. US. Turd, chocolate log. 2. n.* An apprentice *mudhole plumber.*

twin peaks *1. n. prop.* An experimental television series of the early 1990s created by David Lynch. *2. n.* Smashing *tits* like Audrey's in the series. *Dunce's hats, sweatermeat.*

twins, the *n.* A fine pair of *milky swingers* that could prevent a fellow getting a good night's sleep for months on end.

twin tone *n.* A *fart* which suddenly and ominously drops in pitch, indicating something other than *marsh gas* may have been expelled. A *follow through, squench.*

twin tub *n.* Back, then frontal penetration.

twirly *n.* An affectionate term used by omnibus drivers to describe senior citizens who attempt to use their free passes before 9.00am. ie, they are "too early" and have to be thrown off the bus.

twist *1. rhym. slang. US.* Girl. From twist and twirl. *2. n.* Of *carpet munching* relationships, the *carpet,* as opposed to the *muncher*. A passive *lesbo. 3. v.* From the pontoon playing gambit, to risk losing a scoring hand in the hope of getting a better one; thus to turn down the advances of a half decent lady in the hope that one will *cop off* with something better.

twister *n. US.* Pervert, a *nonce.*

twist on nineteen *1. v.* In the world of blackjack - which seems to be a bit like pontoon, but played for money instead of matches - to foolishly risk busting your hand by asking the dealer to turn over another card. To gamble when the odds are stacked against you. *2. v.* In the world of flatulence, to *fart* recklessly whilst *touching cloth. 'Open a window, love. I've had three Guinnesses and a prawn egg foo yung but I'm gonna twist on nineteen. By the way, is there a twenty-four hour Tesco round here that sells underpants?'*

twitcher *n.* A *bird watcher, ie.* one who light-heartedly takes photographs of his female colleagues on his mobile phone in the full knowledge that he will later *wank his knackers flat* at home whilst viewing the snaps. So called because of the involuntary twitches his *knob* makes whilst he's taking the pictures.

twitcher's chin *n.* A very scruffy, chronically untrimmed lady's *front bottom* which resembles the unkempt lower mandible of bino-toting grumpy TV ornithologist and former funnyman Bill Oddie.

twitching Buddah *n.* A short, fat, excitable erection.

twitter *n.* A lady's perineum, that area of the anatomy between the *twat* and the *shitter. Duffy's bridge, biffin bridge, tinter, taint.*

Twix lips *n.* A *front bottom* version of *hungry arse. Knicker sausages.*

two am grab bag *n.* In a night club, the ropey assortment of frankly second-rate *tussage* which is all that is left to choose from at chucking out time. The *floor sweepings, bin rake,* sediment.

two aspirins on an ironing board *sim.* Descriptive of the bosoms of the slimmer-figured lady. Flat *stits, fried eggs, lung warts, TPTs.*

two bagger *n.* Someone so ugly that two bags are required in order to go *quim wedging* with them; one over their head and one over yours, just in case theirs falls off.

two bob billionaire *n.* A young man in an £80 shirt who still lives with his mum and dad.

twoc *v.* Take Without Owner's Consent. To borrow someone's car, not in order to steal it, but merely to drive it through Dixon's window and set it on fire. Also *twock.*

two can Van Damme *n.* In the pub, the jumped-up little *shit* that starts acting like the hardest man on the planet after a couple of drinks. *Tinny mallet.*

twocker *n.* A cheeky rapscallion who *twocks.* A loveable rogue, a lively urchin.

two flush push *n.* An obstinate *digestive transit* which requires a second pull on the *bog* handle before it will set off for the seaside.

two page charlie *n.* The literary equivalent of a *two push charlie.* An overexcited *one-handed reader* who foolishly doesn't take the opportunity to peruse his new *art pamphlet* in a leisurely manner before *squirting his curd.*

two-pot bechamel *n.* A thick, white *bollock sauce* produced by heating up one's *two-pots* without serving. *'The wedding was pucka, but straight after the honeymoon I had to spend a month away filming. By the time I saw Jools again, I was gasping to dish up a bit of the old two-pot bechamel.'* (from *Mockney Rebel*, the autobiography of Jamie Oliver).

two pot screamer *n. Aus.* Someone who cannot hold their beer. A more reserved British equivalent would be *halfpint Harry*.

two puppies fighting in a bag *n.* Large, mobile and unrestrained breasts.

two ring circus *n.* The greatest show on earth. *Over the shoulder boulder holder,* a bra.

twoskin *n.* Half a *fourskin*.

two stroke poke *n.* Similar to a *one pump chump,* only twice as sexually satisfying for his missus. A *two push Charlie.*

two up *n.* A *twos up*, a *threesome* with two gentlemen and a lady.

two wombles looking over a balcony *sim.* Descriptive of *NGT*s.

twunt n. Useful, satisfying yet inoffensive combination of two very rude words which can safely be spoken in the primmest and properest company.

Tyne Bridge *adj.* Descriptive of the position adopted by a dog trying to lay a particularly tenacious *egg*.

tyre *n. medic.* Swollen condition of the *fiveskin* caused by over-zealous *relaxation. 'Did you get your internet sorted out, Clive?' 'Yes, I got it connected yesterday, and I've already got a tyre.'*

Uu

U-bend straightener *n.* A mighty powerful *shit.*

UB40 winks *n.* A mid-afternoon nap taken after a hard morning at the telly face.

U-blocker *n.* A titanic *dreadnought* so big it causes a *jobbie* jam in the foul drainage system. The Moby Dick of *brown trouts, a plumber's bonus.*

udders *n.* Breasts with absolutely no erotic qualities whatsoever.

udderpants *n.* A utility brassiere in which function is more important than form.

udder scudder *n.* A agricultural *sausage sandwich.*

UDI *abbrev.* Unidentified Drinking Injury. Inexplicable damage sustained during a *bender* of which the victim has no recollection. A mystery *binjury.*

ugly as a Thai stripper's scrotum *sim.* Graphic metaphor, descriptive of that moment when something which seems to be going along swimmingly suddenly takes a distinctly unpleasant turn. *'Senna's lap looked perfect until he ran wide into the Tamburello Curve, when things turned as ugly as a Thai stripper's scrotum.'*

ugly bus *n.* A vehicle that mysteriously turns up after one has had 8 pints on a Friday night and takes all the ugly women home, leaving the pub full of beautiful ladies.

ugly duckling *n.* A long-protracted *Exchange & Mart* launched mid-walk, where the benefactor "walks with a quack and a waddle and a quack".

ugly lights *n.* A revealing lighting apparatus which is switched on in pubs at chucking out time.

ugly taxi *n.* The vehicle which mysteriously delivers an unattractive *bird* into one's *fart sack* on a Saturday morning.

Ulrikas *n.* A pair of *kahoomas* that look smashing in clothing, but pitifully saggy when released on a beach.

ummfriend *n.* A *fuck buddy.* From the commonly-heard introduction at parties: "Hi, Gillian. Have you met Kate? She's my ... ummm ... friend."

unblocking the sink *sim.* A vigorous and impatient *wank,* presumably using both hands. *Starting the hornmower.*

Uncle Albert's beard *n. Jelly jewellery.*

Uncle Doug *rhym. slang. Self abuse.* From Uncle Doug = tug. *'I'm just off for an Uncle Doug, but if there's anything you need, just ask one of the stewardesses.'*

Uncle Fester *n.* A *goolie*-ish *bald-headed man* from the *old Adam* family, who occasionally rises up and puts the *willies* up your missus.

uncork the brown champagne *v.* On the morning after a night of strong ale and spicy foodstuffs, to bring in the *pace car,* thus unleashing a frothy torrent of foul, effervescent liquid.

undefuckable *adj. Bust,* damaged beyond repair. *'Oh, and there goes Barricello's engine on the warm-up lap. He'll head straight for the pit lane, but that looks pretty undefuckable. It's certainly the end to his Portuguese Grand Prix, Martin.'* (Murray Walker, commentating as Frentzen's front left wheel came off on the final corner, Belgian Grand Prix 1999).

underbeard *n. Minge.*

undercarriage *n.* Genitals, usually male. *The fruit bowl, family jewels, pudendas.*

underchunders *n. Trolleys, tacklebags.*

undercoat *n.* A soft drink ordered to accompany the first pint of a long session which prepares the stomach's surface for the later layers of alcoholic emulsion. Also *George Best undercoat, Winehouse lining paper.*

undercover cop *1. n.* A plain clothes detective. *2. n.* A crafty spot of *DIY* under the bedsheets whilst the missus is in the ensuite. 3. n. A trivial, opportunistic sexual assault committed on a crowded bus or underground train.

undercrackers *n. Underchunders.*

underdaks *n. Undercrackers.*

underkecks *n. Underdaks.*

under one's wing, take someone *v.* To perform a spot of *bagpiping.* To essay a *Hawaiian muscle fuck.*

under starter's orders *adj.* Suffering from that uncomfortable rising pressure in the lower gastric tract that signals the onset of *arse labour. 'Christ, nan, hurry up and get out of there before I papper me trolleys, will you? I'm under starter's orders here.'*

undertaker, play the *v.* To bury a *stiff. 'Was it okay meeting up with your ex-wife?' 'Yeah, not bad. She let me play the undertaker, anyway.'*

undertaker's privileges *n.* Acts of carnality performed by a *corpse packager* on his recently-deceased clients. Funeral director's perks. *'Wanted. Hard-working young man to train as Mortuary Attendant in a busy London hospital. Must have 4 GCSEs at grade C or above. 35 hours per week, occasional weekends. Starting salary £10,000 plus clothing allowance & undertaker's privileges.'*

under thunder *n.* Ominous rumbles from the bowels of hell.

unit *1. n.* The genitals, usually male, esp. the *veiny bang stick. Pud. 2. n. Bird,* an individual piece of *talent.*

unleash the dobermans *v.* After a night on the Guinness, to let loose with a particularly savage and uncontrollable outburst of *black and tan* from the *back gate.* Let out the *boys from the black stuff.*

unless I could piss petrol *phr.* A humorous codicil to the commonly-used vituperative exclamation "I'd not piss on him if he was on fire," which can be used to rich comic effect, *viz. 'That Bono's a tosser. I'd not piss on him if he was on fire...unless I could piss petrol.'*

unload *v.* To drop a *depth charge* or launch an *air biscuit.* To empty one's *hatchback* of *shopping.*

unmentionables *n.* Roman Catholic word which enables mother-in-laws to mention genitals or underwear. *'Sweet Jesus mother of Mary, stop playing with your unmentionables, will you, and have another slice of cake.'*

unmown crease *1. n.* An unprepared cricket pitch. *2. n.* A particularly hirsute clopper. *Terry Waite's allotment, a biffer, Judith etc.*

unstipation *n.* Medical condition of the *back body* which necessitates trips to the *shitter* every five minutes or so. Usually caused by a heavy night on the beer and curry. *'I went to the doctor and said, "Have you got anything for unstipation?" He said yes, have this fucking bucket.' (Routine by Bernard Stone-Age-Manning,*

Neanderthal stand-up comedian, 500,000 BC).

untidy sock drawer *n.* A *ripped sofa, badly-packed kebab, ragman's coat.*

unwrap the meat *v.* To *let the twins out.* Of Lord Owen, to get *his tits out for the Liberal Democrats.*

up and over like a pan of milk *euph.* Descriptive of a gentleman who is so good at sex that he can ejaculate before he's even got his pants off.

up and twichin' *adj.* The point at which the gentleman is ready to engage in the courses of love.

upchuck *v.* To *laugh at the carpet.*

upgrade *v.* To go to the *chod bin* for a *number one,* but decide to take the opportunity to have a *number two* whilst one is there.

upgrade a fart *v.* To go for a *shit. 'I would love to stand here chatting all day, Your Majesty, but I really must go and upgrade a fart.'*

uphill gardener *n.* He who sows his *seed* on the *backyard allotment.* A pusher of a *cheesy wheelbarrow* up the *lavender* path. A *crafty butcher.*

uphill wanking *n.* Masturbating over somewhat challenging *whack fodder*, for example a knitting pattern or a birthday card from one's granny.

up on blocks *adj.* Of a woman. A monthly *MOTT* failure due to a recurring leak under the *beetle bonnet.*

up periscope *n.* Bathtime game for up to one person. *Polishing the lighthouse, waxing the dolphin, making nylon.*

upstairs *n.* The *rack, top bollocks, top bum. 'What's she got upstairs?' 'Two knockers.'*

up the Beeston ginnel, one *n.* The act of *making love* up the *wrong 'un,* from the name of a narrow, malodorous passage in the environs of the notorious Leeds *shit hole. 'Tamoshanta was powerless to resist. His eyes burnt into hers like agates. His muscular arms enfolded her body as she felt herself being swept away on a dustpan of passion. 'I'm sorry, Your Grace, but you'll have to give me one up the Beeston ginnel this morning as I am up on blocks at present.''* (from *The Milkmaid and the Bishop* by Barbara Cartland).

up the duff *adj. medic. Up the pasture, in the pudding club.*

up the Jimmy Savile, to take a lady *v.* To indulge in a session of *back door work.* So called because of the warbling "eeurgh!-eeurgh!-eeurgh! now then! now then!" noises made by the lucky recipient.

up the pasture *adj. medic. Up the poke, up the duff.*

up the poke *adj.medic. Up the stick, up the pasture.*

up the stick *adj. medic. In the club, up the poke.*

up the Tregenna, take the missus *v.* To do one's good lady up the *coal hole.* A phrase coined with reference to Merthyr's poshest restaurant, where the South Wales man about town takes his wife for birthdays or anniversaries. To have a *once a year special.*

up to the apricots *adj. Up to the back wheels, up to the maker's nameplate.*

up to the back wheels *adj. Up to the apricots, up to the buffers.*

up to the buffers *adj. Up to the bumper, up to the cannon wheels.*

up to the bumper *adj. Up to the cannon wheels, up to the eggs.*

up to the cannon wheels *adj. Up to the eggs, up to the buffers.*

up to the eggs *adj. Up to the maker's nameplate, up to the back wheels.*

up to the maker's nameplate *adv.* An engineering term for being *conkers deep.* Also *up to the boilermaker's nameplate.*

up to the wrist, go for the elbow *phr.* A more imaginative alternative to "in for a penny, in for a pound," which is much in use amongst farm vets, gynaecologists and customs officers.

up to your nuts in guts *adj. Aus.* In a *sausage and doughnut situation*, to throw oneself fully into one's work.

up to your pots *adj.* Amazingly enough, not to be *up to the apricots, wheels, buffers, bumper, cannon wheels, eggs or maker's name plate*, but to be *ripped to the tits* on drink. *Pissed, wankered, shit-faced, arsehoed, refreshed.*

up, in, out and off *phr.* Plot synopsis essential to all *grumble flicks*.

Urals, the *n.* Vague and tenuous British film comedy euphemism for the testicles. See also *the Balkans.*

Uranus *1. n.* A large planet with brown rings around it. With a big smelly *shit* coming out a hairy hole in the middle of it. Sadly, these days it usually pronounced "Ur-arn-us" to save the blushes of Patrick Moore. *2. n. Urarse.*

urban cockerel *n.* A loud, rasping reveille emitted from under the duvet around sunrise, with enough volume to wake everyone in the street. A *dawn chorus.*

uri *rhym. slang.* Premium Belgian lager. From cutlery-fucking man of mystery Uri Geller = Stella. Also *Nelson Mandela.*

urineapple chunks *n.* The fruit-like yellow cubes that nestle around the plughole of a *shark's mouth. Kola cubes.*

urine shroud *n.* A cotton or nylon artefact, clearly showing the miraculous crusty image of a *bearded clam.* ie, a pair of discarded *scads* found sunny side up on a lady's bedroom floor.

UTAH FD *1. acronym.* The people who come to the rescue when the Osmonds catch *ahad. 2. acronym.* An accommodating one-night-stand ladyfriend. Up The Arse Hole First Date.

UTBNB *abbrev.* Up The Bum, No Babies. A reliable, yet malodorous contraceptive device. Opposite of an IUD.

Vv

vadge *n.* A *fadge*. A *fanny*.

vag *acronym.* The Volkswagen Audi Group.

vaggie *n.* An uncomfortable front-tuck for a lady. A vaginal *wedgie*, a *smedgie, vedgie*. *'A major diplomatic row errupted today after the Australian Premier gave the Queen a vaggie when she was attending the State Opening of Parliament in Melbourne.'*

vagilant *adj.* On the sharp-eyed look out for *cunker.*

vagimite *n.* Unpleasant-tasting yeast derivative, most commonly sampled *down under.*

vagimix *n.* Noisy electrical appliance which makes life easier for housewives. Usually has three speeds and is perfect for whipping up a light and frothy *batter.* A *fanny hammer, bob, neck massager.*

vagina decliner *n.* The male equivalent of a *todger dodger*. A *beaver leaver*, a *pie-shy guy.*

vaginosaur *n.* A rather mature actress in a *meat flick.*

vagitarian *n.* He who only eats *hairy pie, fur burgers,* and *vertical bacon sandwiches.* Plus the occasional *fish supper*. An inveterate *diner at the Y.*

vagitation *n.* Agitation of the *meat flower*. *Bean flicking, invisible banjo playing, gusset typing,* female masturbation.

Valentine's day mascara *n. Eyelid glue.*

Valentine's day porridge *n. Semen-o-lina, spaff, spangle, snedge, gunk, liquid pearls.*

valley of decision *1. n.* Literary work penned by late 19th century author Edith Wharton; the story of a man who is forced to choose between two conflicting loyalties during an Italian revolution. *2. n.* The story of a man forced to choose between two conflicting loyalties during a romantic episode, *ie.* the *nipsy* or the *minge.*

vampire *n.* A *big-boned bird* who forces her fat *arse* into tight jeans, because "she obviously can't see herself in the mirror".

vandal grease *1. n.* Substance used to deter Liverpudlians from climbing onto the tops of public buildings. *2. n.* Substance used by *botters* to lubricate their bottoms so that they can be *botted* by other *botters.*

vanilla *n. US.* A term used by sado-masochists to refer to normal, respectable people, *eg.* doctors, lawyers, *etc.* who do not share their perversion. Also *civilian, muggles.*

vanilla strip *n.* The *tinter,* the *carse,* the *taint.* A lady's perineum, named after the vanilla strip which, in a tub of Neapolitan ice cream, is found precisely between the pink and the brown.

varnish the cane *v.* To give the old *walking stick* a one-handed waxing. To *oil the bat.*

Vatican roulette *n. Pull out and pray*. A method of contraception practised by *left-footers* with very large families.

V-bone steak *n.* A sumptuous, meaty meal, eaten off a *hairy plate*.

vedgie *1. n.* A vaginal *wedgie*. Also known as *splitting the twix.*

vein strainer *n.* A *hog's-eye*-popping *diamond cutter* of potentially life-threatening proportions, which could quite easily place intolerable demands on one's circulatory system. *Pink steel* that looks like it's in danger of going off like that bloke's head in *Scanners.*

veiny bang stick *n.* The *slag hammer.*

velcro arse *n. medic.* Descriptive of the condition of the *bum cheeks* after a long, hot day.

velcro triangle *n. Minge, mott, mapatasi.*

Velma *n.* The act of deliberately or accidentally shooting *jitler* into one's *bird's* eyes, reproducing the disorientating effects suffered by Velma from *Scooby Doo* each time she lost her glasses. *Spunkblindness. St. Valentine's Day mascara, Gabrielle, King Harold.*

venetian bind *n.* An awkward situation in which a gentleman finds himself when there isn't a curtain available to wipe his *cock* on.

verandah over the toyshop *n. Aus.* An *ocker's* lovingly-nurtured beer-gut. A *one-pack, party seven, Foster's child.*

verminillionaire *n.* A lottery winner who doesn't deserve it, has a criminal record as long as your arm and spends all the money on helicopters and Ferraris. Mind you, the ones who say it won't change their lives are even worse. Bastards.

versnatche *n.* A designer *cunt.*

vertical bacon sandwich *n.* That which is clearly visible in *hamburger shots.* Also *vertical smile, vertical taco, club sandwich, haddock pastie.*

vertical eyebrow *n.* A *bush* that has been trimmed to within a quarter of an inch of its life. A *Pires's chin.*

vesser *n.* A silent *fart, SBD.*

vesta vespa *n.* The two-stroke engine-like noise one's *anus* makes the morning after eating a box of the foul, dried curry substitute. Accompanied by a puff of blue smoke.

Vesuviarse *n.* A mighty eruption of sulphurous lava from your *fumerole* the morning after a hot curry. Named after Mount Vesuviarse, which erupted on August 24th A.D.79, burying the town of Pompeii under a superincumbent mass of hot diarrhoea. Also *Cackatoa, Stromboweli.*

vet's bin *n.* A grim old *clout.* Like a *butcher's dustbin,* but much more highly-qualified.

V festival *n.* A lesbian *orgy.* A gathering of sweaty *twats* lip-synching.

vibration white fanny *n. medic.* A *plastic-coccupational* hazard. Semi-numbed condition of a *bird's farmyard area,* typically resulting from prolonged use of heavy duty *snatch plant.*

vibration white finger *1. n.* A medical condition which commonly affects miners and people who use powerful drilling machinery. *2. n.* Condition commonly suffered by teenage boys.

vicar's calling card *n.* Sticking the *organ* up the *reredos.* A *sting in the tail. Bumming.*

vicar's piss *n.* Any particularly weak beer.

Victorian photographer *n.* Any *cunning linguist* who performs under the skirts of a lady.

video cripple *n.* One who can normally walk perfectly well, but loses this ability when returning a video to the shop and has to park right outside, even if it's a double yellow line or they are restricting traffic. Similar to a *cashpoint cripple.*

Vin Diesel *1. n. prop.* Gravel-voiced, bald actor who always wears sunglasses. *2. n.* Happy Shopper wine costing less than £2, and which leaves one gravel-voiced, bald and wearing sunglasses. *Screwtop.*

vidiot *n.* A translucent, spotty youth who spends most of his time cooped up in his bedroom kidding himself he's in the magical land of Zelda and not Basingstoke.

Viennetta *n.* A rich and satisfying multi-layered toilet pudding, consisting of several alternating layers of *turd* and *bumwad. Bangers and mash.*

vinegar Joe *n.* The *stick vid* actor responsible for causing *porn trauma*.

vinegar string *n.* The *banjo.*

vinegar strokes n. Of males *on the job*, the final climactic stages of intercourse or masturbation. From the similar facial expression associated with sipping vinegar. *'Would you believe it? The phone rang just as I was getting onto the vinegar strokes. I nearly ran into the car in front.'*

vinegar tits *n.* The sort of miserable, sour-faced woman that looks, one might unfairly judge, like her *lils* would deliver neat Sarson's into the mouth of any unfortunate suckling infant, *eg.* Estelle Morris MP.

viper's tongue *sim.* A figure of speech, or trope, illustrative of the bifurcated stream of micturant which issues from a urethral meatus which is partially occluded by post-coital *sponglement*, fossilised *smegma* or a piece of sweetcorn. *Twin jets.*

virgin oil *n.* The facial grease secreted by *scoobescent* teenagers.

virgin poo *n.* The first *turd* laid at work after the cleaning lady has scrubbed the rim.

visit from aunt Flo *euph. Having the painters in. Sheep sitting, dropping clots.*

visiting day at Preston Prison *euph.* An assortment of rough-looking women, inexpicably dressed as if going to a discotheque at ten-thirty on a Monday morning.

visit the V&A *v.* To spend a leisurely time exploring two of the more interesting exhibits *down south*.

vital organs *euph.* Breasts. *'We've got a female, mid twenties, been in an RTA. Irregular heartbeat, her breathing's erratic and shallow, she's semi-conscious with a weak radial pulse, but her vital organs are looking good.'*

vitamin P *n.* The luminescent lime green *wazz* produced after one has consumed high dose multivitamins.

vitamin S *n.* A naturally-occurring substance which men insist is very good for women when taken orally in 5ml doses. Often added to McDonald's burgers by disgruntled staff.

vixen *n.* Wily *bird*, a young temptress, a foxy *chick, nymph*, *eg.* Stevie Nicks in about 1978.

vogue *1. n.* A briefly-fashionable pose-striking dance made popular by Madonna. *2. v.* To strike an artistic pose prior to *dropping one's guts* in order to amuse friends or charm young ladies into bed.

voice of Winehouse, face of shitehouse *n.* A cumbersome bit of terminology describing a local pub karaoke queen who, despite having a fair voice on her, has a face like a sack of broken bells.

void the warranty *v.* To perform a sexual act with one's partner that is clearly at odds with the maker's intentions. *'Aw go on, Sophie. Let me void the warranty.' 'Go on,* *then. But make it quick, will you? I'm reading the news at six.'*

Volvo, drop a *v.* To do a *poo* that keeps its headlamps on during daylight hours and has very poor aerodynamics, but would score 5 stars in the Euro/NCAP crash tests.

vommunition *n.* Anything eaten to line the stomach before a drinking session. *'Giz some of them scratchings, mate. I need some vommunition.'*

voodoo butter *n.* The raw material of *squid marks. Ghee.*

vote for Tony Blair *v.* To rush enthusiastically into the cubicle expecting big things, only to get a pathetic little *fart.* To be constipated.

vowel and towel *n.* The daily pleasure of relieving one's internal tensions whilst watching quiz-show lexatrix Carol Vorderman going about her business.

VPL abbrev. Visible Panty Line. A dead giveaway that a *bird* is wearing *Alans,* and therefore frigid.

Vulcan bomb doors *sim. RAF.* Huge, gaping *piss flaps,* making the *hairy pie* resemble the underside of the eponymous delta-winged bomber making a low pass over the runway at Port Stanley.

vulvo *n.* A solidly-built *fanny* which is unlikely to set your *heirbags* off, but could nevertheless withstand an offset frontal impact at 40mph and come out reasonably unscathed.

vurp *n.* A burp which brings up a small but foul-tasting quantity of stomach contents which is small enough to be gulped straight back down again. A *broat, Bob's full mouth.*

Ww

wab *n.* The *bald-headed hermit.*

wad *1. n.* The large sum of money which Harry "Loadsamoney" Enfield waved around after he started getting advertising work. *2. n.* That featured in a *money shot.* A small package of *hot fish yoghurt* flying out the end of a *mutton musket.* A *jizzbolt.*

wad chomper *n.* A lady who is anxious to please. One who enjoys a portion of *man pop* and sees no reason to spit it out. A *swallower.*

wade in *1. v.* To move in for the kill immediately prior to pulling a *bird. 2. v.* To walk towards the centre of a *pagga*, with one's arms above one's head in order to join the fun.

Wagon Wheel *1. n.* A sickly, cream-filled confection. *2. n.* A large *cock.* From the 1980s advertising slogan for *1.* "*You've got to grin to get it in*".

wail switch *n.* An excitable lady's *clematis. The devil's doorbell.*

waist height delight *n.* A fun-size lady, ideal for vertical *horatio* or enthusiastic *cowboy.* A *laptop*, a *throwabout.*

wait for the wings, to *v.* To eagerly anticipate the demise of an elderly loved one to fund the purchase of luxury items in their memory. *'Sadly, my granny is very ill at the moment. I'm just waiting for the wings, then I'm going to get some 8 by 18-inch Wolfrace Spirit alloys for my Saxo. And a big exhaust pipe.'*

waiting for the red cheque to clear *euph.* Of a married man, to endure the monthly four to five day period of sexual limbo which occurs whilst *Aunt Flo is visiting* his wife's *below stairs areas.*

wake up with Jake up *v.* To have a *dawn horn, morning glory, motorcycle kickstand.* To *pitch a tent.*

walk in the country *n.* Taking a gentle stroll with the index and middle fingers through, in and around a woman's *ladygarden.* A pubic ramble.

walking condom *n.* Descriptive of a breed of young male who is up to no good in a baggy tracksuit with a hood. An *asbo.*

walking on the Moon *1. n.* The feeling one experiences after depositing a particularly weighty *Thora,* similar to that encountered by astronauts in one-sixth gravity. *2. n.* Autobiographical song written by Sting out of the Police after he'd just done a really big *shit.*

walking stick *1. n.* Long piece of nobbly wood wielded by senior citizens on buses. *2. n.* That old object upon which a fellow gives it *six nowt* whilst *relaxing in a gentleman's way.*

walking tripod *sim.* A well-endowed male, *donkey-rigged* individual. When admiring *buffage* a sexist lady might offensively remark *'Look at the third leg on that. He's a walking fucking tripod.'*

walking wounded *n. milit.* Women who go out on the pull despite the fact that they are *bleeding from a shotgun wound. 'I wouldn't bother buying her a drink, Geordie. She's walking wounded.' 'So? She's got a mooth, hasn't she?'*

walkman shit *n.* Pairs of dead AA or AAA batteries found on bus seats and in other public places.

walk the line *v.* To go for a *Johnny Cash. 'Watch runways three, four, five and seven will you? I'm off to walk the line.'*

walk the plank *1. rhym. slang.* To masturbate. Whilst a jeering monocular unidexter jabs a cutlass in your *arse. 2. v.* To avoid *splashback* at a urinal when doing a high-pressure *gypsy's kiss* by standing three or four feet back, and avancing slowly towards the *shark's mouth* as the flow recedes.

Wallace *rhym. slang.* To vomit. From Wallace & Gromit. *'He's Wallaced all over my new carpet.'*

wall of death *1. n. Attack of the helicopters. 2. n. Last hot dog in the tin.*

wallop *n. Cookin'.* Any beer bought by a hearty *twat* with a beard who calls the barman Landlord or Squire.

walnut *1. n.* The leaky washer in an old man's *waterworks.* The prostrate gland, *doughnut. 2. n.* Those annoying, little bits of feculant that "walnut" come off. *Tagnuts, dangleberries.*

walnut manoeuvre *n.* The legendary method by which good looking nurses are trained to poke one's prostrate in order to obtain an instant *Thelonious* sample.

walnut whip *1. rhym. slang.* A minor operation which removes the *cream*, but leaves the *nuts* intact. The *snip. 2. n.* A firm, cone-shaped stool that has been hollowed out and filled with a sickly cream-like substance, usually whilst a couple is exploring *the third way.*

walrus, the *n.* Another unlikely sounding, probably illegal, and certainly immoral sexual act whereby a fellow gets his ladyfriend to swallow his *mess* before karate chopping her on both sides of the neck, causing "tusks" of *jitler* to run out of her nostrils in a style reminiscent of the popular moustachioed underwater dog. *'Reader, I married him. A quiet wedding we had: he and I, the parson and clerk, were alone present. On the way back from church, I've gave Mr Rochester a nosh in the back of the carriage and he done the walrus on me.'* (from *Jane Eyre Does Milcote* by Charlotte Bronte).

wancunian *1. n.* A *wanker* from Manchester. A *manker. 2. adj.* Descriptive of a *wanker* from Manchester.

wand waver *n. Flasher*, sexual exhibitionist.

wang *n. Wab.*

wangst *n.* Post-masturbatory anguish. A *wank hangover.*

wanic *n.* The state of perturbation that occurs when a wife or girlfriend returns home unexpectedly just as one is reaching the *vinegar strokes* in front of one's favourite *scud mags.* A *wank panic, jazz funk.*

wank *1. n.* A bout of *self help. 'If you have a wank every day you'll go blind.' 2. n.* Rubbish. *'Don't talk wank.' 3. v.* To masturbate. *'Well my brother wanks all the time and he's gone blind.'*

wankache day *n.* A special day which a fellow spends gripping a *panhandle* whilst *tossing hot batter* towards the ceiling.

wank against time *n.* An anxious, *Tarzan cord*-chafing act of *self harm* indulged in during Television X's ten-minute freeview, in the hope of *dropping one's yop* before it becomes necessary to phone in one's credit card details to the topless *scrubber* on the screen.

wankarium *n.* A box room containing a chair, a computer and a sock drawer.

wankathon *n.* A single man's right arm excercise endurance test. Days of frenzied *self abuse* heralded by the arrival of a large brown envelope with a Dutch postmark. Often ends with a dehydrated and disorientated *self-harmer* being wrapped in a large sheet of tin foil.

wank clamp *n.* A hand, *spunky wrench*.

wank crank *n. medic.* Elbow.

wanker *1. n.* One who practises a secret vice. *2. n.* A fellow road user, a motorist at whom one waves.

wankerchief *n.* A *spanky hanky*, *jizz sock*, *toss rag*, *j-cloth*.

wankered *adj.* See *blitzed.*

wanker's badge *n.* A moustache. From the fact that most people sporting moustaches tend also to be *wankers*, *eg.* Steve Wright, Des Lynam, Anne Robinson. *'Short back and sides, is it Sir? Not too much off the top and tapering at the neck? And would you like me to trim your wanker's badge?'*

wanker's block *n.* A complete absence of imagination or inspiration when trying to stimulate a reaction in the *trouser department*. Often occurs when one has the *horn* but is too *pissed* to think of anything rude.

wanker's cocoa *n.* A late night *tug* that induces a restful night's sleep. *Temazepalm*.

wanker's colic *n. medic.* Of seasoned factory/warehouse workers, a humorous diagnosis of the cause of hiccups or burps in their younger colleagues.

wanker's crisps *n.* Brittle, ready-salted tissues found under any healthy gentleman's bed. *Porn crackers*.

wanker's genie *n.* The irresistible force that resides inside one's *magic lamp* and regularly summons one to release it via a quick *magic buff*.

wanker's hankie *sim.* Descriptive of something very brittle. *'Come along to the Curry Capital, where the food is hot, the beer is cold and the popadoms are as brittle as a wanker's hankie.'* (Press release from Abdul Latif, Lord of Harpole).

wanker's rickets *n.* The wobbling movements of the legs caused by orgasmic weakening of the knees.

wanker's tache *n. medic.* The vertical line of hair between the navel and the top of the *pubes*. Develops as a consequence of masturbation, along with spots, hairy palms, shortsightedness, insanity and stunted growth. The *crab ladder*.

wanker's tan *n.* Ghostly pallor effected by young men who spend far too much time alone in their rooms with the curtains shut. *'I've just got Need for Speed ProStreet for Christmas, so I'll be spending the next few months working on my wanker's tan.'*

wankety blank *n.* The state of mental blockage during attempted masturbation when one's *mammary banks* are in the red. *Wanker's block*.

wank handle *n. medic.* In sex, a male erection of the penile shaft and glans. A turgid *crank*.

wank hangover *n.* Post *self abuse* self-loathing. *Wangst* which can only be assuaged by the hair of the dog.

wank holiday *1. n.* An exhausting day off work spent masturbating.

2. *n.* Contrariwise, a period of self-imposed abstention from *bishop-bashing,* brought on through guilt and/or severe cramp.

wankier mâché *n.* The malleable sculputural compound produced when an onanist's *love glue* mixes with his cleaning-up apparatus. *Bedroom popadoms* - also known as *wankerchiefs, porn crackers* or *wanker's crisps* - as well as *monks' trunks, crunchies* and *midget's surfboards,* are made of *wankier mâché.*

wanking chariot *n.* A single bed.

wanking ears *n.* Descriptive of the bat-like, heightened sensitivity of hearing achieved by a fellow indulging in a bit of *self discipline,* allowing him to detect the faint sound of his wife's / girlfriend's / parents' key entering the lock two floors below. *'September 2nd, 1666, Morning. Up betimes, and finding the house deserted, was minded to settle down with a hose for a brief strum over the corsetry pages of Mr Grattan's estimable catalogue. However, Mrs Pepys return'd unexpectly, and, had it not been for my wanking ears, would surely have discovered me in a most compromising situation. Afternoon. London burned down.'* (from *The Diary of Samuel Pepys*).

wanking jacket *n.* Dressing gown.

wanking Jap, grin like a *sim.* To smile broadly in the style of a *spamurai warrior*. To *turn Japanese.*

wanking parlour *n.* Brothel, house of ill repute; any club popular with *gonks.* A *toss parlour, rub-a-tug shop.*

wanking spanners *n. Spunky wrenches, cunt scratchers.*

wanking studs *n. medic.* Warts on the hands or fingers.

wankish *adj.* Slightly useless. *Mouse, Swiss. 'That Eamonn Holmes is a bit wankish, isn't he.'*

wank it dry *v.* To ossessively persevere with something long after it is clear that there is no more benefit to be gained, *eg*. Mohammed Al Fayed going on about his conspiracy theory, the *Daily Express* going on about Mohammed Al Fayed's conspiracy theory, BBC News 24 newspaper reviewers mentioning the headlines on the front of the *Daily Express*. *'Christ, not Norman Collier doing his broken microphone routine again. He wanked that dry thirty years ago on the Wheeltappers' and Shunters' Social Club.'*

wankle *1. n.* A type of rotary engine. *2. n. medic.* The wrist. From wank + ankle.

wank-me-downs *n. Bongo mags* inherited from an elder brother or friend. Also *one-hand-me-downs. Pubic hairlooms.*

wank or bank *n.* The quandary faced by a gentleman who must decide whether to *knock himself about a bit* or conserve his fluids until his ladyfriend's next visit when he can *make a deposit.*

wank outsider *n.* A chap who prefers the hedgerow to the bedroom as a location for a *five knuckle shuffle.*

wank pie *n.* Something third rate, *eg*. any programme with Jimmy Carr in it.

wankquiliser *n.* A self-administered, stress-relieving bedtime *knockout yop.* A *knuckle nightcap, pullaby.*

wank robber *n.* Onanistically speaking, a parent who, returning home unexpectedly early, robs their teenage son of his *money shot*.

wankroll, put her on the *exclam.* Phrase used by a businessman when deciding to employ a pulchritudinous young female, despite the fact that her CV may not be quite as impressive as those of certain other candidates. *'Let's cut the bollocks, darling, you're a lightweight, you're a quitter, you're a schmoozer and you're a bullshitter. And let me tell you this, I don't like lightweights, I don't like quitters and I don't like bullshitters. But when I saw you bending over to open the filing cabinet I thought Alan, do yourself a favour. Put her on the wankroll. Michelle, you're hired.'*

wankrupt *adj.* Descriptive of one who has *spent his wad* and has an empty *pod purse*.

wank seance *n.* Whilst *pulling one's pud*, the eerie feeling that one is being watched disapprovingly by dead relatives. Also *Doris Strokes*.

wank slacks *n.* Type of dirty tracksuit trousers, designed to afford the wearer easy and unencumbered manual access to his *fruit bowl* at short notice. Worn by students, jobseekers and other people who find themselves spending a lot of time lounging round the house. *'Have you seen my smart trousers, Jane? I've got an interview this afternoon.' 'They're in the wash, Jonathan. Why don't you just put your wank slacks on? Your legs will be behind your desk, and everybody will be looking at Madonna anyway.'*

wanksmith *n.* An enthusiastic or workmanlike *onanist*.

wank sock *n.* Cylindrical cloth item tied to a bedpost designed to indicate when wind conditions are suitable for *monkey spanking*.

wank stain *n. Bum scrape, piss flap, dip shit, toss pot*. General purpose insult. *'Oi, I said a Crunchie McFlurry, you fucking wank stain.'*

wankstop *n.* medic. The flange that prevents the *wanking spanner* disengaging from the end of the *shaft* when revving your *single cylinder engine*. The *brim* of the *herman gelmet*. The *sulcus*.

wank tanks *n. Balls, nads, knackers*.

wankticipation *n.* Feeling of hollow, mounting excitement experienced by a man sitting in front of his computer with his trousers round his ankles and his *giggle stick* in his hand, whilst he waits for his *cyber scud* to download.

wanktique *n.* An ancient *rhythm pamphlet*, such as a dog-eared 1978 *Whitehouse* found behind some tins of paint in your late grandfather's garage.

wankton *n.* A unicellular life-form that inhabits the shallow waters of the bath after a session of *dolphin waxing. Dutch jellyfish, nylon squid, frigspawn*.

wankupuncture *n.* Ancient, tried-and-tested alternative therapy self-administered by ailing gentlemen. The belief that the symptoms of an illness can be ameliorated, if not cured completely, by a quick *hand shandy*. The *placebone effect*.

wank window *n.* An opportune moment during which a crafty gentleman can enjoy a swift bout of *relaxation. 'A woman tells her husband she is just popping to the shops to get a pint of milk and a loaf of bread. The shops* *are 4 miles away and her husand knows that his wife's car travels at an average speed of 22 mph. He also knows that his wife will spend ten minutes selecting each of the items from the shelves of the supermarket and a further twelfth of her total journey time queuing at the till. For how long is the man's wank window open?'* (Associated Examining Board GCE Applied Mathematics paper, Summer 1986).

wank xerox *1.n.* One who *knocks one out* repeatedly throughout the day, only to find the quality diminishes as his *toner* runs out. *2. n.* Masturbating over and over again to the same *jazz mag. Groundhog wanking.*

wanky *adj.* Self-indulgent, pretentious, *eg. Newsnight Late Review.*

wannocks *n.* The area of no-man's land between the *nuts* or the *fadge,* and the *ringpiece.* The *biffin bridge, notcher, barse, taint, tintis, twitter, scranus.*

wanquility *n.* The all too brief post-*toss* period of serenity experienced immediately before the loathing, self-hatred, *wangst* and shame set in.

wanxious *adj.* Anxious for a *wank.* Derivation unknown.

wapp off *v.* To masturbate furiously over a two-inch pornographic image on your phone, which has cost you several pounds. One of the many benefits of third generation mobile communications technology.

wap-waps *n. medic.* A lady's mammary glands. *'Now, Mrs Johnson, if you'll just get your wap-waps out, I'll start the examination.'*

warm Norman *n.* A *hotplate, Cleveland steamer.*

warm up the choirboys' breakfast *n.* Of a vicar, to *relax in a gentleman's way.*

warning George and Gracie *n.* To emit a long, drawn-out *basso profundo Bakewell tart* that resembles plangent whalesong and hence could have been used to warn the two humpback cetaceans, George and Gracie, about the whaling vessel they were about to encounter in the film *Star Trek IV.*

war paint *n.* Of *birds* getting ready to go out at night, their make-up. *Fuck dust.*

warren *n.* Generic term for one not blessed with attractive features. From "Warren ugly bastard".

warthog whammies *n.* Fantastic *chudleighs* on an ugly woman. *Hefferlumps.*

wartime searchlights *n.* Descriptive of the amusingly dis-collimated vision of one who is in an advanced *state of refreshment,* whose eyes appear to be independently raking the heavens for incoming Heinkel bombers. *'Look out everyone, Ronnie's got his wartime searchlights on.'*

Warwick Passage fayre *n.* Ugly, rough or slatternly women. A reference to the alley next to the Old Bailey where the wives and girlfriends of the accused traditionally await access to the public galleries of the courtroom, saying "My fella never done nothing, bless", and other lies.

washing machine doors *n.* Swirling, export strength *beer goggles.*

Washington refill *n.* The type of night-time urination carried out in a rush in order to return to the warmth of one's bed as soon as possible. From the speedy nature of petrol station customers in Washington DC and surrounding districts during their 2002 Beltway sniper shenanigans.

wash the cosh *v.* To polish the *love truncheon, oil the bat.*

waste *n.* An attractive feature on an otherwise unattractive individual. *'Jesus. Have you seen the chebs on that Kerry Catona, your grace?' 'I know, Archbishop. What a fucking waste.'*

water babies *1. n.* Aquatic fairies featured in the Victorian novel by Charles Kingsley. *2. n.* Floating clumps of semi-congealed *merry monk* in the bath, toilet, *Sunday Times* restaurant critic's drinking glass *etc. Frigspawn.*

watering can wazz *n.* The uncontrollable multi-directional *gypsy's kiss* taken after a bout of *horizontal jogging* or a *five knuckle shuffle.*

water puppies *n.* Term used by swimming pool lifeguards to draw each other's attention to a large pair of *milky swingers* bobbing playfully up and down whilst their owner does the backstroke.

water sports *n. Recreational Chinese singing.* European way of expressing romantic feelings for another person by *pissing* onto their face, *etc.*

Watney houston *n.* A *discount diva* who, after downing a few pints, will tunelessly belt out pompous tear-jerking anthems over the jukebox. A bit like Whitney Houston, if you believe what you read in the papers.

waving a sausage in the Albert Hall *n.* Sticking one's *cock* in a *fanny* that can seat 5000 people and the London Symphony Orchestra.

wax one's slats *v.* Of a woman, to *play the invisible banjo* until her *blip tap* begins to drip.

wax the bonnet *v.* To *spoff* over a *bird's* bodywork, then lean over and polish it in until the desired shine is achieved.

wax the dolphin *v.* To *polish the lighthouse.*

wazoo *n. Jacksie, anus.*

wazz *v.* Variously to *piss*, to *puke*, to *wank. 'Who's wazzed on the bathroom floor?' Erm...'It might be me, mum. What sense of wazz are you using?'*

wazzed *adj. Pissed* on, *puked* on and *wanked* off. And *pissed up*, come to think of it.

wazzock *n.* Mild northern insult for a great, useless, spawny-eyed, parrot-faced person.

wear a Twyfords collar *v.* To *drive the porcelain bus,* to *shout soup,* to *yoff, call Ralph on the great white telephone.*

Wearside vines *n.* Exposed outcrop of *annabels* which looks for all the world like an attractive bunch of Gamay grapes, glistening on a sun-kissed slope.

wear the beard *1. v.* To perform *cunning linguistics* on a woman. *To impersonate Stalin. 2. v.* Of *bean flickologists*, to be the *stone. 'You can tell which one of them two wears the beard.'*

weathered on *1. adj.* Of North Sea offshore workers, to be unexpectedly stranded on an oil rig due to poor meteorological conditions and have nothing to do but sit about and *wank,* and thus *2. adj.* Descriptive of the dejected mien of a man whose missus has *fallen to the communists.*

webbed tits *n. Frankentits* of elderly Hollywood actresses with a highly-stressed membrane between, caused by the sheer weight of implants.

wedding milk *n. Spingle, spangle, spint, spongle, spadge, spedge, spidge, spodge, spudge, etc. Spunk.*

wedding tackle *n.* The male genitalia. Also *wedding furniture.*

wedge *v.* To pull another's *bills* up the crack of their *arse.*

wedgie *n.* Nickname of politician Anthony Wedgwood Benn, who's *bills* are always getting pulled right up the crack of his arse.

wedgie, atomic *n.* The act of pulling someone's *bills* up the *crack* of their *arse* with a dockyard crane, whilst their shoes are bolted to the floor.

wed zeppelin *n.* A former *looker* who, once she has got married, lets herself go and fills up with hydrogen. And then explodes in a ball of flame at Lakehurst Naval Air Station, New Jersey, killing 36 of the people on board her.

wee heid rules the big heid *phr. Scot.* Descriptive of the moment when a gentleman, usually wearing *beer goggles,* decides that sexual intercourse with the woman he has just met and whose name he does not know is the correct course of action.

wee-hole surgery *n.* Do-it-yourself medical experiments carried out by bored bachelors, involving the insertion of foreign objects into the urethra. *'Is there a man doctor I can see please, nurse? Only it's a bit delicate. I was doing a bit of wee-hole surgery and I've got a propelling pencil lead stuck in my hog's eye.' 'I'll just see if there's anyone available, Mr Brown. It is Mr Brown, isn't it? The former publisher?'*

weekend flat in Brighton, to have a *v.* Of a gentleman, to be a *good listener* on a part-time basis. Likewise of a woman, to be an occasional *consumer of tufted wilton.* To be *half rice half chips.*

weenie *n. US.* Penis. Also *wienie, wiener.*

weenie waggler *n.* A *wand waver.*

weenis *n.* A minuscule *veiny bang stick,* such as those sported by jockeys, Channel swimmers, Arctic explorers and current Lord High Chancellor and Secretary of State for Justices.

weft *n.* Lady's *pubes,* which are all lying in one direction after she has been wearing particularly tight briefs. *Twat nap.*

weggy *adj.* Of a flatulent emission, to be wet and eggy. From wet + eggy. *'Open the window, Buzz. that's a weggy one.'*

weigh anchor *v.* To drop an immensely large *turd,* being careful not to break the porcelain.

we just lost the moon *exclam.* Phrase used by Tom Hanks in the film *Apollo 13,* which can also be used to great effect in everyday life when something goes drastically wrong and you are unable to reach your objective but have to go through the motions nevertheless. For example, when a fellow is having to *bang* his *pissed* wife at her instigation and he knows that there's no way on God's earth that his tadpoles are going for a swim tonight.

welder's bench, face like a *sim.* An ugly woman. Also *blind cobbler's thumb, burglar's dog, box of frogs, sack of chisels, bag of spanners.*

well fair state *n.* The state of drunkenness only achievable for many on Giro day.

well struck Sir! *exclam.* An amusing remark which can be used immediately after someone has hit some methane for six with their *arse.* Also *what's that, Sweep?*

well thumbed *adj.* Much consulted or handled, *eg.* the state of Will Self's Thesaurus and (reference to Ulrika Jonsson removed on legal advice).

welly top *sim.* A term used to describe the larger *billy goat's mouth.* A *yawning donkey. 'That* (reference to Ulrika Jonsson removed on legal advice) *must have a fluffit like a welly top.'*

welly tubbies *n.* Small, fat lasses squeezed into *slag wellies,* and out *on the lash.* So-called due to their similarity to the children's TV characters, in both their appearance and limited vocabulary.

Welsh *n.* Masturbation while listening to a male voice choir.

Welsh letter *n.* Same as a *French letter,* but with a leak.

Welshman's cock *sim.* Descriptive of someone who is short and thick, *eg.* Dennis Wise.

Welsh mist *n.* A particularly dense and clammy *fart* which hovers around ankle level and chills the bones.

Welsh salad, go for a *v.* To urinate, go for a *leak.* From the Welsh national vegetable, the pea.

Welsh shot *n.* The knocking back of the contents of a *smeg cup.* A *Dutch oyster.*

Wendy *n.* An uncomfortable front tuck for a lady. A vaginal *wedgie,* a *vaggie, vedgie.*

Wendy's melt *1. n. US.* A sandwich served at the popular eponymous fast-food restaurant, consisting of two prime strips of beef, bacon strips, cheese and mayonnaise in between. 2. n. A *ladyburger.*

werecow *n.* A nice, pleasant woman who mysteriously transforms into a right *fucking cow* once a month.

west country trim *n.* Yokel alternative to a *Brazilian* or *Hollywood wax* which is situated somewhere between a *landing strip* and *Terry Waite's allotment* on the feminine intimate grooming spectrum. A rudimentary trim of the *spider's legs* sticking out the sides of the large pants before trotting off to the local barn dance. *Luton airport.*

western grip *n.* Manner of *wanking* in which the *cock* is held as a rodeo rider holds onto his steer, *ie.* with the fingers of one hand on top, the thumb underneath and the other hand waving a hat behind his head.

wet as an otter's pocket *sim.* Descriptive of the moistness of an object, *eg.* a face flannel, a raincoat, a *frothing gash.*

wet cress, eat *v.* During an act of man-on-lady, or indeed lady-on-lady, oral-type sex, to munch on a bit of exceptionally moist *gorilla salad.*

wet dream *n.* A night-time reverie which leads to *milmed jim-jams.* Can be avoided either by having a cold bath or a right good *pull* into a sock before retiring.

Wetherspoon's run *n.* A trip to one's nearest Wetherspoon's pub for the sole purpose of *laying a cable* in one of their spotlessly-clean, luxury cubicles, thus avoiding the *shit/puke/*

spunk-covered seats of the average drinking house *bogs*. *'Watch me pint lads, me taxi's here. I'm just off on a Wetherspoon's run.'*

wet Hurst *n.* A *Wolstenholme*. The final bit of *piss* which waits until the *cock* is safely back in the trousers before dribbling out causing a *wet penny in the pocket*. From the commentary describing Geoff Hurst's final goal in the 1966 World Cup final. "They think it's all over... it is now".

wetmare *n.* A dream that is both wet and a nightmare. A *wet scream*.

wet one *1. n.* A pre-moistened cleaning tissue. 2. n. An untrustworthy *fart*, possibly a *twin tone* that would require the use of *1*. A pre-moistened *Bakewell tart*.

wet penny in your pocket *n.* A circular *piss*-stain on the trouser frontage, caused by insufficient shaking of the *wang*.

wet season *n.* That time of the month when the *crimson tide* comes in. *Blow job week*.

wet scream *n.* A nocturnal erotic reverie in which the *vinegar strokes* are marred by the dawning realisation that one's sexual partner is one's mother/granny/Janet Street-Porter *etc*.

wetsuit *1. n.* In sub-aquatic pursuits, a protective rubber garment worn whilst one plumbs the murky depths. *2. n.* In *sub-bridge* pursuits, a protective rubber garment worn whilst one sticks one's *cock* up a *clunge*.

wet the baby's head *v.* To have intercourse with a woman who has a *bun in the oven*. To *tickle the baby*. *'And so it was that Mary and Joseph came to an inn in Bethlehem. And Mary was heavy with child and the innkeeper spake unto them saying, Behold, there is no room at the inn. And Joseph replied unto him saying, Yea, we have travelled from Nazareth, and my wife is heavy with child, and I have great need to wet the baby's head. And he gave unto the innkeeper a wink. And lo the wink was cheeky.'* (from *Matthew*).

whacknicolour *n.* The luridly alluring garishly-hued inks with which *seed catalogues* are printed.

whackpot *n.* A windfall of *grumble* that unexpectedly comes the way of a lucky gentleman. *'I tell you what, I really hit the whackpot when I got the job of clearing the effects of the late poet and lifelong jazz enthusiast Philip Larkin from his house.'*

whacksmith *n.* A workmanlike masturbator who seems intent on beating his *pork sword* into a *ploughshare*. *'Birthdays: Tom Wolfe, journalist and author, 74, Jonathan Ross, TV & radio presenter, film reviewer, interviewer, whacksmith, 48.'* (from *The Times*, March 2nd 2007).

whalesong *n.* A melodic, though slightly eerie sequence of whines, squeaks, clicks and whistles that emanate from a toilet cubicle.

whaletail *1. n.* A laughable aerodynamic feature favoured by the smaller-penissed car driver. 2. *n.* The unsightly effect produced when a lady in ill-fitting jeans's thong rides up her *arse crack*.

whammers *n. Bazoomas, Gert Stonkers, big tits.*

whanger *n.* An extremely large *wang*.

what's that, Sweep? *exclam. interrog.* Amusing rhetorical expression which can be used to fill the silence following a high-pitched, wavering *Bakewell tart.* From the catchphrase of late Yorkshire-based Sooty puppeteer Harry Corbett when responding to his mute star's comedy dog sidekick's squeaky interlocutions. Also *someone's tinkered with Herbie; more tea vicar?*

wheek *v. Scot.* To remove *jobbies* from an aeroplane toilet.

wheelie bint *n.* A woman so ugly that she only gets taken out once a week. In the dark. By dustmen.

whidgey *n. Front bottom.*

whiffhanger *n.* A *dropped gut* so pungent that it clings to your *duds.* A *velcro fart.*

whiff of lavender *n.* Of a marriage, the suspicion of a *beardsome* bride. *'I don't know about Edward. There's a distinct whiff of lavender about that marriage if you ask me, Phil.'*

whip round, to have a *v.* To *relax in a gentleman's way* into a coach-driver's hat.

whirling pits n. Attack of the *helicopters, wall of death.*

whirly wheel challenger *n.* Something which drops to the ground unexpectedly, *eg.* a small nugget of excrement which hits the landing carpet when you are shuffling across to the *bogroll* cupboard.

whisker biscuit *n.* A *fur burger.*

whisker pot *n. Fanny, minge, whidgey.*

whistle down the Y-fronts *v. Fart,* pass wind.

whistling gorilla *n.* An inviting and voluptuous *toothless gibbon.*

whistling in the dark *n. Muff diving,* eating *hairy pie.*

white arrow angels *n.* Van-driving messengers who bring catalogue goods to those ill-equipped to afford them.

whitecastleassitis *n. medic.* Alimentary canal condition afflicting up to 90% of the US population, caused by consumption of that country's most infamous small burgers, six at a time, steamed and lavished with onions. *Whitecastleassitis* is principally symptomised by the passage of stools which are indistinguishable from the said burgers - affectionately known as *belly bombers* - in both appearance and odour.

white knuckle ride *n.* A solo thrill which makes your eyes bulge and lasts about three minutes. *One off the wrist.*

white lightnin' Hopkins *n.* An *al fresco* beverage enthusiast who is wont to sing about his woes to the world in general. Also *blind drunk Lemon Jefferson.*

white mouse *n.* Tampon. A *cotton mouse, fanny mouse, chuftie plug, jampax.*

white-out! *exclam.* When two large, pale breasts are exposed.

white pointers *n.* Extremely impressive *tits* found inhabiting a wet T-shirt.

whitewash the hall *v.* To *spoff* up a lady's *cunt.* A far more fulfilling job than *painting the ceiling.*

whitewater wristing *v.* To rapidly paddle the *skin boat.* To *pull your pud,* masturbate.

white wee-wee *n.* Planet Skaro Dalek term for semen.

Whitney dressed as Britney *n.* Descriptive of a lady who's done a few miles, and is gamely attempting to turn the clock back. *Mutton dressed as lamb.*

Whitfield tan *n.* The blue and red tartan effect often seen on the legs of residents of Dundee's premier housing development, achieved by the simple expedient of sitting in front of a two-bar electric fire. *The Whitfield tan* is a look which is always in fashion amongst those who choose to opt out of the work ratrace.

whiztits *n.* Unusually conicular breasts. Named after the seldom-loved children's television show which featured a crudely-animated magic cone with the voice of balding confabulist Paul Daniels. *Dunce's hats.*

whoof *v.* To *fart* at a burglar.

whoof whoof! *1. exclam.* Term of approval directed at passing *talent. 'Whoof whoof! Give that dog a bone.'* 2. *exclam.* Term of disapproval aimed at passing women who haven't made the effort to look attractive.

whoops a gaysy *n.* Of a gentleman, slipping over in an effeminate manner whilst emitting an unexpectedly girly whimper.

whoopsy *n.* A *piss* or *shit,* usually done by a cat in Frank Spencer's beret.

whore d'oeuvres *n.* The unnecessary appetizers before the main course at a massage parlour, *ie.* the massage.

whore from Fife *n. derrog.* A term of abuse that incorporates the two insults of being a whore and of coming from Fife. *'Hey, you've just taken my last fag, you whore from Fife.'*

whore frost *n.* A *good time girl's* sudden change of attitude once the *dirty deed* is done.

whoreganisation *n.* Of a commercial traveller, the practice of sorting out the order of his evening's entertainment using the contact ads section of the *Daily Sport* and a highlighter pen. Perhaps whilst sitting in a Vauxhall Vectra outside a Little Chef situated just off the A1 north of Newcastle upon Tyne.

whoregasm *n.* The unconvincing appreciative noises made by a *lady of the night* to persuade her customer that he is getting his money's worth, despite sensory evidence to the contrary.

whore licks *n.* Malty bedtime drink for a gentleman or lady, consisting of either warm *spongle* or a *furry cup* of *kitten tears.*

whoremark *n.* A small tattoo on a lady's lower back, aping the classy style originally adopted by porn actresses. A *tramp stamp* or *slag tag.*

whore's bath *n.* An act of personal hygiene practised by ladies of the lower orders; a brief, yet fulsome handwash of the *undercarriage* often performed at a sink. *Rinsing the lettuce.*

whore's brass *n.* The shiny Lizzie Duke *tack* found decorating women in southern pubs. *Bingo clink.*

whoreshoes *n.* Fashionable pink stilettos. *Fuck me shoes.*

whorism *n.* The horizon-broadening practice of travelling the world to experience different and exotic cultures via the medium of going with *pros.*

whoresome *adj.* Heaving with easy *blart. 'Hey lads, it's going to be a great night. I've heard this place is whoresome.'*

who's the daddy? *exclam. interrog.* Another one of those phrases which can be shouted after one has *dropped* a noisily noisome *gut.*

why, are you hungry? *exclam.* Humorous riposte to someone who asks if one has *farted.*

whybrows *n.* The bizarre tonsorial result of a lady armed with a pair of tweezers and an eyebrow pencil, *eg*. Theresa Gorman.

wick *1. n.* Penis. See *dip your wick.* 2. *n.* Nerves, *tit ends. 'I wish that Tim Westwood would fuck off. He really gets on my fucking wick.'*

wicked pisser *n. US.* A good egg or a good show, top notch person or experience. As in *'Thank you very much for your kindness and generosity. You really have been the most wicked pissers. My name's Bing Crosby. Goodnight.'*

wicker basket *n.* A matted and tangled *bush* in which the previous night's *clacker lacquer* has been allowed to dry out.

widdle *1. n.* Childish term for a *wee wee. 2. v.* To do some *wee wee.*

wide on *n.* Female equivalent of a *hard on, a slop on.*

widow wanky *n.* The first despondent, but necessary *act of self violation* indulged in after the wife or girlfriend has left for good.

widow's memories *n.* Penis-shaped sausages, cucumbers *etc.* Indeed, anything vaguely cylindrical in a supermarket which is fingered nostalgically by old ladies.

widower's tears *n.* The involuntary dribble of *spunk* from the end of a long-disused *cock.*

widower's tickle *n.* The short burst of pleasure a man experiences when he flushes whilst in a sitting position and his *three piece suite* is caught in the spray. A thrill of almost Netto cheapness.

wife beater *n.* An unnecessarily strong lager. *Wreck the hoose juice.*

wifectomy *n.* An extremely painful divorce. One invariably experiences an *OPE* during the operation.

wifetamer *n.* An impressive *weapon* that affords one the respect of one's spouse, like a whip and chair would on a lion in a circus. A *cuntbuster.*

wife's radar *n.* A lady's bat-like ability to detect the merest rustle of a *jazz mag* from a hundred yards.

wifestyle *n.* The expensive and excessive level of comfort in which one must keep one's good lady, in order to ensure regular and unencumbered access to her *quim* and *charlies.*

Wigan rosette *n.* The state of the *freckle* after a particularly fierce *Ruby Murray*. A *Johnny Cash.*

wil *n.* A lady's *snarse, tinter, taint, carse,* whatever. Her perineum. So-called because it is situated "between the *Gary* and the *Mott*".

wilfrid *n.* The spontaneous retraction of the prepuce, exposing the *bellend.* Named after the character whose domed head pokes out the top of his pullover in *The Bash Street Kids.*

Wilkinson, to do a *v.* To perform a defecation in a hovering, squatting position over a *pissy*-seated pub *bog.* From the pose's similarity to the hands-clasped, sticky-out-*arsed* stance struck by rugby star Jonny before he makes a kick and goes off injured.

willets *n.* A type of *jugs.*

willie *n.* A ten-foot penis that has to be cut with a rake. *John Thomas, Percy the pork swordsman,* he who gives *Gert Stonkers* a *pearl necklace*. The *tassel,* the *Peter*, the *charlie*. Also *willy.*

willie and the hand jive *n.* Rhythmic, throbbing cork-popping combo who perform the *Bologna bop* among other dances.

willie welly *n. French letter, French safe, English overcoat.*

willie woofter *rhym. slang. Fruit feeler, spud fumbler.*

willipedes *n.* genital arthropods. *Mechanical dandruff.*

willnots *n. Tagnuts, dangleberries.* Toffee entwined in the *kak canyon* undergrowth which simply "will not" come off. *Walnuts.*

willydelphia *n.* Soft, spreadable *knob cheese.* Often to be found on your *crackers.*

willy mid-on *n.* Amusing cricketer's term for a *semi,* such as like what might make it uncomfortably cramped in one's box. *'I say Aggers, the batsman's Holding the umpire's Dickie. If I'm not much mistaken he's getting a willy mid-on.'*

Wilmslow panzer *n.* A large 4-wheel-drive vehicle which is designed to operate in the harshest of terrain and to protect its occupants from the most inclement conditions, but which only ever gets used to drive the hundred yards from a 4-bedroom house on a Balfour-Beatty estate to a Montessori fucking primary school. The north-west equivalent of a *Chelsea tractor.*

Wilton to Stilton, prefer *v.* To be a woman suffering from *lesbicious* tendencies; specifically to be keener on *munching carpet* than chomping down on a savoury mouthful of *blue-veined cheese. 'Sorry pal, you're wasting your time. I prefer Wilton to Stilton.' 'Never mind. I'll just watch instead, then.'*

Wimbornes *rhym. slang.* Haemorrhoids. From the Dorset village of Wimborne St. Garsegrapes.

wimp wiper *n.* In an office or workplace environment, one who takes his/her own toilet tissue in rather than use the rough industrial type.

windchimes *n.* Gravitationally-challenged breasts which sway gently in the morning breeze, occasionally clanging together in a restful and melodic manner.

wind farm *n. milit.* A barracks full of vigorously *farting* squaddies.

wind in the pillows *n.* Unlikely-sounding bedtime practice, involving a squatting gentleman and his very accommodating prostrate ladyfriend.

wind jammer *n.* A *style-conscious* man.

windsock *n.* A particularly low-hanging *fiveskin.* An *anteater's nose, lace curtains.*

window cleaner's pocket *n.* A large, sad, damp, dishevelled *fadge.*

window of plopportunity *n.* That brief period of time in the digestive process when a *turd* comes out just lovely.

window shopping *v.* Of a lady, to go out on the town and give blokes the impression that she is interested when she has no intention of opening her *purse.*

wind that shakes the barley *1. n.* Title of a controversial Ken Loach film depicting the history of the English Black & Tans in Ireland in the early part of the century, and the formation of the IRA. *2. n.* An *air biscuit* so strong that it blows all one's *arse cress* in the same direction, creating the appearance of a dark Irish wheat field in one's *cleft.*

windy pops *n. Bunny-shooting*

bullets, chuffs, anal announcements.

wind your watch *euph.* To commit a disgusting act of *self delight* upon one's generative member. From the similarity of a *relaxing gentleman's* hand movements to the characteristic rapid wrist flicks and rotations which must be performed in order to prime the mainspring of an automatic timepiece. *'What were you doing in there?' 'I was just winding my watch, love.' 'But your watch is at the mender.' 'I know. I meant having a wank.'* (*Bamforth's Seaside Chuckles* postcard, by Donald McGill, 1933).

wingspan *n.* A measure of manual spreadability in *meat mag* models posing for *spam butterfly* shots. *'Have you seen Irene from Walsall in Readers' Wives? What a fugly cow.' 'Yeah, but she's quite a peeler. Just look at the wingspan she's achieved.'*

winking *n.* When preparing to *hack off a lump,* the uncomfortable feeling of the *anus* twitching whilst still undoing the belt. The *point of no return.*

winking the Jap's eye *n.* An emergency cutting-short of an act of micturition. Curtailing a *slash.*

winking walnut *n. Brown eye, chocolate starfish.*

winkle picking *1. v. medic.* Anal sex with one afflicted with piles. *2. v.* Ancient seafarer's practice acheived using special pointed shoes.

winky *1. n.* A tiny *cock. 2. adj.* Having a tendency to wink a lot.

winkybag *1. n.* A tiny scrotum. *2. n.* An ugly old woman with a tendency to wink a lot.

winner *n.* Unit in which *spunk* is traditionally measured in the catering industry. *'Boil 1 small tablespoon of sago in very little water till clear. Dissolve a teaspoonful of meat or vegetable extract in a cup of boiling water. Strain the cooked sago into the made broth. Season to taste, and lastly, if a red-faced cunt is coming to dine, stir in a winner of gentleman's spendings.'* (from *Household Management* by Mrs Beeton).

winner corner *n.* Secluded quarter of a restaurant kitchen, where staff members may retire in order to discreetly prepare *perseverance soup* for their less popular customers.

winnered *adj. Wanked dry.* Term used to describe the *clockweights* of kitchen staff following a sudden rush on *chef's special sauce.*

Winner's sauce *n.* That which, in the food industry, is added to the recipe wherever food critic Michael Winner eats. *Spunk.*

Winner takes all *1. n.* Erstwhile TV quiz programme featuring scouser comic Jimmy Tarbuck. *2. n.* Game played in restaurant kitchens whereby everyone (including head chefs, sous-chefs, waiters, bar staff and the other customers) perform acts of onanistic *self-delight* into the red-faced *Sunday Times* columnist's soup.

Winner widow *n.* The disgruntled wife of a cordon bleu chef whose sexual energies have been entirely redirected into the production of *special sauce* for the consumption of the popular film director and fat *cunt.*

winnet *n. Kling on, dag, dangleberry, willnot, brown room hanger* *on*. Also *winnit*.

winnet picker *n.* Someone of arguably lower social standing than a *jizz mopper. 'I only got three A's and a B at A-Level, so I'm working as a winnet picker.'*

winnie *n.* A lesbian, she who licks the *honey pot*.

winnit *n.* See *winnet*.

Winslet twins *n.* A nice proper pair of buoyant breasts as sported by *Titanic* actress Kate.

wintercourse *n.* Frosty sex, the kind had with a lady who doesn't approve of that kind of carry on. One would imagine Margot and Jerry out of *The Good Life* and the Queen and Prince Philip engage in *wintercourse*.

win the chocolate lottery *v.* To receive a particularly large *milkman's bonus*.

win the speedboat *v.* Having already secured a dead-cert *bang* whilst out *on the pull*, to go for - and miraculously get the go-ahead from - a much better option. From the closing round on TV quiz-show *Bullseye*, where the contestants could gamble their safe sixty-pounds winnings on scoring a hundred-and-one in six darts or less and thus win a mystery prize, which was invariably revealed as a speedboat full of fat-titted, bikini-clad blonde *birds* when they lost. Or a trailer tent if they won.

wipe your feet *v.* To vigorously *beskid* a lavatory *pan. "I is the only nice and jumbly giant in Giant Country! I is the Big Friendly Giant!' 'I don't care who you are,' replied Sophie. 'I'm not using that crapper. It looks like you've wiped your feet in there, you mucky old cunt."* (from *The BFFG* by Roald Dahl).

wire spider *n.* The hairs around the *chocolate starfish* that come to life when you are in a meeting or in the checkout queue at Asda.

Wirral peninsula *1. n.* The area of land which falls between Chester and Liverpool. *2. n.* Them bits of skin that separate *cunts* and *arseholes*. The *taint, notcher, carse, snarse, biffin bridge, Humber Bridge, tinter etc*.

witch doctor's rattle *n.* Descriptive of a woman with a *nice personality*. A *monk's pin-up*.

witch's cave *n.* A *wizard's sleeve, clown's pocket, wall of death*. An enormous *fadge. 'Soldier, soldier, would you marry me / For you are so strong and brave / Oh no, sweet maid, I cannot marry you / You've a twat like a witch's cave'* (Traditional folk song).

witch's lips *n.* The cold kiss of a porcelain toilet bowl on one's *bell end* occasionally felt whilst *dropping off the shopping*.

witch's trick *n.* The phenomenon of a *back beauty, backstabber* or *golden deceiver* who appears stunning from behind, only to reveal herself as looking like Grotbags off *Emu's World* from the front.

witch wagon *n.* Elongated white left-hand-drive vehicle designed to shunt drunk harpies of limited vocal and cerebral capacity to and from, to pick a destination at random, The Black Sheep, Croydon CR0 1NA on a Saturday night. A stretch limo. *'Will you be having pissed up sex in the back of the witch wagon? Only we charge an extra fiver for the hire of a special sheet to keep spunk and vomit off the velour seats.'*

withdrawal symptoms *n. Spangle* on the stomach, *iced buns, iPod earphones, jelly jewellery* and other assorted evidence of *aerial jackrobatics.*

with one's cock out, do something *v.* To perform a task or action badly. *'My right honorable friend would have us believe that he can increase government spending in the health service whilst at the same time delivering tax cuts across the board. Well I'm afraid he must have written this budget with his cock out, because I can tell him that the figures simply do not add up.'* (Rt Hon Michael Howard MP, *Hansard*).

witten *n.* See *winnet.*

wittgenstein, do a *v.* Yet another classical piano-based term for a specific act of *self pollution.* To perform a few *five finger exercises* with the left hand on one's short, pink *upright,* possibly in front of a large audience in the Royal Albert Hall. Named after the unidextrous Austrian concert pianist Paul Wittgenstein (1887-1961), who lost his right arm in WWI, but nevertheless continued his musical career using his remaining limb to play a number of specially-commissioned works. And it always felt like someone else was doing it.

wizard's sleeve *n.* A *witch's cave.* A particularly capacious *sausage wallet. 'I can't feel a bloody thing, Mother Teresa. You must have a fanny like a wizard's sleeve.'*

wizards' hats *n. Dunces' hats, motorway cones.*

WOAT *acronym.* A light-hearted term for a woman at a football, rugby or cricket match. Waste Of A Ticket.

wobbly boots *adj.* Uncontrollable alcoholic footwear. *Seven pint boots* worn when you've got *legs like snapped candles.*

wobbly landing *n.* Trying, when drunk, to manoeuvre your under-inflated *zipper Zeppelin* safely through your wife's *hangar doors.*

wolfbagging *v.* To have sex with a wolf inside a large bag.

wolf bait *n.* An unusually meaty, pungent *fart,* similar to the smell encountered when opening a tin of Butcher's Tripe Mix. A *fyst.*

wolf bite *n.* A really painful *arsehole, eg.* after a curry. *'Would you care to ride with us to Wenlock Edge, Captain Tremaine?' she asked. The Captain winced. 'I regret I must decline your kind offer, Mrs Dugdale,' he replied. 'I lately partook of a monstrous vindaloo with the Lord of Harpole, and I still have a wolf bite upon my postillion.'* (from *Middlemarch,* by George Eliot).

wolf pussy *n.* A nasty, exceptionally hairy *growler* that looks like it could inflict serious damage if provoked. *'Girl, you ain't coming no muthafucking way near me with that goddam muthafucking wolf pussy of yours and mess up my muthafucking dick, bitch. Shiiit.'* (Eddie Murphy in *Nutty Professor II The Klumps*).

woman in comfortable shoes *n.* A *tennis fan,* a *lady golfer.* A *bird* who is *fond of walking holidays.*

women's things *n. medic. Flangina.*

wombies *n. Tits,* breasts, *baps.*

womb strudel *n.* An un-savoury *strawberry* dessert baked once a month in a *hairy pie.*

womfer *n.* The female equivalent

of a *barse*. *Chinrest* used to avoid cramp at a *hairy pie* tasting.

womit *n.* Dribbly sick.

wonderwank *n.* An act of *self abuse* carried out without the use of visual stimulation. Named after the pop singer Stevie Wonder.

wonder woman *n.* A lady with a *lovely personality*. A *boot* that only a blind man could fancy.

wongle *v.* To rive one's *passion cosh* up and down one's wife's *arse* in an attempt to wake her up for a *poke*.

wonk *1. n.* A political researcher. Usually a young man with glasses and a *wanker's tan*. *2. n.* A desperate and ultimately unsatisfying act of *self help* with multiple interruptions. *'Bless me Father for I have sinned.' 'Do you mind coming back in about ten minutes, my son? I'm half way through a wonk in here.'*

wood *n.* Erectification of the peniculastical appendulation.

woodburner *n.* An enthusiastic *masturbatrix* who gives it *six nowt* whilst *playing fives* on a fellow's *walking stick* to such an extent as to cause a certain amount of charring to his *wood*. A woman who goes at it *like Ray Mears starting a fire*.

woodpecker *n.* A woman who performs rapid, hands-free *horatio*. From the movement of the *bird's* head as she hammers your *trunk*.

woody *n.* What a young American surfer dude takes to the beach.

wookie hole *1. n.* Uninspiring tourist attraction consisting of a hole in the ground and a gift shop. *2. n.* A particularly hairy *Mary Hinge*. A *biffer*, a *Judith*.

wool *n. coll. US. Fluff, blart, fanny, totty*.

woolly bird *n. Aus.* A sheep.

woolly wardrobe *n.* A bulky, cavernous receptacle in the bedroom where gentlemen stuff their *roll neck sweaters*.

woolworths *n.* A plain *bird* that will not impress your mates, but who will do absolutely anything you can think of.

work a split shift *v.* Of a lovable, lucky, cheeky chappie, to have two *ladyfriends* on the go at the same time.

working from home *euph.* Spending the day *relaxing in a gentleman's way*.

working in the Tamworth gang *euph.* Descriptive of a homosexual. From a legendary troupe of railway track labourers whose camaraderie reputedly progressed beyond banter and cups of tea.

world of leather *n.* The *parts* of an aged lady. *Granny's oysters, grandma's Wolseley*.

worm's belt, tighter than a *sim.* Descriptive of a particularly unaccommodating *snatch*, a *butler's cuff, mouse's ear, mole's eye*. *'DUCHESS OF BERWICK: My dear Lord Plymdale. I really do not understand why you associate with Mrs Erlynne. She is such a tiresome conversationalist. LORD PLYMDALE: Conversation is, I find, a somewhat over-rated virtue, your ladyship. Besides which, Mrs Erlynne kindly vouchsafed me tops and fingers in Lord Darlington's gazebo last night and believe you me, her twat's tighter than a worm's belt.'* (from *Lady Windermere's Fanny* by Oscar Wilde).

worth a squirt *adj.* Sexually desirable. *Prodworthy*.

WOT *acronym.* An aesthetically-challenged person who nevertheless sports a fine pair of *eye magnets* on their chest, for example Liz MacDonald off *Coronation Street or* Kerry Catona off the Iceland adverts. *Waste Of Tits.*

wounded soldier's walk *n.* The trip a gentleman makes to the bathroom after completing a messy act of *relaxation* when he has nothing to hand with which to clean up the resultant mess. From the fact that cupping a few teaspoonsful of rapidly-cooling *spuffer* to his belly causes him to assume a hunched posture which is very reminiscent of a shot infantryman clutching his injured stomach as he hobbles off the battlefield.

wozny *n. Scots/Ir.* A *bird's* perineum or taint, from the fact that "if it wozny there, you'd be in the shit". The *tinter, carse, Humber bridge, Niftkin's bridge, tisnae, snarse etc.*

WRAC *1. abbrev. milit.* The Women's Royal Army Corps. 2. *abbrev. milit.* Coarse squaddies' argot for Weekly Ration of Army Cunt. *'Good news lads. The WRAC's arrived. Bagsy fog up.'* (General Bernard Montgomery addressing his troops on the eve of the battle of El Alamein, North Africa, October 29th 1942).

wring the rattlesnake *v. Siphon the python.* To *piss, strain the greens.*

wrinkled penny *n. US.* The *ringpiece, balloon knot, tea towel holder, nipsy.*

wrist flick *n.* A *grumble vid*, a *stick film.*

wristicuffs *n.* A bout of *knocking oneself about a bit. Boxing the Jesuit.*

writer's cock *n.* The excuse used by authors caught looking at illegal *grumble* whilst *researching a book. Writer's cock* can be so bad that some of the books being researched take many years to be completed, if they ever appear at all.

write the letter 'M' *v.* To inscribe the thirteenth letter of the alphabet in *arse* sweat on the toilet seat whilst having a *Queensway.*

wrongbow *n.* White cider. A tangy, refreshing apple-based alternative to trampagne, *supermarket smack* or metal polish.

wrong 'un *n.* The *coal hole.* To quote Roy Walker, "it's good, but it's not right."

wuilty *adj.* Descriptive of the sense of shame a fellow experiences when he inadvertently bumps into a lady over the thought of whom he has *knocked himself about a bit* earlier that very day. *'Did you catch Jonathan Ross interviewing that stripper who's married to Marilyn Manson the other night? He didn't half have a wuilty expression on his face.'*

wu-wu *1. n.* Childish name for a *fufu.* *2. n.* The noise a train makes.

wuffle nuts *n.* The fruits of the *dangleberry* tree.

Wurzel *1. n. prop.* A member of the English rock supergroup of the 1970s. *2. n.* An embarrassingly small penis. An *acorn,* a *Jack Straw.*

wysinwyg *acronym.* What You See Is Not What You Get. Computer-talk for flirting on the internet with a pert bit of blonde, A-level *fluff* who turns out to be a 58-year-old *sex case* panel beater masturbating in his mum's spare room.

Xx

X-flow, rough as a cold *sim.* A mechanic's term when referring to an aesthetically unconventional female. Named after Ford's notoriously noisy pushrod engine of the 1970s. *'No, but seriously though, fuck me, she's as rough as a cold X-flow.'* (Dr Rowan Williams, the Archbishop of Canterbury, addressing the reception following the wedding of His Royal Highness the Prince of Wales and Camilla Parker-Bowels, in the cafe of the Wacky Warehouse, Bracknell on 9th April 2005).

X-piles *n.* Mysterious, unidentified throbbing objects from *Uranus*.

X-ray specs *n.* Cheap, cardboard spectacles, available only by mail order from the back of pubescent boys' comics, which enable the wearer to see through women's clothing. A more expensive version, which is available from the back of the *Lancet*, is used to diagnose fractures in hospital Accident & Emergency departments.

XX *adj.* Special video certificate awarded to pornographic films of poor sound and picture quality.

XXX *adj.* Special video certificate awarded to pornographic films of exceptionally poor sound and picture quality.

xylophone *1. n.* Like a piano, but you twat it with little sticks. *2. v.* To move along a line of naked women who are all bending down, and spank their bottoms - which are of varying sizes - with one's penis. To play a tune on women's buttocks. From the Greek xylo = wood & phonnicus = to be hit tunefully by a fat astronomer at a Royal Variety Performance.

Yy

yabba dabbas *n.* In stone age cartoon intercourse, the climactic stages of coitus which immediately precede the *dooooooos*. The *vinegar strokes*.

yachting *n.* The stirring sight of a dog in full sail, tacking its way across the living room carpet, attempting to remove the *barnacles* from its *keel.*

yaffle the yoghurt cannon *v.* To *nosh* voraciously.

yak *1. n.* Big hairy animal of untidy appearance. *2. n.* A big hairy *eskimo's glove* of untidy appearance. A feminist's *beaver*, a *minge* with a *pant moustache*.

yambag *n.* The wrinkled retainer in which the *gourds* are kept.

yang *n. US.* A *wang*.

yank *1. n.* An inhabitant of the northern states of America. *2. n.* A "one-man-band"-type device with which an American sex case attaches his penis to his ankle in order to *pull himself off* whilst walking about.

yank off *v.* To *relax* vigorously *in a gentleman's way*.

yank the plank v. To *tug* one's *wood,* whilst running the risk of getting a hand full of splinters.

yarbles *n.* Testicles. *'He's lost his yarbles.'*

yard *1. n. arch.* Olde Worlde Penis. *2. n.* Confusingly, the *ladygarden* too.

yardbrush *n.* A bristly *fanny* one could sweep out the garage with.

yard high club *n.* The exclusive group of sexual adventurers who have made love in the lavatory of a static caravan.

yard on *n.* An extra large *hard on* achieved when particularly aroused, although probably still smaller than 3 feet. A *faint on.*

Yaris fanny *euph.* A lady's *bodily treasure* which is, like the eponymous Toyota vehicle, "bigsmall". Something you think is going to be like a *mouse's ear* which ends up being like the Albert Hall. A *twat* where you can fold down the seats and get your week's shopping and four sets of skis in.

Yarmouth clam *n.* Similar to a *Viennese oyster,* only performed by a malodorous woman from the Norfolk seaside town.

Yasser *abbrev. US.* Erection. From "Yasser Crack-a-fat". A lame and pointless pun on the name of the late tea-towel-titfered Palestinian Ringo Starr lookalike.

yawnography *n.* Dull, uninspiring *grumble* of the sort shown on the telly, where they don't let you see it *going in* or anything.

Y-bone steak *n.* Female opposite of a *tube steak*. The *beef curtains*.

Y-box *n.* Much more fun than an X-box, and only costs the price of a bunch of flowers from the 24-hour garage.

yellow-fronted brown-backs *n.* *Nether garments* which are in need of a good wash. *'Eeh, we had a smashing night at the Arena. Tom Jones come on for his encore and did Delilah, and your nan got so excited she threw her yellow-fronted brown-backs up on the stage.'*

yellow toilet brush *euph.* The use of a skilfully-controlled stream of high-pressure *wazz* to clean the *bisto skids* off the sides of the *gravy bowl.*

yeti's welly *n.* A voluminous *fadge*, a *donkey's yawn, jade yawning.*

yinyang *1. n. US. Arse, bum. 2. n.*

US. Fuckwit, jerkwad, asswipe, dicksplash.

yitney *n.* One who is *yitten.*

yitten *adj.* Scared of something very tame.

yobble *v.* To *shit* somewhere other than a toilet, usually for the amusement of others. *eg.* onto a cow from a tree.

yodel in the canyon/valley *v.* To *growl* at a very *capacious badger* whilst wearing a small hat with a shaving brush stuck in it.

yodel *v.* To vomit, to *sing a rainbow.*

yoffy's finger *euph. Touching cloth.* From the 1970s children's show *Fingerbobs'.* "Yoffy lifts a finger / and a mouse is there / puts his hands together / and a seagull takes the air / Yoffy lifts a finger / And a scampi darts about / Yoffy bends another / and a tortoise head peeps out".

yoinkahs *n.* A pair of *twin peaks* that cause a volcanic eruption in your *underkrakatoas.*

Yoko *1.* A *bird* who accompanies her boyfriend everywhere, *eg.* down the pub with mates, fishing, the recording sessions for the *Let It Be* album, the *fucking* lot.

yongles *n. US. Clockweights*, testicles.

yoni *n.* Ancient Hindu female genitals, *twat.*

yonks! *exclam.* Popular speech balloon reaction to finding a tenner on a cartoon pavement.

york *onomat.* To vomit, *call Huey.*

Yorkie bar *n.* A *puddle jumper, botter* or *gaylord.* From the popular chocolate confection advertising slogan. "It's not for girls".

Yorkshire flamingo *n.* A tired-looking, malnourished, pink-faced *bird* who, due to the sorry state of her shabby surroundings (*eg.* the Frontier Club, Batley), appears exotic and alluring to the untrained eye.

you'll have to buy that now, you've ripped it *exclam.* Humorous phrase which can be used to great effect after someone has *let rip* in a particularly rip-roaring manner. See *you're only supposed to blow the bloody doors off.*

you milk? *interrog.* A phrase used by far-eastern prostitutes to ascertain whether or not their client has *dropped his yop.*

you still have two wishes left! *exclam. hum.* Amusing phrase which can be used to lighten a ladyfriend's rancorous mien after you have used your *magic wand* to cover her face with *jizz,* for example.

You're only supposed to blow the bloody doors off *exclam.* Post-flatus repartee. *A bit more choke and she would have started; a confident appeal by the Australians there; an excellent theory, Dr Watson; anybody injured?; don't tear it, I'll take the whole piece; how much?; keep shouting Sir, we'll find you; more tea vicar?; someone let him in; someone's tinkered with Herbie; speak on, sweet lips that never told a lie; speak up caller, you're through; taxi for Brown; that's working, now try your lights; well struck Sir!; what's that, Sweep?; you'll have to buy that now, you've ripped it; sew a button on that; catch that one and paint it blue; good health!; pin a tail on that* and *there goes the elephant.*

yo-yo knickers *n.* A *bike,* loose woman; she whose knickers go up and down faster than Richard Branson's hot air balloons.

yummy mummy *1. n.* A middle-aged woman worthy of a good *seeing to*, *eg*. Helen Mirren. *2. n.* A young mother with a fantastic *arse* pushing a buggy. *3. n.* On a cannibal menu, either a delicious, well-cooked mother, or jerky made from an Egyptian pharaoh.

Zz

Zebedee *1. n.* At school, a face, complete with "Julius Pringles"-type moustache, drawn onto the glans with a biro in order to amuse one's classmates or pupils. *2. n.* A tea-time erection that springs up unexpectedly, signalling that it is "time for bed".

zeps *abbrev. Zeppelins.* Large, hydrogen-filled, flammable meat balloons. *Hindenburgs, blimplants.* See also *dead heat in a zeppelin race.*

zerotica *n. Wanking* material of the lowest imaginable potency, *eg.* a thermal underwear catalogue, a picture of a nuns' hockey team or the letters page in the *People's Friend.*

zig-a-zig ahhhh! *onomat. arch.* To have a bloody good *one off the wrist* whilst watching a Spice Girls video.

zilch *n. Fuck all, jack shit.*

Zinzanbrook *rhym. slang. NZ.* Short for *fuck.*

zipper fish *n.* The penis, or *trouser trout.*

zipper sniffer *n.* A keen penis enthusiast of either gender.

zipper Zeppelin *n.* Shiny, cigar-shaped craft which occasionally explodes at its moorings. *'Watch it! Watch it! Oh get out of the way of my zipper Zeppelin! Too late! Oh, the humanity! Oh, the humanity! Let me get you a tissue, Your Majesty.'*

zip snip *n.* An unintentional circumcision and/or vasectomy operation performed using the flies of one's trousers. Usually carried out under about ten pints of general anaesthetic.

zit *n.* A *pluke.*

Zoes *n. Balls, clockweights, gonads,* testicles. From the *Strictly Dance Fever* presenter Zoe Bollocks.

zonked *adj. Pissed, wankered, wazzed. Trousered.*

zoob *n.* Penis.

zook *n.* A prostitute, a *ho'.*

zorba *1. rhym. slang.* To have a *Chinese singing lesson.* From Zorba the Greek = leak. *2. v.* To have sex in the *Grecian* style. *'Oscar Fingal O'Flahertie Wilde, you are charged with zorba-ing a load of jockeys.'*

Zorro mask *n.* A Saturday morning disguise worn by the wife of a big drinker. *Nature's make-up.*

zounds *n. arch.* God's wounds. 17th century swear word banned by Act of Parliament in 1651, but okay now if used in moderation. Also *g*dzooks, fuckanory.*

zucchini *n. US. Cock.* Something stuck into burgers by disgruntled fast food preparation staff. *Dill,* the *man mayonnaise bottle.*

zuffle *v.* To wipe one's *charlie* clean on the curtains after having a *bang,* usually in a posh *bird's* house, *ie.* one that has curtains. *To fly the flag.*

zuffle bag *n.* A dirty woman whose soft furnishings show evidence of substantial previous *zuffling.*

zuffle coat *n.* The topmost item of clothing in the pile on a bed at a party. Used by a male guest to clean the *sloom* off his *three card trick* after a furtive *poke.*

zylophone *n.* Incorrect spelling of *xylophone.*

ZZ bottom *n.* An exceptionally long-haired *muff,* from the resemblance to the unsightly, unkempt beards sported by members of the Texan blues rock band ZZ Top. But not the drummer.

ZZ tops and fingers *n.* The act of *firkyfoodling* one's missus whilst she's asleep.

ZZZ tops and fingers *n.* The act of *firkyfoodling* one's missus whilst she's in a coma.